Lecture Notes in Computer Science 1622

Edited by G. Goos, J. Hartmanis and J. van Leeuwen

Springer

Berlin
Heidelberg
New York
Barcelona
Hong Kong
London
Milan
Paris
Singapore
Tokyo

Michael González Harbour
Juan A. de la Puente (Eds.)

Reliable
Software Technologies –
Ada-Europe '99

1999 Ada-Europe International Conference
on Reliable Software Technologies
Santander, Spain, June 7-11, 1999
Proceedings

Springer

Series Editors

Gerhard Goos, Karlsruhe University, Germany
Juris Hartmanis, Cornell University, NY, USA
Jan van Leeuwen, Utrecht University, The Netherlands

Volume Editors

Michael González Harbour
Universidad de Cantabria, Facultad de Ciencias
Departamento de Electrónica y Computadores
Avda. de los Castros s/n, E-39005 Santander, Spain
E-mail: mgh@ctr.unican.es

Juan A. de la Puente
Universidad Politécnica de Madrid, ETSI Telecomunicacion
E-28040 Madrid, Spain
E-mail: jpuente@dit.upm.es

Cataloging-in-Publication data applied for

Die Deutsche Bibliothek - CIP-Einheitsaufnahme

Reliable software technologies : proceedings / Ada Europe '99, 1999 Ada Europe
International Conference on Reliable Software Technologies, Santander, Spain,
June 7 - 11, 1999. Michael González Harbour ; Juan A. de la Puente (ed.). -
Berlin ; Heidelberg ; New York ; Barcelona ; Hong Kong ; London ; Milan ; Paris
; Singapore ; Tokyo : Springer, 1999
(Lecture notes in computer science ; Vol. 1622)
ISBN 3-540-66093-3

CR Subject Classification (1998): D.2, D.1.2-5, D.3, D.4, C.2.4, C.3, K.6

ISSN 0302-9743
ISBN 3-540-66093-3 Springer-Verlag Berlin Heidelberg New York

Typesetting: Camera-ready by author
SPIN: 10705270   06/3142 – 5 4 3 2 1 0   Printed on acid-free paper

Foreword

The Fourth International Conference on Reliable Software Technologies, Ada-Europe'99, took place in Santander, Spain, from June 7 to 11, 1999. It was sponsored by Ada-Europe, the European federation of national Ada societies, in cooperation with ACM SIGAda and Ada-Spain, and it was organized by members of the University of Cantabria and the Technical University of Madrid, in Spain. This was the 19th consecutive year of Ada-Europe conferences, which have always been the main Ada events in Europe, with their counterparts being the ACM SIGAda conferences in the USA (formerly Tri-Ada).

The conference is not just devoted to the Ada language, but rather to the more general area of reliable software technologies. In this sense, there are papers on formal methods, testing, software architectures and design, software engineering tools, etc. We believe that the role of reliable software technologies is becoming increasingly important, as computer applications control more and more of our everyday systems. The goal of our conference is to contribute to advancing the state of the art of all the technologies that help us in achieving better and more reliable software at a lower overall cost.

After the substantial revision that represented the Ada 95 standard, the Ada language is receiving renewed interest in many research institutes. One of the driving forces behind this interest is the availability of the free software GNAT compiler, as well as other free or low-cost compilers. The fact that researchers have the source code of the compiler and the run-time system available makes it possible for them to "play" with new language constructs, new run-time features, and new alternate implementations. Several of the papers presented at the conference go along these lines.

Certainly, the language is not only used for research. Industry experience with the Ada language is common in the areas where software reliability is a requirement. This typically, but not only, involves safety-critical systems such as aeroplane, train, or nuclear power station control systems. The recently developed Ravenscar Profile for safety-critical systems — a set of restrictions on the tasking model that allows building certifiable run-time systems — is receiving a lot of attention because it allows application programs running under Ada 95's tasking model to be used in systems with very stringent safety requirements. A few of the papers given at this conference discuss safety-critical systems and the role of the Ravenscar Profile.

At this conference, there were also papers on industry's experience with Ada for application areas that are not safety critical. In these application areas, it is recognized that other languages such as C++ and, more recently, Java, receive much more attention from programmers and system developers. However, two factors seem to forecast an increase in the use of the Ada language in those areas. Firstly, as more and more systems become computer controlled, demand for reliable software is increasing. For example we need our mobile phones, TV sets, automobiles, etc., to work reliably; and they rely heavily on computers, and thus on software. Secondly, there are many academic institutions teaching Ada today. This has changed considerably over the last few years because of the low cost of Ada compilers now. And for instructors and students the Ada language is just perfect for teaching and practising. As a first language, a Pascal-like subset of the language can be used; later, more in-depth concepts, such as abstraction, object-oriented programming, concurrent programming, real-time programming, etc., can be experienced using the same robust language that was learnt in the first place.

Experience with distributed systems programmed in Ada is also receiving increasing attention, since many more computer systems are distributed nowadays. In fact, the distributed systems section of this conference is one of the largest in number of papers. There are different approaches available to Ada programmers, who can choose to support distribution through operating system calls, by using middleware such as CORBA, or by using the language-defined Distributed Systems Annex. Papers presented to the conference explore all these possibilities. Also included in the conference are sections traditional to the Ada community such as real-time systems and fault tolerant systems.

This year, the conference included a special section on Hardware/Software Codesign. Although this topic has not been addressed in previous conferences, we thought that it would be interesting for this audience because there are several groups who are proposing Ada as a system-level specification language for hardware/software codesign. It is interesting for the Ada community to learn about these proposals because, if they get enough support, they may represent another important and expanding area in which the language may be used in the future.

The conference presented three distinguished invited speakers, who delivered state-of-the-art information on topics of great importance for now and for the future. Participation of one of the invited speakers had not been confirmed at the time this foreword was written; the other two invited speakers were:

- An Architectural Perspective of Real-Time Ada Applications
  C. Douglass Locke, Lockheed Martin Corporation
- The Evolving Architecture of GNAT
  Edmond Schonberg, New York University & Ada Core Technologies (ACT)

We are very proud to have been able to host these keynote speakers, and are very grateful to them for their efforts.

For this conference a large number of papers were submitted from 17 countries, almost doubling the paper submissions of previous years. The program committee worked hard to review all these papers and the paper selection process proved to be very difficult, since many papers had received excellent reviews. As a result of this process, the program committee selected 36 high quality papers covering a broad range of software technologies:

- Ravenscar Profile and High Integrity Systems
- Software Architectures and Design

- Testing
- Formal Methods
- Education
- Distributed Systems
- Real-Time Scheduling and Kernels
- Tools
- The Role of Ada in Hardware/Software Codesign
- Fault Tolerance
- Case Studies

The conference also included an interesting set of tutorials, featuring international experts who presented introductory and advanced material on reliable software technologies:

- Java for Ada Programmers
  Benjamin M. Brosgol

- Windows Development with Ada
  Orjan Leringe

- Software Interoperability: Principles and Practice
  Jack C. Wileden and Alan Kaplan

- Building Ada Development Tools: ASIS and other GNAT Technologies
  Cyrille Comar and Sergey I. Rybin

- MetaH — An Architecture Description Language for Building Avionics Systems with Ada
  Bruce Lewis and Dennis Cornhill

- High Integrity Ada - The SPARK Approach
  John Barnes

- FUSION: An Object-Oriented Development Method, with Mapping to Ada
  Alfred Strohmeier

- Ada & Java: A Manager's and Developer's Road Map
  Franco Gasperoni and Gary Dismukes

- Using GNAT for the Java Platform
  Emmanuel Briot, Gary Dismukes and Franco Gasperoni

Many people contributed to the success of the conference. The program committee, made up of international experts in the area of reliable software technologies, spent long hours carefully reviewing all the papers, paper abstracts, and tutorial proposals submitted to the conference. A subcommittee formed by Lars Asplund, Johann Blieberger, Erhard Plödereder, Ángel Álvarez, and the program co-chairs met in Santander to make the final paper selection. Some program committee members were assigned to shepherd some of the papers. We are grateful to all of those who contributed to the technical program of the conference.

The work of the members of the organizing committee deserves a special mention. In particular, Ángel Álvarez, who together with John Barnes, Dirk Craeynest, and Stéphane Barbey prepared an extremely attractive tutorial program. Alejandro Alonso worked long hours contacting many companies and people to prepare the conference exhibition. And always helping the organizing committee was Alfred Strohmeier, Ada-Europe's Conference Liaison, who had good advice for us every time we needed it.

We also want to thank the people of the University of Cantabria for the work spent in the local organization. Special thanks to J. Javier Gutiérrez García, for publicising the conference by post and e-mail and by creating the conference Web page and preparing the brochure with the conference program. We also want to thank Mario Aldea Rivas, who worked many hours on the Web server that we used to manage the paper submission and revision process. This Web server was based on the Start Conference Manager, which was provided free of charge by Rich Gerber, and proved to be extremely useful and convenient.

Last but not least, we would like to thank all the authors who submitted their papers to the conference, and all the participants who helped in accomplishing the goals of the conference, providing a forum for the exchange of ideas between researchers and practitioners of reliable software technologies. We hope that they all enjoyed the technical program as well as the social events of the International Conference on Reliable Software Technologies.

March 1999   Michael González Harbour and Juan A. de la Puente

Organizing Committee

Conference Chair

Michael González Harbour, *Universidad de Cantabria, Spain*

Program Co-Chairs

Michael González Harbour, *Universidad de Cantabria, Spain*
Juan A. de la Puente, *Universidad Politécnica de Madrid*

Tutorial Chair

Ángel Álvarez, *Universidad Politécnica de Madrid*

Exhibition Chair

Alejandro Alonso, *Universidad Politécnica de Madrid*

Publicity Chair

J. Javier Gutiérrez García, *Universidad de Cantabria, Spain*

Ada-Europe Conference Liaison

Alfred Strohmeier, *Swiss Federal Institute of Technology in Lausanne*

Ada-Europe Board

John Barnes, *JBI*
Dirk Craeynest, *OFFIS nv/sa, Belgium*
Erhard Plödereder, *University of Stuttgart, Germany*
Björn Källberg, *CelsiusTech Systems AB*
Alfred Strohmeier, *Swiss Federal Institute of Technology in Lausanne*
Lars Asplund, *Uppsala University*
Michael González Harbour, *Universidad de Cantabria, Spain*

Program Committee

Ángel Álvarez, *Universidad Politécnica de Madrid*
Lars Asplund, *Uppsala University*
Paul A. Bailes, *The University of Queensland*
Ted Baker, *Florida State University*
Brad Balfour, *Objective Interface*
Stéphane Barbey, *Swiss Federal Institute of Technology, Lausanne*
John Barnes, *JBI*
Johann Blieberger, *Technical University Vienna*
Jim Briggs, *University of Portsmouth, UK*
Benjamin Brosgol, *Aonix*
Jorgen Bundgaard, *DDC-I*
Alan Burns, *University of York*
Dirk Craeynest, *OFFIS nv/sa, Belgium*
Alfons Crespo, *Universidad Politécnica de Valencia*
Peter Dencker, *Chairman of Ada-Deutschland*
Jesús González-Barahona, *Universidad Carlos III de Madrid*
Michael González Harbour, *Universidad de Cantabria*
Mike Kamrad, *BlazeNet*
Jan Van Katwijk, *Delft University of Technology*
Hubert B. Keller, *Forschungszentrum Karlsruhe*
Yvon Kermarrec, *ENST de Bretagne*
Fabrice Kordon, *Université P. & M. Curie*
Albert Llamosí, *Universitat de les Illes Balears*
Franco Mazzanti, *Istituto di Elaborazione della Informazione , CNR*
John McCormick, *University of Northern Iowa*
Paolo Panaroni, *Intecs Sistemi S.p.A.*
Laurent Pautet, *ENST Paris*
Juan A. de la Puente, *Universidad Politécnica de Madrid*
Erhard Plödereder, *University of Stuttgart, Germany*
Jean-Pierre Rosen, *ADALOG*
Sergey Rybin, *Moscow State University & ACT*
Edmond Schonberg, *New York University & ACT*
Andreas Schwald
Martin J. Stift, *Universität Wien*
Alfred Strohmeier, *Swiss Federal Institute of Technology, Lausanne*
Theodor Tempelmeier, *Rosenheim*
Stef Van Vlierberghe, *OFFIS N.V./S.A.*
Tullio Vardanega, *European Space Agency*
Andy Wellings, *University of York*

Table of Contents

Education

Distributed Systems

Real-Time Scheduling and Kernels

Tools

The Role of Ada in Hardware/Software Codesign

Fault Tolerance

Case Studies

Author Index

An Architectural Perspective of Real-Time Ada Applications

C. Douglass Locke

Lockheed Martin Corporation, Chief Scientist - Systems Support, Owego, NY 13827, USA
doug.locke@lmco.com

Abstract. While there are appear to be many ways in which real-time Ada systems can be designed, it is observed that they can be described using four architectural families: the Timeline, Event-Driven, Pipeline, and Client-Server architectures. This paper describes the principal characteristics of each of these architecture families with respect to their ability to provide bounded application response times, their cost, and safety at a high level. In addition, the use of important Ada constructs for each architecture family is discussed, and examples of application domains that use each of these architectures are identified.

1 Introduction

There are probably as many ways to use the Ada language as there are system and software architects and designers. The Ada language contains a number of very powerful constructs that can be used as tools for the architect. This is especially true for the software architect of a real-time system. The choice of Ada concepts to be used for a real-time application is strongly affected by the underlying software architectural choices.

Regardless of whether Ada is being used as the programming language or not, there are actually very few unique software architectures in general use by real-time software architects. These basic architectures have their roots in various traditional approaches to certain application domains, and they have naturally been carried over into systems for which Ada is the primary language. In many cases, these architectures have become so entrenched that the original reasons for their use has been lost in relative antiquity, and conscious tradeoffs are no longer made when new applications in the same domain are considered.

It is the purpose of this paper to discuss these basic software architectures for real-time systems used with (or without) Ada, comparing and contrasting them along several lines:
- The choices of Ada architectural constructs that are generally used for each
- The ability of the resulting architecture to meet its real-time constraints
- The response of applications using that architecture to errors encountered during system operation
- Costs associated with the architecture

These discussions are, of course, somewhat subjective, but they are based on this author's experience working with a wide variety of systems over a long period of time. Nevertheless, the reasoning on which these discussions are based should become clear, and it is expected that the reader will be able to assess the basis for the conclusions drawn.

It is noted at the outset that virtually all the basic software architectures used in practical real-time systems can be categorized at a high level into only four families, although in practice there are a many variations of these. In this paper, we denote these architectural families as:

1. **Timeline** (sometimes called a cyclic executive)
2. **Event-driven** (with both periodic and aperiodic activities)
3. **Pipeline**
4. **Client-Server**

Each of these four architectural families will be discussed in some detail.

Once a system's software architecture is defined, and when Ada has been chosen as the implementation language, there are many decisions that must be considered. While this paper cannot provide a definitive treatment of all of these, some of the most important architectural decisions involve:

- Ada Tasks (How many? How they should be used?)
- Communication (Shared memory? Messages? Protocols?)
- Synchronization (Protected objects? Rendezvous? Semaphores? Mutexes?)
- Shared Data
- Generics (Should thy be limited in some way?)
- Package Size and Content
- Exceptions (At what level should they be handled? What about "others"?)
- Extent of Application-Specific Types (When should predefined types be used, if at all?)
- Interface to Environment (e.g., POSIX, SQL, Motif, CORBA)

Of these decisions, only the first three will be discussed in this paper due to limited space.

In addition, it is instructive to illustrate how these decisions are frequently made in application domains such as air traffic control, aircraft mission processors, vehicle simulation systems, and flight control.

The remainder of this paper is organized into 4 sections. Section 2.0 contains an overview of each of the architectural families, while Section 3.0 discusses the major Ada decisions involved for each family in the light of these application domains. Section 4.0 then contains a brief summary and conclusion.

2 A Taxonomy of Real-Time Architectures

It is observed that virtually all real-time systems can be classified into four architectural families. Although there are many variations within these families, each of the families can be described in relatively concrete terms regarding the management of system resources (e.g., CPU, memory, I/O, and communications) which characterizes the resulting application's ability to meet its time constraints. Here, we discuss each of these families individually.

2.1 Timeline

The timeline architecture is at once the oldest real-time architecture, and conceptually the simplest. It is sometimes called a **frame-based** architecture because of its use of fixed time frames within which all the application procedures are executed in some predetermined sequence. It is also called a **cyclic executive** architecture because of its use of a simple time-driven executive that manages all application procedure invocation using a frame sequence table.

Essentially, the timeline architecture requires dividing the application into a fixed set of procedures that are called sequentially by a relatively simple executive, triggered by a timer set to expire at fixed intervals. At each time trigger, the executive uses the frame sequence table to call the appropriate procedure to the handle the task that is ready for that interval. The individual time intervals are called *frames* or *minor cycles*. The frames are grouped into a fixed sequence that is then repeated throughout the system execution; such a group is called a *major cycle*.

For example, consider the simple example illustrated in Figure 1. Here, we have a trivial application composed of four periodic procedures, each executing at rates of 40 Hz., 20 Hz., 5 Hz., and 1 Hz., respectively. The architect has chosen a frame, or minor cycle length of 25 ms., which is equal to the fastest procedure's 40 Hz. rate. To meet all the application rate

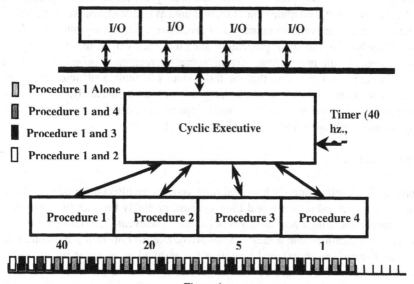

Figure 1

requirements, the procedures are executed in groups as shown, such that procedure 1 is executed every frame, procedure 2 is executed immediately following procedure 1 in the first frame of each major cycle and every other frame thereafter, procedure 3 is executed immediately following procedure 1 in the second frame and in every eighth frame thereafter, while procedure 4 is executed immediately following procedure 1 in the fourth frame and in every 40th frame thereafter. In this way, each procedure is executed at its required rate.

Note that this architecture has several interesting properties. First, there is never any need for two procedures to execute concurrently, so there is no need for explicit synchronization. Because there is no need for concurrency, there is no overhead paid for context switching at the application level. Thus, at first sight, it appears that this architecture is inherently quite efficient, which is generally considered to be a desirable quality for a real-time architecture. Second, because it can be precisely determined at design time exactly when each procedure is to be executed, the system can be said to be deterministic.

However, as noted in [1], these advantages remain largely illusory. Efficiency is not a primary requirement for real-time systems, and neither is determinism. While efficiency and determinism can be useful, they must frequently be compromised (slightly) in favor of creating an architecture with predictable response behaviour. While it is true that a deterministic system will be able to meet its timing constraints, it really isn't necessary to precisely determine when each procedure is to be executed; rather it is sufficient that each procedure be able to predictably meet its own response requirements. Further, while eliminating concurrency and removing context switch overhead seems desirable, it can readily be shown that it is easy to limit the blocking delays caused by synchronization, and to bound the overhead from context switches, particularly using Ada 95, so that it is not necessary to eliminate them.

In fact, eliminating concurrency comes at an astonishingly high price. The timeline architecture requires every procedure to fit comfortably into its frame. Even though there may be (and frequently is) quite a bit of unused time available elsewhere in the schedule, this unused time is unavailable to individual procedures. Thus, long-running tasks must be manually broken into small procedures such that each will fit into the frame. This really amounts to the programmer having to create preemption points manually, then ensure for each resulting point that the task's state will remain sufficiently consistent between invocations. In other words, the programmer must do manually, with error-prone ad-hoc techniques, what any modern real-time operating system is much more capable of doing automatically with fully predictable results[4].

2.2 Event-driven

Although the timeline approach to real-time systems architecture produces the most common architectural style for real-time systems, probably the second most common architectural style is the event-driven architecture. The event-driven design (see Figure 2) waits for indications that a message has arrived, an I/O operation has completed, a timer has expired, or an external operation has resulted in an event such as a button depression. In the Ada language, this is generally seen as a rendezvous accept or a protected procedure invocation. In the event driven architecture, such events trigger the execution of all of the program's computation.

Thus an event-driven architecture consists of a set of tasks, each awaiting an event, where each task is provided with a priority. Task priorities are generally determined using either the time constraints or the semantic importance associated with the job to be done. For example, when an event arrives at a processor, an interrupt handler executing at interrupt priority will typically handle it initially. In the best designs, this interrupt handler will then execute for a minimal amount of time, triggering the execution of a secondary task. This secondary task will then run at a user-defined priority associated either with the time constraint associated with the event or based on its semantic importance alone.

The resulting event-driven architecture involves concurrency at the application level. This means that individual operations running at their correct priorities may preempt each other and results in the need for synchronization using such operations as the POSIX mutex, semaphore, or an Ada protected object. This synchronization adds complexity to the application architecture, but this is counter-balanced by the fact that concurrency increases the resource utilization levels at which the system can operate while meeting its time constraints.

The event-driven paradigm results in a significant problem for the application designer that is frequently overlooked until the later stages of system integration, frequently resulting in unpredictable response times. This problem results from the bursty arrival pattern almost always associated with events (other than events resulting from timer expiration.) The most common mathematical model for such arrivals is the Poisson arrival distribution, in which the system load produced by a burst of arrivals cannot be bounded at a predictable level over any specific time interval, resulting in an unpredictable response time. This generally results in the most common type of real-time systems failure: an intermittent "glitch" that leaves no trail, is unrepeatable, and frequently exhibits different symptoms each time it is observed.

In response to their concerns over the system response time, designers usually try to group together the total utilization generated by these random arrivals over a sufficiently long time interval to show that the system will achieve the average throughput required to handle all of these arrivals. However, this architecture pattern makes it impossible to predict the response time of individual event arrivals. This predictability problem can ameliorated by using any of several bandwidth preserving algorithms such as the sporadic server[6], but otherwise the event-driven paradigm makes it difficult to produce a predictable response time with reasonable levels of utilization.

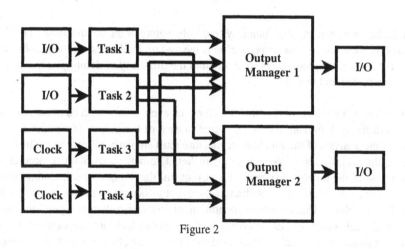

Figure 2

2.3 Pipeline

The pipeline architecture is similar to the event-driven architecture, but is intended specifically to take advantage of a distributed system by a allowing event arrivals to take place at one processor for initial processing, then pushing additional processing off to other tasks, processes, or threads in the same or any other processor in the system. Thus the pipeline architecture initially processes events but sends the remaining processing and the final response to the events to separately scheduled entities elsewhere in the system (see Figure 3.) In the pipeline architecture, it is quite common for a single event to generate processing and many other schedulable entities, resulting in communication across many parts of network, and finally many outputs occurring at various points in the system. From the perspective above, and the time constraints involved, the most important performance parameter is the latency from the initial arrival of the event to the output of each of the resulting responses. This is referred to as the end to end time constraint of the system and may differ for each event or each type of event in the system.

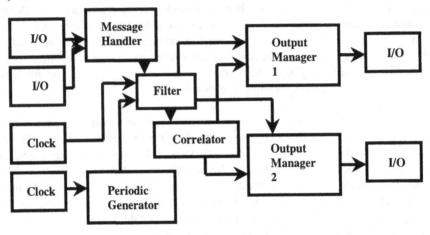

Figure 3

One of the key issues in any distributed system is the nature of the control flow. The flow of control through the system strongly affects the system load balance, the number and nature of the scheduling decisions required, and the difficulty of debugging the system as it is constructed and tested.

In the pipeline architecture, the control flow for each event moves with be event information through the system from the event source to each of the output destinations. This means that the analysis of the pipeline architecture must similarly follow the control flow sequence; the complexity of that sequence makes it somewhat difficult to predict the response time of the pipeline system. This also means that a separate scheduling operation occurs at each point in the pipeline as the event information arrives at each of the stages of the pipeline. This scheduling operation, of course, involves competition among all the schedulable entities in each processor; thus, entities handling a specific event are likely to compete not only with entities handling other events, but also with other entities handling other components of the same event.

Analysis of the resulting scheduling operations is critical to determining the end-to-end time constraints of the pipeline architecture. However because the sequence of schedulable entities handling each portion of the pipeline may, in fact, be handling multiple types of events in separate "pipes" running in opposite directions through the system, it becomes extremely difficult to define the correct priority for each schedule entity. For example, if a system is handling radar contacts eventually displaying them on an operator console, many of the schedulable entities may also be involved in handling operator control operations controlling the behavior of the radar sensors.

For these reasons, task priorities generally play only a minor role in pipeline systems. In fact, the priorities of tasks in a pipeline are frequently defined more by the direction of the pipeline flow than by analysis of the end-to-end time constraints to be achieved. For example, it can easily be shown that if task priorities increase as the event moves through a pipe, the queues of events at each intermediate stage will be minimized. In future systems, it may become possible to have the priority of the stages of the pipeline be adjustable according to the priorities of the arriving messages, thus allowing the system to preferentially a provide good response to some events while pushing others off that exhibit less stringent time constraints. At present, however, this priority handling mechanism is not generally available in commercial system infrastructures.

2.4 Client-Server

The client-server architecture is similar to the pipeline architecture in that events arriving at one or more or nodes of the distributed system are processed throughout the system as needed, based on the event type. Unlike the pipeline architecture, however, the control flow for the client-server model generally remains at the same node as the initial event handler. Although the event still arrives at an initial schedulable entity, the successive processing stages are invoked using remote procedure calls from the initial task, rather than being invoked using a one-way message (see Figure 4.) This means that the locus of control for any given event remains with the initial event handler, and all further processing, including responses, are made by one or more server entities, frequently at other nodes in the system.

Thus, the response time of the client-server architecture can be analyzed in the same way as for the pipeline architecture, but the infrastructure controlling the scheduling of each of the entities involved for each event is somewhat different. This is the architecture used, for example by the CORBA[1] standard. At present, the Object Management Group is completing a significant extension of CORBA, called *Realtime CORBA 1.0* [2], that will provide for priority propagation and scheduling throughout a real-time client-server system. This standard is expected to make the construction and performance analysis of real-time client-server systems significantly more robust.

At present, even with the CORBA real-time extensions, the only mechanism for managing the response time of the client-server system is the use of priorities. As with the other real-time architectures described here, priority can be determined using either response time requirements or semantic importance, but it has generally been found that it is more effective to assign priorities to messages rather than to tasks or threads. The message priorities can then propagated to the clients. This is one of the mechanisms available in the forthcoming CORBA real-time extension.

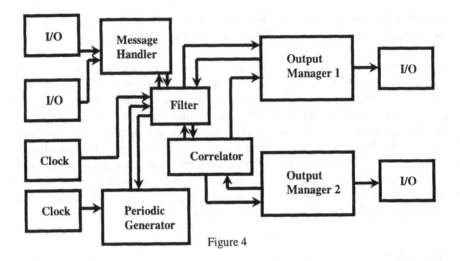

Figure 4

An additional benefit of the client-server architecture is the ease with which the system can be debugged relative to the pipeline architecture. With the pipeline architecture, it is difficult to determine the location of the control flow for a given event at any point in time, so debugging the processing of any event, either to correct response time problems or functional problems, can be very difficult. With the client-server architecture, because the sequence of operations is entirely controlled by a single thread, the location of a malfunctioning element needing further analysis becomes significantly easier to identify.

3 Using Ada in Real-Time Archtectures

There are many ways to utilize the Ada language in the construction of real-time archi-tectures, but there are a few particularly common approaches that can be described for the architecture families described here. For each of the approaches, the Ada constructs commonly considered are briefly described, along with a few sample application domains that use or are considering using each architecture family.

3.1 Timeline

In the timeline architecture, the principal Ada construct used is simply the Ada procedure call. In the simplest systems, a small control program (a cyclic executive) is constructed in a single Ada task that executes periodically at the minor cycle rate. In Ada 95, this task would use the **delay until** statement to control the timing of each minor cycle. The cyclic executive maintains a count of which minor cycle is being initiated at each delay expira-tion, and uses a frame sequence table to determine which procedure(s) should be called for that cycle. Thus, concurrency is avoided and no further Ada tasks are needed. Of course, this also means that there is no need for the priorities, rendezvous, protected objects, asynchronous transfer of control, etc.

This architecture is most commonly used for such applications as aircraft and missile flight control, many avionics mission processors, industrial production controllers, and other relatively simple applications. The minimal use of the more complex Ada features makes this approach quite common for safety-critical systems for which both the application and the run-time infrastructure must be certified.

3.2 Event-Driven

The event-driven architecture is generally constructed in Ada using a set of tasks for each event source or type. For periodic events, the task consists of a loop governed by the **delay until** statement. For aperiodic events, the task will frequently consist of a loop governed by an accept statement driven either by a rendezvous from another task or directly by an interrupt arrival from the run-time environment.

A well-designed event-driven real-time application will use no more tasks than is necessary to handle events with different time constraints. The most common Ada design errors found in event-driven systems is the use of too few tasks (i.e., attempting to handle multiple events with different time constraints in a single task,) or the use of too many tasks (e.g., using the task concept for encapsulation.) Ada tasks introduce overhead in the form of context swapping and synchronization, but when they are used to handle separate time constraints, this overhead is readily bounded and the system's ability to predictably meet its time constraints at high utilization levels is greatly enhanced.

Task priorities should generally be chosen to be consistent with such scheduling methodologies as Rate Monotonic Scheduling[3] or Deadline Monotonic Scheduling, thus providing for analysis leading to a predictable system. Proper use of the Ada protected object for task synchronization and the Ada 95 Real-Time Annex to handle priorities can result in a highly robust system that can meet all its time constraints. For aperiodic events, the use of a sporadic server (generally implemented using a **delay** statement in conjunction with the **accept** statement that triggers the event-driven task, can bound the processor utilization that can otherwise make event-driven architectures subject to timing anomalies under bursty load.

Event-driven system architectures are now frequently supplanting timeline systems because of their greatly increased robustness in meeting time constraints at high resource utilization levels, and significantly lower maintenance costs. Common exceptions are applications requiring safety certification, since the certification agencies commonly mandate the timeline approach. This is expected to change over the next few years as the predictability made possible with the event-driven approach becomes more widely understood, and as tools such as Ada Ravenscar Profile[5] become more widely available.

3.3 Pipeline

The pipeline system, like the event-driven system, is generally constructed using a set of Ada tasks, one for each stage of each of the pipelines. Synchronization between these tasks can be handled using the protected object, but the management of priorities is more difficult. This is because the decomposition of the system functions into tasks is likely to result in tasks that must be executed by event arrivals with multiple time constraints. This is a source of widespread priority inversion, resulting in systems that can miss time constraints even at relatively low utilization levels.

One way to improve the processing of tasks that receive messages from sources with disparate time constraints is to arrange for such tasks to have incoming messages arriving in multiple queues, one for each time constraint. Then the task checks each queue in order of increasing time constraints (non-preemptive Deadline Monotonic order), minimizing the resulting priority inversion. A further useful practice is to perform only minimal processing in tasks characterized by arrivals with disparate time constraints, pushing more extensive processing load to tasks handling activities with single time constraints (and appropriate priorities.)

Presently, the pipeline approach is being used to construct command and control systems, air traffic control, and occasionally vehicle simulation systems. It has also been occasionally used for such application domains as satellite ground systems and submarine combat control systems.

3.4 Client-Server

The client-server architecture is constructed similarly to the pipeline architecture in terms of its use of Ada tasks, but the propagation of messages involves waiting upon a return message to the sender in response to each message sent, thus utilizing a remote procedure call. Ada 95 describes such processing in the Distributed Systems Annex, although implementations have not been quick to support it. In the meantime, systems being built to a client-server architecture are using the Ada bindings available for CORBA, and are expected to use the capabilities provided by the Realtime CORBA 1.0 extensions when they become available. Thus, the client tasks can be expected to be defined as they would be for the pipeline architecture, while the propagation of priorities to server tasks is handled using CORBA mechanisms.

The client-server architecture has not yet been widely used by Ada real-time applications, but with CORBA, it is expected that this architectural model will be used by many of the application domains previously implemented using the pipeline approach. This would include such application domains as air traffic control, command and control, industrial automation, and supervisory systems.

4 Conclusions

The choice of architecture family for a particular system has a major effect on many of the most critical success factors for a real-time system. For uniprocessor or federated processor applications, the most likely candidates are the timeline or event-driven architectures; however, except for safety critical systems, the best choice in terms of application internal complexity, maintainability, reliability, and life-cycle cost, is a well-designed event-driven approach[4]. For distributed applications, the current choice is likely to be the pipeline approach, with careful attention to message priority management, communications latency (generally bounded only stochastically), and processor utilization. This results from the immaturity and lack of resource management support from existing infrastructures for real-time client-server approaches. With the availability of the Realtime CORBA extensions, CORBA will provide a strongly viable client-server alternative for many distributed applications.

Provision of a robust synchronization alternative in Ada 95, the protected object, as well as other Ada 95 changes described in the Real-Time Annex, make Ada highly suitable for either uniprocessor or distributed processor support of real-time systems. The Ada facilities can be used with any of the architectural choices presented here. Of course, not every facility available in Ada should be used in a real-time system, but detailed recommendations are beyond the scope of this paper.

References

1. The Common Object Request Broker: Architecture and Specification, Revision 2.0, July 1996, Object Management Group, Framingham, Massachusetts, USA
2. The Joint Revised Realtime CORBA Submission, March, 1999, Object Management Group, Framingham, Massachusetts, USA
3. Liu, C.L. and Layland, J.W., Scheduling Algorithms for Multiprogramming in a Hard Real Time Environment. JACM 20 (1):46-61, 1973
4. Locke, C. D., Software Architecture for Hard Real-Time Applications: Cyclic Executives vs. Fixed Priority Executives, Real-Time Systems Journal, Kluwer Publishers, vol 4, 1992
5. The Ravenscar Tasking Profile for High Integrity Real-Time Programs, A. Burns, B. J. Dobbing, G. Romanski, in Reliable Software Technologies – Ada-Europe '98, Lecture Notes in Computer Science, Springer-Verlag, June, 1998
6. Sprunt, H. M. B., Sha, L., Lehoczky, J.P., Aperiodic Task Scheduling on Hard Real-Time Systems, Real-Time Systems Journal, Kluwer Publishers, 1989

A Formal Model of the Ada Ravenscar Tasking Profile; Protected Objects

Kristina Lundqvist[1] *, Lars Asplund[1] *, and Stephen Michell[2]

[1] Uppsala University, Information Technology, Dept. of Computer Systems
P.O. Box 325, S-751 05 Uppsala, Sweden
Kristina.Lundqvist@DoCS.UU.SE, Lars.Asplund@DoCS.UU.SE
[2] Maurya Software, 29 Maurya Court Ottawa, Ontario, Canada K1G 5S3
steve@maurya.on.ca

Abstract. The definition of the Ravenscar Tasking Profile for Ada95 provides a definition of a tasking runtime system with deterministic behaviour and low enough complexity to permit a formal description of the model. The complete model of the Protected Object portion of the Ravenscar Model is presented in UPPAAL. Some important properties are verified such as timing of calls to protected procedure. This is the first time a part of an Ada run-time has been formally verified.

Keywords: Ada Tasking, Protected Objects, Ravenscar, Formal Methods, Run-Time System, UPPAAL.

1 Introduction

High Integrity systems traditionally do not make use of high-level language features such as concurrency. This is in spite of the fact that such systems are inherently concurrent. The traditional approach has been to declare concurrency to be a system issue, and to develop alternative methods, such as cyclic executive approaches to solve concurrency issues. The net result has been the creation of non-cohesive systems that are very difficult to analyse, let alone attempt any formal proofs of correctness.

The Ada community has long believed that the static properties of the language, the strong typing facilities, and the relatively few occurances of implementation-dependent and unspecified behaviour could result in the development of provably correct programs in Ada. Indeed the existence of SPARK [Bar97], AVA [Smi92] and Penelope [GMP90] for Ada83 showed that this was possible, although the proof technologies and Ada83 itself made the provable subset somewhat limited. Many in the community have also believed that these proof methodologies could be extended to Ada tasks if a sufficiently predictable and precise tasking subset was specified.

---

* Funded by Swedish National Board for Industrial and Technical Development, Swedish Nuclear Power Inspection, and Swedish Defence Material Administration

Ada95 introduced a number of new tasking-related capabilities that helped to improve the specification of concurrent behaviour, and gave explicit permission to restrict language features to improve performance, predictability or correctness. At the 8th International Real Time Ada Workshop, a concurrency model was developed called the Ravenscar Tasking Model [DB98] [WB97] which could make the verification of tasks in Ada a reality.

2 The Ravenscar Profile

The Ravenscar model eliminates nearly all of the Ada tasking constructs that contain implementation dependencies and unspecified behaviour. The ISO/IEC/-JTC1/SC22/WG9/HRG Ada Safety and Security Rapporteur Group [HRG98] states that the Ravenscar tasking profile increases the effectiveness of the verification of the concurrency aspects of the application, as well as overcoming most of the difficulties associated with timing and scheduling issues.

The specification of the Ravenscar tasking model significantly advances the way of proving concurrent programs in that one can also prove that the tasking runtime system correctly implements the model.

To date there has been one implementation, Raven, [DB98] of the Ravenscar model. This implementation can be certified in conjunction with an application program, but there has not yet been any attempts to formally analyse either the kernel itself, or an application using this kernel. In Raven some emphasis is put on suspension objects, which fits very well into the Ravenscar model.

There has been some previous work done to formally verify different runtime systems e.g. [Tol95] [Hut94]. The development process described in [FW97] attempts to capture all of the temporal properties of a preemptive kernel, and show how an implementation of them can be developed. The formal development of the kernel is done for a simple real-time operating system, designed to support a restricted Ada 95 tasking model. The kernel is specified using the logic of the Prototype Verification System (PVS) [CO$^+$95], with the temporal properties of the system expressed using Real-Time Logic (RTL) [JM86] embedded in PVS. The work is based on a previous work on specifying real-time kernels [FW96]. The subset of Ada that is used is similar to the Ravenscar profile.

2.1 Protected Objects

One of the major capabilities that the Ravenscar model adds to high integrity concurrent systems is a deterministic intertask communication and synchronisation capability. This capability is provided by a "limited" form of Protected Objects, as described below.

The Ravenscar Profile limits Protected Objects in several ways and also limits other tasking features in ways that dramatically simplify PO behaviour.

– There can only be one entry in one PO, and only one task that ever can call the PO entry.

- The entry guard can only ever be a simple boolean.
- Asynchronous Transfer of Control is prohibited.
- Requeue is prohibited.
- Delay and "else" alternatives in entry calls are eliminated.
- The 9th International Real Time Ada Workshop [IRT99] clarified the Ravenscar Model in that implementations must document whether or not they support concurrent protected function calls.
- Tasks cannot be nested inside subprograms, blocks, or other tasks.
- Tasks never terminate.
- Tasks have no entries.
- There is no unchecked deallocation of tasks or Protected Objects.
- There is no relative delay statement.
- The real-time package is mandated, with priority-based scheduling.

These restrictions eliminate virtually all of the non-deterministic behaviour in an Ada runtime. From these restrictions, and the precise Ada specification of the Protected Object, it should be possible to completely specify the behaviour of the PO model, and therefore the behaviour of a set of tasks, each with a unique priority and executing on a single cpu and using POs to implement simple intertask communication and synchronisation.

3   The Mana-project

The aim of the Mana-project is to develop a Ravenscar-compliant Ada RTE using formal development methodologies. A complete Run-Time System will be modelled. The tool, for the formal description and for the formal verification, we intend to use is UPPAAL [LPY97]. With this tool we can prove the correctness of the model, of the kernel, and make it possible to reason about the tasking use of Ada/Ravenscar.

In this paper the Protected Object is described and analysed, including the behaviour of exceptions. In the analysis some timing requirements are modelled. These will later originate from the application software to describe timing behaviour and range from BCET (Best Case Execution Times) to WCET (Worst Case Execution Times).

4   Timed Automata and UPPAAL

UPPAAL is a tool box for modelling [LPY97], simulation and verification of real-time systems, based on constraint-solving and on-the-fly techniques, developed jointly by Uppsala University and Aalborg University. It is appropriate for systems that can be modelled as a collection of nondeterministic processes with finite control structure and real-valued clocks, communicating through channels and (or) shared variables.

UPPAAL consists of three main parts: a description language, a simulator, and a model-checker. The description language is a non-deterministic guarded command language with data types. It serves as a modelling or design language to describe system behaviour as networks of timed automata extended with data variables. The simulator and the model-checker are designed for interactive and automated analysis of system behaviour by manipulating and solving constraints that represent the state-space of a system description. The simulator enables examination of possible dynamic executions of a system during early modelling or design stages and thus provides an inexpensive mean of fault detection prior to verification by the model-checker which covers the exhaustive dynamic behaviour of the system.

There has been some previous work concerning Ada and UPPAAL [Bjo95], where the relation between the Ada tasking model and the formal model timed automata is given, and also some guidelines for translating Ada tasking constructs into timed automatas and vice versa.

4.1 The UPPAAL Model

A timed automaton (TA) [AD90] is a finite automaton [HU79] extended with time by adding real-valued clocks to each automaton, and for each transition adding guards as enabling conditions. A system model in UPPAAL consists of a collection of timed automata modelling the finite control structures of the system. In addition the model uses a finite set of clocks and integer variables.

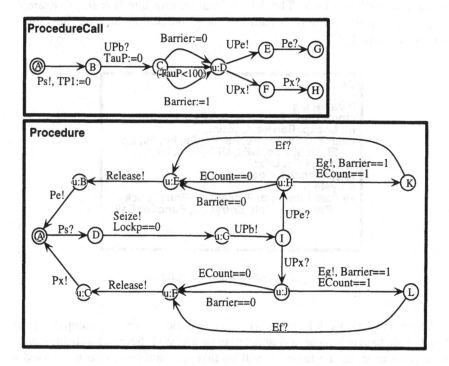

Fig. 1. The ProcedureCall and Procedure Automata.

Consider the model in figure 1. The model consists of 2 components, ProcedureCall and Procedure, with control nodes A, B, C, D, E, F, G, H and A, B, C, D, E, F, G, H, I, J, K, L, and uses two clocks TP1, TauP, and ten channels Ps, Pe, Px, Eg, Ef, UPb, UPe, UPx, Release, Seize. The edges of the automata are decorated with three types of optional labels;

- A guard, expressing a condition on the values of clocks and integer variables that must be satisfied in order for the edge to be taken. For example, the edge between Procedure.J and Procedure.F can only be taken when the value of the variable ECount equals zero.
- A synchronisation action, which is performed when the edge is taken. In figure 1, the two processes may communicate via the channels Ps, Pe, Px, UPb, UPe and UPx. The notation Ps! and Ps? denotes the complementary actions of sending and receiving on channel Ps. (The channels Release, Seize, Eg, and Ef synchronises with other automata.)
- A number of clock resets and assignments to integer variables. In figure 1, the clock TauP is reset to 0 when the transition from ProcedureCall.B and ProcedureCall.C is taken, similarly the integer variable Barrier is set to one, zero or unchanged whenever one of the transissions between nodes ProcedureCall.C and ProcedureCall.D is taken.

In addition to this, the control nodes may be decorated with invariants, which are conditions expressing constraints on the clock values in order for control to remain in a particular node. The default location invariant is *true*. For example, in figure 1, control can only remain in ProcedureCall.C as long as the value of TauP is less than 100.

```
Config

// Variables
clock TauF, TauP, TauE, TP1;
int Lockp, Barrier, ECount;
chan Es, Ee, Ex, Ps, Pe, Px, Fs, Fe, Fx, Eg,
     Ef, UEb, UEe, UEx, UPb, UPe, UPx,
     UFb, UFe, UFx;
urgent chan Release, Seize;
// System
system Function, Procedure, Entry, Lock,
     ProcedureCall, EntryCall, FunctionCall;
```

Fig. 2. Configuration information.

To prevent a network from delaying in a situation where two components are already able to synchronise, a channel may be declared (figure 2) as being *urgent*, i.e. as soon as it can be taken, it will be taken. A state can also be marked as being *urgent* (indicated by the u:-prefix), which is used if a component should make a number of transitions without being interrupted by any other component. For example the atomicity of the action sequence Ef?Release!Pe! in automaton Procedure is achieved by insisting that the urgent locations in between must be left immediately. An *urgent* state must be left in zero time, but it does not prevent other transitions to take place at the same time. If a transition from an urgent state is not possible to take at once, then the transition is considered as being impossible to take.

5 Modelling a Protected Object

The modelling phase can be separated into two steps, the environment (automata FunctionCall, ProcedureCall, and EntryCall), and modelling the PO in itself (automata Function, Procedure, Entry, and Lock). Figure 3 shows a flow-graph of the resulting model. Nodes represent automata and edges represent synchronisation channels.

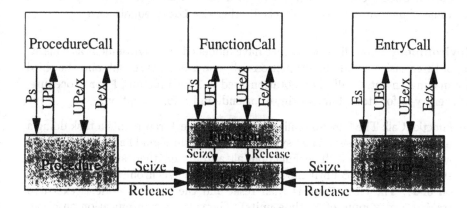

Fig. 3. A Flow-Graph of the Protected Object (shaded boxes) and its Environment.

The system uses six variables, of which three are clocks (TauF, TauE, TauP), and three are state variables (Barrier, ECount, and Lockp). In the following subsections we give a detailed description of the clocks, variables and automata of the system. The clock TP1 is only a decoration of the automata needed to verify properties of the system, see chapter 6.

Clocks Three different clocks are needed to simulate WCET for the protected operations. The clocks do not really measure the CPU time, but rather the real time it takes to execute the code. The WCET for executing the function, entry and procedure are in our example chosen arbitrarily. However, in an application the actual WCET would be used.

– TauF: The time it takes to read the function is bound to be less than 10 time units.
– TauE: The time for executing the entry code is always less than 50 time units.
– TauP: It will always take less than 100 time units to execute the procedure code.

Variables

– Barrier: The action of an entry call is provided by an entry body which has a boolean barrier condition that must be *true*/1 before the entry body can be executed. The value of the barrier is set by the application. If the barrier is *false*/0 then the calling task is queued until the barrier is set to *true* and the lock (see below) is open. The domain of Barrier is {0,1}.
– ECount: The number of tasks queueing for a protected entry. Tasks wait in the queue until the entry's barrier becomes *true*. The Ravenscar profile limits the number of tasks to one per entry, i.e. limiting the domain of ECount to {0,1}.
– Lockp: Each PO has a conceptual lock associated with it. Lockp has the value of one when the PO is locked, otherwise Lockp equals zero.

Environment In our first model, we have modelled the environment as consisting of three tasks, one doing a function call, one a procedure call, and the third one making an entry call. The notation used is F for function, P for procedure, E for entry, s for start, b for begin, e for end, and x for exception.

– FunctionCall: The FunctionCall automaton, figure 4, represents a task doing a function call. The signal Fs! synchronises with the signal Fs? in the Function automaton, figure 6. The FunctionCall automaton then suspends itself in state FunctionCall.B until the lock is seized and synchronisation takes place on UFb!. The clock TauF is then reset and the function code is executed (taking a maximum of 10 time units). Thereafter synchronisation on either UFe! or UFx!, the lock is released and either the synchronisation signal Fe! or Fx! is sent to the FunctionCall automaton depending on if the execution finished without or with an exception.

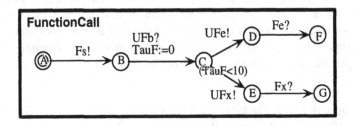

Fig. 4. The FunctionCall Automaton.

- ProcedureCall: The procedure call automaton, figure 1 (ProcedureCall component), starts by sending a synchronisation signal Ps! to the Procedure automaton, also shown in figure 1. It then suspends until the procedure has seized the lock. Thereafter a synchronisation signal UPb! is sent, the clock TauP is reset and the execution (state ProcedureCall.C) of the user code commence. This code may or may not change the value of the Barrier. The time spent executing the code is bounded to be less than 100 time units. If an exception occurs, the signal UPx! is sent, otherwise the signal UPe! is sent and the ProcedureCall automaton again suspends until the procedure has finished, and the PO either sends the signal Px! or Pe! depending on whether an exception should be propagated or not.
- EntryCall: The automaton for the task doing an entry call, figure 5, works much the same as the ProcedureCall automaton, the only differences are the name of the signals, and that the signals now synchronise with the Entry automaton, figure 7, in the PO. Finally the maximum time for executing the entry is bounded to be less than 50 time units.

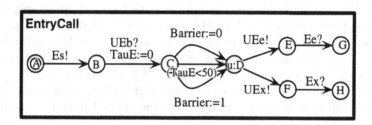

Fig. 5. The EntryCall Automaton.

Functionality The functionality of the PO is modelled by four automata, the Function, Procedure, Entry, and Lock.

- Function: A task that makes a function call, figure 4, synchronise on the signal Fs? between Function.A and Function.C in figure 6. The calling task gets suspended in state Function.C until the lock is free (i.e. variable Lockp is *false*/0). When the lock is free, the lock is seized and synchronisation on UFb! takes place. The Function automaton then suspends in state Function.G until the calling task has finished executing the code. When the signal UFe? or UFx? is received, the lock is released and depending on if there was an exception that should be propagated synchronisation on Fx! takes place, otherwise synchronisation on Fe!.
- Procedure: Inputs on channel Ps? requests a procedure call. The calling task, figure 1, is suspended at state Procedure.D until Lockp is *false*. If the lock is free, the lock is immediately taken (the channel Seize is declared as being an urgent channel, figure 2), the synchronisation signal UPb! is sent to the

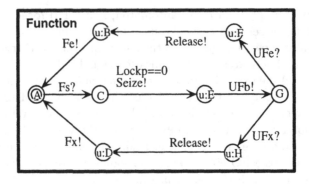

Fig. 6. The Function Automaton.

ProcedureCall automaton and the Procedure automaton suspends until either an exception occurred, which is signalled via UPx?, or until the signal UPe? is received. If there is no task waiting in the entry queue or the barrier is *false*, the automaton finishes by releasing the lock and synchronising on Pe! or Px!. If there is a task in the entry queue and the barrier is *true*, then that task has to be allowed to execute, which is done by synchronising on Eg!. The Procedure automaton then suspends in state Procedure.K or Procedure.L until synchronisation on signal Ef?, where-after it releases the lock and synchronise on Pe! or Px! as before. If there occured an exception while executing the entry code, that exception will be handled by the Entry automaton.

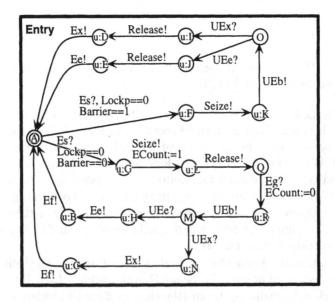

Fig. 7. The Entry Automaton.

– Entry: There is a queue, here represented by the variable ECount, associated
with each protected entry, figure 7. If the Barrier is *false* when a task
makes its entry call, the lock is seized and the task is queued. While waiting
in a queue, a task does not hold the lock, and becomes suspended in state
Entry.Q until a synchronisation on channel Eg? takes place. The entry code
is executed and any exceptions are propagated to the calling task, thereafter
synchronise on the signal Ef! to let the procedure finish its execution. On
the other hand, if the barrier is *true* and the lock is free when the task make
the entry call, the lock is seized at once, and the entry code is executed.
When finished, the lock is released and synchronisation on channel Ex! or
Ee! takes place.

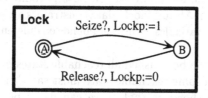

Fig. 8. The Lock Automaton.

– Lock: At the start of a protected operation, the calling task seizes the lock.
Evaluation of barriers, execution of protected operation bodies, and manipulation of entry queues are all done while the lock is held (i.e. Lockp equals
true/1). The handling of the lock is done by a separate automaton, figure 8.
If a task wants to seize a lock, then it has to synchronise on Seize?, the
variable Lockp gets the value of 1 and the task has the lock. To release the
lock the task synchronise on Release?, setting Lockp to zero.

5.1   Requirements on the System

To analyse various properties of the modelled system, the following informal
requirements and desired functionality of the protected object has to be verified.

1. Performance: The WCET for the user code is set to arbitrarily chosen values,
   i.e. 100 time units for the procedure, 50 for the entry code and 10 time units
   for the function code.
2. Predictability: The predictability requirements are to ensure strict synchronisation and control between components. The system should be free from
   dead-locks and live-locks. If there is as task queued, it must be allowed to
   execute if the barrier is *true* when the procedure code is executed. Any order
   between the calling tasks must be allowed.
3. Functionality: It should never be the case that there is more than one task
   executing the body of a protected object.

6 Formal Validation and Verification

In this section we formalise the informal requirements given in Section 5.1 and prove their correctness using the symbolic model-checker of UPPAAL.

UPPAAL is able to check for reachability properties [LPY97], in particular whether certain combinations of control-nodes and constraints on clock and data variables are reachable from an initial configuration. The properties that can be analysed are of the forms:

$$\varphi ::= \forall \Box \beta \mid \exists \Diamond \beta$$

$$\beta ::= a \mid \beta_1 \wedge \beta_2 \mid \neg \beta$$

Where a is an atomic formula being either an atomic clock/data constraint or a component location. Atomic clock/data constraints are either integer bounds on individual clock/data variables, or integer bounds on differences of two clock/data variables.

Intuitively, for $\forall \Box \beta$ to be satisfied all reachable states must satisfy β. Dually, for $\exists \Diamond \beta$ to be satisfied some reachable state must satisfy β.

The first property shown is that there can never be more than one task executing the body of a protected object. This is formulated by the following three logical statements.

1. A[] not(EntryCall.C and ProcedureCall.C)
2. A[] not(EntryCall.C and FunctionCall.C)
3. A[] not(ProcedureCall.C and FunctionCall.C)

The second property shown is that all eight possible end states after executing the PO is possible.

4. E<> (EntryCall.G and ProcedureCall.G and FunctionCall.F)
5. E<> (EntryCall.G and ProcedureCall.G and FunctionCall.G)
6. E<> (EntryCall.G and ProcedureCall.H and FunctionCall.F)
7. E<> (EntryCall.G and ProcedureCall.H and FunctionCall.G)
8. E<> (EntryCall.H and ProcedureCall.G and FunctionCall.F)
9. E<> (EntryCall.H and ProcedureCall.G and FunctionCall.G)
10. E<> (EntryCall.H and ProcedureCall.H and FunctionCall.F)
11. E<> (EntryCall.H and ProcedureCall.H and FunctionCall.G)

To show that a queued task always will be allowed to execute if the barrier is *true* the following formulas are needed.

12. A[] not(Entry.Q and Procedure.E and Barrier==1)
13. A[] not(Entry.Q and Procedure.F and Barrier==1)

The final property shown is that there is always an upper bounded time between when a task makes a procedure call and until the procedure call is finished executing. This property is stated as follows; the clock TP1 in automaton ProcedureCall gets the value of zero while synchronising on the signal `Ps!`. The clock `TP1` will at state `ProcedureCall.E` never be more than the maximum time for a function call, one entry call and the time it takes to execute the procedure call, i.e. clock `TP1` will not exceed 160 time units (10+50+100).

14. `A[] (ProcedureCall.E imply not(TP1 > 160))`

6.1 Verification Results

We have verified totally 14 properties of the system using UPPAAL and when the model checker is invoked it returns

```
Property 1 (line 1) is satisfied.
Property 2 (line 2) is satisfied.
Property 3 (line 3) is satisfied
...
Property 14 (line 14) is satisfied.
```

All 14 logical statements are said to be satisfied.

6.2 Extended Test of the Protected Object

There really is no way of having a general number of tasks in UPPAAL, and indeed not in any other approach based on model checking. We can not make a statement that the PO model is valid for any other number of tasks than the three used in the environment model above. As an experiment we have a model with three tasks executing the function body, two tasks executing the procedure and one task (limited by the Ravenscar model) executing the entry. The same kind of tests as above are made, and also this time all properties are satisfied.

7 Results and Discussion

A Run-Time System for Ada is a complex system. To model it using Formal Methods is not possible today. The Ravenscar restrictions may make it possible to model the complete run-time system in conjunction with a moderate sized application program. This is the expected outcome of the Mana project.

In the Ravenscar model the Protected Object plays an important role in the scheduling of tasks, synchronisation of concurrent activities and exchange of data between communicating tasks. Because of the fundamental role that the PO's play, they are modelled first.

The paper covers all of the semantics of Protected Objects according to the Ravenscar model. The verifications take roughly two seconds to compute on a pentium-class processor.

Although this is only a part of a complete run-time system it gives us good confidence that it is possible to accomplish a full run-time system.

The approach taken, to formally verify a system is adopted by some areas of safety critical applications, such as railway signaling systems [Cha98]. Other areas have taken the approach of certifying the systems. This certification relies upon the products of the development - machine code, executable images and test procedures to do this certification. Because of the significantly different approaches, it is today not clear how well formal verification of a system fits with certification of the system.

Given that the transformation between the formal model and the actual code can be verified, a formal verification must be a stronger evidence than code inspection and testing, especially when concurrency is being verified. In the case of code inspection and testing, the complexity of simultaneous tasks and states make it more or less impossible for a human to cover all possibilities. In the Formal approach a computer can check the whole state-space.

In this work some choices has been made which correspond to implementation choices in order to improve the analysis. The first choice was to model the entry queue as a single variable instead of an actual queue. The Ravenscar constraint that only a single caller be able to call any task entry is not a static property, hence runtime checks or detailed formal analysis of application is needed to prove this property. We have chosen to rely upon the analysis of application code to eliminate the runtime check. The second choice was to eliminate multiple protected function callers.

For a single cpu-system using the Immediate Inheritance Ceiling Protocol, multiple readers are not possible. Thus, there is no need for different locks.

After finalising the work with the Protected Object, the scheduler will be modelled. It will conform to the Immediate Inheritance Ceiling Protocol and we will integrate the scheduling with the model of the Protected Object. The final phase of the Mana project will be to model interrupts, integrate the pieces and do formal verification on small applications that can use the Ravenscar model.

References

[AD90] R. Alur, and D. Dill, "Automata for Modeling Real-Time Systems", Proceedings of the 17th International Colloquium on Automata, Languages and Programming, vol. 443, Springer-Verlag, 1990.

[Bar97] J. Barnes, "High Integrity Ada - The SPARK Approach", Addison Wesley, ISBN 0-201-17517-7, 1997.

[Bjo95] L. Björnfot, "Ada and Timed Automata", In proc. Ada Europe, Frankfurt, Germany, LNCS 1031, pp. 389-405, Springer-Verlag, Oct 1995.

[Cha98] Pierre Chapront, "Ada+B The Formula for Safety Critical Software Development", Ada Europe, Uppsala, Sweden, LNCS 1411, pp. 14-18, Springer-Verlag, June 1998.

[CO+95] J. Crow, S.Owre, J. Rushby, N. Shankar, and M. Srivas, "A tutorial introduction to PVS", WIFT'95: Workshop on Industrial-Strength Formal Specification Techniques, Boca Raton, Florida, April 1995.

[DB98] B. Dobbing and A. Burns, "The Ravenscar Tasking Profile for High Integrity Real-Time Programs", SIGAda'98, Nov 8-12, 1998.

[FW96] S. Fowler and A. Wellings, "Formal Analysis of a Real-Time Kernel Specification", FTRTFT'96, 1996

[FW97] S. Fowler and A. Wellings, "Formal Development of a Real-Time Kernel", 19th IEEE Real-Time Systems Symposium, Dec 1997.

[GMP90] David Guaspari, Carla Marceau, and Wolfgang Polak. Formal Verification of Ada Programs. IEEE Transactions on Software Engineering, vol. 16, no. 9, September 1990, pp. 1058-1075.

[HRG98] ISO/IEC PDTR 15942, Guidance on the Use of the Ada Programming Language in High Integrity Systems,

[HU79] J.E. Hopcroft and J.D. Ullman, "Introduction to Automata Theory, Languages and Computation", ISBN 0-201-02988-X, Addison-Wesley, 1979.

[Hut94] A. Hutcheon, "Safe Nucleus Formal Specification", Project Reference CI/GNSR/27: The Design and Development of Safety Kernel, Aug 1994.

[IRT99] To be published in Ada letters, spring 1999.

[JM86] F. Jahanian and A. K. Mok, "Safety analysis of timing properties in real-time systems", IEEE Transactions on Software Engineering, 12(9):890-904, Sept. 1986.

[LPY97] K.G. Larsen, P. Pettersson, and W. Yi, "UPPAAL in a Nutshell", Int. Journal on Software Tools for Technology Transfer, Springer-Verlag, vol 1, number 1-2, pp. 134-152, Oct 1997.

[Smi92] M.K. Smith, The AVA Reference Manual: Derived from ANSI/MIL-STD-1815A-1983, Computational Logic Inc., Feb. 1992

[Tol95] R.M. Tol, "Formal Design of a Real-Time Operating System Kernel", Ph.D. thesis, University of Groningen, 1995.

[WB97] A. Wellings and A. Burns, "Workshop Report", The Eighth International Real-Time Ada Workshop (IRTAW8), Ada User Journal, vol 18, number 2, June 1997.

An Ada Runtime System Implementation of the Ravenscar Profile for High Speed Application-Layer Data Switch

Mike Kamrad and Barry Spinney

Top Layer Networks, Inc.
2400 Computer Drive
Westborough MA 01581
USA
+1.508.870.1300 x139 and x121
kamrad@TopLayer.com
spinney@TopLayer.com

Abstract. The Top Layer Networks AppSwitch™ is a coordinated hardware and software Layer 7-application switch designed to provide Application Control for data communication networks by automatically prioritizing network traffic according to the user and the application that is generating the messages. The AppSwitch™ software was developed in Ada95 (A companion paper describes how that software was built [1]). The nature of the application and the need for efficiency has dictated that the use of multiple task communication and synchronization be kept simple and straightforward. As a result, the communication and synchronization needs are very similar those defined in the Ravenscar Profile. Top Layer Networks found it necessary to construct an Ada runtime system that efficiently supported the Ravenscar Profile. The paper will describe the details of our Ravenscar Profile and will summarize its impact on the performance of the AppSwitch™ software.

1 Introduction

Top Layer Networks (formerly BlazeNet) is a new data communication product company, whose new product, the AppSwitch™ 2000, uses Ada as its implementation language. Top Layer Networks found it necessary to "build" a bare-machine runtime system that supports the Ravenscar Profile. This goal of this paper is to familiarize the reader with the motivation, design guidelines and decisions and the experience of the effort to build that implementation. The paper is divided as follows: Section 2 gives a brief description of the purpose of the AppSwitch™ 2000; Section 3 provides a short summary of the hardware and software structure of the AppSwitch™ 2000. Together they give the reader some context for motivation and constraints on the implementation. Section 4 describes why Ada was chosen, a short summary of the Ravenscar Profile and the motivation for doing a "custom" implementation. Section 5 lists the guidelines for the Top Layer implementation. Section 6 goes into some details of the implementation by providing an overview of the architecture of the runtime system, comparing it with the previous architecture of the GNAT runtime system and highlighting some interesting features of the implementation. Section 7 concludes the paper with comments on the Top Layer Networks experience in building and using the Ravenscar Profile. The Appendix contains the specification of the major interfaces of the runtime implementation.

2 Quality of Service for the Rest of Us

Usage in enterprise networks often conflicts with business goals. Large database email messages can slow down urgent database queries or bandwidth intensive Web browsing may block e-commerce. While faster networks provide some relief, without network policies enforcing quality of service (QoS), there are no guarantees. By modulating bandwidth consumption between time-critical transactions and less urgent bandwidth hogs, QoS can increase network efficiency and reduce operation costs.

Until recently QoS has been expensive and difficult to implement. The AppSwitch™ family of LAN/WAN switches is designed to change that situation. AppSwitches analyze application traffic and enforce QoS policies automatically, namely, with no human intervention and no changes to PCs or servers. This is accomplished with coordination of hardware to examine and switch traffic at wire speed and software to guide switching, and therefore network performance, according to business goals.

At the same time, monitoring and managing network performance has become extremely complex. With the integrated hardware and software architecture, the AppSwitch™ enables the network administrator to monitor and understand all the elements of the network and to adapt the network to changes, all through a Web-based graphical user interface.

More details on the capabilities of the AppSwitch™ can be found on our Web page at www.TopLayer.com/pdf/whitec.pdf.

3 The Chief Elements of the AppSwitch™ Hardware and Software Architecture

At the core of the AppSwitch™ (see Figure 1) are the hardware and software components that constitute flow classification technology. With this technology, the AppSwitch™ can go deep into the incoming packets, up to Layer 7 headers that applications produce to determine source and destination addresses and application types of that packet. The AppSwitch™ flow classification is supported by the pre-configured Application Profile Library (APL) that is built into every switch and that holds the rules for flow classification and prioritization. The APL is extensible and adaptable to capture future applications and to reflect an enterprise's business requirements.

At the arrival of the first packets of a flow, the AppSwitch™ uses the a connection setup process subarchitecture to select the appropriate "tailored" profile in the APL and to establish pertinent information on the new flow, which is captured in the Session database. After that, remaining packets in the flow are switched through the coordination of the Session data and the selected profile. The state data captured by each flow in the Session database can intelligently adjust QoS as needed to upgrade or downgrade priority. On the output side, there are thousands of queues available to expand the number of flows and priorities among those flows.

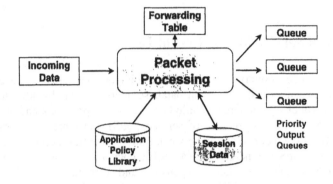

Fig. 1. Application Switching

Completing the picture of the AppSwitch™ architecture, Figure 2 shows the supporting elements to facilitate LAN and WAN data communication and to get the network administrator systematic control of the network.

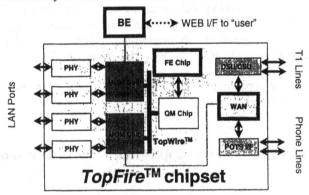

Fig. 2. Overview of AppSwitch™ Major Elements

Besides the components to handle the LAN connections, the AppSwitch™ includes a WAN subsystem to handle both T1 and phone lines in an integrated manner. Incoming packets from both LAN and WAN connections are subjected to proprietary "triage" by the Media Access Control Function (MOM) components to make very broad categorization of the packets and to put the packets into a canonical form that is data link independent. From there, the "categorized" packets flow over the TopWire to the Forwarding Engine (FE Chip + QM Chip) where the Application Switching is performed. Output packets flow back out of the Forwarding Engine to their destination over the TopWire where MOM components reverse the effect of the canonicalization of the packets before they are transmitted to the LAN and WAN connections.

At the top of the AppSwitch™ architecture is the Background Engine (BE) which functions as a backup switch to the Forwarding Engine, the "mission control" computer of the AppSwitch™ and the user interface to the network administrator. In its "mission control" role, the BE has numerous "agents" that monitor and control all aspects of the AppSwitch™. In its user interface role, the BE contains the facilities to serve the Web-based interface that can be displayed on any computer on the network.

There are three programmable processors in the system: the Background Engine, the Forwarding Engine and the WAN subsystem processor. Both processors in the Background and Forwarding Engines are based on the ARC Cores (formerly Argonaut RISC Cores) processor. where it was developed originally for computer games. The ARC is a RISC microprocessor solution for embedded applications, that is provided as a VHDL macro, which has been tailored to meet the specific needs of the AppSwitch™. The WAN subsystem is powered by the MPC860, which is a PPC-based member of the Motorola QUICC family, consisting of the CPU and additional hardware features for handling communications.

Both the Forwarding Engine and the WAN subsystem are singly focused architectures, requiring only a single task (or thread) to do their jobs. Consequently, their software executes without the support of an Ada runtime system and the GNAT compilation adequately supports no runtime system execution with the Restrictions pragma. Conversely, the Background Engine must handle multiple activities concurrently and its software must be supported by an Ada runtime system. It is for the Background Engine that Top Layer Networks built its own Ada runtime implementation.

More details on the architecture of the AppSwitch™ are described in [1].

4 Why Ada and A Custom Ada Runtime System Implementation

Ada was chosen as the programming language for AppSwitch™ software to provide high reliability and portability. This software must work right the first time and continue to execute in the presence of faults and software reconfiguration. The software for the AppSwitch™ is expected to have a long lifetime, therefore the programming language must be able to be ported between different target machines and generations of target machines. Ada has the best combination of language features for both high reliability and portability, including strong typing, object-oriented programming, multi-tasking and exception handling.

GNAT was chosen as the tool chain because it was based on GCC. Only GCC was targeted to the ARC processor. Additionally, Top Layer Network needed to have greater control over the internal mechanisms of the Ada tool chain that only GNAT and GCC provided.

As you will see from a the list of motivations shown below, much about Ravenscar Profile was appealing for the use of Ada on the Background Engine. The appeal of Ravenscar Profile was based on two major points. The nature of the Background Engine software architecture requires a limited use of Ada tasking communication and synchronization features. There is no need for Ada tasks to directly communicate with each other. Any communication between tasks can be done by protected objects.

All protected objects are either entry-less or need only one entry call. The single entry protected objects are best characterized by being used as event queues, which are serviced by only a single task. It became clear that Top Layer's Ada usage nearly matched those of the Ravenscar Profile. The existence of the Ravenscar Profile and the apparent acceptance of it (or slight variations of it) by the Ada community made a compelling argument to following its restrictions, because of the increased likelihood supporting implementations.

Top Layer Networks was motivated to build a custom implementation of Ravenscar Profile Ada runtime system because:

- Due to the nature of the engineering development, the developers require great control of key elements of the architecture. The size and speed of the executable code of the Background Engine is one of those key elements. It simply must be known what is happening in the Ada runtime system to have confidence in its performance.

- The only public domain Ada runtime system targeted to embedded systems, RTEMS [2], was assessed as being too general and excessive for use on the Background Engine. Furthermore the level of effort to integrate RTEMS with our target and to trim it down to meet our simplified usage was considered to be as large as a new implementation of a Ravenscar Profile runtime system. And we would never know as much about it as we would know about the custom implementation.

- Top Layer Networks possessed uniquely experienced engineering talent, capable of tackling an Ada runtime implementation effort.

Consequently Top Layer Networks proceed to build a Ravenscar Profile Ada runtime system for a bare-machine by starting with the existing GNAT Ada runtime system and trimming it down to size.

5   Design Guidelines for the Ravenscar Profile Ada Runtime System Implementation

A set of guidelines was developed that would ensure the resulting implementation would serve the Top Layer current and future needs.

- The underlying "kernel" will be designed from the start to execute on a bare-machine. No consideration will be given to executing overtop another operating system.

- There will no upward dependencies among the layers of software in the Ada runtime system. This makes the design of the Ada runtime system more hierarchical, less complex and more easily portable to new processors.

- The architecture must isolate the specific machine dependencies of the ARC processor not only for technical reasons but also legal reasons as the ARC ISA is considered intellectual property of Argonaut.

- Since building and maintaining Ada runtime systems is not our core competency, the implementation must continue to be supported by the GNAT compilation system. Therefore simplification of the Ada runtime must be constrained so that it still supports the GNAT compiler interface. ACT will be consulted to ensure this compatibility. For their part, ACT has used the Restrictions pragma to simplify the GNAT compiler interface for the Ravenscar Profile usage.

- Ada will be used for new software that will be developed. Consequently, except for the public domain malloc software module and the lowest level machine dependent software, all Ada runtime system code has been implemented in Ada.
- The underlying "kernel" layer of the Ada runtime system must be able to support the execution of modules written in C, for legacy and development flexibility reasons. Consequently, the interface of the kernel must restrict its Ada usage to only those features that C language can use.
- Closely connected to the previous guideline is that the interface of the underlying "kernel" must comply with the POSIX time interface, again for legacy and development flexibility reasons.
- Future growth of the Background Engine architecture includes the dynamic loading and execution of "extension modules". Top Layer determined that the implementation and interactions of these extension modules are best encapsulated as processes or Ada partitions. Consequently, the architecture of the runtime system must accommodate the addition of processes/partitions to the implementation.
- A high level of instrumentation will be provided to support both the development of the runtime system and, later, the usage of resources by the Background Engine software.
- The underlying "kernel" must support both priority-based preemptive scheduling and time-slicing with priority to prevent thread starvation.

6 Overview of the Implementation

6.1 Baseline

Baseline for the implementation of the Ravenscar Profile Ada runtime system was the existing GNAT Ada runtime system. The design of GNAT has been documented in a series of papers by Dr. Ted Baker and his students of Florida State University [3]. At the risk of over simplification, the architecture is divided into four layers:

- an Ada dependent layer at the top where are the Ada-specific runtime semantics are handled; the interface to this layer, called GNARLI, is defined in [3]:
- an intermediate layer, which supports the Ada dependent layer with an operating system independent set of operations; the interface to this layer is called the GNULLI, is defined by the following collection of modules:
- a lower layer which provides a "thin" binding between the intermediate layer and the underlying kernel of operating system primitives; interface and implementation is highly influenced by POSIX standard; the implementation of this layer is usually provided by the supplier of the underlying kernel or operating system.
- the underlying kernel or operating system, which may or may not be a POSIX-like operating system.

6.2 Differences

The construction strategy was to tailor the GNAT runtime system in three ways: (1) Simplify the functionality of the Ada specific layer of the runtime system to support only the Ravenscar-like profile; (2) Reduce number and the "thickness" of layers in GNAT runtime system; and (3) Construct a POSIX-compatible "kernel" that is simplified for bare machine execution. The architecture of Top Layer Ravenscar Profile Ada runtime system, as described by Figure 3, differs from the GNAT baseline in these main ways:

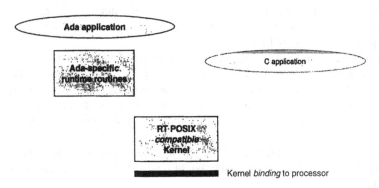

Fig. 3. Architecture of Ravenscar Profile Runtime System

- The Ada-dependent layer has been significantly reduced to only support those features in the Ravenscar Profile; the result is that only the following modules remain in the GNARLI interface:

System.Tasking   System.Tasking.Stages
System.Tasking.Protected_Objects   System.Tasking_Soft_Link
System.Task_Specific_Data   System.Task_Info
Ada.Exceptions   System.Exceptions
System.Exception_Table
System.Standard_Library   System.Parameters

The reduction of the GNARLI is made possible by the strict use of the Restrictions pragma to ensure the compiler does not invoke any of the operations from the module that have been deleted. The specific set of specifications for the Restrictions pragma is:

```
pragma Restrictions
  (Max_asynchronous_select_nesting => 0, Max_select_alternatives => 0,
  Max_task_entries => 0, Max_protected_entries => 1, Max_tasks => n,
  No_asynchronous_control, No_dynamic_priorities, No_task_allocators,
  No_terminate_alternatives, No_abort_statements, No_task_hierarchy)
```

- The intermediate layer has been eliminated. Much of its functionality of this layer has been moved down to the "kernel" and the remaining functionality has been explicitly "inlined" throughout the Ada dependent layer. Some type declarations remain in System.Task_Primitives and a private package System.Task_Objects.
- The underlying kernel is divided among three major modules:

- Kernel.Threads, which performs thread management in a processor independent manner
- Kernel.Process, which performs process management in a processor independent manner
- Kernel.CpuPrimitives, which encapsulates all the machine dependent operations to handle machine state and interrupts and acts as the lowest layer in Ada runtime system. Its specification is known only to the underlying kernel.
- Kernel.Memory, which performs real memory management
- Kernel.Time, which provides low-level time type and operations
- Kernel.Parameters, which contains constants for use only by the Kernel layer.
- Kernel.Exceptions, which performs low-level exception management
- Kernel.Crash, which logs significant machine state before resetting
- Kernel.IO, which is the interface to a flash disk device.

The specification for Kernel.Threads can be found in the Appendix and rest can be found at our Web site (www.TopLayer.com). Note that the specifications for all mdules are defined so that they can be used by C programs.

6.3 Highlights

To go into all the details of implementation would significantly exceed our paper limit, so, instead, the following highlights are presented to provide insight and the flavor of the implementation:

- As expected, the restrictions of the Ravenscar Profile had a significant impact on the size of the Ada-dependent layer. In particular, elimination of these features had the most impact: asynchronous transfer of control, requeue, rendezvous and task hierarchies.
- The implementation does not adhere completely to the restrictions in the Ravenscar Profile. These differences are due in large part to the fact that the Background Engine software is not strictly a hard real-time application. This is not to say that meeting deadlines isn't important but rather elimination of some restrictions permits greater flexibility in our software architecture to accommodate the dynamic nature of data communications The major differences are:
  - Dynamic memory management is permitted; further details are described below.
  - Dynamic allocation of protected objects is permitted.
  - Eventually, dynamic creation and termination of tasks will be permitted as part of the dynamic execution of extension modules.
  - Timed entry and conditional entry calls are permitted.

    It is Top Layer's opinion that permitting these exceptions does not add significant weight to the implementation.
- At this point, the compiler interface prevents further simplification. One example of this is the compiler anticipates that tasks have entries and protected objects having more than one entry; consequently, the underlying system data structures continue to be burdened with unnecessary information about entries. The organization of the Ada-dependent modules could be further simplified with the elimination of unnecessary modules and operations that compiler anticipates

using. Creating a special compiler interface would help but this is a non-trivial decision on the part of any Ada vendor.

- Only a single lock is used to synchronize operations in the Ada runtime system. The paper [4] by Dr. Baker and his students convinced us that in our particular situation, where the Ada runtime will be executing only on a single processor, the saving in eliminating the overhead for multiple locks would offset the blocking costs.

- Thread control blocks are now physically separated from the Ada task control blocks. This permits the underlying kernel to transparently support both Ada tasks and C threads. Furthermore it is transparent as to how the thread control blocks are created. Currently, they are dynamically allocated but they could be easily statically allocated.

- Interrupt handling and management required special attention, in two particular ways:
  – Instead of using a protected procedure to encapsulate the interrupt handler code, the underlying kernel now permits any parameter-less procedure to encapsulate the handler code.
  – Using parameter-less procedures to encapsulate the handler code is supported by the fact that all interrupts that are user-definable have their own thread along with an associated thread control block. This also permits the execution of the interrupt handler code to be scheduled and dispatched like any other thread.

- The interface provided by the underlying kernel is POSIX compliant insofar as the POSIX operation that is supplied takes advantage of the flexibility in the definition of that operation. In particular, the semantics for the POSIX operations use permissions in the POSIX standard to simplify their implementation and use. As an example, there are no spurious wakeup signals permitted in the Ada runtime system when threads are performing a conditional wait. Spurious wakeup signals were permitted in the current GNAT runtime system because it was implemented over the POSIX compliant systems that permitted them. As single processor bare-machine implementation, our underlying kernel does not handle any spurious wakeup signals and passes the simplification along to the rest of the runtime system.

- An idle thread exists to perform background testing and to simplify the queuing of thread control blocks.

- The management of dynamic memory is done on two layers. At the lowest layer, Kernel.Memory manages all heap storage in fixed length blocks of 512 bytes. In doing so, it keeps the mapping of allocated and free blocks separate from the block themselves to minimize the potential of corruption by users. It also keeps track of who has allocated block and how blocks are allocated. Except for requests from the Kernel.Threads module, all other requests to Kernel.Memory come through a malloc module or a dynamic storage pool mechanism. The malloc module supports the standard storage pool requests and it is based on the excellent publicly available implementation by Doug Lea [5] and has been simplified to work with the Kernel.Memory. The dynamic storage pool mechanism is a generic constructed around an extension to Root_Storage_Pool; it enables clients of this generic to micro-manage individual storage pools. Both mechanisms cooperate with Kernel.Memory to keep track of how memory is being allocated.

7 Experience So Far

At the time of this writing, we have just completed and tested the Ada runtime system and it is supporting our AppSwitch™ in beta-testing. Therefore our comments can only reflect that experience:

- The effort to build and test the runtime software took about 16 weeks of time, performed by two engineers. Our investment in instrumentation paid off handsomely in uncovering the sources of some very nasty timing bugs. All in all, we strongly believe that our investment in the whole effort was well justified for both technical and economic reasons.

- Unfortunately there is no other full-semantics Ada runtime system baseline on which to compare the performance savings accumulated by the implementation of our version of the Ravenscar Profile runtime system. Judging by the amount of code that was removed and simplified, we think that the savings are considerable. To quantify the savings would require much more effort than Top Layer can afford to invest.

- Over the next several months, we will continue to improve and extend the implementation. Two examples are optimizing exception handling and adding the process/partition capability.

References

1. Kamrad, M.: An Application (Layer 7) Routing Switch with Ada95 Software, 1999 Ada-Europe Conference.
2. On-Line Application Research Corporation: Real-Time Executive for Military Systems: Ada Applications User's Guide. Release 3.2.X, May 1995.
3. Baker, T., Giering, E.: PART/GNARL Interface Definition. Version 1.24. Florida State University, Aug. 1993.
4. Oh, D., Baker, T.: Optimization of Ada'95 Tasking Constructs, TriAda'97, St. Louis Missouri USA, 1997.
5. Lea, D.: A Memory Allocator. unix/mail. December, 1996.

Appendix A: Specifications for Kernel.Threads, Kernel.Memory and Kernel.CpuPrimitives

```
--    Copyright (C) 1998 Free Software Foundation, Inc.    --
with Kernel.CpuPrimitives, Kernel.Time, System;
package Kernel.Threads is
   package KCP renames Kernel.CpuPrimitives;
   package KT  renames Kernel.Time;

   EAGAIN    : constant := 11;
   EFAULT    : constant := 14;
   EINTR     : constant := 4;
   EINVAL    : constant := 22;
   ENOMEM    : constant := 12;
   ETIMEDOUT constant := 116;

   type thread_t is mod 256;
   subtype ThreadIdType is thread_t;

   function IsValid (threadId : ThreadIdType) return Boolean;

   type mutex_t      is limited private;
   type cond_t       is limited private;

   nullThreadId : constant thread_t;

   type thread_attr_t is
      record
      priority    : Integer;
      stackCheck  : Boolean;
      stackSize   : Integer;
      end record;

   defaultAttr : constant thread_attr_t := (0, true, 0);

   function  thread_create (attr         : thread_attr_t;
                            startRoutine : System.Address;
                            startArg     : System.Address)
                            return         thread_t;
   function  thread_self return thread_t;
   function  thread_get_priority (threadId : thread_t)
             return Integer;
   procedure thread_set_priority (threadId : thread_t;
                                  priority : Integer);
   procedure thread_yield;
   procedure thread_kill (threadId : thread_t);
   procedure thread_exit;  pragma No_Return (thread_exit);

   function thread_get_taskId return System.Address;
   function thread_get_errno  return Integer;
   function thread_get_pid    return Integer;

   procedure thread_set_taskId (taskId : System.Address);
   procedure thread_set_errno  (errno  : Integer);
   procedure thread_set_pid    (pid    : Integer);
```

```
procedure mutex_init      (mutex : in out mutex_t;
                           ceiling_prio : Integer);
procedure mutex_lock      (mutex : in out mutex_t);
procedure mutex_unlock    (mutex : in out mutex_t);
procedure mutex_destroy   (mutex : in out mutex_t);

procedure cond_init       (cond   : in out cond_t);
procedure cond_wait       (cond   : in out cond_t;
                           mutex : in out mutex_t);
procedure cond_timedwait  (cond   : in out cond_t;
                           mutex : in out mutex_t;
                           wakeupTime : in  KT.TimeType);
procedure cond_signal     (cond   : in out cond_t);
procedure cond_destroy    (cond   : in out cond_t);

procedure pause;
procedure sleep   (wakeupTime : KT.TimeType);
procedure resume (threadId   : thread_t);

type HandlerPtrType is access procedure;
function CurrentHandler (id : KCP.Interrupt_ID)
         return HandlerPtrType;
function AttachHandler (id          : KCP.Interrupt_ID;
                        newHandler : HandlerPtrType;
                        taskId      : Address;
                        priority    : Integer)
                        return        ThreadIdType;

--   ThreadCycleCount is a 64 signed integer which represents the
--   total  number of processor clock cycles consumed by a thread
--   as it executes instructions, since the thread was first
--   created.  It should never be negative.
type ThreadCycleCount is new Standard.Long_Long_Integer;
for  ThreadCycleCount'Size use 64;

type ThreadInfoType is
   record
   heapSize  : Integer;
   stackSize : Integer;
   execTime  : ThreadCycleCount;
   end record;
type ThreadInfoPtrType is access all ThreadInfoType;
function  GetThreadTime return ThreadCycleCount;
procedure GetThreadInfo (threadId : thread_t;
                         infoPtr : ThreadInfoPtrType);

procedure UpdateHeapSize (heapSizeChange : Integer);

type ThreadStatsType is
   record
   spuriousCondSignals   : aliased Integer;
   spuriousResumes       : aliased Integer;

   threadPreemptions     : aliased Integer;
   threadYields          : aliased Integer;
   threadBlocks          : aliased Integer;
   threadUnblocks        : aliased Integer;
   threadInits           : aliased Integer;
   threadDestroys        : aliased Integer;
```

```
      changeMyPriorities     : aliased Integer;
      changeOtherPriorities  : aliased Integer;
      timerInserts           : aliased Integer;
      timerRemoves           : aliased Integer;
      timerAwakens           : aliased Integer;
      mutexInits             : aliased Integer;
      mutexDestroys          : aliased Integer;
      mutexLocks             : aliased Integer;
      mutexUnlocks           : aliased Integer;
      condInits              : aliased Integer;
      condDestroys           : aliased Integer;
      condWaits              : aliased Integer;
      condTimedWaits         : aliased Integer;
      condSignals            : aliased Integer;
      pauses                 : aliased Integer;
      sleeps                 : aliased Integer;
      resumes                : aliased Integer;
      attachHandlerCalls     : aliased Integer;
      interruptCallbacks     : aliased Integer;
      timerCallbacks         : aliased Integer;
      timerPreemptions       : aliased Integer;
      timeSliceExpirations   : aliased Integer;
      end record;
   type ThreadStatsPtrType is access all ThreadStatsType;

   procedure GetThreadStats (statsPtr : ThreadStatsPtrType);
private

   type ThreadQueueType is
      record  --  TBD. Should we also keep a thread count?
      first : System.Address;
      last  : System.Address;
      end record;
   pragma Suppress_Initialization (ThreadQueueType);

   type mutex_t is limited
      record
      owner              : System.Address; -- Is non-null when locked.

      -- Holds the priority of locking thread.
      previousPriority : Integer; ceilingPriority  : Integer;
      chain              : System.Address;
      end record;
   pragma Suppress_Initialization (mutex_t);

   type cond_t is limited
      record
      threadQueue : aliased ThreadQueueType;
      chain       : System.Address;
      end record;
   pragma Suppress_Initialization (cond_t);
end Kernel.Threads;
```

Re-engineering a Safety-Critical Application Using SPARK 95 and GNORT

Roderick Chapman[1] and Robert Dewar[2]

[1] Praxis Critical Systems Limited, 20 Manvers St., Bath BA1 1PX, UK,
rod@praxis-cs.co.uk,
http://www.praxis-cs.co.uk/
[2] Ada Core Technologies Inc., 73 Fifth Avenue, 11B, New York, NY 10003, USA,
dewar@gnat.com,
http://www.gnat.com/

Abstract. This paper describes a new development of the GNAT Ada95 compilation system (GNORT) that is appropriate for the development of high integrity embedded systems. We describe GNORT, the motivation for its development, and give some technical detail of its implementation. The latter part of the paper goes on to describe SHOLIS—an existing safety-critical application written in SPARK 83 that has been re-engineered to take advantage of SPARK 95 and GNORT. We assess the benefits of this approach through metrics on the SHOLIS application source and object code. These data may be of interest to engineers who are considering Ada95 for a new project or converting an existing Ada83 application to Ada95.

Keywords. High Integrity Systems. Ada Language and Tools.

1 Introduction

This paper describes GNAT-No-Runtime (GNORT)—a development of the GNAT Ada 95 compiler that is appropriate for the production of high integrity embedded systems. We also describe an existing safety-critical application (SHOLIS) which has been re-engineered using GNORT. This work was carried out with two major goals:

- To evaluate if the subset of Ada 95 allowed by GNORT is a superset of the language supported by SPARK 95,[1] and to provide its developers with early feedback on its performance when used to compile a real-world application.
- To evaluate the improvement (in terms of program size, object code quality etc.) that can be gained from re-engineering an existing application using SPARK 95 and GNORT.

Implementations of Ada95 are now beginning to appear which are (at least claimed to be) suitable for high integrity systems. Engineers may be considering Ada95 for

---

[1] The SPARK programming language is not sponsored by or affiliated with SPARC International Inc. and is not based on the SPARC™ architecture.

new projects, or converting existing applications to Ada95, but there is little empirical evidence to suggest what benefits may be gained from such a change. This paper hopes to address this need, at least within the context of high integrity, embedded systems.

The remainder of the paper is structured as follows. Section 2 describes GNORT, covering its goals, design and implementation, and gives a comparison with other high integrity Ada compilation systems. Section 3 gives a brief outline of the SHOLIS system. Section 4 describes how SHOLIS was re-engineered to take advantage of SPARK 95 and the facilities offered by GNORT. Sections 5 and 6 offer thoughts on further work and conclusions.

2 GNORT

2.1 The motivation for the development of GNORT

The notion of a "run time library" is a relatively new one that has appeared in connection with more advanced high level languages. Certainly there were library routines accessed by a typical Fortran program, but the development of complex language semantics (for example tasking and exception handling) that require run-time code for support of basic language semantics, introduces new considerations into the development of safety-critical code that must be certified.

Two approaches are possible. Either the run-time library must itself be certified, or it must be eliminated. Some other Ada systems have pursued the first approach, but not only is this an expensive process, possibly requiring major reengineering of the run-time, but it is also procedurally awkward, because it means that the ultimate application must depend on a "foreign" certification, and in particular, it is difficult to deal with varying certification requirements.

For these reasons, we decided to adopt the second approach, of eliminating the run-time system entirely. This completely solves the certification problem, since there is no run-time to be certified, and the entire code of the executable image is derived directly from the customer's application, and certified in a manner that meets the particular certification needs of the application.

The only disadvantage of this approach is that it requires the language to be fairly severely subsetted. Front-end features like generics, child packages, derived types etc are not affected, but fundamental run-time facilities such as tasking and exception handling must be eliminated. However, in practice many, if not most, safety-critical applications are already committed to using a small subset of the language for certification reasons, so in practice the limitations introduced by this subsetting may be entirely acceptable. As a measure of this, it is interesting to note that GNORT can handle all the Ada language constructs that appear in the SPARK language[5].

2.2 Potential uses of GNORT in the development of high integrity systems

The use of Ada in high integrity systems is attractive for many reasons. In particular the strong abstraction facilities, and strong typing semantics of Ada, which mean that many errors can be caught at compile time, can substantially contribute to the reliability of applications, and thus the ease of generating high integrity systems. It is important to note that we are concentrating here on the static semantic facilities of Ada that provide compile time security, not on the more elaborate run-time facilities, such as exceptions, which are unlikely to be used anyway in safety-critical systems.

Clearly it is feasible to develop high integrity systems using much lower level languages that completely lack a run-time system, such as C. The use of GNORT means that the run-time model is roughly comparable to that of C, that is it is constrained to be very simple. However, the great advantage of GNORT is that this simplicity can be achieved without sacrificing the careful high-level design of Ada 95 that provides excellent abstraction facilities and strong compile time checking capabilities.

The fact that GNAT is committed to using standard system formats for all generated files, including the output of debugging information means that a very simple compilation model can be used with GNORT. The Ada units are simply compiled, and standard system format object files are produced. These object files can then be processed using any standard tool chain. The use of Ada in this manner does not introduce any Ada-specific difficulties in terms of the tool chain or run-time environment. The debugging information is carefully designed to be usable with a C-style debugger, but contains encodings that a more elaborate Ada knowledgeable debugger can use to provide full access to Ada data structures

2.3   The implementation of GNORT

The first step in the implementation of GNORT was to provide a configuration pragma *No_Run_Time* that restricts the features of the language that can be used. Basically this acts like a set of Restrictions pragmas, and causes fatal errors to be issued if any features are used that would require the run-time library to be accessed. The binder was also modified to check that this pragma is used uniformly on all units in a partition, to eliminate the automatic inclusion of a basic set of run-time routines, and to generate an entirely stand-alone main program.

Once these modifications were completed, a problem became immediately apparent, in that the subset of the language that could be supported depended on whether inlining was active. Inlining is activated in Ada 95 by the use of the *Inline* pragma, but in addition GNAT requires that the *-gnatn* switch be specified. In the presence of *-gnatn*, a number of important features, including dynamic dispatching, could be accomodated in GNORT mode, since the bodies of the run-time routines, consisting of a few machine instructions, could be inlined into the generated code, eliminating the need for the run-time routine itself.

To take advantage of this opportunity to extend the subset that could be accomodated, we implemented a pragma *Inline_Always* that would inline even if *-gnatn* were not specified, and applied this pragma to a number of critical routines, thus significantly extending the subset that could be handled in GNORT mode. A corresponding change was required in the binder, to understand that even though a routine from a run-time library unit had been called, the run-time unit itself was not required after the inlining of the body.

2.4 GNORT and other high integrity Ada compilation systems

GNORT represents a simple and cost-effective approach to meeting the requirement for certified high- integrity code. The subset provided is large enough to allow most of the important facilities of Ada to be used. It is interesting to compare GNORT with the Aonix C-SMART system[4]. Both these systems provide a subset of Ada, and indeed the subsets are very similar. The important difference is that the Aonix approach requires a small run-time system, and certifying even a small run-time system is an expensive proposition, so this approach is definitely not a low-cost one.

Aonix has also recently announced the Raven product, which extends the system to include the Ravenscar profile[6] for limited tasking. This requires additional run-time support. There are two possible extensions to the GNAT technology to provide similar capabilities. The first, called GNARP (GNAT No-Runtime with Ravenscar Profile) relies on the use of the Java VM in the context of the JGNAT (Ada 95 to JVM) product. The native tasking provided by the JVM is very simple, but is powerful enough to support in-line generation of all the Ravenscar tasking constructs. In conjunction with a Java chip that provides this tasking support in hardware, this means that the pure GNORT approach can be extended to cover the Ravenscar Profile.

In other environments, a different approach is required. GNAT now provides a restricted run-time option that corresponds almost exactly to the Ravenscar profile. Our future development will simplify this restricted run-time, and we can either provide a certified component that implements this run-time, or, probably more practically, document the very simple interface required, and expect the application to provide the necessary simple tasking constructs.

One more comment that is relevant here is that the open-source model of software distribution embraced by GNAT is particularly well suited to our no run-time approach. In a proprietary model, the fact that GNORT is in a sense "nothing", would make it difficult to charge money for the product itself. On the other hand, the open source model in which the charge is primarily for support, can accommodate this approach with no difficulty. Ada Core Technologies charges a modest (25% additional) fee over the normal support fee to provide full support for the GNORT feature, to cover the special additional support issues raised by the use of embedded tool chains.

3 SHOLIS

The Ship/Helicopter Operational Limits Instrumentation System (SHOLIS) is a ship-borne computer system that advises ship's crew on the safety of helicopter operations under various scenarios. It is a fault-tolerant, real-time, embedded system and is the first system constructed to meet the requirements of Interim Defence Standard 00-55[1] for safety-critical software.

IDS 00-55 sets some bold challenges: it calls for formalised safety management and quality systems, formal specification of the systems behaviour, formal proof (at both the specification and code levels), fully independent verification and validation, and static analysis of program properties such as information flow, timing and memory usage. This section cannot hope to cover all aspects of the SHOLIS development, but instead concentrates on the construction of the SHOLIS software and its use of Ada.

3.1 The SHOLIS software

IDS 00-55 calls for the use of a small, rigorously defined programming language. To this end, SHOLIS is constructed almost entirely in SPARK 83[2]—a subset of Ada83 augmented with formal annotations which allow static analysis and program proof. SPARK eliminates language features which are not amenable to formal definition, program proof, and static analysis, or which might give rise to unpredictable behaviour in terms of run-time or memory usage. SPARK also eliminates almost all of Ada83's implementation dependencies, so a SPARK program exhibits no dependence on parameter passing mechanism, expression evaluation order, or elaboration order. These restrictions are checked by the Examiner tool, which also performs data- and information-flow analysis, and generates verification conditions for program proof.

SHOLIS is not a trivial program. It comprises some 133000 lines of code, including some 13000 declarations and 14000 statements. The compiler used on the SHOLIS project was the Alsys (now Aonix) Ada83 to 68k cross compiler[3] with the "SMART" runtime system.[4] All optimisation options were disabled.

The principle challenges in the construction of the SHOLIS software were as follows:

Real-Time vs. Provable code. Writing software which is amenable to formal proof and which runs at an acceptable pace proved to be a major challenge. For example, a pure-functional programming style can be useful for proof purposes, but had to be rejected for SHOLIS, since the cost of returning large data structures from functions was deemed to be too expensive, both in terms of execution time and memory usage.

Non-functional implementation dependencies. SPARK eliminates most semantic implementation dependencies from Ada, but we found some non-functional properties which generated unacceptable code. For example, when initialising composite constants with a large aggregate, we found that the compiler generated elaboration code which allocated a temporary object on the heap, even if the aggregate could be evaluated at compile time. This was particularly unfortunate, since SMART does not feature a heap manager by default! These cases had to be "programmed around" by introducing field-by-field initialisation code for these objects, which would normally be considered poor programming style.

Exception freedom. Neither SPARK nor SMART feature exceptions, and the requirements for SHOLIS required static analysis to show that predefined exceptions could not be raised. The SPARK Examiner generates verification conditions, the proof of which ensure that a program is free from Constraint_Error. Tasking_Error and Program_Error are eliminated simply because language features that give rise to these are excluded from SPARK, or through simple static analyses performed by the Examiner. Storage_Error was eliminated through static analysis of the generated code to determine worst-case stack usage. As noted above, SHOLIS was carefully coded to avoid dynamic allocation of objects from a heap. These analyses also allow compiler-generated run-time checks to be justifiably switched off, which improves both the run-time performance of the system, and the developer's confidence in the system!

4 Re-engineering SHOLIS

SHOLIS is essentially constructed using what (to the Ada community) is considered to be "old" technology: SPARK 83 and an old (but well-respected and trusted) Ada83 compiler. We naturally ask "What benefit could be gained from re-working SHOLIS using SPARK 95 and a recent Ada95 compiler, such as GNORT?" The remainder of this paper hopes to address this question, using GNORT as a focus.

4.1 Phase 1 - Minimal port to SPARK 95

In phase 1 of this effort, a self-hosted version of GNORT was used to port the existing SHOLIS software to SPARK 95. Unsurprisingly, this required almost trivial effort: existing implementation-defined pragmas (e.g. *No_Image*) were replaced with their Ada95 equivalents, and address representation clauses were adapted to be compatible with Ada95's package System. Having completed these steps, GNORT compiled SHOLIS "first time." GNORT did not indicate that any language features used in SHOLIS were incompatible with its supported language subset, which lent some evidence to our belief that the language subset compiled by GNORT is a superset of SPARK 95.

4.2 Phase 2 - Taking advantage of SPARK 95

Phase 1 resulted in a version of SHOLIS that was workable, but still offered scope for improvement through the adoption of new features of SPARK 95[5]. For example, SPARK 95 supports the "use type" clause, arbitrary deferred constants, and a partial data-flow analysis option which makes subprogram annotations far smaller and easier to maintain in parts of a system where full information flow analysis is not required or useful. The following subsections report our findings.

Use Type. In SPARK, the "use" clause is not allowed, so explicit operator renaming is normally used in SPARK 83 programs to make the infix operators of a type directly visible as needed. The introduction of the use type clause in SPARK 95 allows such renaming to be eliminated. In SHOLIS, this simplification reduced the size of the application by some 270 source lines.

Atomic. In SHOLIS, approximately 100 library level variables represent registers and buffers of specific I/O devices. Most of these devices only allow access to these registers using specific sizes and alignments, and all input devices and readable control registers must be considered Volatile (i.e. we consider that the value of such a register can be changed by the environment.) Secondly, some I/O registers required multiple reads or writes—care had to be taken to ensure that the intended number of accesses to each device was preserved in the generated code. In the original version of SHOLIS, we simply relied on having the compiler's optimiser switched off and careful coding to ensure that a variable's size, alignment and volatility were respected.

Ada95 provides pragmas *Atomic* and *Volatile* for these purposes. These use of these pragmas preserve the intended dynamic semantics, while (perhaps more importantly) also allowing optimisation to be enabled.

Aggregates in initialisation. In section 3.1, we mentioned that some composite objects in SHOLIS had to be initialised field-by-field, rather than using an aggregate, to avoid the implicit allocation of a large temporary object on the heap. GNORT always allocates such temporaries on the stack, so the original code could be restored. While this change seems trivial, it actually has a beneficial effect upon program proof. Consider initialising an array field-by-field:

```
--# pre True;
for I in A_Index loop
  A(I) := 0;
  --# assert (forall J : A_Index, A_Index'First <= J and
  --#                             J <= I -> A(J) = 0);
end loop;
--# post A = A_Type'(others => 0);
```

In SPARK's model of program proof, this code fragment has 3 basic paths (from the precondition to the assertion, from the assertion to the assertion, and from the assertion to the postcondition) and thus the Examiner generates 3 verification conditions (VCs) which must be discharged to show this fragment partially correct with respect to its precondition and postcondition. The proof of these VCs is actually non-trivial, and cannot be completed by our automatic VC Simplifier, and so must be discharged by hand using our interactive Proof Checker.

The alternative code

```
--# pre True;
A := A_Type'(others => 0);
--# post A = A_Type'(others => 0);
```

is rather better is this respect. This fragment has a single basic path, and the resulting VC is trivially discharged by the simplifier.

Elaboration Control. Through a variety of rules, a SPARK program cannot exhibit any implementation dependence on elaboration order. Nevertheless, it has still been useful to experiment with Ada95's Preelaborate and Pure pragmas to determine their potential usefulness. The various package in SHOLIS fall into roughly one of three classes:

- Those which declare types and simple operations on those types only. These packages are typically "stateless" in that they declare no variables.
- Those which implement device and I/O drivers. These typically declare objects which are mapped to physical I/O devices using address representation clauses.
- Main packages. These implement the core state and operations of the SHOLIS system.

We found that packages in the first class were readily made Pure. This has the added effect of informing the compiler that all functions in such packages are also Pure, and thus have no side-effects. Unfortunately, we found that neither Preelaborate nor Pure could be applied to most packages in the second class. This owes to the normal form of an address representation clause:

```
for A'Address use To_Address(...);
```

The To_Address function is not a static function as defined by the LRM, and so is not pre-elaborable, but remains the only way of turning an integer literal into a value of type System.Address since, following the LRM's advice, System.Address is private.

Another related problem was the elaboration of large composite constants. These are initialised by an aggregate, which is not a static expression in Ada95 terms, and so a compiler is not obliged to even attempt to evaluate this aggregate at compile time. The elaboration cost of such a declaration can be a major source of confusion amongst novice Ada programmers, since it may well be Pre-elaborable, but its cost at runtime may be significant (with some compilers), or zero (with others.) The placement of such a constant (e.g. at library-level or nested within a subprogram) can also have a significant effect on program performance. GNORT does well in this respect—it often goes further than the LRM's requirements, and evaluates such aggregates at compile time.

ROM Data and Deferred constants. SHOLIS includes a database of operational scenarios, which is physically located on a single card containing a bank of FLASH EEP-ROMs. The database can be changed, upgraded, or improved at any time *in situ* without any change to the main application software.

In Ada terms, the database is represented as a single large package, which exports a set of memory-mapped objects. In SPARK 83, the usual idiom of declaring variables with address representation clauses is used. For the analysis performed by the Examiner, though, it is useful to indicate that the objects in question are really constants, and not variables (they are in a ROM after all!), so we introduce a shadow package specification, containing a constant declaration which mimics each database variable declaration. This gives us two versions of the database package: one which is compiled, and one which is submitted to the SPARK Examiner.

This trick is important because constants in SPARK play no role in dataflow or information flow analysis, and thus never appear in SPARK's global or derives annotations. If this trick were not employed, then the annotations for each subprogram in SHOLIS would be significantly larger, but would carry no additional useful information.

While this approach is workable, the analysis time for the shadow package is significant (the Examiner spends a significant time analysing the initialising expressions which are then never needed!). The need to have two package specifications "in sync" also complicates configuration control.

SPARK 95 allows deferred constants of any type, which offers a more elegant solution:

```
ClearScreenC : constant GraphicTypes.GraphicString;
   ...
private
   for ClearScreenC'Address use
         System.Storage_Elements.To_Address(...);
   pragma Import(Ada, ClearScreenC);
```

This approach has the advantage that only a single package specificaiton is required for both compilation and analysis. Analysis time is also improved by a factor of approximately 3 using this approach for SHOLIS's database package, which features over 400 such declarations. Finally, we note that declaring these objects as constants rather than variables might allow an optimiser to improve code generation for some algorithms.

4.3 Phase 3 - Code generation and optimisation

This section considers the improvement (if any) offerred by GNORT in terms of code size, quality and understandability over the project's original Ada83 compiler. Unfortunately, it has not been possible to evaluate the performance of the GNORT-generated system, owing to the unavailability of the SHOLIS target hardware.[2]

Generated code size. This is important in embedded systems where ROM and RAM resources may be tightly constrained. Table 1 shows the size in bytes of the code[3] and data sections for SHOLIS, compiled with the Alsys Ada83 compiler, and GNORT at optimisation levels 0, 1 and 2. The code submitted to GNORT was that resulting from the improvements described in section 4.2. The Alsys compiler had all optimisations turned off—the options that were used for delivery of the system. In all four cases, runtime checks were suppressed, and subprogram in-lining was enabled. Here we see that

Table 1. Code and Data sizes for Alsys vs. GNORT

Compiler	Code	Data	Total
Alsys	174066	78878	252944
GNORT -O0	202412	71052	273464
GNORT -O1	138280	71052	209332
GNORT -O2	135192	71052	206244

GNORT at optimisation level 0 generates approximately 27k more code than Alsys. This reflects the fact that, with optimisation off, GNAT can achieve the goal of absolutely no optimization at all, since the table driven techniques used can be directed to completely avoid optimization. With a hand written code generator like that used by the Aonix compiler, it is relatively difficult to eliminate *all* optimization of any kind.

At higher levels of optimisation, GNORT does significantly better. In particular, at level 1 the GCC backend implements common subexpression elimination, assigns variables to registers where possible, and eliminates many redundant load and store operations. The code is often shorter, and (perhaps more importantly) makes significantly fewer references to main memory. While it has not been possible to measure the execution time of GNORT's code on the real SHOLIS hardware, our manual analysis

---

[2] The prototype SHOLIS system is currently bolted down to a Royal Navy ship, whereabouts unknown!

[3] The code section includes all generated code and constants for the SHOLIS application code. For the Alsys compiler, the SMART runtime system code, constants, and exception tables are not included in this figure.

of several time-critical inner loops suggests that the GNORT code would comfortably out-perform the original system.

Ability of GNORT to take advantage of SPARK. As we pointed out in section 3.1, SPARK enforces several static semantic rules (e.g. no function side-effects, no exceptions, staticness of initialising expressions etc.) If a compiler could recognise these properties of a program, then some improvement in code generation may be possible. These features include:

Exceptions. SHOLIS is proven to be free of all predefined exceptions. GNORT allows exceptions to be raised, but they always result in a simple jump to a single user-defined routine, which can be used to terminate or restart the program. In a totally exception-free program like SHOLIS, GNORT imposes no overhead—it does not generate unwanted handlers or tables, and does not impose any overhead on the subprogram entry/exit sequence. This contrasts with the Alsys compiler, which imposes no run- time overhead for unused exceptions, but still generates 6095 bytes of exception handling tables in the final program image, which are never used.

Staticness. In a SPARK program, constraints are always static, and the expressions initialising constants are always determinable at compile time. As we saw in section 4.2, GNORT does well in this respect. In most cases, it is able to evaluate initialising expressions at compile time, even when the Ada95 definition of "static" does not require it to do so.

Function side-effects. SPARK eliminates all function side-effects, which offers some possibility of improved code-generation. Pragma Pure offers one technique for this, and was successfully applied to a small subset of the packages in SHOLIS. GNORT also offers an implementation-defined pragma *Pure_Function* for this purpose. Experimentation with this pragma did not show any great improvement in generated code, although the algorithms in question simply may not have been amenable to such improvement.

Optimisation. In the safety-critical community, "no optimisation" seems the norm. Reasons often cited for this include the perceived unreliability of optimisers in early Ada83 implementations, and the difficulty of debugging and reviewing optimised object code. GNORT (being based on the GCC back-end) is normally run with its optimiser enabled, though, so there may be a strong argument in favour of its use. If object-code integrity is of concern, three approaches can be taken:

- The use of a formally verified compiler.
- Review of the compiler's in-service history and reliability.
- Manual review of generated code.

The first of these options remains a research topic, and is not an option for a language the size of Ada at present. The second option leads to the question "what compilation options are considered to be most reliable, and therefore most suitable for a safety-critical system?" For GNORT (and other compilers derived from GCC), informal evidence suggests that -O1 is the most reliable option, since this option is normally used by the vast majority of users.

Finally, the manual review of object code remains a necessary (but arduous) task for some safety-critical systems. To determine how well GNORT supports such an activity, a single subprogram from SHOLIS was subjected to a manual review, comparing the code generated by the Alsys compiler with that generated by GNORT at optimisation levels 0 and 1. Pragma Reviewable was applied to the unit in question.

The Alsys compiler produces in its listings file details of record type layout, the stack layout for each subprogram, and an annotated dissassembly of the unit's object code. The annotations include source line numbers, the name of objects accessed by any one instruction, and the Ada name of called subprograms. These annotations and stack-layout information significantly simplify the job of reviewing the generated code.

Similar information is available in the GNORT-generated listings. The GNU *obj-dump* utility can be used to produce a merged listing showing the disassembled code and source. The debugging information can also be reproduced in a human-readable form which reveals the stack layout for each subprogram. At optimisation level 0, the code is as easy to understand as that generated by the Alsys compiler, or better. At level 1, things are slightly more complicated (indeed, pragma Reviewable is not strictly supported at this level.) At this level, the GCC backend can assign objects to registers, and can re-use those registers when the life-times of two such objects do not overlap, so interpreting the code is somewhat more difficult, although not impossible for an experienced user. This increase in difficulty is balanced by the reduction in code volume at this level. Note that at -O1, the GCC optimiser does not perform global re-organisation of the code (which *would* complicate any verification considerably.)

A final observation on this topic is that GNAT allows a level of verification not available with most other compilation systems through the availability of the front-end's intermediate language (IL). The *-gnatD* switch produces the IL as an Ada-like listing for each unit, and places references to the IL in the object code, not to the original source. This implies that the objdump listing for a unit then shows the generated code interspersed with the IL listing rather than the original source. This facility offers the prospect of a 2-step verification of object code. The first step would verify the IL against the source code, which requires a detailed knowledge of Ada, but not necessarily of the target machine. The second step would verify the generated code against the IL. This process might ease verification since the "semantic gap" between the languages being compared in each step is far narrower.

5 Further work

5.1 GNORT

With regard to GNORT, the facilities provided are essentially complete with respect to the SHOLIS requirements. The one technical point is that it is unfortunate that an address clause cannot be written in a pre-elaborable unit, as pointed out in section 4.2. Note that from a code generation point of view, there is no problem here, since the call to To_Address would be inlined and in fact does not generate code at all (it is essentially an unchecked conversion). We propose to add a new implementation defined attribute:

```
for X'Address use Address'Value (...);
```

This special attribute will defined to have the same semantics as To_Address, but will be a static attribute, and thus be allowed in a pre-elaborable unit. This is not strictly a GNORT issue, but for the reasons described in this paper, it is likely to arise in this context. We anticipate similar situations arising in future that may require minor work in the area of additional inlining, or special attributes.

5.2 SHOLIS

As for SHOLIS itself, this work has not attempted to take advantage of child packages, which are permitted in SPARK 95. Introducing child packages implies a complete re-think of the program's structure, which was beyond the limits of this investigation, so this remains a topic for future work. Secondly, SHOLIS remains a totally single-task program, with a cyclic scheduler. While this approach offers some benefits in terms of simplicity and efficiency, it has some serious drawbacks: the program's structure is damaged to "fit" computations into the available system cycles, and some real-time requirements are difficult to meet. An obvious development would be to re-work SHOLIS using the Ravenscar tasking profile[4, 6].

6 Conclusions

From the findings of these investigations, we can conclude:

- GNORT provides a usable and effective means of producing safety-critical applications, and offers a cost-effective alternative to a traditional "small but certified" run-time.
- Careful use of SPARK 95 features can offer measureable improvements (in terms of code size, complexity, performance) when applied to an existing SPARK 83 application. These improvements can be achieved with relatively little effort.
- With optimisaion off, GNORT generates code which is slightly larger than that generated by the project's original Ada83 compiler, but is well suited to debugging and manual review.
- The use of optimisation *can* be justified with a GCC-based compiler like GNORT. This offers significant benefits in terms of code size and performance, without overly detracting from the understandability of the object code (should a manual review be required.)
- GNORT's support for object code review is at least as good as that offered by the original compiler, but also offers the potential for a 2-phase process, based on a program's intermediate language. We note that GNORT's "open source" philosophy makes this style of review possible—an option that may not be available for other proprietary compilers.

References

1. The procurement of safety-critical Software in Defence Equipment, Ministry of Defence, Interim Defence Standard 00-55 (Parts 1 and 2), Issue 1, April 1991.
2. SPARK—The SPADE Ada Kernel, Edition 3.2, Praxis Critical Systems, October 1996.
3. Alsys Ada Compiler Cross Development Guide for UNIX workstations to Motorola 68k Targets. Version 5.5.2. Alsys Ltd. September 1993.
4. Safety Critical Solutions. Aonix Inc. 1998
   http://www.aonix.com/Pdfs/CSDS/safecrit/safe.crit.pdf
5. High Integrity Ada—The SPARK Approach. John Barnes with Praxis Critical Systems Limited. Addison Wesley, 1997.
6. Proceedings of the 8th International Real-Time Ada Workshop: Tasking Profiles. ACM Ada Letters, September 1997.

Acknowledgements. The authors would also like to thank Power Magnetics and Electronic Systems Ltd. and the UK MoD for their permission to publish material relating to SHOLIS in this paper. The first author would like to thank the staff of ACT Inc. and ACT Europe for their patience and support during the practical phase of this work.

The principle developers of the SHOLIS at Praxis Critical Systems were: Andy Pryor (technical authority and project manager), Rod Chapman (software development and proof), Jonathan Hammond (formal specification, proof and safety engineering), Janet Barnes (formal specification and proof), and Neil White (program proof).

An Ada95 Solution for Certification of Embedded Safety Critical Applications

Jacob Frost

DDC International
Gl. Lundtoftevej 1B
DK-2800 Lyngby, Denmark
Tel: +45 45871144
Fax: +45 45872217
Email: jf@ddci.dk

Abstract: The Ada95 programming language is widely used for implementation of embedded safety-critical airborne systems and equipment. The RTCA/DO-178B is a mature standard for certifying such systems and equipment through testing. This paper focuses on the solution DDC-I will provide for RTCA/DO-178B level A certification of Ada95 applications though its new SCORE compiler/debugger product line and associated test tools products. Furthermore, the paper outlines how the DDC-I approach relates to the work in the ESPRIT OMI/SAFE project which aims at establishing a complete software factory for the development and certification of embedded safety-critical applications.

1   Introduction

The use of software in safety-critical systems continues to increase rapidly. In addition to being used in an increasing number of real-time embedded systems, software also plays an increasingly critical role in these systems. Some of the most prominent examples of this trend can be found in the avionics and automotive industry. In both airplanes and cars, software controls an increasing number of safety-critical functions such as flight control and breaking. In addition, the traditional mechanical backup systems are starting to disappear as the industry introduces new systems that rely entirely on software.

Such use of embedded systems place strong demands on the correctness and reliability of the associated software. Formal methods have been suggested to deal with the increased demands to software correctness in embedded systems. However, industry still relies on strict discipline and exhaustive testing to provide the required level of confidence.

The high demands on modern embedded software caught the attention of designers of programming languages and organisations such as the RTCA back in the early eighties. The Ada programming language, which is widely used in safety-critical embedded applications, encourages and enforces a strict and clean style of programming. In its latest incarnation, Ada95 [4], it provides a dedicated safety and security annex (Annex H) supporting the development of safety-critical software. Similarly, the RTCA has published a mature set of guidelines called the RTCA/DO-178B [3] dealing with the requirements to certification of safety-critical software such as that found in airborne systems.

This paper focuses on the solution DDC-I plans to provide for RTCA/DO-178B certification of Ada95 applications through its new SCORE compiler/debugger product line and associated test tools products. In particular, the paper describes the support of Annex H and two dedicated test tools supporting level A (highest level) of certification/testing according to the RTCA/DO-178 guidelines. Furthermore, the paper briefly outlines how the DDC-I approach relates to the work in the ESPRIT OMI/SAFE project which aims at establishing a complete software factory for the development and certification of embedded real-time safety-critical applications.

The rest of this paper consists of two sections and a conclusion. The first section describes how DDC-I plans to provide support for Annex H and DO-178B certification of embedded real-time safety-critical applications. This includes a general overview of the approach and more details about the specific tools developed. The second section provides a brief description of the OMI/SAFE project and its goal to develop a complete software factory.

2 The DDC-I Certification Tools

The goal of the DDC-I software development tools/features described in this section, is to provide software developers with a basic set of no-nonsense tools and features supporting development and certification of safety-critical embedded real-time applications. Each of the tools/features described are designed to complement each other, addressing different issues of software certification. The remaining of this section describes the implementation of Annex H, the CoverCode structural coverage test tool and finally the requirements coverage test tool.

2.1 Ada95 Annex H

The Ada95 core language has a number of features that makes it particular suitable for the development of safe and secure software. The strong typing system, pointer initialisation, extensive run-time checks, a robust exception mechanism, abstract data types, packages are all examples of such features. Annex H adds a number of new features. The main issues are the following: understanding program execution, reviewing object code and restricting the use of certain language features. The SCORE Ada95 compiler from DDC-I will provide a full implementation of Annex H.

Understanding Program Execution. Annex H supports the understanding of program execution through pragma Normalize_Scalars and by documenting implementation decisions.

The use of pragma Normalize_Scalars forces all otherwise uninitialised scalars to be assigned a predicable value initially. If possible an invalid value will assigned to the scalar. As examples of the strategy, consider the declarations in figure 1. The variable A will be assigned the value 11 and B assigned the value 1. No out-of-range value can be assigned to C. Instead the bit-pattern represented by the hexadecimal number 16#DEADDEAD# is assigned. This solution is generalised to scalars of a differ-

```
A : Integer range 2..10
B : Integer range 2..Integer'Last
C : Integer
D : Float
```

Figure 1: variable declarations

ent bitsize. In the case of floats such as D, the compiler will assign a bit-pattern representing not-a-number value. This solution works even when no out-of-range values exist.

The strategy is designed to make it easy to discover common type of errors related to uninitialised variables. The assignment of an invalid value will typically cause a range check to fail and an exception to be raised at runtime. This is what happens in figure 2 when the factorial program is executed with an argument of 2.

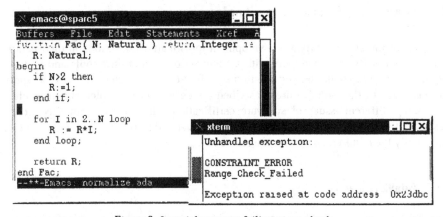

Figure 2: factorial program failing range check

Reviewable Object Code. Annex H provides two pragmas, Reviewable and Inspection_Point, for assisting in reviewing object code. Both pragmas requires various information to be provided about the object code. In additional documentation, the compiler system has been enhanced such that it can generate various listings which contains the required information for the code in question.

Pragma Reviewable provides the required information in two separate listnings: a source code listing annotated with information relevant to the object code and an object code listing with references to the source code. Fragments of such listings for the program in figure 1 are shown in figure 3 and 4 respectively.

```
xterm                                                    ⊟□✕
    15     for I in 2. N loop
                           ^
*** 209W-0: Reviewable: N is known to be initialized

    16       R := R*I;
                  ^
*** 207W-0: Reviewable: run-time support: S_SYSTEM__RTS__EM_RANGE_CHECK_FAILED
                         ^
*** 208W-0: Reviewable: R is possibly uninitialized
                        ^
*** 210W-0: Reviewable: Range_Check generated here
--More--(22%)
```

Figure 3: annotated source code listing

The source code listing provides information about numerous things such as compiler generated initialisation of scalars, run-time checks, implicitly invoked run-time support routines and much more. In general, the source code annotations concerning initialisation are conservative in the sense that variables might be marked "possibly uninitialised" although a static analysis might conclude that they are either initialised or not. The compiler performs a small dataflow-analysis in order to determine how to mark scalars. Essentially, a scalar is marked as initialised if it is initialised directly by declaration, by assignment or through a subprogram call. Formal parameters are also considered initialised. If the scalar is initialised inside an if-statement or other similar construct, then it is considered "possibly uninitialised". Otherwise, it is considered "unitialised". Despite the simplicity, this stategy often yields precise results. The

```
xterm                                                    ⊠□✕
----------------------------------------------------------
    00023D18    80 a6 20 02       cmp       %i0, 2
    00023D1C    04 80 00 03       ble       0x23d28
    00023D20    01 00 00 00       nop
----------------------------------------------------------
    11:    if N>2 then
----------------------------------------------------------
    00023D24    b2 10 20 01       mov       1, %i1
----------------------------------------------------------
    12:        R:=1;
    13:    end if;
    14:
----------------------------------------------------------
    00023D28    b4 10 20 02       mov       2, %i2
----------------------------------------------------------
    00023D2C    80 a6 20 02       cmp       %i0, 2
    00023D30    06 80 00 40       bl        0x23e30
    00023D34    01 00 00 00       nop
----------------------------------------------------------
    15:    for I in 2..N loop
----------------------------------------------------------
```

Figure 4: annotated object code listing

information in figure 3, for example, is spot on. N is clearly initialised as it is the formal parameter to the function, while initialisation of R depends on the value of N. The annotation concerning the range check, reveals the range check causing the exception being raised as shown in figure 2

In the object code listing, each block of object code is related to the source code from which it is generated. Comparing the object code to the source code, it can been seen that register %i0 is used to hold the value of the variable N, %i1 to hold R and %i2 to hold I. Similarly, it can be seen how the if-statement is implemented as a traditional conditional jump past the object code corresponding to branch statement.

Pragma Inspection_Point can be seen as a sort of high-level breakpoint providing a mapping from all inspectable objects (visible objects at the point of the pragma) to the location of their values. This might prevent optimisations such as dead-code elimination as the values of the inspectable objects must be present although not serving any real purpose. The pragma Inspection_Point is supported by generating listings based on the relevant information provided by the DWARF debug information [2] present in the object format.

Restricting the use of Certain Language Features. The use of certain language features can be restricted by using the special Annex H configuration pragma Restrictions. The kinds of restrictions enforced are determined by an optional list of keywords such as No_Task_Hierarchy, No_Floating_Point, No_Exceptions, No_Recursion.

The use of pragma Restrictions should be seen as a guarantee from the developer that the mentioned language features are not used. However, the compiler will detect obvious violations. If, for example, No_Exceptions is in force, then the compiler will check for the presence of raise statements and exception handlers as shown in figure 4.

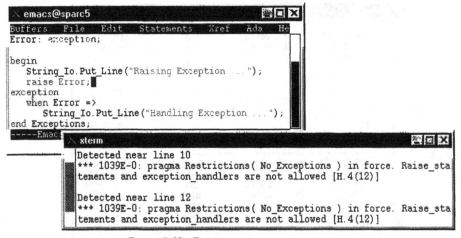

Figure 5: No_Exceptions restriction in force

Restrictions can be used by the compiler to perform a number of optimisations and simplifications. For example, the DDC-I Ada95 compiler is able to select specialised run-time systems (such as a non-tasking variant) based on the restrictions in force. This leads to reduced code size, improved performance and simplified code easing certification.

2.2 CoverCode Test Tool

The CoverCode test tool has been designed specifically to support structural coverage analysis as required for level A certification according to the RTCA/DO-178B guidelines. Structural coverage addresses the general problem of ensuring that testing is sufficiently thorough. As such CoverCode complements the requirements coverage test tool, described later, which is mainly concerned with what is tested rather how well this is done. Due to the general nature of structural coverage analysis, CoverCode is also expected to be an efficient general purpose tool for development of safety-critical software. The remaining of this section presents a simple example of structural coverage analysis performed by the tool and provides a brief description of the architecture and selected tool features.

Example. Structural coverage analysis measures to what extend the program structure has been exercised or covered during program execution. Several definitions of structural coverage can be given, giving rise to different coverage criteria. Furthermore, coverage can be measured on both the object code and source code. A simple and straightforward criteron is statement coverage which measures if, and possibly how many times, each statement of the code has been executed. Figure 6 shows a fragment of a source-level statement coverage report generated by CoverCode.

The statement coverage report consists of a program listing annotated with line numbers and the number of times each statement has been executed (hit). If more than one statement occur on a single line it is broken into multiple lines such as 66A and 66B in figure 6. Statement coverage formalises the well-known principle that tests should be designed to exercise every statement. For that reason, lines with zero hits

```
 xterm                                                           
   65 |     25 |       while I <= 16 loop
   66A|     24 |          if (I >= 1) and (I <= 8) then
   66B|      8 |                                A(I)  := TRUE; end...
   67A|     24 |          if i >= 2 then
   67B|     15 |                      B(I)  := TRUE; end if;
   68A|     24 |          if i <= 7 then
   68B|     15 |                      c(i)  := true;  end if;
   69 |     24 |          i := i + 1;
   70 |     24 |       end loop;
   71 |        |
   72 |      1 |       Try(1, q, b, a);
   73 |      1 |       if not Q then
   74 |     0*|          String_IO.Put_Line( "ERROR" );
   75 |     0*|       end if;
 --More--(32%)
```

Figure 6: statement coverage report

are very interesting as they are more likely to hide errors. Consequently, they are marked with an asterisk such as line 74 in figure 6. Other more complex coverage criteria can be used to catch errors that statement coverage will not find. Branch coverage, for example, will check if every possible branch has been followed at least once. This is particular useful when searching for errors caused by if-statements with no else branch.

Architecture. CoverCode is designed for an embedded environment and consists of the following main components: several coverage reference material generators, a coverage controller, a coverage analyser, a coverage report generator and a coverage monitor. The coverage monitor is downloaded to the chosen target board while all the remaining components reside on the host.

CoverCode performs structural coverage analysis in a non-intrusive way. Instead of instrumenting the code, the tool uses a coverage monitor. The coverage monitor residing on target is a standard DDC-I debug monitor which controls the target program in a transparent way through the use of breakpoints. The monitor is controlled from the host by the coverage controller, typically through a serial or ethernet connection. One responsibility of the coverage controller is the calculation of breakpoints (their addresses) which are subsequently used to generate an execution trace showing which parts of the program that have been executed.

The information needed, in order to calculate the breakpoints is provided by the coverage reference material generators. These generators analyse the code (object and source) and divide it into basic blocks with a fixed flow of control. For example, the Ada95 coverage reference generator reads Ada95 source code, analyses the code using the ASIS standard interface [6] and generates the necessary coverage reference material. In addition to forming the basis for the calculation of breakpoints (after each basic block), the coverage reference material is also used to relate the execution of the target program back to the object and source code.

The actual transformation of the execution trace into a report is done by the coverage analyser and report generator. The analyser performs the basic analysis such as counting hits while the report generator presents the information in a readable format.

CoverCode has been designed to allow easy retargeting and support for new languages. In addition to providing a new reference material generator for the relevant target specific instruction set or source language, changes are normally only needed in the target/language specific parts of the coverage controller and report generator.

The tool supports a number of standard coverage criteria including all those required by the RCTA/DO-178B guidelines. At source-level, CoverCode supports statement coverage (every statement has been executed), call coverage (every subprogram has been executed), branch coverage (each branch of control has been followed), decision coverage (each boolean decision affecting the control flow has been evaluated to both true and false) and MCDC (Modified Condition Decision Coverage, i.e. that each condition of a decision have independently affected the outcome of the condition [1]). Conditions are the atomic boolean expressions of decisions which in turn are the boolean expressions determining the flow of control in for example if-then-else statements. At the object-level, only statement and branch coverage are supported. Roughly speaking, MCDC at the source-level corresponds to branch coverage at the object-level.

In addition to fundamental features, CoverCode provides a special option, allowing coverage to be measured as the accumulated result of several different invocations of the same piece of code. Another feature allows explanations of non-coverage to be added to the report. This is useful because there might be parts of the code that will never be covered for a good reason. For example, code fragments which only serve diagnostic purposes in case of unexpected errors, might never be executed. This is the case for the statement in line 74 of figure 6. Once added, the non-coverage information can be included automatically in future reports.

2.3 Requirements Coverage Test Tool

The requirements coverage test tool has been designed specifically to support requirements-based coverage analysis as required for level A certification according to the RTCA/DO-178B guidelines. The purpose of requirement-based coverage analysis is to ensure that test cases exist for each test case, that they satisfy certain criteria and finally that the necessary test cases have been executed satisfactory. As such the tool addresses a very common problem of software testing and consequently it should also be useful as a general purpose development tool. Furthermore, it complements the CoverCode tool, which measures how well the test cases exercise the code, not what is tested by running the test cases. The remaining of this section first presents a small example illustrating the basics of requirements-based coverage analysis and the support provided by the tool. This is followed by a brief discussion of the tool architecture and selected features.

Example. The basis of requirements-coverage analysis is a description of requirements, test cases and how requirements and test cases relate. In general, fulfilment of a single requirement might depend on several test cases passing. On the other hand a single test case might assist in testing more than one requirement. Given requirements named R1, R2, R3 and test cases named C1, C2 and C3, the situation can be illustrated as in figure 7. The figure shows how, for example, R1 requires both C1 and C2 to pass to be satisfied. Furthermore, requirements have been divided into two catego-

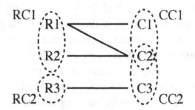

Figure 7: req./test case relation

ries RC1 and RC2 while the test cases belong to one or both of the categories CC1 or CC2. Examples of test case categories could be normal and robustness corresponding to the criteria required by the RTCA/DO-178B guidelines. Similarly, requirements could be categorised as functional, performance, high-level, low-level and so on.

Having prepared the basic information in the format accepted by the requirements coverage test tool, the tool can execute the relevant test programs (each consisting of one or more test cases) and generate a number of different reports. Assuming that test case C1 fails while both the C2 and C3 pass, then the tool will generate the report shown in figure 8. In addition, it is possible to generate specific reports concentrating on a specific category. It is easy to imagine the benefit of such information when working on a real project with hundreds of requirements and many thousand test cases.

```
┌ xterm                                              _ □ ✕ ┐
│Requirement Category : all_requirements : NOT_MET        │
│  Comment : Automatic category with all requirements.    │
│  Number of requirements :  3, tested :  3, met :  2     │
│  Percentage of tested requirements in category met : 66.7│
│  Percentage of requirements in category met      : 66.7 │
│                                                         │
│                                                         │
│  Requirement :  R1 : NOT_MET                            │
│    Associated tests :                                   │
│      jf_test_prog.sh : C1 C2                            │
│                                                         │
│  Requirement :  R2 : MET                                │
│    Associated tests :                                   │
│      jf_test_prog.sh : C2                               │
│                                                         │
│  Requirement :  R3 : MET                                │
│    Associated tests :                                   │
│      jf_test_prog.sh : C3                               │
│--More--(99%)                                            │
└─────────────────────────────────────────────────────────┘
```

Figure 8: requirements coverage report

Architecture. Although integrated in one tool, the requirements coverage test tool really consists of several conceptually different components. The main components are the organiser, the script generator, the executor, the analyser and the report generator. These components are described below.

The task of the organiser is to parse and analyse the initial input to the tool. The organiser parses a description written in a dedicated test language. This dedicated language is designed to allow description of requirements, test cases, categories and the relationship between test cases and requirements. It is also used to specify how test cases are organised in test programs, how the test programs should be executed and to write general comments. Having parsed a syntactically correct description, the organiser makes a number of static sanity and consistency checks. For example it checks that there exists at least one test case for each requirement. The ultimate goal is to use the language to completely formalise both requirements specification and test plan.

Following the application of the organiser, the script generator is invoked to generate an initial script describing which test programs should be executed and which test cases they contain. Typically, the initial test script contains all test programs/test cases. However, it is possible to ask the tool to generate a script containing only a subset of the test programs/test cases such as those corresponding to particular requirements or test case categories.

The test script is used by the executor which is a particular robust part of the tool responsible for the execution and collection of results from the test programs. The test programs are downloaded and executed using standard tools for the target in question.

Test cases report results to executor using a simple target specific package. The end result of running the executor is a file containing the relevant test results.

The test results are used by the analyser which calculates to what extent requirements are satisfied. This calculation is based on the relation between requirements and test cases. The analyser also calculates summary information for each of the requirement and test case categories.

The final presentation is the responsibility of the report generator. In addition to generating a top-level report for all requirements and test cases, it can generate various special reports. For example, it can generate a report focusing on a particular category of requirements. The ultimate goal is to use the report generator to fully automate the generation of test reports.

Often a test run reveals one or more errors. In addition to generation of the initial test script, the script generator is able to generate scripts based on the result of a previous test run. For example it is able to generate a script executing only previously failed test cases. This can be used decrease the time spend on retesting, especially when working with large numbers of test programs/test cases.

3 The OMI/SAFE Software Factory

OMI/SAFE is an ESPRIT project which started in 1997. It involves seven companies from Europe. One of the main goals of this project is to establish a comprehensive ANDF based software factory or tool set aimed at developers of real-time embedded safety-critical applications. The remaining of this section provides an overview of the software factory and briefly describes the status and achievements of the project.

3.1 Software Factory Architecture

The software factory consists of a number of separate tools/components. These can be into a number of different categories depending on the issues being addressed. The description below is structured according to such categorisation.

Low Level Support. The components consist of a new ANDF [5] installer and a number of enhanced low level components (runtime systems and libraries). In particular, the components are enhanced to improve on the issues of numerical deficiencies due to error propagation and mechanisms for automatic error control during calculations. Such issues go beyond RTCA/DO-178B.

Static Code Analysis. The relevant components are the implementation of Annex H described earlier, plus a static code analyser. The static code analyser works at ANDF level being able to perform a number of static checks concerning both program correctness and programming style. This is particular useful in the context of C which has neither the safety enhancing features of Ada95 nor features such as those provided by Annex H.

Safety and Schedulability Analysis. The tools consist of one subsystem for each of the two kinds of analysis. The safety analysis subsystem supports automatic identification of non-safe components of the safety-critical system including construction of hazard/failure lists for the relevant components. The schedulability analysis subsystem is a tool for analysing whether a safety-critical real-time application can meet its timing requirements.

Test and Documentation. The tools consist of the two DDC-I test tools described earlier and a test case generator. The test case generator can generate both traditional test cases useful for automating structural coverage testing and test cases which consider ranges of data instead of single samples.

Formal Verification. The component is a formal verification kernel integrated in a formal verification tool. This component can be used to automatically verify certain properties of embedded safety-critical applications.

3.2 Project Status and Achievements

OMI/SAFE will end in the second half of 1999 and the results are beginning to emerge. Many of the tools/components of the software factory are already at the prototype stage with some even at the product stage and being marketed. In addition to developing the tools, quite some effort is being put into demonstrating the tools through application. For one thing, the many of the tools are being applied in the development of a real-world small embedded real-time safety-critical application. Besides addressing a number of safety-critical issues, the OMI/SAFE consortium has managed reduce the size of this real-world Ada95 application to require less than 256bytes of RAM and less than 16Kbytes of ROM.

4 Conclusion

This paper has presented a number of tools aimed at developers of safety-critical embedded software. In particular, it has described two DDC-I test tools and an implementation of Ada95 Annex H. Furthermore, a brief overview of the components of the software factory being developed in the OMI/SAFE project has been presented.

The DDC-I tools as well as many other components of the software factory are build around established standards and methods. These standards and methods are already being applied by industry in the development of safety-critical embedded software. Similarly, the tools being presented are not tools of the far future. Some are already available and others such as the DDC-I tools will be available shortly.

Acknowledgements. This paper has benefited from the comments of several persons at DDC-I. In particular, Niels Mellergaard and Peder S. Møller have provided valuable information and suggestions to the sections concerning the DDC-I certification tools.

References

1. J.J. Chilenski and S.P. Miller. Applicability of Modified Condition/Decision Coverage to Software Testing. Software Engineering Journal, Vol. 9, No. 5, September 1994.
2. DWARF Debugging Information Format. Industry Review Draft, Unix International, Revision 2.0.0, 27 July 1993.
3. RTCA: Software Considerations in Airborne Systems and Equipment Certification. Document No. RCTA/DO-178B, December 1992.
4. Ada95 Reference Manual: Language and Standard Libraries. S. T. Taft and R. A. Duff (editors). 1997.
5. TDF Specification, Issue 4.0 (DRAFTC), DRA/CIS(SE2)/CR/94/36/40/C. I. F. Currie, June 1995.
6. Ada Semantic Interface Specification (ASIS), ISO/IEC DIS 15291.

Architectural Frameworks: Defining the Contents of Architectural Descriptions

David E. Emery

The MITRE Corporation
1820 Dolley Madison Blvd, MS W538 McLean, VA 22102-3481 USA
emery@mitre.org, +1 703 883 7606 v, +1 703 883 6143 fax

Abstract. This paper describes experiences with several architectural frameworks. An "architectural framework" specifies what is included in the description of an architecture, independent of the specific system being described. The three frameworks are the U.S. DoD C4ISR Architecture Framework, the associated Core Architecture Data Model and the emerging IEEE Recommended Practice on Architecture Description. From these experiences, we speculate on the further evolution of architecture frameworks and architectural descriptions.

1 Introduction

The term "architecture" means many things to many people. Initially, there was no 'formal' defininition of the term. Users of the term relied instead on intuition and the analogy with other disciplines, such as structural architecture and landscape architecture. Within the last two years, though, there have been many attempts to add structure and rigor to the notion of 'architecture', resulting in several different approachs to defining what constitutes an architecture. These attempts have defined "architecture" by defining how to -describe- architectures.

These examples give us a notion of an abstract "architecture" with many possible "architectural descriptions", where the contents of an architectural description (the concrete representation of the architecture) is established by an "architectural framework". Thus an "architectural framework" is a specification of how to describe architectures, rather than the definition of a specific architecture.

This paper relates the author's experience with several different architectural frameworks. There are many architectural frameworks and approaches in the literature; we concentrate here on those that are used to describe the systems aspects of software-intensive systems, rather than the more specific notion of "software architectures." (A survey of architectural frameworks can be found in [9]). Architectural frameworks are important, since the value of architecture comes as a communications medium, and a common "language" (as defined by an architectural framework) is needed to compare architectures.

1.1 Characterizing Architecture Frameworks

An architectural framework tells the user how to describe an architecture. The framework may imply a methodology, but the intent of the framework is to establish the contents of a (conforming) description of an architecture. Generally, a framework consists of a definition of "architecture" and related terms and concepts, along with the definition of one or more "views", or representations. The architecture is described by a set of these views, where each view conforms to the requirements of the framework. Some frameworks may place additional requirements on the set of views (e.g. cross-view consistency rules).

2 DoD C4ISR Architecture Framework Document

This section discusses the U.S. Department of Defense Command, Control Communications and Computers, Intelligence, Surveillance and Reconaissance (C4ISR) Architecture Framework document. [16]

2.1 The C4ISR Architecture Framework

The C4ISR Architecture Framework was developed in response to U.S. Department of Defense need for a coordinated approach for developing, integrating and using Command, Control, Communications, Computers, Intelligence, Surveillance and Reconnaissance (C4ISR) systems. Operation Desert Storm showed both strengths and weaknesses in combining systems developed by each military service into an integrated system for the Commander in Chief. One of the most notable examples from Desert Storm is that the Navy and Air Force were reduced to exchanging air tasking information on floppy disks, rather than through any interactive or automated process.

The Framework document prescribes that architectural descriptions will be oriented around three views, with a series of products for each view. These views are

- Operational View: tasks and activities, operational elements and information flows required to accomplish or support a military operation. (Often abbreviated "OA")
- Systems View: descriptions, including graphics, of systems and interconnections providing for, or supporting, warfighting functions. (Often abbreviated "SA")
- Technical View: minimal set of rules governing the arrangement, interaction and interdependence of system parts or elements, whose purpose is to ensure that a conformant sytsem satisfies a specified set of requirements. (Often abbreviated "TA")

For each of the three views, the Framework document specifies a set of "products". A "product" is a document that contains information relating to some aspect of the architecture. Products are classified as "Essential" or "Supporting", with Essential products containing the minimum information needed to understand a given architecture. Products are specified by examples in the Framework document, rather than through a rigorous Data Item Description. An architectural description is considered conformant with the Framework if it provides all of the Essential products and appropriate Supporting products, and if it uses terms and graphics consistent with the Framework document and normal DoD usage. Thus the C4ISR Framework approach sees architecture as a series of documents.

The Framework document has undergone a trial use and review cycle, producing Version 2.0, which has been mandated for use within the DoD. Each military service is responsible for determining how to implement the Framework document.

2.2 An Implementation of the C4ISR Framework

The U.S. Army has adopted the C4ISR Framework for describing how Army units and their command, control and communications systems are connected. This is described in the Army Enterprise Architecture (AEA) [14] document. The AEA document establishes responsibilities for the three views of the C4SIR Framework. The Operational View is the responsibility of the Army's Training and Doctrine Command (TRADOC), specifically the TRADOC Program Integration Office for Army Battle Command Systems at Ft. Leavenworth, KS. The Technical View is the responsibility of the Office of the Director, Information Systems, Command, Control, Communications, Computers (DISC4) at Army Headquarters in the Pentagon. Responsibility for the System view is spit between the Army Signal Center, Ft. Gordon, GA and the Program Executive Officer for Command, Control and Communications Systems (PEO C3S) at Ft. Monmouth, NJ. The integration responsibility for the Army Enterprise Architecture lies with DISC4 in the Pentagon.

The Army has adopted the notion that each C4ISR Framework View can be done relatively independently of the other views. This is clear by the fact that each view is done in a different location. Furthermore, the Army specifies a relative ordering for the various views. The Technical View, as defined by the Joint Technical Architecture-Army document [13] provides the core interoperability standards for Army systems. The Operational View is focused on the concept of "Information Exchange Requirements", which represent the flow of information from one element to another. For instance, one IER specifies that orders flow from the Battalion Commander to the Company Commanders, and another specifies that periodic spot reports flow from the Company Commanders back to the Battalion Commander. According to the Army's approach [14], both the Operational and Technical Views should be developed before work starts on the System View.

The Army has divided the Systems View into two parts. The first part, which is always completed first, is called the "Conceptual Systems Architecture" ('SA-C'). This part is developed by the Army Signal Center, and identifies organizations and equipment. So, from the example in the previous paragraph, the SA-C would specify that the Battalion Commander and each Company Commander has a radio on the Battalion Command Net which is used to pass the orders from Battalion to Company, and the spot reports back from Company to Battalion. The second part of the Systems view is called the "Detailed Sstems Architecture" ('SA-D'). This work is performed by PEO C3S, and includes all of the specific pieces of equipment needed to implement the actual system architecture. For example, if the Battalion Command Net is implemented using a Packet Radio system such as EPLRS, then the Detailed Systems Architecture must ensure that there are sufficient packet nodes available to cover the battalion area.

With the "digitization" of Army tactical forces, much of the traffic formerly carried via voice radios is now carried as TCP/IP packets. So a Battalion may have both a Voice Command Net and a Digital Command Net. One of the main funtions of the Detailed Systems Architecture is to ensure that these digital nets have an appropriate network structure, including IP subnet definitions, routers, security firewalls, and related digital network gear.

Each architecture View is associated with one or more products. The Technical View is expressed by a single product, the Joint Technical Architecture-Army (JTA-A) document.[13] The JTA-A document extends the DoD Technical Architecture [15] definition by adding additional Army-specific requirements to the DoD baseline. (One notable Army addition is the Army's continuing use of Ada.) In this respect, the JTA-A looks like a profile of the JTA document. The Operational View is captured in a database of IERs and related requirements, along with publications that list the IERs, expected battlefield layouts and related doctrine. The Systems View products are captured using a network diagramming tool called "netViz" [10] that provides an interactive way to view Army organizations, the equipment assigned to organizations, and the networking of that equipment. There is also a database representation of this information with an on-line query capability, and a representation that shows only units and equipment (without network connections). This latter representation is widely used to make sure that the right equipment is being procured and delivered to the using organization. The Army implementation of the C4ISR Framework represents architecture as both documents and CASE tool databases.

3 Core Architecture Data Model

This section describes the C4ISR Core Architecture Data Model (CADM). The CADM captures the intent of the C4ISR Framework Document by describing the various data elements that can be used to describe architectures, and how these data elements interrelate.

3.1 IDEF-1X Data Modelling

Data Modelling is a formal process built on the Entity-Attribute-Relationship (ERA) model. A data model captures the data elements and relationships in a fully normalized form. The most common use for a data model is to capture the requirements for a database, but data models are also commonly used to capture data interchange requirements. [2] [4]

3.2 CADM Goal: Capture C4ISR Framework Architectures

The CADM attempts to capture the core data needed to represent the architecture products defined by the C4ISR Framework Document. The Framework document, as a text document, is subject to substantial interpretation by its users. The CADM represents the belief that ultimately architectural representations are really databases of information about architectures.

The C4ISR Framework document does not specify any particular methodology or approach for producing architectural representations. As previously described, the Army's Enterprise Architecture represents one approach. Other Services and projects can apply other approaches. The intent of the CADM is to capture the underlying data, regardless of approach. In particular, the belief is that two architectures, developed using completely independent approaches, can be combined and/or compared by representing each representation as an instance of a CADM database.

The CADM was developed by a group of experts who analyzed the Framework document, extracting data elements, and working those data elements into an IDEF1X format (using the software tool ERWin.) This produces a "rich" (or "complex") data model. This complexity is managed by having a separate database view for each C4ISR Framework product. Thus, it is possible to view the data model for the product entitled "Node to Node Connectivity Matrix". This data model shows that nodes are related via one or more IER, and also that this relationship can be associated with one or more communications channels (used to pass the messages between the nodes.)

The CADM was also defined to be 'self-describing,' in that the CADM contains a data model for data models. This is not so difficult, since data models follow the Entity-Relationship-Attribute approach. But it allows an architecture description to contain information about itself, or about other architecture descriptions (described as a data model, or as some other form of document.

3.3 Applying the CADM to an Existing Architecture Framework

One of the motivations for the CADM was to serve as a basis for exchanging information among architecture description developers. The Army used the CADM as the basis for exchanging information between the Army Signal Center (SA-C) and PEO C3S (SA-D). This was accomplished by starting with CADM entities that matched data in the netViz representation of the Army System View. The Army then extended the CADM in two directions. One direction contained data that was tool-specific, such as the netViz icon for each organization type or equipment type. More importantly, additional entities were added that reflected Army-specific data requirements. This was done by preserving, as much as possible, the key structures in the CADM. So Army-specific extension to the CADM entity "Organization-Type" has the exact same keys as its parent CADM entity.

This preserves both the CADM core data (by not modifying existing CADM structures), and the structural intent of the CADM, by following existing key structures as much as possible. The result is two entities in the data model. A subsequent physical schema design reduced these two entities (the CADM "Organization-Type" and the Army-specific "Army-Organization-Type") into a single table, producing no performance penalty.

There were a few cases where the Army data model added new entities and keys. The Army System View is very concerned about fully describing the TCP/IP topology of the military Internet. Entities and attributes were added to fully capture the IP addresses for (appropriate) pieces of equipment, along with IP subnet routing data for organizations. These extensions were made in part to support network modelling and simulation activities that verify the behaviour of the resulting TCP/IP network under various loading conditions. It also supports the modelling of how this network will have to be reconfigured when a tactical unit reorganizes, moving organizations and equipment from one subnet to another.

4 IEEE 1471: Recommended Practice for Architectural Descriptions

IEEE Project P1471 for Architectural Descriptions is, at the time of this writing, in final ballot as an IEEE Recommended Practice. The focus of P1471 is specify how to produce an architectural description of a "software-intensive system." [6]

4.1 P1471 Basic Meta-model

P1471 describes an architectural description in terms of views, viewpoints and stakeholders. A viewpoint is the specification of a view, including the methods used to describe the view and the stakeholders and their concerns addressed by the view. The idea is that viewpoints can be shared across descriptions (e.g. a 'data viewpoint' or a 'performance modelling viewpoint'), providing for a common representation of architectural descriptions. In Ada terms, the Viewpoint is like a generic template that is instantiated for each architectural description. Another analogy is that a Viewpoint is a 'pattern' used to specify Views. See [6] more details.

The viewpoint-stakeholder-view approach in P1471 is very close to the method used by MITRE for several architectural products [3]. Thus we use P1471 as a codification of the MITRE method. The P1471 framework can be used to capture other architectural methods, such as ISO RM-ODP [7] and even C4ISR Architecture Framework. The key concept behind P1471 is that architecture is represented by sets of views and viewpoints that capture stakeholder concerns.

4.2 Applying Viewpoint-Stakeholder-View

In each of the MITRE projects, there was a multi-phased approach to developing the architecture description. The first phase determined the basic system requirements, both the functional requirements and the user preferences and trade-offs. At the same time, all of the system stakeholders were identified, along with a set of concerns for each stakeholder.

The next phase selected viewpoints that met these stakeholder concerns. This started by iterating through previous viewpoint descriptions, selecting those viewpoints that would address stakeholder concerns. If all stakeholder concerns were not covered, we defined new viewpoints. For example, we applied this method to the Army's Distance Learning project. One key stakeholder was the training developer (often different from the instructor actually delivering the training.) Training developers were concerned about how their training materials would be distributed to the instructors, and also about gathering feedback from both students and instructors on the effectiveness of their training materials. For this project, we defined a new viewpoint that captured the Training Developer's concerns. This same project reused existing viewpoints for data, security, network/systems management and software development and maintenance.

Once we have the set of viewpoints defined, we then flesh out a view for each viewpoint. This view contains the actual architectural contents for the system. The separation of viewpoint from view allows us to figure out ahead of time the data requirements and framework. With this firm foundation, we concentrate on developing the system-specific contents of each view. Our experience to date is that about 75% of the viewpoints we select for each system are pre-existing viewpoints. But this means that each system has enough system-specific issues that some number of new viewpoints are needed to cover that system, its stakeholders, and their concerns.

5 What Do We Know About Representing Architectures?

We have learned a lot about the representation of architectures over the last several years. In particular, there exists a strong consensus on two points:

- Multiple views are required to capture an architecture.
- There exist definitions of the description ("viewpoints," in IEEE 1471 terms) that exist independent of any particular architectural instance.

These two points are consistent with practice in structural architecture, where floorplans, elevation drawings and architectural models are all used to represent different aspects of a building (multiple views). Each of these representations has a well-defined set of notations and conventions (viewpoints). [5]

5.1 It Takes Multiple Views to Describe an Architecture

There is substantial acceptance in other domains for representing a single description using multiple views. For instance, in structural architecture, floor plans, elevations and architectural models are all widely used representations of a single architecture.

Some representations of 'software architecture' [12] have concentrated on a single view of the software, consisting of the software 'structure'. Recent work [1] has revealed that some essential system properties are not easily determined from a single structural view, including performance and security. In the Army implementation of the C4ISR Framework, security issues are spread across the three Views. Consolidating the security aspects from each view into a coherent discusson of system security is proving difficult. A separate Security view would certainly help capture all of the security issues into a single representation.

5.2 Viewpoints Can Exist Independent of the System Being Described

In each of our examples above, there is the notion of a 'viewpoint' that exists separate from any instance of an architectural description. The C4ISR Architecture Framework document provides a traditional textual presentation of 'viewpoints'. The CADM provides an alternate representation of the same viewpoints, described as an IDEF1X data model. IEEE P1471 codifies this notion of viewpoints, but does not specify the contents of viewpoints, instead leaving this decision to the architect.

Thus we can conceive of one step in an architecting process [11] as the selection of viewpoints to be used in a specific architectural description. There is an implied prior step, that of defining and archiving architectural descriptions. The C4ISR Framework starts with a static set of viewpoints, as do some other architectural methods, such as RM-ODP [7] and "4+1" [8]. The MITRE experience shows that we can define a library of viewpoints, supporting browsing and selection based on stakeholders and concerns.

5.3 Comparing and Analyzing Architecture

Once we have architectural representations, the next step is to compare or integrate these descriptions. Integration is a particular issue within the U.S. DoD, where each military service develops an architecture for its forces (e.g. Army Division, Air Force Wing, Navy Surface Action Group). When we build a Joint Task Force (JTF) with forces from each service, the JTF itself needs an architecture description that shows how each service works in the larger whole.

If two architectural descriptions are based on the same set of viewpoints, comparisons should be much easier. The views can be compared, "like to like", based on the underlying viewpoint. Without this level of consistency, much of the effort in comparing two architecture descriptions will occur in trying to reduce two dissimilar views to some sort of common denominator.

The CADM approach, describing viewpoints through a data model, may yield substantial results in comparing and integrating viewpoints. The underlying database notion makes it easy to extract common elements, or to join elements of two architecture descriptions into a new description. There are some efforts within the U.S. DoD that plan to use the CADM for integrating architectures.

Tools and techniques for comparing architectures are a very promising research area.

5.4 Architecture Descriptions as an Evolving Process

Each of the specification approaches described in this paper are relatively static, in that each defines a "complete set" of architectural description products, without providing any sort of ordering or process. Thus they specify the end-state of an architectural description, without providing any guidance on intermediate representations. The C4ISR Framework Document, as it has been commonly interpreted, generally implies that Operational and Technical view products preceed Systems view products, but this is not specified by the Framework Document itself.

Architecture specifications may be evolving from specifications of "paper products" such as reports and matrices, towards more interactive representations of architectures. Both the C4ISR Framework Document and the IEEE Recommended Practice define "paper products." The CADM, as a data model, lends itself to implementation via a database. The Army implementation of the C4ISR Framework Document uses both a database and a network diagraming tool.

As we gain more experience with architecture as a discipline, our description techniques will evolve to time/event sequences of products. The MITRE Architecture Approach [3] includes a set of preliminary products (Goals, Vision, Needs) that preceed those captured by the IEEE AWG document (viewpoints and views). Thus architectural descriptions will probably evolve towards more dynamic representations, including a process orientation that defines when and how products are produced, and a tool orientation that specifies architectural representations as databases and tool datasets, rather than paper products.

6 Where Are We Going With Architecture Descriptions?

There seems to be two evolving notions, that of "system architectures" as described in this paper, and the notion of "software architecture" as described in [12]. The primary focus of "software architecture" is on the (internal) structure of a software system, while "systems architecture" approaches concentrate more on the role of a given system in its environment. Thus it is common to read of "client-server software architectures" or "pipe and filter software architectures," but no similar terms describing common styles or 'patterns' have evolved in systems architecture representation.

However, the system architecture approaches, such as described in this paper, allow for a wider variety of topics than software architecture representations. There are many properties of systems, such as security, fault tolerance, maintainability, adaptability, etc, that are common in system architecture analyses. A definition of software architecture that focuses solely on structure is less suited to capture such non-structural properties of systems.

Both communities are investigating tools, particularly tools that capture the dynamic properties of systems and software. The tools used in the author's projects have concentrated on capturing the data behind the description, to allow various representations of the architectural description. One of the motivations for a data-centric representation is that the database containing a specific architectural representation has been used as input to other efforts attempting to model or simulate the resulting architecture. These models have included classic network performance analysis, military simulations (wargames), and to a lesser degree, as inputs for testing systems that are components of the architecture.

Thus the future of architecture descriptions should include:

- Representations that cover non-structural aspects of systems
- Common sets of viewpoints.
- Increased tool support, particularly for interactive specification and analysis of architectural representations.
- "Interoperability" of architectural representations based on common viewpoints and underlying descriptions of the information in these viewpoints.

Both "system architecture" and "software architecture" approachs will contribute to this evolution.

7 Summary

The evolution of 'architecting' has reached the point where there is wide acceptance that 'architectures are important', but that previous ad-hoc methods for describing architectures are insufficient. Thus there have been several recent efforts to describe the contents of architectures, independent of any specific architecture.

This paper has described the author's experiences with several of these 'architecture description technologies', including the textual description of the US DoD's C4ISR Architecture Framework document, the associated Core Architecture Data Model and the IEEE Recommended Practice for Architectural Description. All of these approaches acknowledge the need for multiple views to describe a single architecture. They vary in how they define the contents of the views, and their relative focus on 'documents', 'databases' and 'viewpoints' as key architectural framework decisions.

Once we capture architectural representations, the obvious next step is to compare them. The current state-of-the-art in such comparisons, supporting a variety of methods that produce architectural descriptions, is based on data modelling. We require more experience with architectural analysis to know if architectural data models are sufficient to permit analysis and comparison of architectures.

The evolution of the architectural process will produce changes in our architectural specification technologies. In particular, current practice tends to imply paper-based static representations. With the evolution of tools and interactive representations (such as the World Wide Web), architectural meta-techologies will move towards process and behavior models. Methods for defining the contents and meaning of architectural descriptions should continue to evolve. We have captured here a snapshot of current efforts; stay tuned for further developments.

References

1. Allen, Robert J. "A Formal Approach to Software Architecture." PhD Thesis, Carnegie-Mellon University (CMU-CS-97-144), May 1997.
2. Bruce, Thomas A; "Designing Quality Databases with IDEF1X Information Models," Dorset House Publishing, 1992.
3. Emery, David E, Hilliard, Richard F II and Rice, Timothy B; Experiences Applying a Practical Software Architedture Method, in A. Strohmeier (ed), "Reliable Software Technologies - Ada Europe '96." Springer-Verlag: Lecture Notes in Computer Science 1088, 1996. $http$: $//thomas.pithecanthropus.com/awg/CaseStudies.pdf$
4. Federal Information Processing Standards (FIPS) Publication 184, Integration Definition for Data Modeling (IDEF1X), 21 December 1993.
5. Hoke, John Ray (ed), "Architectural Graphic Standards," John Wiley & Sons, 1994
6. Institute of Electrical and Electronic Engineers; "IEEE Recommended Practice for Architecture Descriptions, Draft 4.1; IEEE, 1998. See $http$: $//www.pithecanthropus.com/awg.$
7. Internationl Standards Organization; ISO/IEC 10746-3, Open Distributed Computing - Reference Model Part 3: Architecture. ISO, 1995. $http$: $//www.iso.ch$: $8000/RM-ODP$
8. Kruchten, Philippe; "The 4 + 1 View Model of Architecture", IEEE Software, 28 (11), 42-50, November 1995. $http$: $//www.rational.com/sitewide/support/white-papers/dynamic.jtmpl?doc\_key = 350$
9. Mowbray, Thomas J; "Will the Real Architecture Please Sit Down?" Component Strategies, December 1988.
10. "netViz 3.0." netViz Corporation. $http$: $//www.quyen.com$
11. Rechtin, Eberhard and Maier, Mark; "The Art of System Architecting" CRC Press, 1996.
12. Shaw, Mary A and Garlan, David; "Software Architecture: Perspectives on an Emerging Discipline" Prentice-Hall, 1996.
13. U.S. Department of the Army; Joint Technical Architecture - Army Version 5.0, Washington, DC 1999. $http$: $//www.usace.army.mil/inet/functions/im/lcmis/ata/ata.htm$
14. U.S. Department of the Army; Army Enterprise Architecture Guidance Document, Washington DC 1999. $http$: $//arch-odisc4.army.mil/aes/html/aeagd.htm$
15. U.S. Department of Defense; Joint Technical Architecture version 2.0, Washington, DC 1998. $http$: $//www-jta.itsi.disa.mil/jta/jtav2\_dnld.html$
16. U.S. Department of Defense; C4ISR Architecture Framework, Version 2.0, Washington, DC. $http$: $//www.rl.af.mil/programs/jcaps/download.html\#FRAME$
17. Walker, Robert (editor); C4ISR Core Architecture Data Model (CADM), Arlington, VA: Institute for Defense Analyses 1999. $http$: $//www.rl.af.mil/tech/programs/jcaps/cadm.html$

Acknowledgements: The Army System Architecture team was led by LTC Angel Colon and LTC Jim Travis. The CADM team was led by Dr. Robert Walker and Dr. Francisco Loaiza of IDA. Jim Perry, EER Corporation and Tim Anderson and Jack Garhart, BDM Corporation defined the Army System Architecture extensions to the CADM. Teams led by Steve Schwarm, Tim Rice and Kevin Heidemann produced the series of MITRE architecture projects. Basil Sherlund led the P1471 Architecture Working Group. Thanks to Karl Nyberg, Rich Hilliard and Olimpia Velez

Mapping Object-Oriented Designs to Ada

Alfred Strohmeier

Swiss Federal Institute of Technology, Department of Computer Science
Software Engineering Laboratory, 1015 Lausanne, Switzerland
email: alfred.strohmeier@epfl.ch

Abstract: The paper explains how an object-oriented design can be mapped to an implementation using the Ada 95 programming language. Object-oriented designs, whatever the method, UML or Fusion, are not programming-language specific, and there is therefore a gap between the design models and the implementation. This paper is a comprehensive study of all of these gaps for the Ada programming language. The approach is illustrated by an example, complete enough to illustrate most of the implementation decisions.

Keywords: Object-Oriented Software Development, Fusion Method, Ada Programming Language.

1. Introduction

Fusion is a systematic object-oriented software development method [6]. It can be used to develop sequential reactive systems, and certain restricted kinds of concurrent systems. The method is based on a concise but comprehensive set of well-defined models, and proposes a process for software development. During the last phase of the Fusion process, a detailed design, consisting in class descriptions and high-level algorithmic designs of the methods, is mapped to a programming language. In order to remain programming-language independent, and like many other software development methods, Fusion provides only a general mapping strategy. Although we very well understand the idea of language independence, we think it also leads to underestimating the difficulties of the implementation phase.

This paper shows how a Fusion design can be mapped to the Ada 95 programming language [10]. It expands and enhances earlier work of Barbey [2]. The material has previously been presented during tutorials [9] and to students at the Swiss Federal Institute of Technology in Lausanne, who used it successfully in projects. We are convinced that our ideas do not only apply to the Fusion method, but also to object-oriented designs resulting from other methods.

We propose to explain the implementation phase on a case study. We will first show the models of the Fusion process that are necessary for understanding translation to Ada. General rules and guidelines for this mapping are then given. In some length, we deal with mutual dependencies between classes, a subject entirely neglected by the method. We conclude by a short overview of our additions to the Fusion method and a comparison with work of other authors.

Finally a word about terminology. We will avoid the use of the word object as defined by Ada, and use the term variable instead. The meaning of object will therefore be "instance of a class".

2. Case Study Problem Statement: Bank Transactions

A bank manages accounts. There are two kinds of accounts: checking accounts and savings accounts. An account is owned by exactly one customer, who can in turn own a checking account, or a savings account, or both. The bank processes financial transactions: get the balance of an account, withdraw cash from an account, deposit cash in an account, and transfer money from one account to another. A transaction can therefore involve one or two accounts. The transactions are recorded, because at the end of each month reports are sent to all customers showing all transactions performed for their accounts during the last period.

To simplify, we will suppose that all transactions are performed by the clerks of the bank on behalf of the customers. The customers receive later on confirmation of the transaction and its outcome by postal mail.

The transfer operation withdraws an amount of money from one account and deposits it in another account. The operation can be performed only if the withdrawal is authorized. A withdrawal from a savings account is authorized if it does not exceed the balance. A withdrawal from a checking account is authorized if the credit limit will not be overrun. The operation is completed by recording the transaction and by notifying the account owners. The other financial transactions are carried out in a similar way.

3. Analysis Phase

According to the Fusion process, the concepts in the problem domain are modeled by a class model (Fig. 1), using the notation and semantics of the well-known entity-relationship approach [5]. It is important to notice that at this stage of the process, classes have only value attributes, such as the name and address of a customer.

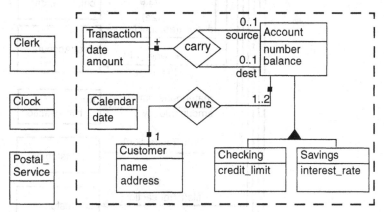

Fig. 1 System Class Model

The next step in the process is to identify external agents and their interaction with the system by exchange of events. The problem statement tells us that the system interacts with two external agents, the bank clerk and the postal service. Input events to the system trigger system operations. For sake of simplicity, the same name is used for both of them; e.g. the clerk sends the input event withdraw_cash to the system, which triggers the system operation withdraw_cash. For the purpose of this paper, it is enough to know that the application must provide the system operations retrieve_balance, deposit_cash, withdraw_cash, transfer, and generate_monthly-_report.

Finally, following the Fusion method, each system operation, e.g. transfer, is specified by a schema. Such a schema describes by pre- and postconditions how an operation changes the state of the system and what output events it sends to external agents. When analyzing the creation of a financial transaction, we discovered that the date of the day was needed. We decided to add the class Calendar to the class model and to trigger update of the Calendar.date attribute by the input event new_day sent by the clock agent to the system.

4. Design Phase

4.1. Interaction Graphs

At the end of the analysis phase, we know the main classes of the system and all the operations it will provide, but the operations are not yet attached to classes. Fusion, rightly in our opinion, postpones this step to design. For each system operation, an interaction graph is designed (Fig. 2). This graph shows the controller of the operation,

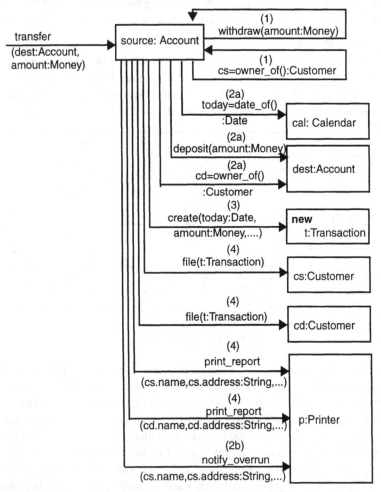

Fig. 2 Interaction Graph for transfer

the source account of the transfer operation in the example, and how the controller achieves the effect of the operation by collaborating with other objects. Collaboration is systematically performed by message sending. E.g. the source account sends the message "file the transaction t" to the customer cs who is the owner of this source account. It is important to note that interaction graphs model control flows, not data flows. As a consequence, data may flow in both directions: parameters follow the direction of the arrow, whereas results flow in the opposite one. There is no need to add an arrow to hand back a result.

4.2. Visibility Graphs

Once the designs of all system operations, and recursively of all methods called by system operations, have been described by interaction graphs, the next step will yield the visibility graphs. In order for a client object to send a message to a server object, the former one must "know the name" of the latter one. If this reference is stored in the client object, then Fusion says the visibility is permanent, and uses a solid arrow. Otherwise, the visibility is called dynamic; this is especially the case if the server object is passed as a parameter to the client object just for the duration of a method invocation. Dynamic visibility will induce dependence between classes, whereas permanent visibility will make the client object have a so-called object attribute, i.e. a component which holds a reference to the server object. It is important to note that in this second case, there is anyway a dependence between the classes.

Fig. 3 shows the visibility graphs for the bank transaction system. It takes into account the visibility needs of all system operations. According to the interaction graph of the transfer operation, the source account needs a permanent reference to its owner, since the owner_of function returns that very owner. The source account also needs a dynamic reference to the owner of the destination account, called cd. Because the permanent visibility link already makes the client class depend on the server class, we can drop this dynamic reference from the visibility graphs. Also, we decided that the printer and calendar objects are global to the system, i.e. visible to all objects.

Fusion also distinguishes between shared and exclusive server objects, shown in a double box. As expected, at any given time, only one object can hold a reference to an exclusive server object. The collection of transactions of a customer, note the keyword **col** for a collection, is an example of an exclusive server object. If the lifetime of the server object is bound to that of the client object, then the server is graphically enclosed in the client, as shown for the checking and savings account belonging to a customer. Finally, if a reference cannot be changed, the name of the server object is preceded by the keyword **constant**.

5. Class Descriptions

We are now ready to record the interfaces of the classes in class descriptions. This is almost a mechanical task, and no new creative work is needed. Classes and value attributes come from the system class model, e.g. account and balance of an account (Fig. 1). Object attributes have their origin in the visibility graphs, e.g. the owner of an account (Fig. 3). The keywords **bound/unbound**, **shared/exclusive**, **constant** and **col** have the same meanings as for the visibility graphs (4.2.). The interaction graphs show the operations and methods, including their parameters, the class must provide (Fig. 2).

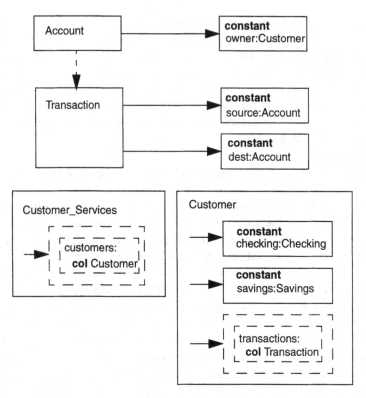

Fig. 3 Visibility Graphs

Finally, generalization-specialization relationships, also called interface inheritance, originate from the system object model, e.g. a savings account is a sort of account. Sometimes when scrutinizing the class descriptions, patterns common to several classes might be discovered. It is then possible to factor the common features and create new parent classes. The result will be implementation inheritance.

5.1. Class Account

```
abstract class Account
    attribute Number: Account_Number;
    attribute Balance: Money;
    attribute constant Owner: unbound shared Customer;
    method Check_Balance (): Money;
    method Deposit_Cash (Amount: Money);
    method Withdraw_Cash (Amount: Money);
    method Transfer (Dest: Account; Amount: Money)
    method Owner_Of (): Customer;
    local method Deposit (Amount: Money);
    local abstract method Withdraw (Amount: Money);
endclass
```

5.2. Class Checking

```
class Checking isa Account
    attribute Credit_Limit: Money;
    local method Withdraw (Amount: Money);
```

```
    -- Raises Overrun_Error if withdrawing would
    -- exceed the credit limit.
endclass
```

5.3. Class Savings

```
class Savings isa Account
    attribute Interest_Rate: Rate;
    local method Withdraw (Amount: Money);
    -- Raises Overrun_Error if withdrawing would
    -- result in an overdraft.
endclass
```

5.4. Class Customer

```
class Customer
    attribute Name: Name_Type;
    attribute Address: Address_Type;
    attribute constant Owned_Checking: bound shared Checking;
    attribute constant Owned_Savings: bound shared Savings;
    attribute Transactions: col Transaction;
    method Checking_Account_Of (): Checking;
    method Savings_Account_Of (): Savings;
    method File (T: Transaction);
endclass
```

5.5. Class Transaction

```
class Transaction
    attribute Date: Date_Type;
    attribute Amount: Money;
    attribute constant Source: shared Account;
    -- Source is undefined for a cash deposit.
    attribute constant Dest: shared Account;
    -- Dest is undefined for a cash withdrawal.
endclass
```

5.6. Class Customer_Services

```
class Customer_Services
    attribute constant Customers: col Customer;
    method Generate_Monthly_Reports;
endclass
```

6. Mutual Dependencies

Enhancing the Fusion method, we propose to finish the design phase, or to start implementation, by looking out for mutual dependencies between classes, and to decouple them whenever possible, for the following three reasons.

Relationships between classes first appear in the class model during analysis. These relationships are then "designed away". Object attributes and collection attributes are often the rest of such relationships. E.g. the object attribute Owner of Account together with the Owned_Checking and Owned_Savings attributes of Customer originate from the owns relationship (Fig. 1). However, independent unidirectional links can neither ensure consistency nor enforce cardinality constraints of the underlying relationship. E.g. when navigating from a Customer to her savings account by using the Owned_Savings account and then further along to the Owner, there is no guarantee that we come back to the starting point. Consistency between links is called referential integrity by data base people.

An implementation with many interdependent classes is difficult to maintain. Indeed, to fully comprehend a class, all classes it depends on must also be understood, and a change made to a class might impact all dependent classes.

Finally, in Ada, mutual dependencies between package specifications are not allowed. As a result, mutually dependent classes must be declared in the same package specification. They are therefore a hindrance to physical modularization.

To find out about mutual dependencies between classes, it suffices to look out for circularities in the (union of the) visibility and inheritance graphs. For the bank transaction case, the graph is depicted in Fig. 4. It contains three cycles, one being

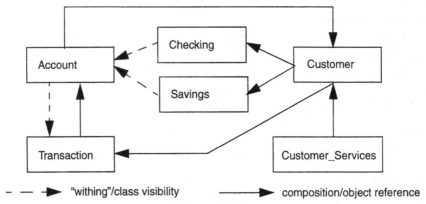

Fig. 4 Class Dependencies according to the Visibility and
Inheritance Graphs

Account - Customer - Transaction - Account. Whereas it is easy to diagnose mutual dependencies, it is more difficult to deal with them.

Some mutual dependencies are a sign of bad design. Beware especially of data flow semantics in object interaction graphs! Revise them if possible to remove circularities in message passing. For instance when a directory object messages a file for changing its protection, confirmation can be modeled as a result parameter of messaging, and there is no need for the file object to message back to the directory. We consider therefore the example in figure 4.5 of the Fusion book [6] to be incorrect.

Sometimes, a mutual dependency is coincidental. E.g. the owner of a house is a person and a person lives in a house, but the two persons are unrelated. There is then no referential integrity problem and the links can be exposed (but don't have to be) without much harm, since they are independent:

```
type House_Type;
type House_Ref is access all House_Type'Class;
type Person_Type;
type Person_Ref is access all Person_Type'Class;
type House_Type is tagged record
   Owner: Person_Ref;
   ...
type Person_Type is tagged record
   Residence: House_Ref;
   ...
```

But otherwise, and whenever possible, a mutual dependency should be traced back to a relationship in the class model. The relationship will then expose the consistency and cardinality constraints that must be maintained. We propose to hide the unidirectional links and to provide operations to create, to update consistently all links, and to navigate along them. Forgetting for the moment the different sorts of accounts, we could write:

```
type Account_Type is tagged private;
type Account_Ref is access all Account_Type'Class;
type Customer_Type is tagged private;
type Customer_Ref is access all Customer_Type'Class;
procedure Associate (Account: in Account_Ref; Customer: in
Customer_Ref);
-- all kinds of consistency checks might be performed by Associate
function Owner_Of (Account: Account_Type) returns Customer_Ref;
```

This approach provides for referential integrity, but in general, the classes remain still mutual dependent, and have to be implemented in the same package.

In a first step, it might be worth to determine if class dependencies in the visibility graphs are dependencies between their interface or their implementation. E.g., according to the interaction graph of Fig. 2, only the implementation of the Account class depends on the Transaction class. We propose to depict this finding in the dependency graph (Fig. 5). When mapping to Ada, the specification of the Transaction

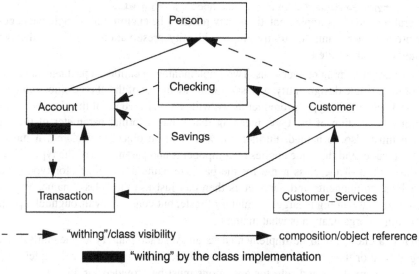

Fig. 5 Class Dependencies after Decoupling

class will depend on the specification of the Account class, but only the body of the Account class depends on the Transaction specification.

As a next step we propose to examine if any of the mutually dependent classes is rather a role of the relationship, and to look out for a class that can be factored out of that role. As a result, links will be added by type extension. In the example, being a customer is indeed a role of a person. This Person class has all the features of any person, e.g. a name, an address, etc. The class Customer inherits from Person (Fig. 5), and adds all the properties specific to a bank customer, e.g. links to the owned accounts. Note that as a result of this kind of decoupling, potential reuse is increased, e.g the Person class can be used in other applications, whereas the Customer class is more specific.

The disadvantage of breaking the cyclic dependency is a loss in descriptive knowledge, i.e. owners of an account should really be customers, and a weakening of the static type checking that goes along with the tighter attribute type. As we will see later (10.2.), it is possible to add code for a run-time check.

If all of the above does not work, the mutual dependency might be left untouched, or a purely artificial class could be added to break it.

7. Mapping Class Descriptions

In order to provide for possible future "inheritance", a (root) class will usually be implemented as a tagged type within a package.

```
package Accounts is
    type Account_Type is abstract tagged ...
```

A subclass is implemented by a type extension, i.e. by deriving from a tagged type, and is usually included in a child package:

```
package Accounts.Savings is
    type Savings_Account is new Account_Type with ...
```

Several related class implementations may possibly be enclosed in a single package. If the programmer wants to strictly enforce identity preservation of objects, the types should be made limited.

A word about naming conventions. Two implementation entities, a package and a type, stand for a single design entity, a class. But the identifier of the class cannot name both the package and the type. Moreover as we will see, any method of the class becomes a primitive operation of the type, meaning that it has a formal parameter of the type, which must also be named. Further on, whenever an object is declared, it must be given a name, and the same applies to components and parameters of the type. We will use the plural of the class name for the package name and suffixes for type names. Variables, components and parameters then can just use the "class" name. We must recognize that naming is largely a matter of taste, but consistency throughout a project or within an organization is what matters.

Usually, a class should be implemented as an Abstract Data Type, meaning that the tagged type or the extension part is made private. As for any ADT, a complete set of constructor, modifier and selector operations must be provided for all attributes. E.g. for a person, operations for setting and retrieving the name, setting, changing, and retrieving the address must be available. The major drawback of private components is that there is no way to pass them as parameters to operations, except when of mode in. Therefore, when all or some attributes are completely independent from each other and from all other attributes, it might be better to make them public components. Making public only some of the components of a tagged type is a little bit trickier in Ada than in C++, where it is part of the language.

Value attributes, e.g. Balance of Account, become components of the tagged type, or of its private view. They are of some data type, predefined or defined by the programmer. Sometimes a value attribute may be implemented by a method, e.g. the age of a person is best computed from his birthday. Collection attributes are similar to value attributes: the collection itself is usually the component (and not an access value to the collection).

An object attribute is implemented by a component holding a reference to the object. Using a reference is required because the identity of the object must be preserved. To provide for this possible need, but also for a future use as a parameter, a tagged type declaration should therefore come with a general access type to the class-wide type.

```
type Person_Type is tagged ...;
type Person_Ref is access all Person_Type'Class;
type House_Type is tagged record
   Owner: Person_Ref;
   ...
```

In some special cases, it might be that an object attribute can be implemented by a specific-type reference, or even by embedding the object.

A method will usually be mapped to a primitive operation of the tagged type which implements the class. This tagged type becomes an explicit parameter of the operation. As an advantage of this particularity of Ada, compared to C++ or Java e.g., access control to this parameter can be specified by its mode. To decide upon the access needs, we have to go back to the design documentation, especially to the interaction graphs, and see what the needs are for implementing the operation. Clearly in out and access parameters fit all needs, but then Ada's special charm is lost. Local methods, i.e. visible only within the class and its heirs, should be mapped to private operations, i.e. declared in the private part of the package.

A primitive function should not return the tagged type; it would become abstract when inherited, and is usually difficult to override with a sensible implementation. Better make the function return an access value (or sometimes a class-wide type):

```
function Retrieve (N: Name) return Person_Ref;
```

Binary primitive operations of a tagged type are possible, and no problem at all (whereas they are in C++):

```
procedure Marry (Bride, Groom: in out Person_Type);
```

But beware: it's not enough to have two parameters of the same class to be a binary operation. For an example, see the Transfer operation of the Account class (10.2.).

Parameters of other tagged types will usually be references:

```
type House_Type is tagged private;
procedure Set_Owner (House: out House_Type; Person: in Person_Ref);
function Owner_Of (House: House_Type) return Person_Ref;
```

For mapping implementation inheritance, the best is to use private/hidden inheritance, i.e. the parent type is derived in the private part of the package:

```
type Automobile_Type is tagged private;
private
   type Automobile_Type is new Motor_Vehicule_Type with ...
end;
```

Sometimes a class is rather a mixin. The Fusion method will then display multiple inheritance. The best practice in Ada is to use a combination of generic instantiation together with type derivation. E.g. a versioning mixin is used to derive a versioned file type from a regular file type [3] [4].

A constant object attribute, i.e. the reference is constant, not the object itself, can sometimes be mapped to an access discriminant. The use of an access discriminant also has the advantage that the component is always defined, never null.

A bound object attribute can be implemented by a controlled access value: control over the access value is used to control the referenced server object itself and to synchronize its lifetime with that of the enclosing object; e.g. in 10.5. we ensure that an account does not outlive its owner, since it is bound to him as stated in 5.4.. Controlled types can be used to achieve other integrity checks.

Exclusive access to a server object can be enforced in two ways. There is only one access path to the server object, and this access path is hidden in the private part of the client object. A less restrictive schema is to use a protected type for implementing the server's class. However, inheritance is then no longer available as a built-in feature of the language, and some work-arounds must be used if needed.

8. Collections

Collections are mapped onto the classical data structures sets, lists, queues, stacks, etc. depending on the needed operations and the required performance. It is important that a collection of objects holds references to these objects and does not enclose the objects themselves. The rationale is again object identity, and yet again we see the need for associating a general access type with the tagged type. The transactions related to a customer are a collection attribute (5.4.) (10.5.).

9. Method Bodies

Most of the information required for the implementation of method bodies is contained in the object interaction graphs. The main remaining issues to deal with are iterations over collections and error handling. Exceptions are there for error handling. Iterations can be implemented by the well-known implementation patterns: passive generic iterator, passive iterator with access-to-subprogram parameters, and active iterators.

10. Mappings for the Bank Transaction Case

Most of the preceding recommendations and rules can be nicely shown on the bank transaction case study. To simplify, we will declare data types next to the "class" declarations which use them for their value attributes or as method parameters.

The class Person is mapped to an "open" type, whereas Account is an Abstract Data Type. It is important to notice that Transfer is not a binary operation, because transfers are allowed between different kinds of accounts. As expected, checking accounts are derived from accounts, and the same holds for savings accounts, not shown here.

The mapping of Transaction uses discriminants for constant object attributes and shows functions returning access-to-object values.

Finally, Customer has a collection attribute. Moreover, a customer controls the lifetime of his/her accounts by encapsulating their references in a controlled type.

Mapping of Customer-Services is straightforward, and not shown. Because there is only a single Customer_Services object in the system, a package with state, a so called Abstract State Machine, instead of a type, could be used for its implementation.

10.1. Person

```
package Persons is
    type Name_Type...; type Address_Type...;
    type Person_Type is abstract tagged limited
    -- could be non limited, and even non abstract
        record
            Name: Name_Type;
            Address: Address_Type;
        end record;
    type Person_Ref is access all Person_Type'Class;
end Persons;
```

10.2. Account

```
with Persons; use Persons;
package Accounts is
    type Account_Number_Type is ...;
    type Money_Type is ...; type Rate_Type is...;
    type Account_Type is abstract tagged limited private;
    procedure Create (Account: in out Account_Type; Owner: in
Person_Ref);
    -- Can be called only once. A check is made that Owner is not null,
    -- and that s/he is in Customer'Class.
    -- The account then gets a unique account number.
    function Owner_Of (Account: Account_Type) return Person_Ref;
    function Account_Number (Account: Account_Type)
                                    return Account_Number_Type;
    function Check_Balance
        (Account: Account_Type) return Money_Type;
    procedure Deposit_Cash
        (Account: in out Account_Type; Amount: in Money_Type);
    procedure Withdraw_Cash
        (Account: in out Account_Type; Amount: in Money_Type);
    procedure Transfer
        (Source: in out Account_Type; Dest: in out Account_Type'Class;
        Amount: in Money_Type);
    -- Dest must not be limited to the specific type!
    Overrun_Error: exception;
private
    procedure Deposit
        (Account: in out Account_Type; Amount: in Money_Type);
    procedure Withdraw
        (Account: in out Account_Type; Amount: in Money_Type) is abstract;
    -- Raises Overrun_Error if withdrawing is impossible.
    type Account_Type is abstract tagged limited
        record
            Owner: Person_Ref;
            Number: Account_Number_Type := 0;
            Balance: Money_Type := 0.0;
        end record;
end Accounts;
```

10.3. Checking

```
package Accounts.Checking is
   type Checking_Type is new Account_Type with private;
   type Checking_Ref is access all Checking_Type'Class;
   procedure Set_Credit_Limit
      (Account: in out Checking_Type; Amount: in Money_Type);
   function Credit_Limit_Of
      (Account: Checking_Type) return Money_Type;
   Overrun_Error: exception renames Accounts.Overrun_Error;
private
   procedure Withdraw
      (Account: in out Checking_Type; Amount: in Money_Type);
   -- Raises Overrun_Error if withdrawing would
   -- exceed the credit limit.
   type Checking_Type is new Account_Type with record
      Credit_Limit: Money_Type := 0.0;
   end record;
end Accounts.Checking;
```

10.4. Transaction

```
with Accounts; use Accounts;
package Transactions is
   subtype Date_Type is Ada.Calendar.Time;
   type Transaction_Type(Source: in Account_Ref; Dest: in Account_Ref)
         is tagged limited private;
   type Transaction_Ref is access all Transaction_Type'Class;
   procedure Create
      (Transaction: out Transaction_Type; Amount: in Money_Type);
   -- The transaction is timestamped with the help of the clock.
   function Date_Of
      (Transaction: Transaction_Type) return Date_Type;
   function Amount_Of
      (Transaction: Transaction_Type) return Money_Type;
   function Source_Of
      (Transaction: Transaction_Type) return Account_Ref;
   function Dest_Of
      (Transaction: Transaction_Type) return Account_Ref;
private
   type Transaction_Type
      (Source: in Account_Ref; Dest: in Account_Ref) is tagged limited
record
         Date: Date_Type := Ada.Calendar.Clock;
         Amount: Money_Type;
      end record;
end Transactions;
```

10.5. Customer

```
with Sets_G; with Transactions; use Transactions;
package Transaction_Sets is new Sets_G (Transaction_Ref);

with Ada.Finalization; use Ada.Finalization;
with Persons; use Persons;
with Accounts.Savings; use Accounts.Savings;
with Accounts.Checking; use Accounts.Checking;
with Transactions; use Transactions; with Transaction_Sets;
package Customers is
```

```
type Customer_Type is new Person_Type with private;
type Customer_Ref is access all Customer_Type'Class;
procedure Open_Checking
    (Customer: in Customer_Ref; Checking: in Checking_Ref);
-- Will check that Checking.Owner = Customer_Ref.
-- If needed, we can enforce that Open_Checking is
-- called only once for a given Customer.
function Checking_Account_Of
    (Customer: Customer_Type) return Checking_Ref;
-- Open_Savings and Savings_Account_Of are similar, and omitted.
procedure File
    (Customer: in out Customer_Type;
    Transaction: in Transaction_Ref);
private
    type Controlled_Checking_Ref is new Controlled with
    record
        Reference: Checking_Ref;
    end record;
    procedureFinalize
    (Checking_Ref: in out Controlled_Checking_Ref);
-- will close the checking account hold by the customer.
-- Similar for Savings.
    type Customer_Type is new Person_Type with record
        Owned_Checking:Controlled_Checking_Ref;
        Owned_Savings:Controlled_ Savings_Ref;
        Transactions: Transaction_Sets.Set_Type;
    end record;
end Customers;
```

11. Modifications made to Fusion

Fusion uses the term object model, where we prefer class model. Fusion usually forgets about dynamic visibility, and is not aware that it implies dependencies between classes. To keep this information, but in order to avoid overly complex graphs, we propose the simplification rule that permanent visibility makes dynamic visibility redundant.

Fusion does not know about abstract classes in class descriptions. Whenever the subclasses partition the parent class, the parent class should be declared as abstract. Also, when a method can only be defined for the subclasses, the method should be declared as abstract in the parent class. For an example (5.1.), the method Withdraw can only be defined when the sort of the account is known, because the rules governing checking and savings accounts are not the same. Finally, if a method is never called from the outside, we propose to mark it as local. For examples, see the Withdraw and Deposit methods of Account (5.1.).

12. Comparison with Work of Other Authors

In [9], we made a proposal of how to depict messaging of collections, which is inspired by Kris Oosting [7]. Oosting names the class of the collection, e.g. files: List (File). We think it is premature to decide upon a specific data structure when designing the object interaction graphs. Indeed, only the full set of object interaction graphs can show the methods required from a given collection.

Martin van Amersfoorth [1] proposes to show in the visibility graphs that links are inverse of each other. Design and implementation can then use this information to guarantee referential integrity.

Mutual dependency between classes and packages is sometimes called the "with-ing" problem in Ada. It has been studied in-depth by John Volan [13].

Rosen [8] discusses extensively the naming issue for Ada. He also explains the suffix notation we use in this paper, but rejects it in favor of generic identifiers. It leads to difficulties when several types are directly visible.

Acknowledgments

Many thanks to Erhard Ploedereder and the anonymous reviewers for carefully reading a first version of this paper and for their very useful comments and remarks.

References

[1]   Martin van Amersfoorth; Family Ties - Or How to Survive Mutual Relationships; *in* Fusion Newsletter, May 1997, pp. 5-8.

[2]   Stéphane Barbey; Ada 95 as Implementation Language for Object-Oriented Designs; *in* Proceedings of TRI-Ada '95, Charles B. Engle, Jr. (Ed.), Anaheim, California, November 5-10 1995, pp. 212-225.

[3]   Stéphane Barbey and Alfred Strohmeier; Object-Oriented Programming with Ada 95; *in* International Conference on Reliable Software Technologies, Ada-Europe'97, London, U.K, June 1-6 1997, Tutorial Notes, 1997. (This tutorial was given the first time in 1994.)

[4]   Stéphane Barbey, Magnus Kempe and Alfred Strohmeier; Programmation par objets avec Ada 9X; *in* TSI (Techniques et Sciences Informatiques), vol. 13, no. 5, 1994, pp. 639-669.

[5]   P. P. Chen; The entity-relationship model: towards a unified view of data; *in ACM TODS*, 1(1), 1976.

[6]   Derek Coleman *et alii*; Object-Oriented Development: The Fusion Method; Prentice Hall, 1994.

[7]   Kris Oosting; The Collective - resistance is futile; *in* Fusion Newsletter, February 1997, pp. 4-7.

[8]   Jean-Pierre Rosen; A naming convention for classes in Ada 9X; *in* ACM Ada Letters, XV(2):54-58, Mar.-Apr. 1995.

[9]   Alfred Strohmeier; The Fusion Method, with Implementation in Ada 95; *in* TRI-Ada'97 Tutorial Notes, St. Louis, MO, USA, ACM Press, 1997, and *in* SIGAda'98 Tutorial Notes, Washington D.C., USA, ACM Press, 1998.

[10] S. Tucker Taft, Robert A. Duff (Eds.); International Standard ISO/IEC 8652:1995(E): Ada Reference Manual; Lecture Notes in Computer Science 1246, Springer Verlag, 1997.

Electronic resources

[11] WEB site for the Fusion method: http://www.hpl.hp.com/fusion

[12] UML documentation: http://www.rational.com/uml/documentation.html

[13] John Volan: http://bluemarble.net/~jvolan/WithingProblem/FAQ.html, Version 2.06, June 3, 1997.

Efficient and Extensible Multithreaded Remote Servers[*]

Ricardo Jiménez-Peris[1], M. Patiño-Martínez[1],
F. J. Ballesteros[2], and S. Arévalo[1]

[1] Technical University of Madrid
[2] Madrid Carlos III University

Abstract. In many cases, servers must impose a protocol of calls to their clients, and at the same time handle multiple client requests. The MT-Rendezvous design pattern greatly simplifies both tasks: separate server threads handle separate clients or sessions, and each different call protocol is handled by means of rendezvous.

One of the most significant performance problems in this kind of system is the latency introduced by network messages exchanged between clients and servers. Another design pattern, CompositeCalls, has been used to achieve dramatic performance improvements. With CompositeCalls clients send entire *programs* to the server so that the number of messages exchanged can be greatly reduced. Moreover, servers can be dynamically extended by using CompositeCalls.

Therefore, an *expressive and efficient* server model can be obtained by mixing both patterns within the same framework. However, as both patterns overlap, its integration is not a trivial task.

In this paper we describe how can both patterns be combined, including a brief description for its instantiation in Ada 95. Besides, we show concrete applications where the compound pattern, CompositeRendezvousCalls, can be employed, including a transactional framework for distributed Ada applications, *TransLib*.

1 Introduction

One of the mechanisms proposed for client-server interaction is rendezvous. It has some advantages over the RPC model. In particular, servers can easily impose a protocol of calls to their clients. Consider a server design that imposes a protocol for client calls, which is the common case; e.g. open must be called first, then a sequence of read and/or write, and finally close[1]. Rendezvous is probably the best way to go, because enforcing call protocols with RPC is somewhat awkward and error prone. With RPC, it is necessary to record results from

---

[*] This work has been partially funded by the Spanish Research Council(*CICYT*), contract number *TIC98-1032-C03-01* and the Madrid Regional Council (*CAM*), contract number *CAM-07T/0012/1998*.
[1] A more involved protocol results when considering different (specialized) open primitives: openRead, openAppend, openModify.

previous calls, test those results in following calls, and maintain shared data structures to associate session state with client identifiers (or addresses).

However, using rendezvous also posses some drawbacks. In particular, it is hard to implement multithreaded servers, using different call protocols for different clients. The MT-Rendezvous design pattern [2] simplifies such task providing support for multithreaded rendezvous. The server code just deals with a single client. That is, when the first call from a client is received a server thread is created. That call and future calls from the same client will be managed by the same server thread. Thus, server development is greatly simplified. Some scenarios where multithreaded rendezvous-based servers are convenient are transactional environments [4]; like *Transactional Drago* [3, 2], and DVM [10].

In a distributed environment, typical client/server interactions require many network messages. For instance, to copy a file within the same server the whole file will cross the network twice. Reducing the number of messages required to perform a given task can dramatically improve latency. The CompositeCalls design pattern [5] allows a client to send multiple calls, bundled together, to a given server (they will be referred as composite calls or programs). Simple control structures, such like *"while I can read, write what I have read"* can be submitted to the server. Every call made to a server entry point, within a composite call, is actually a local procedure call. Finally, results are returned back to the caller node. Therefore, by using CompositeCalls, a lot of network traffic can be avoided, improving the latency for the service. An additional benefit of CompositeCalls is that it allows dynamic extension of the server (e.g. a copy service could be added by building upon the primitive read, and write services).

Improvements in server latency, expressiveness and simplicity can be achieved by careful integration of the CompositeCalls and MT-Rendezvous patterns. Such integration presents several difficulties because both patterns intersect, addressing common issues in rather different ways (e.g. they model server calls in different ways). Despite that, combining both patterns brings clear benefits in distributed applications:

1. Servers need to include just basic (primary) services. Thus, its design is simplified. Later, they can be extended dynamically by means of composite calls.
2. Client/server interaction can be more cleanly structured, by using the expressive power of rendezvous.
3. Client/server interaction can be more efficient. All server calls made within a composite call do not cross the network.
4. Server code is more easily written, as it has to deal with a single client; while, at the same time, more throughput can be obtained on multiprocessors by servicing in parallel different clients (i.e. due to multithreading).
5. A single call, expressing an entire rendezvous-based session, can be built; i.e. separate steps in a call protocol enforced by rendezvous can be combined in a single entity.

In what follows, we will show the patterns involved in sections 2 and 3. Section 4 shows how to the CompositeCalls pattern can be mixed with MT-Rendezvous in a distributed environment. We will also show what difficulties we found, and how to tackle them. Some Ada 95 specific implementation issues we had to address are described too in section 5. Example applications for the new compound pattern are given in section 6. Section 7 comments related design patterns. Finally, section 8 describes some conclusions.

2 The MT-Rendezvous Design Pattern: Multithreaded Servers

As we have already mentioned, one of the advantages of using rendezvous is that servers can impose, in an easy way, a protocol of calls to their clients. However, in the traditional rendezvous model of interaction, a single server thread deals with all the clients. The MT-Rendezvous design pattern [2] supports a variant of rendezvous where each client[2] is served by a different server thread (ServerXTask and ServerYTask in figure 1). This design pattern allows the use of passive remote servers that use rendezvous to attend multiple clients, which it is unfeasible with traditional rendezvous.

In MT-Rendezvous calls proceed as shown in figure 2 (see also section 2.1). Client calls are encapsulated in the Call class hierarchy (fig. 1). As calls are handled as abstract entities, they can be changed independently. The state of a call consists of the actual values of the parameters (or results).

When a request is received at the server side, the Forwarder, or more concretely its Process method, will check whether there is a server thread (ServerTask) for that client. If there is none, it creates one of the appropriate type. It can do so, by calling the StartServerTask method of the call received.

The newly created server thread will be used for the session held with that client. The forwarder can store a reference to it as reference to an abstract ServerTaskObject (fig. 1).

Task creation is performed by calls, because forwarders must not know concrete server interfaces. The only objects which really know what kind of the server is being called are calls themselves. In particular, the forwarder delivers calls to the appropriate server task, without any knowledge about the actual server interface.

The Forwarder class encapsulates the forwarding policy (concurrent, sequential[3], etc.). This has the additional advantage that it can be changed independently of the rest of the system.

CourierTasks are used to prevent blocking the forwarder, and make the actual call asynchronously. They do so by calling the MakeCall method of the call, that makes the actual call. This method dispatches to a concrete entry of an agreed-upon[4] ServerTask.

---

[2] Note that MT-Rendezvous clients can be concurrent and/or distributed.

[3] In particular, this policy is useful to build deterministic, replicated servers.

[4] It can be set with the SetDestinationTask method. In fact, the forwarder calls this method when it finds out the associated (to the client who has submitted the call) server task.

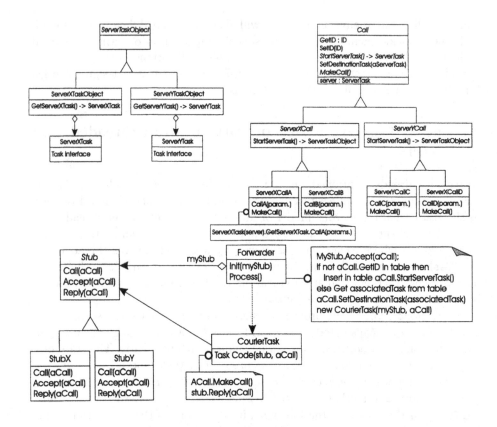

Fig. 1. MT-Rendezvous Pattern

Calls are built by the client and sent to the server by means of the communication layer. Such layer is represented as an Ada 95 stream, named Comm, what allows the flattening and unflattening of calls being sent.

Concrete stubs are used to enforce server interface to the client, as well as for flatenning, sending, receiving, unflattening and replying calls.

2.1 Using MT-Rendezvous Design Pattern

A single call in the MT-Rendezvous pattern goes through the following path (figure 2):

1 The client makes the request to the client stub.
2 The client stub flattens the call and submits it using the comm object.
3 The flattened call crosses the network.
4 The server stub gets the call from the comm object and unflattens it.
5 The forwarder takes the call from the local stub. If a server thread does not exist for the client, it creates a new one.

6 The forwarder creates a courier task to make the call asynchronously.
7 The courier task makes the call and the server thread accepts it.

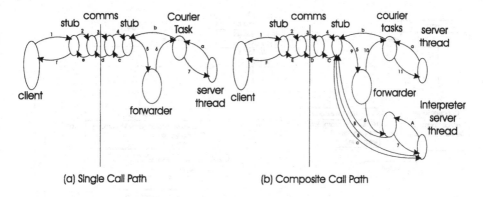

(a) Single Call Path   (b) Composite Call Path

Fig. 2. Using `CompositeRendezvousCalls`.

Once the call is processed the result returns through this path:

a The rendezvous between the courier task and the server thread finishes.
b The courier task sends back the results of the call to the local stub.
c-f The result comes back from the server stub to the client.

3 Reducing Domain Crossings: The `CompositeCalls` Design Pattern

The `CompositeCalls` design pattern [5] has been proposed to reduce the number of cross-domain calls as much as possible, and to provide dynamic server extension. In this pattern, the client code that performs the interaction with the server is encapsulated in an object, and submitted to the server. Once in the server domain, it is interpreted so that local procedure calls suffice.

The pattern (fig. 3) contemplates the possibility of using different languages to build submittable client code. No matter the language used, the client code being sent to the server is termed `program` (it is also known as a composite call). Each kind of `program` is made out of a kind of `commands`. For instance, high-level programs are composed of high-level commands and low-level programs are made out of low-level commands.

A variable table, `VarTable`, is used to keep program state, an also to hold both input and output parameters for the program. Therefore, variables are tagged with a mode which can be either `In`, `Out`, `InOut`, or `None`. `In` and `InOut` variables have an initial value set by the client, so they must be transmitted to the server along with the submitted `program`. `Out` and `InOut` variables contain values generated or updated by the server; the client is interested in them, as

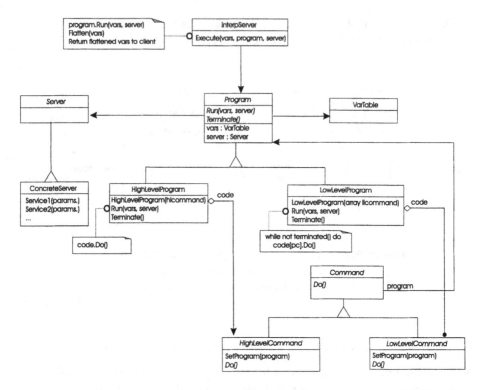

Fig. 3. CompositeCalls Pattern

outcome of the service. Thus, Out and InOut variables are delivered back to the client as soon as the program completes. Variables tagged as None are temporal (local) variables, only used within the server domain.

For each server, the command hierarchy is extended with the set of services the server provides, named ServerCalls (in figure 4). Values for ServerCall parameters are not known at submission time, but at interpretation time. This is an important difference with respect to the MT-Rendezvous pattern, where parameter values are known when calls are being built, i.e. at submission time. Such difference is similar, in some sense, to the one between actual and formal parameters. Parameters supplied in CompositeCalls calls behave as formal parameters which are filled later on, during program execution; parameters given to MT-Rendezvous calls, are actual parameters.

When a ServerCall is created, its constructor takes, as parameters, those variables which should be used as parameters at interpretation time. Then the call is submitted to the server.

Once in the server, the interpreter of the program is invoked by calling the Run program method. In turn, Run calls the Do method of involved commands. That is, each command has its interpretation built-in.

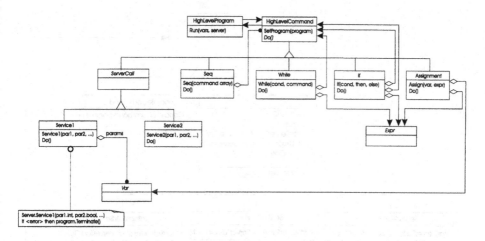

Fig. 4. High-Level Command Hierarchy

To accept legacy servers, the server is encapsulated in a `ConcreteServer` class (fig. 3), which can be either the actual server, or a wrapper for it.

4 Efficient, Extensible and Expressive Multithreaded Servers

At first sight, the `CompositeCalls` pattern fits very naturally in a rendezvous-based client-server interaction (particularly in `MT-Rendezvous`). Clients will submit composite calls or programs to the server for execution. If there is no server task associated to the client, the server will create a new one for it. The program is interpreted on the server side, and calls are issued locally to the associated server task. When program execution finishes, results are sent back to the client.

Efficiency is improved, because many remote calls are now implemented as local ones. Moreover, the server is now "extensible", as new entry points can be added *on the fly* by means of `CompositeCalls`. `MT-Rendezvous` provides expressivenes.

4.1 Building the `CompositeRendezvousCalls` Design Pattern

As we previously mentioned, one of the main differences between `MT-Rendezvous` and `CompositeCalls` design patterns is the way calls are handled. In `MT-Rendez-vous`, calls encapsulate the actual parameters, and the service to be called. On the other hand, in `CompositeCalls` actual parameters are not known on the client side, but on the server side—when the program is interpreted.

Another important difference, involving the server side, is structural. In `CompositeCalls`, the server structure can be very simple, just a thread that receives programs and executes them. However, `MT-Rendezvous` has a much

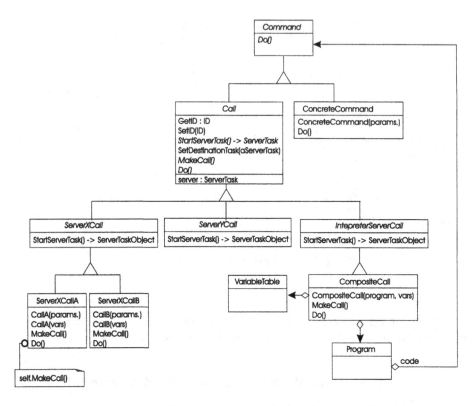

Fig. 5. Integration of `MT-Rendezvous` and `CompositeCalls` Patterns

more complex framework, as it has to deal with multiple server threads, and a request forwarding policy (it can forward the requests sequentially, in groups, in parallel, etc.).

After we noticed both patterns would not mix cleanly, by simple cut-&-paste, we defined several guidelines to aid the integration:

- The `Call` class hierarchy, which was different in both patterns, should be unified both to avoid redundancies and to prevent conflicts.
- No flexibility should be lost due to the integration: encapsulation of the forwarding policy; the ability of using different languages/interpreters for different servers; reusing existing languages/interpreters for new servers; concurrent clients support ... all should be preserved.
- Clients should be able to submit single calls, as well as composite calls.

From the different alternatives[5] for unifying the call hierarchies we chose to keep the `MT-Rendezvous` abstract `Call` as a subclass of the `CompositeCalls` abstract `Command` (of the language chosen by the server). The symmetric alternative (that we discarded) is to embed `MT-Rendezvous` calls in programs. This

---

[5] Which we omit due to space constraints.

has the disadvantage that the user is forced to use composite calls even for single calls, which is more inefficient. Besides, the stub must discriminate between single and composite calls to prevent creation of interpreter servers for single calls. It was just simpler and cleaner to embed composite calls into MT-Rendezvous calls.

The solution adopted consists in preserving the MT-Rendezvous architecture, by adding a new kind of server call, the InterpreterServer (see Interpreter-ServerCall in fig. 5). Thus, composite calls are managed (by MT-Rendezvous) as single calls, and delivered to the InterpreterServer. Where InterpreterServer interprets the program and, as a "side-effect", some single calls are issued. Those single calls are sent back to the stub, so they follow the same path traversed in MT-Rendezvous calls.

Therefore, when the forwarder takes a new call from the stub, it can be a call issued from either the client, or the interpreter server. The stub remembers from where the call originated, so it can be returned to the caller (the client or the interpreter server).

4.2 Using the CompositeRendezvousCalls Design Pattern

To illustrate the resulting system, we will now describe how are both single and composite calls handled in the new environment.

A composite call in CompositeRendezvousCalls follows the same path followed by a single call in MT-Rendezvous. To achieve that, we have created a new kind of server, the InterpreterServer. All composite calls are aimed to it. However, single calls are generated while interpreting the composite call (or program) received at the server side (and not at the client side as happened in MT-Rendezvous).

As can be seen in figure 2, the path for a composite call or program (fig. 2.b, arrows 1-7) is the same as the one for a single call (fig. 2.a, arrows 1-7). Single calls originated from a CompositeCall follow the path below:

8 The interpreter passes the call to the server stub.
9 The forwarder takes the call from the stub.
10 The forwarder creates the courier task to make the call asynchronously.
11 The courier task makes the call and the server thread accepts it.
a The server thread finishes rendezvous and sends back the results of the call.
b The courier task finishes and returns the results back to the stub.
c The stub sends the results to the interpreter server (instead of the client, as happens with calls generated by the client).

When the interpretation of the composite calls finishes, the results follow this path:

A The results (Out and InOut variables of the variable table) are sent back to the calling courier task.
B The courier task returns the results to the server stub.

C-F The same than for c-f.

One of the achievements of our integration is that it keeps almost the same path for single calls—no matter their originator. Calls originated within `Composite-Calls` follow the same path they follow in the `MT-Rendezvous`.

5   `CompositeRendezvousCalls` in Ada 95

We have implemented the pattern in several languages, namely, C, C++, and Ada 95. There are some interesting details, regarding the Ada 95 implementation, which are worth discussing.

Streams was one of the mechanisms most welcomed in Ada 95, as the predefined flattening methods `Read` and `Write` were. These methods save a lot of work when instantiating the pattern. The communication layer was modeled as a stream, which made easier object flattening and unflattening needed to send calls across the network. Moreover, being Ada streams typed, they allow type-safe communication over an unstructured medium, such like a network connection.

It should be noted, though, that type-safeness can be assumed only when both the client and the server are trusted. Otherwise, the server should check received requests for integrity, or be prepared to handle invalid data (any ill-behaved sender could send malformed messages). In particular, when the pattern instance must tolerate multi-lingual applications (e.g. C++ mixed with Ada 95), callers should not be trusted by callees. However, this is not a specific issue of the proposed pattern, as it also happens on RPC-based distributed systems.

The design pattern proposed is going to be used in *TransLib* [3, 2], an Ada 95 framework for building transactional applications. `MT-Rendezvous` fits naturally in a transactional framework, where each transaction is considered to be a client. There, predefined `Read` and `Write` are used for loading and storing persistent objects. They are also used to undo during transaction abortion. In *TransLib*, clients are transactions identified by means of transaction identifiers (tids). In order to alleviate the programmer from the tedious task of tid handling, we have used the systems programming annex operations for task attributes handling. Thus, tasks executing transactions are tagged with their tid. In this way the system always knows which transaction a given task is working for.

The ability to store tags in a stream allows to instantiate the pattern without stub generators. Streams take care of object tags and behave as "automatic" stubs.

- *Generics* are useful to create templates for pattern participants. They can be later instantiated for concrete applications. In particular, they allow to instantiate different interpreters without extra cost, at run time, for dynamic dispatching.
- *Dynamic tasks* have been helpful in several places (where its number was not known a priori). Tasks used for the server and courier tasks are both dynamic. Task discriminants further simplified task creation.

– *Requeue statement* can be used as a forwarding mechanism between the stub, the forwarder, and the courier. If the former two were tasks instead of objets, the forwarder could use a requeue statement to delegate the call to the courier task. Besides, it does not need to pass the stub as a task discriminant.

– *Protected objects* are useful to implement the stub state as it must process calls concurrently issued from both the forwarder and courier tasks.

6 Applications

There are many potential applications for the composite pattern, `Composite-RendezvousCalls`. To name a few, it can be used on:

Translib and other transaction frameworks, to implement commitment, abortion, and crash recovery.

Distributed storage (or checkpointing) facilities, as illustrated by the file system example in the introduction.

Disconnected Ada 95 partitions [6] could employ them to defer calls until eventual reconnection.

Wireless and expensive-communication environments can prefer to save some network messages.

Extensible Ada 95 partitions could rely on the pattern to allow downloading of new composite operations.

Distributed debugging can use the interpreter as an indirection level, which can be used as a hook for a debugger (e.g. small `CompositeRendezvousCalls` programs can be used as standard entry points into a given service; "just call" programs could be exchanged with "trace and call", or "cause breakpoint and call", or "conditionally trace and call", ...).

7 Related patterns and Ada 95 antecendents

Many other patterns can also help to address issues raised by the development of a multithreaded distributed service. In particular, both `MT-Rendezvous` [2], and `CompositeCalls` [5], describe some patterns related to each of them.

A `Reactor` [8] can be used to decouple multithreading from request handling. However, `Reactor` does not address call protocols, and does not save network messages, as `CompositeRendezvousCalls` does. A thorough description of multithreading issues in (ORB) servers can be found in [9]. An `Interpreter` [1] can support the language used for `CompositeCalls`.

In the past, some patterns have been instantiated on Ada 95 environments [6, 7]. We tried to go further by addressing interaction between several pattern instances within the same application. Moreover, our target application domain considers a fully distributed environment.

---

[6] Assuming an implementation for Annex E is being built to tolerate disconnected operation.

8 Conclusions

In this paper we have presented CompositeRendezvousCalls, an integration of MT-Rendezvous and CompositeCalls design patterns. By using such pattern, flexible, efficient and expressive distributed applications can be built.

Efficiency is achieved by means of composite calls that are executed locally on the server side saving network crossings. Rendezvous provides expressiveness by allowing the server to impose a call protocol. Dynamic server extension provides flexibility.

Besides, this is the first time CompositeCalls has been used in a distributed object-oriented programming language, Ada 95.

This pattern will be used in the implementation of *TransLib*, an Ada 95 framework to program distributed transactional systems. We have also discussed how Ada 95 features affected the pattern instantiation process. Finally, some other applications for the pattern have been suggested.

References

1. E. Gamma, R. Helm, R. Johnson, and J. Vlissides. *Design Patterns. Elements of Reusable Object-Oriented Software.* Addison Wesley, 1995.
2. R. Jiménez, M. Patiño, and S. Arévalo. Multithreaded Rendezvous: A Design Pattern for Distributed Rendezvous. In *Proc. of ACM Symposium on Applied Computing.* ACM Press, Feb. 1999.
3. M. Patiño, R. Jiménez, and S. Arévalo. Integrating Groups and Transactions: A Fault-Tolerant Extension of Ada. In *Proc. of International Conference on Reliable Software Technologies, Ada-Europe'98*, volume LNCS 1411, pages 78–89. Springer, June 1998.
4. M. Patiño, R. Jiménez, and S. Arévalo. Synchronizing Group Transactions with Rendezvous in a Distributed Ada Environment. In *Proc. of ACM Symposium on Applied Computing*, pages 2–9. ACM Press, Feb. 1998.
5. M. Patiño, Ballesteros F. J., R. Jiménez, S. Arévalo, Kon F., and Campbell R. H. Composite Calls: A Design Pattern for Efficient and Flexible Client-Server Interaction. In *http://www.gsyc.inf.uc3m.es/~nemo/off/interp.ps*, 1998.
6. B. I. Sandén. The State-Machine Pattern. In *Proc. of ACM Tri-Ada'96.* ACM Press, 1996.
7. J. M. Sasine and R. J. Toal. Implementing the Model-View-Controller Paradigm in Ada 95. In *Proc. of ACM Tri-Ada'95.* ACM Press, 1995.
8. D. C. Schmidt. Reactor. An Object Behavioral Pattern for Concurrent Event Demultiplexing and Event Handler Dispatching. In J. Coplien and D. C. Schmidt, editors, *Pattern Languages of Program Design.* Addison Wesley, 1995.
9. D. C. Schmidt. Evaluating Architectures for Multithreaded Object Request Brokers. *Communications of the ACM*, 41(10):54–60, Oct. 1998.
10. C. J. Thompson and V. Celier. DVM: An Object-Oriented Framework for Building Large Distributed Ada Systems. In *TriAda Conference.* ACM Press, 1995.

Report on the VERA Experiment

Bruno Hémeury

Marconi Research Centre
England - UK

Abstract. The rising cost of testing is driving industry to revise its processes and techniques in order to be able to verify in an economical way the complex systems demanded by current and future applications. The Marconi Research Centre devised a software testing experiment called VERA with the aim of finding a cost-effective verification process. Four mainstream techniques were selected: code review, Fagan inspection, static analysis and automated test-case generation. An independent team applied these techniques on a typical piece of software developed at Alenia Marconi Systems. Metrics originating from 65 other Marconi projects were also analysed. Of the possible combinations of these four verification techniques, our results suggest that Fagan inspection with static analysis is the most cost-effective process.

1 Introduction

Software testing is key to improving and gaining confidence about the correctness of the code, but for a typical project, it can absorb up to 50% of the overall budget. Testing techniques are labour-intensive and pressure is growing within industry to optimise the testing process and determine the effectiveness for testing techniques.

The aim of the Verification Evaluation and Review Analysis (VERA) experiment was to evaluate four verification techniques: code review, Fagan inspection, static analysis and automated test-case generation, in order to determine a cost-effective verification process for Ada software. The motivation behind the VERA experiment was the belief that costs of testing could be reduced by using greater automation and by concentrating effort where it is most likely to find errors. Within Alenia Marconi Systems (AMS), currently over half the errors found are detected during the integration phase. Detecting and correcting errors at this stage in the life-cycle is expensive and on average each error takes 22 hours. Automating the testing process and applying a more rigorous review process should help reduce this cost.

2 The VERA Experiment

VERA is a European Systems and Software Initiative (ESSI) funded Process Improvement Experiment (PIE) which aimed to derive a cost effective V&V

process for a given piece of software. The project involved two Marconi Electronics System companies: the Marconi Research Centre and Alenia Marconi Systems (AMS) Ltd.

Three software engineers, with varied backgrounds took part in the experiment. Only one had expert level knowledge in Ada and static analysis. The two others had experience of software development in other languages as well as testing (see Table 1).

Table 1. Experience (years) of VERA experimenters

Experimenter	Ada	Static analysis	Software testing
X	0·2	0	1
Y	0	0	2
Z	6	6	4

2.1 Baseline Project

AMS primarily develops radar-control systems, and a recent project was chosen as the baseline for this experiment. Because the whole system would be too large for the resources and time-frame available for the experiment, a self-contained module of 60 KLOC was selected. The whole system was written in Ada83 and although such software has real-time constraints and uses dynamic task allocation, the experiment was only concerned with functional correctness.

2.2 Experimental Protocol

The baseline software had been reviewed by the AMS development team. Within the VERA experiment, the software was subjected to static analysis using Rational's Ada Analyzer and automated test-case generation using Rational's Test-Mate.

All defects were categorised using the Fagan defect classification scheme where defect severity is expressed as major, minor or investigations, as in table 2:

Table 2. Fagan Defect Severity Classification

Major	A defect that could cause operational failure within the specified range of operation.
Minor	A defect in workmanship, spelling, or a violation of the standard code of programming that will not cause operational failure.
Investigation	A defect whose actual classification could not be resolved at the time and needs further investigation to determine whether it is a major or a minor defect, or should simply be discarded.

The techniques were assessed in terms of efficiency, to determine the effort involved, and effectiveness, to estimate the average number of defects found in a piece of software.

3 Selected techniques

3.1 Code review

Review is the main verification process used within the Radar Systems Division for finding defects in the code prior to the integration phase. Definitions of code review and the rigour with which they are applied vary greatly. Within Marconi Electronic Systems (MES) code review is defined as follows:

> The Purpose of a code review is to ensure that the code is a correct interpretation of its software design specification. The review also checks for conformance to good programming principles and adherence to coding standards as defined by project plans. The review should be performed after successful compilation of the code and before formal software testing. It is preferable that the review be carried out by persons not involved in the writing of the source code but with a good understanding of the design. Throughout the review, errors identified are recorded for correction which should also be reviewed.

AMS uses a relatively well-defined process, but the analysis of twelve years of project metrics has highlighted the lack of consistency and rigour in the application of reviews. The main symptoms are:

− the use of checklists is often neglected;
− the selected participants have sometimes been involved in the writing of the software under review;
− and the pace of review is too fast.

The evidence that an alternative to code review must be found is the fact that over half of the total number of defects are found during integration testing. As a result of the rising costs of fixing and correcting errors [1], an alternative to code review was introduced in 1997: Fagan inspection.

3.2   Fagan inspection

In 1976, Fagan published a paper [3] describing a more rigorous way of reviewing software, which he called inspection. Fagan experimented with his process while a project manager on an IBM operating system upgrade. He observed that use of inspections caused coding productivity to increase by 23% and the quality of the delivered code to improve. Fagan's paper was well received and despite resistance to adopting new processes, the use of inspection spread in the industry.

Inspection is a formal review-based process in which the seven phases of the process are rigorously defined (see Table 3).

Table 3. The seven steps of the inspection process

Planning	A management activity that involves selection of the inspectors, setting a schedule and checking that the subject document meets the entry criteria.
Overview	A short presentation during which the author describes the content and purpose of the document to be inspected.
Preparation	Each inspector reads the document and prepares for their role. Obvious defects can be recorded, but the aim of this step is to understand the document.
Inspection meeting	The moderator ensures each participant plays their role and the team focuses on finding defects. Unless a correction is obvious, there must be no attempt to derive a solution.
Process improvement	The inspection leader calls a meeting to discuss ways to improve the development process.
Re-work	The moderator and the author review the list of issues recorded, decide which issues generate an action and identify issues to be investigated.
Follow-up	Corrections implemented by the author are checked in order to avoid introducing bad fixes.

Another difference between reviews and inspections is the existence of entry criteria. Before passing through an inspection a document should satisfy certain criteria to ensure that no effort will be wasted on a poor quality document. One of these entry conditions is usually that the source documents should have passed a Fagan inspection. Hence specification and design documents should be inspected before the code. A typical entry condition for code is that it must compile without errors or warnings.

The assignment of a role to each participant is a key characteristic of the inspection process. The recommended team size for an inspection is four with the main roles being:

Moderator: The moderator is the inspection leader who ensures that the process is followed.

Reader: The reader paraphrases the code and any software products, a few lines at a time.

Author: The author explains his decisions if required or corrects misinterpretations from the reader.

Tester: The tester devises ways to test the software and suggests them during the meeting.

4 Static Analysis with Ada Analyzer

Ada Analyzer is the static analysis tool developed by Little Tree Consulting and distributed by Rational Corporation. Rational advertises Ada Analyzer as "a versatile tool to improve code quality"[2]. Its capabilities range from the analysis of code correctness and conformance to programming standards to code efficiency. The choice of Ada Analyzer was motivated by its functionality, ease of use, and position in the market place.

The tool is well integrated into the Apex development environment, and retains the consistency of the Apex user interface; the same development environment used by AMS to develop the baseline project.

4.1 Selected Analysis

Ada Analyzer includes 75 functions that can satisfy various quality objectives. Its capabilities include the detection of defects, the analysis of the program content, the computation of complexity metrics, and the identification of efficiency and portability issues. Ada code is unlikely to suffer from the sorts of problems which would be encountered in other languages such as FORTRAN or C (e.g. spaghetti goto's or type violations). But there are statically determinable errors which are not detected by Ada compilers. A trial period was organised to evaluate and assess Ada Analyzer capabilities and the following analyses were selected:

Data-flow analysis: The purpose of data-flow analysis is to highlight any discrepancies in the use and setting of variables. Ada Analyzer's current implementation is limited to detecting data-flow inconsistencies in scalar variables and records only. Two functions were used to detect when a variable is used before being set, or a variable is set twice before use. Multiple initialisation of a variable can increase code size and execution, but it can also give a clue that code is missing.

Control-flow analysis: The tool capability is limited to detecting a path in a function which does not return a value and to detecting an exception propagating outside its scope. There are no checks for non-executable code.

Static constraints analysis: Static constraint errors are the most critical, since this class of errors will automatically cause operational errors. Division by zero and array indices outside boundaries are detectable, but not necessarily in all cases.

Standard code of practice check: Ada Analyzer implements rules to verify that the software analysed complies with the standard code of programming set by the Software Productivity Consortium on Ada Quality and Style ?ith additional rules devised by Little Tree Consulting. For example, this function detects:

- LTC-107: Unchecked conversion mismatch;
- LTC-205: Inconsistent representation specifications;
- LTC-404: Use of the package `Text_io`;
- LTC-514: Use of unqualified references.

This function is considered to be the most useful in the Ada Analyzer arsenal to find defects. Over one hundred rules are checked covering code correctness, maintainability, efficiency, readability and portability.

Customisation By design, Ada Analyzer is highly customisable. Ada Analyzer uses the Ada Semantic Interface Specification (ASIS) to build its analyses. ASIS is a standardised and compiler-independent interface to semantic and syntactic information of compiled Ada programs. ASIS greatly facilitates the development and the porting of code analysis tools. Since the source code for these analyses is distributed as part of the product, it is possible to modify or add analyses.

4.2 TestMate

TestMate is a complete test management environment for all levels of software testing. The particular function of interest within the VERA experiment was the automatic generation of unit test data. The tool can generate data to satisfy code or branch coverage. Alternatively it can generate test data for Rational's "functional testing" which tests the combination of the lower, middle, and upper value of each input variable. Once the tester has set the expected outputs, TestMate can create the corresponding test script, run the compiler, execute the script and indicate which test cases have passed or failed, along with the test coverage obtained. The scripts are generated in Ada and are, in principle, customisable. However, editing the scripts means that testing is less easy to maintain and re-run. The script would need to re-edited if test data were modified.

Three options (All, Each, Min) govern the level of combinations between the generated parameter values. The "All" option generates all the possible combination of the lower, middle, and upper bound of each variable. The expected benefit for automated test-case generation is two-fold:

- good code coverage is facilitated with automated test-case generation;

– the tester does not need to write test scripts and can concentrate on producing specific test cases.

5 Results

5.1 Comparison Between Code Review and Fagan Inspection

AMS adopted Fagan inspection in 1996 and the VERA experiment was an opportunity to evaluate its impact on testing productivity. At present, 511 code inspections have been collected in the Fagan Inspection Metrics Database and in MARS (Metrics Analysis and Reporting System).

The results show that the more formal process delivers improved code quality and more consistent results than the less formal process. On average, Fagan inspection finds two and a half times more major defects than code reviews (see Fig. 1). It is believed that the distinct roles for each inspector (the process structure which leads its participants to focus on one task at any one time), as well as constraints to limit the rate of review and the size of the document to be examined are responsible for this improvement.

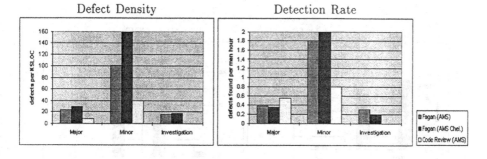

Fig. 1. Average effectiveness and productivity of code review and Fagan inspection

Fagan (AMS)	Code inspection results from the AMS division.
Fagan (AMS Chel.)	Code inspection results from the AMS Chelsmford division where the baseline project originates.
Code Review (AMS)	Code review results from the AMS division.

Finding defects early in the life-cycle is paramount and although Fagan inspection requires additional resources compared to reviews, this cost is recouped during test integration. A defect found during test integration costs 4 to 5 times more than one found during the implementation phase. The impact of individual engineers on any process is also extremely important. Our evidence suggests that the more experience engineers have in the language and application domain, the more defects are found. This result contradicts the generally accepted view that any competent engineer can review effectively.

5.2 Comparison Between Static Analysis and Code Review

Static analysis is the activity of verifying software without executing it. Tool supported static analysis performs checks to detect automatically coding violations and control-flow anomalies. Three participants took part in the static analysis experiment using Ada Analyzer (from Rational) on the baseline code. A trial period was required to familiarise the experimenters with Ada Analyzer; two of whom had no previous experience of static analysis. The results of the static analysis were then compared with the results of the code review carried out by the team who had designed and implemented the system.

The static analysis took 140 man hours to complete (see Fig. 2). This figure excludes the computation time to generate reports since it was generated overnight and even a low-end Unix workstation needed no more than two and a half hours to generate the most detailed report on the largest module. As a matter of comparison, the development team reviewed the same software in 249 hours.

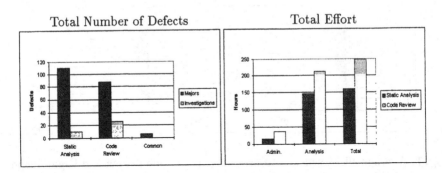

Fig. 2. Number of defects found and effort expanded in static analysis and code review.

With no prior knowledge of the application, the experimenters completed the analysis 34% faster than code review and detected 26% more major defects. However, a significant number of the defects were found, not by the tool, but by the experimenter while analysing the code. Code review and static analysis seem complementary because they target different types of defects. This is a major finding of the VERA experiment; only 5% of the defects found were common to both techniques.

Static analysis was found to be effective and complementary to code review. Only seven major defects were detected by both code review and static analysis. Our hypothesis is the two techniques tend to find different types of defects. Table 4 indicates that reviewers have mainly concentrated on the logic of the code, whereas static analysis focused on the misuse of data.

Table 4. Types of defects detected by code review and static analysis

Defect type	Code Review	Static Analysis
Logic	75%	24%
Data	5%	55%
Interface	11%	5%
Comment	3%	6%
Other	6%	10%

It is also worth noting that the three experimenters generally found different defects from each other. Only 25 percent of the defects detected were common to two or more experimenters. This may seem surprising since the process was automated, however Ada Analyzer reports potential defects, and the user needs then to investigate the code and the corresponding design. Experience indicated that some classes of potential defects highlighted by Ada Analyzer were unlikely to be actual defects. The user may not investigate all reports of these classes of potential defects thoroughly and as a consequence may miss actual defects.

A further explanation for the different defects detected by the experimenters is the difference in their attitudes to detecting additional defects while investigating a particular problem flagged up by the tool.

Within the VERA experiment, Ada Analyzer was used retrospectively to detect defects in code which had already entered the V&V phase. Static analysis tools, such as Ada Analyzer, could also be used by the programmers or designers of the code to check the code as it is developed. If programmers and designers statically analyse their own code they are unlikely to detect the full range of defects detected by the static analysts within the VERA experiment but they could potentially remove classes of defects, such as data-use anomalies and some control-flow checks and coding violations, before the code enters the V&V phase. This would leave inspectors or reviewers to concentrate on the verification of the design.

5.3 Experience with automated test-case generation with TestMate

On many large projects, unit testing is regarded as laborious and, therefore, expensive. The view that unit testing is not cost-effective is fuelled by the very positive results obtained by formal review processes, such as Fagan inspection. The goal of the experiment was to evaluate if the automatic generation of test data could improve the productivity of unit testing.

At present, the automated test case generation of TestMate (version 2.4.6) is applicable to a limited subset of Ada. The baseline software used the whole Ada language causing technical difficulties which severely limited the scope of the experiment, and only 7% of all units were unit tested.

From a total of 130 hours effort, 99 hours were spent solving problems and incompatibilities between TestMate and the baseline software. During the remaining 31 hours four major defects were found.

The nature of the baseline software, a real-time control system exchanging complex messages with its sub-systems, was perhaps ill-suited for TestMate. This was aggravated by the lack of flexibility to modify test scripts generated by TestMate and problems in the tool's user interface (for example, to enter test data for nested records or arrays which the baseline software used extensively). Scalar variables and enumerated types are the only types supported by TestMate.

6 Conclusion

The lack of a theoretical framework to objectively determine how much testing is required is problematic for the verification of complex software systems. The results of the VERA experiment provide guidance on which techniques are more cost-effective; the main lessons learned are:

- Fagan inspection improves the correctness of the code and promotes a culture of process improvement.
- The additional cost of inspection compared to code review is recouped at a later stage in the life-cycle.
- On the baseline project, static analysis was more effective (by 60%) and more efficient (by 26%) than code review.
- Static analysis is complementary to code review; only 5% of the defects were found by both techniques.
- The benefits of automated test-case generation with TestMate are limited for software using the full range of Ada language features.

From a business point of view the results of the VERA experiment show that:

- The most cost-effective V&V process for software is static analysis coupled with Fagan inspection. On a typical piece of code, this combination of techniques is likely to detect three times as many defects as performing code review alone (the main V&V activity previously performed at AMS prior to testing integration).
- The experience of the inspectors is a factor in the effectiveness of inspections.
- Static analysis, using Ada Analyzer, can be performed by competent engineers who have little or no domain knowledge. This is useful since there is often a shortage of such domain experts.

– A formal process only produces consistent results if the rules of the process are followed. Similarly, automating a process only produces repeatable results if use of the tools is controlled (for example, by a code of practice).

Our results were found through experimentation on Ada code, further work would be required to see if they were also relevant to code implemented in other languages.

7 Follow-up work

The results from the VERA experiment suggest that static analysis contributes significantly to improve code quality. Based on our experience with Ada Analyzer, software engineers are now using a batch program which drives Ada Analyzer and generates a single report of issues to be resolved before the review or inspection meeting.

8 Acknowledgement

The VERA team would like to thank ESSI for the opportunity to perform the experiment, Andy Warman from AMS Frimley who provided the Fagan Inspection Metrics Database and the participants of the three VV&T workshops for their inputs to the project.

References

[1] B.W. Boehm. *Software Engineering Economics*. Prentice Hall, 1981.

[2] Little Tree Consulting. *Ada Analyzer User's Guide*. Little Tree Consulting, 1996.

[3] M.E. Fagan. Design and code inspections to reduce errors in program development. *IBM Systems Journal*, 15(3):182–211, 1976.

Acceptance Testing of Object Oriented Systems

Jose L. Fernández

Area de Arquitectura (Caja Madrid)
28230 Las Rozas (Madrid) Spain
phone 34.91.5588477
fernadezjl@acm.org

Abstract

A rigorous approach for acceptance testing of object oriented systems is proposed. The approach combines use cases for requirements modeling and cause-effect graphing for the design of test cases. The formal characteristics of this approach guarantee a complete functional coverage not easily found in the state of the practice "adhoc manner" acceptance testing. This approach was applied in an object oriented application developed for the financial domain. The approach is independent of the implementation language.

1. Introduction

For years, many organizations have accepted software errors in their systems as a cost of doing business. When you built a system you assumed it would have defects. They would be annoying, but you just had to live with them. However, the problem of system errors has grown far beyond the annoying stage. System quality has now become the major factor in the success or failure of an organization.

From a quantifiable perspective, typical test efforts are very ineffective. Most software is released with only 30-50% code coverage and 40-60% functional coverage [1].

The major opportunity for improving the way software systems are tested lies in improving the process in which requirements specifications are developed and functional tests are designed.

We proposed an approach where user requirements, modeled by use cases, provide an excellent start at the formulation of an acceptance test plan. A test case design technique called cause-effect graphing [2] is used to transform rigorously use case scenarios into a formal logic model using a limited set of symbols representing logical operators: "and", "or", "nand", "xor" and negation.

Section 2 provides a brief explanation of use cases and the notation we used to model them. Section 3 deals with the cause-effect graphing technique. Section 4 is a description of the FUM object oriented application we developed, including some of the test cases designed and the results obtained.

2. Use Cases

Functional requirements are modeled in terms of actors and use cases. An actor is an external entity that uses or interacts directly with the system. An actor can be either a human user or another software or hardware system. A use case is a set of interactions between the system and one or more actors in order to achieve some specific business related goal. Thus, the purpose of a use case is to yield a result of measurable value (provide a service) to an actor in response to the initial request of that actor.

A use case diagram (Figure 1) is a graph of actors, a set of use cases enclosed by the system boundary, communication (participation) associations between actors and use cases, and generalization among the use cases [3].

The term scenario is related to use cases. An scenario refers to a single flow through a use case, one that shows a particular combination of conditions within that use case. For example, if we want to order some goods, we would have a single use case with several associated scenarios: one in which all goes well; one in which there are not enough goods; one in which credit is refused; and so forth [4]. Use Case is the level of granularity we consider to design acceptance test cases.

A use case description can be rather difficult to overview if it contains too many alternative, optional or exceptional flows of events that are performed only if certain conditions are met as the use case scenario is carried out. Jacobson suggests that a way of making the description clearer is to extract some of these subflows and let them form a use case of their own. This new case is said to extend the old one [5]. Jacobson also suggests to apply the uses relation, for helping to avoid redundancy by letting use cases share subflows [5].

We use two templates for the description of user requirements; one is applied at use case level and the other at scenario level. Use cases and scenarios are labeled for traceability purposes. Use cases are represented graphically by the use case diagram. Use case description based on templates guarantees the consistency in requirements specification. The templates used in FUM are described below.

Use case template:
- name
- type
- primary actor
- secondary actors
- relations to other use cases
- description

Scenario template:
- preconditions
- postconditions
- description (flow of events)
- notes

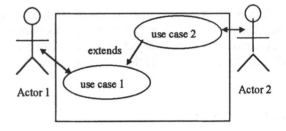

Fig. 1. Use Case Diagram Notation

3. Cause Effect Graphing

Cause effect graphing is a test-case design methodology that can be used within the scope of functional testing. It is used to select in a systematic manner a set of test cases, which have a high probability of detecting errors that exist in a system [6].

This technique explores the inputs and combination of inputs to the system (causes) in developing test cases. A boolean graph is used to represent the links from inputs to the outputs. A boolean graph is a formal logic model using a limited set of symbols representing logical operators: "and", "or", "nand", "xor" and "not" (negation). Each graph should start with invokable inputs (inputs that the tester can put directly into the system such as an input transaction) and end in observable events (outputs that the tester can check externally such as elements on a screen or in a database).

Cause-effect graphs are built with the notation shown in figure 2. The nodes represent causes and effects, and the links represent cause-effect transformations or logic combinations of causes. Causes and effects can be chained; thus an intermediate effect can also represent an intermediate cause.

It is important to distinguish primary cause nodes, those nodes which are not an effect of another cause, and primary effect nodes, those nodes which are not a cause to another effect. Both types of node are implicitly observable. All other nodes are referred to as intermediate effects. Typically, primary cause nodes are shown on the left side of the graph and primary effect nodes are shown on the right side of the graph.

The graph is annotated with constraints describing combinations of primary causes that are impossible because of syntactic or environmental issues.

By methodically tracing conditions in the graph, it is converted into a limited entry decision table. A limited-entry "decision table" determines which input conditions will result in each identified output. The set of test cases can be easily derived from this table.

The process of creating a cause-effect graph to derive test cases is described briefly:
- Carefully analyze each use case and its scenarios to identify all primary causes and effects in the specification. A cause is a distinct input condition; an effect is an

output condition or an observable change in the system state. An error message should be considered an effect.

- Assign each cause and effect a unique identification number.
- Analyze the semantic content of each use case and the specification of its scenarios, and transform it into a boolean graph linking the causes and effects; this is the cause-effect graph modeling the analyzed use case.
- For each effect, trace back through the graph to find all combinations of causes that will set the effect to be true. Each such combination is represented as a column in the decision table.
- Convert the columns in the decision table into acceptance test cases.

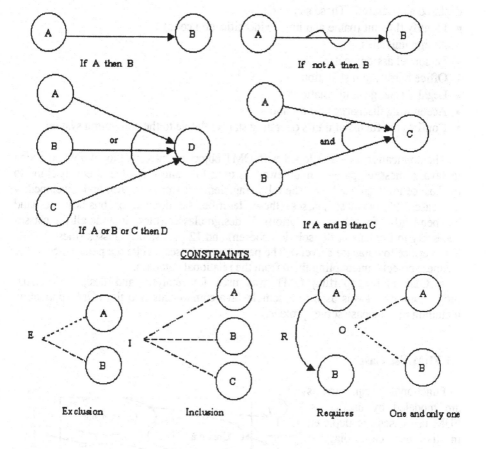

If A then B

If not A then B

If A or B or C then D

If A and B then C

CONSTRAINTS

Exclusion

Inclusion

Requires

One and only one

Fig. 2. Cause-effect Graph Notation

4. Acceptance Testing of the FUM Application

The Financial Units Management (FUM) application provides the services to update and consult information related to the organization units of the bank. An organization unit is a party which is a component of an organization; for example, Consumer Services Division, Legal Department, Branch Office #12. The bank is structured into financial units performing different activities: selling financial products, customer services, support services and so on. The typical financial unit is a branch. Caja Madrid has more than 1500 branches in different locations all over Spain.

Once a new unit is created, there are several steps to accomplish before it can be declared as operative. These steps are:

- Identify the unit (name and unique identification code)
- Assign unit sites
- Personnel assignment
- Office hardware installation
- Legal discharge confirmation
- Accounting discharge confirmation
- Confirm the financial unit's operating status relative to the computing system

The application was developed with OMT object oriented methodology and coded in Java; a message passing middleware is used for connecting the client machine to the host centralized database. The following elements were designed and developed: 4 use cases, 23 business classes (these describe the domain or business at hand independently of a software solution), 53 design classes (these include all the classes necessary to implement the solution chosen) and 12 persistence classes (these handle the interface to database servers). The persistence classes handle the persistence of the business objects, uncoupling them from the relational database.

A Case tool supporting OMT was used for analysis and design. A visual programming tool was used to assemble Java components into the FUM application including the database server proxies.

4.1 FUM Use Cases

Functional requirements are modeled by use cases. FUM use cases are depicted in the use case diagram (figure 3).

For the sake of brevity, we illustrate the approach with only one FUM use case, describing the Financial Unit Creation.

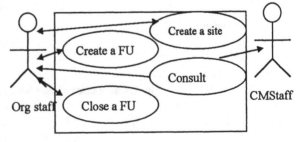

Fig. 3. FUM Use Case Diagram

The use case is documented using the following template:

Use case Name: Create FU

Use Case Id.: UC1

Type : Real

Primary Actor: Organization staff

Secondary Actors: Caja Madrid staff (Personnel staff, accounting staff, real estate staff, systems staff)

Relation to other use cases: not applicable

Description:

A user from organization department starts the use case in order to create a new financial unit for the bank and establish its relations to other units.

UC1 Create FU use case contains 7 scenarios (independent execution paths). A full description of the use case scenarios can be found elsewhere [7]. As an example the personnel assignment scenario is shown:

Name: Personnel assignment

Id: E1-3

Preconditions:

The unit must be identified.

The unit site where the person is going to be assigned has been already created.

Description:

This scenario performs the assignment of employees belonging to the Caja Madrid group to a unit. The main steps of the scenario are described below.

- The user enters the employee number of the person to assign.
- The system checks the employee already exists.
- The user enters the job assignment (as a percentage) of the employee related to that unit.
- The system shows the existing unit sites in a list.
- The user selects the unit site.
- The user can assign as many employees as he/she considers necessary.

Notes:

A job represents a significant role that is played in Caja Madrid organization.

4.2 Acceptance Testing Outputs

The acceptance testing process described in section 3 produces diverse outputs. Here only those related to the Create FU use case are shown.

4.2.1 Causes and Effects identified for UC1

Causes and effects listed below are identified for the complete UC1 including its seven scenarios. Personnel assignment scenario, described above, contributes to cause 5: enter employee description, and effect 104: erroneous employee identifier. Executing the other UC1 scenarios triggers causes 1, 2, 3, 4, 6, 7,8 and 9. Same effects may be produced by several scenarios, for example effect 105: wrong interaction sequence.

Causes
1. Enter Financial Unit Code
2. Select Financial Unit code from the code list
3. Enter Financial Unit description
4. Select site from the site list
5. Enter employee description
6. Confirm legal discharge
7. Confirm accounting status
8. Confirm operating status relative to the computing system
9. Confirm office hardware installation

Effects
100. Correct partial discharge
101. Correct total discharge
102. Erroneous FU code
103. Errors in FU description
104. Erroneous employee identifier
105. Wrong interaction sequence

4.2.2 Cause-Effect Graph for UC1

Use case 1 is translated into a boolean logic diagram (figure 4) representing constraints between causes and cause-effect sequences. Logical operators such as "and", "or", "not " (negation) and constrains such as "E" (cause exclusion) are used.

The temporal sequence of events is represented in the graph using intermediate nodes (20, 30, 50, 60) combining later causes with earlier non-primary effects.

4.2.3 Decision Table for UC1

Determining in the previous graph, which input conditions result in each identified output condition, yields the decision table. Each column in the table represents an independent test case.

Causes	1	2	3	4	5	6	7	8	9	10	11	12	13
1. Enter financial unit code	F	T	T	-	-	F	F	F	F	F	F	F	T
2. Select financial unit code from the code list	--	--	--	T	T	T	F	F	F	F	F	F	--
3. Enter financial unit description	--	F	T	--	--	--	--	--	--	--	--	--	T
4. Select site from the site list	--	--	--	T	--	--	T	--	--	--	--	--	T
5. Enter employee description	--	--	--	--	F	T	--	T	--	--	--	--	T
6. Confirm legal discharge	--	--	--	--	--	--	--	--	T	--	--	--	T
7. Confirm accounting status	--	--	--	--	--	--	--	--	--	T	--	--	T
8. Confirm operating status relative to the computing system	--	--	--	--	--	--	--	--	--	--	T	--	T
9. Confirm office hardware installation	--	--	--	--	--	--	--	--	--	--	--	T	T
Effects													
100. Correct partial discharge	F	F	T	T	F	T	F	F	F	F	F	F	F
101. Correct total discharge	F	F	F	F	F	F	F	F	F	F	F	F	T
102. Erroneous financial unit code	T	F	F	F	F	F	F	F	F	F	F	F	F
103. Financial unit information errors	F	T	F	F	F	F	F	F	F	F	F	F	F
104. Erroneous employee identifier	F	F	F	F	T	F	F	F	F	F	F	F	F
105. Wrong sequence	F	F	F	F	F	F	T	T	T	T	T	T	F

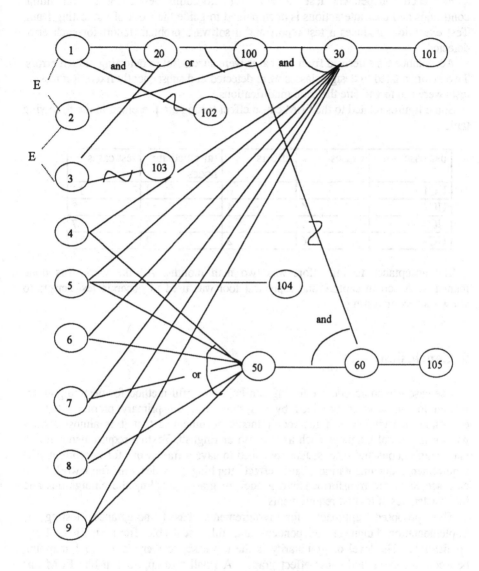

Fig. 4. FUM Cause-Effect Graph

Effects related to errors result from invalid data inputs or an incorrect sequence of operator inputs.

For each independent test case, a test procedure describing system initial conditions and user interactions is documented to guide the work of the testing team. Test execution produces a test report and a software problem report for each error detected.

Acceptance tests derived from use cases were successful in detecting hidden errors. Two errors related to design classes were detected and subsequently fixed. Regression tests were run to validate the code modifications.

Some figures related to the FUM cause effect testing are presented in the following table.

use case	causes	effects	intermediate nodes	test cases
UC1	9	6	4	13
UC2	4	4	1	5
UC3	7	4	2	7
UC4	6	2	2	6

The acceptance testing effort was two man months. All the work was done manually. A screen capture and reply test tool was used to generate test scripts to allow regression testing.

5. Conclusions

Use case driven acceptance testing can be a powerful method for detecting errors related to the services provided by a system. But the primary problem that we encounter in trying to test the requirements document is that it is almost always written in natural language such as Spanish or English. Textual requirements are by nature ambiguous and inconsistent. We need to have a framework for interpreting the requirements documentation. Cause-effect graphing provides this framework. Use case scenarios are transformed into a boolean graph, avoiding the ambiguities and inconsistencies of textual requirements.

The proposed approach for requirements based acceptance testing is implementation language independent and fully scaleable from small to large applications. The level of granularity is the use case, so there is a 1 to 1 mapping between use cases and cause-effect graphs. A small size application like FUM has less than a dozen use cases/cause-effect graphs.

This technique to create test cases has not yet been totally automated. However, conversion of the graph to a decision table is an algorithmic process, which could be automated by a computer program. Some tools support the technique and are useful in avoiding the tedious work of converting graphs for medium and large applications [8]. Once a cause-effect graph is developed, the tool can then apply the path sensitizing algorithms to design test cases. For a use case with n inputs, there are 2 to the power of n possible ways to combine the input data into test cases. Due to temporal ordering and constraints, the number of independent test cases is small. It turns out that is a small subset of the input combinations that can be derived using these algorithms to fully test the use case.

Test case design takes a disciplined approach that is not only methodical, but one which is also truly rigorous. Thus acceptance testing functional coverage is considerably improved. We conclude that the approach here described to map use cases to cause-effect graphs can be very beneficial to achieve acceptance testing in object oriented systems.

Acknowledgments

The author likes to express his gratefulness to Teresa Martínez and Esther Camarero. He is also indebted to the FUM project team. The reviewers comments and advice have helped to improve this paper.

References

[1] Bender and Associates Inc. : Why a Disciplined Approach Means a Competitive Approach to Software Quality. White Paper. October 1998.

[2] Myers G. : The Art of Software Testing. Wiley-Interscience Publication 1979.

[3] Rational : Unified Modeling Language. Notation Guide
Rational Software Corporation, Version 1.0, Jan. 1997

[4] Fowler M., Scott K., and Booch G. : UML Distilled: Applying the Standard Object Modeling Language. Addison Wesley 1997.

[5] Jacobson I., Ericsson M. and Jacobson A. : The Object Advantage: Business Process Reengineering with Object Technology. Addison Wesley 1995.

[6] Presson E. : Software Test Handbook, Software Test Guidebook Volume II (of two). Boeing Aerospace Company/Rome Air Development Center, Technical Report TR-84-53, March 1984.

[7] Sanjuan I., Lestau L., Martínez T., and Fernández J. : Piloto de Aplicación de Centros. Requisitos. Caja Madrid Version 1.1 (in Spanish), April 1998.

[8] Bender and Associates Inc. : Softest Users Tutorial Release 5.1. August 1996

Environment for the Development and Specification of Real-Time Ada Programs

Apolinar González[1], Alfons Crespo[2]

[1]Universidad del Valle (Calí, Colombia)
apogon@eiee.univalle.edu.co
[2]Universidad Politécnica de Valencia (Spain)
Camino Vera s/n; 46072 Valencia
alfons@disca.upv.es

Abstract. The use of formal methods for real-time system provides an analysis and a validation of the accomplished specifications, however, the complexity encumbers their interest in the industrial developments. This causes a gap between the real needs of the practical users (industrial) and the scientific community. The design based on components emerges as a design technique to reduce the complexity and the validation process of software development. Moreover, in the real-time system design where the object oriented design has demonstrate its validity, the use of predefined components can strongly improve and reduce the design, implementation and validation phases. In this paper we present an tool to design real-time control systems from a set of specific components. The tool provides a graphical interface to define component levels. Each component has associated a High Level Time Petri Net and an Ada code which are composed to build a prototype and a design specification.

1. Introduction

The use of formal methods for real-time system provides an analysis and a validation of the accomplished specifications, however, the complexity encumbers their interest in the industrial developments. This causes a gap between the real needs of the practical users (industrial) and the scientific community. Recently, several works have proposed solutions based on languages that conjugate what is informal with a rigorous notation and the analysis of the formal methods. The main idea consists of linking generated specifications in a friendly language to a formal validation method.

The methods and tools used to produce requirements and specifications analysis directly determine the quality of the software development [1]. In real time systems, these methods and tools provide formalism and mechanism concepts. These concepts allow to capture, in a high abstraction level, the concurrence of the activities, the synchronisation and the communication between them and the internal and external events management. The specification inconsistencies and completeness can be solved or amended during the development process of the final design. Another problem that should be considered before the final design is the validation. To reach the final goal of the process it is necessary to predict the behavior of the system taking into account the timing constraints [2] [3] [4].

The global specification of the system allows the capture and validation of the global behavior of the system using any of the formal available methods. However, once the specification is validated, a detailed design of the system is performed and the code is generated. It is very complex to connect the initial validation of the system with the generated code. In our criteria, it is very relevant to the designer to use similar abstractions during the different development phases (specification, design, implementation). The design process of a new development environment should take into account the following decisions:

- To select the appropriate components to be offered to the user as high level abstractions
- To select the formal model to support these abstractions
- To translate individual components to formal components
- To build a library of components and translations
- To provide a global model to build complete specifications
- To test the specification
- To produce a prototype in the selected language

There is reasonable agreement regarding the main components or abstractions to be used in the development of real-time systems. In the works of [5] [6] [7] [8] some components are analysed and proposed. With respect to formal models, Petri Nets have been extensively studied and used as a formalism for specifying concurrent systems. However, in the past they were extended in several different directions, with the goal of making them suitable for specifying other aspects, such as data, functionality, and timing. In this sense, High Level Timed Petri Nets allow the specification of concurrent systems with timing constraints. On the other hand, Ada is recognised as an appropriate language to implement real-time systems.

In order to connect the global specification of the system with the generated code a common method should be used. In this paper we attempt cover the first step in this process. From an architectural design based on predefined components, a specification, based on High Level Petri Nets, and an Ada code are generated. It will allow the validation of some properties of the final implementation. In the IPTES project [9], the ideas about connecting a formal specification with the code and the process validation have been developed and implemented [10] [11]. In this paper the application framework has been forcibly reduced to real-time control systems. In a future step, this specification should be connected with the global specification in order to validate the behavior of the final implementation. A description of the components, their translation to HLPN and the environment to define the architectural levels are detailed in this paper. This method or process, can be used with other design methods like HRT-HOOD [12].

In this paper we present an environment to design real-time control systems from a set of specific components. The environment provides a graphical interface to define component levels. Each component has associated a High Level Time Petri Net and an Ada code which are composed to build a prototype and a design specification.. A description of the main components, their translation to HLTPN and the Ada code is described in the following sections.

2. Design based on components

The design based on components emerges as a design technique to reduce the complexity and the validation process of software development. Moreover, in the real-time system design where the object oriented design has demonstrate its validity, the use of predefined components can strongly improve and reduce the design, implementation and validation phases. HOOD design method is an excellent example of the hierarchical system decomposition based on objects or components. Moreover, HRT-HOOD provides extensions to represent the common hard real-time abstractions.

An intensive work has been done in order to automatically translate from a software design to a final language. The following figure (fig. 1) shows the design process and the expected results in this work.

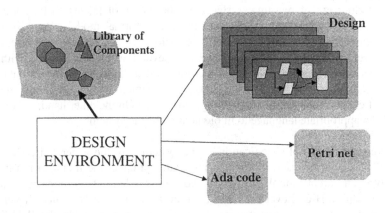

Fig. 1. Design phase and result of this process

The design environment handles objects, defined in a library of components, and allows the definition of layouts (levels in the hierarchy) with the objects and their relationships. The result of this process is the set of the design levels, an Ada prototype and a Petri net. The prototype and the Petri net are automatically generated from the user design.

As defined in the HRT_HOOD method, the logical design of the system is based on the explicit concurrence of active objects. The developed environment provides graphical components to define hierarchical levels in the system instantiating classes of components and parameter. The following aspects are basic in the process:

-   Applications are based on explicit concurrency. Active objects have a flow control (thread) and can invoke operations in other objects. On the other hand passive objects have not a flow control, so their operations are executed as consequence of other object invocations.
-   Aspects as the activity sequence and the communication and synchronisation mechanism are very relevant in the process.
-   Automatic generation of High Level Timed Petri Nets (HLTPN) [13]. The link between the architecture components and the HLTPN allows to obtain a formal model of the system design that can be formally validated.
-   Automatic generation of Ada code. In the same way, the environment can build an Ada prototype from the architectural components that can be executed.

Taking into account some previous works [4] [5] and the functional requirements of real-time systems, a great variety of components have been identified and modeled. The proposed components can be classified as follows:

2.1 Activities

Real-time system activities are built around periodic and sporadic:

-   Periodic tasks: Periodic activities are used to model repetitive actions executed at fixed timing intervals. The period, mode and the timing constraints are determined in the instantiation.
-   Periodic tasks with optional computation. This task defines a periodic task with a mandatory part and an optional computation. The period, mode and timing constraints are fixed in the instantation.
-   The environment provides a graphical interface to define component levels. Each component has associated a High Level Time Petri Net and an Ada code which are composed to build a prototype and a design specification. Aperiodic tasks: Aperiodic activities allow to define actions to be executed as response to an event. The event, mode and timing constraints are defined at instantiation time.

Other activities without timing constraints are also offered in this group.

2.2 Coordination mechanisms

In this group of components several mechanisms for synchronisation and communication have been defined. The Barrier, Signal, Lock, Event, Pulse are some of the modeled synchronisation mechanism. These components allow to synchronise activities using Ada protected types.

The Buffer, Data Store, Buffer Timed, Mailbox, Blackboard are some of the components that allow data communication. Some of these components can be used by one or several activities. In consequence, two different versions, shared and not shared, are supplied.

2.3 Specific components

To build real-time control applications specific application components are required. These components allow to access to external analog and digital data. As in the other group, two versions of most of them (shared and not shared) are provided.

In the same context, several classes or Regulator implementing different control algorithms are defined. Other modules to process data, (fusion, filtering, etc.) or some predefined computation have been also considered.

To include new user defined objects, a generic protected object with several procedures, entries and functions can be used. When it is instantiated, the number of procedures, entries and functions has to be defined to build the appropriated structures.

2.4 The design tool

All the above components have been considered as the basis of an environment for the design of real time system. Figure 1. shows the graphical interface of this environment.

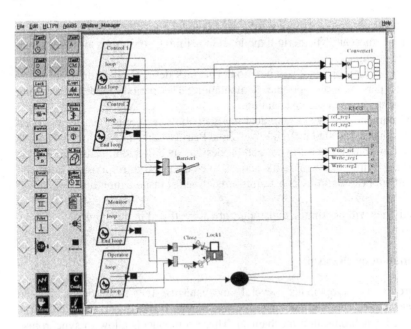

Fig. 2. Graphical interface

In the left hand side of the figure, there a list of the components that can be instantiated during the design phase. The user can create new levels to include components of the groups described above. The objects are allocated in the right hand side window establishing the appropriated relations or connections. Each component can be zoomed to define the internal components corresponding to their design.

3. Translating Ada components to High Level Timed Petri Nets (HLTPN)

High-Level Timed Petri Nets have been chosen to validate the design of real-time systems by its simplicity and clear operational semantics. In [13], a HLTPN is defined as an unified formalism for Petri nets through a tuple (P, T, To, I), where P is a finite set of places that permits to contain tokens. The tokens carry out two classes of data: a time t indicating the instant of creation of the token and variables that contain data whose types have been defined in the places. T is a finite set of transitions that allows to represent the behavior attaching to each transition t a predicate and an action. The predicate is a boolean function whose parameters correspond to the variables associated with the tokens in the input places of the transition t. The predicate selects a subset of token tuples (called functionally enabling tuples) among all the possible token tuples in the input places of the transition t. Not all functionally enabling tuples may be chosen for firing the transition.

The action is a procedure whose input parameters correspond to the variables associated with the tokens in the input places that can be chosen to fire the transition t and whose output parameters correspond to the variables associated with the tokens in the output places of the transition t produced by the firing. The action defines the values associated with the tokens produced by the firing of the transition t, except for time information.

The validation of the HLTPN in this work is concentrated in two different analysis: bounded invariance and bounded response properties. Bounded invariance is associated to the detection of undesirable states within a given interval. Bounded response properties detects desirable states in the interval. These properties are equivalent to safety and liveness but restricted to a temporal interval.

Each layout or level in the process design is the result of the addition of individual components interconnected among them. At the end of the design phase, it is required to translate the whole structure obtained into a HLTPN and an Ada prototype. To describe the translation process, for each component, we detail the Ada code and the associated HLTPN. We will identify the interconnection states with other components in each structure.

3.1 Periodic activities

A periodic activity has the following code

```
task body Periodic_Task_1 is
      Period : constant Duration := P;
      Next : Time;
   begin
```

```
Barrier1.Wait;
Next := Clock + Period;
loop
   -- actions
   Next := Next + Period;
   delay until Next;
end loop;
end Periodic_Task_1;
```

The following figure (fig. 3) shows the translation of the periodic task to a HLTPN structure.

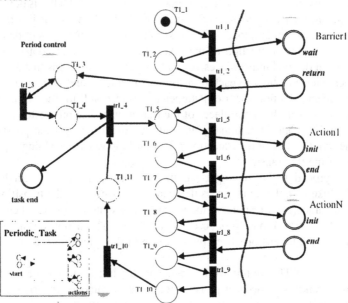

Fig. 3. HLTPN of a Periodic task

The resulting HLTPN has defined several groups of places and transitions to handle the control period, synchronisation and action execution. The control period is modeled by places T1_3, T1_4, T1_11 and transitions tr1_3, tr1_4, tr1_10. Places T1_1 and T1_2 along with tr1_1 and tr1_2 allow the initial synchronisation of the task using an external component that can be shared by several tasks. Places T1_5 to T1_10 and the corresponding transitions allow the external action execution. The last group can be enlarged depending on the number of actions in the tasks. In the figure only two actions (Action1 and ActionN)) have been drawn. Double circled places represent places that permit the component connection. In this sense, the whole HLTPN can be seen as it is drawn in the bottom-left of fig. 3.

If the periodic task has defined an optional computation the Ada code generated is the following:

```
task body Periodic_Task_Optonal_1 is
   Period : constant Duration := P;
```

```
      Next, Deadline : Time;
begin
    Barrier1.Wait;
    Next := Clock + Period;
    loop
        -- mandatory actions
      select
          delay until D; -- Deadline
        then abort
            --- optional actions ;
        end select;
        Next := Next + Period;
        delay until Next;
      end loop;
end Periodic_Task_Optional_1;
```

Next figure shows the HLTPN obtained for this component.

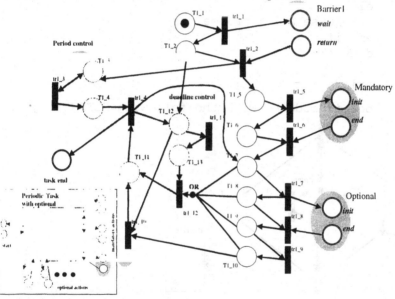

Fig. 4. HLTPN of a periodic task with optional part

This HLTPN is a similar to the described for periodic tasks. In this case, the actions are organised in two set of actions, a first associated to the mandatory part and a second one to the optional part. The deadline associated to the optional part is watched over the deadline control (places: T1_12 and T1_13; transitions: tr1_12 and tr1_13). In the figure , only one action (mandatory and optional) has been considered. In the bottom-left part of the figure is drawn a representation of this component with a control (start) connection and several possible connections for mandatory and optional parts.

The place T1_12 is labelled as *weak*, it means that can be fired or not when it is enabled. The OR node is not implemented as it is shown in the figure due to the lack of space. Moreover, some places can not be directly aborted. It happens when some action is accessing to a protected operation waiting for an entry call.

3.2 Coordination mechanisms

In section 2., several coordination mechanisms have been enumerated and considered as components for real-time applications. In this subsection, the code and HLTPN of the component Barrier will be described.

The Barrier component has been used as a task synchronisation mechanism. The specific code for the access control is shown in the following figure.

```
protected body Barrier is
    entry Wait when Wait'Count=Needed or Release_All is
      begin
        if Wait'Count > 0 then
          Release_All := True;
        else
          Release_All := False;
        end if;
      end Wait;
      . . . . .
end Barrier;
```

This code is modeled with the following HLTPN (fig. 5).

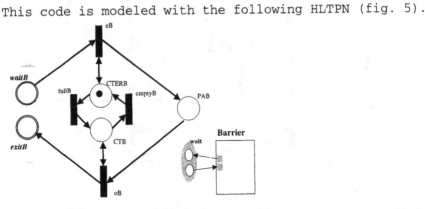

Fig. 5. HLTPN of the access control of a Barrier component

In this HLTPN several parts can be detected: the places to access and abandon the Wait entry (*waitB* and *exitB*), and the control of a counter to block the threads. The place CTERB takes control of the number of threads, and PAB gets the thread identity inside of the Barrier. When the number *Needed* has been reached, the place CTB enables the output of the threads.

3.3 Application components

In this subsection, a basic component to perform the analog-digital conversion is presented. The object provides two basic operations (Read and Write) to get or send data values to external devices. This object is used

```
protected body Converter is
procedure READ(channel: INDEX; value: out NATURAL) is
    begin
    .....
    end READ;

procedure WRITE(channel: INDEX; value: NATURAL) is
    begin
    .....
    end WRITE;
end Converter;
```

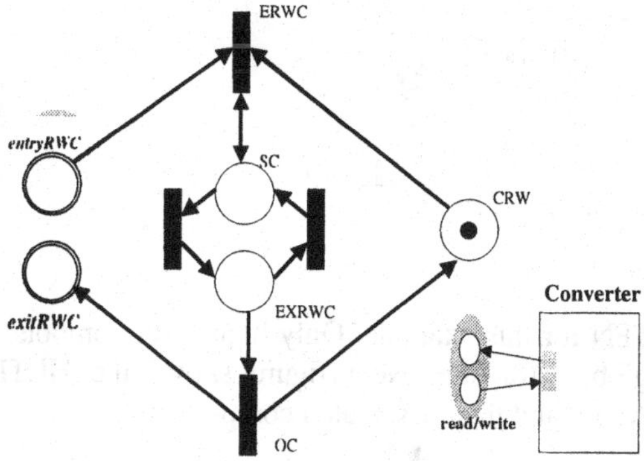

Fig. 6. HLTPN of the Converter

Both operations (read and write) are modeled in the same way. Places SC and EXRWC control the exclusive access to the object. When the operation is finished, the transition OC is fired and the token is returned to the caller and recovered the initial state in the HLTPN.

4. Example

In order to illustrate the process design an experimental process control has been designed and tested. The process control is a pilot plant of residual water [14]. The process control has defined two control loops (level and temperature) as well as an operator interface and a graphical interface.

Four tasks have been identified in the system: two periodic control tasks which are synchronised by means of a *Barrier* component, a periodic task that updates the graphical interface and a sporadic task to accept commands from the operator. Data values are stored and shared in a common structure (*Blackboard*) which provides mechanisms to write and read values. Sensors and actuators use the shared object *Converter*.

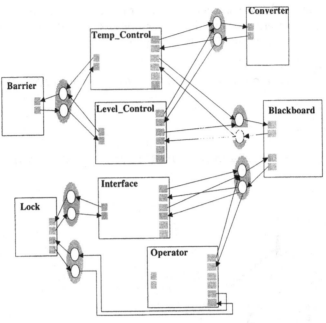

Fig. 7. HLTPN at component level

Figure 7 shows the generated HLTPN for this example. Only high level components have been drawn to show the global structure. Next figure shows the HLTPN generated for the specific *Temp_Control* and their associated components.

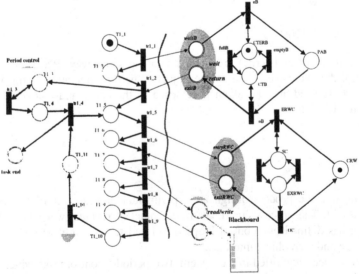

Fig. 8. HLTPN of the Temp_Control.

5. Conclusions

In this paper, a tool to design, prototype and validate real-time using specific components has been presented. The components set has been selected from previous works and the authors experience in the development of real-time control systems. The ambit of this work is restricted to real-time control systems.

From each selected component an Ada implementation and a Petri net specification has been defined. The design tool provides a graphical interface to define objects in a given level of the design hierarchy. From this design levels, a system prototype as well as a whole Petri net are automatically generated.

The obtained Petri net can be analysed in order to validate the generated code. The code can be executed to test the application functionality. The application can be completed adding actions to the specific objects without changing the external relation of objects.

References

1. Bucci G., Campanai M., Nesi P., (1995) Tools for Specifying Real-Time Systems. Real-Time Systems, Vol 8, Number 2/3. pp 117-172.
2. Baresi L., Orso A, and Pezzè M., (1997) Introducing Formal Specification Methods in Industrial Practice,. Proceedins of the First KIT125 Workshop Formal Methods for the Design of Real-Time Systems, Italy.
4. Fernández J. L., (1997) A Taxonomy of Coordination Mechanisms Used by Real-Time Processes, ACM Ada LETTERS, Volume XVII, Number 2, pp 29-54
5. Burns A. and Wellings A, (1995) Concurrency in Ada,.Cambrige University Press.
6. ARTEAWG, (1993) Ada Run-Time Environment Working Group. Catalogue of Interface Features and Options for the Ada Runtime Environment. ACM, Draft Release.
7. Fernández L.(1997) Arquitectura Software Genérica para Sistemas de Tiempo Real, Tesis Doctoral.
8. Miguel Cabello M. A. De (1997), Diseño de Sistemas de Tiempo Real mediante Objetos Ejecutables, Tesis Doctoral.
9. Pulli P. and Elmstrom.R. (1993) IPTES: A concurrent engineering approach for real-time software development. Real-Time Systems. Vol 5, No 2/3
10. León G., Dueñas J.C., de la Puente J.A.. (1993) The IPTES Enviroment: Support for incremental heterogeneous and distributed prototyping. Real-Time Systems. Vol 5, No 2/3
11. de la Puente J.A.., Alonso A., León G., Dueñas J.C., (1993Distributed execution of specifications. Real-Time Systems. Vol 5, No 2/3
12. Burns A. Wellings A.J. (1994) HRT_HOOD: A Structured Design Method for Hard Real-Time Systems. Real-Time Systems. Vol 6, No 1.
13. Carlo Ghezzi, Dino Mandrioli, Sandro Morasca, And Mauro Pezzè. A Unified High-Level Petri Net Formalism for Time-Critical SystemsIEEE Transactions On Software Engineering, Vol. 17 No. 2 February 1991.
14. Crespo A., García A., Angulo H., González A., (1996) A practical exercise on the use of Ada 95 for proces control developments. Workshop on Real-Time Programming WRTP'96. Gramado, Brasil.

Interprocedural Symbolic Evaluation of Ada Programs with Aliases

J. Blieberger[1], B. Burgstaller[1], and B. Scholz[2]

[1] Institute for Computer-Aided Automation (183/1),
Technical University Vienna,
Treitlstr. 1/4, A-1040 Vienna, Austria
{blieb,bburg}@auto.tuwien.ac.at
[2] Institute for Software Technology and Parallel Systems,
University of Vienna,
Leichtensteinerst. 22, A-1090 Vienna, Austria
scholz@par.univie.ac.at

Abstract. Symbolic Evaluation is a technique aimed at determining dynamic properties of programs. We extend our intraprocedural data-flow framework introduced in [3] to support interprocedural symbolic evaluation. Our data-flow framework utilizes a novel approach based on an array algebra to handle aliases induced by procedure calls. It serves as as a basis for static program analysis (e.g. reaching definitions-, alias analysis, worst-case performance estimations, cache analysis). Examples for reaching definitions- as well as alias analysis are presented.

1 Symbolic Evaluation

In this section we introduce the basics of interprocedural symbolic evaluation as it is used throughout the paper. We abstract from intraprocedural evaluation details such as conditional or repetitive statements in order to be concise. Treatment of intraprocedural symbolic analysis of Ada programs can be found in [3].

Symbolic evaluation is a form of static program analysis in which symbolic expressions are used to denote the values of program variables and computations (cf. e.g. [5]). In addition a path condition describes the impact of the program's control flow onto the values of variables and the condition under which control flow reaches a given program point. The underlying program representation for symbolic evaluation is usually the *control flow graph (CFG)*, a directed labelled graph. Its nodes are the program's basic blocks (a basic block is a single entry, single exit, sequence of statements), whereas its edges represent transfers of control between basic blocks. Each edge of the CFG is assigned a condition which must evaluate to true for the program's control flow to follow this edge. *Entry* and *Exit* are distinguished nodes used to denote start and terminal node.

Program State and Context

The *state* S of a program is described by a set of pairs $\{(v_1, e_1), \ldots, (v_m, e_m)\}$ where v_i is a program variable, and e_i is a symbolic expression describing the value of v_i for $1 \leq i \leq m$. For each variable v_i there exists exactly one pair (v_i, e_i) in S.

A program consists of a sequence of statements that may change S.

A *state condition* specifies a condition that is valid at a certain program point. It directly relates to the conditions of the CFG edges. If conditional statements are present, there may be several different valid program states at the same program point. A different state condition is associated with each of them.

States S and state conditions C specify a *program context* which is defined by

$$\bigcup_{i=1}^{k} [S_i, C_i] \in \mathbb{C}$$

where k denotes the number of different program states valid at a certain program point, and $\mathbb{C}$ represents the set of all possible contexts. A program context completely describes the variable bindings at a specific program point together with the associated state conditions.

Arrays

Besides being an efficient and well-established compound data structure arrays lend themselves nicely to the modelling of memory space (e.g. caches, virtual memory, cf. [4]). In the latter way they can be used to track the adverse effects of *aliasing* on interprocedural analysis.

An array is represented as an element of an array algebra $\mathbb{A}$. For sake of simplicity we describe only one-dimensional arrays with it[1].

The array algebra $\mathbb{A}$ is defined inductively as follows:

1. If n is a symbolic expression, then $\perp_n$ in $\mathbb{A}$.
2. If $a \in \mathbb{A}$ and α, β are symbolic expressions then $a \oplus (\alpha, \beta)$ is in $\mathbb{A}$.
3. Nothing else is in $\mathbb{A}$.

In the state of a context an array variable is associated to an element of the array algebra $\mathbb{A}$. Undefined array states are denoted by $\perp_n$, were n is the *size* of the array and reflects the number of array elements. A write access to an array is defined by $\oplus$-function. The semantics of $\oplus$-function is given as follows

$$a \oplus (\alpha, \beta) = (v_1, \ldots, v_{\beta-1}, \alpha, v_{\beta+1}, \ldots, v_n),$$

where β denotes the index where the value α is written.

An element a in $\mathbb{A}$ with at least one $\oplus$-function is a $\oplus$-chain. Every $\oplus$-chain can be written as $\perp_n \bigoplus_{k=1}^{m} (\alpha_k, \beta_k)$. The length of a chain (also written as $|a|$) is the number of $\oplus$-functions in the chain.

---

[1] Extending the algebra to the multi-dimensional case is left to the reader.

Simplification Intuitively, a simplification is needed to keep the symbolic description of an array as short as possible. Although the equivalence of two symbolic expressions is undecidable in general [7], a wide class of equivalence relations can be solved in practice.

A partial simplification operator θ is introduced to simplify $\oplus$-chains. It is defined as follows

$$
\theta\left(a\bigoplus_{l=1}^{m}(\alpha_l,\beta_l)\right) = \begin{cases} \perp_n \bigoplus_{l=1,l\neq i}^{m}(\alpha_l,\beta_l), & \text{if } \exists 1 \leq i < j \leq m : \beta_i = \beta_j \\ \perp_n \bigoplus_{l=1}^{m}(\alpha_l,\beta_l), & \text{otherwise} \end{cases}
$$

The partial simplification operator θ seeks for two equal β-expressions in a $\oplus$-chain. If a pair exists, the result of θ will be the initial $\oplus$-chain without the $\oplus$-function, which refers to the β-expression with the smaller index. If no pair exists, the operator returns the initial $\oplus$-chain; the argument could not be simplified. Semantically, the outer β-expression relates to the later assignment; if a previous assignment exists and the index of the previous statement is equal to the current one, the inner $\oplus$-function can be reduced. The value of the array element is overwritten by the outer assignment statement. The partial simplification operator θ can only reduce one redundant $\oplus$-function. Moreover, each $\oplus$-function in the chain is a potentially redundant one. Therefore, the chain can be potentially simplified in less than $|a|$ applications of θ. A complete simplification is an iterated application of the partial simplification operator and it is written as $\theta^*(a)$. If $\theta^*(a)$ is applied to a further application of a partial simplification operator θ will not simplify a anymore: $\theta(\theta^*(a)) = \theta^*(a)$.

Please note that for ease of readability we have presented array simplification as this iterated application of the θ operator. However, in practice more efficient algorithms to do this exist.

Array access The ρ operator accesses an element of an array a, which is described as an element of the array algebra $\mathbb{A}$.

If $a = \perp_n \bigoplus_{l=1}^{m}(\alpha_l,\beta_l)$ is element of $\mathbb{A}$, then

$$
\rho\left(\perp_n \bigoplus_{l=1}^{m}(\alpha_l,\beta_l),i\right) = \begin{cases} \alpha_l, & \text{if } \exists l = \max\{l \mid 1 \leq l \leq m \wedge \beta_l = i\} \\ \perp, & \text{otherwise} \end{cases}
$$

If index i cannot be found in the $\oplus$-chain, ρ yields the undefined value $\perp$ – this means that either the element was never written or that we have failed to prove the equality of index i with some β inside a $\oplus$-function. If a is not completely simplified, more than one β can be found in the $\oplus$-chain. The β with the highest index is taken.

A Data-Flow Framework for Symbolic Evaluation

We define the following set of equations for the symbolic evaluation framework:

$$
\text{SymEval}(B_{\text{entry}}) = [S_0, C_0]
$$

where S_0 denotes the initial state containing all variables which are assigned their initial values, and C_0 is true,

$$\text{SymEval}(B) = \bigcup_{B' \in \text{Preds}(B)} \text{PrpgtCond}(B', B, \text{SymEval}(B')) \mid \text{LocalEval}(B)$$

(1)

where $\text{LocalEval}(B) = \{(v_{i_1}, e_{i_1}), \ldots, (v_{i_m}, e_{i_m})\}$ denotes the symbolic evaluation local to basic block B. The variables that get a new value assigned in the basic block are denoted by $v_{i_1}, \ldots, v_{i_m}$. The new symbolic values are given by $e_{i_1}, \ldots, e_{i_m}$. The *propagated conditions* are defined by

$$\text{PrpgtCond}(B', B, \text{PC}) = \text{Cond}(B', B) \odot \text{PC}$$

Denoting by PC a program context, the operation $\odot$ is defined as follows:

$$\text{Cond}(B', B) \odot \text{PC} = \text{Cond}(B', B) \odot [S_1, p_1] \cup \ldots \cup [S_k, p_k]$$

$$= [S_1, \text{Cond}(B', B) \wedge p_1] \cup \ldots \cup [S_k, \text{Cond}(B', B) \wedge p_k]$$

Definition 1. *The semantics of the $\mid$ operator is as follows:*

1. *We replace*

$$\{\ldots, (v, e_1), \ldots\} \mid \{\ldots, (v, e_2), \ldots\}$$

by

$$\{\ldots, (v, e_2), \ldots\}.$$

The pair (v, e_1) is not contained in the new set.

2. *Furthermore*

$$\{\ldots, (v_1, e_1), \ldots\} \mid \{\ldots, (v_2, e_2(v_1)), \ldots\},$$

where $e(v)$ denotes an expression involving variable v, is replaced with

$$\{\ldots, (v_1, e_1), \ldots, (v_2, e_2(v_1)), \ldots\}.$$

For the situations discussed above it is important to apply the rules in the correct order, which is to elaborate the elements of the right set from left to right.

3. *If a situation like*

$$[\{\ldots, (v, e), \ldots\}, C(\ldots, v, \ldots)]$$

is encountered during symbolic evaluation, we replace it with

$$[\{\ldots, (v, e), \ldots\}, C(\ldots, e, \ldots)].$$

4. *For arrays $A \in \mathbb{A}$*

$$\{\ldots, (A, \perp), \ldots\} \mid \{\ldots, (A, A \oplus (\alpha, \beta)), \ldots\}$$

is replaced by

$$\{\ldots, (A, \perp \oplus (\alpha, \beta)), \ldots\}.$$

And for the general case,

$$\{\ldots,(A,A\bigoplus_{l_1=1}^{m_1}(\alpha_{l_1},\beta_{l_1}),\ldots\}|\{\ldots,(A,A\bigoplus_{l_2=1}^{m_2}(\alpha_{l_2},\beta_{l_2}),\ldots\}$$

is replaced by

$$\{\ldots,(\theta^*\left(A,A\bigoplus_{l_1=1}^{m_1}(\alpha_{l_1},\beta_{l_1})\bigoplus_{l_2=1}^{m_2}(\alpha_{l_2},\beta_{l_2})\right)\ldots\}.$$

This data-flow framework has been introduced in [2], cf. also [3]. The array algebra has been introduced in [4].

2 Aliasing

Call-by-Reference parameter passing between procedures introduces *aliases*, an effect where two or more *l-values* (cf. [1]) refer to the same storage location at the same program point. [10] shows that solving the may-alias problem for $k > 1$ level pointers is undecideable. However, from this proof it follows that determining $k = 1$ (aka single) level pointers is almost trivial - [9] solves this problem with polynomial effort whereas the algorithm we use (cf. [11]) is almost linear w.r.t. time.

Aliases and Ada95

In [8] (6.2) it is stated that parameters in Ada95 are either passed by-copy or by-reference. If a parameter is passed by-copy, any information transfer between formal and actual parameter occurs only before and after execution of the subprogram. By-copy parameter types are elementary types, or descendants of a private type whose full type is a by-copy type.

All other types (e.g. tagged types) are either passed by reference (in which case reads and updates of the formal parameter directly reference the actual parameter object) or the parameter passing mechanism is undefined.

Access types also contribute to the generation of aliases. Line 10 of our *Main* example procedure (cf. Fig. 3) generates a second access path to variable V from within procedure *Do_It*. For this particular invocation of *Do_It* the updates of both V and $P.all$ refer to the same storage location.

Treatment

We model the semantics of access values by treating the memory space in which the program is symbolically evaluated as an array A, element of the array algebra $\mathbb{A}$. The address of a given variable V is denoted by $\$V$. The example given in Section 4 utilizes this notation. For the ease of reading we not only give the address and the corresponding symbolic value of an access of A, but also the variable affected by that access. Only for that reason we introduce the $^\wedge$ operator used for dereferencing access values. Note that $^\wedge\$V = V$. This translates to a slightly modified use of the $\oplus$ function as

$$a \oplus (\alpha, \beta, \gamma) = (v_1, \ldots, v_{\beta-1}, \gamma, v_{\beta+1}, \ldots, v_n),$$

where α denotes the entity being updated, β denotes the corresponding address, and γ represents the update value.

3 Interprocedural Analysis

Each procedure call may change a symbolic context in two ways:

1. By passing back values from the callee to the caller (e.g. by means of *out* parameters).
2. Through side effects within the callee (e.g. by assigning values to variables not local to the callee).

Topic 1 is achieved by devoting a CFG node to each procedure call. Within this node, parameter passing between caller and callee is handled.

Moreover, the effect of the callee on the current symbolic context (Topic 2) is incorporated at this node. This requires intraprocedural symbolic evaluation of the callee (for details cf. [2]). It is denoted as $LocalEval(B) = Proc(ap_1, .., ap_n)$ (cf. Equation 1, Section 1) in our data-flow framework (ap_n denoting the *actual* procedure parameters). Intraprocedural symbolic evaluation of the callee utilizes the callee's *formal* parameters, it results in a functional description of the callee's effects on the symbolic context that is then appended to the callers context under consideration of the parameter passing mechanism. Since we restrict ourselves to acyclic procedure call graphs[2], it is possible to evaluate every callee before its callers (post order traversal of the procedure call graph).

The parameter passing mechanism is modelled as it is specified in [8]. A parameter that is passed by-copy is treated as follows:

- Mode *in*: This entity is not allowed to be used as an l-value. Thus it is sufficient to replace such a formal parameter by the corresponding actual parameter (or *default_expression*) at the CFG node representing the call site (cf. the example in Section 4).
- Mode *out*: A formal parameter of mode *out* introduces a new l-value in the program context of the callee. [8] (6.4.1(13)-(15)) defines how such an entity is initialized. For elementary types we have considered so far this is $\perp$ (they are uninitialized).

  To pass back the value of the formal parameter to the actual parameter at the call site we replace the l-value occurrences of the formal parameter in the symbolic description of the callee by the corresponding actual parameter.

---

[2] Thus excluding recursive calls.

```
1    package P1 is

2        type Int_Pointer is access all Integer;
3        V: aliased Integer := 1;

4        procedure Do_It(P : Int_Pointer);

5    end P1;
```

Fig. 1. Package Spec P1

```
1    package body P1 is

2        I: Integer := 0;

3        procedure Do_It(P : Int_Pointer) is
4        begin
5          P.all := P.all + 1;
6          V := V + 1;
7          I := I + 1;
8          P.all := P.all + V + I;
9        end Do_It;

10   end P1;
```

Fig. 2. Package Body P1

- Mode *in out*: Basically the sum of the two modes given above: l-value occurrences as well as occurrences within (right-hand side) expressions of the formal parameter are replaced by the actual parameter.

A parameter that is passed by-reference involves a single-level pointer to the entity of the parameter itself. This can be treated by the approach introduced in Section 2.

4 Example

X_{Exit} of procedure *Do_It* contains the functional description in terms of the *formal* parameter on the symbolic context. For procedure *Main* we give the SymEval equations for each of its CFG nodes. X_1 corresponds to the entry to the program where all entities are assigned their initial value. X_2 corresponds to lines 6 to 8 of *Main*. X_3 calculates the effect of the first procedure call (line 9), X_4 of the second call. The solution of this set of equations is depicted in X_{Exit} of *Main*. Note that Y stays initialised to *null* throughout this program due to

```
1   with P1, Text_IO;

2   procedure Main is
3       X: P1.Int_Pointer := new Integer'(1);
4       Y: P1.Int_Pointer;
5   begin
6       if False then
7           Y := X;
8       end if;
9       P1.Do_It(X);
10      P1.Do_It(P1.V'access);
11  end Main;
```

Fig. 3. Procedure Body Main

the *False* condition[3] in line 6. This fact is handled correctly by our data-flow framework. For that reason we differ from e.g. [6] where the above case would introduce a so-called *may-alias*.

It is shown in [3] how our framework can be exploited for reaching definition analysis where we can detect if Y was referenced somewhere in the code.

Do_It

$$X_{Exit} = X_1$$
$$= X_{Entry} \mid \{(A, A \oplus (^\wedge P, P, \rho(A, P) + 1) \oplus (V, \$V, \rho(A, \$V) + 1)),$$
$$(I, I + 1), (A, A \oplus (^\wedge P, P, \rho(A, P) + \rho(A, \$V) + I)\}$$

Main

$$X_1 = X_{Entry} \mid \{(A, \bot \oplus (V, \$V, 1) \oplus (^\wedge X, X, 1) \oplus (^\wedge Y, Y, \bot)), (I, 0)\}$$

$$X_2 = False \odot X_1 \mid \{(A, A \oplus (Y, \$Y, X))\}$$

$$X_3 = (True \odot X_1 \cup False \odot X_2) \mid P1.Do\_It(X) = X_1 \mid P1.Do\_It(X) =$$
$$= X_1 \mid \{(A, A \oplus (^\wedge X, X, \rho(A, X) + 1) \oplus (V, \$V, \rho(A, \$V) + 1)),$$
$$(I, I + 1), (A, A \oplus (^\wedge X, X, \rho(A, X) + \rho(A, \$V) + I)\}$$

$$X_4 = X_3 \mid P1.Do\_It(\$V)$$
$$= X_3 \mid \{(A, A \oplus (^\wedge \$V, \$V, \rho(A, \$V) + 1) \oplus (V, \$V, \rho(A, \$V) + 1)),$$
$$(I, I + 1), (A, A \oplus (^\wedge \$V, \$V, \rho(A, \$V) + \rho(A, \$V) + I)\}$$

---

[3] Contrary to Dead Code Elimination, Symbolic Evaluation can handle arbitrary complex expressions as conditions. Only to keep the example simple and expressive we chose *False*.

$$X_{Entry}, X_1, X_2, X_3, X_4 \to X_{Exit}$$

$$
\begin{aligned}
X_{Exit} = {}& X_{Entry} \mid \{(A, \bot \oplus (V, \$V, 1) \oplus (^\wedge X, X, 1) \oplus (^\wedge Y, Y, \bot)), (I, 0)\} \\
& \mid \{(A, A \oplus (^\wedge X, X, \rho(A, X) + 1) \oplus (V, \$V, \rho(A, \$V) + 1)), (I, I + 1), \\
& \quad (A, A \oplus (^\wedge X, X, \rho(A, X) + \rho(A, \$V) + I)\} \\
& \mid \{(A, A \oplus (^\wedge \$V, \$V, \rho(A, \$V) + 1) \oplus (V, \$V, \rho(A, \$V) + 1)), \\
& \quad (I, I + 1), (A, A \oplus (^\wedge \$V, \$V, \rho(A, \$V) + \rho(A, \$V) + I)\} \\
= {}& X_{Entry} \mid \{(I, 2), (A, \bot \oplus (^\wedge X, X, 5) \oplus (V, \$V, 10) \oplus (^\wedge Y, Y, \bot))\}
\end{aligned}
$$

By solving these SymEval equations according to the algorithm presented in [11] we derive for X_{Exit} the program context valid after executing procedure *Main*. Note that this corresponds exactly to the result obtained by executing *Main* on a *real* CPU.

5 Conclusion

We have presented an extension of the intraprocedural data-flow framework introduced in [2] to support interprocedural symbolic evaluation. Aliases due to by-reference parameter passing are handled by using an array that models the underlying memory. At present we are investigating the use of this concept for general pointers. A prototype implementation of the framework presented is under way.

References

1. A. V. Aho, R. Seti, and J. D. Ullman. *Compilers: Principles, Techniques, and Tools*. Addison-Wesley, Reading, MA, 1986.
2. J. Blieberger. Data-flow Frameworks for Worst-Case Execution Time Analysis. (submitted), 1997.
3. J. Blieberger and B. Burgstaller. Symbolic Reaching Definitions Analysis of Ada Programs. Proceedings of the Ada-Europe International Conference on Reliable Software Technologies, 238-250, June 1998.
4. J. Blieberger, T. Fahringer, and B. Scholz. An Accurate Cache Prediction for C-Programs with Symbolic Evaluation. (submitted), 1999.
5. T. E. Cheatham, G. H. Holloway, and J. A. Townley. Symbolic Evaluation and the Analysis of Programs. *IEEE Trans. on Software Engineering*, 5(4):403–417, July 1979.
6. J. D. Choi, M. Burke, and P. Carini. Efficient Flow-Sensitive Interprocedural Computation of Pointer-Induced Aliases and Side Effects. *ACM PoPL*, 1/93:232–245, 1993.
7. M. Haghighat, C. Polychronopoulos. Symbolic Analysis for Parallelizing Compilers. *ACM Trans. Prog. Lang. Sys.*, 18(4):477-518, July 1996.
8. ISO/IEC 8652. *Ada Reference manual*, 1995.
9. W. Landi, and B. G. Ryder. Pointer-induced Aliasing: A Problem Classification. *Conference Record of the Eighteenth Annual ACM Symposium on Principles of Programming Languages*, 235-248, 1992

10. G. Ramalingam. The Undecidability of Aliasing. *ACM Trans. Prog. Lang. Sys.*, 16(5):1467–1471, 1994.
11. V. C. Sreedhar. *Efficient Program Analysis Using DJ Graphs*. PhD thesis, School of Computer Science, McGill University, Montréal, Québec, Canada, 1995.

Automatic Verification of Concurrent Ada Programs

Eric Bruneton[1] and Jean-François Pradat-Peyre[2]

[1] INRIA Rhône-Alpes
Projet Sirac
Eric.Bruneton@inrialpes.fr
[2] Conservatoire National des Arts et Métiers
Laboratoire CEDRIC
peyre@cnam.fr

Abstract. The behavior of concurrent Ada programs is very difficult to understand because of the complexity introduced by multi-tasking. This complexity makes classical test techniques unusable and correctness can only be obtained with the help of formal methods. In this paper we present a work based on colored Petri nets formalism that automates the verification of concurrent Ada program properties. The Petri net is automatically produced by a translation step and the verification is automatically performed on the net with classical related techniques. A prototype has been developed and first results obtained allow us to think that we will be able in a near future to analyze realistic Ada programs.

1 Introduction

Ada is the reference language when building software for critical computer systems. The design and the construction of these softwares require the use of concurrent programming. Although Ada provides well structured patterns for concurrent programming (such as task, protected object, rendez-vous and requeue statements), it is often very difficult to predict the behavior of such programs due to their non determinism. It is now established that only formal methods can ensure the respect of safety and liveness properties of concurrent programs. However, the use of these formal methods needs the knowledge of different formalisms and a sound experience in modeling.

In this paper we present a work allowing a non expert in formal methods to verify automatically liveness properties of concurrent Ada programs. This work uses high level Petri nets and is based on a three steps methodology:

1. *translation*: the Ada program is translated into an equivalent high level Petri net;
2. *verification*: liveness or safety properties are verified on the Petri net using structural methods and model checking;
3. *report*: when a property is not verified, the tool tries to show in the Ada program parts that are relevant to the non respect of the property.

Some previous works have already investigated this approach (analysis of Ada concurrent programs by a translation to Petri nets) [MSS89], [TSM90], [SMMW89],[HL85],[MZGT85]. These works used ordinary Petri nets and then, they were not able to take into account realistic Ada programs. Indeed, ordinary Petri nets cannot model general assignment, structured data or boolean conditions that can appear in synchronizations.

Our approach is based on high level Petri nets and theoretically we can translate any Ada programs. The main problem is to define translation rules that take into account complex program patterns but that produce simple nets i.e. nets that can be automatically analyzed. We try to achieve this goal by first removing all parts of the program that are not relevant to concurrency; secondly by defining for each case (variable declaration, protected object declaration, assignment expression, call to an entry, ...) a simple rule of transformation; thirdly by removing parts of the net that have been generated but are not used; fourthly by applying high level Petri nets reductions in order to obtain a smaller but equivalent net (related to the checked property); fifthly by applying modern verifications techniques such as partial order state space reductions.

We have developed a first version of a tool that automates these different steps. This tool (which is still under construction) seems to prove that this approach will be usable in the analyze of realistic concurrent Ada programs.

The following of the paper is organized as follow : in section 2 we present briefly Petri nets and high level Petri nets; in section 3 we present the translation step; in section 4 we show how the resulting high level net can be analyzed; in section 5 we give an example and in section 6 we conclude and discuss worthwhile future works.

2 High level Petri nets

High level Petri nets (also called colored nets) allow the modeling of more complex systems than ordinary Petri nets because of the abbreviation provided by this model. In a colored net, a place contains typed (or colored) tokens instead of anonymous tokens in Petri nets, and a transition may be fired in multiple ways (i.e. instantiated). To each place and each transition is attached a type (or a color) domain. An arc from a transition to a place (resp. from a place to a transition) is labeled by a linear function called a color function. This function determines the number and the type (or the color) of tokens that have to be added or removed to or from the place upon firing the transition with respect to a color instantiation.

Generally, color domains are compositions of basic ones, called *classes*, and color functions are tuple of basic functions defined on these classes. A class is a finite and non empty set and its size may be parameterized by an integer. The particular class ϵ contains the only item $\bullet$: $\epsilon = \{\bullet\}$.

The most usual color functions for a class C are the identity (or selection) denoted X_C (or $Y_C, Z_C, \ldots$), the diffusion or the global synchronization over the class C, denoted All_C, and the successor mapping denoted $X_C + +$.

2.1 An example

We propose here to model a solution of the dining philosophers problem. In this solution, a philosopher requests the resources all at once (i.e. its chopstick and that of its right-hand side neighbor) and waits for them since it cannot proceed with a subset of the requested resources (i.e. a philosopher cannot eat with only one chopstick, or cannot do another activity when he is hungry); the server allocates them globally when they are available.

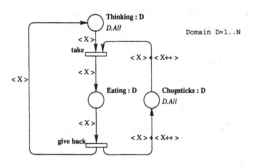

Figure 1: *A model of the dining philosophers problem*

This net is composed of three places (*Thinking, Eating* and *Chopsticks*) and of two transitions (*take* and *give back*). Places *Thinking* and *Eating* model the two different visible states of the N philosophers. For instance, a philosopher x is in the state eating when a token of color x is in the place *Eating*. Place *Chopsticks* models the available chopsticks.

Initially, all philosophers are in state thinking and all chopsticks are free. This is modeled by the definition of the initial marking $M_0(Thinking) = D.All$, $M_0(Eating) = 0$, $M_0(Chopsticks) = D.All$.

Transition *take* can be fired for a color x when place *Thinking* contains at least one token of color x and when place *Chopsticks* contains at least one token of color x and one token of color $x + 1 \, mod \, N$. Upon firing, the needed tokens are removed and a token of color x is added to place *Eating*.

Transition *give back* is fireable when place *Eating* contains at least one token of color x (the philosopher x is in state eating). This firing produces the two tokens x and $x + +$ in place *Chopsticks* (the chopsticks x and $x + 1 \, mod \, N$ become free again) and one token x in place *Thinking* (the philosopher x is now in state thinking).

3 Translation

Turing machines, High Level Petri nets, Ada programs... all have the same expressive power. It is therefore theoretically possible to automatically translate an Ada program into an equivalent Petri net. The difficulty is to define translation rules that produce useful nets, i.e. nets that can be analyzed by standard tools such as the prod tool [VJKT95].

Some Ada programs have been translated, by hand, into Petri nets [KPP97]. The resulting Petri nets are very small and easy to analyze and, ideally, the automatic translation should produce similar results. The analysis of these examples lead us to the following conclusions:

- the resulting Petri nets do not model all aspects of the source program, but only what is relevant to concurrency.
- they model Ada constructs with very simplified nets, which are valid for each particular case, but not in general.
- they are extremely small: for example, a 60 lines program can be translated into a 4 places net.
- the Ada code is represented by a Petri net, and its execution by the movement of tokens (one per task) in this net.
- Ada statements are generally represented by transitions, and their execution by the firing of these transitions.
- local variables of a task are translated into a color in the token representing this task.
- protected variables are modeled by a colored place.

This lead us to define a three steps translation mechanism. The *simplification* step simplifies an Ada program by removing all parts that are not relevant to concurrency. The *translation* step translates this simplified Ada program into a Petri net, by replacing the various Ada constructs with Petri net fragments that model their full semantic. Finally, the *cleaning* step removes the parts that are unused.

The rest of this section presents the simplification and translation steps. For simplicity reasons, the algorithms given below are limited to a subset of the Ada language. In this subset, a program consists of a single procedure which contains types, variables, subprograms, tasks, and protected objects definitions, and a body. Only basic types, expressions and instructions constructs are handled. Most of Ada's advanced features are not handled: genericity, overloading, exceptions, object oriented features, pointers, many type features, imbricated tasks . . . . Of course, almost all concurrency constructs are handled: tasks, protected objects, entry calls, select[1] and requeue statements, guards and barriers, the count attribute. . .

3.1 Simplification step

To study the concurrent behavior of an Ada program, and especially to detect deadlocks and fairness, we do not need to translate all the logic of the program, which can be very complex, but only the management of concurrency (i.e. creation, communication and synchronization of tasks).

The *simplification* of an Ada program P is another Ada program P' obtained from P by removing as much code as possible, and such that P and P' have the same concurrent behavior. It seemed at first that this simplification could not be

---

[1] only the selective accept form is supported, without else and terminate alternatives

automated, because we did not see how to know if a given part of a program can be removed without modifying its concurrent behavior. Fortunately, it is easier to answer to the opposite question. There is indeed a function that, given some parts of a program to keep, returns other parts to keep. Therefore, instead of directly removing useless parts, we iterate this function from initial parts that must trivially be kept, until all useful parts have been found. We can then remove the other parts.

The simplification algorithm uses a stack and an iterative process. *By hypotheses*, each node of the program's abstract syntax tree can be pushed in the stack at most once [2], and a node that has been pushed must be kept. During initialization, the nodes that must trivially be kept are pushed in the stack. At each iteration, a node is popped and analyzed. This analysis can push other nodes in the stack. When the stack is empty, the nodes that have not been pushed can be removed.

Let study a trivial example to better understand how the algorithm works. The program below is made of a task that returns consecutive numbers, and several other tasks that use the first one to get an identity number. This program can be represented by the tree on the middle.

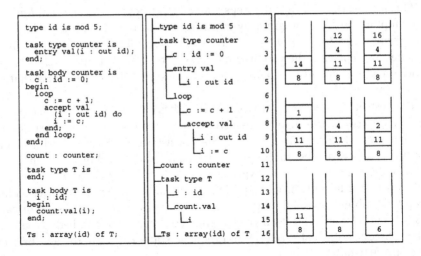

Figure 2: *An example of the simplification algorithm*

Initially, the accept (8) and the entry call (14) statements are pushed, as potentially blocking operations that can directly lead to deadlocks or famines. At the first iteration, the node 14 is popped and analyzed: its parent node (12) and the declarations of count (11) and val (4), used in the entry call, are pushed. At the second iteration, the analysis of node 12 pushes node 16, which creates tasks of a potentially problematic task type. This declaration uses the definition of the id type (1), which is pushed at the next iteration. Node 1 does not need any other nodes, but node 4 needs its parent node (2). The analysis of node 2

---

[2] each node contains a boolean indicating if it has already been pushed or not.

does not push node 11, already pushed. Node 8 needs its parent node (6), which in turn needs its parent node (2), already pushed. The stack is now empty: the nodes 3,5,7,9,10,13 and 15, which correspond to the computation of the identity numbers and have never been pushed, can be removed.

More generally, during initialization, all potentially blocking code is pushed (entry calls, protected calls, and accept statements) as well as code that *may* not terminate (some loops and calls to recursive code). At each iteration, the analysis of a node x can push a node y. The node y is pushed when it is x's father, when it is necessary for x (e.g. x uses a variable that is declared in y), when it modifies a variable used in x (e.g. a variable used in a guard), when it modifies the flow of control in x (e.g. y is a return statement), when it creates a variable that contains tasks of type x, when it is a call to x...

This algorithm is relatively simple and efficient. It should be noted however that it may keep unnecessary parts of some programs, because it is not always possible to be sure if a node must be kept or not (some problems are indeed undecidable, e.g. termination). In order to avoid removing useful parts, when in doubt, we suppose that a node must be kept.

3.2 Translation step

The translation step is like the code production step in a compiler, but it produces Petri nets instead of assembly code. The algorithm is defined by a limited number of rules, one for each Ada construct (expressions, statements, procedures...). It is therefore simple to understand but it can produce unnecessary large nets. It will be dull to present here each of these rules. We present instead how the nets they produce work.

Ada code is represented by a Petri net, and its execution by the movement of *task tokens* (one per task) in this net. Simple statements are translated into transitions, and their execution corresponds to the firing of these transitions. A task token conveys the identity of a task and the local variables this task can access at a given time. For example, in the body of a task, this token contains the local variables of this task. In a procedure, it contains the procedure's local variables and parameters (the task's local variables are not accessible within a procedure). During a call, the token is duplicated. One copy remains in the caller, with the local variables of the caller, while the other moves in the callee, with the callee's local variables. The stacks used at runtime by Ada tasks are therefore represented, but in a distributed and fragmented manner.

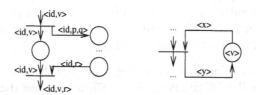

Figure 3: *A sample call and a sample assignment translation*

Shared data (protected or not) is represented by *data tokens*. Unlike task tokens, these tokens are not attached to a specific task, and they do not move. They just represent the current value of a shared variable.

A task entry e is translated into three places. The first one, e.queue, models the queue of this entry. It contains the tokens of the tasks waiting for a rendez-vous on this entry. The place e.count models the count attribute of this entry (i.e. the number of tokens in e.queue). The place e.return contains tokens corresponding to completed calls. The caller must atomically deposit a token with the actual parameters in e.queue, and increment e.count. It must then wait for the result in e.return. The callee must decrement e.count when it takes a token from e.queue during an accept.

Two places are used per protected object to ensure its mutual exclusion properties. They contain anonymous tokens and serve as read and write locks. The read lock place contains one token per task executing a protected function. The write lock place contains a token if and only if a task is executing a protected procedure or entry. To enter in a protected function, the write lock place must be empty. To enter a protected procedure or entry, both places must be empty. We use inhibitor arcs to ensure this (i.e. in figure 4, transition enter can be fired only if place .RW contains no token). The figure 4 shows the translation of a protected function: the read and write lock places are on the left.

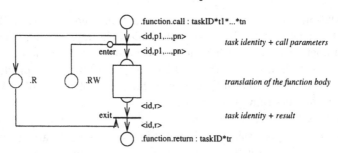

Figure 4: *A sample protected function translation*

4 Verification

The colored Petri net obtained by the translation step can be analyzed by classical techniques related to Petri net verification. We restrict us in our prototype to the verification of absence of deadlock and fairness but we are developing interfaces to pick up properties expressed in temporal logic.

The major difficulty to be faced is the complexity of the set of reachable markings of the net (states of the program). In order to cope with this problem we combine two kind of verification techniques :

- first, we use reduction techniques that transform the net into a smaller but equivalent one [Ber86] [Had91], [BHPP97]. Reductions that can be applied depend on the property that the user wants to check. Principal reductions have been implemented in our prototype.

– second, we apply direct analysis of the reachability graph or we use stubborn sets or sleep sets techniques that combat the state space explosion problem by using partial order state space reductions. Our prototype uses theses techniques by an interface to the prod tool [VJKT95].

We combine these two kind of techniques because they are complementary : reductions techniques use local structures of the net in order to transform it in a smaller one. They can reduce considerably the net (and then the size of the set of reachable marking), they are efficient (complexity depends only of the arcs number of the net) but they cannot be used alone because they produce a new net that must be analyzed. Analysis of the reachability graph cannot be used on large model because even with advanced optimizations, the size of this graph remains very important. In counterpart, they are very efficient for the verification of general properties when the size of the model is small. Using firstly reductions techniques and then reachability graph analysis allows us to verify general properties on big models.

Let us consider a small example on the well known dining philosophers problem and suppose that we want to check if there is or not a deadlock :

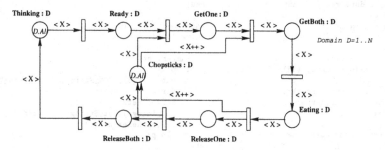

Figure 5: *A model of the dining philosophers problem*

With 5 philosophers, the size of the reachability graph is of 6874 nodes and 30120 arcs. Using sleep sets and stubborn sets techniques this size is limited to 126 nodes and 152 arrows.

If we reduce first the net using structural reductions we obtain the following net (5 agglomerations have been done). By definition, this net is equivalent for the deadlock property to the initial one. The differences between these two nets are that some local states (not relevant with the deadlock property) have been hidden by transitions agglomerations.

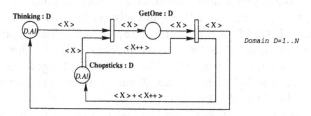

Figure 6: *The equivalent reduced model*

With 5 philosophers, the size of the reachable graph is now of only 32 nodes and 120 arrows. Using sleep sets and stubborn sets techniques this size is further reduced to 22 nodes and 48 arrows.

5   Example

Let us consider the following implementation of the dining philosophers problem.

```
with Common; -- some basic definitions
use  Common;
procedure Main is
   type Id is mod 5;
   type Tforks is array (Id) of boolean;

   protected type resource_server is
      entry Get1 (Id);
      entry Get2 (Id);
      procedure Release (x : in Id);
   private
      Resource:Tforks:=(others=>true);
   end;

   protected type number_server is
      procedure get (x : out Id);
   private
      num : Id := 0;
   end;

   task type philo;
   type Tphilo is array (Id) of philo;

   Server : resource_server;
   Number : number_server;
   Philos : Tphilo;

   protected body number_server is
      procedure get (x : out Id) is
      begin
         x := num; num := num + 1;
      end;
   end;

   protected body resource_server is
      entry Get1(for X in Id) when Resource(x) is
      begin
         Resource(x) := false;
      end;

      entry Get2(for X in Id) when Resource(X+1) is
      begin
         Resource(X+1) := false;
      end;

      procedure Release(X : in Id) is
      begin
         Resource(x) := true; Resource(x+1) := true;
      end;
   end;

   task body philo is
      ego : Id;
   begin
      number.get(ego);
      loop
         put_id(ego); Put_String("is thinking");
         Server.Get1(ego);
         Server.Get2(ego);
         put_id(ego);Put_String("is eating");
         Server.Release(ego);
      end loop;
   end;

begin -- of procedure Main
   null;
end;
```

Program 1: *A sample Ada concurrent program*

After the simplification step, the program obtained is identical except that all Put instructions have been removed.

The high level net produced by the translation step is composed of 54 places and 45 transitions (9 places and 5 transitions have been suppressed by the cleaning step because they were non used). The figure 7 shows a part of the Petri net obtained. This part models the behavior of the tasks Philos.

All task philo (indexed by Id) are initially ready to start (a token I is in place Philos[].$Start$ for each value of Id). A task I first acquires a system identifier (X on transition t38), and begin its body (after the fire of transition t40). The state of a task is now defined by a token (I,X,Ego) that moves from place to place (I models its array index, X models its system identifier and Ego the value of its local variable Ego).

The body of a task (I,X,Ego) consists first in a call to the procedure Get of Number (transition t42) by deposing a token (X,Ego) in place Number.Get.Call.

This task waits until this call ends (place `Number.Get.return` must contains a token `(X,Y)`), then fires transition t43 and modifies its state token with the value Y produced by `Number`. It enters a loop in which it calls successively, entry `Get1`, entry `Get2` and procedure `Release` of the protected object `Server`. The meta-transition 34 (that corresponds to a call of the task `(I,X,Ego)` to the entry `Get2`) is depicted in the left of figure 7.

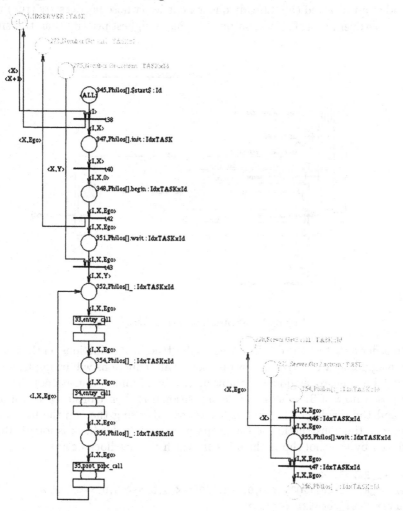

Figure : 7 *Translation of the array task Philos[]*

The model of the entry `Get2` of the protected object `Server` is depicted in figure 8. In this net, one can remark the lock of `Server` (place `Server.RW`), the queue of blocked calling tasks (place `Server.Get2.queue`) and the count of this entry (place `Server.Get2.count`).

When a task (identified by its system identifier and by the value of its local variable Ego) `(X,Y)` calls this entry, it must first obtain the lock (transition t11) and then accesses state ready. If the guard is evaluated to true, (if the place `Server.Resource[]` contains a token `(Y+1,true)`) then this task enters the body of `Get2` (transition t15); otherwise, the calling task is put in the queue, it releases the lock and the variable count is incremented (transition t13).

A task waiting in the queue accesses the body of `Get2` by firing transition t14. In order to take into account the processing policy of protected objects (at the end of a protected call, already queued entries (whose barriers are true) take precedence over new calls), transition t14 is has a highest priority than transition t11.

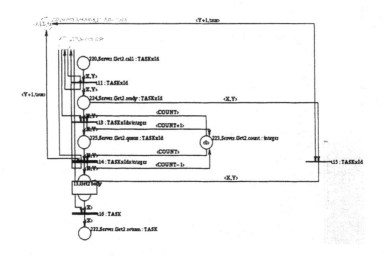

Figure 8: *Translation of the Get2 entry*

In order to detect the deadlock, we apply structural reductions on the net and we can agglomerate 17 transitions (as soon as all reductions will be implemented, we will be able to agglomerate automatically 17 more transitions). The net (composed now of 37 places and 28 transitions) is then transfered to the prod tool and the deadlock is found in a few seconds using the "on-the-fly" option that stops the construction of the graph as soon as a deadlock is found. Result produced by the tool shows the state in which the deadlock occurs:

```
Server_RW207: <.0.>
Server_ResourceTT208: <.0,0.>+<.1,0.>+<.2,0.>+<.3,0.>+<.4,0.>
Server_Get1_count212: <.0.>
Server_Get2_count223: <.5.>
Server_Get2_queue225: <.1,4.>+<.2,3.>+<.3,2.>+<.4,1.>+<.5,0.>
PhilosTT_wait355: <.0,5,0.>+<.1,4,1.>+<.2,3,2.>+<.3,2,3.>+<.4,1,4.>
```

In this state, all tasks `Philos` are calling entry `Get2` of the protected object `Server`. The variable count of the entry `Get2` has the value 5 (modeled by the place `Server_Get2_count223`); no resources are available (the marking of the place `Server_ResourceTT208` equals $\sum_{x \in 0..5} < .x, 0. >$) and all the philosophers are waiting for the return of the call to `Get2` (place `PhilosTT_wait355`).

These results are not yet automatically reported in the Ada code, but naming conventions and links made between the Petri net and the Ada code at the translation step allow us to believe that this report can be easily done.

6 Conclusion

In this paper we have presented a work concerning the verification of the behavior of concurrent Ada programs. We try to combat the inherent complexity of such verification by using high level Petri nets that offer a good power of modeling, as well as numerous theoretical and practical tools.

We have developed a tool that automates the different steps lied to this verification: simplification, translation, and analysis. The first results that we obtained seem to prove that we will be able in a near future to verify realistic concurrent Ada programs. However, in order to validate our approach, we have to extend the subset of the Ada language which is accepted by our tool and we have to complete the implementation of verification techniques.

Acknowledgment We would like to thank Professor Claude Kaiser for his careful reading of a first draft of this paper, and for his helpful comments.

References

[Ber86]   G. Berthelot. Transformations and decompositions of nets. In *Advances in Petri Nets*, number 254 in LNCS, pages 359–376. Springer-Verlag, 1986.

[BHPP97] F. Breant, S. Haddad, and J.F. Pradat-Peyre. Characterizing new reductions by means of language and invariant properties. Technical Report 97-04, Conservatoire National des Arts et Métiers, laboratoire Cedric, 1997.

[Had91]   S. Haddad. A reduction theory for colored nets. In Jensen and Rozenberg, editors, *High-level Petri Nets, Theory and Application*, LNCS, pages 399–425. Springer-Verlag, 1991.

[HL85]   D. Helmbold and D. Luckham. Debugging Ada-tasking programs. *IEEE Transactions on Software Engineering*, Vol. 2(No. 2):45–57, 1985.

[KPP97]   C. Kaiser and J.F. Pradat-Peyre. Comparing the reliability provided by tasks or protected objects for implementing a resource allocation service : a case study. In *TriAda*, St Louis, Missouri, november 1997. ACM SIGAda.

[MSS89]   T. Murata, B. Shenker, and S.M. Shatz. Detection of Ada static deadlocks using Petri nets invariants. *IEEE Transactions on Software Engineering*, Vol. 15(No. 3):314–326, March 1989.

[MZGT85] D. Mandrioli, R. Zicari, C. Ghezzi, and F. Tisato. Modeling the Ada task system by Petri nets. *Computer Languages*, Vol. 10(NO. 1):43–61, 1985.

[SMMW89] S.M. Shatz, K. Mai, D. Moorthi, and J. Woodward. A toolkit for automated support of Ada-tasking analysis. In *Proceedings of the 9th Int. Conf. on Distributed Computing Systems*, pages 595–602, June 1989.

[TSM90]   S. Tu, S.M. Shatz, and T. Murata. Applying Petri nets reduction to support Ada-tasking deadlock detection. In *Proceedings of the 10th IEEE Int. Conf. on Distributed Computing Systems*, pages 96–102, Paris, France, June 1990.

[VJKT95] K. Varoaaniemi, Halme J., Hiekanen K., and Pyssisalo T. prod reference manual. Technical Report 13, Helsinki Univ. of Tecnologies, Finland, 1995.

Translating Time Petri Net Structures into Ada 95 Statements *

F.J. García[1] and J.L. Villarroel[2]

[1] Universidad de La Rioja, Dpto. Matemáticas y Computación,
C/ Luis de Ulloa s.n., 26004 Logroño, Spain
fgarcia@dmc.unirioja.es
[2] CPS, Universidad de Zaragoza, Dpto. de Informática e Ing. de Sistemas,
C/ María de Luna 3, 50015 Zaragoza, Spain
JLVillarroel@mcps.unizar.es

Abstract. The intention of this paper is to show how real-time systems modeled with time Petri nets can be implemented in Ada 95. To achieve this objective, we use models of the Ada 95 tasking statements. Using reduction rules the model of the statement is reduced in order to make it recognizable in the net which models the system. Thus, we can build a catalogue of the reduced models of the Ada 95 tasking statements so that they can be used in the translation of net structures into Ada programs.

1 Introduction

This work is a part of a wider study whose main aim is the use of a formal method for the whole life cycle of a real-time system (RTS) development. The complexity of the design, analysis and implementation of real-time systems is well known; a complexity that is further amplified if reliability aspects are considered. In these systems, reliability is essential due to the possible catastrophic effects that a failure could produce. Therefore, any attempt to apply a formal method to the life cycle of an RTS must be welcome so that the reliability requirement can be met. If, in addition, the use of a automated tool to generate the code for the system is considered, this is a double advantage, because in addition to the obvious reduction in the coding mistakes, we add a reduction in the cost of the development. Bearing this idea in mind, our proposal is to use the *Time Petri Net* (TPN) formalism to model, analyze and generate the code for an RTS. In this paper we are concerned with the latter part of this development, that is, the automatizable code generation for an RTS. Ada 95 was chosen as the target language because of its tasking and real-time features.

Petri nets are suitable for the modeling of real-time systems because the net can naturally model concurrency, resource sharing with mutual exclusion, synchronizations, etc. In order to model an RTS with a Petri net, some kind of extension to classical Petri nets involving time must be used. There seems to be some consensus in using the Time Petri Net formalism [1][2] among the

* This work has been partially supported by the CICYT (project TAP97-0992-C02-01)

authors who have dealt with this subject in the recent past. See for example [3][4][5], or [6][7] where only classical nets are used. Nevertheless, other related formalisms, such as the interval timed coloured Petri nets [8] or the time environment/relationship nets (TER nets) [9] must not be dismissed, above all the latter in the modeling of absolute delay statements. We have chosen time Petri nets due to their high expressive power (with the only limitation being the modeling of absolute delay) and, from our point of view, it is more intuitive and suitable for the specification of the systems which are the object of our study.

The idea of bringing together the worlds of Ada and the Petri nets is not new. Several authors have already used Petri nets for the modeling of Ada and Ada 95 tasking statements, mainly with two objectives: to define precise behaviour for tasking semantics and to support the automated analysis of concurrent software, above all in deadlock detection. For the first objective, see for example [3][4] where formal models for the main tasking statements are shown. The second line of interest is the subject matter in [5][6][7].

The intention of this paper is to show how a model of an RTS in terms of time Petri nets can be implemented in Ada 95 and demonstrate that the code generated for this implementation is correct, in the sense that it has the same semantics as the model that is being implemented. To achieve this objective, we use models of the Ada 95 tasking statements, models similar to those in [3][4]. Using reduction rules for classical or time Petri nets ([6][10][11]) we reduce the model to the minimum net structure that can be directly recognized in a time Petri net. Once we have a catalogue of the reduced models of the Ada 95 tasking statements, implementing the software skeleton of an RTS modeled with a time Petri net requires only that we isolate and recognize the reduced models in the net, and put the corresponding Ada statements together in the program that will implement the system. This last part can be automated. In addition to this main objective, this work can be seen as a contribution in two additional ways: it complements the definition of the models of the Ada 95 statements, as in [3][4], and it helps with the proposal described in [6] since it provides reduced models of the tasking structures that can reduce the size of the model of the system to be analyzed.

The organization of this paper is as follows. Section 2 summarizes basic concepts about time Petri nets and their relation with real-time systems. In section 3, we describe how a time Petri net can be decomposed into a set of concurrent processes, each of which will be implemented in a different Ada task. Section 4 shows an example of implementation of a real-time system modeled with a TPN and the next section explains how the code of the example was built.

2 Basic Concepts about Time Petri Nets

A Time Petri Net ([2]) is a tuple $(P, T; F, B, M_o, SIM)$, where $(P, T; F, B, M_o)$ defines a marked classical Petri net, the *underlying Petri net*[1]; and SIM is the

---

[1] We assume a basic knowledge about classical Petri nets (see [10] for a survey)

mapping called the static interval $SIM : T \to \mathbb{Q}^* \times (\mathbb{Q}^* \cup \infty)$, where $\mathbb{Q}^*$ is the set of positive rational numbers. Thus, TPNs can be seen as Petri nets with labels: two time values (α_i, β_i) which are associated with transitions. Assuming that transition t_i is enabled at time θ_0, and is continuously enabled, the first time value represents the minimum time, starting from θ_0, that t_i has to wait until it can be fired, and the second is the maximum time that t_i can remain enabled without firing. These two time values therefore allow the calculation of the firing interval for each transition t_i in the net: $(\theta_0 + \alpha_i, \theta_0 + \beta_i)$. Once the transition is to be fired, the firing is instantaneous. This work assumes that a transition with no associated time interval has an implicit time interval of $(0, 0)$, that is, the transition is immediately fired as soon as it becomes enabled. The need to implement the net inspired this decision, against the approach taken in [2], where a time interval of $(0, \infty)$ was considered for these transitions. In addition, we use predicates associated with transitions and inhibitor arcs which connect places and transitions in our models of Ada statements (see [10]).

All transitions in TPNs have the same functionality, but the different situations that appear in an RTS must be focused on in our models. Therefore, and with the aim of implementing the model, we distinguish three kinds of transitions:

- CODE transitions (filled in segments) together with their input places, represent the code associated with an activity, which starts its execution when the transition is enabled, i.e. the input places are marked. The two time values (α, β) represent the execution time of the activity. At best, the code execution will finish at time α, and at worst the execution will take until β. The firing represents the end of the code.
- TIME transitions, (unfilled segments) are those with an associated time event, e.g. a time-out. They also have associated time information, described with an interval (α, α), where α represents the event time. The firing of this kind of transition represents the occurrence of the event.
- SYCO transitions (thin segments) are those with no temporal meaning used to perform synchronization (SY) and control (CO) tasks. The firing of a SYCO transition leads to simple state changes.

As an example, Fig.1 shows a TPN modeling a periodic process that executes a piece of code and communicates with another process. This communication has an associated time-out. Three elements have been highlighted (a piece of Ada code with the same behaviour is provided for a better understanding of the model). Box A models the periodic activation of the process. Every 10 time units, the transition fires and causes the execution of the process. Box B shows an action, i.e. code, to be executed by the process. The execution starts when the input place is marked. The computation time of this activity is between 4 and 5 time units. Box C shows a communication with another process which has an associated time-out. Let us suppose that the place is marked at time τ. If the transition labeled with $entry\_A$ does not fire (start the communication) before $\tau + 1$ (expiration time of the time-out), then transition $(1, 1)$ will fire, aborting the starting of the communication.

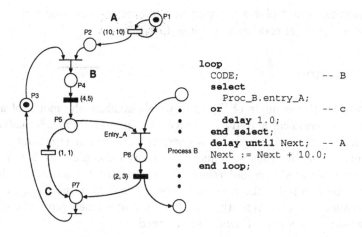

```
loop
    CODE;                    -- B
    select
        Proc_B.entry_A;
    or                       -- c
        delay 1.0;
    end select;
    delay until Next;   -- A
    Next := Next + 10.0;
end loop;
```

Fig. 1. Example of TPN model

3 Decomposing Petri Nets into Processes

A time Petri net can describe the behaviour of an RTS. Several concurrent activities or processes can usually be recognized in this behaviour. Thus, the first step in the implementation of an RTS modeled with a time Petri net is to isolate these processes and their inter-connections. A brief description about how this decomposition can be achieved is given here (see the details in [12][13][14][15]). The basis is to merge a set of transitions in mutual exclusion (ME) into a single process (two transitions are in mutual exclusion if they cannot be fired simultaneously). A set of transitions which are in ME are not concurrent, so guaranteeing that a process is made up only of sequential activities. The existence of ME between transitions can be determined by a computation of *monomarked p-invariants*[2] because they describe a set of places in ME which obviously implies a set of transitions in ME (the input and output transitions of the places). In addition, the p-invariant can be used to describe the control flow of the process. In this way, the only transitions which are able to fire are those whose input place belonging to the p-invariant is marked (see for example Fig. 1, where a token passes through places p_3, p_4, p_5, p_6 and p_7, determining the flow of the process).

Eventually some places will remain which do not belong to any process. These places model asynchronous communications between the processes which they link. The other way of communication is a shared transition which represents a synchronous communication (rendezvous). Moreover, it is possible to share

---

[2] A monomarked p-invariant is a set of places interconnected with transitions through which a single token flows (monomarked) and that holds that in every reachable state the token is always in one of these places, i.e., the sum of the tokens in the places is always one (invariant)

sets of transitions and places grouped in a subnet; this subnet represents the execution of a piece of code in an extended rendezvous.

4 An example

Let us consider the example of Fig. 2 in which we show the model of an RTS made up of a periodical activity (Activity 1) of period *Period_Activation* that executes a code (*code 1*) which has an associated time-out (*time-out 1*). After this execution, a rendezvous with another activity takes place. This rendezvous has another associated time-out (*time-out 2*). Activity 2 executes a code (*code 3*) that can be aborted if the time-out of *code 1* is fired. Otherwise, Activity 2 makes a rendezvous with Activity 1 and later executes a new piece of code (*code 4*). The whole system stops if *time-out 1* is fired.

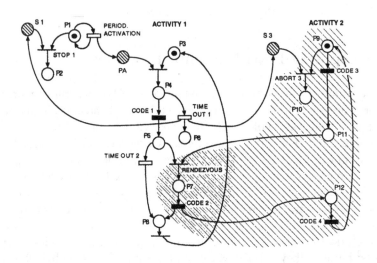

Fig. 2. A real-time system modeled with a TPN. The processes are highlighted

A computation of monomarked p-invariants reveals the existence of three of them which cover all the transitions of the net. They are: $I_1 = \{p_1, p_2\}$; $I_2 = \{p_3, p_4, p_5, p_6, p_7, p_8\}$; $I_3 = \{p_7, p_9, p_{10}, p_{11}, p_{12}\}$. With these p-invariants, three processes can be built (they are highlighted in Fig. 2). One of them (*Proc_1*) represents the periodical activator of Activity 1, another (*Proc_2*) is the body of Activity 1 and the last (*Proc_3*) corresponds to Activity 2. Fig. 2 also shows the way in which the processes communicate with each other. Three shared places (S_1, PA and S_3) act as a medium for asynchronous communication and one shared subnet ({rendezvous, p_7, code 2}) acts as a synchronous communication medium in which *code 2* is executed.

Due to the fact that in the decomposition technique the temporal information is not taken into account, the periodical activity is split into two processes.

We are currently studying how to include temporal mutual exclusion in the recognition of processes. Observe that if time were considered the transitions of *Proc_1* would all be in mutual exclusion with the ones in *Proc_2*, and the two processes could therefore be brought together.

The implementation will be made up of three Ada tasks and the implementation of the shared places. Here is the Ada 95 code that we propose for the processes and the shared places:

```
task body S1 is
begin
  accept Mark;
  Proc_1.Demark_S1;
end S1;
-- The same structure for
-- the place PA

task body Proc_1 is
  L_E: Time; -- Last_Event
begin
  L_E := CLOCK;
  loop
   select
    accept Demark_S1;
    L_E := CLOCK;
    exit;
   or
    delay until L_E + PERIOD_ACT;
    L_E := L_E + PERIOD_ACT;
    PA.Mark;
   end select;
  end loop;
end Proc_1;

task body Proc_3 is
begin
  loop
   select
    S3.Demark;
    exit;
   then abort
    CODE_3;
   end select;
   Proc_2.Rendezvous;
   CODE_4;
  end loop;
end Proc_3;
```

```
task body Proc_2 is
  L_E: Time; -- Last_Event
begin
  L_E := CLOCK;
  loop
   accept Demark_PA;
   L_E := CLOCK;
   select
    delay until L_E + Time_out_1;
    L_E := L_E + Time_out_1;
    S1.Mark; S3.Mark; exit;
   then abort
    CODE_1;
    L_E := CLOCK;
   end select;
   select
    accept Rendezvous do
     CODE_2;
    end Rendezvous;
    L_E := CLOCK;
   or
    delay until L_E + Time_out_2;
    L_E := L_E + Time_out_2;
   end select;
  end loop;
end Proc_2;

protected body S3 is
  entry Demark when Marks > 1 is
  begin
   Marks := Marks - 1;
  end Demark;
  procedure Mark is
  begin
   Marks := Marks + 1;
  end Mark;
end S3;
```

5 Software implementation

This section describes how the code of the previous example was built. Each process can be implemented in an Ada task that has a loop structure. The flow of the token through the p-invariant that generates the process reveals the execution order of the transitions. Basically the implementation of the transitions are as follows:

- The existence of a SYCO transition means that decisions are taken inside a process or that synchronous communication between processes occurs, as will be shown below.
- The existence of a CODE transition involves the execution of its associated code.
- The existence of a TIME transition represents a delay in the execution of the process. The model of a relative delay statement corresponds to a TIME transition.[3] Therefore, as a first approximation, a TIME transition is implemented with a delay statement. However, the implementation of a TIME transition with a simple delay can provoke cumulative drift in the implemented process. This can be avoided if a time variable is associated with each process containing TIME transitions. This variable (Last_Event) records the time at which the last marking update occurred in the process. Each time a transition is fired, the time at which this firing occurs is recorded in the variable. This time is used in the computation of the expiration time of the delays. Thus, the implementation of a TIME transition with an associated time interval (D, D) corresponds to these two instructions:

```
delay until Last_Event + D;
Last_Event := Last_Event + D;
```

The use of this variable can be seen in the code of the example in processes *Proc_1* and *Proc_2*.

The implementation becomes more complex when conflicts appear, i.e. there are several transitions at the output of a place. More complex Ada statements must be used. At this point we begin the proof that the proposed code for the example net is correct, i.e. that it has the same semantics as the model itself. The procedure followed for the proof consist of modeling the semantics of each Ada statement used in the implementation code. By means of a reduction process, we reduce the model of the statement to the structure of the net that was translated into that Ada statement. During the reduction, we must preserve all the CODE and TIME transitions and merge a sequence of SYCO transitions firings to a single transition with the same behaviour, in such a way that the original model and the reduced one are equivalent. Several rules that obey these restrictions

---

[3] The modeling of a delay until statement is not possible using TPN, because all the time values involved are relative to the instant of the enabling of the transition. To model an absolute delay statement, it would be necessary to consider the use of TER nets [9]

have been taken from [6][10][11] for use in the reduction process. Lack of space prevented us from presenting all the models for every Ada structure. We show some of the more representative models, without considering the occurrence of exceptions, aborts or requeue statements.

5.1 Modeling the select statement with a delay branch

The net in Fig. 3.(1) is proposed to model the behaviour of a select statement that has several accepts and a delay branch. The model corresponds to the situation in which only one client calls the server. The model is not valid if different clients can call all the entries.

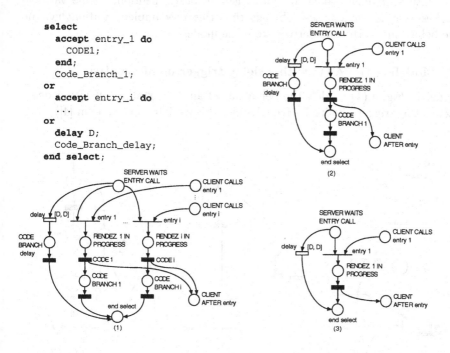

Fig. 3. Model and reduction of the select statement with a delay branch

The server that executes the select statement must wait in the *server waits entry call* place until one of its output SYCO transitions becomes enabled due to a client issuing a call to one of its entries by marking a *Client calls entry i* place. The SYCO transition is then fired, representing the start of the rendezvous in which *code i* is executed. Once the code finishes, the client can continue and the server can execute an optional code (*code branch i*) before finishing the select. If the marking of some *client calls entry i* place does not take place in a time D, the TIME transition corresponding to the *delay* fires, removing the token from the *server waits entry call* place and aborting the possibility of making any rendezvous.

The model can be simplified if we consider only one client and one entry (Fig. 3.(2)), as in the case of our example. If, in addition, the select does not have the optional code after either the accept or the delay branches, then the *code branch delay* and *code branch 1* transitions can be removed (Fig. 3.(3)). This structure can be seen in the example net involving the *rendezvous, time-out 2* and *code 2* transitions. This corresponds to the select of *Proc_2* and the entry call of *Proc_3*. Moreover, if no code is executed in the accept, the same structure can be recognized in the *stop 1* and *period. activation* transitions corresponding to *Proc_1*.

With the aim of avoiding cumulative drift, for example in *Proc_1*, we substitute the delay statement which corresponds to the TIME transition with the delay until statement which includes the previously mentioned time variable *Last_Event*. It is immediately obvious that this new implementation has the same behaviour as the one derived from the model.

5.2 Modeling the ATC with a delay triggering alternative

The net in Fig. 4.(1) models the behaviour of an ATC statement with a delay statement as triggering alternative (the model is similar to the one in [4]).

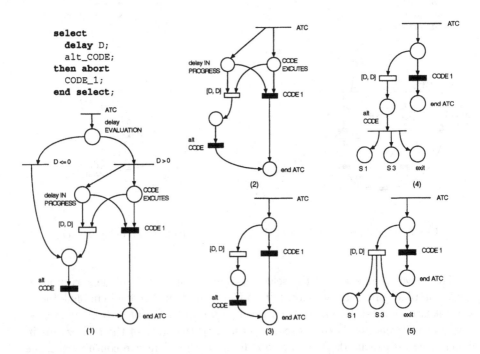

Fig. 4. Model and reduction of the ATC statement with a delay as triggering alternative

Once the ATC begins, the delay expression must be evaluated. If the expression is positive, the *delay in progress* and *code executes* places are marked, involving the enabling of the TIME and CODE transitions. These two transitions compete to remove the tokens from both places. If the CODE transition *code 1* fires before time D expires, the tokens will be removed and the TIME transition will be disabled (this means aborting the delay statement). The code of the delay alternative is then executed. On the other hand, if time D expires before the CODE transition fires, the tokens are removed and the CODE transition disabled (this means that the code execution is aborted). If the expression in the delay is negative or zero, the code of the delay alternative is directly executed. This case has not been considered in the reduction process because, within the scope of this study, the delay expression is always positive (Fig. 4.(2)).

Applying reduction rule 6 of [11] (parallel redundant places) the *delay in progress* and *code executes* places can be reduced to one (Fig. 4.(3)). In the case of our example, the code that must be performed if the delay alternative is triggered is the marking of two places (S_1 and S_3) and the execution of an exit statement that breaks the normal flow of the process, avoiding the place *end ATC* being marked. This is shown in Fig. 4.(4). In Fig. 4.(5) the final structure is obtained by applying rule 3 of [11] (post-fusion). The resultant model can be recognized in the net of the example involving place p_4 and transitions *code 1* and *time-out 1* that are implemented in *Proc_2*. Once again, the delay is substituted with the corresponding delay until using the *Last_Event* variable.

5.3 Modeling the ATC with an entry call triggering alternative

The net in Fig. 5.(1) models the general behaviour of an ATC statement with an entry call as triggering alternative. This model corresponds to the general real situation, where both the triggering alternative and the abortable part can evolve in parallel. However, we consider only monoprocessor implementation platforms, and static priorities. With these restrictions, the model can be simplified because it is impossible for both parts to be executed at the same time. In this case, the server that accepts the entry call must have a higher priority than the client, since this is the only way in which the server can have a chance of interrupting the abortable part. Once the entry is accepted, the abortable part is preempted and the ATC finishes before it can execute again. This simplification leads us to the model in Fig. 5.(2).

When the ATC begins, *abortable part* and *wait for accept* places are marked. This involves *code 1* starting its execution while the marking of the *server accept* place is being waited for. If this is already available, the transition *rendezvous* fires, removing the token from the *abortable part* place and aborting the starting of the code. Otherwise, the code execution will be aborted in the same way at the moment in which the *server accept* place is marked. If this place is not marked, the code can finish removing the token from the *wait for accept* place and then abort the entry call.

For the reduction rule 2 of [6] is used (pre-fusion of transitions). This leads us to the net in Fig. 5.(3). Rule 6 of [11] (parallel redundant places) can then be used to eliminate the *wait for accept* place (which is the same as *abortable part*). The code that is executed after the entry call consists of an exit statement

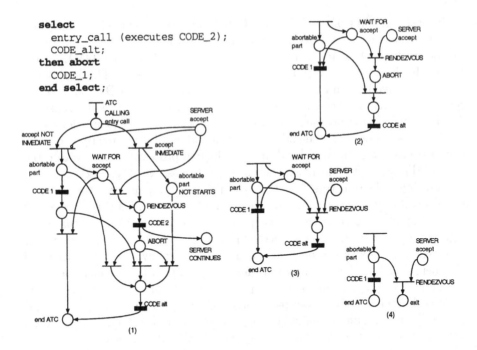

Fig. 5. Model and reduction of the ATC statement with an entry call as triggering alternative

that breaks the normal flow of the process and avoids the *end ATC* place being marked. The product of these last steps is shown in Fig. 5.(4). This structure can be directly seen in the net of the example involving p_9, S_3 and p_{10} places, and *abort 3* and *code 3* transitions.

6   Conclusions and Future Work

The Petri net formalism is directly executable. This paper demostrates how the code which implements the net can be obtained. Moreover it has been shown that the translation into Ada 95 code is correct, i.e. it has the same behaviour as the net. This allows us to enrich the Petri nets formalism, which has been traditionally used for the specification and analysis of behavioural and timing properties in real-time systems. We have now shown how to implement this, and so making time Petri nets an alternative method for the whole life cycle of a real-time system.

Future work will be devoted to the study of several optimizations for the generated code. Firstly a study must be carried out on how to include temporal restrictions in the recognition of the processes embedded in the time Petri net. This will avoid situations such as the one in the example of section 4, where a periodic activity had to be split into two processes. In the second place, the use of the time variable *Last_Event* in order to avoid cumulative drift must be optimized. In the current implementations it is used in every process with TIME transitions but should anly be necessary in process where there is at least one sequence of execution only with TIME transitions and no external interaction.

References

[1] P. Merlin and D.J. Farber. Recoverability of communication protocols. *IEEE transactions on Communication*, 24(9), September 1976.

[2] B. Berthomieu and M. Diaz. Modeling and verification of time dependent systems using time Petri nets. *IEEE transactions on Software Engineering*, 17(3):259–273, March 1991.

[3] D. Mandrioli, R. Zicari, C. Ghezzi, and F. Tisato. Modeling the Ada task system by Petri nets. *Computer Languages*, 10(1):43–61, 1985.

[4] R.K. Gedela and S.M. Shatz. Modelling of advanced tasking in Ada-95: A Petri net perspective. In *Proc. 2nd Int. Workshop on Software Engineering for Parallel and Distributed Systems, PSDE'97*, Boston, USA, 1997.

[5] U. Buy and R.H. Sloan. Analysis of real-time programs with simple time Petri nets. In *Proc. Int. Symp. on Software Testing and Analysis*, pages 228–239, 1994.

[6] S.M. Shatz, S. Tu, T. Murata, and S. Duri. An application of Petri net reduction for Ada tasking deadlock analysis. *IEEE Transactions on Parallel and Distributed Systems*, 7(12):1307–1322, December 1996.

[7] S. Duri, U. Buy, R. Devarapalli, and S.M. Shatz. Application and experimental evaluation of state space reduction methods for deadlock analysis in Ada. *ACM Transaction on Software Engeeniering Methodology*, 3(4):340–380, December 1994.

[8] W.M.P. van der Aalst and M.A. Odijk. Analysis of railway stations by means of interval timed coloured Petri nets. *Real-Time Systems*, 9(3):241–263, November 1995.

[9] C. Ghezzi, D. Mandrioli, S. Morasca, and M. Pezze. A unified high-level Petri net formalism for time-critical systems. *IEEE transactions on Software Engineering*, 17(2):160–171, February 1991.

[10] T. Murata. Petri nets: properties, analysis, and applications. *Proceedings of the IEEE*, 77(4), April 1989.

[11] R.H. Sloan and U. Buy. Reduction rules for time Petri nets. *Acta Informatica*, 43:687–706, 1996.

[12] J.M. Colom, M. Silva, and J..L. Villarroel. On software implementation of Petri Nets and Colored Petri Nets using high level concurrent languages. In *Proc. of 7th European Workshop on Application and Theory of Petri nets*, pages 207–241, Oxford, England, January 1986.

[13] F. Kordon. Proposal for a Generic Prototyping Approach. In *IEEE Symposium on Emerging Technologies and Factory Automation*, Tokyo, Japan, number 94TH8000, pages 396–403. IEEE Comp Soc Press, 1994.

[14] F. Bréant and J.F. Peyre. An improved massively parallel implementation of colored Petri nets specifications. In *IFIP-WG 10.3 working conference on programming environments for massively parallel distributed systems, Ascona, Switzerland*, 1994.

[15] F.J. García and J.L. Villarroel. Decentralized implementation of real-time systems using time Petri nets. application to mobile robot control. In D.F. García Nocetti, editor, *Proc. of the 5th IFAC/IFIP Workshop*, Algorithms and Architectures for Real Time Control 1998, pages 11–16. Pergamon, 1998.

Railway Scale Model Simulator

Pierre Breguet[1] and Luigi Zaffalon[2]

[1]*University of Applied Sciences HES-SO,*
School of Engineering Vaud (EIVd),
Route de Cheseaux 1
CH-1400 Yverdon-les-Bains, Switzerland
Pierre.Breguet@eivd.ch

[2]*University of Applied Sciences HES-SO,*
School of Engineering Genève (EIG),
4, Rue de la Prairie
CH-1202 Genève, Switzerland
Zaffalon@eig.unige.ch

Abstract: The Ada programming language has been used for more than 12 years in our classes of concurrent and real time programming. This teaching includes also programming assignment based on various equipment and in particular on railway scale models. Moreover, students have had inexpensive Ada 95 programming environments on PC/Windows at their disposal for several years. They are therefore able to prepare the assignment at home and use the laboratory equipment intensively. The last step was to provide them with a simulator of a railway scale model. This software completely simulates the behaviour of real models and like real models, it illustrates the concepts inherent of concurrent and real time programming. Furthermore, the students are very enthusiastic about its use. The writing of programs controlling trains is based upon the Ada tasks and the new features provided with the 95 version of the language (protected objects, requeue, System Annex).

Keywords: Education and training, simulation, concurrency, resource management, protected objects, rendez-vous.

1   Introduction

Railway scale models induce a very high interest to the students although their use and access is limited to the equipped laboratories. Moreover it is not possible to increase the number of such equipment in the restricted space of the laboratories, and students may not generally use it at home. Furthermore not all students can access it simultaneously during regular laboratory hours. These reasons justified the definition of a railway scale model simulation program and its implementation in Ada 95 [5]. The current version of the program enables users to simulate two types of real *Märklin Digital* scale models available at RTL (*Real Time Laboratory* at EIVd):

- 2 scale models of type A (Fig. 1) which includes 17 switches and 26 contacts;
- 2 scale models of type B (Fig. 3) which includes 24 switches and 36 contacts.

The simulator, entirely written in Ada 95, also enables the students to prepare assignments on a third scale model placed at IIL (*Industrial Computer Science*

Laboratory at EIG). That model includes 45 switches and 2*96 reed-relay type contacts. Because the description of the model is also an input to the simulator, it is possible to easily create as many models as needed [10].

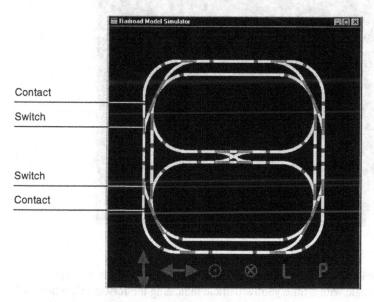

Contact

Switch

Switch

Contact

Fig. 1 Railway scale model of type A

2 View of the simulator

A *console window* (Fig. 2) provides the textual user interface, the tracing of events and the reporting of errors such as collisions and derailments.

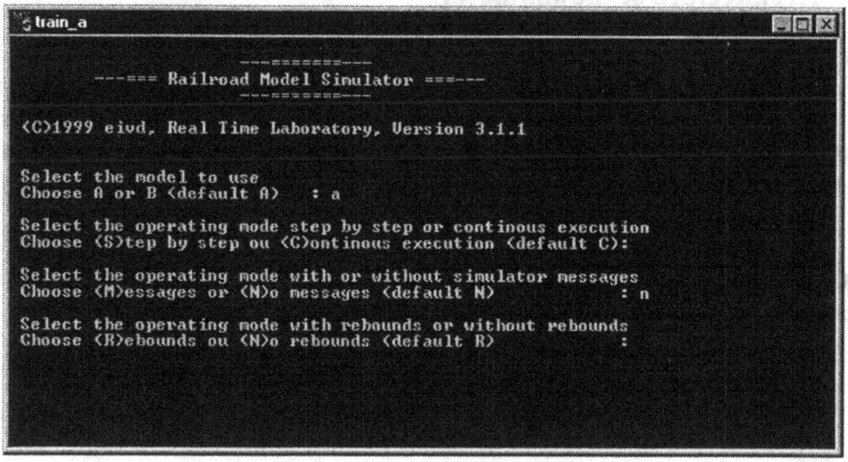

Fig. 2 Console window

The traces generated by the simulator are also written in a text file.

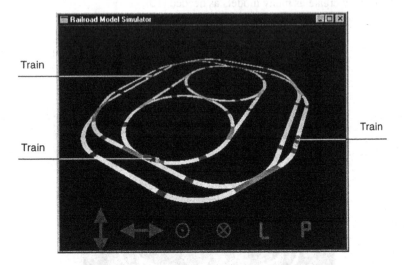

Fig. 3 Graphic window, railway scale model of type B

A *graphic window* (Fig. 3) shows the model in use, and the trains that are represented by a mauve rectangle with a little yellow particle indicating the forward direction. All train positions are drawn in that window. It allows also to command the simulator by clicking with the mouse on one of the six icons placed at the bottom of the window. The two left icons move the point of view and rotate the model. Zooming forward and backward is possible by clicking on the two middle icons. The two last icons act upon the course of the simulation by changing the speed and by providing a step by step mode.

3 Architecture of the simulator

As mentioned previously, the simulator is written in Ada 95 [6]. The development environment used is *ObjectAda* [4] and the software runs on PC under Windows NT or 95. The graphic interface has been implemented with *OpenGL* [11] which is included with the operating system and interfaced with the simulator. That interface is provided with the ObjectAda environment by Aonix.

The data structures used to implement the model and to manage the trains are in the packages grouped together with the name Model on Fig. 4. Concurrent accesses are handled by a protected object for mutual exclusion.

The task Window controls the graphic display of the model and trains. The task also handles the actions of the mouse on the icons.

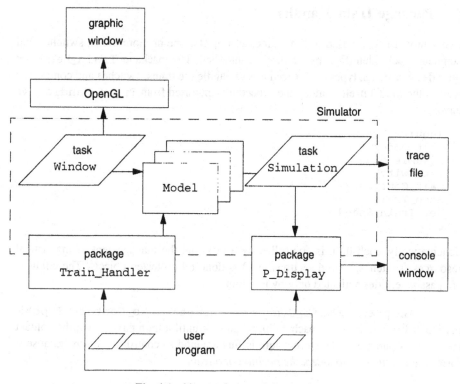

Fig. 4 Architectural view of the simulator

The task Simulation simulates the progress of the trains considering their speed during a simulation step. At each step it displays textual information on the state of the model and the trains and updates the corresponding data structures.

The tasks Window and Simulation synchronize each other in order to update, at each simulation step, the graphic window and to modify the behaviour of the simulator at each action of the mouse on the two right icons (Fig. 1 and 3). The synchronization is implemented as usual by a protected object internal to Model.

The package Train_Handler [5] enables the users to control a real *Märklin* scale model or the simulator. Indeed, in both cases, the specification of the package is the same. The behavior is also identical, especially regarding the trains passing over the contacts.

The package P_Display has a specification that is a subset of Ada.Text_IO. As the specification of Train_Handler is unique, the user program is *identical* if it runs with the simulator or if it controls a real model. As P_Display handles the messages coming from several tasks, the mutual exclusion on the console window must be done by a protected object.

4 Package Train_Handler

Every model is composed of three kinds of objects: one or more trains, switches and contacts, each identified by an unique number. The package `Train_Handler` provides constants, types and procedures to handle the trains, switches and contacts as well as the model itself. Among the procedures exported from `Train_Handler`, we have:

```
Inquire_Train,
Init_Model,
Disable_Model,
Set_Switch,
Wait_Contact,
Stop_Train
Set_Train_Speed,
etc.
```

Schematically, each train is controlled by a task and the management of the critical resources (switches, shared sections, etc.) is done by protected objects. The contacts are passive entities activated only by the trains.

The procedure `Wait_Contact (Contact: in Nb_Contact_Type)` is particular because it blocks each calling Ada task until a train passes over the contact specified as parameter. This procedure is fundamental to control the trains because it forms *the unique way to detect the position of a train.*

Generally the number and the speed of each train are provided by the user when executing `Inquire_Train`. Each train is then placed between two contacts and the first specified contact defines the forward direction.

5 Modeling the routes of the trains

The first step of the student work consists mainly of modeling in Ada 95 the route of the trains. These routes can be decomposed into a *sequence of contacts* provided that the sequence defines entirely the route:

```
Commercial_Speed: constant Speed_Type := 12;
Low_Speed:        constant Speed_Type := 6;

type Segm_Type is
   record
      Contact: Nb_Contact_Type;   -- At the end of the segment
      Speed:   Speed_Type;        -- Speed on the segment
   end record;

type Journey_Type is array (Natural range <>) of Segm_Type;

First_Journey: aliased Journey_Type:=
   ( (Contact=>19, Speed=> Commercial_Speed),
     (Contact=>20, Speed=> Low_Speed),
     ...
     (Contact=>22, Speed=> Low_Speed),
     (Contact=>13, Speed=> Commercial_Speed) );
```

```
Second_Journey:  aliased Journey_Type:= ...;
Third_Journey:   aliased Journey_Type:= ...;
Fourth_Journey:  aliased Journey_Type:= ...;
```

6 Modeling the behaviour of the trains

In our example each train is modeled by a task object of the same task type because the trains all have the same behavior, only their routes differ. The routes are defined by a discriminant with a value that is a pointer on a static *aliased* structure (see Sect. 5).

```
task type Train (Journey: access Journey_Type);
task body Train is
    Nb_Train:     Nb_Train_Type;
    Speed_Train:  Speed_Type;
    Next_Resource, -- A resource is always bounded by contacts
    Current_Resource: Model_Controller.Nb_Resource_Type;
begin
    Inquire_Train (Journey(Journey'First).Contact,
                   Journey(Journey'Last).Contact,
                   Nb_Train, Speed_Train);
    Model_Controller.Allocate (Journey(Journey'Last).Contact,
                               Journey(Journey'First).Contact,
                               Current_Resource);
    for Nb_Current_Journey in 1..Max_Journey loop
        for Index in Journey'First..Journey'Last loop
            declare
                Current_Segment:Segm_Type renames Journey(Index);
                Next_Segment: Segm_Type renames
                    Journey((Index+1) mod Journey'Length);
            begin
                Stop_Train(Nb_Train,Speed_Train);
                Model_Controller.Allocate
                    (Current_Segment.Contact,Next_Segment.Contact,
                    Next_Resource);
                -- Switches setting done in Model_Controller.
                Set_Speed_Train(Nb_Train,Speed_Train);
                Wait_Contact(Current_Segment.Contact);
                Model_Controller.Release(Current_Resource);
                Current_Resource := Next_Resource;
            end;
        end loop;
    end loop;
    Stop_Train(Nb_Train);
end Train;
begin
    Init_Model;
    declare                 -- One task per train.
        Santa_Fe:          Train(First_Journey'Access);
        Western_Union:     Train(Second_Journey'Access);
        Union_Pacific:     Train(Third_Journey'Access);
        Western_Pacific:   Train(Fourth_Journey'Access);
    begin
        null;
    end;
    Disable_Model;
end;
```

It is interesting to notice that the handling of the switches is included in Model_Controller in our example (see also Sect. 7). Indeed the switches will be set to the direction taken by the train if the resource defined by its contacts has been allocated to that train.

Since Model_Controller handles the switches, it can *optimize the allocation* of shared track segments. As illustrated in Fig. 5, two trains can share the same resource ((6) for example) if their routes are parallel (10, 11, 12, 13 and 14, 15, 16 for example), but only one train is authorized on the shared tracks if one of these trains takes the way 10, 15, 13.

7 Modeling a scale model and resource management

Naturally, the routes can have common segments. Consequently the latter must be modeled as resources that are bounded by contacts (Fig. 5) so that collisions may be avoided. The allocation and release of *segment* resources must be handled as *critical resources*. Note that the train tasks are unware of the modeling of the resource. The only information available to them is the route (sequence of contacts)..

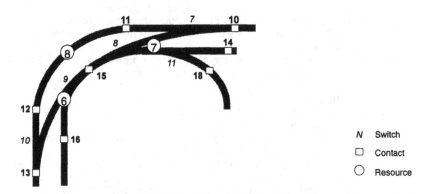

Fig. 5 Definition of a segment resource

Several kinds of resource allocation algorithms are possible to illustrate the paradigms and features of Ada. The first solution for resource management is based on an *entry family* of a Controller task. However a first announce is necessary to implement this solution and consequently a deferred blocking appears if the segment resource has already been allocated to another train task. The algorithm (not presented here) is a typical Ada 83 algorithm.

The second solution is also based on a Controller task and uses the requeue on a *private entry* of that task. This new possibility was introduced with Ada 95. This time the call handled by the controller is easier and potentially blocking:

```
Wait_Contact(Current_Segment.Contact);
Stop_Train(Nb_Train);
Controller.Allocate(Current_Segment.Contact,
                    Next_Segment.Contact);
```

```
-- Switches setting done in Controller.
Set_Speed_Train(Nb_Train,Speed_Train);
... -- Pass the railroad segment.
Wait_Contact(Current_Segment.Contact);
Controller.Release;
```

In the parameter profiles of the above calls, the absence of the `Resource` parameter in the `Allocate` and `Release` entries must be noticed. The train tasks provide only a (partial) route to the controller. It is indeed possible to use the `Caller` attribute or the `Current_Task` function (*System Annex*, [3]) to obtain the identity of the calling task for which the resource is being allocatedor released.

The resource allocation protocol can be the same for an active controller task and for a passive controller implemented with a *protected object*. The package body of `Model_Controller` details the internal structure of such a controller and the calling algorithms and `requeue` mechanism described previously:

```
with Ada.Task_Identification;  use Ada.Task_Identification;

package body Model_Controller is

   type Path_Type is
      record
         State:          State_Type := Free;
         -- Switches on the route crossing a resource:
         Nb_Switches:  Nb_Switches_Type := 0;
         Switches_List:Switches_List_Type;
      end record;
   type All_Paths_Type is array (Nb_Resource_Type) of Path_Type;
   All_Paths: All_Paths_Type;
   -------------------------------------------------------------
   protected Controller is

      entry Allocate (Entry_Contact,
                      Exit_Contact: in     Nb_Contact_Type;
                      Nb_Resource:    out Nb_Resource_Type);
      procedure Release;

   private
      entry Wait_Resource (Nb_Resource_Type)
                      (Entry_Contact,
                      Exit_Contact: in     Nb_Contact_Type;
                      Nb_Resource:    out Nb_Resource_Type);
      ...
   end Controller;

   protected body Controller is
      function Search (Entry_Contact,
                      Exit_Contact: Nb_Contact_Type)
                      return Nb_Resource_Type is ...;
      procedure Hold(Nb_Resource  : in Nb_Resource_Type;
                     Calling_Task : in Task_Id) is ...;
      procedure Make_Free is ...;
      function  Path_Free (Path: Path_Type) return Boolean is...;
```

```
   entry Allocate(Entry_Contact,
                  Exit_Contact: in    Nb_Contact_Type;
                  Nb_Resource:     out Nb_Resource_Type)
      when True is
   begin
      Nb_Resource := Search(Entry_Contact, Exit_Contact);
      if not Path_Free(All_Paths(Nb_Resource)) then
         requeue Wait_Resource(Nb_Resource);
      end if;
      Hold(Nb_Resource, Allocate'Caller);
   end Allocate;

   entry Wait_Resource (for Nb_Ress in Nb_Resource_Type)
                  (Entry_Contact,
                   Exit_Contact: in    Nb_Contact_Type;
                   Nb_Resource:     out Nb_Resource_Type)
      when Path_Free(All_Pathes(Nb_Ress)) is
   begin
      Hold(Nb_Ress, Wait_Resource'Caller);
      Nb_Resource := Nb_Ress;
   end Wait_Resource;

   procedure Release is
   begin
      Make_Free;  -- Function Current_Task used.
   end Release;
end Controller;
-------------------------------------------------------------
procedure Allocate(Entry_Contact,
                   Exit_Contact: in Nb_Contact_Type) is
   Nb_Resource: Nb_Resource_Type;
begin
   Controller.Allocate(Entry_Contact, Exit_Contact,
                       Nb_Resource);
   Set_Resource_Switches(Nb_Resource);
end Allocate;

procedure Release is
begin
   Controller.Release;
end Release;

end Model_Controller;
```

During an allocation, the Search function returns the resource bounded by two contacts. The resource is next allocated by the Hold procedure if the path crossing the resource is free. Otherwise the call is requeued on the Wait_Resource private entry. The call is accepted when the resource becomes free. The Release operation liberates the mutual exclusion granted to the train.

8 Use of the simulator in the laboratory

Generally the students take a deep interest in simulation. In the case of the railway scale model simulator, the *play aspect* reinforces the software attraction and many students are very enthusiastic. Graduate students often remember the programming work with the simulator as a nice and interesting activity.

The dynamic aspect of the directing trains materializes typical abstract phenomena from the concurrent programming field. The students appreciate these situations, not only when the trains are correctly managed but also when collisions are unavoidable and showing conceptual or implementation errors lurking in their algorithms.

As opposed to the real models, the simulator provides debugging facilities because of the strong interaction between the simulation and the code of the applications. Error detection is then much easier.

Finally the developing time and the test of the applications for the real models is dramatically reduced with the use of the simulator. This is also true for the conception and the correction of the assignments.

9 Conclusion

The railway scale model simulator presented in this paper allows to:

- work out solutions based on semaphores, protected objects, rendez-vous and any other mechanism feasible in Ada 95 [1] [2] [3];

- implement numerous paradigms found in concurrent programming [7] [8] [12];

- implement different and incremental methods resulting in the elaboration of solution of complex problems (resource management, deadlock prevention, etc.) by reusing entirely or partially existing modelisations;

- illustrate in a attractive and dynamic way the implementations.

The visual and play aspects reinforce the student's interests and generate an outstanding motivation in seeking original solutions.

We thank the author of the simulator, Mr. Philippe Girardet presently an assistant at EIVd for his excellent work carried out in 1997, mainly during his diploma work [9].

References

[1] Ada, Manuel de référence du langage de programmation, Presses polytechniques et universitaires romandes (1987)

[2] Ada 95 Rationale, The Language, The Standard Libraries, Intermetrics Inc. (1995)

[3] ANSI/ISO Standard, Ada 95 Reference Manual, The Language, The Standard Libraries, Intermetrics Inc. (1995)

[4] ObjectAda for Windows 95 and Windows NT, Aonix (1997)

[5] Breguet P., Girardet M.: Simulateur de maquette v. 3.1, Documentation utilisateur, Poly-copié (1999)

[6] Breguet P., Zaffalon L.: Analyse et programmation en Ada 95, Polycopié (1998)

[7]   Burns A., Wellings A.: Real-Time Systems and Programming Languages, Addison-Wesley (1997)

[8]   Burns A., Wellings A.: Concurrency in Ada, Cambridge University Press (1998)

[9]   Girardet Ph.: Interface graphique pour un simulateur de maquettes de trains, Polycopié (1997)

[10] Girardet Ph.: Documentation pour le créateur de fichiers décrivant les maquettes, Polycopié (1998)

[11] Neider J., Davis T., Woo M.: OpenGL Programming Guide, Addison-Wesley (1995)

[12] Zaffalon L., Breguet P.: Programmation concurrente et temps réel en Ada 95, Polycopié (1998)

Ada 95 as a Foundation Language in Computer Engineering Education in Ukraine

Alexandr   Korochkin

National Technical University of Ukraine -
"Kiev Polytechnical Institute,   Kiev, Ukraine
Department of Computer Systems
NTUU- KPI,   KPI - 2002
Pr. Pobedy 37,
Kiev, 252057
Ukraine
cora@comsys.ntu-kpi.kiev.ua

Abstract. The paper presents a proposal for introducing Ada 95 as the major teaching language for courses in computer engineering education in Ukraine.

1 Introduction

Ukraine is a country situated in eastern Europe. It has a population of about 50 million people. The country is probably best known now for the football club Dynamo Kiev and, less fortunately, for Chernobyl. However the country has a large potential for economic and scientific growth.

Both the development of computer science and the computer industry have a long tradition in the Ukraine. In 1951 the MESM computer was developed in Kiev by Professor S. Lebedev's group. This computer was the second in Europe and the first in continental Europe.   In 1963 the world-renowned Academic Glushkov Cybernetic Center (Institute of Cybernetic of Academy of Science of Ukraine) was created. The Ukraine has since developed and manufactured many indigenous computers including Mir-1, Mir-2, Dnipro, PS-2000, PS-3000, SM-2, SM-4 and many special computers, which were used in military, industrial and space applications.

The computer industry in Ukraine is currently not a world player, but it is developing rapidly. Today there are more than one million computers of different kinds in use: PC, workstations, servers and multi-processors systems. More than 250,000 computers were sold in 1998. Companies such as IBM, DEC, Hewlett-Packard, Siemens and others have divisions in the Ukraine. In Kiev alone there are more than 470 companies involved in the manufacture and sale of computers. The country is a huge prospective market for modern hardware and software and consequently needs many specialists in computer science and computer engineering.

2 The Computer Engineering Education in Ukraine

Since 1957, computer education in Ukraine was provided by Kiev Polytechnical Institute. When Ukraine became independent in 1991, education was reformed and bachelor, specialist and magistr degrees were created. After this reform, computer education was divided into computer science and computer engineering. In 1994 the first standard of computer engineering education was created. This standard prescribes the structure, list and contents of major courses in computer engineering education for bachelor of computer engineering only. By 2002, a new full standard of computer engineering education will be created through the national program called "Education - 21st Century".

Today Ukrainian Computer Engineering Education is offered by more then 25 technical universities in Kiev, Lvov, Charkov, Donetsk, Odessa, and Dnepropetrovsk. The degrees available in computer engineering in Ukraine are:

- Bachelor of Computer Engineering (4 years)
- Specialist (Engineer) (1 - 1,5 years)
- Magistr (Master) (1,5 - 2 years)

The standard list of courses in the bachelor program include Mathematics, Physics, Economics and Social Issues, Computer Electronics, Computer Logic, Computer Arithmetic, Theory of Circuits, Digital Computers, Computer Networks, Computer Systems Architecture, Real-Time Systems and a block of software courses. There are also elective courses.

The graduate programs of Specialist and Magistr are provided in three different areas:

1. Computer Systems and Networks
2. System Programming
3. Special Computer Systems.

Currently, there are no standard curriculums for the specialist and magistr degrees. Every university has its own set of courses. Standards will be created by the year 2002.

The computer engineering curriculum in Ukraine is a combination of computer science and computer engineering that provides the education and training necessary to design, implement, test and utilize the hardware and software of digital computer systems. Within the curriculum students study all aspects of computer systems from electronic design through logic design, VLSI concepts and device utilization, machine language design, implementation and programming, operating system concepts, system programming, networking fundamentals and application of these systems. As a result of historical developments, students in the computer engineering department take many of their courses in the departments of computer science and electrical engineering.

Education in software development includes Programming, Object-Oriented Programming, Modeling, System Programming, Parallel Programming, Operating System, Programming Real Time and Embedded Systems, Programming Distributed Systems and so on. Programming languages currently used in these courses are summarized in a table in a later section of this paper.

3 Ada in Ukraine

Ada is becoming more popular in Ukraine. There are many perspective areas of the Ada using : Avionics (Antonov - "Mria AN-124", AN-140, AN-70), Space (Yuzhmash - "Zenit"), Banking Systems, Medicine, Metallurgy, Metro and Railways.

Ukrainian teachers and researchers are looking at Ada 95 materials outside of Ukraine. They are active participants of Ada-Europe and next year they will begin participation in ACM/SIGAda activities. The Ukrainian Ada users are currently creating a society - "Ada in Ukraine". We believe that Ada has a bright future in Ukraine.

4 Ada 95 in Computer Engineering

We now have experience of using and teaching Ada in Ukrainian classrooms. Ada is taught by several universities in Ukraine. The Department of Computer Systems at the National Technical University of Ukraine - "Kiev Polytechnical Institute" has used Ada since 1986. Ada is also taught at Charkov, Odessa, Kremenchug, and Kirovograd. The main problems with teaching Ada in Ukraine are the absence of a good textbooks with Ada 95 and knowledge of modern pedagogy for teaching and using Ada 95 in the classroom. While there is a Ukrainian Ada 95 textbook for beginning programmers [3], there are no Ada 95 based books for the remainder of the curriculum.

There are many academic and financial arguments for using one core language in software education [1, 2]. They are equally valid in Ukrainian education. Until the arrival of Ada 95 there was no programming language which supports the concepts taught in the majority of software courses offered in Ukraine. I am proposing that we use Ada 95 as the core language of Ukrainian computer engineering.

The table given below presents computer engineering software courses and the use of programming languages in these in Kiev National Technical University. It is typical for Ukrainian universities.

Courses	Languages
Programming	Pascal, C
System Programming	Assembler, C
Modeling	Pascal
Parallel Programming	Ada
Object-Oriented Programming	C++
Numerical Methods	Pascal
Real-Time Systems	Pascal
Embedded Systems	Assembler, Pascal
Security	Pascal
Distributed Computing	Ada, Java

As can be seen from the table above, Ukrainian students have experience with a variety of languages. Currently, Ada is used only in the parallel and distributed computing courses. How can we add "Ada" to other lines of the language column of the table? The course "Programming" is the first programming course taken by computer engineering students. A successful choice of programming language is very important here. As demonstrated by studies at U.S. military academies [4], using Ada in this course will allow us to improve our students' foundation in computer science so they will be better prepared to understand modern software concepts such as abstractions of different kinds, modules and libraries, object oriented, exceptions, separate compilations and so forth.

Ada will be a good vehicle in "System Programming". The "Modeling" and "Numerical Methods" courses will also benefit from the power of Ada. Finally Ada remains an excellent choice in such courses as "Parallel Programming" and "Distributed Computing".

5 Main goals of project

The goals of our project "Ada 95 as a Foundation Language in Computer Engineering Education in Ukraine" include:

- the study of experience in European and American universities using the Ada language in teaching
- adaptation of Ada in the Ukrainian universities
- development of methods of Ada 95 teaching in Computer Engineering curriculum
- writing (in collaboration) and publishing in the Ukraine new Ada 95 textbooks.

We are developing this project as a part of the national curriculum project "Education - 21ˢᵗ Century". The schedule for completing this major education system reform is

1998	– new list of education directions
1999 - 2000	– full Standard for bachelor
2000 - 2001	– full Standard for specialist
2001 - 2002	– full Standard for magistr.

The full Standards prescribe the qualification characteristic of graduates, the structure, list and contents of major and elective courses and the tests.

A Working Group in the Ministry of education of Ukraine, is creating the full Standard in Computer Engineering. The author of this paper is a member of the group and also the secretary of the committee "Computer Engineering". The National Technical University - KPI is the basic university in charge of the creation of this new Standard.

The use of Ada in Computer Engineering Education is planned in two steps. The first step is to include Ada in the new Standard as compulsory programming language for beginning students. The second step is using Ada in most other courses. The major obstacles we face are that many of our teachers 1) don't know Ada 2) believe that Ada is a very complicated language and 3) don't know of the latest Ada standard: Ada'95.

The work of adopting Ada in Ukrainian universities is now underway. Teachers from Ukrainian universities have learned Ada at the National Technical University – KPI. Therefore we will plan Ada classes and seminars in several universities in Ukraine. (In April and May we will have such classes in Odessa and Kirovograd).

6 Summary

This project is one more step in bringing Ukrainian education up to that of the best education systems in the World. Using the Ada 95 programming language as a foundation language in computer engineering education in Ukraine will allow us:

- to study modern outstanding programming language
- to enter in the world of modern information technologies
- to use international experience of teaching and using Ada
- to participation in joint projects
- to exchange students and teachers

We guess if only Ada was used at the Ukrainian nuclear stations we did not have the tragedy in Chernobyl.

7 Acknowledgements

Thanks are due to Professor Erhard Ploedereder and Professor Dan Simpson, who supported an idea of project.

Many thanks are due to Professor John McCormick, who helped me in this project.

References

1. Feldman, M.: Ada 95 as a Foundation Programming Language. Ada User Journal 3(17) (1996) 144-145
2. Simpson D. : Ada and Software Engineering Education. Ada User Journal 4(18) (1997) 144-147
3. Korochkin A.: Ada 95: An Introduction to Programming. Svit Kiev (1998)
4. Murtagh, J., Hamilton, J. : A Comparison of Ada and Pascal in an Introductory Computer Science Course, Proceedings ACM SIGAda '98, Washington, DC, (1998) 75-80

yaRTI, a Ada 95 HLA Run-Time Infrastructure

Dominique Canazzi

CS-SI, 3 rue Le Corbusier, SILIC 232
94528 RUNGIS CEDEX – France

Abstract. HLA stands for High Level Architecture. It is a standard developed by the US Department of Defense to achieve the interoperation and the reuse of simulations. The formal definition of the HLA comprises three main parts: the HLA rules, the HLA interface specification (I/F Spec) and the HLA Object Model Template (OMT). A HLA Run-Time Infrastructure is a middleware that implements the I/F Spec, allowing a set of simulations (a federation) to interoperate. The standardization process for the HLA is in progress (IEEE P1516). For the time now, the DoD has sponsored the development of RTI prototypes, and commercial products begin to appear. All are developed in C or C++. yaRTI is the first pure Ada 95 implementation of the HLA I/F Spec, taking advantage of the powerful distribution and tasking features of the language. The paper mainly focuses on a general description of the HLA, a more precise description of the I/F Spec, the presentation of the architecture of yaRTI and the major implementation characteristics, the main issues encountered and the lessons learned.

1 HLA overview

1.1 Vocabulary and concepts

A Federate is a HLA compliant simulation application. A federate manages simulation actors (objects). Objects are instances of object classes. Object classes have attributes (their public data) and are organized into an inheritance hierarchy. It also exchange messages (interactions) with other federates. Interactions are instances of interaction classes. Interaction classes have parameters (the message data).

A Federation is a set of Federates, a distributed simulation application built from the capabilities of the federates.

A SOM (Simulation Object Model) is the formal description of the capabilities of a federate, mainly in terms of:

- Simulated actors or part of actors (object classes attributes that the federate will publish), interesting actors or parts of actors (object classes attributes that the federate will subscribe). The responsibility of updating an attribute (ownership) may be transferable.

- Interactions it can initiate, interactions which it reacts to or which it is interested in (sense). Interactions are from federate to federate, and not explicitly related to object classes.

A FOM (Federation Object Model) describes what may be actually exchanged within a Federation. Roughly, the FOM is a negotiated subset of the intersection of the SOMs of the Federates. This negotiation takes place at the beginning of the design time of the federation.

A communication atom is either an object class attribute or an interaction. Interaction parameters are not atoms. An atom has a transportation mode ("reliable" or "best effort") and a delivery or ordering mode ("receive ordering" or "time stamp ordering").

The FED (Federation Execution Data) is a subset of the FOM data including the object classes tree, the Interactions tree and, for each communication atom, the transportation and ordering modes.

OMT stands for Object Model Template. It describes how the FOMs and the SOMs must be written. In addition, the OMT defines the base data types available for Attributes and Parameters, and how to construct and describe complex data types.

The RTI (Run–Time Infrastructure) covers everything conceptually lower than the application layer of the federates. That includes API, RTI middleware, networking software and devices, and the wires. The RTI API is described by the Interface Specification (I/F Spec.). The RTI API is the **only RTI part** that is described by the standard. Implementation and low–level protocols are not specified.

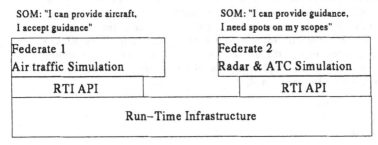

SOM: "I can provide aircraft, I accept guidance"

SOM: "I can provide guidance, I need spots on my scopes"

| Federate 1 Air traffic Simulation | Federate 2 Radar & ATC Simulation |
| RTI API | RTI API |

Run–Time Infrastructure

FOM: aircraft (object class) and guidance messages (interaction class) are exchanged

Fig. 1. A simple ATC federation.

Though naive, the figure above illustrates the concept: Federate 1 will publish the object class "aircraft" (probably with position and velocity as periodic attributes and flight plan as static attribute) and subscribe the "guidance message" interaction. Federate 2 will subscribe "aircraft" and publish "guidance message". If Federate 1 is purely constructive and Federate 2 is manned, we have an ATC training federation.

In this example the FED data looks like this:

```
(FED
  (objects
    (class objectRoot
      (attribute privilegeToDelete reliable timestamp)
      (class flyingObject
        (attribute position reliable timestamp)
        (attribute velocity bestEffort receive)
        (class Aircraft
          (attribute flightPlan reliable receive)
        )
        (class FlyingSaucer¹
        )
      )
    )
  )
```

---

¹ Flying saucers *never* have a flight plan.

```
    )
    (interactions
        (class interactionRoot
            (class guidanceMessage reliable timestamp
                (parameter recipientId
                (parameter radioFrequency
                (class turnMessage
                    (parameter newHeading)
                )
                (class changeAltitudeMessage
                    (parameter newAltitude)
                )
            )
        )
    )
)
```

We can see that there is no information about data types. The RTI does not have to know about data that it transports, but only *how to* transport it. For each atom (object class attribute or interaction), there is a transportation mode and a delivery mode.

1.2 HLA benefits

The most evident capability of the HLA is to break a complex simulation problem into more simple ones, or, according to the point of view, to put together distant simulations to make a large one. This allows:
- CPU load breakdown,
- not to transport heavy hardware like big simulators or real systems,
- secret protection (a classified model may run on a federate located in a protected area and elaborate and exchange unclassified data with other federates), etc.

Moreover, the formal description of the capabilities of each federate brings increased reusability and the formal description of the federation (communications between federates), and the use of a unique communication mechanism (the RTI) allows easier integration and verification.

The main goal of the DoD, when promoting HLA, is to reduce the cost of military simulation by the intensive reuse of simulations and simulators, then considered as components.

A parallel program, named SEDRIS (Synthetic Environment Data Representation and Interchange Specification) addresses environment (terrain, atmosphere, sea) representation issues.

1.3 The three Standard parts

The HLA Standard (IEEE P1516) has three parts: HLA Rules, HLA Interface Specification and Object Model Template.

Rules *(short rationale)*

The standard defines a set of 10 rules, 5 for federations, 5 for federates.
The Federation Rules are:

1 Federations shall have an HLA FOM, documented in accordance with the HLA OMT. *(we must have a formal description of what is exchanged between the federates)*

2 In a federation, all simulation–associated Object instance representation shall be in the federates, not in the run–time infrastructure (RTI). *(the RTI must be application–independent, so it may not have any simulation semantics, not even know about)*

3 During a federation execution, all exchange of FOM data among federates shall occur via the RTI. *(we want our applications to be reusable in a standardized way, so we cannot allow specific backchannels)*

4 During a federation execution, federates shall interact with the RTI in accordance with the HLA interface specification. *(they must use the RTI API)*

5 During a federation execution, an instance attribute shall be owned by at most one federate at any given time. *(ownership is the right to send data updates: imagine two federates trying to tell where is the same aircraft...)*

The Federate Rules are:

1 Federates shall have an HLA SOM, documented in accordance with the HLA OMT. *(we want a formal description of the capabilities of the federate...)*

2 Federates shall be able to update and/or reflect any attributes and send and/or receive interactions, as specified in their SOMs. *(...and it should not lie)*

3 Federates shall be able to transfer and/or accept ownership of attributes dynamically during a federation execution, as specified in their SOMs. *(Id.)*

4 Federates shall be able to vary the conditions (e.g., thresholds) under which they provide updates of attributes, as specified in their SOMs. *(Id.)*

5 Federates shall be able to manage local time in a way that will allow them to coordinate data exchange with other members of a federation. *(the time of the models that the federate manages must be coherent with the RTI Time Management)*

More detailed rationales for all the rules may be found in [1].

Interface Specification

The Interface Specification (I/F Spec.) is the description of the services that federates must use to communicate. It describes all the primitives that any implementation of the run–time infrastructure (RTI) must offer:

- In a textual form (arguments, pre- and post–conditions, exceptions),
- In several languages (IDL, C++, JAVA, Ada 95).

We give more details below.

Object Model Template

The Object Model Template is the metastructure for SOMs and FOMs. It defines the basic description elements (Object Classes, Attributes, Interactions, and Parameters) and, for each of them, the properties that must or may be given in a SOM and a FOM.

The OMT describes also the exchange formats for FOM and SOM data (DIF, Data Interchange Format).

1.4 The I/F Spec Services

A more extensive definition of all the services may be found in [2].

Federation management
Federation Management offers the federate primitives for:
- Creating and destroying a federation execution,
- Joining and resigning a federation execution,
- Synchronizing federation execution with other federates,
- Saving and restoring federation state in a coordinated way.

In the HLA, there is no specification about communication between different federations[2]. A RTI may be used to run multiple federation executions, which are still independent.

Declaration management
With these services, a federate can:
- Publish object classes (indicating that it will create Object Instances of the class, and update their attributes),
- Subscribe object classes (indicating that it is ready to "reflect" attributes of object instances of the class, created elsewhere),
- Publish interaction classes (indicating that it will send interactions of the class),
- Subscribe interaction classes,
- Stop any publication or subscription.

The federate may provide services (callbacks) if it wants to know when other federates subscribe to something it publishes.

In our example Federate 1 publishes "Aircraft" and subscribes "guidanceMessage". Then Federate 2 subscribes "flyingObjet" because it wants to see everything on its radar scopes. Federate 1 is then informed that it can begin to create Aircraft, because Aircraft are "flyingObjects". Federate 2 also subscribes "Aircraft" because it wants also to know about idents and flight plans, and says that it can provide guidance: is publishes all the guidance interactions. Federate 1 subscribes them. The order of the different declarations is indifferent.

Object management
The Object Management allows:
- Object instances creation and deletion for the federates that have published the corresponding object class,
- Object instance discovery and removal (callbacks) for the federates that have subscribed the corresponding object class,
- Instance attributes values update (for publishers) and reflection (callback, for subscribers),

---

[2] This may be different in the future. Anyway, an application may join more than one federation execution and may be used as a "bridge" between them. Coordination of the time managements then becomes a very hard problem.

- Interaction sending and receiving.

In addition, a federate can explicitly request updates for a class that it has subscribed.

In our favorite example, if Federate 1 creates an Aircraft, Federate 2 discovers an Aircraft. But if Federate 1 creates a FlyingSaucer, Federate 2 discovers a "flyingObject" (it has subscribed the superclass).

Ownership management

These services offer primitives for exchanging the right to update instance attributes. Ownership acquisition may be negotiated or not. It obviously interacts with Declaration Management and Object Management.

Time management

These services allow the coordinated advancement of the simulated time. Time management is based on two notions:

- Attribute and Interaction *delivery ordering*: it may be *Receive Ordering* (RO: delivered as received, time does not matter) or *Time Stamp Ordering* (TSO: delivered only when there is no message in the federation with an inferior time stamp),
- The Time Management mode of a federate: it may be Time Regulating (TR: the federate can send TSO messages) and/or Time Constrained (TC: the federate can receive TSO messages).

A federate can request for a time advance. It will be granted that time (if the federate is TC) when the RTI can guarantee that no TSO message will be delivered with a time stamp less than the requested time. The current time of a federate is the last granted time.

Coordination is achieved by time–stamp ordering reception of the Object Management messages. For a non–TC federate, time advance grants are trivial.

A TR federate defines a positive delay named lookahead: the federate is committed not to emit TSO messages with a time stamp less than its current time, plus its lookahead. This feature increases the parallelism of the different federates execution.

In a completely coordinated federation, all federates are both TC and TR.

Data Distribution management

The DDM is based upon the notion of routing space. A routing space is a named set of named scalar dimensions with no a priori semantics. A routing space can be associated with any communication atom of a FOM (class attribute or interaction). An extent is a set of intervals in all the dimensions of a routing space (for a 2-dimensions space, it is a rectangle). A region is a collection of extents (union of the rectangles).

A federate may subscribe a class attribute with a region (this is an interest region). If another federate updates this attribute with a region (the manifestation region), the subscriber gets the reflection only if the regions intersect. The same can be done for interactions.

It is the responsibility of federates to manage the bounds of the regions, so the semantics of the routing space is in the federates.

This mechanism can allow considerable bandwidth saving if, for example, there are many object instances with poor sensors modeled.

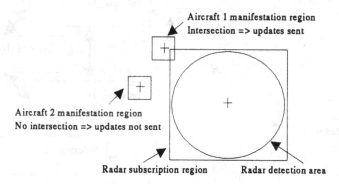

Fig. 2. Simple DDM example

In our example, the most useful routing space is the geographical space. If Federate 2 manages a radar, it may subscribe aircraft with a subscription region centered on the radar position and including its detection area. Federate 1 updates its aircraft with tiny or punctual manifestation regions centered on their position. The RTI transmits the update only if the regions intersect. Of course, this filtering method is not perfect: in the example, Federate 2 has to check if the reflected aircraft is really inside the radar detection range (this is not the case in the above scheme).

Support services
Support services provide miscellaneous primitives to deal with names and handles of object classes, attributes, interactions, parameters, spaces, dimensions, etc.

2 yaRTI architecture

2.1 Overview

yaRTI is based on GLADE, an implementation of the Distributed Systems Annex. yaRTI can handle multiple federations executions.
The architecture is based on 3 or more partitions: rtid (federations manager), fedex (federates manager), and federates. The real kernel is distributed in federates. It is about 75% of the RTI software.

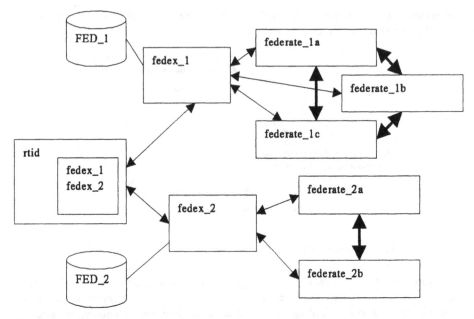

Fig. 3. Overall architecture

The only RCI package is in rtid. Other communications (between federates and between a federate and its fedex) use the RACW (Remote Access to Class Wide) mechanism. Most communications (thick arrows) are between federates, via the distributed RTI kernel. The most complex algorithms (Declaration Management, Object Management and especially Time Management) are distributed.

2.2 Creating and joining a Federation Execution

The rtid partition must have been launched anywhere first. When a federate wants to create a federation execution, it asks its RTI kernel, which asks rtid in turn. If a fedex with the right name exists, the kernel raises Federation_Already_Exists (which the federate is supposed to handle). If no fedex exists, rtid locks federation creation and reserves a fedex slot and the kernel spawns a fedex and waits for federation creation to be unlocked. The newly created fedex gives rtid its RACW. Then rtid fills the fedex slot and unlocks federation creation. When the fedex starts, it reads the FED (Federation Execution Data) and makes it ready for federates which will join and ask for it.

This mechanism was needed because there is no federate dedicated to federation creation. So all federates can have the same connection scheme:

```
begin
    Create_Federation_Execution ( <args> );
exception
    when Federation_Already_Exists => null;
end;
Join_Federation_Execution ( <args> );
```

Joining is simple: the federate first obtains from rtid the access to the fedex, then tells the fedex it joins. In return, the fedex provides the federate with a unique Id and the pairs (access, Id) of already joined federates. The first thing that the RTI kernel of the federate does is to initialize its internal data with the FED provided by the fedex.

2.3 Distributed Declaration Management

Federates which publish or subscribe object classes attributes or interaction must notify all other joined federates for the following reasons:

- Another federate may have subscribed what it publishes before it joins. It is necessary for the kernel of a publishing federate to know exactly who is subscribing because we do not want to spend bandwidth in sending all further updates to all joined federates. When a federate kernel is notified a publication, it checks if it matches some of its subscriptions[3]. If so, it informs the kernel of the publishing federate of its interest.

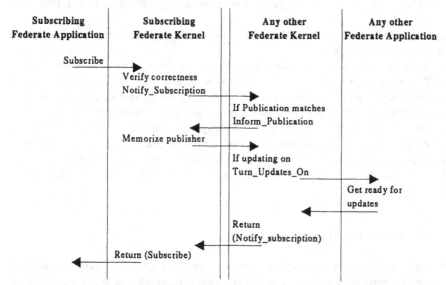

Fig. 4. Subscription scheme.

- The kernel of a subscribing federate has to inform the kernels of publishing federates that they have to send their updates to it. In addition, it has to know the publishing federates for DDM considerations (it must know who to notify of the subscription region changes). When a federate kernel is notified a subscription, it informs the notifying kernel if some of its publications match.

---

[3] Object classes attributes match if some of the published attributes are subscribed for the same class or any superclass. An interaction class matches if the class or any superclass is subscribed.

The control flow scheme above shows the subscription mechanism. The publication mechanism is quite similar. All these remote calls use synchronous RACW.

2.4 Distributed Object Management

Each federate kernel handles an object instance dictionary. This dictionary contains instances created by the federate application, and some other remote instances that are *discovered*. The discovery mechanism has two steps:

- The kernel discovers a remote instance if the application has subscribed the class or some superclass,
- The federate application discovers the remote instance just before the first related attribute update that has to be reflected, according to the subscription match and the current reflection policy.

The class of a discovered instance is the lowest subscribed superclass of the actual class of the instance, including the actual class.

Incoming atoms are stored in two queues: a FIFO queue for "receive ordering" atoms (the RO queue), and a sorted queue for "time stamp ordering" atoms (the TSO queue).

Outgoing atoms are put into a unique FIFO queue. This queue is consumed as fast as possible by a sending task.

The "reliable" transportation mode is implemented by synchronous calls (normal RACW remote calls). The Distributed Systems Annex guarantees that the callee is executed "exactly once" and says that the caller waits for the remote call completion, so it can be sure that the data has been delivered when the remote call returns.

The "best effort" mode is implemented by asynchronous calls (remote calls using RACW with pragma Asynchronous). The language guarantees that the callee is executed "at most once". By the way, it cannot be sure that the data has been delivered, but the process is much faster because the caller does not wait for the remote call completion.

2.5 Distributed Time Management

The time management mechanism involves the TSO queue of each constrained federate (a constrained federate can receive TSO messages), and the "time status" of each regulating federate (a regulating federate can send TSO messages).

Each federate must be able to compute a Lower Bound Time Stamp (LBTS), i.e. the highest time such that there is no TSO message in the federation with a time stamp lower than it.

In order to do that, each regulating federate diffuses to the other federates its "time status", i.e. its current time, its lookahead, the current time advance request (if there is one pending), and the lowest time stamp in its TSO queue (if it is also regulating).

So, any other federate receiving such status can deduce the lowest time stamp that the emitter can ever emit:

- If no request is pending, it is the current time plus lookahead,
- If a time advance request is pending, it is (according to the request type), either

the requested time plus lookahead, or the lowest time stamp in the TSO queue plus lookahead.

For a given constrained federate, LBTS is the minimum of the lowest time stamps among all other regulating federates.

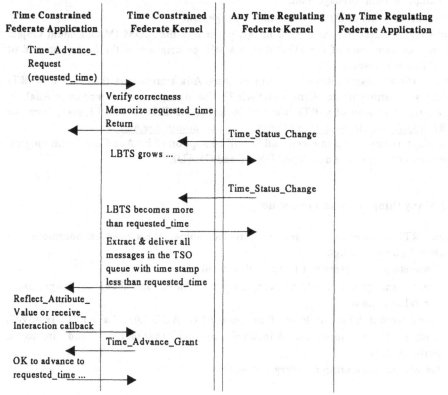

Fig. 5. Time advance scheme

For the time now, time status change notifications are queued on the emitter side, which implies the use of a centralized resource (a counting semaphore located on the fedex) to be sure to get the right LBTS in time.

3 Conclusions

3.1 It works at a very low cost

Initially aimed at research and concept evaluation, yaRTI has proven its efficiency with a pre-existing real-time federation as testbed. The integration of yaRTI in this federation was done in a couple of hours and led to major improvements in yaRTI algorithms.

The development cost of yaRTI is very low: about 18,000 lines of code including comments, for about 90% functionality implemented, including:

- complete Federation Management,
- complete Declaration Management,
- complete Object Management,
- complete Time Management,
- important parts of Data Distribution Management,

and some features not mentioned in this paper like the MOM (Management Object Model, an extension of the FOM that is a self–description of the federation and of the RTI mechanisms).

yaRTI allows easier integration with existing Ada simulations than any C++ RTI (many simulations in the Military and Air Traffic Management are written in Ada).

The current version of yaRTI is available, under the GNU Public License, from the URL http://perso.wanadoo.fr/dominique.canazzi/dominique.htm .

If enough people show interest, yaRTI will be supported by Ada Core Technologies, the company who have developed GNAT and GLADE.

3.3 Many things remain to be done

Some RTI services are not yet implemented, some others need enhancements, or more enlightened design:

- Ownership management is to be implemented,
- Time management should be completely distributed, and should no longer use a central semaphore,
- Some workarounds due to the limitations of GLADE 1.03p have to be removed, leading to a more straightforward message management and improved performance,
- Orderly federate crash recovery is desirable.

Bibliography

[1]   HLA Rules, version 1.3 dated 5 Feb. 1998, available at http://hla.dmso.mil Select "HLA Technical Specifications", then "Rules".

[2]   HLA Interface Specification, version 1.3 draft 1 dated 2 April 1998, available same way.

[3]   Object Model Template Specification, version 1.3, dated 5 Feb. 1998, available same way.

[4]   Ada 95 Language Reference Manual, especially Annex E: Distributed Systems.

[5]   GLADE user guide, available in the GLADE public distribution.

The HLA IEEE standard elaboration process is underway, so the documents [1], [2] and [3] above are slightly obsolete. Nevertheless, they are very close to the expected final standard.

General information about HLA is also available at hla.dmso.mil.

An Ada95 Implementation of a Network Coordination Language with Code Mobility

Emilio Tuosto

Dipartimento di Informatica, Università di Pisa
Corso Italia 40, 56100 Pisa - Italy
e-mail: etuosto@di.unipi.it

Abstract. One of the principal aims of distributed programming research is the definition of paradigms which permits the description of *Global Computation*, as Cardelli calls them, i.e. computations on a net of heterogeneous sites. In this context, it seems that code mobility is a good paradigm for limiting network traffic.
Here we will describe the implementation, in Ada95, of Klaim, a kernel language that uses code mobility and gives the possibility of coordinating the activity of processes running on a net.

Keywords. Ada Language and Tools, Ada Experience Reports, Case Studies and Experiments, Ada and other Languages, Distributed Systems.

1 Introduction

Defining suitable languages for writing *global computations* (computations operating on resources distributed on *global computers* [Car96]) is one of the aims of distributed programming research [Car95, Car96, CG97, DFP97a, DFP97b, DFP98, GV97, Whi94]. In these languages three fundamental aspects must be considered:

1. Network Traffic Minimization;
2. Network Heterogenity;
3. Network Security.

In this paper, the third aspect will not be considered.

Recently, the interest in paradigms which can specify some form of code mobility has grown thanks to their intrinsic ability in limiting, at least in some cases, network traffic. For example, a distributed application which elaborates a large quantity of data (distributed on different physical sites) can be made more efficient if a paradigm that allows *agent* [1] movement on the sites containing data is used.

As in [Vig98], we divide the distribution models in two classes: *Traditional Distributed Systems* (Fig. 1) and *Mobile Code Systems* (Fig. 2). In a traditional distributed system, the *True Distributed System* layer (TDS) hides the physical

---

[1] Here we use the term *agent* to indicate the code that can be moved accross a network.

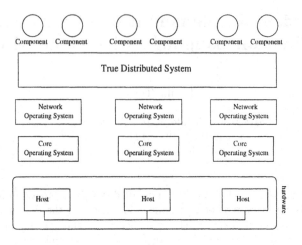

Fig. 1. Traditional Distributed System.

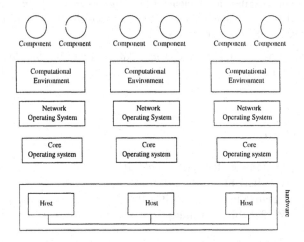

Fig. 2. Mobile Code System.

structure of the network (its sites and connections) from the application layer. A tipical example of TDS is the mechanism adopted in CORBA [OMG95] which renders an object visible on a net. In a mobile code system, the TDS layer is replaced by the *Computational Environment* (CE) layer, which is an abstraction of sites for the applications.

In this paper **Klada**, an implementation of **Klaim** [DFP98], will be presented. **Klaim** is a kernel coordination language of agent interaction and mobility which derives from **Linda** [CG89] and **Llinda** [DFP97a], **Klaim** processes interact via a "blackboard" communication model. In fact, the data are exchanged by visiting a multiset of tuples (finite sequences of values and variables). This multiset is called *Tuple Space* (TS) and it is distributed on network sites. Processes can be used as fields of tuples. Language communication primitives select the TS to use by an explicit notion of locality. Localities are first class objects, as processes are, so they can be exchanged in communications. **Klaim** processes can be composed by a non-deterministic choice operator and by a parallel operator.

We will provide a compiler which transforms **Klada** programs to **Ada95**. Given a **Klada** program, the compiler generates :

1. the partitions of the corresponding **Ada95** distributed program;
2. a configuration file which when passed to **Glade**, a tool developed by GNU organization that implements the directives described in [ARM95], permits the execution of **Ada95** programs on (heterogeneus) networks.

The principal features of **Klada** that require some peculiarities of **Ada95** are those regarding the dynamic characteristics of **Klada** nets. In particular, implementing the **newloc** primitive requires the use of remote access type objects and the introduction of a *Name_Manager*.

The languages that provide code mobility may be divided in two classes: *strong mobility* and *weak mobility* languages. The first class includes the languages in which it is possible to move execution threads of control among sites. An example of a strong mobility language is **Telescript** [Whi94]. The languages in which the remote code execution is obtained by activating a new thread that is indipendent from the thread that moves the code, belong to the second class. **Klada** is a weak mobility language. In the implementation, mobility is obtained by introducing a **Klada** interpreter, kvm. Each **Ada95** partition implementing CE of **Klada** sites is linked to kvm.

The definition and the implementation of **Klada** are part of a thread of research in the field of concurrent and distributed languages. Other models of concurrency and distribution have been proposed and implemented. For example we can indicate **Pict** [PT97], an implementation of (a variant of) the π-calculus described in [MPW92], **Obliq** [Car94, Car95], a lexically-scoped untyped interpreted language that supports distributed object-oriented computation, **FACILE** [GMP89, TLG92] an extention of the **ML** functional language with communication primitives. Moreover, **Klaim** has also a **Java** implementation defined in [BDFP98].

2 Klada

An informal description of the actions of **Klaim** processes follows:

- **in**(t)@ℓ: evaluates the tuple t and searches for a matching tuple t' in the TS denoted by locality ℓ. Whenever t' is found, it is removed from the TS and the its values are assigned to the corresponding variable fields of t, then the operation terminates. If no matching tuple is found, the operation is suspended until one is available.
- **read**(t)@ℓ: similar to **in**, but after the assignment to the variables of t, the tuple t' is not removed from the TS.
- **out**(t)@ℓ: evaluates the tuple t and adds it to the TS located at ℓ. The **out** primitive needs no synchronization: it is an asynchronous action.
- **eval**(P)@ℓ: agent P is executed on the site named ℓ. This corresponds to the remote code evaluation. Like **out**, **eval** is asynchronous.

– **newloc**(u): creates a "fresh" site that can be accessed via the locality variable u. Also **newloc** is a non-blocking instruction.

A distinguished logical locality, **self**, is used by **Klaim** processes to denote their execution site.

From this informal description, it can be noted that **Klaim** specifies two code mobility mechanisms: the first is the possibility of exchanging processes as data (**in**, **read/out**) and the second one is the remote evaluation of processes (**eval**). An important aspect to note is that the localities used by a **Klaim** process are logical names: a programmer, therefore, has an abstract view of the net.

Klaim uses both static and dynamic scoping strategies to evaluate the logical localities of the agents. The agents that occurr in tuples fields are evaluated with a static scoping discipline, but, for the code moved using **eval**, a dynamic scoping is adopted. In particular, a table which maps the logical localities on physical sites is associated to the CE representing the **Klaim** sites. When an agent is moved through tuple spaces, the starting CE constructs a "closure", i.e. a couple of code and a (partial) mapping from logical localities to sites. When the code is executed on a new site and a locality is evaluated, this mapping will be used before the one of the site CE. On the other hand, for **eval**, the closure built by the starting CE has a void mapping and so only the site environment of the executing site will be searched. Moreover, it must be observed that a **Klaim** network may dynamically grow by adding new sites with **newloc**.

Klada processes may be derived from the grammar in Table 1. In Table 2 we give the sintax of **Klada** nets. Types, localities and tuples are specified in Table 3. The usual boolean, numeric and string expressions are not specified. We can see that **Klada** is an extension of **Klaim** with some constructs typically used in imperative programming (**if**, **while**, :=). This extension, in any case, does not give more expressive power because it is possible to prove that **Klaim** can simulate the new constructs [Tuo98]. In **Klada**, a new choice operator is defined, Ext_Ch, similar to the guarded command of CSP [Hoa85]. Ext_Ch is used for deriving the external choices, i.e. the choices that need an external synchronization to be resolved. Int_Ch, the **Klaim** choice operator, is used to choose non-deterministically among some branches without external conditioning. Moreover, the declaration constructs of variables and constants are expressed.

We have used the following shorthands:

– productions such as $A ::= B \mid \epsilon$ will be abbreviated to $A ::= [B]$;
– $[A]^\star$ is $\overbrace{A \ldots A}^{n}$, where $n \geq 0$;
– $[A]^+$ is $A[A]^\star$;
– **id** stands for a generic identifier.

Let's make some considerations on the grammar given in Table 2.

A *Net* is a set of *Nodes* that may be preceeded by some definitions of process constants (used to define recursive processes). A *Node* is composed by an **id** (the name of a network machine), an allocation environment, *Env*, and the processes allocated on the node. *Env*, the sintactic category for the allocation environment,

$$
\begin{array}{ll}
Task & ::= Ext\_Ch \;\square\; Ext\_Ch \;\big|\; Int\_Ch \\[4pt]
Ext\_Ch & ::= \mathbf{in}(\,Tuple)@L\_exp.Seq[\square\,Ext\_Ch] \\
& \quad \big|\; \mathbf{read}(\,Tuple)@L\_exp.Seq[\square\,Ext\_Ch] \\[4pt]
Int\_Ch & ::= Seq \;\big|\; Seq\;\#\; Int\_Ch \\[4pt]
Seq & ::= Com \;\big|\; Com;\,Seq \;\big|\; \mathbf{call}\;\mathbf{id}\;[(\,Tuple)] \;\big|\; \mathbf{id'} \;\big|\; \mathbf{nil} \\[4pt]
Com & ::= \mathbf{eval}(\,Task)@L\_exp \;\big|\; \mathbf{out}(\,Tuple)@L\_exp \\
& \quad \big|\; \mathbf{in}(\,Tuple)@L\_exp \;\big|\; \mathbf{read}(\,Tuple)@L\_exp \;\big|\; \mathbf{newloc}(L\_exp) \\
& \quad \big|\; \mathbf{if}\;Exp\;\mathbf{then}\;Task\;\mathbf{else}\;Task\;\mathbf{fi} \;\big|\; \mathbf{while}\;Exp\;\mathbf{do}\;Task\;\mathbf{od} \\
& \quad \big|\; \mathbf{id} := Exp \;\big|\; (\,Task)
\end{array}
$$

Table 1. Grammar of Klada processes

$$
\begin{array}{ll}
Net & ::= [\mathbf{define}\;\mathbf{id}[[[\mathbf{id}:Type;]\,^*]]\;\mathbf{as}\;Const\;\mathbf{on}]\;\mathbf{net}\;Node\;\mathbf{quit} \\[4pt]
Const & ::= NamedProc \;\big|\; NamedProc;\,Const \\[4pt]
NamedProc & ::= \mathbf{rec}\;\mathbf{id}\;[(\,\mathbf{id}:Type[;\mathbf{id}:Type]\,^*)]\;\mathbf{declare}Dec\;\mathbf{begin}\;Task\;\mathbf{end} \\[4pt]
Node & ::= \mathbf{id}::\{[Env]\}ProcDef \;\big|\; Node\;\|\;Node \\[4pt]
Dec & ::= \mathbf{const}\;\mathbf{id} := Exp \;\big|\; \mathbf{id}[,\mathbf{id}]\,^*:Type\;[:=Exp] \\[4pt]
Env & ::= \mathbf{id}\;\tilde{}\;\mathbf{id} \;\big|\; Env,Env \\[4pt]
ProcDef & ::= \mathbf{declare}Dec\;\mathbf{begin}\;Task\;\mathbf{end} \;\big|\; ProcDef\,|\,ProcDef
\end{array}
$$

Table 2. Sintax of the Klada nets

is a list of pairs of **id**: the first is the (name of) the logical locality and the second represents the (name of) the physical machine (IP address).

In Table 3, the distinguished locality **screen** is used to model the data output on external devices (for the time being, only the screen) using the same philosophy of the tuple spaces. A screen may be thought of as a particular kind of TS, i.e. when we write **out**(t)@**screen**, we will be able to printout the data in the tuple t on the screen.

$$
\begin{array}{ll}
Type & ::= \mathbf{int} \;\big|\; \mathbf{bool} \;\big|\; \mathbf{str} \;\big|\; \mathbf{location} \;\big|\; \mathbf{process} \\[4pt]
Exp & ::= \cdots \\[4pt]
Tuple & ::= Exp \;\big|\; L\_exp \;\big|\; \mathbf{!id} \;\big|\; \mathbf{begin}\;Task\;\mathbf{end} \;\big|\; Tuple,Tuple \\[4pt]
L\_exp & ::= \mathbf{self} \;\big|\; \mathbf{id} \;\big|\; \mathbf{screen}
\end{array}
$$

Table 3. Types, expressions, tuples and localities

3 Klada semantics: a programming example

To clarify the Klada semantics, it's better to give an example that shows most of the features of the language. For a formal definition the reader is referred to [DFP98].

We will provide an electronic commerce application. We want to program an agent that visits the camera shops which are "nearest" to a distance d, searching for a camera with the lowest price. Camera shops will be modelled by processes such as the following:

$shop \equiv$ **begin**
$\quad$ **out**("camera$_1$", $price_1$)@**self**; ... ; **out**("camera$_k$", $price_k$)@**self**;
$\quad$ **end**

The *MarketPlaceClient* in Fig. 3, asks the local server *MarketPlace* for the list of camera shops nearest to d (line 5). Once *MarketPlaceClient* has received

```
1.   rec MarketPlaceClient (Cam: str; RLoc: loc; d: int) declare
2.       var ShopList, FirstShop: loc;
3.       var NumShop: int
4.   begin
5.       out("Shop list", d)@self;
6.       in(!ShopList)@self;
7.       in(!NumShop)@ShopList;
8.       if NumShop = 0
9.          then out(Cam, "NO SHOP", -1)@RLoc
10.         else
11.            in(!FirstShop)@ShopList;
12.            out(NumShop - 1)@ShopList;
13.            eval(call ShopAgent (Cam, ShopList, RLoc, 0))@FirstShop
14.      fi
15.  end
```

Fig. 3. *MarketPlaceClient*

the (locality of the) list (line 6), if there is a shop to visit, it remotely evaluates the *ShopAgent* by passing to it the camera type, the list of shops, the locality where the results are to be returned and the current obtained price (lines 7 - 13).

The server *MarketPlace* (Fig. 4) has the list of shops with their distances (line 5) and executes an endless loop waiting for a request (lines 6 - 7). To satisfy a request, *MarketPlace* creates a new site where the shop list will be allocated (line 8), constructs the list (lines 9 - 15), returns the (locality of the) list to the client (lines 16) and prints a message on the screen (line 17).

When *ShopAgent* (Fig. 5) starts its execution on the site of a new shop, it reads the price of the camera (line 5) and, if the new price is lower than the old one, it removes the old price from the TS at RLoc and replaces it with the new price (lines 9 - 15). Then *ShopAgent* reads the number of shops that must be examined (line 17) and, if a shop exists, it updates the number of shops, takes the address of the next shop and executes a copy of itself on the new shop (lines 21 - 23). The new copy of *ShopAgent* will continue the search in the remaining shops.

```
1.  declare
2.      var Dist, ShopDist, Pos, PosList: int := 0;
3.      var ShopLoc, ShopList: loc
4.  begin
5.      out(1, "shop₁", d₁)@self; ···; out(h, "shopₕ", dₕ)@self;
6.      while true do
7.        in("Shop list", !Dist)@self;
8.        newloc(ShopList);
9.        while Pos ≤ h do
10.          read(Pos + 1, !ShopLoc, !ShopDist)@self;
11.          if ShopDist < Dist
12.            then out(ShopLoc)@ShopList; PosList:= PosList + 1; Pos:= Pos + 1
13.            else Pos:= Pos + 1
14.          fi
15.        od;
16.        out(PosList)@ShopList; out(ShopList)@self;
17.        out("List builded...")@screen
18.      od;
19. end
```

Fig. 4. *MarketPlace*

4 Ada95 Distribution Model and Glade

The **Ada95** distribution model [ARM95] (Annex E) defines the *partition*, the principal distribution unit, as a set of structures and/or algorithms which can be allocated on the nodes of a net. A partition can be considered the union of two logical components. The first component implements the algorithms for the application that one wants to obtain. The second component defines the communication interfaces to/from the other partitions. In the algorithm implementation phase, an **Ada95** programmer must satisfy only some constraints required by the language distribution model. Problems concerning partition distribution and communications are application-independent, so they may be faced in a separate phase. During the application developement, there is no need for hypotheses about the architecture on which the program will be executed; the association node-partitions are established in the configuration phase.

Partition cooperation is based on a *Remote Subprogram Call* mechanism enriched by the possibility of *dynamic dispatching* which, at run-time, permits the establishment of procedures which are to be executed, according to the values of some actual parameters.

The distributed systems annex does not describe how a distributed application should be configured. The tool **Glade** and its configuration language have been purposely designed to allow to specify the partition definition and the machines where each partition must be executed. **Glade** combines the distributed

```
1.  rec ShopAgent (Cam: str; ShopList: loc; RLoc: loc; Price: int) declare
2.    varNewPrice, NumShop: int;
3.    varOldShop, NextShop: loc
4.  begin
5.    read(Cam, !NewPrice)@self;
6.    if Price = 0
7.      then out(Cam, self, NewPrice)@RLoc
8.      else
9.        if NewPrice < Price
10.          then
11.            in(Cam, !OldShop, !Price)@RLoc;
12.            out(Cam, self, NewPrice)@RLoc;
13.            Price:= NewPrice
14.          elsenil
15.        fi
16.    fi;
17.    in(!NumShop)@ShopList;
18.    if NumShop = 1
19.      then out("go")@RLoc
20.      else
21.        out(NumShop - 1)@ShopList;
22.        in(!NextShop)@ShopList;
23.        eval(call ShopAgent (Cam, ShopList, RLoc, Price)@NextShop
24.    fi
25. end
```

Fig. 5. *ShopAgent*

and object-oriented features of **Ada95**, it reads a configuration file and builds several executables, one for each partition. Using **Glade** it is possible to create applications where objects are physically distributed over a network of heterogeneous machines (without having to interface to any low-level communication layer), to support different network protocols, and to provide replication and fault-tolerance.

Therefore, it can be stated that the **Ada95** distribution model is a traditional distributed system, whereas **Klaim** may be considered an hybrid between traditional systems and mobile code systems because the application programmers have an abstract view of the network and can address network nodes using logical localities.

The choice of **Ada95** to implement **Klaim** is an attempt to study the "natualness" of programming a support of the mechanisms offered by a mobile code system by using a traditional distributed system.

5 Implementation

In this section we will present some of the implementation choices adopted in order to realize **Klada**. In particular we will discuss the implementation of code mobility and **newloc** primitive. Other aspects, like external choice and the representation of the tuple spaces, will not be faced here.

5.1 The compiler

A **Klada** program N describes a net on which some processes are (statically) allocated. For example, the commerce system described in section 3 may be organized as shown in Fig. 6 (the only agent is *ShopAgent*). To make the execution

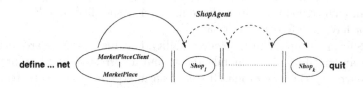

Fig. 6. The electronic commerce net.

of N more efficient we have developed a compiler that generates, for every node expressed in N, an **Ada95** partition in which the code part corresponds to the processes allocated on the node. This also permits some static controls such as **ids** must be declared before use and can't have more than one delcaration, all variables must be initialized before use, no assignament to costants is allowed, formal and actual parameters in recursive process calls match, etc. Furthermore, the compiler also performs type checking.

Every partition implementing a node of N is referred by a locally declared remote access object belonging to the class declared by

$$\textbf{type } \textit{Locality} \textbf{ is abstract tagged limited private}$$

these remote access objects may be considered the **self** counterparts of **Klada**. The methods of *Locality* implement the **Klaim** primitives that may be referred by a remote process (**in/read**, **out**, **eval**). For example the code generated by the compiler to translate **in**$(t)@\ell$ is

> $\langle$ evaluate t $\rangle$;
> $\langle$ get s, the remote access object associated to (the name) ℓ $\rangle$;
> _in$(s, \ldots)$;

where _**in** is the method that implements **in**. Depending on s, the **Ada95** runtime support will execute the _**in** procedure of the partition where s has been created (possibly a remote machine). This is the *dinamic dispatching* mechanism of **Ada95** and it provides remote subprogram calls in which the subprogram is determined at run-time.

As we shall see in the **newloc** implementation, these remote access objects are also used to provide new physical sites to the net.

5.2 Code Mobility

The most important task of the CEs of a MCS language is the preparation of the execution environment that an agent needs during its migrations. When the runtime support of a MCS language has to move an agent from site s_1 to site s_2, the CE of s_1 will provide the allocation on (CE of) s_2 of the complete environment the code needed for his execution. For example, if on s_1 the following code is running:

$$A : \ldots; \ B : \ldots; \ \textbf{begin} \ldots \ \textbf{eval}(C)@s_2; \ \ldots \ \textbf{end};$$

and C uses A but not B, then the CE of s_1 must construct, on (the CE of the) site s_2, an environment in which the value of A is specified and B may not be defined or have a different definition.

Ada95 has no support for the code mobility. For this reason we are compelled to define an encoding of the mobile agents and a corresponding interpreter for such an encoding (i.e. the Klada CEs need an interpreter to execute agents).

In our implementation, an agent has the following representation:

```
type Agent_Type is record
   Code : Code_type;
   Env : Environment_Type;
   Mem : Memory_Type;
end record
```

When the compiler detects an agent A (code appearing in a field of a tuple or in an **eval** instruction), it generates a *closure*, a representation of A (its parse tree) and the environment for the evaluation of the logical localities referred by A (if it is moved with **eval**, the environment part will be void). Furthermore, the compiler also attaches a "memory" (a private address space) to the closure in which the agent can store and retrive the values of its variables.

The implementation of code migration is obtained by making a remote call to kvm, the Klada interpreter, and by passing it an object, A, of type *Agent_Type*. By visiting the tree A.Code and using A.Env and A.Mem, kvm is able to execute the agent represented by A. Therefore, kvm also may be thought of as a method of the class *Locality*.

5.3 Dinamic site creation

A new (physical) site may be added to a preexisting network executing a *void_site* command from an operating system shell. The *void_site* command executes an Ada95 partition that simply generates its site-address (by allocating a new remote access object), sends it to the *Name_Manager* and waits for a partition that uses the new site.

The *Name_Manager* handles L, the list of new added sites that can be given to the **newloc** invocation it receives (Fig. 7). It must be said, however, that if L is void, *Name_Manager* will create a new "virtual" site on the caller machine. This behaviour is due to the non-blocking semantics of the **newloc** operation

Fig. 7. Creating new sites.

Referring to Fig. 7, once $Site_i$ has received the new site-address, it may, for example, use the new tuple space and its underlying machine for tuple exchanging of remote code evaluations respectively.

The tool we use to distribute the **Ada95** programs on a network is **Glade**. The compiler creates an **Ada95** partition for every **Klada** site. Furthermore, a configuration file for **Glade** is generated. According to this configuration file, **Glade** will compile and distribute the partitions on the phisycal sites specified.

6 Conclusions

We have introduced some aspects of an **Ada95** implementation of **Klada**, a coordination language with code mobility. The purpose of this implementation is to study the "naturalness" that TDS models, like the **Ada95** distribution model, have when they are used to realize MCS. What we can say is that **Ada95** was quite suitable for the realization of all the features of **Klada**, but the lack of any support for code mobility compels us to provide an interpreter of **Klada** agents. Furthermore, the **Ada95** distribution model and **Glade** allow us to concentrate on the implementation of **Klaim** primitives, without worrying about the communications among different partitions, therefore avoiding low level programming.

Some improvements, that in this first release have been neglected, may be introduced. In this connection, it is possible to add a new functionality to the *Name_Manager*: when a site S asks for a new physical site (**newloc**), if there are no available machines, *Name_Manager* allocates on M_S, the machine of S, a new site. In this manner, if the processes on S execute **newloc** many times, M_S would be overloaded. We can modify *Name_Manager* to take account of the network load and select the less used machine. In such a way *Name_Manager* can distribute the load on the whole network.

Klaim and its implementations (**Klada** and X-**Klaim** [BDFP98]) have been proposed for the study of the usefulness of code mobility at the application level. However, some work must be done to provide a true programming language; for example, new types or tools like a debugger or sintax driven editors may be implemented. From this point of view, an interesting direction is the definition of an **Ada95** library that simply implements the **Klaim** primitives and can be used in **Ada95** programs. In this way it would be possible to write large distributed applications in **Ada95** that use code mobility as programming paradigms.

References

[ARM95] International Standard ISO/IEC 8652:1995(E). Annotated Ada Reference Manual: Language and Standard Libraries. Intermetrics, Inc., 1994.

[BDFP98] L. Bettini, R. De Nicola, G. Ferrari, R. Pugliese. Interactive Mobile Agents in XKlaim Proceedings of WETICE'98, IEEE, 1998. (To appear)

[Car94] L. Cardelli. Obliq: A language with distributed scope. SRC Research Report 122, Digital Equipment Corporation Systems Research Center, June 3, 1994.

[Car95] L. Cardelli. A Language with Distributed Scope. Computing Systems, 8(1):27-59, MIT Press, 1995.

[Car96] L. Cardelli. Global Computation. ACM Computing Surveys, Vol. 28, Number 4es, pp. 163-163, December 1996.

[CG89] N. Carriero, D. Gelernter. Linda in Context. Communications of the ACM, 32(4):444-458, April 1989.

[CG97] L. Cardelli, A. D. Gordon. Mobile Ambients. FoSSaCS, LNCS 1378, pag. 140-155, 1998

[DFP97a] R. De Nicola, G. Ferrari, R. Pugliese. Locality based Linda: programming with explicit localities. FASE-TAPSOFT'97, Proceedings (M. Bidoit, M. Dauchet Eds.), LNCS 1214, pp. 712-726, Springer, 1997.

[DFP97b] R. De Nicola, G. Ferrari, R. Pugliese. Coordinating Mobile Agents via Blackboards and Access Rights. COORDINATION'97, Proceedings (D. Garlan, D. Le Metayer, Eds.), LNCS 1282, pp. 220-237, Springer, 1997.

[DFP98] R. De Nicola, G. Ferrari, R. Pugliese. Klaim: a Kernel Language for Agents Interaction and Mobility. IEEE Transactions on Software Engineering, 24(5), pp. 315-330, 1998.
(Available at the URL http://www.di.unipi.it/~giangi/papers). ·

[GMP89] A. Giacalone, P. Mishra, S. Prasad. Facile: A Symmetric Integration of Concurrent and Functional Programming. Internation Journal of Parallel Programming, 18(2), 1989.

[GV97] C. Ghezzi, G. Vigna. Mobile Code Paradigms and Technologies: A Case Study. Proceedings of the First International Workshop on Mobile Agents (MA97), Berlin, Germany, April 1997.

[Hoa85] C.A.R. Hoare. Communicating Sequential Process. Prentice Hall Int., 1985.

[MPW92] R. Milner, J. Parrow, D. Walker. A Calculus of Mobile Processes, (part I and II), Information and Computation, 100:1-77, 1992.

[OMG95] Object Management Group. CORBA: Architecture and Specification, August 1995.

[PT97] B. C. Pierce, David N. Turner. Pict: A Programming Language based on the Pi-Calculus Technical Report, Computer Science Department, Indiana University, Number CSCI 476, March 1997.

[TLG92] B. Thomsen, L. Leth, A. Giacalone. Some Issues in the Semantic of Facile Distributer Programming. REX Workshop "Semantics: Foundations and Applications" (J. W. de Bakker, W-P. de Roever, G. Rezenberg), LNCS 666, pp. 563-593, Springer, 1992.

[Tuo98] E. Tuosto. Semantica e Pragmatica di un Linguaggio di Coordinamento di Attività su reti. Master Thesis in Computer Science, University of Pisa, Italy. 1998.

[Vig98] G. Vigna. Mobile Code Technologies, Paradigms, and Applications. Ph.D. Thesis, Politecnico di Milano, 1998.

[Whi94] J. E. White. Telescript Technology: Foundation for the Electronic Market Place. General Magic White Paper, 1994.

CORBA & DSA: Divorce or Marriage?

Laurent PAUTET, Thomas QUINOT, and Samuel TARDIEU

{pautet,quinot,tardieu}@enst.fr
ENST
Paris, France

Abstract

This paper presents a comparison between CORBA and the Ada 95 Distributed Systems Annex. We also focus on the latest developments made by the ENST research team to GLADE that are related to CORBA services.[1]

1 Introduction

Before comparing two models for distributing heterogeneous applications, one must realize that they have very different goals. The Object Management Group (OMG) was formed to promote standards for the development of distributed heterogeneous applications. The Common Object Broker Request Architecture (CORBA) is the key component of its Object Management Architecture (OMA). CORBA [2] is an architecture for interoperable distributed object systems.

The Distributed System Annex (DSA) of Ada 95 pursues a different objective. It provides a model for programming distributed systems within the disciplined semantics of a language that supports type-safe object-oriented and real-time programming. From our experience, DSA has very powerful features compared to CORBA and offers an interesting balance between abstraction and performance. CORBA specifies a flexible architecture based on interoperable and reusable components. Our general objective is to propose the interesting features of CORBA to DSA users.

---

[1] The current release of GLADE, the implementation of Annex E of the Ada Reference Manual for the GNAT compiler, has been developed by the ENST team and is maintained by ACT Europe. See http://www.act-europe.fr/.

1.1 Programming models for distributed systems

Using OS network services In [11] we present several programming techniques for developing distributed applications. These applications have traditionally been developed using network programming interfaces such as TCP or UDP sockets. Programmers explicitly have to perform calls to operating system services, a task that can be tedious and error-prone. This includes initializing socket connection and determining peer location, marshalling and unmarshalling data structures, sending and receiving messages, debugging and testing several programs at the same time, and porting them on several platforms to account for subtle differences between network interfaces.

Of course, this code can be encapsulated in wrappers to reduce its complexity but it is clear that most of it could be automatically generated [12]. Message passing diverts developer's attention from the application domain. The query and reply scenario is a classical scheme in distributed applications; using message passing in such a situation could be compared to using a "goto" mechanism in a non-distributed application. This is known to cause significant problems with respect to modern programming languages. A more robust design would be to use a structured approach based on procedure call.

Using a middleware environment A middleware environment is intended to provide high level abstractions in order to ease development of user applications. Environments like CORBA or Distributed Computing Environment (DCE) offer an approach to develop client/server applications using the Remote Procedure Call model (RPC). The RPC model [3] is inspired from the query and reply scheme. Compared to a regular procedure call, arguments are pushed into a stream along with some data specifying which remote procedure is to be used. The stream is then transmitted over the network to the server. The server decodes the stream, does the regular subprogram call, then put the output parameters into another stream along with the exception (if any) raised by the subprogram, and sends this stream back to the caller. The caller decodes the stream and raises the exception if needed.

CORBA provides the same enhancements to the remote procedure model that object languages provide to classical procedural languages. This includes encapsulation, inheritance, type checking, and exceptions. These features are offered through an Interface Definition Language (IDL).

The middleware communication framework provides all the machinery to perform, somewhat transparently, remote procedure calls or remote object method invocations. For instance, each CORBA interface communicates through an Object Request Broker (ORB). A communication subsystem such as an ORB is intended to allow applications to use objects without being aware of their underlying message passing implementation. But the user may also require a large number of complex services to develop the distributed application. Some of them are definitively needed like a location service that allows clients to reference remote services via higher level names instead of a traditional scheme for addressing remote services involving Internet host addresses and communication port numbers. Other services provide domain independent interfaces that are frequently used by distributed applications like naming services.

Using a distributed language Rather than defining a new language like an IDL, an alternative idea is to extend a programming language in order to provide distributed features. The distributed object paradigm provides a more object-oriented approach to programming distributed systems. The notion of a distributed object is an extension to the abstract data type that permits the services provided in the type interface to be called independently of where the actual service is executed. When combined with object-oriented features such as inheritance and polymorphism, distributed objects promote a more dynamic and structured computational environment for distributed applications.

Ada 95 includes a Distributed Systems Annex (DSA) which defines several extensions allowing a user to write a distributed system entirely in Ada, using packages as the definition of remote procedure call or remote method call on distributed objects [5]. The distributed systems models of Ada 95, Java/RMI [9], and Modula-3 [4] are all very close, and all replace IDL with a subset of the language. The language supports both remote procedure calls and remote object method invocations transparently.

A program written in such a language is supposed to communicate with a program written in the same language, but this restriction also yields useful consequences. The language can provide more powerful features because it is not constrained by the smallest common subset of features available in all host languages. In Ada 95, the user defines a specification of remote services and implements them exactly as he would for ordinary, non-distributed services. The Ada 95 environment compiles them to produce a stub file and a skeleton file that automatically includes calls to the actual service *body*. Creating objects, obtaining or registering object references or adapting the object skeleton to the user object implementation are transparent because the language environment has a full control on the development process.

2 DSA *vs.* CORBA comparison

2.1 Overview of DSA

The Ada Distributed Systems Annex provides a solution for programming distributed systems. An Ada application can be partitioned for execution across a network of computers so that typed objects may be referenced through remote subprogram calls. The remotely-called subprograms declared in a library unit categorized as remote call interface (RCI) or remote types (RT) may be either statically or dynamically bound, thereby allowing applications to use one of the following classical paradigms:

Remote subprograms: for the programmer, a remote subprogram call is similar to a regular subprogram call. Run-time binding using access-to-subprogram types can also be used with remote subprograms.

Distributed objects: particular access types can be defined, which designate remote objects. When a primitive dispatching operation is invoked on an object designated by a remote access, a remote call is performed transparently on the partition on which the object was created.

Shared objects: data can be shared between active partitions, providing a repository similar to a shared memory, a shared file system or a database. Entryless protected objects allow safe access and update on shared objects. This feature is orthogonal to the notion of distributed objects, which are only accessed through exported services.

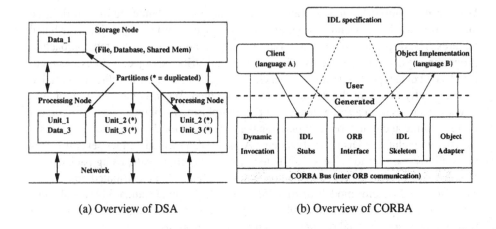

(a) Overview of DSA   (b) Overview of CORBA

Fig. 1. Comparing the two architectures

An Ada 95 distributed application is a set of partition executed concurrently on one or more machines; each partition is constituted of one or more compilation units which together constitute an executable binary.

2.2 Overview of CORBA

CORBA is an industry-sponsored effort to standardize the distributed object paradigm via the CORBA Interface Definition Language (IDL). The use of IDL makes CORBA more self-describing than any other client/server middleware. [10] describes the main features of CORBA, which are Interface Definition Language, Language Mappings, Stubs, Skeletons and Object Adapters, ORB, Interface Repository, Dynamic Invocation, ORB protocols and CORBA services.

The IDL specifies modules, constants, types and interfaces. An object interface defines the operations, exceptions and public attributes a client can invoke or access. CORBA offers a model based solely on distributed objects. In some respects, it can be compared to Java, as this language only provides an object-oriented programming model, and ignores the classical structured programming model.

An IDL translator generates client stubs and server skeletons in a host language (e.g., C++, C, Java, Ada 95) [2]; a language mapping specifies how IDL entities are implemented in the host language. Depending on the features available in the host language, the mapping can be more or less straightforward. When an IDL feature is not defined in the host language, the mapping provides a standardized but complex way of simulating the missing feature. Although the user works with the generated code, a good understanding of the language mapping is often necessary.

When the host language does not provide object-oriented features, the user has to deal with a complex simulation of those functions. A C++ programmer has to follow several rules related to parameters passed by reference. Defining whether the callee or the caller is responsible for parameter memory allocation can be considered as C++

programming conventions. The most difficult parts of the Ada mapping, that an Ada programmer should avoid when possible, are multiple inheritance and forward declarations.

The IDL translator produces several host language source files depending on the language mapping: client files called *stubs* and server files called *skeletons*. These files are specific to a vendor and product, as they make calls to a proprietary communication subsystem, but their structure and interface are supposed to follow a standard canvas. The client stubs convert user queries into requests to the ORB, which transmits these requests through an object adapter to the server skeleton (figure 1(b)).

2.3 Interface Definition Language

In DSA, the IDL is a subset of Ada 95. The user identifies interface packages at compile time. Some library-level packages are categorized using pragmas:

Remote Call Interface (RCI): Library units categorized with this pragma can declare subprograms to be called and executed remotely. This RPC operation is a statically bound operation. In these units, clients and servers do not share their memory space.

Dynamically bound calls are integrated with Ada capabilities to dereference subprograms (remote access to subprogram — RAS) and to dispatch on class-wide operands (remote access on class wide types — RACW). These remote access types can be declared in an RCI package.

A remote access type can be seen as a fat pointer — a structure with a remote address and a local address. The remote address can describe the host on which the entity has been created; the local address describes the service in the remote address space.

Remote Types (RT): Unlike RCI units, library units categorized with this pragma can define distributed objects and remote methods on them. They can also define the remote access types described above. A subprogram defined in a RT unit is not a remote subprogram. Unlike RCI units, a RT unit are not to be placed on only one partitions, they act like regular units instead.

Shared Passive (SP): the entities declared in such library units are to be mapped on a shared address space (file, memory, or database). When two partitions use such a library unit, they can communicate by reading or writing a common variable. This corresponds to the shared variables paradigm. Entry-less protected objects declared in these units provide atomic access to shared data, akin to in a transaction.

In RT or RCI units, variables are forbidden and non-remote access types are allowed only as long as their marshalling subprograms are provided. Any exception raised in a remote method or subprogram call is propagated to the caller.

An additional pragma All_Calls_Remote in a RCI unit can force a remote procedure call to be routed through the communication subsystem even for a local call. This allows debugging of an application in a non-distributed situation that is close to the distributed case.

A pragma Asynchronous allows statically and dynamically bound remote calls to be executed asynchronously. An asynchronous procedure doesn't wait for the completion of the remote call and lets the caller continue its execution path. The procedure must have only *in* or *access* parameters, and any exception raised during the execution of the remote procedure is lost.

All such categorized units can be generic. Instances of these generic packages can be either categorized or not. In the latter case, the unit loses its categorization property.

Each categorization pragma has very specific dependancy rules. As a general rule, RCI ≻ RT ≻ SP ≻ Pure. That means that a Remote_Types package declaration can only depend on other Remote_Types, Shared_Passive and Pure units.

The example shown on figure 2(a) highlights several DSA features. This system is based on a storage and a set of factories and workers. Each one of these entities is a partition itself. A factory **hires** a worker from a pool of workers and **assigns** a job to him. The worker performs the job and **saves** the result in a storage common to all the factories. The worker **notifies** the factory of the end of his job.

The worker produces a result corresponding to a query. When needed, a factory consumes this result. To do this, we define a protected area in the SP package Storage (sample 2(d)). An entryless protected object ensures serialized access on this area.

Types is a Remote_Types package that defines most of the remote services of the above system (sample 2(f)). First, we define a callback mechanism used by a worker to notify the end of his job to a factory. This is implemented using RAS *Notify*.

We define an abstract tagged type *Worker* which is intended to be the root type of the whole distributed worker hierarchy. *Assign* allows a factory to propose a job to a worker and a way to notify its employer the end of this job. *Any_Worker* is a **remote access to class wide** type (RACW). In other words, it is a reference to a distributed object of any derived type of Worker class.

G1_Worker is derived from type Worker and Assign is overridden (sample 2(c)). Sample 2(e) shows how to derive a second generation of workers G2_Worker from the first generation G1_Worker. As mentioned above, this RT package can be duplicated on several partitions to produce several types of workers, and also workers at several remote locations.

In sample 2(g), we define a unique place where workers wait for jobs. *Workers* is a Remote_Call_Interface package with services to hire and free workers. Unlike Remote_Types packages, Remote_Call_Interface packages cannot be duplicated.

In order to use even more DSA features, *Factory* is defined as a generic RCI package (sample 2(b)). Therefore, any instantiation defines a new factory (sample 2(h)). To be a RCI itself, this instantiation has also to be categorized.

In CORBA, the IDL is a descriptive language; it supports C++ syntax for constant, type and operation declarations. From IDL descriptions, a translator can generate client header files and server implementation skeletons.

An IDL file starts by defining a *module*. This provides a name space to gather a set of interfaces. This is a way to introduce a level of hierarchy whose designation looks like (*<module>::<interface>::<operation>*). The Ada 95 binding maps this element into a (child) package. *#include* statements make any other name spaces visible.

A module can define *interfaces*. An interface defines a set of methods that a client can invoke on an object. An interface can also define exceptions and attributes. An exception is like a C++ exception: a data component can be attached to it. An attribute is a

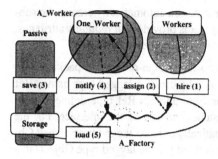

(a) Global picture

```
with Storage; use Storage;
generic
package Factory is
    pragma Remote_Call_Interface;

    procedure Notify (Q : Integer);
    pragma Asynchronous (Notify);
end Factory;
```

(b) Generic remote unit

```
with Types, Storage; use Types, Storage;
package One_Worker is
    pragma Remote_Types;

    type G1_Worker is
        new Worker with private;

    procedure Assign
        (W : access G1_Worker;
         Q : Integer;
         N : Notify);
private
    -- Declaration not shown
end One_Worker;
```

(c) First generation worker

```
package Storage is
    pragma Shared_Passive;

    protected Queue is
        procedure Save (Q, R : Integer);
        procedure Load
            (Q : in Integer;
             R : out Integer);
    private
        -- Declaration not shown
    end Queue;
end Storage;
```

(d) Shared memory data

```
with Types, Storage; use Types, Storage;
with One_Worker; use One_Worker;
package Another_Worker is
    pragma Remote_Types;

    type G2_Worker is
        new G1_Worker with private;

    procedure Assign
        (W : access G2_Worker;
         Q : Integer;
         N : Notify);
private
    -- Declaration not shown
end Another_Worker;
```

(e) Second generation worker

```
with Storage; use Storage;
package Types is
    pragma Remote_Types;

    type Notify is
        access procedure (Q : Integer);
    pragma Asynchronous (Notify);

    type Worker is
        abstract tagged limited private;
    procedure Assign
        (W : access Worker;
         Q : in Integer;
         N : in Notify) is abstract;

    type Any_Worker is
        access all Worker'Class;
    pragma Asynchronous (Any_Worker);

private
    -- Declaration not shown
end Types;
```

(f) Several DSA features

```
with Types; use Types;
package Workers is
    pragma Remote_Call_Interface;

    procedure Free (W : in Any_Worker);
    procedure Hire (W : out Any_Worker);
end Workers;
```

(g) Static and unique workers pool

```
with Factory;
package One_Factory is new Factory;
pragma Remote_Call_Interface (One_Factory);
```

(h) Remote unit instantiation

Fig. 2. A complete DSA example

component field. For each *Attribute*, the implementation automatically creates the subprograms Get_*Attribute* and Set_*Attribute*. Only Get is provided for *readonly* attributes. An interface can derive from one or more interfaces (multiple inheritance).

The Ada 95 binding maps this element into a package or a child package. For the client stub, the implementation will automatically create a tagged type named Ref (which is derived from CORBA.Object.Ref or from another Ref type defined in another interface) in a package whose name matches the one of the interface. For the server skeleton, the implementation will automatically create a tagged type named Object (which is derived from an implementation defined private tagged type Object) in a package named Impl, which is a child package of a package named after the interface name (⟨*interface*⟩.*Impl*).

A method is defined by a unique name (no overloading is allowed) and its signature (the types of its formal parameters). Each parameter can be of mode *in, out* or *inout*, whose meanings are comparable to their Ada homonyms. Every exception that can be raised by a method must also be declared as part of the method signature (section 2.4 for the rationale).

The *oneway* attribute can be applied to a subprogram, giving it at-most-once semantics instead of the exactly-once default. This precludes a method from having output parameters, a return value, or raised exception. It is not portable to assume that the caller resumes its execution once the input parameters are sent.

Most CORBA data types map in a straightforward way onto predefined Ada types, with the exception of *any* and *sequence. any*, that can designate any CORBA type, is mapped onto a stream type with *read* and *write* operations. A *sequence* holds a list of items of a given type and is represented in Ada using a pair of lengthy generic packages. One may note that the CORBA *string* type is mapped onto the *Unbounded_String* Ada 95 type. The IDL does not provide an equivalent to unconstrained arrays.

The Ada 95 mapping provides special mechanisms to implement two difficult-to-map CORBA features. First, it provides a translation of multiple inheritance. As described above, an Ada 95 package defines a type derived from the first interface, and extends the list of its primitive operations to achieve inheritance from other interfaces (this solution is quite similar to mixins, as described in [14]). Another unnatural feature of CORBA for an Ada programmer comes from forward declarations. In Ada, two package specifications cannot "with" each others, but this can occur between two IDL interfaces. To solve this, the mapping proposes to create "forward" packages. This can result in a very non-intuitive situation where the client stub does not "with" its usual interface packages but "forward" packages instead.

When developping a distributed application with CORBA, two situations may appear. On the server side, the programmer is responsible for the IDL file. He has to understand the Ada 95 language mapping in order to avoid structures with a non-trivial implementation whenever possible, such as forward declaration and multiple inheritance. On both the server and the client side, the programmer has to deal with the generated code. A good understanding of the mapping is useful to get back and forth from the IDL file to the generated code in order to keep an overview of the distributed application. Understanding this mapping can be a tedious task depending of the host language.

IDL interface information can be stored on-line in a database called Interface Repository (IR). A CORBA specification describes how the interface repository is organized and how to retrieve information from it. The reader will note that this information is close to what the Ada Semantic Interface Specification (ASIS, see [6]) can provide.

The interface repository allows a client to discover the signature of a method which it did not know at compile time. It can subsequently use this knowledge together with values for the method's parameters to construct a complete request and invoke the method. The set of functions that permits the construction of a method invocation request at run time is the Dynamic Invocation Interface (DII).

The IR API allows the client to explore the repository classes to obtain a module definition tree. From this tree, the client extracts subtrees defining constants, types, exceptions, and interfaces. From an interface subtree, the client can select an operation with its list of parameters (type, name and mode) and exceptions.

A client has then three ways to make a request. As in the static case, he can send it and wait for the result; he can also may a one-way call and discard the result. With dynamic requests, a third mechanism is offered: the client can send the request without waiting for the result, and obtain it later, asynchronously.

The DII has a server-side counterpart, called Dynamic Skeleton Interface. Both mechanisms are powerful but very complex and tedious to use. In some respects, they also violate the Ada 95 philosophy, because strong typing is not preserved. Most users will keep working with static invocations.

2.4 Communication Subsystem

The communication subsystem is one of the key points of a distributed system: it offers basic services such as the capability to transmit a message from one part of the distributed program to another. Those elementary services are then used by higher level services to build a fully functional distributed system.

The limit between what belongs to the communication subsystem and what belongs to an external service may sometimes be difficult to draw. Moreover, something considered as a service in CORBA may be viewed as purely internal in DSA.

In the DSA world, everything that is not done by the compiler in regard to the distribution belongs to the partition communication subsystem (PCS). For example, figuring out on which partition a package that will be called remotely is located is part of the PCS's responsibility.

The PCS entry points are well defined in DSA, and described in the System.RPC package declaration. By looking at this package, one can notice that there is nothing related to abortion of remote subprogram calls, although the Annex states that if such a call is aborted, an abortion message must be sent to the remote partition to cancel remote processing. That means that the PCS is in charge of detecting that a call to one of its entry points has been aborted and must send such an abortion message, without any help from the compiler.

Another interesting characteristic of the PCS is its behavior regarding unknown exceptions. When an exception is raised as a result of the execution of a remote subprogram call, it is propagated back to the caller. However, the caller may not have any visibility over the exception declaration, but may still catch it with a *when others* clause. But if the caller does not catch it and let it be propagated upstream (maybe in another partition), and if the upstream caller has visibility over this exception, it must be able to catch it using its name. That means that the PCS must recognize that a previously unknown exception maps onto a locally known one, for example by being able to dynamically register a new exception into the runtime.

In CORBA, a much more fragmented approach of services was adopted: they are essentially defined externally. For example, the naming service (which maps object names to object references) is a distributed object with a standard IDL interface.

While this approach seems more pure, it has performance drawbacks. Being itself a distributed object, the naming service cannot be optimized for the needs of a specific ORB. A special case is also required in the ORB for it to be able to locate the naming service itself (chicken and egg problem): in order to get a reference on a distributed object (an IOR, Interface Object Reference) to start with, the programmer needs to have an IOR for the naming service. This IOR can be retrieved from the command line, from a file or by invoking the ORB Interface, depending on the CORBA version.

Regarding exception propagation, an ORB is not able to propagate an exception that has not been declared in the IDL interface. This restriction, although annoying because it restricts the usage of exceptions, is understandable given the multi-language CORBA approach: what should be done, for example, when a C++ exception reaches a caller written in Ada? Note that an implementation may provide more information in the CORBA exception message, such as the C++ or Ada exception name.

2.5 Application development

The DSA does not describe how a distributed application should be configured. It is up to the user (using a partitioning tool whose specification is outside the scope of the annex) to define what the partitions in his program are and on which machines they should be executed.

GLADE provides a Configuration Tool and a Partition Communication Subsystem to build a distributed application. The GNATDIST tool and its configuration language have been specially designed to let the user partition his program and specify the machines where the individual partitions will be executing [7]. The Generic Ada Reusable Library for Interpartition Communication (GARLIC) is a high level communication library [8] that implements the interface between the Partition Communication Subsystem defined in the Reference Manual and the network communication layer with object-oriented techniques.

The CORBA ORB provides a core set of basic services. All other services are provided by objects with IDL. The OMG has standardized a set of useful services like Naming, Trading, Events, Licensing, Life Cycle,... A CORBA vendor is free to provide an implementation of these services. The Naming Service allows the association (*binding*) of object references with user-friendly names. The Events service provides a way for servers and clients to interact through asynchronous events between anonymous objects.

2.6 Summary

CORBA provides an outstanding and very popular framework. The IDL syntax is close to C++. The object model is close to Java: CORBA defines only distributed objects. Furthermore, when using the Ada mapping, the stub and skeleton generated code is close to Java with two root classes, Ref for clients and Object for servers.

DSA provides a more general model. This includes distributed objects, but also regular remote subprograms and references to remote subprograms. Shared passive packages can be defined as an abstraction for a (distributed) shared memory, a persistency support or a database. Basically, the IDL is a subset of Ada 95 and the remote services are defined in packages categorized by three kinds of pragmas (RCI, RT, SP). The distributed boundaries are more transparent as the application is not split into IDL and host language sources. host languages.

In DSA, any Ada type can be used except access types, but this can be solved by providing the marshalling operations for such a type. The exception model is entirely preserved. Overloading is allowed in DSA (not in CORBA). The user can also define generic packages and use mixin mechanism to obtain some kind of multiple inheritance.

The DSA user can design, implement and test his application in a non-distributed environment, and then switch to a distributed situation. With this two-phase design approach, the user always works within his favorite Ada 95 environment. The use of pragma All_Calls_Remote also facilitates debugging of a distributed application in a non-distributed context.

To work on client stubs or server skeletons, the CORBA user will have to deal with generated code. In any case, understanding the host language mapping is always very useful. It can be required for some languages like C++. An Ada programmer should avoid using forward declaration or multiple inheritance (and in some respects, sequence).

The CORBA user has to re-adapt his code to the code generated by the translator from the IDL file anytime the latter is modified. He also has to use the predefined CORBA types instead of Ada standard types; he has to call ORB functions or a naming service to obtain remote object references.

As Ada 95 is its own IDL, the user does not deal with any generated stub or skeleton code. The configuration environment takes care of updating object, stub and skeleton files when sources have been updated. The system automatically provides some naming functions like declaring RCI services. It also takes care of aborting remote procedure calls, detecting distributed termination, checking version consistency between clients and servers, and preserving and propagating any remote exception.

The RM does not require a DSA implementation to work on heterogeneous systems but GLADE, like any reasonable implementation, provides default XDR-like marshalling operations. This feature can be inhibited for performance reasons. An ORB is required to implement a Common Data Representation (CDR) to ensure safe communications between heterogeneous systems.

CORBA is a very rich but very complex standard. Its drawbacks include the high learning curve for developing and managing CORBA applications effectively, performance limitations, as well as the lack of portability and security [13]. These drawbacks are the price to pay for language interoperability, a facility the Ada 95-oriented DSA does not provide.

Interoperability between compilers is not yet an issue with DSA because there is only one implementation available (GLADE). But it is a validation requirement to permit a user to replace his current PCS with a third-party PCS. We can note this issue was not resolved in CORBA until revision 2.2. For the same reasons, we can expect future DSA implementations to ensure PCS compatibility.

Using its IDL, the OMG has described a number of *Common Object Services* (COS) [1] that are frequently needed in distributed systems. Unfortunately, these specifications are limited to IDL descriptions, and most of the semantics are up to the vendor. The DSA misses such user-level libraries, including basic distributed software components. More generally, the lack of component libraries has always been a problem for Ada.

Implementing CORBA services as native Ada 95 distributed objects, taking advantage of the standard language features, yields a simpler, easy to understand and use specification. We have already implemented the Naming service, the Events service and a service close to the Concurrency one with DSA. Developping the CORBA services was an interesting experience. We realized that although those services are nicely specified by an IDL file, their semantics is quite vague in such a way portability is dramatically broken. This work will be described in a future paper.

Another major goal of the GLADE team is to export DSA services to the CORBA world. The idea is to translate all DSA features to equivalent IDL features using ASIS. This would allow a DSA user to connect his DSA server to an ORB. This would also allow applications written in other languages to invoke DSA features. We are also seeking to use this approach to offer a DII mechanism for DSA (subsection 3.4).

3 DSA services for CORBA users

3.1 Objective

Services implemented as RT or RCI packages can currently be invoked only from other Ada 95 code using the DSA mechanisms: remote procedure calls and distributed objects. This may be considered a drawback by software component developers when they consider using the DSA to implement distributed services, because this limits the scope of their products to Ada 95 application developers.

In order to promote the use of Ada 95 as a competitive platform for the creation of distributed services, we aim at providing a means for CORBA applications to become clients of DSA services. This requires:

– an automated tool to generate an IDL specification from a DSA package declaration; this specification shall be used by CORBA client developers to generate stubs for calling the services exported by the DSA package;
– any necessary interface code to map CORBA requests onto Ada primitive operation invocations; this code shall be replicated on each program partition that instantiates the DSA package, so that its distributed object instances can receive method invocation requests from the CORBA software bus.

3.2 From DSA specification to IDL file

ASIS [6] is an open, published, vendor-independent API for interaction between CASE tools and an Ada compilation environment. ASIS defines the operations such tools need to extract information about compiled Ada code from the compilation environment.

We are seeking to generate an IDL interface specification from a DSA package declaration using the ASIS API and an ASIS-compliant compilation environment. The ASIS interface allows the tool developer to take advantage of the parsing facility built in the compiler; it provides an easy access to the syntax tree built by the compiler from the package specification.

We will use it to obtain a list of Remote Access to Class-Wide (RACW) types declared in Remote_Types packages. These types are the Ada 95 constructs that denote distributed objects. We will then retrieve the attributes and primitive operations of the corresponding classes, and translate them into IDL interface specifications, with one IDL module corresponding to one DSA package, and one IDL interface corresponding to one RACW. To the extent possible, we will do so in accordance with the standard mapping between Ada and CORBA constructs.

We seek to define a mapping of all languages constructs permitted in a RCI or RT package to IDL constructs. We will develop an automated tool that performs the translation of a DSA package declaration to an IDL interface specification; ASIS will be used to inter-operate with a compliant compilation system. Independence between our tool and the underlying environment implementation will thus be assured.

3.3 Binding DSA entities with CORBA

In the previous section we exposed how we sought to produce an IDL interface definition from the declaration of a DSA package. In order to allow CORBA clients to make calls to DSA services, we also have to provide a mechanism to translate CORBA requests to DSA method invocations at run-time.

To this effect, we are considering a two-step approach. We will first generate a CORBA server skeleton in Ada using traditional ORB software: using an IDL definition generated by the automated tool described in 3.2 and a preexistent IDL translator, we will produce a CORBA skeleton in Ada. We will fill in this skeleton by implementing CORBA request handling as invocations of primitive operations on DSA objects. Each instance of a Remote_Types package will be accompanied with an instance of the skeleton code, and will act as a CORBA server: it will provide access to its local DSA object instances for all clients on the CORBA software bus (figure 3).

We will therefore have to map the DSA addressing space (RACW i. e. fat pointers — section 2.3) into the CORBA addressing space (CORBA object references). Each DSA object instance will thus be referable in the CORBA address space; clients that want to obtain services from the DSA objects will send requests to the associated CORBA objects, in accordance with the generated IDL definition.

We seek to provide an automatic code generation tool that will produce "glue" code to map CORBA requests to DSA object primitive invocations. The necessary adaptation code to interface with the underlying ORB shall also be provided; this includes a mapping of Ada data types to CORBA types, including a translation of DSA fat pointers into CORBA object references.

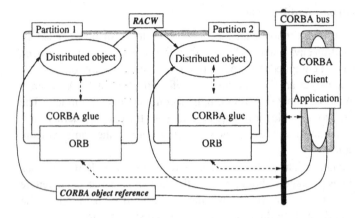

Fig. 3. Calling DSA objects from CORBA

3.4 DII using DSA

CORBA's Interface Repository service allows clients to retrieve a method's signature at run time from an interface repository, and to invoke that method even though its specification was unknown to the client at compile time using the DII mechanism (see 2.3). The DSA does not define a similar mechanism. However, a similar service can easily be provided using an RCI package that will act as a DSA interface repository, an ASIS tool that will automate the registration process of offered services, and a utility package for dynamic request construction.

The interface repository will be a straightforward RCI server that offers two kinds of services. For DSA service providers (i. e. other RCI or remote types packages), it will provide a means to register an interface, comprising a set of primitive operation names and their signatures. For clients, it will offer a means of retrieving the description of the primitive operations of a distributed object, given a reference to this object.

ASIS greatly simplifies the registration process on the server side: using ASIS, one can automatically traverse the specification of a DSA server package, and generate the corresponding calls to the interface repository's registration function. After this registration process is completed, the interface is known to the repository. In the case of the registration of the primitive operations of a distributed object (designated by a RACW), for example, any client that obtains an access value designating an object of this type can retrieve the description of its primitives even though it knew nothing of it at compile time, and does not semantically depend on the server's specification.

A function will finally construct a request message from an interface description retrieved from the repository, and actual parameters provided by the client. This message will be sent to the server using the PCS, just like a normal remote call generated by the compiler in a "static" service invocation. Apart from the generated registration functions, no IR or DII-specific code is required on the server side; it should be noted in particular that from the server point of view, a dynamically constructed request is treated exactly in the same way as a traditional, static request. The dynamic interface discovery and invocation mechanisms are confined in the DSA interface repository and the client dynamic request construction library.

This system is going to be implemented at ENST in the next few months; DSA users will thus gain the same flexibility with dynamic invocation as is currently available to CORBA programmers.

4 Conclusions

We have offered a comparison of the CORBA and Ada Distributed Systems Annex models for distributed heterogeneous applications. We have described a future tool for exporting DSA services to the CORBA world. Our general objective is to propose the interesting features of CORBA to DSA users.

Acknowledgments: The authors would like to thank Brad Balfour (Objective Interface) and Frank Singhoff (ENST) for their fruitful comments. They also would like Top Graph'X for their free release of ORBAda.

References

1. *CORBAservices: Common Object Services Specification.* November 1997. OMG Technical Document formal/98-07-05.
2. *The Common Object Request Broker: Architecture and Specification, revision 2.2.* February 1998. OMG Technical Document formal/98-07-01.
3. A.D. Birell and B.J. Nelson. Implementing remote procedure calls. *ACM Transactions on Computer Systems*, 2(1):39–59, February 1984.
4. Andrew Birell, Greg Nelson, Susan Owicki, and Edward Wobber. Network objects. Technical Report 115/94, Digital Systems Research Center, February 1994.
5. ISO. *Information Technology – Programming Languages – Ada.* ISO, February 1995. ISO/IEC/ANSI 8652:1995.
6. ISO. *Information Technology – Programming Languages – Ada Semantic Interface Specification (ASIS).* ISO, 1998.
7. Yvon Kermarrec, Laurent Nana, and Laurent Pautet. GNATDIST: a configuration language for distributed Ada 95 applications. In *Proceedings of Tri-Ada'96*, Philadelphia, Pennsylvania, USA, 1996.
8. Yvon Kermarrec, Laurent Pautet, and Samuel Tardieu. GARLIC: Generic Ada Reusable Library for Interpartition Communication. In *Proceedings Tri-Ada'95*, Anaheim, California, USA, 1995. ACM.
9. Sun Microsystems. *RMI – Documentation.*
10. Robert Orfali, Dan Harkey, and Jeri Edwards. *The Essential Distributed Objects Survival Guide.* John Wiley & Sons, Inc, 1996.
11. Laurent Pautet and Samuel Tardieu. Developping distributed Ada application in Ada 95. In *Tutorials of Tri-Ada'97*, Saint-Louis, Missouri, 1997.
12. Douglas C. Schmidt and Steve Vinoski. Comparing alternative client-side distributed programming techniques. *SIGS C++ Report*, Col 3:1–9, May 1995.
13. Douglas C. Schmidt and Steve Vinoski. Comparing alternative server programming techniques. *SIGS C++ Report*, Col 4:1–10, October 1995.
14. Alfred Strohmeier, Stéphane Barbey, and Magnus Kempe. Object-oriented programming and reuse in Ada 9X. In *Tutorials of Tri-Ada'93*, volume 2, pages 945–984, Seattle, Washington, USA, September 1993.

How to Modify the GNAT Frontend to Experiment with Ada Extensions*

J. Miranda, F. Guerra, J. Martín, and A. González

Dpto. Ingeniería Telemática
University of Las Palmas de Gran Canaria. Canary Islands, Spain.
{jmiranda, fguerra}@cma.ulpgc.es

Abstract. This paper describes how we modified GNAT to experiment with one Ada extension. Our proposed extension, named Drago, is designed to support the implementation of fault-tolerant distributed applications. It is the result of an effort to impose discipline and give linguistic support to the main concepts of the Isis communication toolkit, as well as to experiment with the group communication paradigm. In this paper we briefly introduce Drago, and describe the modifications made to the GNAT scanner, parser, and semantic analyzer.

Keywords: Compilers, Ada, Distributed Systems, Fault-Tolerant Systems.

1 Introduction

GNAT (GNU NYU Ada Translator), is a frontend and runtime system for Ada 95. The overall structure of the GNAT system (figure 1) is described in [1]. It is composed by the compiler (which by means of the Run-Time generates the object code), the binder (which verifies the consistency of the objects that are to be assembled and determines a valid order of elaboration for the units in the program) and the linker (which combines all the objects into one executable file).

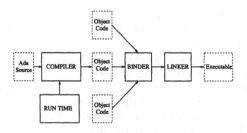

Fig. 1. GNAT Structure.

---

* *This work has been partially funded by the Spanish Research Council (CICYT), contract number TIC98-1032-C03-02.*

The frontend of the compiler is written in Ada 95 and uses the GCC backend as a retargettable code generator (see figure 2).

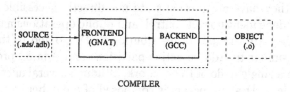

COMPILER

Fig. 2. GNAT Compiler.

The frontend comprises five phases, which communicate by means of a rather compact Abstract Syntax Tree (AST): lexical analysis phase, syntax analysis phase, semantic analysis phase, expansion phase (tree transformations that generate a tree close equivalent to C), and finally GIGI phase (transformation of the tree into a GCC tree). See figure 2.

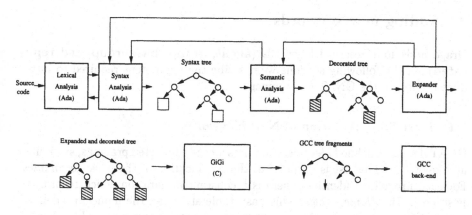

Fig. 3. Frontend phases.

Drago[2, 3] is an experimental language developed as an extension of Ada for the construction of fault-tolerant distributed applications. The hardware assumptions are: a distributed system with no memory shared among the different nodes, a reliable communication network with no partitions, and *fail-silent* nodes (that is, nodes which once failed are never heard from again by the rest of the system.) The language is the result of an effort to impose discipline and give linguistic support to the main concepts of Isis[4], as well as to experiment with the group communication paradigm. To help build fault-tolerant distributed applications, Drago explicitly supports two process group paradigms, *replicated process groups* and *cooperative process groups*. Replicated process groups allow the programming of fault-tolerant applications according to the active replication model[5], while cooperative process groups permit programmers to express parallelism and therefore increase throughput.

A process group in Drago is actually a collection of *agents*, which is the way processes are named in the language. Agents are rather similar in appearance to Ada tasks (they have an internal state not directly accessible from outside the agent, an independent flow of control, and public operations named *entries*). Furthermore, they are the unit of distribution in Drago and in this sense they perform a role similar to Ada 95 active partitions and Ada 83 programs. Each agent resides in a single node of the network, although several agents may reside in the same node. A Drago program is composed of a number of agents residing at a number of nodes.

This paper briefly describes the modifications made to the GNAT 3.10p sources in order to support the Drago language. It is organized as follows: Section 2 describes the integration of Drago keywords into the GNAT environment; section 3 describes the addition of a new pragma and one attribute; section 4 illustrates the addition of Drago syntax rules; section 5 illustrates the addition of Drago semantic checks; and section 6 describes the tree expansion. Finally, section 7 closes with some conclusions and references to related work.

2 Adding new keywords

Drago adds four reserved keywords (**agent**, **group**, **intragroup**, and **replicated**). In the following sections we describe the main steps required to introduce them into the GNAT environment.

2.1 First Step: Addition of New Keywords

GNAT list of predefined identifiers contains all the supported pragmas, attributes and keywords. This list is declared in the specification of the package *Snames*. For each predefined identifier there is a constant declaration which records its position in the *Names Table*. This hash table stores all the names, predefined or not. Keywords are classified in two main groups: keywords shared by Ada 83 and Ada 95, and exclusive Ada 95 keywords. Each group is delimited by means of a subtype declaration. Depending on the GNAT compilation mode, Ada 83 or Ada 95, this subtype allows the scanner to properly distinguish user identifiers from Ada keywords.

In order to introduce Drago keywords we added a third GNAT mode, Drago mode, and one new group with Drago exclusive keywords. The result was as follows:

```
-- Drago keywords.

First_Drago_Reserved_Word       : constant Name_Id := N + 475;
Name_Agent                      : constant Name_Id := N + 475;
Name_Group                      : constant Name_Id := N + 476;
Name_Intragroup                 : constant Name_Id := N + 477;
Name_Replicated                 : constant Name_Id := N + 478;
Last_Drago_Reserved_Word        : constant Name_Id := N + 478;
```

```
subtype Drago_Reserved_Words is
    Name_Id range First_Drago_Reserved_Word .. Last_Drago_Reserved_Word;
```

We also updated the value of the constant *Preset_Names*, declared in the body of *Snames*, keeping the order specified in the previous declarations. This constant contains the literals of all the predefined identifiers.

2.2 Second Step: Declaring the New Tokens

The list of tokens is declared in the package *Scans*. It is an enumerated type whose elements are grouped into classes used for source tests by the parser. For example, *Eterm* class contains all the expression terminators; *Sterm* class contains the simple expressions terminators[1]; *After_SM* is the class of tokens that can appear after a semicolon; *Declk* is the class of keywords which start a declaration; *Deckn* is the class of keywords which start a declaration but can not start a compilation unit; and *Cunit* is the class of tokens which can begin a compilation unit. Members of each class are alphabetically ordered. We have introduced the new tokens in the following way:

```
type Token_Type is (
```

– Token name	Token type	Class(es)
...		
Tok_If,	– IF	Eterm, Sterm, After_SM
Tok_Intragroup,	– INTRAGROUP	Eterm, Sterm, After_SM
Tok_Pragma,	– PRAGMA	Eterm, Sterm, After_SM
...		
Tok_Agent,	– AGENT	Eterm, Sterm, Cunit, Declk, After_SM
Tok_Function,	– FUNCTION	Eterm, Sterm, Cunit, Declk, After_SM
Tok_Generic,	– GENERIC	Eterm, Sterm, Cunit, Declk, After_SM
Tok_Group,	– GROUP	Eterm, Sterm, Cunit, Declk, After_SM
Tok_Package,	– PACKAGE	Eterm, Sterm, Cunit, Declk, After_SM
...		
Tok_Private,	– PRIVATE	Eterm, Sterm, Cunit, After_SM
Tok_Replicated,	– REPLICATED	Eterm, Sterm, Cunit, After_SM
Tok_With,	– WITH	Eterm, Sterm, Cunit, After_SM
...		
No_Token);		

Classes associated to tokens are specified in the third column. Our choices were based on the following guidelines:

- **Intragroup** must always appear after a semicolon (see the specification of a Drago group on section 4).
- **Agent** and **Group** start a compilation unit and a new declaration.
- **Replicated** qualifies a group (similar to Ada 95 private packages, where the word *private* preceding a package declaration qualifies the package; they are otherwise public). Therefore they were placed in the same section.

---

[1] All the reserved keywords, except *mod, rem, new, abs, others, null, delta, digits, range, and, or xor, in* and *not*, are always members of these two classes (*Eterm, Sterm*).

According to the alphabetic ordering, *Tok_Agent* is new first token of *Cunit* class. Therefore we updated the declaration of the corresponding subtype *Tok_Class_Unit* to start the class with *Tok_Agent*. Finally we modified the declaration of the table *Is_Reserved_Keyword*, which records which tokens are reserved keywords of the language.

2.3 Third Step: Modifying the Scanner initialization

The scanner initialization (subprogram *Scn.Initialization*) is responsible for stamping all the keywords stored in the *Names Table* with the byte code of their corresponding token (0 otherwise). This allows the scanner to determine if a word is an identifier of a reserved keyword. This work is done by means of repeated calls to the procedure *Set_Name_Table_Byte* passing the keyword and its corresponding token byte as parameters. Therefore we added the following sentences to the scanner initialization:

```
...
Set_Name_Table_Byte (Name_Agent,      Token_Type'Pos (Tok_Agent));
Set_Name_Table_Byte (Name_Group,      Token_Type'Pos (Tok_Group));
Set_Name_Table_Byte (Name_Intragroup, Token_Type'Pos (Tok_Intragroup));
Set_Name_Table_Byte (Name_Replicated, Token_Type'Pos (Tok_Replicated));
```

We also modified the scanner (subprogram *Scn.Scan*) in order to recognize the new keywords only when it is compiling a Drago program. This allows us to preserve its original behaviour when it is analyzing Ada source code.

This was the last modification required to integrate the new keywords into GNAT. In the following section we describe the modifications made to add one new pragma and one attribute into the GNAT scanner.

3 Adding one pragma and one attribute

Drago provides one new attribute *Member_Identifier* and one new pragma (*Drago*). When *Member_Identifier* is applied to a group identifier it returns the identifier of the current agent in the specified group. When pragma *Drago* is applied the compiler is notified about the existence of Drago code (similarly to GNAT pragmas *Ada83* and *Ada95*). For integrating them into GNAT we had to modify the package *Snames* in the following way:

1. To add their declaration to the list of predefined identifiers keeping the alphabetic order. According to the ARM [6], GNAT classifies all pragmas in two groups: configuration pragmas, those used to select a partition-wide or system-wide option, and non-configuration pragmas. The pragma Drago was placed in the group of non-configuration pragmas.
   GNAT classifies all attributes in four groups: attributes that designate procedures (*output*, *read* and *write*), attributes that return entities (*elab_body* and *elab_spec*), attributes that return types (*base* and *class*), and the rest of the attributes. *Member_Identifier* was placed in this fourth group.

2. To insert their declarations in the enumerated *Pragma_Id* and *Attribute_Id* keeping the order specified in the previous step. Similarly to the tokens associated to the reserved keywords, these types facilitate the handling of pragmas and attributes in later stages of the frontend.

3. To add their literals in *Preset_Names*. Similarly to the introduction of the keywords, we must keep the order specified in the list of predefined identifiers.

4. To update the C file *a-snames.h*. This file associates a C macro to each element of the types *Attribute_Id* and *Pragma_Id*. This work can be automatically done by means of the GNAT utility *xsnames*.

4   Adding New Syntax Rules

In this section we describe, by means of an example, the modifications made in the parser in order to support Drago syntax. The example is the specification of a Drago group, whose syntax is similar to the one of an Ada package specification:

group_declaration ::= group_specification

group_specification ::=
    [replicated] **group** defining_identifier **is**
        {basic_declarative_item}
    [**intragroup**
        {basic_declarative_item}]
    [**private**
        {basic_declarative_item}]
    end [*group*_identifier];

Replicated groups are denoted by the reserved keyword **replicated** at the heading of the group specification. Cooperative groups do not require any reserved word because they are considered the default group specification. The first list of declarative items of a group specification is named the *intergroup section*. This part contains all the information that clients are able to know about this group. The optional list of declarative items after the reserved word **intragroup** is named the *intragroup section*. It contains information that only members of the group are able to know, and it can be declared only in a cooperative group specification[2]. The optional list of declarative items after the reserved word **private** is named the *private section* and provides groups with the same functionality as the private part of Ada packages. The following sections describe the steps made in order to add this syntax to the GNAT parser.

4.1   First Step: Addition of New Kinds of Nodes

GNAT stores all the semantic and syntactic information of the source program in one Abstract Syntax Tree (AST) [1]. The AST has two node formats: extended

---

[2] Replicated groups do not have this facility because their members are assumed to be replicas of a deterministic automaton and thus they do not need to exchange their state —all the replicas have the same state.

nodes, and non-extended nodes. Extended nodes are used to represent the entities (identifiers, operators and character literals found in the declarations of the Ada source program). Non-extended nodes are used to represent all the other aspects of the Ada source program. All nodes, extended or not, are classified into node kinds. Associated to every Ada syntax rule there is a kind of node which represents it.

GNAT node kinds are declared in the enumerated *Sinfo.Node_Kind*. Similarly to *Token_Type* elements, all its elements are grouped into classes (i.e. nodes that correspond to sentences, nodes which correspond to operators, ...), and elements of each class are alphabetically ordered.

The addition of the rules of a Drago group required two additional kinds of nodes: *N_Group_Declaration* and *N_Group_Specification*. Due to the similarity of a Drago group specification and an Ada package specification we placed the *N_Group_Declaration* node in the class associated with *N_Package_Declaration* node, and *N_Group_Specification* in the class associated with *N_Package_Specification*.

We repeated this work for every additional syntax rule of Drago.

4.2 Second Step: Addition of New Templates

The specification of package *Sinfo* contains templates that define the syntactic and semantic information handled by each kind of node. These templates have the structure of Ada comments, but obey the following strict rules:

1. The first line must specify the associated node kind (one of the node kinds specified in the previous step).
2. The second line specifies the value of the node field *Sloc*. All nodes have this field. It is an index to the word of the source code which forced the creation of the node.
3. The following lines specify the aliases associated to node fields and their corresponding initial values (if any). Non-extended nodes have several general-purpose fields and flags named *Field1..Field5* and *Flag1..Flag18* respectively. GNAT allows us to assign them an alias and, therefore, facilitate their handling.

   When we define a new node we have two possibilities: to reuse aliases predefined by other nodes, or to define new aliases. In the first case we must keep all its features: field number and data type. In the second case we must carefully analyze the field to which we associate the new alias because once it is stated it remains fixed for all nodes.

For each alias we must declare two subprograms in *Sinfo*: one procedure (used to set the value of the field), and one function (to get the stored value). Their names must be the name of the alias (for the function) and the same name prefixed by the word *"Set_"* (for the procedure). All these subprograms have one associated pragma *assert* which verifies the usage of the alias. Therefore, if we reuse some alias we must update the corresponding pragmas.

The templates associated with *N_Group_Declaration* and *N_Group_Specification* are:

```
-- N_Group_Declaration
-- Sloc points to GROUP
-- Specification (Node1)

-- N_Group_Specification
-- Sloc points to GROUP
-- Defining_Identifier (Node1)
-- Visible_Declarations (List2)
-- Intragroup_Declarations (List3) (set to No_List if no intragroup
-- part present)
-- Private_Declarations (List4) (set to No_List if no private
-- part present)
```

This means that the value of *Sloc* in a *N_Group_Declaration* node points to the source code word **group**, and the first field of the node (*Field1*) points to a specification node. On the other hand, the value of *Sloc* in a *N_Group_Specification* node also points to the same word **group** (because the reason for the creation of both nodes was the same word), its first field (*Field1*) points to a defining identifier node, and its second, third and fourth fields (*Field2..Field4*) point to lists which contain respectively its visible, intragroup and private declarations (figure 4).

Similarly to GNAT handling of private packages, the handling of replicated groups only requires to add one new flag in the AST root node (*Flag15* for a private package, and we chose *Flag16* for a replicated group).

4.3 Third Step: Automatic Modification of the Frontend

The templates specified in the previous step are used by three GNAT utility programs (*xsinfo, xtreeprs* and *xnmake*) to automatically generate four frontend source files involved in the handling of nodes: *a-sinfo.h, treeprs.ads, nmake.ads* and *nmake.adb* (see figure 5).

4.4 Fourth Step: Update of the Parser

The GNAT parser is implemented by means of the well known recursive descent technique. All its code is inside the function *Par* which is composed of several subunits (one per ARM chapter [6]). According to this philosophy we decided to add the subunit *Par.Drag* to group all the parser code that syntactically analyzes Drago rules (figure 6).

The functionalities of the GNAT parser are:

1. To check the syntax of the source code and generate the corresponding errors (if any).
2. To create the corresponding subtree.

We have given the name *P_Group* to the function associated with the parsing of a group specification. We used the fragment of the parser that analyzes a

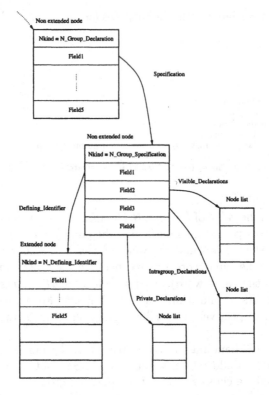

Fig. 4. Subtree of a group declaration and specification.

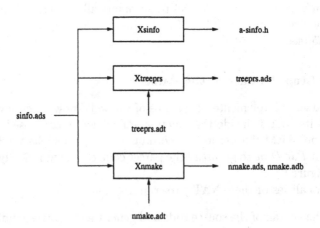

Fig. 5. GNAT utility programs.

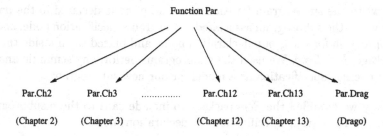

Fig. 6. New parser structure.

package specification as a reference for its development. Finally we modified the parsing of a compilation unit to include a call to this function when it is analyzing Drago source code and it detects a group token.

5 Verification of the Semantics

When the parser finishes its work, the semantic analizer makes a top-down traversal of the AST and, according to the kind of each visited node, it calls one subprogram that semantically verifies it. These subprograms are structured as a set of packages. Each package contains all the subprograms required to verify the semantic rules of each ARM chapter (packages *Sem_Ch2..Sem_Ch13*). There is one subprogram for each node type created by the parser and the main package that derivates the calls is named *Sem*.

For the semantic verification of a Drago group specification we made the following modifications to the GNAT sources:

1. To add one new package: *Sem_Drag*. This package contains all the Drago subprograms that make the semantic verifications.
2. To add one new semantic entity. A GNAT entity is an internal representation of the identifiers, operators and character literals found in the source program declarations. Therefore, the identifier of a group specification must have its corresponding entity. We added the element *E_Group* to the enumerated *Entity_Info* (inside the *Einfo* package) to represent the new group name entity.
3. To update the C file *a-einfo.h*. This work is automatically done by means of the GNAT utility program names *xeinfo* (figure 7).

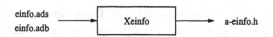

Fig. 7. GNAT semantic utility program

4. To write one subprogram for each new kind of node declared in the parser. We wrote the subprogram associated to the group specification node, and the subprogram for the group declaration node, and placed them inside the new package *Sem_Drag*. We used the subprograms performing semantic analysis of a package specification as a model for our new subprograms.

Finally we modified the *Sem* package to include calls to these subprograms when analyzing a group specification (or declaration) node.

6 Tree expansion

The tree expansion is interleaved with the semantic phase. When GNAT verifies the semantics of one node, it calls one procedure which expands it (if necessary). The expansion of the tree consists of the substitution of one high level node (one node which represents one task, one protected object, ...) by one subtree which contains nodes of a lower level of abstraction and provides the functionality of the high level node.

In the general case, to generate code there is no need to access the GIGI level, and our work finishes at the expansion phase. In our case, we create a mirror of the tree, transform the Drago nodes into Ada 95 nodes which call several added Run-Time subprograms, and finally call the original gnat expansor which expands this Ada 95 tree into the GIGI source tree.

7 Current work

Currently we have a modified version of GNAT which makes all the static verifications (syntax and semantics) required for the Drago language. We are close to finish the integration of the Drago run time system. This implementation reuses the GNAT Run-Time library and is intended to run on a Linux network. It also uses a library of Ada packages that provides reliable atomic broadcast using an original consensus protocol[7][8].

The current distribution requires users to follow all the steps described in the GNAT distribution to recompile and install the system. We intend nevertheless to modify the script of the gnat binary distribution in order to facilitate the installation.

8 Conclusions

This paper has described the integration of Drago into the GNAT frontend. Drago is a language designed as an Ada extension to experiment with the active replication model of fault-tolerant distributed programming. We have focused our attention on the lexical, syntactic and semantic aspects of the integration. For lack of space the abstract syntax tree expansion and code generation have not been discussed here.

Our experience with the GNAT sources has been very positive. We found a complex, high quality product whose source files are very well structured and documented. These features enabled us to study and modify it in order to introduce our Drago language.

9 Acknowledgments

We wish to thank R. Dewar and J. Barahona for their help with the GNAT utility programs. We also wish to thank the members of the Distributed Systems Seminar in the University of Las Palmas de Gran Canaria for their help in clarifying the ideas contained in this paper. Finally we also wish to thank A. Alvarez and Andy Wellings for their help with the final version of this paper.

References

1. Comar, C., Gasperoni, F., and Schoberg, E. *The GNAT Project: A GNU-Ada9X Compiler.* Technical report. New York University. 1994.
2. Miranda, J., Álvarez, A., Guerra, F. and Arévalo, S. *Drago: A Language for Programming Fault-Tolerant and Cooperative Distributed Applications.* Reference Manual. *http://www.cma.ulpgc.es/users/gsd/*
3. Miranda, J., Álvarez, A., Arévalo, S. and Guerra, F. *Drago: An Ada Extension to Program Fault-Tolerant Distributed Applications.* Reliable Software Technologies. Ada-Europe'96. 1996. pp.235–246.
4. Birman, K., R. Cooper, T. Joseph, K. Marzullo, M. Makpangou, K. Kane, F. Schmuck, and M. Wood. The Isis System Manual. Version 2.1. September 1990.
5. Schneider, F.B. Implementing Fault-tolerant Services Using the State Machine Approach: A Tutorial. *ACM Computing Surveys*, **22**(4), December 1990.
6. Intermetrics, Inc. 1995. *Ada 95 Language Reference Manual.* Intermetrics, Inc., Cambridge, Mass. (January).
7. Guerra, F., Arévalo, S., Álvarez, A., and Miranda, J. A Distributed Consensus Protocol with a Coordinator. *International Conference on Decentralized and Distributed Systems ICDDS'93.* IFIP, Palma de Mallorca (Spain). September 1993.
8. Guerra, F. and Miranda, J. and Álvarez, A. and Arévalo, S. *An Ada Library to Program Fault-Tolerant Distributed Applications.* Reliable Software Technologies. Ada-Europe'97. 1997. pp.230–243.

On the Use of Controlled Types for Fossil Collection in a Distributed Simulation System

Helge Hagenauer

Institut für Computerwissenschaften
Universität Salzburg
Jakob-Haringer-Straße 2
A-5020 Salzburg
Austria
hagenau@cosy.sbg.ac.at

Abstract. In the field of distributed discrete event simulation the time warp algorithm is well known. For a generalization, called split queue time warp, a prototype using Ada 95 was built. The present paper describes an implementation of an add-on for fossil collection needed to prevent from memory overflow during a simulation run. The method is based on determining the simulation time, called global virtual time, by respecting the special submodel structure of the prototype. A discussion about the usefulness of Ada's concept of controlled types for such a purpose is included.

1 Introduction

In parallel/distributed discrete event simulation the well established *time warp* algorithm avoids a central simulation clock and use of global state (an introduction is given in [12], [5] and [4]). The system to be simulated is seen as a set of loosely coupled *physical processes*, which are represented by so called *logical processes*, LPs, interacting solely by sending and receiving timestamped messages.

Time warp is an *optimistic* strategy, which means that a LP sets its next step on the base of input received so far. There is no waiting for possible further input which should have been considered earlier. Detecting such a causal error, a LP has to roll back to a former state and all unjustified interim output must be canceled.

An increasing number of rollbacks causes a decrease in efficiency. In standard time warp all messages sent to a LP are inserted into and read from a single input queue that is maintained in ascending timestamp order. In [6] a generalization was proposed, *split queue time warp* (SQTW for short), which allows several input queues per LP. Each input queue corresponds to a message type and is read only when necessary for progress. Thus currently unneeded information can be postponed to reduce the risk of rollbacks.

A first pseudo-parallel one-processor prototype written in Ada 83 (see [7]) showed a decrease in rollback numbers. Therefore a more adequate implementation based on Ada 95 and its capabilities for distributed programming followed. It is described in [8].

Being able to do rollbacks requires from a LP to save state information, as for example keeping track of read messages, actions set and messages sent to other LPs. So this is needed over the entire simulation it is obvious that running out of memory will occur. To prevent from memory overflow a *fossil/garbage collection* has to be added to the system. It is responsible for determining which parts of data are no longer required and thus freeing of the corresponding memory can take place. Since such a distributed simulation system does not have a central clock or a global state a method for computing the simulation time, known as the *global virtual time* in this field, is necessary.

This paper contains in Sect. 2 a brief overview of the SQTW algorithm and the implemented system structure. In Sect. 3 the basic snapshot algorithm for approximation of global virtual time is described. Section 4 discusses the functioning of fossil collection and the ability of using controlled types. First results are given in Sect. 5.

2 Split Queue Time warp

2.1 Algorithm

In time warp a LP reads its arriving messages from a single input queue where they are inserted and consequently processed in strict timestamp order. This leads to two main disadvantages: First, the LP has to save currently unwanted information in its internal state. And second, the early reading of not-yet-needed messages inflates the past of the LP, which increases the risk of rollbacks.

In [6] it is proposed that a LP can have several input queues each of which corresponds to a message type and is read only when necessary for progress. This "lazy" or "by need" processing is called *split queue time warp*, SQTW for short. In Fig. 1 a simple delivery station example illustrates this behavior: At each station parcels arrive from customers and are loaded into vans for delivery. When a van's capacity is reached, the van departs for a delivery tour and returns empty to some station in the system. A LP simulating such a delivery station needs two input queues for parcels and returning empty vans.

2.2 System structure

LPs are the main building blocks of a SQTW system. Their actions are composed primarily into two parts. The first one serves for error-recovery needs such as self-examination for consistency and saving its present state for later recovery or rollbacks. The second one is model-specific, the LP step, and carries out the simulation of the appropriate physical process' behavior. Sending of messages belongs to the LP step.

```
LOOP
   IF waiting_parcels < van_capacity
   THEN
      get(message, parcel_channel);
      waiting_parcels := waiting_parcels + 1;
      local_time := max(message.timestamp, local_time);
   ELSE
      get(message, van_channel); - - looking for an empty van
      local_time := max (message.timestamp, local_time);
      send((van, local_time + delivery_time), some_station);
      waiting_parcels := 0;
   END IF;
END LOOP;
```

Fig. 1. Delivery station model for SQTW

But having the focus on an implementation for workstations connected via a network, some additional structural refinements are necessary. Generally there will be many more LPs than available processing nodes (e.g. processors), so several LPs have to be assigned to the same processing node. Such a group of LPs is called a *submodel*. Figure 2 shows the structure of the prototype implementation where each submodel possesses a submodel manager (realized as a single task) which has to do the scheduling of its associated LPs. Furthermore the submodel manager is responsible for setting up its LPs at system start and for close down and result gathering at the end of a simulation run. The LPs are implemented as passive objects for increasing the scope and flexibility of use. In addition a main program serves as the interface to the experimentator and an address server holds the addresses of all LPs. A detailed description of these topics in conjunction with distribution is given in [8].

3 Global Virtual Time

The state saving of each LP requires a steady increasing amount of memory. So it is clear that during a simulation the available memory will exhaust. To prevent this a *fossil* or *garbage collection* is necessary to free memory for states not needed anymore. Therefore a simulation time or global state of the whole system is required. But in absence of a central clock or event list in a distributed simulation system such a value can be computed by looking at all the LPs and is called *Global Virtual Time, GVT. GVT* can also be used to show the progress of a simulation (e.g. displaying intermediate results).

The simulation time to which LP_i has advanced at real time t is denoted *Local Virtual Time, $LVT_i(t)$*. For all i the function $LVT_i(t)$ is not monotonic increasing due to the possibility of rollbacks. The Global Virtual Time at real time t, $GVT(t)$, must ensure for each LP_i that a rollback to a state with $LVT_i(t) < GVT(t)$ is not possible. Therefore the minimum of all $LVT_i(t)$ (de-

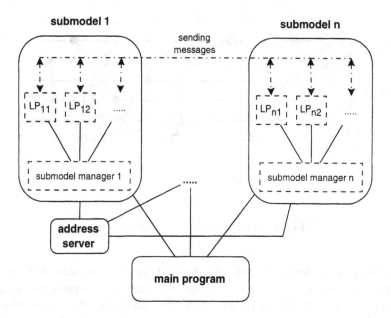

Fig. 2. Submodel structure

noted $LVT_{min}(t)$) and the minimal timestamp of messages in transit at real time t (denoted $ts_{min}(t)$) is needed. Then the formula is

$$GVT(t) = \min(LVT_{min}(t), ts_{min}(t)) .$$

To avoid a general interruption of the simulation a GVT value is approximated by a computation superimposing the simulation. A general algorithm is introduced by Mattern [11] and is based on so-called *cuts*, which divide for each LP the process line into two parts – the past and the future. A cut is triggered by cut events which have no direct influence on the underlying simulation. In a time diagram a cut can be shown as a zigzag line (see Fig. 3). To guarantee the essential properties for GVT a *consistent* cut is needed, which means that no message is sent in the future of some LP_i and is received in the past of some LP_j ($i = j$ allowed).

Obviously a consistent cut C together with M_C, the set of all messages crossing the cut line, defines a global state of the system and therefore can be used for GVT approximation. The main problem is determining M_C. Mattern proposed to use two cuts C and C' (see Fig. 3) where C' is later than C. Additionally C' should be delayed until all messages which cross cut C have reached their destination LP. Then the minimal timestamp of all messages sent after cut C is an approximation for messages crossing cut C'. Hence a status information is necessary (here the colors white and red) and it is piggybacked onto messages.

Using the specific submodel structure described above the main program is the GVT-manager responsible for initiating a new GVT-approximation and

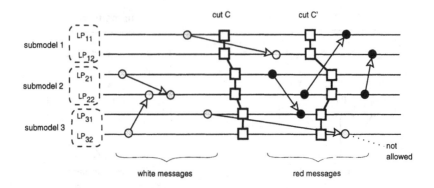

Fig. 3. Principle of *GVT* approximation

controlling if cut C' fulfills the desired criteria. It gets the necessary data from the submodel managers. A submodel manager determines on request the minimal LVT-value of its LPs. Furthermore it holds the differences of sent and received messages and the minimal timestamp of sent messages for both colors. A LP updates after each step these values. No auxiliary means like control messages among LPs are needed. The necessary additional communication is kept at a low level and is concentrated between main program and submodel managers.

Subsequent to the computation of a new valid GVT value the main program submits this value to all the submodel managers, which are now able to perform fossil collection.

4 Fossil Collection and Controlled Types

4.1 Data Structures for State Saving

Being able to do rollbacks requires from a LP to save state information, which includes keeping track of read messages, actions set and messages sent to other LPs. Dynamic data structures such as lists and stacks are employed for this purpose. Details are shown in Fig. 4.

Each LP has one or more input queues which are implemented as double linked lists using access values. The elements in each input queue are inserted in non decreasing timestamp order. A pointer to the last read element marks the "past" of this queue. A read element is not deleted because in the case of a rollback it may be needed again. In Fig. 4 only one input queue is shown for simplicity.

A so called state stack is associated to each LP. It is a classical stack with push and pop operations and saves information needed for rollbacks. Besides some model specific data and the current LVT value these are the last read messages per input queue and all messages sent during a specific step. As indicated in Fig. 4 an access value as part of a stack element represents the last read element of each input queue by pointing to the appropriate position.

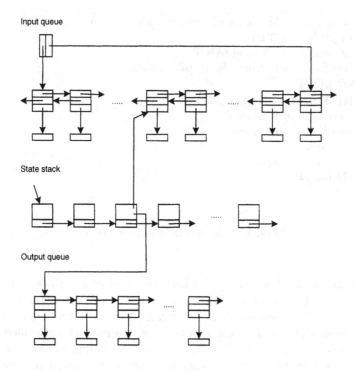

Fig. 4. Data structures affected by fossil collection

All sent messages during one step together with their receiver addresses are copied to an output queue that is part of a stack element. Also realized as a linked list it is needed in the case of rollbacks.

In both, input and output queues, each element is composed of structural information (pointers to the next and if necessary previous elements) and an info component, which is a pointer to a message object.

The actual valid GVT value determines which "end part" of the stack is no longer needed. The first element with $LVT < GVT$ marks this border. Beginning at this point the rest of the stack can be deallocated including each output queue per stack element. For each input queue the pointer to the last read element indicates how far it is possible to delete arrived messages. (Note that a LP may have several input queues which have been read up to different time values; so this pointer technique is really necessary.) Altogether the deallocation includes a front part of each input queue, the whole output queue per stack element and an end part of the state stack.

Figure 5 shows the general algorithm for fossil collection applicable to each LP. After finding the uppermost stack element with $LVT < GVT$ in each input queue the appropriate front parts can be deallocated. For safety reasons the uppermost but one stack element is taken. Then the end part of the stack can be freed including the output queues.

```
fossil := uppermost but one stack_element with LVT < GVT;
IF fossil /= NULL THEN
    FOR each input_queue iq LOOP
        free from begin of iq to fossil.last_read(iq);
    END LOOP;
    WHILE fossil /= NULL LOOP
        next_fossil := fossil.next
        free fossil.output_queue;
        free fossil;
        fossil := next_fossil;
    END LOOP;
END IF;
```

Fig. 5. Algorithm for fossil collection

There are two further situations where allocated memory has to be deallocated. First, in the case of a rollback one or more previous states are popped from the stack. The appropriate memory can be freed, but no release of input queue elements takes place. Second, in the case of a rollback unjustified interim sent messages have to be cancelled. This is done by sending an *antimessage* (indicated by a special tag) with the same information as the original one. In the recipient's appropriate input queue a "real" message and the corresponding anti message cancel each other and again memory has to be deallocated.

4.2 Controlled Types for State Saving?

At first sight Ada's concept of controlled types seems to be very useful here. Especially the complete control over finalization appears to promise a smart and efficient way for nearly automatic deallocation. But a closer examination manifests some details which disagree to this. In the following a short discussion about the usefulness of controlled types for the various data elements is given.

State Stack: This represents the heart of fossil collection. The stack as data structure exists as long as the appropriate LP. Only particular stack elements have to be released during fossil collection and therefore using a controlled type for them seems to be reasonable. But this would raise the requirement of two kinds of finalization:

1. With included deallocation of associated output queues only;
2. Additionally partly deallocation of input queues (a front part).

The second one is only needed during fossil collection (see Fig. 5) whereas the first one is called when rollbacks occur and states are popped too.

Output Queue: It is a component of each stack element, more exactly the output queue's head element is part of the appropriate stack element. Therefore deallocation of the stack element includes releasing of the complete output queue which is also not needed anymore. No pointers to other data structures occur and so controlled types may be used. But caution, *finalize* is invoked in many situations, mainly during assignment or upon creation of temporary objects. A supplementary *adjust* operation is required primarily for doing a so called *hard copy* of linked lists. Lengths of output queues are not predictable and hence this extra work could be too costly and resulting in an efficiency reduction.

Input Queue: Here the same reason as for state stacks applies. An input queue has the same life time than its LP, which, in general, is a complete simulation run. During fossil collection a front part is released and therefore controlled types may be suitable for single queue elements. But there are some other access values pointing to them and deallocation during finalization bears the risk of introducing dangling pointers.

Elements for Input and Output queues: As shown in Fig. 4 these objects are constructed in the same way. The stored message is appended by a pointer which necessitates deallocation of message objects during freeing queue elements. At first sight a typical application for controlled types — but there are several assignments and creations of temporary objects that lead to unwanted behavior. The following example shows one case:

Given are declarations for a simplified queue element using a controlled type in Fig. 6. Further it is assumed that the associated finalize operation comprises a deallocation of the message object pointed to.

```
TYPE element_type;
TYPE element_pointer IS ACCESS element_type;
TYPE element_type IS NEW controlled WITH
  RECORD
    next : element_pointer := NULL;
    info : .....;
    data : message_pointer := NULL;
  END RECORD;

ep : element_pointer;
mp : message_pointer := some_message;
```

Fig. 6. Simplified declarations for queue elements

Now creation of a new element with a given message object represented by an access value may be achieved by using

```
ep := NEW element_type'(controlled WITH mp, info_data, NULL);
```

The result is illustrated in Fig. 7. By elaborating the aggregate a temporary anonymous object is installed with a pointer to the message object. The allocator creates also an object of `element_type` and the "value" of the aggregate is assigned to it. Then the aggregate's object is finalized including deallocation of the message object and the dangling pointer is born.

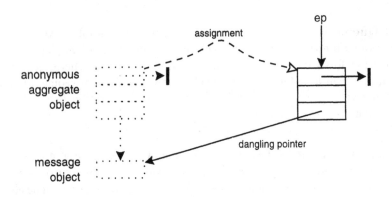

Fig. 7. Dangling pointer situation

Summary: The use of controlled types for such a system has primarily two drawbacks:

1. Finalization operations in a complex data structure with strongly linked elements can cause unwanted deallocations which lead to system failures or give incorrect results. Especially in simulations it is hard to prove the correctness of the final outcome.
2. In some cases one general finalization operation for a type is not sufficient. Depending on the situation when finalize is invoked two or more different methods can be necessary (e.g. see state stacks).

So a fossil collection based on deallocation operations was added to the prototype. They are called in several situations as described above.

5 First Results

First results obtained by experimenting with the prototype are very promising. The example used consists of 200 delivery station LPs (see Fig. 1) and 200 associated source LPs (in the the delivery station example they only generate parcel messages and have no input). The whole system is divided into two submodels. Since measuring the used memory is simpler on one processing node (no distribution) first experiments with and without fossil collection were made on a workstation with one processor. In doing so the required memory during a simulation run compared to GVT advance was measured. Figure 8 shows a nearly linear increase when no fossil collection is active. The slight growth of the curve with fossil collection comes from a rather simple scheduling strategy for source LPs

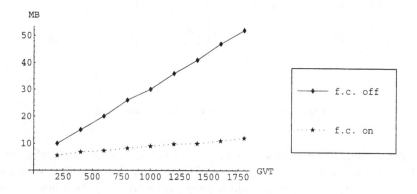

Fig. 8. Memory use (in MB) without/with fossil collection

To support the usefulness of the idea described above the total number of state stack elements in the complete system was determined at various instants during a simulation run. Figure 9 shows an oscillating behavior with no tendency for overall increasing.

6 Conclusion

This paper describes a method of fossil collection for a distributed simulation system and its implementation for a prototype written in Ada 95. After showing the idea a discussion about the usefulness of controlled types leads to the following result: due to the complex data structures involved and considering all situations where special operations (mainly finalize) are invoked, the risk of errors gets very high. A standard deallocation is used by instantiating the predefined unchecked_deallaction procedure.

The prototype is based on the Ada 95 model of programming distributed systems using the GNAT/GNATDIST tools. Language and tools allowed quick and rather smooth progress. Especially the fact that the distributed programmer does not have to deal with low-level details or special linguistic constructs gives room to concentrate on design and coding the distributed system.

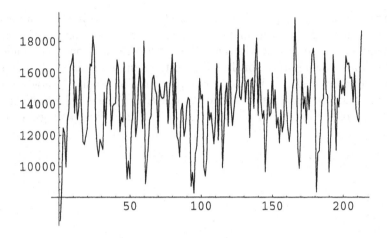

Fig. 9. Stack lengths during a simulation run

The system shows plausible behavior so far, but to show the usefulness of SQTW some "greater" simulations are still necessary. A comparison with standard time warp will show for which model categories SQTW leads to more efficiency. There is also need for a user interface to allow easy application for a distributed simulation system.

References

1. Barnes, J.G.P. 1994. *Programming in Ada*. Addison-Wesley, Reading, Ma.
2. Burns A. and A. Wellings. 1995. *Concurrency in Ada*. Cambridge University Press, New York.
3. Chandy, K. N. and J. Misra. 1989. *Parallel Program Design*. Addison-Wesley, Reading, Ma.
4. Ferscha A. 1996. "Parallel and Distributed Simulation of Discrete Event Systems". *Parallel and Distributed Computing Handbook* (A.Y. Zomaya ed.). Mc Graw-Hill.
5. Fujimoto, R. M. 1990. "Parallel Discrete Event Simulation". *Communications ACM* 33(10), pp.31-53.
6. Hagenauer, H. and W. Pohlmann. 1996. "Making Asynchronous Simulation More Asynchronous". Proc. 10th European Simulation Conference, Budapest.
7. Hagenauer H. and W. Pohlmann. 1996. "Prototyping a Parallel Discrete Event Simulation System in Ada". Proc. ACM TRI-ADA96 (S. Carlson ed.). Philadelphia.
8. Hagenauer H. and W. Pohlmann. 1998. "Ada 95 for a Distributed Simulation System". Proc. Conference Reliable Sortware Technologies – Ada-Europe'98 (Lars Asplund ed.), Uppsala. Lecture Notes in Computer Science 1411, Springer.
9. Hagenauer H. 1999. "Global Virtual Time Approximation for Split Queue Time Warp". Proc. 4th International Conference of the ACPC – ACPC'99 (P.Zinterhof, M.Vajteršic, A.Uhl ed.), Salzburg. Lecture Notes in Computer Science 1557, Springer.

10. Kempe M. 1994. "Abstract Data types are under full control with Ada 9X". Proc. ACM TRI-ADA'94. Baltimore, MD.
11. Mattern, F. 1993. "Efficient Algorithms for Distributed Snapshots and Global Virtual Time Approximation". Journal of Parallel and Distributed Computing 18, no 4.
12. Misra, J. 1986. "Distributed Discrete Event Simulation". *ACM Computing Surveys* 18(1), p.39-65.
13. Pohlmann, W. 1987. "Simulated Time and the Ada Rendezvous". Proc. 4. Symposium Simulationstechnik. Zuerich. J. Halin ed., pp.92-102.

An Application (Layer 7) Routing Switch with Ada95 Software

Mike Kamrad

Top Layer Networks, Inc.
2400 Computer Drive
Westborough MA 01581
USA
+1.508.870.1300 x139
kamrad@TopLayer.com

Abstract. The Top Layer Networks AppSwitch[TM] is a coordinated hardware and software Layer 7-application switch designed to provide Application Control for data communication networks by automatically prioritizing network traffic according to the user and the application that is generating the messages. Ada was chosen as the programming language for AppSwitch[TM] software because it possessed the best combination of language features to provide both high reliability and portability, specifically, language. The AppSwitch[TM] is a multiprocessor system and the software architecture is designed to take advantage of Ada's distributed system features as Distributed System Annex implementations mature. Top Layer faced significant obstacles to make Ada succeed: a huge learning curve, an incomplete Ada tool chain for the processors in the system and the construction of the Ada runtime system to efficiently support the Ravenscar.

1 Introduction

Top Layer Networks (formerly Top Layer) is a new data communication product company, whose new product, the AppSwitch[TM] 2000, uses Ada as its implementation language. Ada is not the traditional programming language for building data communication product software. As such, Top Layer had to overcome significant obstacles to realize its full benefits. The goal of this paper is to describe the software architecture of the AppSwitch[TM] and how well Ada supported the architecture and to reflect on the Top Layer experience in effectively using Ada and overcoming obstacles to its effective use. The paper is divided as follows: Section 2 gives a brief overview of the AppSwitch[TM] 2000, in particular the software architecture of the AppSwitch[TM] 2000. Section 3 describes why Ada was chosen, an overview of the software development environment and how Ada features enhanced that software architecture. Section 4 describes the obstacles Top Layer faced and the lessons learned.

2 The Overview of the AppSwitch^{TM} Hardware and Software Architecture

The AppSwitch^{TM} family of LAN/WAN switches is designed to change that situation. AppSwitches analyze application traffic and enforce QoS policies automatically, namely, with no human intervention and no changes to PCs or servers. This is accomplished with coordination of hardware to examine and switch traffic at wire speed and software to guide switching, and therefore network performance, according to business goals.

At the same time, monitoring and managing network performance has become extremely complex. With the integrated hardware and software architecture, the AppSwitch^{TM} enables a network administrator to monitor and understand all the elements of the network and to adapt the network to changes, all through a Web-based graphical user interface.

At the core of the AppSwitch^{TM} are the hardware and software components that constitute flow classification technology. With this technology, the AppSwitch^{TM} can go deep into the incoming packets, up to Layer 7 headers that applications produce to determine source and destination addresses and application types of that packet. The AppSwitch^{TM} flow classification is supported by the pre-configured Application Profile Library (APL) that is built into every switch and that holds the rules for flow classification and prioritization.

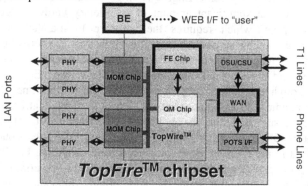

Fig. 1. Overview of AppSwitch^{TM} Major Elements

At the arrival of the first packets of a flow, the AppSwitch^{TM} uses the a connection setup process subarchitecture to select the appropriate "tailored" profile in the APL and to establish pertinent information on the new flow, which is captured in the Session database. After that, remaining packets in the flow are switched through the coordination of the Session data and the selected profile. The state data captured by each flow in the Session database can intelligently adjust QoS as needed to upgrade or downgrade priority. On the output side, there are thousands of queues available to expand the number of flows and priorities among those flows.

Completing the big picture of the AppSwitch^{TM} architecture, Figure 1 shows the supporting elements to facilitate LAN and WAN data communication and to give the network administrator systematic control of the network.

The AppSwitch™ includes a WAN subsystem to handle both T1 and phone lines in an integrated manner. Incoming packets from both LAN and WAN connections are subjected to proprietary "triage" by the Media Access Control Function (MOM) components to make very broad categorization of the packets and to put the packets into a canonical form that is data link independent. From there, the "categorized" packets flow over the TopWire to the Forwarding Engine (FE Chip + QM Chip) where the Application Switching is performed. Output packets flow back out of the Forwarding Engine to their destination over the TopWire where MOM components reverse the effect of the canonicalization of the packets before they are transmitted to the LAN and WAN connections.

At the top of the AppSwitch™ architecture is the Background Engine (BE) which functions as a backup switch to the Forwarding Engine, the "mission control" computer of the AppSwitch™ and the user interface to the network administrator. In its "mission control" role, the BE has numerous "agents" that monitor and control all aspects of the AppSwitch™. In its user interface role, the BE contains the facilities to serve the Web-based interface that can be displayed on any computer on the network.

For more details see [1] or our Web page, www.TopLayer.com.

2.1 The Forwarding Engine Software Architecture

The architecture of the Forwarding Engine is singly focused on routing packets at wire speed. There is a significant amount of proprietary hardware technology to support the switching, which requires the software to maintain a very close relationship with the operations and action of the hardware. The software must act in a highly predictable manner, which means that the overall structure of the software is one polling loop and there are no interrupts in the Forwarding Engine. There are several paths through the polling loop, largely based on the lifetime of a message flow. One path handles the set up necessary for a new flow by identifying significant attributes of the message including the application that generated it. This enables the appropriate "tailored" Application policies to be applied to the routing of the remaining packets in the message flow. A second path, called the FastPath, handles the bulk of the routing for the remainder of the message flows by consulting with the Session database to intelligently apply the appropriate Application policies to the routing of the packets . Additionally, there are paths to maintain the Session database which is used to adjust the routing of all message flows in real-time. While all paths must be high performance, the FastPath must truly be high performance.

2.2 The WAN Subsystem Software Architecture

The architecture of the WAN subsystem is also singly focused on managing "circuits" between T1 and phone lines and the rest of the **AppSwitch**™, using PPP or Frame Relay protocols. Just like the Forwarding Engine, The software must act in a highly predictable manner, which means that the overall structure of the software is one polling loop. There is only one interrupt, to update the internal clock.

2.3 The Background Engine Software Architecture

Unlike the other two subsystems, the Background Engine is multiply focused on many activities. Execution of these activities is triggered by events, of which there are three classes of events:

- Arrival of message packets
- Expiration of time periods, triggering a specific action at a specific time
- Execution of a deferred action, triggering a specific action at a later time

The message packets are either destined for the Background Engine to service, such as driving the user interface to the AppSwitch^{TM}, or they are being routed through the Background Engine, as a backup to the Forwarding Engine. The expiration of time periods is generated internally within the Background Engine to control these various activities found in the Background Engine, such as message flows and application servers. Deferred actions enable a long activity to be divided in a sequence of shorter deferred actions. The Background Engine has a multi-threaded structure, where there is usually a thread assigned to a unique event that the Background Engine handles.

Figure 2 provides an overview of the major components of the Background Engine architecture. All independent entities (either equipment or tasks) are shown as circles. All (independent) software modules are shown in rectangles/squares. The "pipes" are queues. The small letters on some independent activities or queues describe the priority of that entity where 'I' means interrupt level, 'H' means highest application level, L means lowest application level; entities without priority are assigned some priority level between highest and lowest application level. Objects with dashed lines are implemented with hardware and objects with dotted lines are features to be added.

The most important thread in the system is the Packet/Event Processor. This thread is responsible for handling all the message packets, timer events and delayed actions in the Background Engine that are queued collectively in the JobJar. Packet/Event Processor handles a message packet by directing it to either an application/service module or protocol/session module. The protocol/session modules route the message packets according to the appropriate protocol for that message packet, finally exiting out the Background Engine through the DMA output. Queues in the application/service modules accept the message packets as requests for their service; the result of their service may be new messages that are routed as deferred actions through JobJar to their destination. Both set of modules may also produced timer events that are also routed through the JobJar. All the modules without a thread use the Packet/Event Processor's thread for their execution. Those modules with their own threads use them to service the message packets that are enqueued. The clock in the Background Engine is used for cycling modules directly or to generate internal timer events.

The Background Engine must be prepared to sustain the occasional spikes of high communication activity without being overwhelmed and locking up. To prevent this, the Packet/Event Processor will filter out lower priority message packets and, based on saturation measures of DMA interrupts, will retard the number of DMA interrupts, thus bundling the arrival of message packets for more efficient processing.

To ensure adequate scheduling of all tasks in the system, all tasks must be assigned a specific priority. The first and most important task in the system, Packet/Event

Processor, which is assigned the highest priority in the system will execute except when its JobJar is empty or when Packet/Event Processor is timed out to let other tasks in the Background Engine run. All queues and protected objects that Packet/Event Processor accesses (either directly or indirectly through a Module's interface) must have Packet/Event Processor's priority as its ceiling priority. All operations on all queues and protected objects that Packet/Event Processor accesses must be designed not to block Packet/Event Processor.

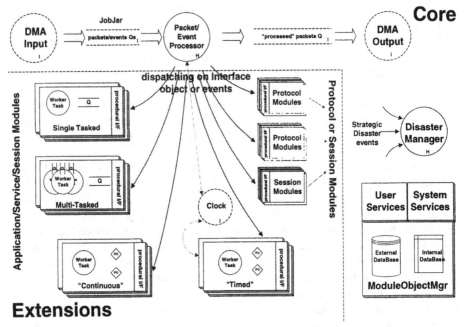

Fig. 2. The Software Architecture of the Background Engine

The architecture divides the major modules of the system into the core modules or extension modules. The Core modules are always present in the Background Engine, providing a set of services that are directly accessible to any module in the system. The Extension modules supply services to the Packet/Event Processor and other modules through one or more procedural Interfaces. All Interfaces that Extension modules provide are found in the Interface class and are concrete type extensions of existing Interface "template" types. The extension modules can only directly reference core modules; they can only reference other extension modules through an Interface object (aka, a handle) provided by the ModuleObjectMgr. Through the Interface object, the client module can access the services it wants from the server module. The ModuleObjectMgr acts like a name server in that it knows where all the extension modules in the AppSwitch™ are located and provides an Interface object to an extension module upon request. When an extension module is not located in memory, the ModuleObjectMgr will be responsible for getting it loaded and prepared for execution. In the future, extension modules will be replaceable or added to the Background Engine dynamically by downloading the new modules directly into the

AppSwitch™. The Disaster Manager is a (place holding) capability that will be responsible for making strategic decisions in the presence of strategic disaster events that can not be handled by the Packet/Event Process or any individual module.

3 Why Ada and How It Was Applied

Ada was chosen as the programming language for AppSwitch™ software to provide high reliability and portability. This software must work right the first time and continue to execute in the presence of faults and software reconfiguration. The software for the AppSwitch™ is expected to have a long lifetime, therefore the programming language must be able to be ported between different target machines and generations of target machines. Ada has the best combination of language features for both high reliability and portability, including strong typing, object-oriented programming, multi-tasking and exception handling.

GNAT was chosen as the tool chain because it was based on GCC and GCC was targeted to the ARC processor. The Ada tools are hosted on Solaris and Linux and targeted to the Motorola MPC 860, the ARC and Linux. The tool chain is designed to operate over a network by connecting the Solaris to an AppSwitch™ through a separate PC which is running either Linux or WindowsNT™; the PC acts as a logical console to the AppSwitch™. Typically, control of the execution of the AppSwitch™ software is done with one window to the console PC for low level load and monitor control and with a second emacs window running gdb for language level load and monitor control.

3.1 Ada on the Forwarding Engine

Ada was applied very straightforwardly to the Forwarding Engine architecture. Since the main software structure is a polling loop and no interrupts are handled, only one thread is needed and, thus, the Forwarding Engine software is encapsulated in one main Ada subprogram. This requires no underlying Ada runtime system. For performance reasons, all the Application policy routines and the FastPath through the polling loop is highly optimized, hand-crafted assembly code; the rest of the software is written in Ada. The split is approximately 10% assembly code and 90% Ada.

3.2 Ada on the WAN Subsystem

Ada was also applied very straightforwardly to the WAN subsystem architecture. An Ada main subprogram encapsulates the polling loop. The interrupt to update the internal clock is handcrafted in assembly language and operates transparently to the Ada main subprogram. Consequently, there is no underlying Ada runtime system. Approximately 90% of the code is written in Ada and the rest is split between assembly code and C code.

3.3 Ada on the Background Engine

The Background Engine architecture is well suited to the use of the Ravenscar Profile. All tasks in the architecture are statically defined and never nested inside any other subprogram or task. As the overview of the architecture illustrates, the Background Engine requires a limited use of Ada tasking communication and synchronization features. There is no need for Ada tasks to directly communicate with each other, since all communication between tasks can be done by queues and signals, all of which can be implemented as protected objects. All protected objects are either entry-less or need only one entry call. The single entry protected objects are best characterized by being used as event queues, where events are enqueued by one or more tasks and are serviced by only a single task. Conforming to simple boolean variables in barrier expressions was not considered particularly onerous and there is no anticipation that requeue will be necessary. It became clear that Top Layer's Ada usage nearly matched those of the Ravenscar Profile. The existence of the Ravenscar Profile and the apparent acceptance of it (or slight variations of it) by the Ada community made a compelling argument to following its restrictions, because of the increased likelihood there will be supporting implementations.

Yet the architecture of the Background Engine differs from the Ravenscar Profile in several ways, due in large part to the fact that the Background Engine software is not strictly a hard real-time application. This is not to say that meeting deadlines isn't important but rather elimination of some restrictions permits greater flexibility in our software architecture to accommodate the dynamic nature of data communications. For more details, please refer to [1].

3.4 Extension Modules and OOP

The handling of extension modules in the software architecture makes an interesting use of the OOP features of Ada. It provided a more natural expression of the circular relationship among the extension modules, their interfaces and the ModuleObjectMgr that maintains knowledge of modules and supplies access to those modules through Interface objects. Modules provide their services through the definitions of concrete extensions of abstract Interfaces. These modules in turn register themselves with the ModuleObjectMgr. The ModuleObjectMgr then honors requests for accesses to Interfaces that the modules supply by returning the Interface objects that is generated by the requested modules. The client modules, which initiated the request for an Interface object from the server module, accesses the operations of the server module through the use of that Interface object.

3.4.1 Construction and Execution of Extension Modules

An Extension module is represented in Ada as a package. All Extension modules must have elements that identify the module, define the Interfaces it provides and support its execution. To identify an Extension module, all modules must have a Module name, which is its Ada package name and a Module version number, which is its 'Body_version attribute. To identify the services an Extension module provides, all modules must have one or more Interfaces, which are concrete type extensions of

Interface "template" types. To support the registration of the Extension module as being active, all modules must have a ModuleBody, which is a type extension introduced to enable the ModuleObjectMgr to obtain the Interfaces that the Extension module provides. The sequence of statements in the module's package body does the actual call to register the Extension module with the ModuleObjectMgr, after it has completed its own elaboration. To support the implementation of the Extension module and its services, modules will also need StateBlock objects which are structures that contain execution state and, optionally, tasks, queues, other protected objects to support the implementation of the module.

The package will contain the following elements:

- One or more concrete extensions of Interface "template" types that the module provides (such as MyStreamDispatchIF or MyStreamClientIF)
- One or more concrete type extensions of StateBlockType to hold module state data (such as MainStateType and ConnectionStateType)
- Concrete type extension of the ModuleBody type (MyModuleBody)

Note the visible package specification must NOT contain any declaration of state, namely, no variables, constants or named numbers. The package body will contain the following elements:

- All implementations of concrete Interface "template" type extensions (such as MyStreamDispatchIF or MyStreamClientIF)
- All implementations of concrete StateBlockType extensions (such as MainStateType and ConnectionStateType)
- Implementation of the concrete ModuleBody type extension (MyModuleBody)
- (optionally) Tasks, queues and other protected objects
- Global values that describe the name and other attributes of the module
- Elaboration code to register the ModuleBody object for the module (Elaboration)

Additional library packages/subprograms may be imported ("with'd") to support the module's implementation. Of course, no extension module may be imported ("with'd") by any other modules.

3.4.2 ModuleBody Type and Class

ModuleBody roots a class of objects that are uniquely associated with all the Extension modules. For each Extension module, there will be a concrete type extension of the root type, ModuleBody, called MyModuleBody and there will be one MyModuleBodyObject declared for that module. It is MyModuleBodyObject that is used to complete the registration of the active Extension module. There are two abstract operations defined for all ModuleBody objects:

- MakeAnInterface: Creates an Interface object (in an Interface "template" class) that enables the client to access the module's implementation of that Interface "template"; the client must submit the ID of the Interface "template".
- IsAnInterface: Validates whether the module produced that Interface object.

No additional operations or additional components are permitted in any extension of ModuleBody type. All operations dispatch on access to an object in the ModuleBody class.

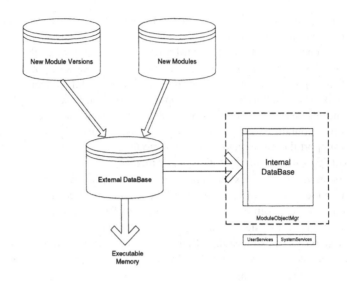

Fig. 3. The Module Object Manager

3.4.3 Module Object Manager

The ModuleObjectMgr is the Core software component that makes Extension modules active and accessible to other Extension modules through Interface objects that the modules provide. The figure above shows the major elements that ModuleObjectMgr handles. ModuleObjectMgr performs the following major services:

- Creates an Internal DataBase of ModuleObjects for all Extension modules from the External DataBase of all Extension modules.
- Downloads and dynamic binds all the executable code of all requested (active) ModuleObjects. The dynamically binding is limited to resolving all external references in the loaded executable code and to finding the adainit and adafinal entry points for the executable code.
- Adds, upon request, new Extension modules and new versions of existing Extension modules to both the External and Internal DataBases.
- Deletes, upon request, Extension modules from the External and Internal DataBases.
- Supports interface services to other modules

A ModuleObject is fully active when its execution code is loaded and bound in memory and there is a valid reference to its ModuleBodyObject.

The usual interface provides the average client module with the following important operations:

- GetIF: Return an Interface object (in the class associated with an Interface "template" type that is identified by its InterfaceID) from the ModuleBody for the ModuleObject, which is identified by the Ada package name for that module.

- GetAnotherIF: Return another Interface object (in the class associated with an Interface "template" type that is identified by its InterfaceID) from the ModuleBody for the ModuleObject through the use of an existing Interface object.
- RegisterModuleBody: Notify the ModuleObjectMgr that the module has completed elaboration and the ModuleObject is fully active.

3.4.4 Interfaces

All Interfaces that a module provides are concrete type extensions of Interface "template" types in the Interface class. This section explains the relationship among Interface class, Interface "template" types, Interface objects and modules.

3.4.5 Interface Class

The abstract Interface type roots a hierarchical class of Interface objects and defines what the Interface objects contain and specifies a basic set of very general operations that all Interface objects must have. All Interface objects contain a reference to the ModuleObject that provides the actual Interface and a reference to the StateBlock object of state data that supports the implementation of that Interface. Among basic set operations that all Interface objects provide are:

- GetState: Return the StateBlock object for the Interface object
- GetModule: Return the ModuleObject for the Interface object
- Release: Deallocate the Interface object

All of the basic operations have meaningful implementations and none of them are permitted to be overridden by type extensions of the Interface class.

At the next level in the Interface class are the abstract Interface "template" types. These "template" types are where the unique operations for module Interfaces are defined. Each "template" type (an example is StreamDispatchIF) defines all the operations that concrete type extensions of this "template" type must provide; thus the "template" type roots the "subclass" of Interface objects that support concrete implementations of those operations defined by the "template" type. Like the Interface type, Interface "template" types are abstract and no object of an Interface "template" type can be declared. The operations defined for each "template" type may be either to be abstract or to be a "null" implementation. The choice is dependent on how often the operations of the concrete type extensions of the "template" type are overridden. If the operations are going to be overridden most of the time then that should indicate that the primitive "template" operation should be abstract.

At the bottom level of the Interface hierarchy are the concrete type extensions of the Interface "template" types. If a module wishes to provide an Interface like that defined by a Interface "template" type, it must declare a concrete type extension of that Interface "template" type. Each concrete type extension (an example is MyStreamDispatchIf, an extension of StreamDispatchIF) of an Interface "template" type provides the actual implementations for all "template" operations it overrides. The Interface objects are typed by exactly one of these concrete type extensions.

In this manner when a client module wishes to use an operation defined by an Interface "template" type and implemented by a specific Extension module, the client simply calls that operation on the Interface object provided by that Extension module and the operation will dispatch to the corresponding implementation.

3.4.6 Final Note on the Extension Modules

The concept of the extension module bears a lot of similarities to the partition concept in Ada. Top Layer intends to take advantage of that similarity. Top Layer will expand the implementation of our Ada runtime system to handle extension modules like partitions by adding processes to encapsulate the execution of the extension module. Whether the extension module/partition/process expands to handle distribution remains to be seen.

4 Lessons Learned

Ada has contributed to success meeting our nine-month development. But it required effort to make Ada successful. This last section describes how Top Layer Networks faced challenges to using Ada and some of the lessons that have been learned.

4.1 Obstacles

Top Layers faced three significant challenges to successfully use Ada:
- Learning curve
- Incomplete tool chain for the ARC processor
- Inadequate runtime system operating system for the ARC

Ada is not the programming language for building data communication product software. Here, C rules. Outside of the CTO, there was no one who had any knowledge let alone experience using Ada. To the very experienced and talente software engineers, Ada was an unnecessary challenge that would not add value to their resumes. Considering these circumstances, the learning curve was indeed steep.

Top Layer faced this challenge in three ways. First, the founders convinced themselves that Ada was the appropriated choice and then stuck with it. There was a top down and unwavering commitment to Ada. Second, a full-time Ada expert was hired to provide intensive internal training in Ada and advocacy, among other duties. The result was nearly a personalized education for all the software engineers. It helped that the Ada expert was working along side the other engineers and "felt their pain". Finally, Top Layer went to extra lengths to make Ada work technically on the target systems, thereby providing a trusted and well-performing tool chain avoiding further resistance and frustration to learning.

The Ada tool chain was not complete for the ARC processor. At the beginning of 1998, there did exist a GCC back end targeted to the ARC processor, in the Free Software Foundation archives, but it was only partially completed. After investigating several alternatives, Top Layer decided in the early Fall of 1998 to shoulder the completion of the GCC backend on its own but not without the able assistance of two experienced consultants on GCC technology. The development of the GCC backend was done in two stages. Patches were made to the existing GCC backend tables to correct the most egregious problems. Then, a whole new set of GCC tables were created to more systematically and efficiently target the GCC to the ARC. At the time of this writing, the new GCC target was being tested. The effort has paid off, with both technical and morale benefits.

The only public domain Ada runtime system targeted to embedded systems, RTEMS [2], was assessed as being too general and excessive for use on the Background Engine. Furthermore the level of effort to integrate RTEMS with our target and to trim it down to meet our simplified usage was considered to be as large as a new implementation of a Ravenscar Profile runtime system. And we would never know as much about it as we would know about the custom implementation. After careful consideration, Top Layer decided that it possessed uniquely experienced engineering talent along with having close cooperation with Ada Core Technologies, capable of tackling an Ada runtime implementation effort. The effort to build and test the runtime software took about 16 weeks of time, performed by two engineers [1]. All in all, we strongly believe that our investment in the whole effort was well justified for both technical and economic reasons.

4.2 Lessons Learned

The following is a partial collection of lessons and experienced learned, appearing in no specific order:

- Beside the restrictions of the Ravenscar Profile, here is a partial list of other features of the language that are either not used or have very limited use:
  - Real types - floating point operations are too expensive; Duration is permitted for use in the predefined time operations
  - Annexes F, G - not applicable to this application.
  - Predefined I/O - too heavyweight; instead a low-level I/O package was built atop the existing flash disk device module.
  - Annexes E, H - not yet applicable to this application; depending on the direction of our product line and the implementing technology, Top Layer may revisit this decision.
  - Function returning unconstrained objects - these function must use a secondary stack which is considered unnecessarily expensive; this prevents the use of the catenation operator on dynamically sized strings.
  - Dynamic slices and aggregates - lack of optimizations makes these features very expensive
  - Length attribute - Surprisingly, when this feature is applied to dynamically sized arrays, it becomes very expensive due to testing for zero length arrays
- The following features have seen limited use, due in large part to lack of user confidence in their knowledge of the feature
  - Child generic units
  - Formal package parameters
  - Use type clauses
- The following features have received significant use:
  - OOP - reinforced relationships among modules, interfaces and state blocks

- Root_Storage_Pool class - important mechanism for supporting total memory management
- Controlled and Limited_Controlled class - another important mechanism in managing memory
- Interfacing to C - there is lots of legacy and third-party software
- All the representation and hardware interface features - obvious
- Assert pragma - GNAT implementation defined feature that has proven its worth during testing time and time again

- Ada provides too many choices for the new and average user of the language. It is frustrating to the new user to understand the subtleties of the many language choices. Too many times, new users make incorrect choices, which results in poor performances and reinforces the image that Ada is a bloated language. Therefore it is imperative to define guidelines for successful use of Ada that are tailored to the application area and the tool chain.
- There are no free compilers for industrial strength software development, as Top Layer has clearly demonstrated. Deal with it...by buying proper support maintenance and by dedicating singly focused resources to make the tool chains work for software development.
- Workstation-based tool chains are not necessarily compatible with the needs of embedded software. A tool chain that is targeted to a work station simply has more horsepower and resources and a lack of demand that highly influence the implementation choices in the tool chain. Those implementations choices deprive the embedded software product the optimizations that are dearly need. The result is that embedded software development must make unnecessary restrictions on language features to get the job done.
- New language users find the Ada compiler very frustrating to use. They are used to other languages whose compilers are less niggling. It is important to support the new user through this period of adjustment with constant assurance that all this niggling will be worth it when the software is being debugged and tested. Also, more informative compiler diagnostics and starting the user with guidelines for good language feature choices are very useful too.
- Be wary of the size of the footprint of generic instantiations. A generic that is instantiated often can consume lots of memory. In this case, it is worthwhile re-examining the design of the generic implementation to find a "shared" code kernel, to reduce the footprint of the instantiations.

References

1. Kamrad, M, Spinney, B.: An Ada Runtime System Implementation of the Ravenscar Profile for High Speed Application-Layer Data Switch
2. On-Line Application Research Corporation: Real-Time Executive for Military Systems: Ada Applications User's Guide. Release 3.2.X, May 1995.

Ada Binding to a Shared Object Layer

Johann Blieberger[1], Johann Klasek[1], and eva Kühn[2]

[1] Institute of Computer-Aided Automation, Technical University Vienna,
Treitlstr. 1/1831, A-1040 Vienna, Austria ({blieb,jk}@auto.tuwien.ac.at)
[2] Institute of Computer Languages, Technical University Vienna, Argentinierstr. 8,
A-1040 Vienna, Austria (eva@complang.tuwien.ac.at)

Abstract. CORSO, a coordination system for virtual shared memory, allows bindings to different programming languages. Currently C, C++, Java, VisualBasic, and Oracle's Developer2000 are supported. We implement an Ada binding to CORSO, thus opening the area of virtual shared memory to the Ada world. Our Ada CORSO binding enhances Ada with transaction-oriented, fault-tolerant, distributed objects in a straight-forward way without having to extend the Ada language.

1 A Layered Approach

In distributed and heterogeneous environments some technique is desirable to shield the attributes of distributed objects like location, replication, representation and persistency from the programmer. Different approaches exist and the relation between them points to some kind of orthogonality. The most common pattern seem to be the message passing versus virtual shared memory (VSM) paradigm.

VSM neither intends to replace nor to exclude message passing architectures like CORBA or DCOM. In contrast, VSM should be seen as an additional layer providing enhanced mechanisms to the programmer.

Specifically in Ada's case, a binding to a VSM increases functionality and facilitates developing distributed applications, despite the fact that a variety of Ada built-in features and annexes in the Ada standard are available. The following issues are to mention:

- Communication, data sharing, and persistence has not to be implemented by means of standard Ada but can be put under coordination of a VSM system where several other languages and system architectures are glued together.
- The symmetric property of a VSM covers the actual needs of an application well. Particular subtasks can be implemented by the best-suited language, e.g. core development in Ada for safety critical parts and GUI development using Java.

The remaining paper is organised as follows: Section 2 overviews shared object paradigms. Section 3 presents concepts of CORSO, a virtual shared object layer developed at the *Institute of Computer Languages* at the *Technical University Vienna* and now made available commercially by *Tecco Coordination*

Systems, Vienna. Technical aspects of CORSO are revealed in Section 4. Our Ada binding to CORSO is described in Section 5. Pros and cons of our binding can be found in Section 6 where we also compare our binding to other language bindings and conclude the paper.

There have been other implementations of VSM in Ada, namely of the Linda tuple space (cf. [5–7]). All these implementations are stand-alone Ada implementations which lack the multi-language support of CORSO. In addition, the features offered by Linda are only a subset of CORSO's functionality.

2 Shared Objects

For the communication and synchronisation of distributed systems there exist two paradigms: *Message Passing* versus a *Virtual Shared Memory.*

2.1 Message Passing

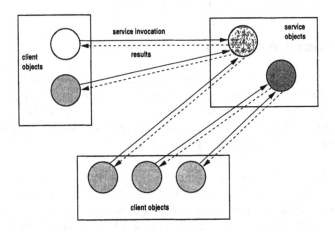

Fig. 1. Message Passing Paradigm

The classical and commercially wide-spread approach is the message passing paradigm. Processes communicate through the explicit (a-)synchronous sending and receiving of messages. The remote procedure call (RPC) is a two-way communication. The highest abstraction of the message passing paradigm are *distributed object* systems like CORBA and DCOM, where object methods can be invoked at remote sites which also results in a two-way communication pattern. Ada's Distributed Systems Annex (see [4]) also favours message passing. Application programs need to be aware of message sending or remote service invocation which means that e.g. fault tolerance has to be implemented explicitly into each distributed application. Adding and/or removing sites from the network of the distributed application has also to be considered explicitly

Moreover, such systems do not cache data fields locally which makes data field access expensive, because it requires an expensive remote procedure call.

Even if the same data fields have been used before by a client or by other clients at the same site, they must be fetched again. Because of the lack of replication and caching support, hierarchical client/server structures are built, although, they bear the disadvantage of a bottleneck w.r.t. performance and availability.

2.2 Virtual Shared Memory

Virtual shared memory offers a conceptually higher level of abstraction than message passing. It provides the vision of a common shared object space to which all participating, distributed and parallel executing processes have a consistent view. The *shared data objects* are used for communication between and synchronisation of parallel and distributed processes. VSM extends local memory to the memories of all sites where processes are running. This approach naturally hides heterogenous parts of the network from the programmer. Shared data objects relieve the application programmer from caching and replication issues. They allow the design of symmetric application architectures, thus avoiding the client/server bottleneck.

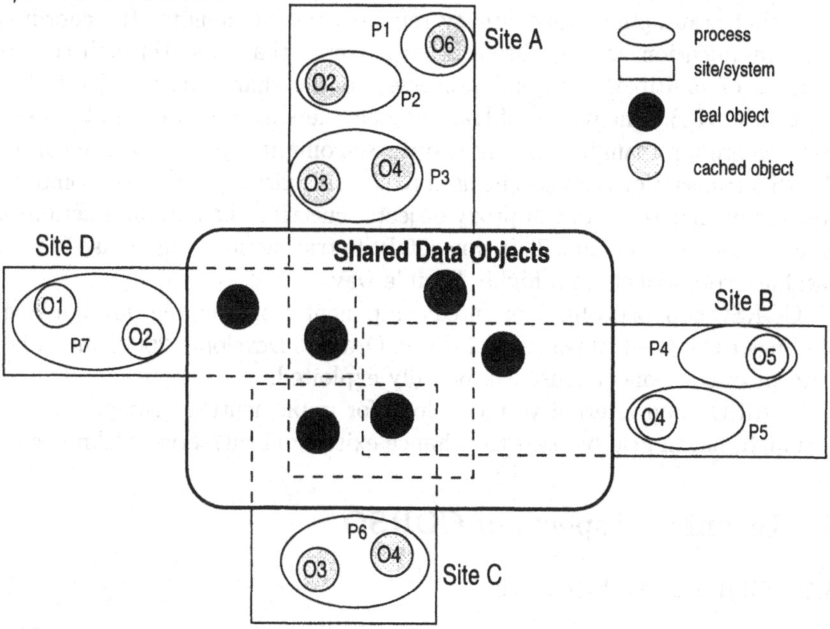

Fig. 2. Virtual Shared Memory Paradigm

Virtual shared memory is a new technology that goes beyond the possibilities offered by message passing. Its advantages concerning its conceptually higher abstraction of the underlying hardware, and its advantages concerning caching and replication have intensively been discussed in scientific literature (see e.g. [1–3]). An obvious tendency towards virtual shared memory replacing or accompanying client/server technology can be observed.

3 CORSO concepts

CORSO is a layered software component for the development of robust and parallel applications that supports the virtual shared memory paradigm. It has been developed at the *Institute of Computer Languages* at the *Technical University Vienna* and now commercially made available by *Tecco Coordination Systems, Vienna*. The granularity of sharing are data objects instead of entire memory pages, which makes CORSO suitable for all different kinds of distributed application scenarios. The shared objects serve for the communication and synchronisation between the parallel, concurrent and distributed processes.

CORSO is not only a pure memory model. It also supports complex coordination patterns on the shared objects through an advanced transaction and process model. Transactions serve to coordinate accesses to shared objects and to make shared objects persistent. Processes are used to reason about concurrency and parallelism and define the checkpoints for recovery.

CORSO meets the following requirements posed by the heterogeneity of distributed applications: It shields location, migration, replication, access, transaction, failure, representation, and persistency requirements from the programmer. Note that transaction transparency refers to transactions for the coordination of communication and synchronisation patterns that arise through concurrent accesses of multiple users and processes to the shared data objects. In contrast, in CORBA the notion of transactions refers to transactions at application level, where for example existing two-phase-commit components are controlled. CORSO transactions can also be used to control existing two-phase-commit components in that they control proxy objects reflecting the data and actions to be taken by the components. This way, CORSO transactions can be used to control database components in a highly flexible way.

CORSO supports object-oriented component programming through language bindings to C, C++, Java, Visual Basic, Oracle's Developer 2000, and Ada. The concept of component reuse can be fully exploited.

CORSO is an alternative technology for implementing distributed systems, although, it can also be used to enhance existing client/server technologies.

4 Technical Aspects of CORSO

4.1 CORSO Architecture

A distributed CORSO application consists of local software systems (LSYS) on which application processes are running. These application processes can use the functionality offered by CORSO and are termed CORSO processes. They are written in one of the programming languages, to which CORSO supports language bindings. A programming language "L" extended by CORSO features is termed "L&Co" which stands for "L plus Coordination". Currently, C&Co, C++&Co, Java&Co, VisualBasic&Co and Developer2000&Co are supported. The language bindings come in form of CORSO language libraries/classes. We are adding Ada&Co to the above list.

4.2 Interface Definition Language (IDL)

CORSO objects can be shared between different language paradigms across heterogeneous platforms that may differ in their representation of data. To make sure that data are understood correctly at each site, internally an interface definition language (IDL) is used. The Coordination Kernel automatically interprets and converts all information it receives from other Coordination Kernels. If a LSYS connects to a Coordination Kernel from a remote site that uses other data type formats, it also automatically converts these data. Application programs are thus portable across all platforms.

Depending on the capabilities of the host language, the employment of the IDL is more or less visible for the programmer. For example, in Java&Co un-/marshalling is done completely automatically so that the existence of the IDL is not evident at all, whereas in C&Co, the marshalling and unmarshalling is done via format commands. The IDL supports data terms of the following basic types:

- Integer: 32-bit integer value.
- Character: 8-bit byte value.
- String: 0-terminated character string.
- Raw: character string that may contain also the 0-character.
- Object identification (OID): unique reference to an object in the VSM. Pointers in local memory are generalised to OIDs.
- Structure: data structure that optionally may be given a name and that is composed of n members. Each member is an IDL-term.
- Stream: data type that is in particular useful for communication purposes. Internally it is a structure consisting of 2 components. The first component is termed head and the second one is termed tail. The head is of any IDL type and contains the user data. A single OID in the tail part acts as link to the next element in the stream. Streams can be conceptually seen as infinite coordination structures that are useful for communicating objects from a producer to a consumer in an obvious "UNIX pipe"-like way.

4.3 Object Sharing

The IDL is used to access and manipulate CORSO objects. Since these objects are usually cached—which is a big performance gain over simple two-way communication—the transaction concept ensures consistency with global virtual shared memory. Arbitrary communication patterns can be defined by selecting the proper coordination data structures composed of shared and nested objects. Different caching strategies are provided which may be selected on a per-object basis depending on the actual access frequency. For example if an object which is rarely written has been (partially) changed, it is automatically propagated to the cache of all current readers.

A variant of CORSO transactions are subtransactions which allow nesting of transactions. Every distributed task can be put under transaction control according to the ACID properties (atomicity, consistency, isolation, durability). Instead of dealing with a big single transaction which may fail or not, one can subdivide it into several subtransactions. The transaction scenario can be spread over several sites, where so called transaction dependent processes are responsible for handling such remote subtransactions. A successful subtransaction is able to provide its results independently of the success of all enclosing transactions. As a consequence a normal rollback of an enclosing transaction is no longer feasible. To guarantee atomicity of the transaction the effects of subtransactions must be compensated at least in a semantic manner. For this purpose special compensate actions can be defined.

Another aspect of transactions is synchronising CORSO processes. CORSO styled interprocess communication is based on transactions upon shared objects in a symmetric kind. CORSO stream objects can be used to implement a communication with properties similar to queues or pipes. Write operations under transaction control in conjunction with synchronous reads are the main constructs to obtain this kind of communication (comp. Section 5.4). CORSO processes can also be used to simulate a remote procedure call: a shared object incorporates input data, a method identification for the remote site, and the result from the method invocation.

5 Ada Binding to CORSO

The primary task in implementing a binding to CORSO is to build a LSYS in Ada. This task can be subdivided into

1. Declaring Ada-conforming IDL data types as can be found in Section 4.2.
2. Implementing marshalling and unmarshalling operations for these types*.
3. Providing an Ada interface to CORSO processes and transactions.

Task 1 is done by defining an abstract tagged CORSO base type, from which the IDL types are derived.

Task 2 is done by implementing read and write attributes for all IDL types. Currently we do not support input and output attributes because the CORSO IDL types are elementary types only which do not profit from Ada's higher representation issues of input and output attributes. Details can be found in Section 5.1.

We implement Task 3 via a "thin binding" which is based on C&Co and is generated semi-automatically with help of the c2ada-tool developed by Intermetrics. This however is not directly presented to the programmer.

5.1 IDL Types and Marshalling

This section describes how the CORSO IDL types are implemented in the Ada binding. How this is done is shown by one example, the type CoKeInt. For the other types listed in Section 4.2 the binding is similar. Package CoKe shown in

---

* These operations are needed to convert IDL types to their "internal" representation.

269

Program 1 Package Coke

```
package CoKe is
  type Comm_type is (const, var, stream);
end Coke;
```

Program 1 gives the root of the Ada CoKe library tree and also contains the declaration of the communication types of CORSO objects. These are `const`, which means the object is written only once, but can be read arbitrarily often, `var`, which means it can be read and written arbitrarily often, and `stream`, which allows for communicating objects from a producer to a consumer in an obvious "UNIX pipe"-like way. Program 2 shows the declaration of type

---

Program 2 Package Coke.Base.Attribute

```
with Ada.Streams, CoKe.Base.Streams;
package CoKe.Base.Attribute is
  type CoKeBaseAttribute is abstract new CokeBase with private;
private
  type CoKeBaseAttribute is abstract new CokeBase with
    record
      Strm: CoKe.Base.Streams.CoKe_Stream_AD;
    end record;
  procedure Read(
      Stream: access Ada.Streams.Root_Stream_Type'CLASS;
      Item: out CoKeBaseAttribute);
  for CoKeBaseAttribute'Read use Read;
  procedure Write(
      Stream: access Ada.Streams.Root_Stream_Type'CLASS;
      Item: in CoKeBaseAttribute);
  for CoKeBaseAttribute'Write use Write;
end CoKe.Base.Attribute;
```

`CoKeBaseAttribute` which forms the base type of all IDL types. Note the procedures `Read` and `Write` in the private part. These and similar procedures defined for the other IDL types perform marshalling and unmarshalling, such that the user of the Ada binding to CORSO can do reading from and writing to the shared memory pool via Ada's read and write attributes in a fairly transparent way.

Package `CoKe.Base.Streams` contains the declaration of type `CoKe_Stream` and some internals of the Ada binding, which is not shown explicitly.

Program 3 shows the generic package for creating objects of type `CoKeInt`, the type used for handling integer types in CORSO. Our current binding does not support operations for IDL types. Thus they can only be used for communication purposes. A later release, however, will provide suitable operations for all IDL types.

Package `Shared` shown in Program 4 is used for building instances of objects being in the shared memory pool. Objects of type `shared` can be equipped with an OID. In contrast to the `Read` and `Write` operations in Program 2 the

---

Program 3 Package Coke.Base.Attribute.CoKeInt

```ada
generic
   type Int is range <>;
package CoKe.Base.Attribute.CoKeInt is
   type CoKeInt is new CoKeBaseAttribute with private;
   procedure Int_to_CoKeInt(from: Int; to: out CokeInt);
   function CoKeInt_to_Int(from: CokeInt) return Int;
private
   type CoKeInt is new CoKeBaseAttribute with
      record
        I: Int;
      end record;
   procedure Read(
        Stream: access Ada.Streams.Root_Stream_Type'CLASS;
        Item: out CoKeInt);
   for CoKeInt'Read use Read;
   procedure Write(
        Stream: access Ada.Streams.Root_Stream_Type'CLASS;
        Item: in CoKeInt);
   for CoKeInt'Write use Write;
end CoKe.Base.Attribute.CoKeInt;
```

Program 4 Package Shared

```ada
with Ada.Streams, CoKe.Base.Attribute, CoKe.Base.Attribute.CoKeOid;
generic
   type Base is new CoKe.Base.Attribute.CoKeBaseAttribute with private;
   Comm_type: CoKe.Comm_type;
package Shared is
   package Oid renames CoKe.Base.Attribute.CoKeOid;
   type Shared is new Base with private;
   procedure Set_Oid(
        Obj: in out Shared;
        the_Oid: Oid.CoKeOid := Oid.Create_Oid);
   function Get_Oid(Obj: Shared) return Oid.CoKeOid;
private
   type Shared is new Base with
      record
        the_Oid: Oid.CoKeOid;
      end record;
   procedure Read(
        Stream: access Ada.Streams.Root_Stream_Type'CLASS;
        Item: out Shared);
   for Shared'Read use Read;
   procedure Write(
        Stream: access Ada.Streams.Root_Stream_Type'CLASS;
        Item: in Shared);
   for Shared'Write use Write;
end Shared;
```

---

corresponding procedures in this package not only perform (un-)marshalling, but they also read/write the corresponding objects from/to the shared memory pool, where they are identified by their unique OID. The basic IDL type Oid is defined in package CoKe.Base.Attribute.CoKeOid which is not explicitly shown here.

5.2 Transactions

Shared objects can be combined with transactions. This is again done using standard object-oriented features of Ada, i.e., using generics and tagged types (cf. Program 5). In general all transactions are put under control of the trans-

---

Program 5 Package Tx

```
with Ada.Streams, Shared, Transaction_Mgt;
generic
  with package Some_Shared is new Shared(<>);
package Tx is
  type Txed is new Some_Shared.Shared with private;
  procedure Set_Tx(
      Obj: in out Txed;
      the_Tx: Transaction_Mgt.Tx);
  function Get_Tx(Obj: Txed) return Transaction_Mgt.Tx;
private
  type Txed is new Some_Shared.Shared with
    record
      the_Tx: Transaction_Mgt.Tx;
    end record;
  procedure Read(
      Stream: access Ada.Streams.Root_Stream_Type'CLASS;
      Item: out Txed);
  for Txed'Read use Read;
  procedure Write(
      Stream: access Ada.Streams.Root_Stream_Type'CLASS;
      Item: in Txed);
  for Txed'Write use Write;
end Tx;
```

---

action manager in package Transaction_Mgt. This manager provides the basic types and functionality to control transactions. By means of the generic package Tx the transaction semantics can be attached to any shared object type. Accessing an object of this new type (using Read and Write operations) remains the same, except of adding transaction properties to it.

To establish a transaction at first a transaction object has to be aquired from the transaction manager using function Create_TX (as shown in Program 9 later). Procedure Set_Tx binds this newly opened transaction to the shared object. Get_Tx is provided as counterpart to procedure Set_Tx for completeness only.

5.3 The LSYS

In order to implement a CORSO application, one has to register the processes in the LSYS. Our binding allows this to be done via package `CoKe.Entries` shown in Program 6. All CORSO processes are in fact Ada procedures of the form

---

Program 6 Package CoKe.Entries

```
with CoKe.Base.Attribute;
package CoKe.Entries is
  type Proc_Ptr is access
    procedure(Param: CoKe.Base.Attribute.CoKeBaseAttribute'CLASS);
  type CoKeBaseAttribute_AD is
    access all CoKe.Base.Attribute.CoKeBaseAttribute'CLASS;
  procedure Add_CoKe_Entry(
    Name: string;
    Run: Proc_Ptr);
  procedure Start_CoKe_Entry(
    Name: string;
    Param: CoKeBaseAttribute_AD);
end CoKe.Entries;
```

`Proc_Ptr`. The parameter `Param` can be used to pass arbitrarily complex data structures using the IDL type `CoKeStruct`.

How these pieces fit together is shown in Section 5.4 where the well-known producer/consumer problem is solved via the Ada CORSO Binding.

5.4 The Producer/Consumer Example

The procedures `Producer` and `Consumer` are given in Program 9 and 10, respectively. The instance of `CoKeInt` used in Program 9 is depicted in Program 7, equipping this type with a transaction is shown in Program 8.

Program 7 Package My_SharedCoKeInt

```
with Coke, My_CoKeInt, Shared;
package My_SharedCoKeInt is new Shared(My_CoKeInt.CokeInt,CoKe.stream);
```

Program 8 Package My_TxedSharedCoKeInt

```
with My_SharedCoKeInt, Tx;
package My_TxedSharedCoKeInt is new Tx(My_SharedCoKeInt);
```

Via calls to `CoKe.Entries.Add_CoKe_Entry` these procedures are registered as CORSO processes. Before that, connection to the LSYS has been established by a call to `LSYSConnect`. The procedures (CORSO processes) are then executed by `CreateIndependentProcess` which is given the name-strings "producer" and "consumer", respectively. In addition to that an identical OID is passed to both processes, which identifies the shared object stream used for communication.

Program 9 Procedure Producer

---

with CoKe.Base.Attribute.CoKeOid, CoKe.Base.Streams, My_SharedCoKeInt,
My_TxedSharedCoKeInt, Transaction_Mgt;
use CoKe.Base.Attribute.CoKeOid, CoKe.Base.Streams, My_SharedCoKeInt,
My_TxedSharedCoKeInt, Transaction_Mgt;

```
procedure Producer(Param: CoKe.Base.Attribute.CoKeBaseAttribute'CLASS)
is
   data: My_TxedSharedCoKeInt.Txed;
   CoKe_Strm: aliased CoKe_Stream;
   Oid: CoKeOid := CoKeOid(Param);
begin
   Set_Oid(Shared(data), Oid);       -- attach Oid we have got from Param to data
   for i in 1..3 loop
     Int_to_CoKeInt(from => i, to => data);
     declare
       topTx: Tx := Create_TX;              -- create and open a transaction
     begin
       Set_Tx(data,topTx);                  -- attach transaction to data
       loop
         Txed'WRITE(CoKe_Strm'access, data);      -- write data to VSM
         exit when Commit(topTx);            -- exit if everything is okay
         Cancel(topTx);           -- cancel transaction if something went wrong
       end loop;
     end;
   end loop;
   Process_Commit;                          -- exit in commit state
end Producer;
```

Program 10 Procedure Consumer

---

with CoKe.Base.Attribute.CoKeOid, CoKe.Base.Streams, My_SharedCoKeInt,
Text_IO;
use CoKe.Base.Attribute.CoKeOid, CoKe.Base.Streams, My_SharedCoKeInt;

```
procedure Consumer(Param: CoKe.Base.Attribute.CoKeBaseAttribute'CLASS)
is
   data: shared;
   CoKe_Strm: aliased CoKe_Stream;
   Oid: CoKeOid := CoKeOid(Param);
begin
   Set_Oid(Shared(data), Oid);       -- attach Oid we have got from Param to data
   for i in 1..3 loop
     Shared'READ(CoKe_Strm'access, data);         -- read data from VSM
     Text_IO.Put_Line(integer'IMAGE(CoKeInt_to_Int(data)));
   end loop;
   Process_Commit;                          -- exit in commit state
end Consumer;
```

The calls to `CreateIndependentProcess` can even be done from programs not written in Ada. Note that the two procedures `Producer` and `Consumer` may reside on different sites in the network, too. Procedure `Process_Commit` serves as indication for the transaction manager how to proceed with the transaction.

6 Discussion and Conclusion

There is only one disadvantage of our Ada CORSO binding, namely that Ada's tasks cannot be used directly as CORSO processes. Nevertheless tasks can be used freely within a CORSO process. By the way, Java&Co suffers from the same problem.

We have found that Ada's read and write attributes are very useful to incorporate access to objects in a shared memory pool.

Transactions have not been considered in the Ada Reference Manual until now. Our Ada CORSO binding enhances Ada with transaction-oriented, fault-tolerant, distributed objects in a straight-forward way without having to extend the Ada language.

Compared to other language bindings, we see that Ada's generics and tagged types provide an excellent means to correctly model the interdependency between IDL types, the shared object paradigm, and transactions. For example Java&Co lacks multiple inheritance and thus cannot model this interdependency in an accurate way. C++&Co heavily uses multiple inheritance for this purpose but is less readable than Ada (at least for an Ada person).

The CORSO layer supports a comprehensive programming model for distributed, parallel and concurrent programming. It supports the virtual shared memory approach and in addition an advanced transaction/process model. Providing an Ada binding to CORSO opens the area of virtual shared memory to the Ada world.

References

1. D. E. Bakken, *Supporting fault-tolerant parallel programming in LINDA*, Ph.D. thesis, University of Arizona, Department of Computer Science, 1994.
2. M. R. Eskicioglu, *A comprehensive bibliography of distributed shared memory*, Tech. Report TR96-17, University of Alberta, Edmonton, Canada, 1996.
3. eva Kühn and Georg Nozicka, *Post-client/server coordination tools*, Proc. of the Second Asian Computer Science Conference on Coordination Technology for Collaborative Applications, LNCS, Springer-Verlag, 1997.
4. ISO/IEC 8652, *Ada reference manual*, 1995.
5. Y. Kermarrec and L. Pautet, *Ada-Linda: A powerful paradigm for programming distributed Ada applications*, Proceedings of the TRI-Ada'94 conference (Baltimore, Maryland), 1994, pp. 438–445.
6. Kristina Lundqvist and Göran Wall, *Using object oriented methods in Ada 95 to implement Linda*, Proceedings of Ada-Europe'96 (Montreux, Switzerland), Springer-Verlag, 1996, pp. 211–222.
7. Göran Wall and Kristina Lundqvist, *Shared packages through Linda*, Proceedings of Ada-Europe'96 (Montreux, Switzerland), Springer-Verlag, 1996, pp. 223–234.

The Ceiling Protocol in Multi-moded Real-Time Systems

Jorge Real[1] and Andy Wellings[2]

[1]*Dept. de Informática de Sistemas y Computadores. Universidad Politécnica de Valencia, Spain*
[2]*Department of Computer Science. University of York, UK*
email: jorge@disca.upv.es, andy@cs.york.ac.uk

Abstract. Fixed-priority scheduling has become a very important approach for implementing real-time systems. Two key aspects of the method are its support for resource management using priority inheritance protocols and its ability to model modes of operation. In this paper, we discuss the impact of mode changes on the immediate inheritance priority ceiling protocol. We show that the approach adopted in Ada can result in an increased blocking time for tasks that can unnecessarily jeopardise their schedulability. We propose several solutions to help solve this problem.

1. Introduction

In 1973, Liu and Layland [1] presented the Rate Monotonic scheme for assigning fixed priorities to tasks in a real-time system. This approach provides a relative ordering for the tasks depending on their period of execution. Fixed-priority pre-emptive schedulers are not difficult to implement and this approach has thus become very important. The initial Rate Monotonic method imposed several restrictions to the set of tasks, such as task independence, no sporadic tasks, periods equal to deadlines, etc. Several researchers have dropped these restrictions. One of the most important restrictions was task independence, which prevented tasks from sharing resources, leading to an unrealistic model. The work by Sha *et al* [2] removed this restriction by using priority inheritance protocols, that is, dynamically increasing the priority of tasks when they are locking a resource, allowing them to rapidly releasing the resource, and finally restoring the original task's priority. Among the priority inheritance family of protocols, the *Immediate Inheritance of the Priority Ceiling Protocol* [3] (IIPCP, for short) is based on using a priority for the resources that will be immediately inherited by the tasks when they access the resource. This priority is chosen to be equal to the highest priority of the tasks that share the resource and it is called the *ceiling priority* of the resource. The IIPCP prevents unbounded priority inversion from happening at run time, allowing a static analysis to account for the worst-case blocking time for a task, due to the effect of resource sharing. This approach has influenced the design of the Ada 95 [4] and POSIX® 1003.1 [5] standards, both of which have included priority inheritance protocols in some way.

In addition, many real-time systems have various mutually exclusive operating modes [6]. In our view, an operating mode is characterised by a set of active tasks.

J. Real is partially funded with a grant from the *Vicerrectorado de Investigación* of the *Universidad Politécnica de Valencia* and by the Valencian Government's project GV-C-CN-05-085-96. It was mostly undertaken during a visit of J. Real to the RTS Research Group in the University of York.

These tasks might or might not be active in other operating modes. Furthermore, a task can have different temporal behaviour across operating modes, such as a different period or deadline. This approach allows one to deal with the design of a complex system by decomposing the system into multiple operating modes in which it can work; these modes being analysable as separate, simpler systems, in which only the needed components appear. A common example is the control system for an aircraft, which can work in modes like take-off, level flight and landing, making use of different software components which act upon different resources such as the brakes, automatic pilot, trimming, etc.

The existence of different operating modes can lead to different ceilings for the resources, as some tasks are active and some others are not in different operating modes. Furthermore, the ability to change task attributes such as the deadline or the period can lead to a task having different priorities in different modes. One approach for managing ceiling priorities in multi-moded real-time systems is to apply the so-called *ceiling of ceilings*, that is, the highest ceiling derived from the analysis of the system in all possible operating modes. As we will show, this can lead to an excessive (though bounded) priority inversion that can make a system unschedulable.

In Ada, shared resources are implemented by means of protected objects (POs). They are both efficient to implement and secure with respect to preventing inconsistencies or race conditions. An Ada pragma allows an implementation to support IIPCP and a priority figure (the *ceiling*) can be statically assigned to each PO. When a task locks the PO, it immediately inherits its ceiling priority. In this way, the maximum time a task will have to wait because the resource is locked is bounded to the worst-case execution time of the service provided by the PO. It is important to stress that, in Ada, the PO priority can only be assigned in its specification, but it cannot be changed at run time. The reason for this is the excessive complexity and semantic ambiguities that immediately arise when trying to provide this facility. Dynamically changing a task priority is relatively easy to implement and has a very concrete meaning, affecting only that task. But changing a ceiling priority could affect the tasks queued in that object and also other objects (and queued tasks) with a former priority lower (or higher) and a new priority higher (or lower) [7].

In POSIX®, the PRIO_PROTECT option is mentioned in the standard. This option provides, among other things, the function *pthread_mutex_setprioceiling*(). According to the standard, when this function is called, the ceiling of a mutex is changed dynamically to a new value given as a parameter. Unfortunately, it is very frequent to find that POSIX implementations either do not implement the PRIO_PROTECT option or their implementation of *pthread_mutex_setprioceiling*() just changes the ceiling figure, but doesn't take into account the state of the system at the moment at which the change of ceiling is requested. Actually, when *pthread_mutex_setprioceiling*() is called, a number of tasks could be waiting queued in one or more condition variables related to the mutex (for the implementation of, say, a monitor). To implement safe and predictable ceiling changes, the implementation should review a potentially large number of queues and also provide semantics for the tasks that are queued whilst the mutex they are trying to access has changed its ceiling. Specially if the ceiling has been lowered and the task priority is higher than the new ceiling. This operation could introduce long delays. A reading of [8] can give an idea of how complex this can be for mode changes.

In summary, consistently changing the ceiling priority of a resource either introduces long delays or is not allowed by current technologies. The existence of different operating modes could make this operation desirable as having a different set of tasks in a new mode may change the priority figure for a resource's ceiling in that mode.

In the rest of this paper, we will discuss these problems in more depth and provide different ways to work around them. Section 2 presents the QUISAP model, the framework for our investigations in real-time systems. In Section 3, an example serves to illustrate how the schedulability of a system can be affected by using the IIPCP in a multi-moded system and a workaround is provided. In Section 4, a special situation that escapes the workaround is described and a new solution for the general case is proposed. Section 5 summarises our conclusions.

2. System Model and Implementation Notes

From our point of view, a real-time system is formed by *tasks*, both periodic and sporadic, and *objects*, which represent the resources and which can be shared by the tasks. This model has been implemented as an architecture for building real-time systems, named QUISAP and is described with detail in [9]. Tasks are allowed to share objects, it being the system's responsibility to provide mutual exclusion to protect them against race conditions. In practice, this feature is implemented by means of Ada protected objects. On the other side, tasks are implemented with Ada tasks. A task type defines the behaviour of tasks which are then instantiated as new tasks with their own parameters such as temporal data (period, deadline) and the procedures that comprise the cyclic actions and handlers for deadline misses and mode changes.

Defining operating modes is also allowed in QUISAP. Operating modes differ in the subset of tasks belonging to each mode (i.e., tasks that can become active while the system is running in a mode) and/or in the temporal attributes of the tasks comprising the mode. Tasks perform the same actions each time they activate, despite what the current operating mode is. Actions are user supplied as separate Ada procedures, which are restricted in the sense that they can not use tasking, protected objects or dynamic memory allocation. The synchronisation needs of the application must be covered by means of QUISAP objects.

Determinism is achieved by means of two predefined Ada pragmas. We use the pragma Task_Dispatching_Policy(Fifo_Within_Priorities) to ensure that a higher priority task will always pre-empt lower priority tasks when it becomes active. With regard to protected objects, the pragma Locking_Policy(Ceiling_Locking) is used, which ensures that the objects will behave as the IIPCP determines, to avoid unbounded priority inversion. It is to be noted that these pragmas are predefined in Ada, thus allowing a portable implementation, valid for a range of platforms.

Finally, with regard to QUISAP tasks support, a protected object with the highest priority is used to control the proper execution of the tasks and to detect and undertake mode changes when requested. We make use of the Asynchronous Transfer of Control (ATC) facility of Ada for providing mode changes. Both abortive and non-abortive models can be applied to tasks so that when a mode change occurs, running tasks can be aborted or allowed to terminate.

3. Combining the Use of Ceiling Priorities and Mode Changes

3.1 Description of the Problem

According to the model described above and its implementation in Ada, a problem arises when trying to combine both mode changes and the use of the priority ceiling protocol. We shall describe the problem by means of an example.

Table 1 shows the data for a real-time system in terms of operating modes, active tasks in each mode, their priorities and whether they use or do not use a protected object (PO) that is also present in the system. There exist two operating modes ($M1$ and $M2$), four tasks ($T1$ to $T4$) and the protected object PO. Figure 1 shows this graphically and adds timing information for the task set. For simplicity, task T_i has a priority i. The bigger the index i, the higher the priority of the task. In this figure, C, T and D represent, respectively, the worst-case computation time, the period for periodic tasks (or minimum inter-arrival time for the activation event of sporadic tasks) and the deadline.

Task	Priority in mode *M1*	Priority in mode *M2*	Uses Protected Object
T1	1	1	Yes
T2	2	2	Yes
T3	3	3	No
T4	Inactive	4	Yes

Table 1. The example task set.

The static analysis of the system would assign a ceiling priority of 2 for the protected object in mode $M1$ ($CP_{M1} = 2$). The same analysis for mode $M2$ would give a ceiling priority of 4 to the same protected object in mode $M2$ ($CP_{M2} = 4$). But this is not feasible to implement in Ada, because it implies that we are able to change the priority of the protected object dynamically, when a mode change is requested by some task.

The problem here is that a priority that applies to mode $M2$ interferes with the analysis for mode $M1$. Thus the solution to this problem has necessarily to consider the analysis of the system in all its operating modes. We have to assign a unique ceiling priority for each protected object and it has to be valid for all the operating modes.

Let M be the set of operating modes of the system. For a given protected object, let CP_m be the ceiling priority for that object when the system is executing in the operating mode m. The only priority ceiling that could be valid for all the operating modes is the so-called ceiling of ceilings, that corresponds to:

$$CP = \max_{m \in M}(CP_m). \tag{1}$$

If we choose a priority higher than CP, then we shall add blocking time to other higher priority tasks unnecessarily. If we choose it to be lower, then we are not properly applying the IIPCP. Furthermore, in Ada it is considered a program error to have a task calling a protected object whose ceiling priority is lower than the priority of the task. This situation would denote a bad analysis of the system, and thus it is caught at run time by means of a Program_Error exception.

In our example, applying equation (1) yields a priority ceiling of 4 for the protected object. This is indeed valid for mode $M2$, but not for $M1$. The consequence of having a unique ceiling priority of 4 is that in mode $M1$, task $T3$ will potentially have to wait for $T2$ or $T1$ to release the protected object because, while using PO, they will be executing at a priority 4. This is contrary to the priority assignment obtained from the static analysis for mode $M1$. Furthermore, if $T3$ has to be blocked by the use of PO by $T1$ or $T2$, then it will be unschedulable. To see this, notice $T3$'s computation time is 100. If we add the 120 time units of blocking time introduced by PO, then we have a worst-case response time of $100 + 120 = 220$ time units, which is greater than the 200 time units deadline for $T3$ in mode $M1$. Nevertheless, if $T3$ always executes at a priority higher than that of $T1$ and $T2$, then these tasks will never block $T1$ and all the tasks in this example will meet their deadlines. This example is not unrealistic: there have been described real-time systems presenting blocking times of up to 135% the computational time of a task [10].

Thus the solution begins by applying equation (1), but it does not end there. The application of (1) has no effect on the analysis for mode $M2$ because it does not affect any of the priority assignments. The negative effects are restricted to mode $M1$. In

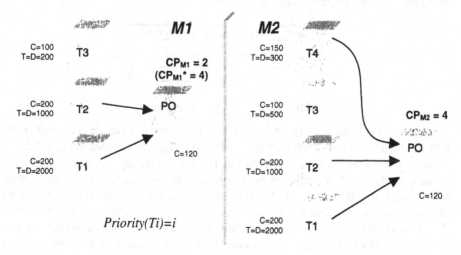

Fig. 1. The example system. CP_{M1}^{*} corresponds to re-assignment after applying Equation (1) (see below).

general, these effects will appear in all modes except those modes m, in which $CP = CP_m$, i.e., modes in which it is not necessary to change the original ceiling.

Table 2 shows the priorities of the tasks for mode $M1$ before and after re-evaluating the ceiling priority of PO according to (1). The column *Max Priority* represents the maximum active priority the task can have during its execution, which is the highest ceiling priority of the objects that the task can use.

Before (1)			After (1)		
Task	Max Priority	Priority	Task	Max Priority	Priority
T3	3	3	T3	3	3
T2	2	2	T2	4	2
T1	2	1	T1	4	1

Table 2. Effect of applying (1) in mode M1.

We see that *T3* has lost importance as a side effect of applying (1). This means at run time, that *T3* can be blocked because *T2* or *T1* are holding the resource represented by *PO* and, as a consequence of this, it could miss its deadline as shown above.

3.2. First Solution: Re-Assigning Tasks Priorities

To avoid the inversion of importance of *T3* in our example, we should assign it a new priority figure so that *T3* recovers its importance with respect to *T2* and *T1* in mode *M1*. For our purpose, the new priority has to be greater than 4. Let that new priority be 5, that is, just what we need to restore the original priority ordering of tasks for mode *M1*. Table 3 shows the new situation.

Task	Max Priority	Priority
T3	5	5
T2	4	2
T1	4	1

Table 3. Re-evaluating the priority of *T3*.

This new assignment solves the problem for this simple example: the priority for task *T3* should be 5 instead of 3 for mode *M1*. No changes are needed in mode *M2*.

In a more general situation, care must be taken when raising the priority of *T3*, because it could affect other higher priority tasks. For instance, if there were another task, say *T5*, which in mode *M1* has priority 4 and which does not use the protected object, the two units increment would wrongly make *T3* become more important than *T5*. To avoid this, we must reassign priorities for *all* the tasks with an original priority higher than *PO*'s original ceiling for mode *M1*. A similar increment in the priorities of these tasks should be made. If we have raised the priority of *T3* by Δ units (in this case $\Delta = 5 - 3 = 2$) we should do the same for *T5* which means, in this case, that *T5*'s new priority should be $4 + \Delta = 6$. This would keep the original relative priority ordering between tasks.

Assuming there exists task *T5*, we would assign tasks *T1*, *T2*, *T3* and *T5* priorities 1, 2, 5 and 6, respectively. It appears a gap in the figures of priority assignments, that is, there will be no tasks having priority 3 or 4 in mode *M1*. But the important thing is that the relative ordering between tasks is correct. A problem arises if there are too few priority levels available. If this is the case, other approaches can be followed, as presented in next section.

Another important effect is that assigning a new priority to a task could result in other priority ceilings being affected if the task uses other (shared) protected objects. If *T3* of the example shares another protected object (*PO'*) with *T1*, then the ceiling priority for *PO'* is, initially, the original priority of *T3* (i.e., 3). But if we apply (1) and afterwards we increase the priority of *T3* by Δ, then the new ceiling priority for *PO'* should be $3 + \Delta = 5$. This situation will force applying the revision again, till there are no changes in the ceiling priority of any protected object in any operating mode.

Essentially, the problem is how to preserve the relative ordering between tasks with an assignment of priority figures that does not contradict the figures calculated for the (fixed) ceiling priorities.

3.3. Generalisation of the First Solution: the Re-Scaling Algorithm

This section proposes a systematic way of reassigning priorities to tasks sharing objects in different operating modes. The solution is presented here as an algorithm. This algorithm has been implemented in Ada, as a part of the static analyser developed for QUISAP. The whole analysis consists of:

1. Sorting the task set for each mode, according to periods or deadlines, depending on the preferred policy: rate monotonic or deadline monotonic, respectively. As a result of this ordering, an initial priority assignment is given, despite the blocking problem.
2. Decide what *numerical* priority the tasks and objects should be given. Here is where the priority re-scaling algorithm helps, giving a figure for each task's priority and object's ceiling so that the system keeps consistent with its specification in all its operating modes. The sorting of step 1 is preserved but the new priority figures will avoid low priority tasks unnecessarily blocking higher priority ones due to applying the ceiling of ceilings.
3. Calculate the response times of all tasks, as described in [11].
4. For each task, compare its response time with its deadline to determine whether the task will or will not be able to respond within its deadline in the worst case. This completes the schedulability analysis.

The response time analysis is performed after re-scaling priorities in step 2, so the calculated blocking time is not affected by the application of the ceiling of ceilings (Equation (1)) to the protected objects. Figure 2 shows the re-scaling algorithm applied in step 2.

Calculate the maximum ceiling priority for each object applying (1) $CP = \max_{m \in M}(CP_m)$

loop
  Modified : = False
  For *M* in every operating mode **loop**
    For *Obj* in every object (in maximum ceiling priority decreasing order) **loop**
      if the maximum ceiling for *Obj* is greater than mode *M*'s ceiling **and**
        Obj is used by some task in mode *M* **then**
        Modified := True
        Δ := Maximum ceiling - Ceiling for this mode
        Raise the ceiling of *Obj* for this mode by Δ
        Also raise by Δ the priority of tasks which both:
          1.- Are active in this mode and
          2.- Their priority is greater than *Obj*'s old priority
        Recalculate the ceilings for all the objects in mode *M*
        Calculate the maximum ceiling priority for every object applying (1)
      end if
      exit this *for* loop if *Modified* = True
    end of for loop
    exit this *for* loop if *Modified* = True
  end of for loop
  exit this loop if *Modified* = False
end of loop

Fig. 2. The re-scaling algorithm. It calculates the numerical priorities for tasks and ceilings for shared objects in a multi-moded real-time system.

It is important to note that this algorithm will not terminate if there are crossed relationships between the ceilings of different objects in different modes, which represents a special case. We deal with this in the next section.

4. A Special Case and a Different Solution

4.1 Description of the Case

There is a special situation that can not be solved by means of the re-scaling algorithm. This situation is important enough to detect it before executing the re-scaling analysis and warn the user in consequence or apply another solution. It can be described as follows: *if an object has a ceiling higher than another object's ceiling in one mode and the reverse situation is given in any of the other modes then the re-scaling algorithm cannot be applied.* This description itself explains how to detect the situation by means of an automated procedure.

Assume we have the system shown in Figure 3. As in previous sections, each task T_i has a priority *i*. The higher the *i*, the bigger the priority. There exist two operating modes, named *M1* and *M2*. In mode *M1*, tasks *T3* and *T1* use object *O2*, while task *T2* uses the object *O1*. Both *O1* and *O2* are implemented as Ada protected objects[2]. The

---

[2] Although it is not necessary to implement *O1* as a protected object, because it is not shared, it is easy to imagine the existence of another task, say *T0*, with a priority lower than *T1*'s, and which also uses *O1*.

283

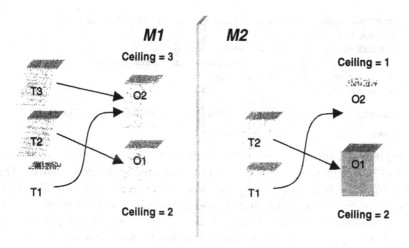

Fig. 3. A special case example.

ceiling priorities for *O1* and *O2* in mode *M1* are 2 and 3, respectively. That is, *O2*'s ceiling is higher than *O1*'s. In mode *M2*, task *T3* is not active, and thus the ceilings for *O1* and *O2* are respectively 2 and 1. So, in *M2* the reverse situation applies: *O2*'s ceiling is lower than *O1*'s.

If we blindly apply the re-scaling algorithm, the ceiling for *O1* will be 2 and the ceiling for *O2* will be 3. While this is correct for mode *M1*, in mode *M2* an excessive blocking will happen when *T2* becomes ready to execute and *T1* has just began to execute the call to *O2*, having its priority raised to 3 by the effect of the IIPCP. So we have moved the situation from mode *M1* to mode *M2*. In fact, the re-scaling algorithm can never terminate for the system in Figure 3. This is because raising the priority of *T1* in mode *M2* to 3, would imply raising the priority of *T2* in mode *M2* to (at least) 4, giving a ceiling of 4 for *O1* in mode *M2*, which would affect its ceiling in mode *M1* and so on. As we said before, the blocking time introduced by *T1* on *T2* in mode *M2* is bounded to the worst-case execution time of *O2*, but it must be taken into account to compute the response time of task *T2* in mode *M2*. So one solution is to live with it, in the case it does not affect the system schedulability, just applying the ceiling of ceilings. But, what can be done if the blocking time makes some task unschedulable and the re-scaling algorithm cannot be applied?

4.2. Second Solution: Implementing Different Versions of the Resources

In the case that applying the ceiling of ceilings makes the system infeasible and the re-scaling algorithm cannot be applied, another approach can be taken. It consists in having different implementations of the object, one for each mode, each with a different ceiling priority. In the case presented in Figure 3, we would have a protected object $O2_{M1}$ that operates in mode *M1* and runs at a ceiling priority 3. An identical object $O2_{M2}$ would exist for mode *M2*, but with a ceiling priority 1. In Ada terms, a protected type can be defined and, for each mode, create a protected object with a different priority as an instance of the type. This can be done by using a discriminant in the definition of the type that represents the object's priority for the corresponding mode. For example, we can define a protected type to provide the implementation of a sensor:

```
protected type Sensor_Type (Ceiling: System.Priority) is
  pragma Priority(Ceiling);
  procedure Read(Value: out Sensor_Range);
  procedure Set_Upper_Limit(New_Value: in Sensor_Range);
  -- Other operations of the sensor
end Sensor_Type;
```

The instantiation of a concrete sensor with a priority ceiling 5 would look like:

```
Sensor : Sensor_Type(Ceiling => 5);
```

Having different versions of the object for the different modes gives raise to the question of how to preserve consistency between the state of different versions. The way of doing this is by having just one state that will be accessed by mutually exclusive operations. For instance, if a variable Upper_Limit is part of the state of our sensor, it will be allocated in a package (e.g., Sensor_State). A protected procedure to set the variable Upper_Limit to a determinate value will be implemented as follows:

```
procedure Set_Upper_Limit(New_Value: in Sensor_Range) is
begin
  Sensor_State.Upper_Limit := New_Value;
end Set_Upper_Limit;
```

In this way, the data of the object exist just in one place (the State package) and is protected by the Ada rules. In particular, the rule that states that, outside the rendezvous or protected objects, it is safe to access a shared variable when one task writes/reads it whilst executing a protected procedure body or entry, and the other task reads/writes the variable as part of a later execution of an entry body of the same protected body (section 9.10(9) of [4]). As this is the case, additional protection mechanisms need not be provided for the steady state.

Replicating the protected object introduces the cost of having several pseudo-replicas (copies with different priorities). This implies a memory cost and also a computational cost, as a method call should take into account what the current mode is before choosing the adequate replica. For example, suppose that the tasks that operate on a sensor have a maximum priority 4 in a "Normal" mode while in "Emergency" mode their maximum priority is 2. To cope with this, we would declare two sensors:

```
Normal_Sensor    : Sensor_Type(4);
Emergency_Sensor : Sensor_Type(2);
```

A call to the method Read(Value) can then be implemented as follows:

```
case Current_Operating_Mode is
  when Normal    => Normal_Sensor.Read(Value);
  when Emergency => Emergency_Sensor.Read(Value);
  -- More cases if needed
end case;
```

Both calls operate on the same state (the *sensor's* state) but with a different interface regarding the ceiling priority that will be inherited by the calling task.

Another possibility is to have the different versions of the protected object in an array, indexed by the operating mode number, thus adding an indirection level in each call but avoiding the need for the case statement. For example:

```
-- Instantiation
Sensor : array(1..Modes_Nr) of Sensor_Type(Suitable_Ceiling);
-- Method call
Sensor(Current_Operating_Mode).Read(V);
```

It is supposed that the mode change operation updates Current_Operating_Mode so that the method call is always consistent with the current system mode. The identifier Suitable_Ceiling may well be a function that returns the ceiling for each version of the object, picking it for instance from a previously filled table. The scheduling analyser should provide these values.

The solution presented in this section (having different versions of the objects with different ceiling priorities) introduces some runtime overhead. Therefore, we propose using it just in the case that re-scaling cannot be applied because of interdependencies (case shown in section 4.1) or because there are not enough priority levels available. Re-scaling introduces no direct cost at run time, acting only during the static analysis of the system, thus being more appropriate whenever it can be used.

Replication of protected objects can be applied in all cases, so it can be regarded as a more general solution, despite the cost it introduces. In any case, the introduced overhead does not involve unpredictably long operations. On the contrary, they just represent an indirection level or a case statement with a known number of cases. Both overheads are easily measurable. The implementation of the mode change and the corresponding schedulability analysis and design of this solution requires special care. Discussion of this issue exceeds the space available for this paper, but it is the subject of current research and will adhere to the analysis shown in [12].

5. Conclusions

The IIPCP represents an efficient and safe method of sharing resources in fixed priority pre-emptive scheduled real-time systems. On the other side, mode changes permit this kind of systems to gain an important degree of flexibility, allowing them to focus only on the important tasks to do, depending on the system's operating mode. In this paper, we have shown how combining both approaches can result in temporarily inverted priorities which, in the worst case, could lead to miss deadlines. In multimoded real-time systems, the analysis of the system could give different ceilings for the same resource in different operating modes. But changing a resource's ceiling priority at run time is a rather difficult task, with many possible secondary effects, semantically difficult to bound and affecting not only the resource's priority but also the state of the tasks that are queued waiting to operate on the resource. The inversion of the priority is bounded in time, but it is necessary to know about its existence to consider it in the schedulability analysis. The amounts of time this priority inversion can last depend on how long it takes for the resource to complete its operation (in the worst case). This time should be bounded, so it can be taken into account in the schedulability analysis, but references have shown that this time can be of considerable importance. So, the schedulability of a task may depend on the blocking factor and this can be sometimes produced because of applying a unique ceiling to a resource for all modes.

A method has been proposed for systematically working around the problem in the analysis phase, statically. The re-scaling algorithm assigns new priorities to tasks depending on their relation with resources and with the rest of tasks, preserving their relative ordering of importance despite what resources they use. The limit for the re-scaling algorithm is the number of priority levels that the system provides and also the special case of inverted relative priorities between resources across different modes.

A different, more costly method has been proposed. It consists in implementing different versions of the resources, one for each mode, thus avoiding the limitation of having just one priority figure for each object. This method can be applied in all situations, including the cases in which re-scaling is not feasible, thus being a more general solution. Replicating objects eliminates the unnecessary blocking problem, with the memory cost of replicating objects and the time cost of checking what the current operating mode is before acting upon a resource, to choose the correct version. Both the static solution (re-scaling) and the objects replication can be integrated with the static schedulability analysis of the system, being perfectly compatible with well known and proven methods such as the Rate Monotonic or Deadline Monotonic approaches.

References

1. C.L. Liu and J.W. Layland. *Scheduling algorithms for multiprogramming in a hard real-time environment.* Journal of the ACM **20**(1), pp 46-61. 1973.
2. L. Sha, R. Rajkumar and J.P. Lehoczky. *Priority inheritance protocols: an approach to real-time synchronisation.* Technical report CMU-CS-87-181. Computer Science Department, Carnegie-Mellon University. Pittsburgh, Pennsylvania. 1987.
3. R. Rajkumar, L. Sha and J.P. Lehoczky. *An experimental investigation of synchronisation protocols.* Proceedings of the 6th IEEE Workshop on Real-Time Operating Systems and Software, pp. 11-17. May, 1989.
4. Information Technology — Programming Languages Ada 95. International standard ISO/IEC 8652:1995. (Ada Reference Manual). 1995.
5. Information technology — Portable Operating System Interface (POSIX®) ISO/IEC 9945-1:1996(E) ANSI/IEEE Std 1003.1, 1996 Edition.
6. K.W. Tindell, A. Burns and A.J. Wellings. *Mode changes in priority pre-emptively scheduled systems.* Proceedings of the Real Time Systems Symposium, Phoenix, Arizona. 1992.
7. Private comments from Offer Pazy and Ted Baker.
8. L. Sha, R. Rajkumar, J.P. Lehoczky and R. Ramamritham. *Mode change protocols for priority-driven preemptive scheduling.* The Journal of Real-Time Systems, **1**, 243-264. 1989.
9. J. Real, A. Espinosa and A. Crespo. *Using Ada 95 for prototyping real-time systems.* In A. Strohmeier (Ed.) Reliable Software Technologies. Proceedings of the Ada-Europe'96 Conference. Lecture Notes in Computer Science vol. 1088, pp. 262-274. Springer Verlag.
10. C.D. Locke, D.R. Vogel and T.J. Mesler. *Building a predictable avionics platform in Ada: a case study.* Proc. of the IEEE 12th Real Time Systems Symposium. Dec 1991.
11. N. Audsley, A. Burns, M. Richardson, K. Tindell, A.J. Wellings. *Applying new scheduling theory to static priority pre-emptive scheduling.* Software Engineering Journal. **8**(5) pp. 284-292. 1993.
12. P. Pedro and A. Burns. *Schedulability Analysis for Mode Changes in Flexible Real-Time Systems.* Proceedings 10th Euromicro Workshop on Real-Time Systems. Berlin, June 1998.

A "Bare-Machine" Implementation of Ada Multi-tasking beneath the Linux Kernel

Hongfeng Shen[1], Arnaud Charlet[2] and T.P. Baker[1]

[1] Department of Computer Science, Florida State University
Tallahassee FL, USA 32306-4019
baker@cs.fsu.edu
[2] Ada Core Technologies, Inc.

Abstract. An Ada tasking kernel is implemented as a layer beneath the Linux operating system. This provides low overhead and precise control of execution timing for real-time Ada tasks, which execute within the Linux kernel address space, while allowing the Linux operating system to execute non-real-time tasks in the background. The Ada tasking kernel is derived from Yodaiken's Real-Time Linux kernel, with new scheduling and synchronization primitives specifically to support the GNAT Ada runtime system. Implementing the Ada tasking primitives directly on the hardware does not just lower execution overhead and improve control over execution timing; it also opens the door for a simple restricted-tasking runtime system that could be certified for safety-critical applications.

1 Introduction

This paper describes how the GNAT multi-tasking runtime system (GNARL) has been ported to execute directly over the hardware of a generic Intel PC-compatible architecture, as a layer *underneath* the Linux[6] operating system.

The GNAT Ada compilation system[8] has been very successful, and has been ported to many processor architectures and operating systems, but until recently its multi-tasking runtime system (GNARL) has not been implemented on a bare machine. The tasking model of the Ada 95 programming language was intended to permit a light-weight bare-machine implementation, and so was the GNARL. The components of GNARL that are dependent on a particular machine and operating system are isolated by a low-level tasking interface, called GNULLI. Previously, GNULLI has always been implemented as "glue code" to the services of an existing thread library, which in turn is layered over an underlying operating system. The performance of Ada tasking has been limited by the threads library and operating system, which in no case were designed to support Ada, and in most cases were not intended for real-time applications. Thus, it has remained an open question how well the tasking implementation would work if it were supported by a small, simple, and highly predictable implementation of the GNULLI, executing directly on the hardware.

The rest of this paper tells more about this project. Section 2 explains the motivation and background, including RT-Linux. Section 3 explains the design of the implementation. Section 4 reports on the outcomes of functional and performance tests.

2 Background

There are two independent motivations for doing a bare-machine implementation of the GNULLI. The first motivation is to achieve the kind of efficiency and predictable execution timing needed for hard real-time applications. In versions of the GNULLI where Ada tasks are implemented using the concurrent programming primitives of a commercial operating system, the activities of the operating system can compete with the tasks in the application, and cause unpredicable variations in their execution timing. The second motivation is to lay the groundwork for the kind of small, certifiably-safe implementation of a restricted subset of Ada tasking that was proposed at the 1997 International Real-Time Ada Workshop at Ravenscar [3]. A simple bare-machine implementation is needed for this because the added complexity of a full off-the-shelf operating system would be an obstacle to certification.

The target hardware architecture for our bare-machine implementation of GNULLI is a generic PC-compatible machine with an Intel 486/586 processor. This was chosen for its wide availability and low cost.

A tasking kernel by itself is not very useful. Interesting applications do input and output, and that requires device drivers. The complexity of a single device driver can exceed that of a tasking kernel. Moreover, hardware device interfaces are often poorly documented or even secret, and subject to frequent changes. Therefore, development and maintenance of an adequate collection of hardware device drivers is very daunting. One way to avoid putting a lot of new work into device drivers is to reuse the device drivers of an existing operating system, such as DOS or Linux. A problem is that these operating systems were not designed for real-time use, and their device drivers are sources of timing unpredictability. Reuse of non-realtime device drivers is possible, but only if they are run in the *background*, at low enough priority that they cannot impede the progress of hard-real-time tasks.

Support for background-foreground separation is generally a useful thing, since all but the simplest real-time systems include a combination of hard and soft real-time or non-real-time processing. For example, a system might have hard-real-time periodic tasks with tight jitter constraints to serve sensors and actuators, and soft-real-time or non-real-time tasks to perform actions that have inherently variable time delays, such as communicating over a network and logging data to a disk. In such a situation, the I/O drivers for the sensors and actuators would need to meet hard-real-time constraints, but the I/O drivers for the network and disk I/O might be reused from a non-real-time operating system.

A traditional way to implement foreground and background processing is for the foreground task scheduler to have single background task, which in turn executes the background task scheduler and all the background tasks. This model was followed by a series of low-level Ada kernels developed at The Florida State University during the late 1980's and early 1990's, in which the DOS operating system ran as the background task. More recently, this model has been followed by Yodaiken's Real-Time Linux[5]. Linux has many advantages over DOS for the role of background operating system, including support for concurrent threads of control and separate virtual address spaces.

Real-Time Linux is a layer of software that is added to the Linux kernel, as a dynamically loaded module. RT-Linux catches hardware interrupts before they get to the regular Linux interrupt handlers. This allows the RT-Linux layer to not only preempt regular Linux tasks, even when they are executing in the Linux kernel, but also to postpone the execution of the hardware interrupt handlers installed by the Linux device drivers. The RT-Linux kernel provides for the creation and scheduling of very light-weight foreground tasks, which execute entirely in the kernel address space. The regular Linux operating system kernel and all the tasks that it schedules run in the background, at a lower priority than all of the RT-Linux tasks. The background tasks have access to the full services of the Linux operating system, but do not have predictable timing. The foreground processes have predictable timing, but cannot use the conventional Linux I/O or make other conventional OS service calls, since they execute below the level of the OS. Communication between the foreground and background is possible only using the bounded FIFO buffer structures supported by the RT-Linux kernel. RT-Linux also provides fine-grained ($0.8\ \mu s$) clock and timer services, which can be used to precisely schedule time delays and periodic execution.

3 Design and Implementation Issues

3.1 Basis in RT-Linux

For this project, we chose to use Linux as the background operating system, and reuse as much code as possible from RT-Linux. RT-Linux support for multiple processors is only in an experimental stage, but we had already decided to restrict our attention to single-processor systems, since our objective was a very simple Ada kernel. All the machine-dependent and OS-dependent code of RT-Linux could be reused, including the mechanisms for inserting RT-Linux into the foreground, the context switching code, and the timer driver. The FIFO's could also be reused directly. Only the task scheduler and synchronization primitives needed rewriting, to support the Ada dispatching and locking policies. We chose to rewrite them in Ada, but to simply define Ada interface to import the original RT Linux C-language code for the timer driver and FIFO buffers.

3.2 Living Inside the Kernel

Execution within and beneath the Linux kernel imposes some restrictions on what an "application" can do. In particular, it cannot perform operations, like calling the standard C `malloc` to allocate memory or the standard C libraries to do input and output, that are implemented using kernel traps. Lower-level substitutes must be found for these services, or they must be done without. Dynamic memory allocation can be done within the kernel address space via calls to `kmalloc`, but for predictable performance these should be limited to a few calls done during initialization of each kernel module. Input and output can be done directly, by means of custom low-level device drivers, or else must be routed through buffers to and from background servers, which can use the full I/O capabilities of the Linux operating system.

Conceptually, an application that includes both foreground and background tasks has multiple partitions. The foreground tasks exist in a real-time partition that executes in the kernel address space using the bare-machine runtime system. The background tasks exist in one or more non-real-time partitions, each of which corresponds to a Linux process, and which each use a runtime system layered over the Linux operating system.

3.3 Ada 95 Rationale Implementation Model

The Ada 95 Rationale[1] describes a very simple model for implementation of task scheduling and protected object locking on a single processor, based on the notion of priority ceiling locking[2]. Our objective was to reimplement that GNAT tasking primitives according to this model. The model is based on a few simple principles:

1. Scheduling is strictly preemptive, according to task active priority. A task can only execute if it is the task at the head of the list of highest-priority ready tasks.
2. Only ready tasks can hold locks. A task that is holding a lock must give up the lock before it goes to sleep.
3. A task is not permitted to obtain a lock if its active priority is higher than the ceiling of the lock.
4. A task that is holding a lock inherits the priority ceiling of the lock, (only) while it holds the lock.

It follows that whenever a task executes an operation to obtain a lock there will be no other task holding that lock. (Otherwise, either the priority ceiling would be violated or the task that is holding the lock should be executing.) Thus, for the implementation of the GNAT tasking primitive `WriteLock` it is sufficient to simply update the active priority of the current task to the ceiling priority of the lock object referenced as parameter. For the implementation of the primitive `Unlock`, the active priority of the current task needs to be restored, and a check may need to be done to see whether some other task should preempt the current task.

3.4 Task Control Blocks

In the GNARL each task is represented by a record object called a *task control block* (ATCB). The ATCB contains a target-dependent component LL. which is a record containing private data used by the GNULLI implementation. When the runtime system is layered over a thread library, this target-specific data includes a thread ID. A thread ID amounts to a reference to another record object in the underlying thread implementation, which might be called a *thread control block*. For our bare-machine implementation, the task implementation is done directly, so there is no separate thread ID and no thread control block; all the necessary information about a task is stored directly in the ATCB.

3.5 Lock Operations

ATCB's, and other GNARL objects for which mutual exclusion must be enforced, are protected by *locks*. When the runtime system is layered over a thread library, locks are implemented using the *mutex* objects of the thread library. For example, consider the code in Figure 1. In the code, L.L is a reference to a POSIX mutex object, and pthread_mutex_lock and pthread_mutex_unlock are imported C functions that that lock and unlock a mutex.

```
procedure Write_Lock
   (L : access Lock; Ceiling_Violation : out Boolean) is
   Result : Interfaces.C.int;
begin
   Result := pthread_mutex_lock (L.L'Access);
   Ceiling_Violation := Result /= 0;
end Write_Lock;
procedure Unlock (L : access Lock) is
   Result  : Interfaces.C.int;
begin
   Result := pthread_mutex_unlock (L.L'Access);
end Unlock;
```

Fig. 1. Locking operations using POSIX thread operations.

In the bare-machine runtime system, this is replaced by code that directly implements the operations, as sketched in Figure 2. The code assumes that there is a single ready queue, ordered by priority and linked via the ATCB component Succ. All queues are circular and doubly linked. (Some type conversions have been omitted from the original code, for brevity.)

Due to the priority ceiling policy, as explained further above, there is no need to record the owner of the lock, or to use any looping or special atomic hardware operation (like test-and-set) to obtain the lock. That makes these operations much simpler to implement than the POSIX thread mutex operations.

3.6 Sleep and Wakeup Operations

The GNAT runtime system uses primitives Sleep and Wakeup to block and unblock a task, respectively. Sleep is only allowed to be called while the current task is holding the lock of its own ATCB. The effect of the operation is to release the lock and put the current task to sleep until another task wakes it

```
procedure Write_Lock
   (L : access Lock; Ceiling_Violation : out Boolean) is
   Prio : constant System.Any_Priority :=
      Current_Task.LL.Active_Priority;
begin
   Ceiling_Violation := False;
   if Prio > L.Ceiling_Priority then
      Ceiling_Violation := True;
      return;
   end if;
   L.Pre_Locking_Priority := Prio;
   Current_Task.LL.Active_Priority := L.Ceiling_Priority;
   if Current_Task.LL.Outer_Lock = null then
      -- If this lock is not nested, record a pointer to it.
      Current_Task.LL.Outer_Lock := L.all'Unchecked_Access;
   end if;
end Write_Lock;
procedure Unlock (L : access Lock) is
   Flags : Integer;
begin
   -- Now that the lock is released, lower our own priority.
   if Current_Task.LL.Outer_Lock = L.all'Unchecked_Access then
      -- This lock is the outer-most,
      -- so reset our priority to Current_Prio.
      Current_Task.LL.Active_Priority :=
         Current_Task.LL.Current_Priority;
      Current_Task.LL.Outer_Lock := null;
   else
      -- If this lock is nested, pop the old active priority.
      Current_Task.LL.Active_Priority := L.Pre_Locking_Priority;
   end if;
   -- Reschedule the task if necessary.
   -- We only need to reschedule the task if its Active_Priority
   -- is less than the one following it.
   -- The check depends on the fact that the background task
   -- (which is always at the tail of the ready queue)
   -- has the lowest Active_Priority.
   if Current_Task.LL.Active_Priority
      < Current_Task.LL.Succ.LL.Active_Priority then
      Save_Flags (Flags); -- Saves interrupt mask.
      Cli;                -- Masks interrupts
      Delete_From_Ready_Queue (Current_Task);
      Insert_In_Ready_Queue (Current_Task);
      Restore_Flags (Flags);
      Call_Scheduler;
   end if;
end Unlock;
```

Fig. 2. Direct implementation of locking operations.

up, by calling **Wakeup**. When the task wakes up, it reacquires the lock before returning from **Sleep**.

When the runtime system is layered over a thread library, these operations are implemented as shown in Figure 3. The ATCB component LL.CV is a POSIX condition variable, and LL.L is a POSIX mutex. The operation **Sleep** corresponds directly to the POSIX operation pthread_cond_wait, and the **Wakeup** operation corresponds directly to the POSIX operation pthread_cond_signal.

```
procedure Sleep (Self_ID : Task_ID; Reason  : Task_States) is
   Result : Interfaces.C.int;
begin
   if Self_ID.Pending_Priority_Change then
      Self_ID.Pending_Priority_Change := False;
      Self_ID.Base_Priority := Self_ID.New_Base_Priority;
      Set_Priority (Self_ID, Self_ID.Base_Priority);
   end if;
   Result := pthread_cond_wait
      (Self_ID.LL.CV'Access, Self_ID.LL.L.L'Access);
   pragma Assert (Result = 0 or else Result = EINTR);
end Sleep;
procedure Wakeup (T : Task_ID; Reason : Task_States) is
   Result : Interfaces.C.int;
begin
   Result := pthread_cond_signal (T.LL.CV'Access);
   pragma Assert (Result = 0);
end Wakeup;
```

Fig. 3. Sleep and wakeup using POSIX thread primitives.

In the bare-machine runtime system, these operations are implemented directly, as shown in Figure 4. **Wakeup** is a little bit more complicated than **Sleep**, because the task being awakened could be on a **Timed_Sleep** call (like a **Sleep** call, but with a timeout). Sleeping tasks with timeouts put on the timer queue, which is ordered by wakeup time. When a timeout expires, the timer interrupt handler moves the timed-out task from the timer queue to the ready queue. Otherwise, if a task is awakened before the timeout expires, it is the responsibility of **Wakeup** to remove it from the timer queue and possibly disarm the timer. Note that **Timer_Queue** is implemented as a dummy ATCB, so **Timer_Queue.LL.Succ** is the first true task in the timer queue.

3.7 Dynamic Priorities

When GNULLI is layered over a thread library, priority changes are done via calls to the thread library. For POSIX threads, these calls are very general and so are necessarily rather heavy weight, since the position of the thread in the ready queue may need to be changed, and the scheduler may need to be called. However, the way these are used in the GNAT runtime, the normal case can be much lighter weight.

It is a policy of the GNAT runtime system that whenever the priority of a task is changed the current task must hold the ATCB lock of the affected task.

```
procedure Sleep
    (Self_ID : Task_ID; Reason : System.Tasking.Task_States) is
    Flags : Integer;
begin
    --  Self_ID is actually Current_Task, that is, only the
    --  task that is running can put itself into sleep. To preserve
    --  consistency, we use Self_ID throughout the code here.
    Self_ID.State := Reason;
    Save_Flags (Flags);
    Cli;
    Delete_From_Ready_Queue (Self_ID);
    --  Arrange to unlock Self_ID's ATCB lock.
    if Self_ID.LL.Outer_Lock = Self_ID.LL.L'Access then
        Self_ID.LL.Active_Priority := Self_ID.LL.Current_Priority;
        Self_ID.LL.Outer_Lock := null;
    else
        Self_ID.LL.Active_Priority := Self_ID.LL.L.Pre_Locking_Priority;
    end if;
    Restore_Flags (Flags);
    Call_Scheduler;
    --  Before leaving, regain the lock.
    Write_Lock (Self_ID);
end Sleep;
procedure Wakeup (T : Task_ID; Reason : System.Tasking.Task_States) is
    Flags : Integer;
begin
    T.State := Reason;
    Save_Flags (Flags);
    Cli;  --  Disable interrupts.
    if Timer_Queue.LL.Succ = T then
        --  T is the first task in Timer_Queue, further check.
        if T.LL.Succ = Timer_Queue then
            --  T is the only task in Timer_Queue, so deactivate timer.
            No_Timer;
        else
            --  T is the first task in Timer_Queue, so set timer to T's
            --  successor's Resume_Time.
            Set_Timer (T.LL.Succ.LL.Resume_Time);
        end if;
    end if;
    Delete_From_Timer_Queue (T);
    --  If T is in Timer_Queue, T is removed. If not, nothing happened.
    Insert_In_Ready_Queue (T);
    Restore_Flags (Flags);
    Call_Scheduler;
end Wakeup;
```

Fig. 4. Direct implementation of sleep and wakeup.

This means the current task is inheriting the priority ceiling of that lock. ATCB locks have the highest (non-interrupt priority) ceiling. Thus, the current task will be inheriting sufficient priority that it cannot be preempted (unless the new priority is an interrupt priority). It follows that unless we are raising the priority of a task other than the current task, and raising it to an interrupt priority, there is no need to move the affected task in the ready queue, or call the scheduler; changing the priority of a task becomes a simple assignment statement.

4 Testing and Performance

A set of functional tests were devised to ensure that all the operations in the kernel-module implementation of GNULLI are functionally correct. Then, simple performance tests were developed for the GNULLI primitives, using direct calls, outside the context of the rest of the GNARL.

The primary performance test comprises a set of six independent, periodic tasks with harmonic periods and rate monotonic priorities (the shorter the period of a task, the higher the priority it has). The deadline for each task is equal to its period. Rates for the six tasks are 320, 160, 80, 40, 20 and 10 cycles per second. The simulated workload of each task is repetition of a simple assignment operation. By changing the number of times this simple operation has to be repeated in each task, the execution time of the task can be adjusted. A single parameter, which we call the *load level*, is used to control this change so that the execution times for all six tasks can be ajusted simultaneously, but linearly, while keeping the relative distribution of the load between tasks unchanged. Starting from a low load level at which all the tasks are schedulable, the load level is then increased gradually and the test is repeated until the maximum load level is reached. Any further increase in the load level beyond this maximum value will cause the task non-schedulable. Once this maximum load level is reached, the utilization limit is calculated.

Theoretically, a utilization limit of 100% can be obtained for this set of tests, since the periods are harmonic. The result on the current implementation running on a 90MHz Pentium PC is 97%, meaning that the scheduling overhead for the tasks is 3%.

The same test was attempted using the Ada tasking implementation based on the Linux native thread library, and it failed miserably. The tasks could never meet their hard real-time requirements even at the lowest load level. The reason, of course, is that the Linux operating system would preempt the processor from the application tasks at arbitrary times. The kernel-module GNULLI demonstrably solves this problem, by running real-time tasks at higher priority than the Linux OS kernel and device drivers.

Performance testing was also carried out on lock and unlock primitives alone, to determine their absolute execution times. The average execution time for a pair of lock/unlock calls on a 90MHz PC is 1.06 microseconds on the current implementation.

We then merged the low-level tasking implementation described above with a restricted version of the rest of the GNARL, so that we could compile and execute tests written using the Ada tasking syntax. (The previous tasks made direct GNULLI calls.) These tests were performed on a 166MHz Pentium PC, and measured the average execution time of three operations: (1) a protected procedure call on a protected object with no entries; (2) a protected procedure call on a protected object with one entry; (3) a pair of protected entry calls that forces alternation of execution between two tasks, similar in effect to a rendezvous. The tests were performed using three versions of the GNULLI, based on FSU user-level threads, "native" kernel-supported Linux threads, and the new kernel-module threads. The results are shown below:

	FSU threads	Linux threads	RT-Linux threads
simple protected procedure	$2.3\ \mu s$	$3.1\ \mu s$	$1.1\ \mu s$
protected procedure	$3.5\ \mu s$	$4.7\ \mu s$	$1.4\ \mu s$
po "rendezvous"	$4.6\ \mu s$	$9.7\ \mu s$	$3.1\ \mu s$

Conclusion

We have coded an implementation of the task primitives, run tests of the primitives both by themselves, integrated the primitives with a restricted version of the rest of the GNARL runtime system, and then tested the combination. The predictability of real-time execution and resulting ability to guarantee deadlines, is exactly what we had hoped to achieve. The absolute peformance results are also very encouraging. Further improvements in performance and convenience will be possible as we continue to simplify the restricted GNARL and improve the compiler's ability to optimize for the restricted cases.

The prototype version of the RT-Linux GNULLI described in this paper, as implemented by Hongfeng Shen, is available at ftp://ftp.cs.fsu.edu/pub/PART/. Arnaud Charlet later integrated the RT-Linux GNULLI with a restricted version of the GNARL developed to support the Ravenscar Profile by Mike Kamrad and Barry Spinney (see another paper in these same conference proceedings) and merged them with the GNAT sources, which are maintained by Ada Core Technologies, Inc.

Like the rest of the GNAT sources, the restricted runtime and RT-Linux port are under a modified form of the Gnu Library General Public License. When they are better tested and are believed to be stable, we expect they will appear as part of a publicly GNAT source distribution.

References

1. Ada 9X Mapping/Revision Team, Annex D of the Ada 95 Rationale, Intermetrics, Inc. (January 1995).
2. T.P. Baker, Stack-based scheduling of real-time processes, in Advances in Real-Time Systems, IEEE Computer Society Press (1993) 64-96.

3. A. Burns, T. Baker, T. Vardanega, Session Summary: Tasking Profiles, Proceedings for the 8th International Real-Time Ada Workshop, Ada Letters XVII, 5 (September/October 1997) 5-7.

4. ISO/IEC: ISO/IEC 8652: 1995 (E) Information Technology – Programming Languages – Ada. (1995)

5. V. Yodaiken, The RT-Linux approach to hard real-time, paper available at http://rtlinux.cs.nmt.edu/~rtlinuxwhitepaper/short.html.

6. Linux operating system web page, http://www.linux.org.

7. Real-Time Linux operating system web page,http://luz.cs.nmt.edu/~rtlinux/.

8. Ada Core Technologies, Inc., GNAT web page, http://www.gnat.com.

Implementing a New Low-Level Tasking Support for the GNAT Runtime System*

José F. Ruiz[1] and Jesús M. González-Barahona[2]

[1] Departamento de Ingeniería de Sistemas Telemáticos,
Universidad Politécnica de Madrid,
28040 Madrid (Spain)
jfruiz@dit.upm.es
[2] Grupo de Sistemas y Comunicaciones, Departamento de Informática,
Universidad Carlos III de Madrid,
28911 Leganés, Madrid (Spain)
jgb@computer.org

Abstract. This paper describes the main design goals and implementation choices of JTK, a library which provides simple tasking support, loosely based on POSIX threads. It has been designed to provide the low-level tasking support for GNAT, it is completely written in Ada, and it is usable on top of a traditional operating system (providing user-level threads) as well as layered over a bare machine. Its main design motivation is the desire to experiment with a low-level tasking implementation that fits well with GNAT tasking requirements.

Currently, JTK provides a priority driven threading model, with preemptive scheduling, facilities for signal handling, and primitives to provide mutual exclusion and synchronized waiting. The long-term target of JTK is to provide all the facilities that GNAT needs to satisfy full Annex D semantics.

Keywords: GNAT, tasking, runtime system, Ada, real-time system.

1 Introduction

When porting an Ada compiler to a new architecture, one of the hardest jobs is to port the Ada tasking implementation. Many compilers (notably GNAT) simplify this problem by implementing an architecture-independent tasking system which runs on top of a well defined interface. In the case of GNAT, this interface is called GNULLI (GNU Lower-Level Interface)[1], which runs on top of native threads (usually POSIX threads) for the given architecture. All the implementor has to do is to implement a GNULLI-like interface for the native threads.

Although this approach has many advantages, it also presents some problems, being some of them the presence of abstraction inversion, some difficulties when

---

* This work was supported in part by the CICYT, Project TIC96-0614.

both tasking models (Ada and POSIX) do not fit well, and some performance penalties, due to the duplication of work in some cases[10, 2].

Our idea, presented in this paper, was to design and build a low-level tasking system, as simple as possible, and directly targeted at being the implementation for the GNULLI. Therefore, our system just "fills the holes" needed by GNARL[1], and does not try to replicate all the facilities already provided by it. We call our system JTK (from Jose's Tasking Kernel).

Currently, JTK provides a priority driven threading model, with preemptive scheduling, facilities for signal handling, and primitives to provide mutual exclusion and synchronized waiting. The long-term target of JTK is to provide all the facilities that GNAT needs to satisfy full Annex D semantics. JTK is completely written in Ada[2].

The remainder of this paper is organized as follows. Section 2 explores the ideas that led us to start this work, as well as the basic goals of the system. Section 3 is a brief overview of some core issues of JTK. Section 4 explains the main details of JTK and how they are implemented. Section 5 describes our design of a new real-time kernel that we are developing to use GNAT and JTK on top of a bare PC machine. Section 6 shows some performance results to endorse the feasibility of our approach. Section 7 concludes with a summary of the JTK implementation status and its availability. Finally, Annex A shows a few lines of some specification packages as an example of its interface.

2 Motivation and Goals

The idea of designing a new low-level tasking system when there are plenty of thread implementations is based on several assumptions:

- The burden and overhead of using GNARL on top of POSIX threads is too high[10, 2], leading to many abstraction inversions. Many aspects of POSIX threads and Ada tasks are at a similar level of abstraction. This forces to ignore (and/or replicate in GNARL) functionality provided by POSIX threads. In fact, the GNAT tasking implementation is so complete and specific[4] that the functionality it really uses from POSIX threads is quite minimal.
- Sometimes, the exact details of a thread implementation are hard to know (specially when its source code is not available). Indeed, in some cases a given implementation of threading facilities directly conflicts with the needs of GNAT. The implementation of Ada ATC (Asynchronous Transfer of Control) in several architectures is a well known case of this problem[3, 12].
- A library written in Ada is much more understandable, specially when used with the rest of GNARL, also written completely in Ada.
- The implementation of GNAT tasking on top of native threads in each architecture leads to portability problems[6]: the work for porting the GNAT tasking system to a new platform is not negligible, with many efforts having to be devoted to understand how the thread implementation really works.

---

[1] GNARL is the runtime system of GNAT.
[2] About 1000 lines of code, not including test programs.

- Sometimes there is no thread support easily available. This is true in the case of many embedded systems, where a full-blown implementation of threads is usually considered to be too expensive.

Of course, implementing GNAT on top of native threads has many advantages[9, 10, 2], not to be described here. But in some situations, considering an alternative can be interesting.

JTK has been designed to directly fit GNARL requirements, while at the same time providing an easy way to extend and modify its implementation. Its main goals are:

- To avoid all the needless facilities to improve the performance and predictability of GNARL.
- To provide the required functionality with an eye set on the specific use made by the GNAT tasking system. The JTK implementation can be very simple because GNARL is in charge of much of the work involved with tasking.
- To allow for an easier way for bounding the runtime execution time, by using a well known (and simple) low-level tasking layer.
- To obtain an easily understandable code.
- To enhance the portability of the library.
- To reduce the number of the time-consuming system calls[11], needed with kernel-space implementations of threads.

3 Internal Architecture

JTK handles all the internal information required to manage the low-level tasks. The set of critical sections of the library code will be referred to as the kernel. JTK uses a single-threaded kernel, inside which the structures used by the low-level tasks must be protected from being inconsistently modified during handling of asynchronous events (signals). The technique used is called a monolithic monitor[8]. The mutual exclusion is provided by a flag which indicates when the kernel is in use (this technique is also used by some POSIX threads implementations[11]). If a signal arrives while the kernel is being used, its management is delayed until the kernel is left (see section 4).

JTK offers a priority driven scheduler with preemption. It has a FIFO queue for each priority to decide the next task to execute.

It also provides two basic synchronization methods: mutual exclusion and conditional synchronization. For the mutual exclusion two mutex objects are provided: one operating as a simple binary semaphore and other using the Immediate Priority Ceiling Protocol[8], which offers the possibility for read and write locking. For the conditional synchronization, JTK implements condition variables, used by the timer and the protected objects.

There are two scheduling policies currently implemented in JTK:

- Simple scheduling, in which tasks are run until they are blocked or until another task with a higher priority becomes ready.

- Round Robin (preemptive) scheduling. In this case, each task has an associated time slice. If there are more than one task with the same priority, each one runs only during its corresponding time slice.

These two ways of using the library are implemented separately to prevent an excessive overhead while using the basic scheduler without Round Robin support. Real-time systems do not use Round Robin scheduling, so they can bypass that extra processing.

The low-level tasks and schedulers have been defined as tagged objects, so there is a very easy and clean way of extending the implementation with a new scheduling policy. Annex A contains source code which shows the format of these objects and the patterns of the methods which use them.

4 Implementation Details

Although JTK has many similarities with POSIX threads implementations, there are some aspects where they strongly differ due to the influence of GNAT semantics. The low-level tasks implemented by JTK are intended to be entities with a minimal weight, at an abstraction level not overlapped with Ada tasks. It avoids the overhead and semantic restrictions imposed by other tasking implementations.

4.1 Timer Support

A clear example of the JTK approach is the timer support. Both GNARL and POSIX threads provide timers and associated facilities for handling timers[1]. One important aspect of GNARL is that it can be modified to issue only one timer request at a time (using a timer server task), and therefore does not need that the underlying library considers more than one simultaneous request. POSIX threads do support multiple timer requests (with their queue management and related aspects). Therefore, POSIX threads have a strong overhead involved with managing the waiting list and serving timer requests that are overlapped with more recent requests (these overlapped timers will never be used by GNARL). JTK knows that this job is done by GNARL and does not implement it again.

GNARL is in charge of ordering the different requests from the tasks and it performs the petitions to the operating system or the underlying kernel. This is the reason why GNARL does not need to request simultaneous timer operations.

The final purpose of the JTK library is to be layered over a specialized kernel (see section 5), designed to fit JTK requirements. This kernel does not need to furnish its own queues for the low-level time management and therefore its implementation has been simplified.

4.2 Signal Management

Signal management is a key issue for improving POSIX threads functionality. GNARL has a very specific way of managing signals[14], similar in many senses to the way used by POSIX threads. What happens is that GNARL executes almost all the job on its own, and uses the low-level support in a minimal mode. But POSIX threads do not offer the possibility of a reduced use, and the result is a lot of redundant processing made by POSIX threads with no benefits in the Ada use. Again, JTK tries to fit to this reduced functionality.

It is done by using an unique signal handler for all the signals that have been requested by the tasks. When a task wants to wait for one signal, it is registered inside a table where the task identifier is stored in the place corresponding to the requested signal. There is a one-to-one correspondence between the waiting tasks and their related signals. The next step is to block the task until the signal arrives. Notice that the GNARL implementation only allows a task to wait for a single signal (the abort signal is a special case and will be explained afterwards). Consequently, a signal waiting request is performed in a very simple and straightforward manner in the JTK approach. The POSIX thread implementation allows a thread to wait for a set of signals at a time. Therefore, the receiving thread must be determined according to a quite complex signal delivery model in the POSIX model.

The mechanism for sending signals is a little more complex. In order to maintain the integrity of the internal data care must be taken about the places where an asynchronous signal can be handled, and hence the signal manager may be delayed.

The signal management is different depending on whether we are accessing protected data or not. This protection is achieved using two procedures (*Enter_Kernel* and *Leave_Kernel*) that bound the code inside which signals cannot be delivered. When a signal arrives while executing this protected code, the signal is stored inside a list of pending signals. When leaving the kernel, if the list is not empty, the managing of these delayed signals is performed.

There is only one thing to be done for the signal processing, that is waking up the waiting task by introducing it inside the scheduler's ready queue.

It has been said previously that a task only waits for a single signal. It is not completely true, because the abort signal can be sent to any task, regardless of whether the task is waiting for a signal or not. But it is not a problem, because if a task is waiting for any signal, it can be sent the abort signal by waking it up and passing the abort signal identifier. This mechanism allows the receiving task to recognize the signal that has arrived. The different tasks furnished by GNARL to wait for the different signals know what to do when receiving the abort signal.

4.3 Asynchronous Transfer of Control

GNARL implements Ada ATC (Asynchronous Transfer of Control) raising a special exception in any specified task[12]. Where GNARL is layered over POSIX threads, it implements this operation using a per-thread signal. On operating systems that do not support per-thread signals, the effect of ATC is delayed until execution reaches a polling point. The latter leads to a non immediate effect of the ATC, and the former is a very time-consuming operation. JTK knows that unless a task is trying to abort itself (if abort is not deferred it can begin processing the abort immediately) it must already have preempted the target task. If the task to abort is waiting for a signal, it is just sent the abort signal. But in any other case, instead of using any signal operation (such as fake calls), it suffices modifying the saved state of the target task to redirect control; the target task will begin processing the abort as soon as it is next scheduled to execute[3].

5   Further Work: Porting to Bare PC

The next step on this work is the porting of the JTK library, together with the GNAT runtime system, to a bare PC target. The purpose is to obtain a cross compiler platform to develop real-time embedded software, fitting a minimal real-time system profile. It will provide a freely available test-bed for experimentation in language, compiler, and runtime support for real-time embedded systems.

Ada is so specific in its requirements, that it is extremely unlikely that a generic operating system or kernel will make its services available in a form that they can be directly used by Ada programs[4]. It is also clear that an efficient and tight real-time performance is very difficult to achieve for an implementation layered over a conventional operating system[5]. There is an important source of unpredictable delays on top of these systems, due to preemptions by interrupt handlers and operating system processes.

Therefore, in order to provide an easily predictable low-level support for GNARL and JTK, we are developing a new real-time kernel with this objective in mind, from hardware up.

This kernel is being designed to fit Ada tasks semantics as tightly as possible. It does not support multiple processes (it will operate in single virtual address space) and it does not have a file system. In the beginning the only devices supported are the timer and the serial port. These simplifications eliminate unpredictable time delays due to page faults, waiting for completion of I/O, and I/O completion interrupt processing[5].

There is a basic set of functionalities needed to support the functions that a minimal real-time operating system should provide. The design of this implementation could be divided into these three main components:

1. Machine-specific support. This includes code to save and restore register windows for context switches, boot up the kernel, and provide time-keeping services. The boot code involves initializing memory mapping hardware and installing trap handlers.
2. Environment interface support. Here it is included memory allocation, signal and interrupt management, minimal timer services and I/O routines to

communicate with the user. This provides the basic interface for the upper layers (GNARL and JTK).

3. Platform support. This implements the mechanisms to transfer the kernel code to the target machine and the support for the remote debugging of the applications. Currently, the system can boot directly from floppy, using a boot loader (such as LILO or GRUB) or using network booting. The debugging method is through the serial line, but this feature is still under testing.

These are the topics that we are following to design and implement the minimal real-time kernel which will provide support for JTK and GNAT.

It also has an important advantage with the interfaces. As we have no constraints in the design of the kernel interface we selected to provide the same interface as is used for Linux. Hence no modifications have to be made to the JTK system, regardless of being on top of Linux or this specialized kernel.

6 Performance

To evaluate the performance and hence the feasibility of this implementation it has been designed a simple test. It consists of two tasks which only performs context switches calling the procedure *Yield* contained in the package *System.Task_Primitives.Operations*. Figure 1 shows the time taken for a context switch. The times reported are averages taken over 100 000 iterations of each task.

The test has been executed on the same machine (Pentium II at 233 MHz). The measurements have been taken over three different GNAT portings:

1. GNAT 3.10p over JTK using the embedded kernel
2. GNAT 3.10p over Linux, using the FSU implementation of Pthreads
3. GNAT 3.10p over DOS, using the FSU implementation of Pthreads

Context switch time is a very important feature in real-time systems, with a high influence on timing behaviour. The notion of cheap concurrency has been around in Pthreads and related works, which try to offer lightweight processes.

7 Conclusions and Availability

JTK was designed to strictly fit the GNAT runtime system needs. This design criterion led to a very simple and efficient implementation.

Flexibility is another issue that has been reached with this library. An easy way of extending the functionality has been established, based mainly on the object oriented techniques available in Ada 95. For example, the design of a new scheduler is a type extension that can reuse by inheritance many of the primitive operations.

Tasking is one of the strengths of Ada, but people still renounce to use it in safety-critical schemes for fear of complexity. Therefore, all the work made

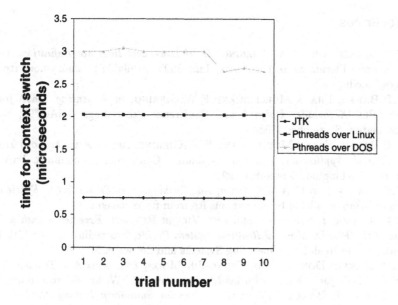

Fig. 1. Time taken by a task context switch

in order to enhance the efficiency, reliability and even more, the simplicity and comprehensiveness of the tasking implementation could lead to an increased use of Ada tasking in a more extended environment, since it is easier to trust in a simple, readable and understandable implementation. It has some similarities with the successful Ravenscar Profile[7] design purposes, but this approach is quite different.

Summarizing, JTK offers to GNARL all low-level tasking features: priority driven scheduling with preemption and support for dynamic priorities, dynamic task creation, support for Asynchronous Transfer of Control (ATCs), mutex object with immediate priority ceiling protocol, signal management and simple timer management.

JTK has been tested in the following architectures:

- Linux/i386, 2.x kernels, with GNAT-3.10p (should also work with 1.x kernels).
- MS/DOS, with GNAT-3.10.

JTK is available from:

> `ftp://ftp.dit.upm.es/str/software/jtk/`

and is covered by a modified GPL license. More information about the JTK library can be consulted at:

> `http://www.dit.upm.es/~jfruiz/jtk.html`

References

1. T.P. BAKER AND E.W. GIERING, *GNU Low-Level Interface Definition*, Technical Report, Florida State University, June 1993. Available by anonymous ftp from ftp.cs.fsu.edu.
2. T.P.BAKER, FRANK MUELLER AND E.W.GIERING, *Implementing Ada9X features using POSIX threads: design issues*, Conference Proceedings, TriAda'93, Seattle, Washington, September 1993.
3. T.P.BAKER, FRANK MUELLER AND E.W.GIERING, *Ada9X Asynchronous Transfer Of Control: Applications And Implementation*, Conference Proceedings, TriAda'93, Seattle, Washington, September 1993.
4. T.P. BAKER AND G.A. RICCARDI, *Ada Tasking: from Semantics to Efficient Implementation*. Available by anonymous ftp from ftp.cs.fsu.edu.
5. T.P. BAKER, FRANK MUELLER AND VIRESH RUSTAGI, *Experience with a Prototype of the POSIX Minimal Realtime System Profile*, Proceedings of the 11th IEEE Workshop on Real-Time Operating Systems and Software, May 1994.
6. T.P. BAKER, DONG-IK OH, SEUNG-JIN MOON, *Low-Level Ada Tasking Support for GNAT-Performance and Portability Improvements*, Wadas'96 Proceedings, 1996.
7. A. BURNS, T. BAKER, T.VARDANEGA, *Session Summary: Tasking Profiles*, In Proceedings for the 8th International Real-Time Ada Workshop, Ada Letters XVII, 1997.
8. ALAN BURNS AND ANDY WELLINGS, *Real-Time Systems and their Programming Languages (2nd Edn)*, Addison-Wesley, 1996.
9. E.W. GIERING AND T.P. BAKER, *Using POSIX Threads to Implement Ada tasking: Description of work in Progress*, TRI-Ada '92 Proceedings (Nov 1992) pages 518-529.
10. E.W. GIERING AND T.P. BAKER, *POSIX/Ada Realtime Bindings: Description of Work in Progress*, In Proceedings of the Ninth Annual Washington Ada Symposium,ACM, July 1992.
11. FRANK MUELLER, *A Library Implementation of POSIX Threads under UNIX*, 1993 Winter USENIX.
12. DONG-IK OH AND T.P. BAKER, *Gnu Ada'95 Tasking Implementation: Real-Time Features and Optimization*, In Proceedings of the 1997 Workshop of Languages, Compilers and Tools for Real-Time Systems (LCT-RTS), Las Vegas, Nevada, 1997.
13. DONG-IK OH AND T.P. BAKER, *Optimization of Ada'95 Tasking Constructs*, Tri-Ada'97, St. Louis, Missouri, 1997.
14. DONG-IK OH, T.P. BAKER AND SEUNG-JIN MOON, *The GNARL Implementation of POSIX/Ada Signal Services*, In Ada-Europe '96 Proceedings, pages 276-286.

A Structure of the JTK Scheduler

```
package Schedulers is
   ...
   -- Sched_Task is the foundation for the class of types used as
   -- low-level tasks.
   type Sched_Task is abstract tagged
      record
         ...
      end record;
   -- Sched_Task_CA is the low-level task descriptor.
   type Sched_Task_CA is access all Sched_Task'Class;
   -- Scheduler contains the list of ready tasks and the
   -- descriptor of the task that is executing currently.
   type Scheduler is abstract tagged limited
      record
         Ready_List : Sched_List;
         Current    : Sched_Task_CA;
      end record;
   procedure Insert (A_Sched_Task : Sched_Task_CA;
                     Sched : in out Scheduler) is abstract;
   procedure Remove (A_Sched_Task : Sched_Task_CA;
                     Sched : in out Scheduler) is abstract;
   procedure Change_Priority (A_Sched_Task : Sched_Task_CA;
                              Prio : System.Any_Priority;
                              Sched : in out Scheduler)
      is abstract;
   procedure Next (Sched : in out Scheduler) is abstract;
   type Scheduler_FIFO_Prio is new Scheduler with null record;
   ...
end Schedulers;

package Schedulers.Basic is
   ...
   type Basic_Sched_Task is new Sched_Task with null record;
   ...
end Schedulers.Basic;

package Schedulers.RoundRobin is
   ...
   type Timed_Sched_Task is new Sched_Task with
   record
      Time_Slice : Duration := Default_Slice;
   end record;
   ...
end Schedulers.RoundRobin;
```

MetaScribe, an Ada-based Tool for the Construction of Tranformation Engines

Fabrice Kordon

LIP6-SRC
Université P.&M. Curie
4 place Jussieu, 75252 Paris Cedex 05, France
email: Fabrice.Kordon@lip6.fr

Abstract : This paper presents MetaScribe, a generator of transformation engine designed to help the implementation of program generators or transformation of a specification to another one. MetaScribe defines a meta-data description scheme suitable for the internal representation of various graphical and hierarchical description.
MetaScribe is fully implemented in Ada and uses the language facilities to enforce type checking and handling of errors in the manipulated descriptions.

Keywords : Meta-data description, Semantic transformation, Code generation.

1 Introduction

Software engineering methodologies rely on various and complex graphical representations such as OMT, UML, etc. They are more useful when associated to CASE (Computer Aided Software Engineering) tools designed to take care of constraints that have to be respected. Such tools help engineers and facilitate the promotion of such methodologies.

Now, CASE tools gave way to CASE environments that may be adapted to a specific understanding of a design methodology. A CASE environment can be defined as follow [12] : it is a set of cooperative tools. CASE environments are built on a platform that allows tool plugging. Communication and cooperation between tools must subsequently be investigated.

Implementation of CASE environments is a complex task because they need various functions like graphical user interface, database and communication facilities. Experimentation over large projects has outlined the difficulty to maintain them, especially when tools come from various origins. In a project like Ptolemy [10] , the software bases for the project have largely changed in order to ease maintenance as well as new development. Such work (in particular, the Tycho interface system [6]) takes into account the definition of evolutionary interfaces between major components.

To implement methodologies and experiment them on large case studies, we have elaborated FrameKit [7] , a framework for the quick implementation of CASE environments. It is parameterized in order to provide a framework for the customization of CASE environments dedicated to a given method (Fig. 1). FrameKit is mostly integrated in Ada (a small amount of C is used to interface Unix) and provides enhanced Ada Application Program Interfaces (API) to operate this customization procedure.

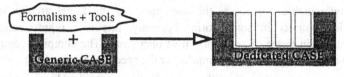

Fig. 1 From a Generic CASE to a dedicated one.

We have used FrameKit to implement CPN-AMI2, a Petri net based CASE environment with satisfactory results. To do so, we have described the Petri net formalism and declared a set of coherent tools that can be applied on Petri net specifications [8] . Doing so, we have noticed there is a major problem to provide data sharing facilities between tools coming from various origins. This problem is even more difficult for an environment like FrameKit where we cannot use specificity of a formalism to ease the implementation (FrameKit is supposed to be generic). There is a need to provide FrameKit with facilities to easily manage *secondary standards*. Secondary standards in FrameKit are communication-based data representations dedicated to a formalism (for example the description of Petri net results potentially exploited by other tools).

CPN-AMI2 implements the MARS method [3] in which both transformations (from a representation to another one) and program generators have to be implemented. We noticed there were a lack of tools to ease such implementations. Parser generators are useful to help the syntactical analysis of input specification but the transformation rules have to be described using a programming language. It is then difficult to reuse transformation rules. On another hand, Expert systems provide good facilities for the definition of transformation rules but are poor for I/O and efficient management of complex data structures. So, there is also a need for a tool providing facilities to the implementation of *transformation engines*. A transformation engine is a program that parses an input specification and produces an output specification by applying transformation rules.

This paper presents MetaScribe, a tool suitable for the two purposes outlined above. MetaScribe is fully implemented in Ada and uses the language facilities to enforce type checking and handling of errors. Section 2 presents MetaScribe and Section 3 discuss its implementation.

2 MetaScribe

MetaScribe solves problems similar to the ones identified in hardware/software codesing of embedded systems where specific processors are built in very limited series. There is a need for designing specific compilers at low-cost. Retargetable compilers are designed for this task and can be classified as follow [1] :

- Automatically retargetable compilers: they contain a set of switches that need to be set to specify the target architecture. Essentially, all possible target architectures that the compiler is intended to be used for are already built in;

- User retargetable compilers: the user specifies the target architecture to the compiler-compiler in some form. Typically, this is a representation of the instructions in terms of some primitive operations. The compiler-compiler takes this as input and generates a compiler for the specified architecture;

- Developer retargetable compilers that is a way to handle machine specific optimizations that go beyond instruction selection is to permit the developer to modify the compiler to target the given architecture. The difference between retargeting and writing a new compiler for any architecture is rather low. For a compiler to be considered retargetable in this scenario, no new processor dependent optimization capabilities are added to the compiler during retargeting.

MetaScribe fits the needs outlined by the two last points. Like a parser generator such as flex/bison [5, 9] , it enables the use of rules applied on input specifications according to a customized scheme. However, because it focuses on the management of hierarchical and graphical like specifications, its philosophy is quite different from the one of a parser generator and the transformation scheme is made of rules contained in a semantic pattern. Like a retargetable compiler, it enables the application of a customized output according to a given syntax format. It is then possible to associate discrete syntactic patterns to a given semantic pattern (e.g. apply Ada or Java code on an object program description). Its parameterization procedure is then similar to the concept of hypergenericity [2] .

2.1 Architecture of MetaScribe

In order to increase reusability of transformation engine's elements, input description, as well as semantical and syntactical aspects of a transformation are separately defined. To be operated, MetaScribe requires three elements to be described (Fig. 2):

- Formalism definition: it is expressed using the MSF meta-description language. Users have to declare any entity that can be found in the formalism;

- Semantic pattern: it is expressed using the MSSM language. Users define the transformation rules to be applied on the associated formalism;

- Syntactic rules: it is expressed using the MSST language. Users define the syntactic representation associated to constructors declared in the corresponding semantic pattern.

The semantic pattern is composed of rules that produce a polymorphic semantic representation similar to the one of ASIS [11] called *semantic expression-trees*. Semantic expression-trees are expression trees expressing the semantic of a description without syntactic information (like a parsed program in a compiler).

Semantic patterns are not dedicated to a given programming language and can be customized. They declare a list constructors that make the connection with a syntactic pattern describing how these constructors will be represented.

Input specifications must be written using the MSM data description language automatically customized according to the entities declared in the MSF description. Checks are enforced at execution time of the transformation engine.

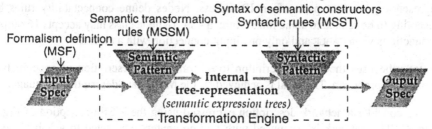

Fig. 2 Structure and components of a transformation engine generated with MetaScribe.

MetaScribe generates a transformation engine from a triplet *<input formalism, semantic pattern, syntactic pattern>*. Such a mechanism enables the reuse of components in any of the involved elements. Thus, MSF, MSSM and MSST languages allow separate definition of pattern components

2.2 Formalism description

The MSF meta-description language allows users to declare entities potentially found in a type of specification. MSF (MetaScribe Formalism) is an object based description language where classes are either nodes or links. A node is a piece of specification. A link relates some nodes together. Both nodes and links may carry local information stored in attributes. Global information is specified in attributes that are related to the specification (and not to a specific entity). Attributes contain typed expressions (characters, strings, integers, etc.).

```
formalism ('NETWORK_DSC');              node (HUB_16) is
// nodes and linkss                        attribute_list
entity_list                                  attribute string  : NAME;
   COMPUTER : node,                          attribute expression : IP_ADDRESS;
   HUB_16 : node,                         end ;
   CABLE : link;                          connectability_list
// Global attributes                         with CABLE
global_attributes                               direction out ,
   attribute string  : NET_ID;                  maximum 16 ;
end;                                         with CABLE
// parsed expressions for IP-address description    direction in ,
construction_list (DYNAMIC, STATIC);            maximum 1 ;
// description of nodes and linkss           end ;
node (COMPUTER) is                       end HUB_16 ;
   attribute_list
      attribute string  : NAME;          link (CABLE) is
      attribute expression : IP_ADDRESS;     attribute_list
   end ;                                        none
   connectability_list                      end ;
      with CABLE                         end CABLE ;
         direction in ,
         maximum 1 ;
   end ;
end COMPUTER ;
```

Fig. 3 Example of formalism description with MSF.

Let us illustrate MSF possibilities with a small example. Fig. 3 presents a simple formalism description: a network composed of computers and hubs related by means of communication cables. Both computers and hubs are reference using a name and an IP-number. The name attribute is a string and the IP-number attribute is an expression tree composed of a root (tagged STATIC or DYNAMIC) and, if STATIC, four sons representing the four parts of an IP-address. Nodes define connectability rules by accepting to be related to some links. Here, a HUB_16 node class may accepts 16 output connections via a CABLE and only one input connection with a CABLE.

MetaScribe uses the MSF description to customize the description of specification using this formalism. This goal is achieved by the MSM data-description language.

Let us consider a network description expressed using the MSF description of Fig. 3 (Fig. 4). The network is composed with two computers connected to a hub via two cables. The hub and one computer have static IP-addresses and the second computer has a dynamic one.

```
formalism ( 'NETWORK_DSC' ) ;
// Global attributes
where (attribute NET_ID => 'my_net') ;
// hub list
node 'hub_1' is HUB_16
   where (attribute NAME => 'hub_one',
              attribute IP_ADDRESS => sy_node (STATIC:
                                          sy_leaf (10),
                                          sy_leaf (10),
                                          sy_leaf (10),
                                          sy_leaf (10)));
// host list
node 'host_1' is COMPUTER
   where (attribute NAME => 'host_one',
              attribute IP_ADDRESS => sy_leaf (DYNAMIC)) ;
node 'host_2' is COMPUTER
   where (attribute NAME => 'host_two',
              attribute IP_ADDRESS => sy_node (STATIC:
                                          sy_leaf (10),
                                          sy_leaf (10),
                                          sy_leaf (10),
                                          sy_leaf (11)));
// connections
link 'cable_1' is CABLE
   where (none)
   relate HUB_16:'hub_1' to COMPUTER:'host_1';
link 'cable_2' is CABLE
   where (none)
   relate HUB_16:'hub_1' to COMPUTER:'host_2';
```

Fig. 4 Description of a specification using teh formalism defined in Fig. 3.

The major advantage of MSM (MetaScribe Model) is to clearly describe a data-structure that can have a memory equivalent. It is a polymorphic data-description language because it does not take side on any aspect of the specification and only carries out its description.

A transformation engine generated with MetaScribe first parses the MSM description of a model and maps it to data structures in memory. Then, actions defined in both semantic and syntactic patterns are applied on this memory representation.

2.3 Semantic patterns description

The MSSM description language allows users to define transformations to be applied on an input specification. Such a description is related to a formalism (i.e. a MSF description) where entities to be manipulated are described. A MSSM (MetaScribe SeMantic) descriptions is composed with three elements:

- *Constructors* that are links to a given syntactic pattern,
- *Rules* that process entities found in the input specification (nodes, links, attributes),
- *Static trees* that corresponds to constant semantic expression-trees.

MSSM is a functional based language. Program units are rules (actions to be applied on the memory image of an input specification) and static-trees. It is possible to build a semantic pattern from separate files.

The goal of a semantic pattern is to produce semantic expression trees. Semantic expression trees are trees where nodes contains at least one of the three following fields:

- A constructor,
- A string,
- An integer.

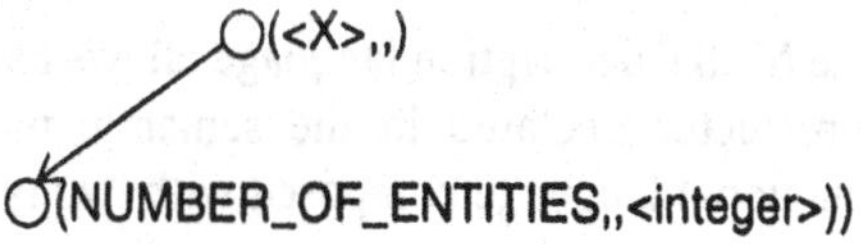

```
...
constructor_list is ...
    NUMBER_OF_ENTITIES,
    TYPE_COMPUTER,
    TYPE_HUB;
...
semantic_tree ONE_OBJECT (TYPE    : semantic_constructor,
                          NUMBER : integer) is
    semantic_node ([$smc (TYPE) # #]:
        semantic_leaf ([NUMBER_OF_ENTITIES # # $int (NUMBER)]))
end;
```

Fig. 5 Example of a static-tree in a semantic pattern.

Fig. 5 presents an example of semantic expression tree and its corresponding description as a static-tree. Let us assume that, to produce a textual display of a network description, three semantic constructors have been declared: NUMBER_OF_ENTITIES, TYPE_COMPUTER and TYPE_HUB. The semantic-tree ONE_OBJECT corresponds to the tree on the upper right where <X> is a predefined constructor (either TYPE_COMPUTER or TYPE_HUB) and <int> a natural value. Thus, the definition of a syntactic form for such an expression can be easily performed. Here, the tree's root only contains a predefined constructor and its son a predefined constructor and an integer.

Fig. 6 presents an example of semantic rule and shows how semantic and syntactic patterns are connected. The rule produces an expression-tree that references all computers in a network. First, it creates the root of a result expression-tree and applies the rule A_RULE to any COMPUTER node in the description. Then, it invokes the syntactic pattern and applies it to the resulted tree. Note that the syntactic pattern is not explicitly named (the association <*MSF description, MSSM description, MSST description*> is set by users when they invoke MetaScribe to build a transformation engine). The application of the syntactic pattern is written in the file a_file as asked in the generate directive.

```
semantic_rule LIST_COMPUTERS (none) return void is

TREE : semantic_tree;

begin
    // Create the root of the result expression-tree
    TREE := create_sm_tree ([ANALYSIS_RESULT #
                                $atrv_str (attribute NET_ID)#]);
    // linking a computer to the description
    message ('Analysis the network...');
    if nb_node_instance (COMPUTER) > 0 then
        for COMP in 1 .. nb_node_instance (COMPUTER) do
            TREE := add_sm_son ($smt (TREE),
                                sm_rule A_RULE (get_node_reference (COMPUTER,
                                                                $int (COMP))));
        end for;
    end if;
    // Applying the syntactic pattern to the result expresion-tree
    generate $smt (TREE) in 'a_file';
    message ('Done...');
    return;
end;
```

Fig. 6 Example of a rule in a semantic pattern.

2.4 Syntactic patterns description

The MSST description language allows users to associate a syntactic expression to any constructor declared in the semantic pattern. MSST (MetaScribe SynTactic) is a functional language composed with two types of rules:

- *External rules* are associated to predefined constructors. Such rules can be either implicitly invoked according to the constructor tag of a semantic expression-tree node or explicitly invoked;

- *Internal rules* are not associated to predefined constructors. Thus, they can only be explicitly invoked from external rules. Usually, an external rule is a "front end" for several internal rules.

```
syntactic_rule TYPE_COMPUTER is
begin
    put ('number of computers in the network :');
    apply ($1);
end;

syntactic_rule TYPE_HUB is
begin
    put ('number of hubs in the network      :');
    apply ($1);
end;

syntactic_rule NUMBER_OF_ENTITIES is
begin
    put_line ($str_int (0));
end;
```

Fig. 7 Abstract of a syntactic pattern.

Fig. 7 contains a set of external rules dedicated to textual display of the semantic tree defined in Fig. 5. Any declared constructor has to be related to a syntactic rule in the pattern. TYPE_COMPUTER and TYPE_HUB implicitly refer to rule NUMBER_OF_ENTITIES using the apply instruction. It invokes the rule associated to the predefined constructor found in the root of the tree transmitted as a parameter.

Fig. 8 presents the execution scheme of the rules presented in Fig. 7 on a tree that respect the required format. TYPE_NUM implicitly invokes the rule associated to the semantic constructor located in the first son of the semantic expression tree transmitted as a parameter (here, NUMBER_OF_ENTITIES). This invoked rule converts the integer value into a string that is written in the output declared in the corresponding semantic pattern (via the generate directive). The result for this expression-tree should be:

```
number of hub in the network        : 4
```

Of course, the «apply» directive can be used to explicitly apply a syntactic rule to a semantic-expression-tree. Then, the rule identifier is also transmitted.

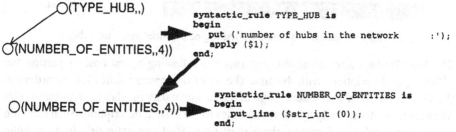

```
syntactic_rule TYPE_HUB is
begin
    put ('number of hubs in the network        :');
    apply ($1);
end;
```

```
syntactic_rule NUMBER_OF_ENTITIES is
begin
    put_line ($str_int (0));
end;
```

Fig. 8 Execution of the syntactic pattern on a given expression-tree.

3 About MetaScribe implementation

Implementation's principles of MetaScribe are rather simple: it is a program generator. We first investigated an interpreted approach but it raises two problems:

- it should be slower,
- execution time checks have to be implemented.

Thus, transformation engines produced by MetaScribe are specific programs implementing a particular transformation. Then, the choice of Ada is obvious: it provides good mechanisms for execution time type checking. Then, all execution time checks are supported by the Ada runtime. Exceptions are caught in a handler and the propagation mechanism is used to provide the program stack (soon or later, this function should be supported by all compilers).

3.1 Structure of a generated transformation engine

The structure of a transformation engine generated by MetaSCribe is shown in Fig. 9. There are six components (the Ada runtime is not a part of MetaScribe):

- the MetaScribe runtime that performs input/output operations and defines all data structures suitable for a transformation engine. For example, it contains a generic semantic expression-tree manager to be instantiated for the constructors defined in the semantic pattern;
- a MSM parser that interpret the input specification and built a memory representation on which semantic rules will operate;

- a MSF parser to dynamically interpret the input formalism's description;
- the implementation of the semantic pattern;
- the implementation of the syntactic pattern;
- the MetaScribe starter.

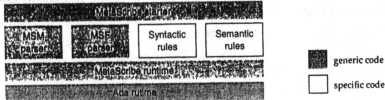

Fig. 9 Structure of a tranformation engine produced by MetaScribe.

The MetaScribe starter basically performs the following operations: a) parsing the MSM input description (with dynamic checks of the input specification according to the MSF description[1]), b) «launching» of the semantic pattern. «launching» means that MetaScribe systematically applies some rules to the current description. Such rules are called «main rules», of course, there must be at least one main rule in a semantic pattern.

Transformation engines designed with MetaScribe are ready to be plugged in FrameKit, our generic CASE environment. Thus, it is a simple way to prototype transformation tools as well as program generators and experiment them in a given methodology.

3.2 Implementation of a semantic pattern

The semantic pattern is composed with two packages : the first one defines data structures, the second one implements the semantic pattern.

```
with GEN_RTM_SEM_TREE;
package STATISTICS_SEM_TREE_MNGR is
    -- ==================================================================
    -- The type that contains all the predefined semantic constructors
    type STATISTICS_SEMANTIC_CONSTRUCTOR is (XXX_SEM_TREE_NO_ITEM,
                                STATISTICS_RID_ANALYSIS_RESULT,
                                STATISTICS_RID_NUMBER_OF_ENTITIES,
                                STATISTICS_RID_TYPE_COMPUTER,
                                STATISTICS_RID_TYPE_HUB);
    -- ==================================================================
    -- Instanciation of the generic unit that defines semantic expresion-trees
    package INTERNAL_STATISTICS_SEM_TREE_MNGR is
            new GEN_RTM_SEM_TREE (STATISTICS_SEMANTIC_CONSTRUCTOR);
    -- ==================================================================
    -- The exception used to generate the propagation stack of errors
    PROPAGATE_ERROR : exception;
end STATISTICS_SEM_TREE_MNGR;
```

Fig. 10 Example of generated code: the main data structure to operate the semantic.

Fig. 10 provides the specification of the package defining data structures. It declares an enumerative type containing all constructors (STATISTICS_SEMANTIC_CONSTRUCTOR)

---

1. To speed up execution, it is possible to disable these execution time check.

and uses it to instance the semantic expression-tree manager. This enables the use of primitives dedicated to the handling of semantic tree-expressions for a specific transformation engine.

The package implementing the semantic pattern groups procedures and functions corresponding to rules and static semantic-trees. The body of these primitives is located in a separate file in order to avoid big files. Fig. 11 shows the code generated for the static semantic-tree presented in Fig. 5. primitives of the instantiated semantic expression-tree manager are used to build a specific tree. Exception handlers are generated to either signal a problem or propagate it. In debug mode, traces are automatically generated at both the beginning and the end of the subprogram.

```
separate (STATISTICS_SEM_ENTITIES)

function SMT_STATISTICS_ONE_OBJECT (TYPE : in STATISTICS_SEMANTIC_CONSTRUCTOR;
                                    NUMBER : in INTEGER) return RTM_SEM_TREE is
    TMP_TAB : SUB_SEM_TREE_STORAGE;
begin
    TMP_TAB := CREATE_RTM_SEM_TREE (CREATE_RTM_SEM_NODE (ITS_TYPE => TYPE,
                                                         ITS_INT_VALUE => NUMBER));
    TMP_TAB := ADD_SON_TO_CURRENT_NODE (TMP_TAB, CREATE_RTM_SEM_TREE (
               CREATE_RTM_ST_NODE (ITS_TYPE => STATISTICS_RID_NUMBER_OF_ENTITIES)));
    return TMP_TAB;
exception
    when PROPAGATE_ERROR =>
        FK_PUT_MSG (MESSAGE => "propagated in ->SMT_STATISTICS_ONE_OBJECT");
        raise ;
    when others =>
        FK_PUT_MSG (MESSAGE => "Huge problem in ->SMT_STATISTICS_ONE_OBJECT");
        raise PROPAGATE_ERROR;
end SMT_STATISTICS_ONE_OBJECT;
```

Fig. 11 Example of generated code: static semantic-tree ONE_OBJECT (Fig. 5).

3.3 Implementation of a syntactic pattern

The syntactic pattern is composed of a package that groups all syntactic rules. As for semantic patterns code generation and to avoid large files, rules bodies are located in separate units. Because they never return any value (they are used to print strings in an output), syntactic rules are implemented via procedures.

```
with STATISTICS_SEM_ENTITIES,
     SYN_GENERATOR_RUNTIME;
use  STATISTICS_SEM_ENTITIES,
     SYN_GENERATOR_RUNTIME;

separate (SYNT_PATTERN_TEXT_DISPLAY_FOR_STATISTICS)
procedure SYR_STATISTICS_TEXT_DISPLAY_TYPE_COMPUTER (SEM_TREE : in RTM_SEM_TREE) is
begin
    SYN_RTM_PUT (FILE_IN_MEM, TO_VSTRING ("number of computers in the network :"));
    APPLY_SYNTACTIC_RULE (CURRENT_GOTO_SON (SEM_TREE, 1));
exception
    when PROPAGATE_ERROR =>
        FK_PUT_MSG (MESSAGE =>
                    "propagated in ->SYR_STATISTICS_TEXT_DISPLAY_TYPE_COMPUTER");
        raise ;
    when others =>
        FK_PUT_MSG (MESSAGE =>
                    "Huge problem in ->SYR_STATISTICS_TEXT_DISPLAY_TYPE_COMPUTER");
        raise PROPAGATE_ERROR;
end SYR_STATISTICS_TEXT_DISPLAY_TYPE_COMPUTER;
```

Fig. 12 Example of generated code: syntactic rule for constructor TYPE_COMPUTER (Fig. 7).

Fig. 12 shows the code generated for syntactic rule TYPE_COMPUTER in the syntactic pattern (Fig. 7). A parameter is necessary that was implicit in the syntactic pattern description: the semantic expression-tree on which the rule is applied. Because rules are sequentially invoked, the output file is not provided, a «current output» is set each time the syntactic pattern in invoked by a semantic rule.

Display functions that put message to a default output set via the generate directive belongs to the MetaScribe runtime (like SYN_RTM_PUT which behaves like PUT). navigation directives (like $1 in the syntactic rule) are implemented by the instantiated semantic expression-tree manager (for example, CURRENT_GOTO_SON implements the $<int> directive).

Exception handlers are set to detect problems in expression-trees construction (they correspond to bugs in the semantic pattern description). A trace mode allows tracking of all input semantic expression-trees of syntactic rules.

```
-- The function that perform dynamicaly the application of the rule tag referenced in the current
-- node of a semantic tree.
procedure APPLY_SYNTACTIC_RULE (SEM_TREE : in RTM_SEM_TREE) is
begin
    case GET_RTM_ST_NODE_TYPE (CURRENT_CONTENT (SEM_TREE)) is
        when STATISTICS_RID_ANALYSIS_RESULT =>
            SYR_STATISTICS_TEXT_DISPLAY_ANALYSIS_RESULT (SEM_TREE);
        when STATISTICS_RID_NUMBER_OF_ENTITIES =>
            SYR_STATISTICS_TEXT_DISPLAY_NUMBER_OF_ENTITIES (SEM_TREE);
        when STATISTICS_RID_TYPE_COMPUTER =>
            SYR_STATISTICS_TEXT_DISPLAY_TYPE_COMPUTER (SEM_TREE);
        when STATISTICS_RID_TYPE_HUB =>
            SYR_STATISTICS_TEXT_DISPLAY_TYPE_HUB (SEM_TREE);
        when XXX_SEM_TREE_NO_ITEM =>
            raise SYNT_PTRN_APPLY_ERROR;
    end case ;
exception
    when PROPAGATE_ERROR =>
        FK_PUT_MSG (MESSAGE => "propagated in ->APPLY_SYNTACTIC_RULE");
        raise ;
    when others =>
        FK_PUT_MSG (MESSAGE => "Huge problem in ->APPLY_SYNTACTIC_RULE");
        raise PROPAGATE_ERROR;
end APPLY_SYNTACTIC_RULE;
```

Fig. 13 Example of generated code: automatic apply function.

One point is the implementation of the apply function. The explicit apply corresponds to a standard procedure call. The implicit apply is implemented by means the procedure shown in Fig. 13. It contains a case based on the enumerative type that describes all constructors declared in the semantic pattern (remind that internal rules cannot be implicitly invoked).

4 Conclusion

We have presented in this paper MetaScribe, a tool to quickly produce transformation engines. A transformation engine is a program that parses an input specification and produces an output specification by applying transformation rules. It can be used to build program generators or to ease standardization of data representation in a CASE environment like FrameKit.

MetaScribe is operational, information can be found on <http://www-src.lip6.fr/ metacribe>. It has been experimented to generated Petri nets or Java programs from high-level semi-formal specification **[13]**. Results of these experimentations are satisfactory. We are currently using it to handle transformation from High Level Agent oriented specification into Petri nets in the ODAC project **[4]**.

References

[1] G. Araujo, S. Devadas, K. Keutzer, S. Liao, S. Malik, A. Sudarsanam, S. Tjiang & A. Wang, "Challenges in Code Generation for Embedded Processors", Chapter 3, pp. 48-64, in "Code Generation for Embedded Processors", P. Marwedel and G. Goossens editors, Kluwer Academic Publishers, ISBN 0-7923-9577-8, 1995

[2] P.Desfray, "Object Engineering, the fourth dimention", Addison-Wesley, 1994

[3] A. Diagne, P. Estraillier & F. Kordon, "Quality Management Issues along Life-cycle of Distributed Applications", in the proceedings of CARI'98, pp 753-763, Dakar, Sénégal, October 12-15, 1998

[4] A. Diagne & M.P. Gervais, "Building Telecommunications Services as Qualitative Multi-Agent Systems: the ODAC Project", in Proceedings of the IEEE Globecom'98, Sydney, Australia, November 1998

[5] C. Donnelly & R. Stallman, "Bison: The YACC-compatible Parser Generator", GNU documentation, <http://www.cl.cam.ac.uk/texinfodoc/bison_toc.html>, November 1995

[6] C. Hylands, E. Lee & H. Reekie, "The Tycho User Interface System", The 5th Annual Tcl/Tk Workshop '97, Boston, Massachusetts, pp 149-157, July 14-17, 1997

[7] F.Kordon & J-L. Mounier, "FrameKit, an Ada Framework for a Fast Implementation of CASE Environments", in proceedings of the ACM/SIGAda ASSET'98 symposium, pp 42-51, Monterey, USA, July 1998

[8] MARS-Team, "the CPN-AMI2 home page", <http://www.lip6.fr/cpn-ami>

[9] V. Paxson, "Flex: A fast scanner generator, Edition 2.5", GNU documentation, <http://www.cl.cam.ac.uk/texinfodoc/flex_toc.html>, March 1995

[10] Ptolemy Team, "The Ptolemy Kernel-- Supporting Heterogeneous Design", RASSP Digest Newsletter, vol. 2, no. 1, pp. 14-17, 1st Quarter, April, 1995

[11] S. Rybin, A. Strohmeier & E. Zueff, "ASIS for GNAT: Goals, Problems and Implementation Strategy", In M. Toussaint (Ed), Second International Eurospace - Ada-Europe Symposium Proceedings, LNCS no 1031, Springer Verlag, pp 139-151, 1995

[12] D.Schefström, "System Development Environments: Contemporary Concepts", in Tool Integration: environment and framework, Edited by D.Schefström & G. van den Broek, John Wiley & Sons, 1993

[13] P. Vidal, "Comparison between implementation and code generation for multi-agent systems : application to the Personnal Travel Assistant", Master thesis in an ERASMUS program, University of Olso and University P. & M. Curie, 1999

An Adaption of our Ada95/O2 Binding to Provide Persistence to the Java Language: Sharing and Handling of Data between Heterogeneous Applications Using Persistence

Thierry MILLAN, Myriam LAMOLLE

Frédéric MULATERO

IRIT - CNRS (UMR 5055)
Université Paul Sabatier
118, route de Narbonne
31062, Toulouse Cedex FRANCE
Tel. (+33) (0)5 61 55 86 32
Fax. (+33) (0)5 61 55 62 58
E-mail: (millan, lamolle)@irit.fr

MIRA
Département de Mathématiques
Université Toulouse Le Mirail
5, allée Antonio MACHADO
31058 Toulouse Cedex
Tel. (+33) (0)5 61 50 42 20
E-mail: mulatero@univ-tlse2.fr

Abstract. This paper sets out the results of our research relating to persistence in Ada and interoperability between applications written using heterogeneous languages. In this paper, we compare the different features of Ada, Java and O2. By making this comparison, we aim to propose a general framework in order to interconnect different applications using the persistence concept. In addition, we propose an example of the co-operation between Ada and Java using O2. We conclude our paper by comparing our approach with the different approaches proposed by other studies on the same subject.

Keywords. Persistence, Ada 83, Ada 95, Java, Object Oriented Database Management System, O2, interoperability, data environment

1 Introduction

The aim of our project is to propose an efficient solution to save, restore and exchange data [1]. We use the concept of persistence to save the application's context in an object oriented database and retrieve it from the database. The object oriented database management system (OODBMS) O2 manages the database. We use the interconnection capability provided by O2 to exchange data. A prototype of an interface [2] between Ada and O2 has been developed to validate our studies in this area. This prototype use an O2 database management system version 4.6 and Ada version 95 (gnat compiler 3.10p). It runs on a sparc station ultra 1 with solaris 2.5. Performance tests have been performed and are presented in [1, 2]. In addition, we extend the results of our previous studies on persistence in order to propose a solution to manage persistent environment with other object oriented languages (e.g. C++, Java). The aim of this generalization is to permit the exchange of data between applications written using heterogeneous languages. The main advantage of this approach is the possibility to delegate certain treatments to applications written in a more appropriate language. For example, it is possible to delegate to a Java application the visualization of the data created by an Ada application. In this way the use of Java makes the realization of an application that accesses data through a network more easy.

This paper proposes a comparative study between the Java language, the Ada language and the O2 OODBMS. This comparison aims to show that the O2 OODBMS could be used as a common platform between Java and Ada in order to exchange data. Besides, O2 respects the recommendations of the Object Database Management Group [3] recommendations. These recommendations provide the features that an OODBMS must respect in order to facilitate interconnection between several OODBMS, or between an OODBMS and applications using the CORBA standard. In this paper, we only present the features concerning the handling of data. However, we do not propose to take into account the persistence of "Ada task", "Java thread" or "Java AWT classes". In this paper, we also propose an example that shows the advantages of such co-operation between heterogeneous applications.

In the first part of this paper, we will present our experience concerning persistent environments. We will also provide our definitions of persistence. We will also provide a short presentation of the binding between Ada and O2. In the second part of this paper, we will propose a comparative study of Ada 95, Java and O2. The aim of this comparison is to demonstrate that the Ada 95/O2 binding can be an interesting base for a Java/O2 binding. In the third part of the paper, we will provide an example of how these bindings can be applied to manage the data handled by an airplane simulator. Finally, we will conclude by presenting a quick discussion concerning studies carried out in relation to persistence for the Ada and Java languages. We will also present the advantages of such a binding when used to facilitate data exchange independent of the language that creates and handles data. This exchange can be performed independent of the medium (DBMS, OODBMS, etc.) used as interconnection platform.

2 Persistence and persistent environment

Our previous work on this subject

The emergence of new applications (computer-assisted design, technical management of documents, Internet, Intranet, etc.) needs to be supported by both database functionality and advanced treatment capacities.

The database management systems offer high storage and data handling functionality. However, they are not sufficient when complex algorithms are required. The Ada language enables one to write complex algorithms; However, the Ada programmer remains totally in charge of the efficient storage and handling of high volume of data. That is why couplings between databases management systems and programming languages are valuable.

3 Definitions

Persistence using Ada 83

The method we propose relies on the following principle [5]: **each data to be handled, has to be linked to a typed identifier.** Ada is a strongly typed language, which means all identifiers require a type which is statically set at compile time. In addition, in order to maintain a strong typed system, which is necessary to set up reliable applications, persistent data should be separated neither from the identifier to which it is linked nor from the **type** of this identifier. **Thus, we consider the concept of persistence at the identifier level rather than at the data level.**

In Ada, we define persistence as the property that allows the triplet (**identifier, data, type**) to survive after the program run-time.

In that context, the program data environment [5] is the set composed of the identifiers declared in the program, the identifiers' type and the data linked to these identifiers.

A persistent data environment is a part of the program data environment which survives once the program run-time ends.

The entire environment of a program is not necessarily persistent. A distinction should therefore be made between the **persistent environment** and the **non-persistent (transient) environment.** With such a persistent environment, it becomes possible to re-use part of the program's data environment. It simplifies the design of applications and improves, among other things, the quality of the software.

It is possible to represent the program data environment by an oriented graph structure [5] where identifiers and data are the graph nodes, and where links between them are the graph edges. A persistent environment is a sub-graph defined by the identifiers, all the data linked to the identifiers and the identifiers' type.

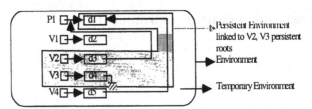

Fig. 1. Persistent environment

Note:

In our definition of a persistent environment, we do not distinguish between data built with the access constructor and the other data. With regard to non access data, we consider that there is only one link between the data and its identifier (see V1 in Figure 1).

Persistence using Ada 95

The object concept is important because it makes the application design easier and it improves the integration between the Ada language and the OODBMS O2.

In Ada, the addition of object concepts allows us to:

- extend types by addition of new attributes and new operations ;
- identify types at run-time ;
- handle values of several specific types and choose an operation at run-time [6].

For this reason, we must improve the rule of "propagation of persistence by reachability" in order to take this new characteristic into account:

– *To be persistent, a data 'd' must be linked to an identifier or a data whose type is the same as, or an ascendant of, the type of the data 'd'.*

To apply this rule, we must re-define persistence through the quadruplet (identifier, type, data, tag of the data):

– *persistence is a property that lets a quadruplet (identifier, type, data, tag of the data) exist after run-time.*

This addition permits the coherence of programs to be retained at the time of the re-use of the environment. Besides, for the persistence instance to exist, all the attributes of a type must be persistent. By way of illustration, we provide the following example: Let a type A derive from a type B and type A uses the types C and D; if persistent instances can exist in type A, persistent instances must also exist in types B, C and D.

Persistent environment properties

In [4], M. Atkinson proposes some properties that a persistent system must respect in order to be transparent for users. These rules are the following:

1. orthogonality to the type system and to creation;
2. propagation of persistence by inheritance or by reachability;
3. behavioral transparency;

Our persistent environment respects the two lasts rules and the orthogonality to creation. However, our persistent environment is not completely orthogonal to the type system. A special Ada code must be included in the corresponding package to have persistent instance. We ensure orthogonality only for new types' creations. In addition to the rules proposed by Atkinson, we add a fourth rule specially for the Ada language. This rule is the following:

4. integration of persistence into a programming language should not involve any changes in the language.

This rule is essential for standardized languages. Compliance with this rule avoids all the problems that arise when modifications are made to a standardized language (i.e. loss of the standard, ensuring that releases are coherent with new languages releases, etc.).

4 Our prototype

Principle

We chose to use an object-oriented database management system (O2) because Ada is closer to the object-oriented data model than the relational data model is. Moreover, O2 [9] complies with the object database management group (ODMG) standard [3]. This increases the interoperability between applications.

The Ada/O2 coupling is based on the use of the O2's application program interface (API). The application program interface is a library of functions which allows interaction with the database management system, insofar as the language which interfaces with the system (here, Ada) supports a C language interface.

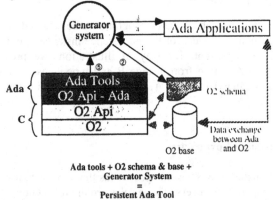

Ada tools + O2 schema & base +
Generator System
=
Persistent Ada Tool

Fig. 2: implementation of Ada persistence

At first, a set of tools has to be designed and implemented in order to connect an Ada application to the O2 database management system (⑤) (see Figure 2). These tools allow the physical connection to O2, the management of transactions, lists, sets and bags; they also solve the impedance mismatch between Ada and O2 types. It is then necessary to provide programmers with two generator systems. The first generator system generates a set of Ada packages (③) corresponding to a set of O2 classes and to an O2 database (①). The second one generates O2 classes and persistent identifiers (an O2 base) (②) corresponding to a set of Ada packages and to a package containing the database (④).

Communication between the Ada Application and the Database Management System

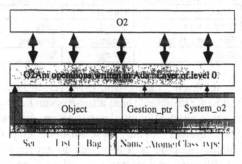

Fig. 3. interface architecture

The architecture [1] set up here (see figure 3) is modular and is composed of two layers. The first one contains all the API operations written in Ada; it represents the exact image of the O2's API written in C. The second layer contains a set of modules providing the services necessary to connect an Ada application with an O2 database. Each module is strongly typed and provides specific services. For example, some modules are used to define sets, lists and bags.

5 From Ada 95 to Java: adaptation of the persistent environment concept to Java using O2

In the previous part of our paper, we provided a short presentation of the work done in relation to the Ada 83 and 95 languages. Now, we are going to present the similarities and the differences between O2, Ada 95 and Java [7].

At present, new object oriented systems are built around the same concepts (inheritance, polymorphism, abstract class, ...). However, Ada 95, Java and O2 are different because they include specific functionality that represent their valuable specificity. Our aim is to show the possible similarities between an Ada/O2 binding and a Java/O2 binding by reference to the common and specific features of Ada and Java.

In the following two sub-sections, we draw a difference between the functionality that affects the data representation (inheritance, polymorphism, abstract class, ...) and the functionality that does not affect this representation (Ada task, Java thread, Java internet functionality, ...).

Similarities between Ada 95, Java and O2

The following table presents a quick overview of the similarities between the two languages [6, 7, 9] and O2.

Description	Ada 95 functionality	Java functionality	O2 functionality	Affects the data representation?
Inheritance	Tagged type (simple)	(simple)	(multiple)	yes
Parallelism	Task	Thread	-	no
Dynamic data type	Access type	Object	class	yes
Polymorphism	Static and dynamic	dynamic	dynamic	yes
Data typing	Strong	Strong	Strong	yes

In this paper, we do not discuss parallelism. However, in Java, a class can extend the thread class and add new attributes. These attributes can have values that generate a persistent environment consistent with the definition that we have previously provided. In this case, we consider that only these attributes are pertinent.

O2 allows to create values and objects. The values do not have identifiers. It is the values themselves that differentiate between two values. The objects have distinct identifiers. It is the identifiers that differentiate between two objects. In Ada 95, we can define both values and objects. Objects are created using access types. We can consider as values those types that do not use access. In Java, all are capable of being objects. Indeed, we can use the "wrapper class" to encapsulate the primitives types. This feature simplifies the binding because all data structures are identified using a reference. Only one kind of data (object) is implemented.

Ada 95 allows for both static binding and dynamic binding. Java, like O2, only provides for dynamic binding.

Differences between Ada 95, Java and O2

Description	Ada 95 functionality	Java functionality	O2 functionality	Affects the data representation?
Generic	Generic	-	-	yes
Classes' variables and methods	-	static	-	yes
Interface	-	Interface	-	no
Collection	-	-	Set, bag, list	yes
Exception management	Exception,raise	Throw, try, catch	-	yes
Package	Package	Package	-	yes/no
Abstract methods and classes	Abstract	Abstract	-	yes

Our interface between Ada 95 and O2 uses many generic units. This solution is better than using inheritance, because using inheritance can generate type incoherence [8]. This incoherence may affect the behavior of the methods.

Java does not provide collection builders as part of the language. The collections are required to access high volumes of data. These builders are part of the O2 language. In Ada 95, this feature can be efficiently replaced using **generic abstract data types**. In Java, we need to use inheritance [8].

Java enables several classes to be grouped in a package. Packages are not used to implement an abstract data types. In Ada, a package is used to create an abstract data type, to group several abstract types or to specify libraries of sub-programs. In our study, the Java package is **not a pertinent concept** influencing persistent environments. We ignore the Java package's concept in this paper.

O2 does not support abstract classes. Ada and Java support this kind of classes. The Ada 95 and Java compilers checks that no instance of such classes is instantiated. An abstract class can be easily mapped into an O2 class without instance. In our definition of persistence we state that "persistence is a property that lets a quadruplet (identifier, type, data, tag of the data) exist after run-time": **a "type" can be an abstract class, but the "tag of the data" cannot**.

Java and Ada support management of exception, and they consider the exception as data. In O2, we can only save the value of an exception. In this case, we do not take into account the specificity of the exceptions.

Java permits to define the interface of a class. This interface is a set of methods that must be implemented in the classes using this interface. A class can implement several interfaces. This concept does not exist in Ada 95 and O2. In addition, an interface is a set of methods and cannot be used as type of a variable. We consider this concept as **not pertinent** because an interface has no effect on the environment.

Like in C++, developer can declare static variables and methods in Java. These variables and methods are global to all the objects of the class. Only one instance of these variables is present in the system. Static methods permit to handle static variables. Static variables avoid the use of global variables that can generate problems due to side effects. However, the only possibility of storing a persistent environment that includes static data is to define an O2 persistent root for each static variable and to define O2 functions for each static method. In such a case, the developer must find a way of managing the problem due to the side effects. In Ada 95, we can define variables in the package body. These variables can be handled directly by a public sub-program provided in the package specification.

In a word

In this part of our paper, we present the similarities and the differences between Ada 95, Java and O2. This study allows us to compare the concept and functionality provided by each language. The fundamental concepts of the object languages are covered by Ada 95, O2 and Java. It is easy to define, set, bag and list abstract data types similar to the collection builders present in O2 using inheritance or generic units. The main difficulty of adapting this interface for Java is the transformation of our generic packages into classes using inheritance instead of genericity. The specific functionality (static, abstract, exception, interface) cannot be considered as pertinent to the definition of persistent environment; this is because some of them can be easily simulated in O2.

6 Example

The example that we present in this paper concerns the development of a airplane simulator. This simulator used the Ada language to implement the treatments of data. It used the O2 OODBMS save the scenarios and the historics of the users.

In this example, we show how to develop a cost efficient solution for the treatment of the data stored in the simulator database (visualization, capture of new scenarios, etc.). We use the Java language to develop these specific applications.

Framework

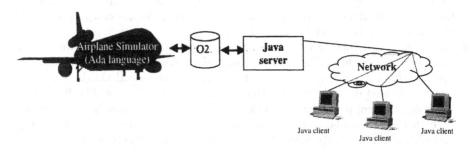

Fig. 4. General framework of the system

The Java server manages the transactions between distant clients. It can decrypt and/or encrypt data, control access and verify the scenario proposed.

The Java client can decrypt and/or encrypt information provide by the Java server. It also provides statistical tools to treat the data provided by the Java server. The main advantage of this application is that the Java client can be easily implemented into different platforms without any need for recompilation. The realization of the Java client and server is relatively easy because Java provides specialized tools which facilitate design and realization of the client-server applications. However, applications written with Java are slower than applications written with Ada. In addition, Ada is a standardized language.

Example of code

Ada code

```
package SCENARIO is
        type T_SCENARIO is record
         ...;
        end record;
        type C_SCENARIO is access T_SCENARIO;
        ... -- Operations for the type C_SCENARIO
end SCENARIO;
```

```
with SCENARIO, SET...;
package PERSISTENT_ENV is
          type SET_SCENARIO is limited private;
          S1 : SET_SCENARIO; -- Persistent Data
          procedure COMMIT();
          procedure ABORT();
private
          package PKG_SET_SCENARIO is new SET(...);--A1
          subtype SET_SENARIO is PKG_SET_SCENARIO.T_SET;
end PERSISTENT_ENV ;
```

Java code

```
class SCENARIO {...;
} //end SCENARIO
package MYTOOL.PERSISTENT; //J1
          import MYTOOL.PERSISTENT_TOOLS.SET;
          class SET_SCENARIO extend SET {
            void put (SCENARIO SCN) {//J2
              super.put(SCN);};
            ...};
          public final class PERSISTENT_ENV { //J3
            static SET_SCENARIO S1; //J4 Persistent Data

            PERSISTENT_ENV(){...}; //J5
            public static void COMMIT() {...}; //J6
            public static void ABORT()  {...};
            ....} //end PERSISTENT_ENV
// End package
```

O2 code

```
class SCENARIO type tuple {...};
...;
end;
name SET_SCENARIO : set (SCENARIO); //O1
```

Discussion

We use an instantiation of the generic package "Set" (*A1*) to simulate the set constructor provided by the O2 language (*O1*).

Java does not provide generic classes . Thus, we create a class "Set " that uses the class "Object" as element. We use a Java package (*J1*) that contains the specialization of the class "Set" to "SET_SCENARIO". The re-definition of the "put" method (*J2*) could be useful to avoid type mismatch when a programmer inserts values into the SET_SCENARIO. Indeed, only the class "PERSISTENT_ENV" can be exported outside the package.

We declare the class "PERSISTENT_ENV" as "final" to avoid its specialization (*J3*) of this class. The persistent roots are declared "static", because there is only one persistent environment in an application. "Static" guaranties that only one occurrence of the persistent environment exists, even if there are several instantiations of the class "PERSISTENT_ENV" (*J4, J6*). A constructor is inserted into the "PERSISTENT_ENV" class to initiate the persistent environment. In the Ada language, this initialization (*J5*) is achieved by adding code into the package body. Indeed, it is possible to run a piece of code when the generic package is instantiated.

In this example, we see that there are several differences between the different implementations. The general software framework is similar but the implementation requires a special effort. It is important to carry out studies concerning solutions using design methods (OMT, UML) to palliate this effort.

The first part of our work aims to validate a generic software framework independent of the language features. A second part of our work must generalize the study presented in the third part of this paper "from Ada 95 to Java" for other languages. The last part of our work seeks to propose different modules according to the language features. For example, we must take into account the fact that languages support parameterized types while others do not.

6 Conclusion

Other studies have been carried out in relation to persistence. Up to now, these studies have related to the persistence of the Java language [10, 12]. However, an Australian team has presented a solution for managing persistent Ada object [11]. [10, 11, 12] propose solutions 100% pure Java or 100% pure Ada. These solutions provide an outstanding result with no type mismatch. However, these solutions are very restrictive and do not provide solutions for exchange data. Thus, interconnection between heterogeneous applications is difficult.

The Java solutions allow the class schema to be saved with the persistent environment. This feature avoids problems of incoherence between applications class schema and the corresponding persistent environment class schema when classes are modified. This solution implies a verification of the coherence at each run-time. The solution that we propose in this paper provides the same feature but we do not provide for any verification. This verification will be implemented later. In addition, the solution [12] can be easily connected with the ObjectStore database. In this case, we will have also a coupling between a high level language and a database which complies with the ODMG recommendations.

The first prototype has shown the feasibility of a such coupling. The test we performed has shown that performance is good when the number of transient data handled is greater than the number of persistent data handled. At present, we are carrying out a study to generalize the previous work to all languages supporting abstract data type implementation. After this study, we will perform tests concerning the performances of our system, when we distribute data and treatment through a network. Indeed, we want to perform tests in relation to a system in which the treatments are distributed through heterogeneous applications. In addition, we are thinking of replacing the O2 OODBMS by ObjectStore in order to carry out study and which will allow us to compare the Ada/O2 binding and the Ada/ObjectStore binding.

Acknowledgments

The authors would like to thank Julian Cockain for reviewing this paper and for suggesting a number of helpful linguistic improvements.

References

[1] **T. Millan**
Ada et les Systèmes Orientés objets: les Environnement Persistants au Travers d'un Système de Gestion de Bases de Données Orienté Objets
University Paul Sabatier Thesis; 14 September 1995 – Toulouse (France)

[2] **T. Millan, P. Bazex**
Ada/O2 Coupling: A solution for an Efficient Management of Persistence in Ada 83 -
Reliable Software Technologies - Ada-Europe'96 - Lecture Notes in Computer Science 1088; Springer-Verlag - Page 396-412; 10-14 June 1996 - Montreux (Switzerland)

[3] **R. Cattel**
ODMG 93: The Object Database Management Group - Edition Morgan Kaufmann, 1994

[4] **M. Atkinson & O. Peter Buneman**
Type and Persistence in Database Programming Languages - ACM Computing Surveys - vol. 19, n° 2 - June 1987

[5] **T. Accart Hardin T. & V. Donzeau-Gouge Viguié**
Conception et outils de programmation. Le style fonctionnel, le style impératif avec CAML et Ada - InterEditions, 1992

[6] **J. Barnes**
Programming in Ada 95 - Addison-Wesley Publishing Company, Inc., 1996

[7] **P. Niemeyer, J. Peck**
Exploring Java - Edition O'Reilly & Associates, Inc., 1996

[8] **B. Meyer**
Conception et Programmation par Objet : pour un Logiciel de Qualité -
Edition InterEditions, 1990

[9] **O2-Technology**
The O2 User Manuel version 4.6

[10] **M. J. Oudshoorn, S. C. Crawley**
Beyond Ada95: The Addition of Persistence and its Consequences -
Reliable Software Technologies - Ada-Europe'96 - Lecture Notes in Computer Science 1088; Springer-Verlag - Page 342-356; 10-14 June 1996 - Montreux (Switzerland)

[11] **M. Atkinson; L. Daynes; M.-J. Jordan; T. Printezis; S. Spence**
An Orthogonally Persistent Java - ACM SIGMOD Record, December 1996

[12] **G. Landis; C. Lamb; T. Blackman; S. Haradhvala; M. Noyes; D. Weinred**
ObjectStore PSE: a persistent Storage Engine for Java
Object Design, Inc. (Internet document)

Browsing a Component Library Using Non-functional Information[†]

Xavier Franch[1], Josep Pinyol[1], and Joan Vancells[2]

[1] Universitat Politècnica de Catalunya (UPC),
c/ Jordi Girona 1-3 (Campus Nord, C6) E-08034 Barcelona (Catalunya, Spain)
franch@lsi.upc.es, josep.pinol.molas@arthurandersen.com
[2] Universitat de Vic (Barcelona),
c/Sagrada Família, 7 E-08500 Vic (Catalunya, Spain)
joan.vancells@uvic.es

Abstract. This paper highlights the role of non-functional information when reusing from a component library. We describe a method for selecting appropriate implementations of Ada packages taking non-functional constraints into account; these constraints model the context of reuse. Constraints take the form of queries using an interface description language called NoFun, which is also used to state non-functional information in Ada packages; query results are trees of implementations, following the import relationships between components. We define two different situations when reusing components, depending whether we take the library being searched as closed or extendible. The resulting tree of implementations can be manipulated by the user to solve ambiguities, to state default behaviours, and by the like. As part of the proposal, we face the problem of computing from code the non-functional information that determines the selection process.

1   Introduction

Software components can be characterised both by their functionality (what the component does) and by their non-functionality (how the component behaves with respect to some quality factors like efficiency, reliability, etc.). Both aspects should be considered during their specification, design, implementation, maintenance and also reuse. If we focus on reusability, a component retrieved from a library regarding only its functional behaviour may not fit into the non-functional requirements of the environment, hindering or even preventing its actual integration into the new system.

Despite this, usual software reuse methods (see [1] for a survey) take only functional characteristics of components into account. The main reason behind this limitation is that non-functional information does not appear in components; furthermore, it often cannot be easily computed (or even cannot be computed at all) from the func-

---

[†] This work has been partially supported by the spanish CICYT project TIC97-1158.

tional part. As a result, retrieval of components cannot guaranty success with respect to non-functional constraints (for instance, constraints about efficiency).

Our approach cope with this problem by coupling three different strategies. On the one hand, we have designed an interface definition language called *NoFun* aimed at stating non-functional aspects of software components in the components themselves. This notation allows to introduce software attributes characterising components, libraries and whole systems; to put constraints on them; and also to establish how component implementations behave with respect to them. On the other hand, we have defined a method for retrieving software components from a library, based on the satisfactibility of some non-functional constraints encapsulated in queries. The method examines component implementations from a non-functional point of view; it will be defined in two different scenarios depending on whether we require to solve the query using just the implementations of the library or not. Last, a framework for computing non-functional information of implementations from code has also been formulated. The framework seems to be able to handle a relevant subset of quality factors (among them, we remark efficiency) in a uniform way.

The paper focuses on the last two parts (especially the second one) and not on the language, which have been formerly described in [2] and later in [3]. A first prototype running on Linux is currently implemented.

2   The Framework

In the rest of the paper, we will view a software component as a pair built up from an *interface* and an *implementation*. In our approach, the interface (enclosed in an Ada package) optionally includes an Anna *specification* (see [2] for details). In the general case, there will be components with the same specification but different implementations (enclosed in Ada package bodies), each one designed to fit a particular context of use. Our reuse method will be on charge of selecting one or more functional-equivalent components with the most appropriate implementation for a given context represented by a query.

On the other hand, components are considered encapsulations of abstract data types. Implementations will consist then of data structures as lists, trees and graphs. This framework affects the kind of relevant non-functional attributes of components; for instance, we measure efficiency with asymptotic notations [4] and not by response time, throughput or number of accesses to disk, which are measures of interest when considering other type of systems.

Non-functional information of software components will be actually integrated into Ada packages by means the NoFun interface description language (lines starting with "--|"). We classify this information into three kinds (see [3] for details):

- *Non-functional attribute* (short, *NF-attribute*): definition of software attributes which serve as a mean to describe components and possibly to evaluate them. Among the most widely accepted we can mention efficiency, maintainability, reliability and usability.

- *Non-functional behaviour* of an implementation (short, *NF-behaviour*): assignment of values to the NF-attributes bound to the component.

- *Non-functional constraint* on a software component (short, *NF-constraint*): constraint on the set of the NF-attributes bound to the component.

In fig. 1 we show an example of definition of an NF-attribute for reliability, which relies on three other NF-attributes: test degree (integer from 0 to 5), error recovery and portability (both boolean).

```
package RELIABILITY is
   --: with ERROR_RECOVERY, TEST
   --: properties
   --: boolean FullyPortable;     -- platform independence
   --: enumerated ordered Reliability [none,low,medium,high]
   --:     depends on Test, ErrorRecovery, FullyPortable
   --:     defined as
   --:       not ErrorRecovery and not FullyPortable =>
   --:                 Reliability = none
   --:       ErrorRecovery and not FullyPortable =>
   --:                 Reliability = low
   --:       not ErrorRecovery and FullyPortable =>
   --:                 Reliability = low
   --:       ErrorRecovery and FullyPortable =>
   --:                 Test in [0..1] => Reliability = low
   --:                 Test in [2..3] => Reliability = medium
   --:                 Test in [4..5] => Reliability = high
end RELIABILITY;
```

Fig. 1. A package introducing a NF-attribute for reliability

This attribute can be used in component packages, as shown in fig. 2; *NETWORK* is a component modeling geographical networks, which establishes connections between items. We assume that items in the network are integers, and that the cost of a connection is also an integer. The *measurement units* stand for data volume sizes: *NbItems* for the number of items, and *NbConns* for the number of links. These units are used later to establish efficiency results.

```
package NETWORK is
   ... declaration of interface
   --: with RELIABILITY
   --:     measurement units NbItems, NbConns
end NETWORK;
```

Fig. 2. A package for a component using the NF-attribute of fig. 1

Fig. 3 includes a NF-behaviour module giving values to these NF-attributes (*Short-estPath* is a procedure computing shortest paths in the network). Note that the value of the *Reliability* NF-attribute is not explicitly given, because it can be computed from the other ones (we say it is *derived*). The *implemented with* construct labels the package body for further package selection.

```
package body NETWORK is
  --| implemented with ADJACENCY_MATRIX
  --| behaviour
  --|      ErrorRecovery; FullyPortable; Test = 3
  --|      -- this implies Reliability = Medium
  --|      space(Network) = pow(NbItems, 2)
  ...
  procedure ShortestPath ...
  --|      time(ShortestPath) = pow(NbItems, 2)
  --|      space(ShortestPath) = NbItems
  ...
end NETWORK;
```

Fig. 3. A package implementation for the component in fig. 2, including NF-behaviour

3   Queries

In our method, a query is the basic retrieval operation. It is aimed at selecting components whose implementation fit better in the new system from a non-functional point of view, identifying which conditions must hold in order for this selection to be correct. Query process relies on the NF-behaviour of implementations; this is why in the rest of this section we talk about implementations instead of components. For every NF-attribute in the scope of the implementation, the NF-behaviour states its value, either implicitly or not, depending on whether the attribute is basic or derived; the NF-constraints appearing in the behaviour module are used to fix the additional conditions. One of the most important basic attributes is efficiency, whose can be computed with the help of a tool (see section 7); we plan to extend the set of basic NF-attributes computed in this way.

In order to combine queries later on, we assume that the selection is made from an initial set of candidate implementations; so, queries may be viewed as mappings that bind sets of implementations. More precisely, given a query q_M and a set S of implementations for an interface M (such that for every $s \in S$, the pair $<M, s>$ is a component from our point of view), the evaluation of q_M over S, written $q_M(S)$, yields:

– A set $T \subseteq S$ such that implementations in T satisfy the conditions appearing in q_M.

– A T-indexed family $Q_T = (q_t)_{t \in T}$, such that q_t is in turn a V-indexed family of queries, $q_t = (q_{t,v}(R_v))_{v \in V}$, being V the set of components imported by t and R_v the set of all the implementations of the component v. The query $q_{t,v}(R_v)$ represent the conditions that the imported implementation v must fulfil in order for t to be selected by the original query.

We call the queries in Q_T *subordinated queries* and then q_M becomes the *main query*. When referring to the result of the evaluation of q_M, eval(q_M), we will write as eval(q_M).T the set T and by eval(q_M).Q_T the family of queries Q_T.

From the syntactic point of view, a query is defined as a list of *atomic queries*, $q_M(S) = aq_{M,1}(S_1) \oplus ... \oplus aq_{M,k}(S_k)$. Items in the list represent conditions in decreasing order of importance; so, the initial set S can be restricted little by little until obtaining the final result. Atomic queries are very close to NF-constraints, except that we require them appearing in conjunctive normal form (CNF) and that we can use a pair of useful operators to select implementations maximizing or minimizing the value of a given NF-attribute. The operator $\oplus$ is called *restriction operator*, and it is defined in 3.2.

3.1   Atomic Queries

We define an atomic query $aq_M(S)$ as an expression given in CNF, possibly negated, $aq_M(S) = A$ or $aq_M(S) = \neg A$, such that $A = A_1 \wedge ... \wedge A_r$; de Morgan laws are applied to eliminate disjunctions, and so A_i may become also negated, $A_i = B_i$ or $A_i = \neg B_i$. Logical connectives are in fact interpreted as set operators. Every B_i can be:

− A relational expression, comparing expressions of a measurable attribute domain. Given the input set S, the evaluation of the relational expression $E_1 < E_2$ (for any defined ordering $<$), denoted by eval($E_1 < E_2$), is defined as ($E[R]$ stands for the evaluation of E with the values appearing in the behaviour module bound to R):

$$\text{eval}(E_1 < E_2) = \{ R \in S \, / \, E_1[R] < E_2[R] \}.$$

− A quantification of the form *max* or *min*, to select a subset of implementations inside S maximizing or minimizing a given expression E, defined as:

$$\text{eval}(\max(E)) = \{ R \in S \, / \, (\forall T \in S: E[T] \le E[R]) \}.$$

$$\text{eval}(\min(E)) = \{ R \in S \, / \, (\forall T \in S: E[T] \ge E[R]) \}.$$

The evaluation eval($aq_M(S)$) of the atomic query $aq_M(S)$ is as follows:

− Computation of T requires the evaluation eval(B_i) of all B_i, which results in sets $S_i \subseteq S$. If $A_i = B_i$, then evaluation eval(A_i) of A_i equals S_i; if $A_i = \neg B_i$, it equals $S - S_i$. Then, we define the evaluation of A as eval(A) = eval(A_1) $\cap$ ... $\cap$ eval(A_r). Finally, we define eval($aq_M(S)$) = eval(A) if $aq_M(S)$ = A, and also eval($aq_M(S)$) = S - eval(A) if $aq_M(S) = \neg A$.

− The T-indexed family $Q_T = (q_t)_{t \in R}$ results in a V-indexed family of queries, $q_t = (q_{t,v}(R_v))_{v \in V}$, such that V is the set of all imported components in t, R_v is the set of all the implementations of v, and $q_{t,v}$ is the NF-constraint stated on v inside t, which will be assumed to be *true* if no such NF-constraint exists.

3.2 Combination of Atomic Queries

We define here the meaning of the restriction operator $\oplus$ that combines atomic queries to give the result of the main query. In fact, we give two different definitions considering two cases. In the first case, we focus on obtaining the best implementations for the component of interest, even if there are not implementations for the imported components in the library; we call it *open case*. In the second one, the *closed case*, the restriction operator assumes that the implementations in the library are enough to satisfy not only the main query but also the subordinated ones.

The Open Case. The main idea behind open query computation is to evaluate atomic queries in order of appearance, until obtaining a single implementation for the abstract data type being reused and thus the component is uniquely defined; the result of an atomic query is considered as the input of the following one. However, there are two cases that do not fit into this scheme:

- Even after processing all atomic queries, more than one implementation is still possible. In this case, all of them are considered as the result of the query.

- An atomic query is not satisfied by any of the implementations resulting from the previous one. In this case, we consider as the result of the query the implementations obtained in this previous atomic query.

In both situations, some user interaction is required for selecting one of them (see section 6).

The evaluation is defined in two steps. First, we define the connection between two consecutive atomic queries by connecting their input and output sets:

$$S_1 = S.$$
$$S_i = \text{eval}(aq_{M.i-1}(S_{i-1})).T, \ 1 < i \leq k.$$

Now, the evaluation of the query $q_M(S)$ is stated as:

$$\text{eval}(q_M(S)) = \text{eval}(aq_{M.i}(S_i)), \ 1 \leq i \leq n, \text{ such that:}$$
$$\mid \text{eval}(aq_{M.i}(S_i)).T \mid = 1 \wedge (i > 1 \Rightarrow \mid \text{eval}(aq_{M.i-1}(S_{i-1})).T \mid > 1$$
$$\vee$$
$$\mid \text{eval}(aq_{M.i}(S_i)) \mid > 1 \wedge (i < k \Rightarrow \mid \text{eval}(aq_{M.i+1}(S_{i+1})).T \mid = 0).$$

The computation of the family of queries is straightforward from the set.

As a correctness condition for evaluation of queries, it must hold that $\text{eval}(aq_{M.1}(S_1)).T \neq \emptyset$.

The Closed Case. If we choose to obtain a result such that all the queries are solved with the existing implementations, it could be the case that restricting excessively the set of implementations in a query processing leads to unsolvable subordinated queries. So, we redefine the evaluation of query $q_M(S)$ preventing this case. The definition uses a predicate *solvable* that checks if there is a unsolvable subordinate query; as subordinated queries may activate others, the predicate takes a recursive form:

$$\text{eval}(q_M(S)) = \text{eval}(aq_{M,i}(S_i)), \ 1 \le i \le n, \text{ such that:}$$
$$\forall q: q \in \text{eval}(aq_{M,i}(S_i)).Q_T: \text{solvable(q)}$$
$$\wedge$$
$$\{ \ | \text{eval}(aq_{M,i}(S_i)).T \ | = 1 \wedge (i > 1 \Rightarrow | \text{eval}(aq_{M,i-1}(S_{i-1})).T \ | > 1$$
$$\vee$$
$$| \text{eval}(aq_{M,i}(S_i)).T \ | > 1 \wedge (i < k \Rightarrow | \text{eval}(aq_{M,i+1}(S_{i+1})).T \ | = 0 \vee$$
$$\exists q: q \in \text{eval}(aq_{M,i+1}(S_{i+1})).Q_T: \neg\text{solvable(q)} \ \}.$$

Being:

$$\text{solvable}(q) \equiv \text{eval}(q).T \ne \emptyset \wedge \forall q': q' \in \text{eval}(q).Q_T: \text{solvable}(q').$$

As a correctness condition for the evaluation of queries, it must hold both that $\text{eval}(aq_{M,1}(S_1)).T \ne \emptyset$ and $\forall q: q \in \text{eval}(aq_{M,1}(S_1)).Q_T: \text{solvable}(q)$.

4 Selection Trees

As the evaluation of queries is defined in a recursive form, it is natural to use trees of implementations to represent its result; we call them *selection trees*. One could think also to use directed graphs, but it would be incorrect since an implementation selected in two different queries may use different implementations for one or more of its imported components.

Selection trees consist of the following elements:

– *Nodes*. We distinguish two types of nodes: *interface nodes*, represented by ellipses, and *implementation nodes*, represented by rectangles. There is a special implementation node, called *void*, that appears when there are not implementations satisfying a particular query.

– *Branches*. There are two types of branches: *import branches*, going from implementation nodes to interface ones, and represented by arrows; and *selection branches*, going from interfaces to implementations and represented by undirected lines.

In fact, component nodes are not strictly necessary, but we include them for clarity reasons and also to support some kinds of user interaction.

5 An Example

Let *NETWORK_USER_IMPL* be a package using *NETWORK* as defined in figure 2. Let's assume that this new component is mainly devoted to compute shortest paths in the network by means of the operation *ShortestPath*. Also, let's assume that the network is nearly fully connected.

There exist different implementations for *NETWORK*, which differ in two points: the strategy to represent the underlying graph (we focus in adjacency lists and adjacency matrix) and the algorithm that implements the operation *ShortestPath*. With respect to the first point, an additional fact must be considered: how the data structure is indexed using items (integers). Note that we have three different cases: the items are known in advance; the items are not known but the number of items is bounded; and there is no information about the items. Let's assume the second case.

Under this assumption, implementations will use instances of a generic *MAPPING* component to access the data structure via items. In the case of an adjacency list, the mapping associates lists to items; in the adjacency matrix case, it returns integers between 1 and *N* to access the matrix.

Operations on mappings are insertion, deletion and retrieval using the item as a key. So, standard mapping implementations will be useful here: hashing, AVL trees, ordered lists, etc. In the case of hashing, chained strategy will use in turn the generic *LIST* component to link synonymous keys.

Lastly, note each of these implementations will also use the *LIST* component, to build adjacency lists when necessary and to build the result of *ShortestPath*.

To keep the example in a reasonable size, we restrict the set of implementations of the components introduced so far (see fig. 4): three implementations for lists (ordered, unordered with pointers and unordered with arrays), two for mappings (chained hashing and AVL trees) and also two for priority queues (heaps and AVL trees with access to minimum element), which are used in some versions of the *ShortestPath* implementation (improved Dijkstra algorithm).

We are going to process the query below, which can be read as: first, minimizing the time of finding shortest paths with a reasonable reliability (the reliability can be relaxed if we are just building a first prototype of the application); next, minimizing type representation space; last, maximizing reliability. As initial set for the query, we take the set of all *NETWORK* implementations introduced above. All of this, with the (asymptotic) relationship $NbConns = power(NbItems, 2)$ (being *NbConns* and *NbItems* the representation in NoFun sentences of the number of connections and items, necessary to state efficiency), coming from the fully connected characteristic of the network (in the query, the semicolon stands for the composition operator):

> min(time(ShortestPath)) and Reliability >= medium ;
> min(space(Network)) ; max(Reliability)

Fig. 5, left, shows the selection tree of the query; its generation follows from the non-functional characteristics of the components. Two ambiguities arise which correspond to the existence of two pairs of siblings. To make them more visible, we draw an ambiguity sphere linking all the selection branches that stem from the same node. Explicit interaction with the user is needed, either to provide an additional query to solve every ambiguity, or to choose an implementation directly by name. In this case, *UNORDERED_POINTERS*, which is valid in both contexts, seems to be preferable.

```
------------ Implementations for NETWORK
--  All of them require:
--  from MAPPING, fast accessing time;
--  on lists, the first two ones dynamic storage
--       (to avoid wasting space), and all of them
--       require fast insertion time for building the
--       result of ShortestPath.
```

ADJ_LISTS_1: -- adjacency lists and Dijkstra algorithm
                 -- with priority queues.
  space(Network) = NbItems + NbConns
  time(ShortestPath) = (NbItems+NbConns) * log(NbItems)
  Reliability = medium
  requires on MAPPING: min(time(Insert, Delete, Get))
            on LIST: min(time(Put)) and DynamicStorage
            on PRIORITY_QUEUE:
                    time(Put, First, RemFirst) <= log(NbElems)

ADJ_LISTS_2: -- adjacency lists and Dijkstra algorithm
  space(Network) = NbItems + NbConns
  time(ShortestPath) = power(NbItems, 2)
  Reliability = medium
  requires on MAPPING: min(time(Insert, Delete, Get))
            on LIST: min(time(Put)) and DynamicStorage

ADJ_MATRIX: -- adjacency matrix and Dijkstra algorithm
  space(Network) = power(NbItems, 2)
  time(ShortestPath) = power(NbItems, 2)
  Reliability = high
  requires on MAPPING: min(time(Insert, Delete, Get))
            on LIST: min(time(Put))

```
------------ Implementations for LIST
```

ORDERED: -- keep elements in order; makes use of pointers.
  time(Put) = NbElems; DynamicStorage

UNORDERED_POINTERS: -- keep elements without order;
                       -- makes use of pointers.
  time(Put) = 1; DynamicStorage

UNORDERED_ARRAY: -- elements stored in an array, linking
                  -- them, without any order.
  time(Put) = 1; not DynamicStorage

```
------------ Implementations for HASHING
```

CHAINED_HASHING: -- hash table linking synonymous with lists
  time(Insert, Delete, Get) = 1; not DynamicStorage
  require **on** LIST: DynamicStorage   -- number of collisions
                             -- not known in advance

AVL: -- an AVL tree making use of dynamic storage.
  time(Insert, Delete, Get) = log(NbElems); DynamicStorage

```
------------ Implementations for PRIORITY QUEUE
```

HEAP: -- elements stored in an array managed as a heap
  time(Put, First, RemFirst) = log(NbElems)
  not DynamicStorage

AVL_WITH_MIN: -- an AVL with an additional pointer to the
                -- minimum element.
  time(Put, First, RemFirst) = log(NbElems)
  DynamicStorage

Fig. 4. Non-functional behaviour (highlights) for some components

To illustrate the importance that relationships between different efficiency parameters have during selection, we reformulate the same query in a different situation, considering networks with a few connections. This situation can be modeled with the (asymptotic) relationship *NbConns = NbItems*, and then the query selects as network implementation the first one, because Dijkstra algorithm takes profit of the use of priority queues. Now, implementation for lists is uniquely determined due to the additional constraint of using dynamic storage for them, while implementation for mappings do not vary. Concerning priority queues, both existing implementations satisfy the NF-constraints, and so both appear in the resulting selection tree (fig. 5, right).

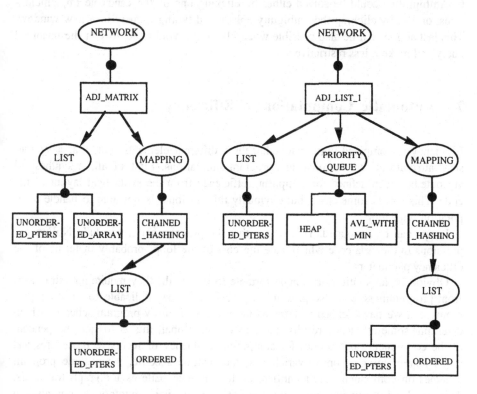

Fig. 5. Two selection trees for a query

6 User Interaction

In order to make our proposal more useful, the method that we have presented is complemented with the ability to guide the process and eventually affect its result. There are many reasons supporting this decision:

– As seen in the example, query evaluation may yield ambiguous selection trees. Users should then choose one of the existing alternatives, or else an additional query may be formulated on the involved component.

– Some users may prefer not to fully rely on the query processing algorithm but only to guide the process and processing atomic queries little by little, perhaps stopping the process before than expected or switching from one type of query to another to compare results.

– Correctness conditions may be violated either in the main query or in subordinate ones. In the first case, the query should be relaxed and the process started again. We do not allow selection of implementations violating queries.

To carry out this interaction, the selection tree is depicted in the screen as seen in fig 6. Ambiguities could be solved either by clicking one of the candidate implementations, or else by clicking the ambiguity sphere and typing a query in a new window. This last action will be also possible when clicking a void node, to edit the unsolved query and make it less restrictive.

7 Automatic Computation of Efficiency

Efficiency is computed putting together three different elements: patterns, a synthesized attribute in the grammar, and program annotations. First of all, a synthesized attribute has been defined for computing efficiency from the syntactical layout of the code. This solves some cases, but obviously this attribute is not able to handle computation with loops.

Loops can be annotated. This means that the programmer can include NoFun expressions in the Ada code which state the cost of the loop, probably in terms of the efficiency parameters.

Obviously, annotations are uncomfortable to deal with; they require an extra effort from programmers, and also prevents our scheme to be applicable to existing programs. So, we have defined patterns as the mean to identify program schemes which determine some efficiency results. Patterns can be global, this is to say, independent of the component, as the ones for computing efficiency of recursive procedures and loops incrementing a control variable; or they can be specific, when some program schemes on components are identified, as for instance patterns for graph traversals. This last kind of patterns are of interest not only to avoid annotations, but also to obtain more accurate results.

Once asymptotic expressions are obtained, we can apply a simplification calculus to obtain reduced expressions, which are the final results to be assigned to the NF-behaviour of components.

8 Conclusions

A proposal for software reuse that takes non-functional issues into account has been presented. The proposal consists of a language to state non-functional attributes, behaviour and constraints; a method for reuse which takes the form of queries written with the same notation; and a framework for computing some quality factors, presently efficiency. The result of the query is a tree of implementations, modifiable by the user, which follows the import relationships between components. Reuse has been studied in two different situations, depending on whether we force the resulting tree to be completed using just the implementations of the library or not. The efficiency of the selection method is not a function on size of the library, but on: 1) the average number of component implementations, 2) on the average height of selection trees, and 3) the amount of atomic queries that appear in non-atomic ones; these factors will generally be moderate enough to assure a good response time.

The most related approach to ours is the faceted-classification scheme presented in [5] and which is the basis of other proposals, many of them implemented on the WWW [6, 7]. In [5], facets are mostly used to select components by the functionality their provide; however, the ideas can be applied to non-functionality by considering facets as enumerated NF-attributes, which are a particular domain constructor in No-Fun. In this sense, our approach generalizes facets by allowing other kind of domains. Another difference is that [5] incorporates a notion of similarity between components; we have not adopted this idea because the language presents other features that allow to rank components (ordered domains) and to retrieve those ones maximizing / minimizing the value of one or more NF-attributes. Lastly, [5] does not allow to retrieve trees of components but just individual ones. On the other hand, there is an interesting feature which we do not provide at the moment, namely the fuzziness quality of some NF-attributes.

References

1. Mili, H.; Mili, F.; Mili, A.: Reusing Software: Issues and Research Directions. IEEE Transactions on Software Engineering 21, 6. IEEE Computer Society (1995)
2. Franch, X.: Including Non-Functional Issues in Anna/Ada Programs for Automatic Implementation Selection. Proceedings of Ada Europe 97 (London, UK). Lecture Notes in Computer Science, Vol. 1251. Springer-Verlag, Berlin Heidelberg New York (1997)
3. Franch, X.: Systematic Formulation of Non-Functional Characteristics of Software. Proceedings of International Conference on Requirements Engineering (ICRE) (Colorado Springs, USA). IEEE Computer Society (1997)
4. Brassard, G.: Crusade for a better Notation. SIGACT News, 16, 4 (1985)
5. Prieto-Díaz, R.: Classifying Software for Reusability. IEEE Software 4, 1. IEEE Computer Society (1987)
6. Boisvert, R.F.: A Web Gateway to a Virtual Mathematical Software Repository. Proceedings of 2nd International WWW Conference, Chicago (Illinois, U.S.A.) (1994)
7. Poulin, J.S.; Werkman, K.J.: Melding Structured Abstracts and the WWW for Retrieval of Reusable Components. Proceedings of Symposium on Software Reusability (Seattle, U.S.A.) (1995)

Hw/Sw Codesign of Embedded Systems

William Fornaciari and Donatella Sciuto

Politecnico di Milano, Dipartimento di Elettronica e Informazione, P.zza L. Da Vinci, 32
20133 Milano, Italy.
{fornacia, sciuto}@elet.polimi.it

Abstract. The architecture of systems tailored for a specific application frequently requires cooperation among hardware and software components. The design of these systems is typically a compromise among a number of factors: cost, performance, size, development time, power consumption, etc. To cope with increasing possibilities offered by nowadays integration technology and steady demanding of shorter time-to-market, a comprehensive strategy aiming at gathering all the involved aspects of the design is becoming mandatory. This new discipline, called *codesign*, considers in a concurrent manner all the activities involved in the design of a mixed hw/sw dedicated system: capturing of design specification and requirements, mapping of the design onto hardware and software domains, system synthesis and design verification. The paper introduces the key factors involved in the design of an embedded system, together with a description on how codesign is overcoming such problems, opening the way to a new generation of CAD frameworks supporting system-level design.

1. Introduction

Applications in the domain of telecommunication, multimedia, automotive and consumer markets make wide use of embedded systems as an important component of the global product. Embedded systems work as part of a larger system with which they interact for control or for performing specific computing intensive tasks [1].

Usually, embedded systems are constituted by one or more microcontrollers or microprocessors to provide programmability of the system, and interact with other digital or analog components to receive data from the external environment and possibly to perform fast manipulations. The functionality of an embedded system is often fixed, as defined by the system interaction with its environment. They are usually characterized by a large number of operation modes, by a high degree of concurrency and by the capability of quickly responding to exceptions.

Programmability is a an important feature of these systems, providing the possibility of implementing in software all those tasks that could be changed in future versions, without having to re-design the entire system.

Different application domains define the different degrees of importance for other types of requirements that can be imposed on an embedded system [20]. In particular, we can mention cost, which is of paramount importance in consumer electronics, performance, real-time response, power consumption, integration level, flexibility, reliability, availability and safety.

Embedded systems can be implemented with different levels of integration: from boards to system on a chip, depending on the type of application. While lower levels of integration, such as boards, allow a reduced cost in the realization and greater flexibility, the higher level of integration, i.e. systems on a chip, allow lower power consumption, higher performance, but higher complexity and chip sizes.

Embedded systems can be characterized by the function they perform. Basically, embedded systems can act as control systems or as data processing systems. Control systems are reactive systems, in the sense that they react to the inputs provided by the external environment. Often, these systems are characterized by real time requirements. In fact, most reactive systems, when they receive the inputs must execute their function before a given deadline, in a predefined amount of time, defined by hard or soft time constraints.

Control-dominated embedded systems include the core of a controller, whose size and capabilities strictly depend on the requirements of the embedded system in terms of performance, power consumption, availability, reliability, safety.

Embedded systems whose main function is to perform data processing, are usually classified as data-dominated systems and can be found in many telecom and multimedia systems, where they execute specific digital or video signal processing algorithms. Here, the starting point is the algorithm to be performed by the system. Then, in most cases, ASIPs (Application Specific Instruction Set Processor) are included to speed up the execution. In fact, in this case, the hardware is chosen in order to support the execution of the embedded software application. ASIPs are specific programmable cores, whose instruction set architecture and underlying hardware has been chosen to improve the performance of specific algorithms with specific instruction profiles.

Therefore, in general, the main components found in embedded systems include some or all of the following: software, firmware, ASICs (Application Specific Integrated Circuits), general-purpose or domain-specific processors, core-based ASICs, ASIPs, memory, FPGAs (Field Programmable Gate Arrays), analog circuits and sensors. Hence, the design of complex embedded systems is a difficult problem, requiring designers with skills and experience in order to identify the best solution.

Unfortunately, designers have little assistance from electronic design automation tools to perform such tasks. In fact, most system designers work in an ad-hoc manner, given the fact that, in most cases, products that must be designed represent enhancements of prior systems. There are no widely accepted methodologies or tools available to support the designer in the definition of a functional specification and then in the mapping phase onto a system architecture. Therefore, the designers usually rely on manual techniques, mainly driven by experience, allowing them to explore only a limited set of alternative solution architectures. An exception is represented by Digital Signal Processing systems, for which there is a longer design tradition and better tools supporting them.

The problem is worsened by the rapid evolution of most markets in the telecom, multimedia, and consumer electronics application domains, which require a drastic reduction in the time to market. This implies that the system design time must be reduced and the design made flexible to modify it in a short time, while, however always improving the performance and their basic characteristics. This has led to a shift to software of most of the system functionality, with dedicated hardware as a support for those fixed functionality delivering a greater speedup in performance, implemented on a single chip which integrates a programmable core.

This evolution requires a careful choice of such a core, in terms of size, functionality and performance, and a careful management of the entire design process. A concurrent design process is necessary to try to balance all requirements that the embedded system must comply with. Such a concurrent design process requires synchronization between the team developing the system architecture, the software and hardware design teams, to meet the short deadlines, possibly avoiding any long re-cycle.

This difficult process must be supported by specific EDA (Electronic Design Automation) tools, which can provide help both to the system, hardware and software designers in the entire design flow. The academic research in this area started only a few years ago, while commercial tools have been made available on the market only recently, covering few specific parts of the complete design flow [21]. This research area is today known as *hardware/software codesign*, providing a global view of the design of embedded systems (mainly completely digital ones). We should note that this field of research derives from the EDA community, and therefore mainly from the hardware perspective, with influence from the software community in the system specification.

Basically, the automation of the global hw/sw design approach, that concurrently considers hardware and software development, synchronizing the two processes aims at providing a unified view of the system in all the design phases. This allows an easier exploration of different alternative solutions that can be more easily verified and tested, before the actual hardware and software components are designed. System integration in this case is improved with respect to the traditional separate design flows, because the co-design flow maintains an alignment between software and hardware developments. Furthermore, a global framework allows management of the documentation in a global manner, thus keeping track of all modifications that could occur in later design stages in a unified format, after the specification phase.

The goal of this paper is to provide an overview of this design process, showing the characteristics of the main tasks and the main issues involved. Then, an overview of the main approaches presented in the academic world and the commercial tools today available will be presented, showing the variety of solutions proposed, based on the type of application they consider.

2. Embedded system design flow

For many years, design teams had to face the realities of combining hardware systems with software algorithms to deliver the system capabilities and performance. The traditional design flow of embedded systems starts from a requirements document, usually leading to an incomplete specification of the system. Given this document, system architects define the set of system functions that must cooperate in order to satisfy the system requirements.

Modeling and validation of these functions is performed by simulating the system, often through an executable specification described in a programming language and executed with different data inputs in order to validate the functionalities. This however, does not allow verification of the timing constraints or any of the other non-functional relevant parameters of the system, such as power consumption, performance of the entire system, safety, reliability and so on. Furthermore, this phase is error prone, since prototyping is usually manually performed, and therefore it is not possible to formally guarantee the equivalence between the specification and the software prototype.

Then, the definition of which functions will be implemented in software and which ones will be performed by dedicated hardware components is performed. In the traditional design flow, this initial partitioning is performed manually by the system designer, helped only by his experience.

From this step on a separate path for the software and hardware components design is followed. Interface design requires the participation of both hardware and software designers for the specification.

Integration and test of hardware and software is performed after all components have been separately developed. This is the actual phase when system design faults are discovered, thus requiring a re-cycle in the hardware or software design paths. Furthermore, the integration phase, i.e., the verification of the correctness of the interaction between the hardware and software components has required, until recently, the building of the actual hardware prototype.

This strategy penalizes the time to market, since errors are discovered at the very end of the design process. In most cases, these errors could have been identified in earlier stages of the process, if a different organization of the work had been chosen.

The process of designing concurrent hardware/software systems thus consists of consecutive phases of modeling and verification, starting from the specification level, followed by the first refined specification, after partitioning, followed by the specification and validation of the hardware, software and interface architectures, down to the implementation level.

The application of the correct modeling strategy at the right time is the key to quickly identify design errors. However, no single approach can be applied in the different phases of the design, and no single modeling technique is suitable for all possible application domains.

The solution to this problem is in the definition of a methodology for system design, from the concept of the product to the final implementation. These tasks are common to all the embedded system designs, while the design flows differ in the techniques they apply for the different classes of application domains.

In particular, co-design can be subdivided into the following main tasks.

1. *Specification capture*. The desired system functionalities are expressed in a formal model and the description is validated by simulation or verification techniques. The result is a functional specification, without any implementation details.
2. *Exploration*. The formal model is used as input to analyze different design alternatives to identify the best one that satisfies all design constraints, both functional and non-functional. The result of this phase is the definition of the hardware and software architectures and partitioning.

3. *Hardware software and interface synthesis.* An implementation is created for each component of the system architecture defined in the previous step. The result is the software code for the software components and the RT-level implementation for the hardware parts.

4. *Coverification.* This step, prior to the physical design phase, allows verification that all components do in fact satisfy all requirements in terms of performance, area, costs, real-time constraints, power consumption, reliability, availability and safety.

The next section will show how in fact co-design methodologies have organized these main phases and which tasks must be performed to obtain a suitable, at least partially automated, design flow for the different classes of embedded systems.

3. Hw/Sw Codesign

Hardware/software codesign in not a recent idea. It has been an industrial practice for a long time but only recently gained attention in the research and EDA communities. For decades, design teams have been faced with the necessity to combine low cost and flexible computing capabilities, such as those provided by microprocessors, with dedicated hardware (e.g., ASICs) in order to cope with systems requirements such as cost, performance, design modifiability, energy saving, size, time to market, etc.

Current trends in embedded systems has both exacerbated the problem of keeping close hw and sw development as well as opened new potential solutions, since now entire systems can fit on a single chip. In addition, increasing time-to-market pressure is making more and more important the availability of *virtual* (possibly executable) models of the system, in order to verify the compliance of the design constraints during the earlier stages of the design, before building the actual prototypes. The shifting of many of the verification activities toward the top part of the design flow, enables the possibility of evaluating alternative hw/sw architectural solutions, instead of committing to conservative (but risk-free) realizations, far from the optimal system implementation.

Codesign is becoming a very comprehensive term, currently research teams and EDA producers are addressing only some of its aspects. However, the ultimate goal is to bridge the gap between functional specification, architectural tuning, the development of hardware and software and system-level verification. In this and in the following section, we will discuss only the aspects related to the R&D process, regardless of the market, product definition, support and any other business-related issue. An approach aiming at covering also these factors, is still a long way to come.

The main application field for hw/sw codesign is the area of embedded systems; the main tasks necessary to support a system-level design are depicted in Fig.1 and the involved aspects are briefly summarized next.

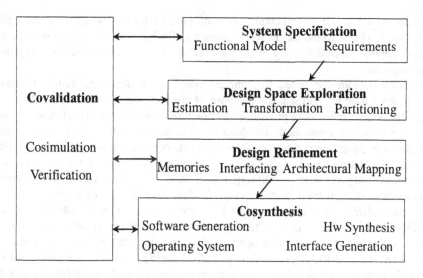

Figure 1. A general system-level hw/sw codesign flow.

3.1 Specification formalism

The description of a system can be performed at any of the abstraction levels, each of which has a specific purpose. For example, describing the system at the component level allows the designer to capture the "pure" functionality, while the logic or Register Transfer (RT) levels are useful to specify also the system structure. Specification formalisms tailored for codesign, should increase the possibility for the designer to describe a more conceptual view of the system in terms of executable specification languages, capable to capture both functionality and design constraints in a readable and simulatable form. Due to the necessity of managing complex systems, the cross dependencies between specification formalism and EDA tools (both for design specification and synthesis) are becoming crucial, and the use of graphical versions of formal languages is becoming a key factor at the higher level of abstraction. On the bottom side, VHDL and C/retargetable assembler formats seem to be the target level to interface with existing and well assessed final synthesis flows. Furthermore, self-documentation capability is also achieved, since the entire design flow is managed with integrated EDA tools, and the split of the system design onto different teams and implementation domains should require reduced integration effort.

The main features of a conceptual model, are traditionally partitioned in three classes: *control*, *data* and *timing*. These three main characteristics, sometimes called "codesign cube" can be used to compare different models of computation and to identify the suitable implementation domain.

Finite state machines are probably the most widely used model, both for hardware and software to represent and design controllers, control units of microprocessors and control logic. This model has been recently extended in terms of hierarchy and communication, in order to prevent the explosion of the state count [18]. Other formalisms are based on customizations of process level models, such as CSP, OCCAM, LOTOS, ADA, etc. In some cases, e.g. DSP applications, there may be no need of control, since data are produced at regular rates, processed and sent out in the same manner.

As far as data are concerned, the simplest model uses boolean constraints to control the variables used to represent the behavior of controllers and control units. In some cases this is not sufficient to provide a clear picture of the functions performed by the rest of the system controlled. To describe also the datapath, complex arithmetic functions can be introduced to specify assignments of values to integer, floating point or arrays. However, complex systems cannot be managed at the clock-cycle level and the computation performed at each step (e.g., a state), is specified by using procedures and processes of high-level languages such C, C++, Java, VHDL, or Verilog.

Timing-related issues can be captured in terms of constraints on rate, delays and deadlines on specific system activities. Synchronous formalisms greatly simplify such a task, in particular when the description will be mapped onto an actual architecture. There exist other formal approaches, e.g., formal timing diagrams, more focussed on the definition and verification of system properties as well as customizations of process-level formalisms, where the related EDA graphical environments simplify the allocation of timing constraints onto sections of the specification.

Models are called synchronous when all the steps of the computation are performed and synchronized by dividing the time into regular intervals, as it is popular in the DSP community. In case the transitions are triggered by external events, the model of time is called event-driven or asynchronous. Such a model is particularly suitable to represent reactive systems, whose behavior is determined as a response to stimuli coming from the environment; as a consequence, the related description formalisms must be able to support exceptions or interrupts.

Differences exist when timing related issues influence not only the performance but the behavior correctness, as it happens for real-time systems. In this case, the ideal specification formalism should allow the designer to capture in a unified manner the functionality and timing constraints defined over "critical sections" of the system's description.

3.2 Target architectures

As recalled in the previous sections, embedded systems implementations can be classified according to the chosen architecture, defined by the type and amount of its *components*, the *connectivity* and the realization *technology*.

The use of standard parts has been the typical solution for many years, while recently ASIC implementations for volume production and FPGAs are becoming the preferred target technology. FPGAs do not offer performance and silicon density as the ASICs, but for prototyping and for systems requiring partial modifiability falling in the range of 100Kgates/100MHz they can be a viable solution.

The basic elements to be connected, range from basic RT-components (registers, counters, memories, ALUs, etc) up to microprocessor cores. Controllers can be hard-wired or microprogrammable and are characterized by their Instruction Sets (IS). On the opposite side, datapaths differ in terms of number and type of functional units and interconnection bus topologies. Each processor consists of one control unit driven one or more datapaths which can be pipelined or non pipelined.

Two basic types of connections can be envisioned: point to point, preferred for shorter on-chip communication and bussed when the distance is longer and intra-chips. Specific data transfers (DMA, Channels) can be occasionally managed through dedicated components.

Architectures for codesign, typically consist of one ore more custom processors connected through busses to a processor acting as the master. Shared memory protocols are frequently adopted for data exchange. Multiple processors architectures are also present, in these cases custom coprocessors are connected via multiple buses or a switching network. Access to system's resources by each processor is regulated by an arbiter and usually takes place using message-passing and data queuing.

Current progress in silicon technology enabled the realization of a system-on-a-chip, and for many applications the "low power" part of the entire system, i.e. the processors surrounded by one or more hardware coprocessors, can be integrated in the same package. For this purpose, a number of companies are marketing core cells (hard of soft macros) for embedded applications, to be integrated and partially customized according to the design needs. Examples are DSP microprocessor cores, standard bus interfaces (PCMCIA, PCI, ...), decoder/encoder (MPEG, GSM, ...), etc.

3.3 Design space exploration

Comparative analysis of alternative solutions can be accomplished by evaluating different aspects: hw/sw partitioning, architecture tuning, constraints fulfillment.

The goal of partitioning is the selection of parts of the specification to be executed either on the microprocessor or through a custom hw implementation. Software is usually cheap, flexible but poor in performance if compared with hardware. Many partitioning algorithms have been presented in literature, mostly derived from the hw/hw existing partitioning strategies. The novelty consists of gathering in a unified goal function, different constraints and cost/performance models specific of the hw or sw domains. Additional problems have to be considered during the split of specification onto the implementation domains; in particular the presence of only a "virtual" task parallelism on the microprocessor with respect to hardware and the bus traffic originated by hw-sw communication.

The selection of the architecture relies on both selecting the proper components and the interconnections. In many proposals it is necessary to tune prediction strategies to identify the proper processor for software execution and a suitable style for algorithm implementation. The exploration includes restructuring at the algorithmic level and scheduling of operations. One of the major problems in exploration relates to early verification of properties and constraints of the system operation. At such an abstraction level, in many cases, it is more important to quickly compare alternative solutions with respect to obtain the absolute precision in the evaluation; approximate prediction-based strategies, both for cost and performance, are currently a hot topic of codesign.

3.4 Concurrent Synthesis

Cosynthesis consists of obtaining software code and schematics by transforming the optimal high-level design descriptions identified during design space exploration. Synthesis is also the step where domain-specific optimization can be performed, and some manual intervention is again necessary. The goal of codesign is to interface existing standards and, at the same time, to manage in a unified way both the hw and sw synthesis flows. One of the most important goals is to reduce the impact on the final system integration, which traditionally can account up to 50% of the global design time, and to possibly generate the hw/sw interface automatically.

Concerning the software synthesis, three main components have to be considered: instruction set, compilation, operating system support [19]. The goal of considering the instruction sets as a variable of the design space is targeted to better tailor the microprocessor to the application needs; ASIP processors and retargetable compilers are good examples of such a research effort. The tuning of an instruction set requires to profile the application code to discover which IS will produce the best performance. However, some limitations must be considered since datapath resources and connectivity affect the IS implementation. Since the realization of a compiler for a specific microprocessor requires a big effort, researchers are working on retargetable compilation strategies able to generate optimized code for different instruction sets, starting form intermediate descriptions of the code and of the resources available to implement the instruction sets.

Operating systems for embedded systems typically require real-time support and compactness. Differently from other general purpose commercial products, they implement scheduling policies conceived for hard real time which, in some cases, can be statically determined. Many customizations are typically present, and their code is deeply joined with the application code.

Hardware synthesis is a threefold activity concerning behavioral, RT-level, and interface synthesis. The goal of RTL synthesis is to select proper units from libraries to store the variables and to perform the proper operations assigned to them. To improve performance, pipelining can be applied. Behavioral synthesis is a step forward in terms of abstraction, even if the results are less predictable with respect to RTL synthesis. In this case algorithms written through high-level formalisms, are converted into an internal representation onto which scheduling of operation and resources allocation can be globally performed. Allocation aims at finding out the suitable amount of resources to tradeoff cost, performance or power constraints. Scheduling typically produces an assignment of the algorithm operations to the different clock cycles.

The generation of interfaces requires simultaneous design of hw and sw components and the adherence to standard strategies such as DMA or memory mapping under the bus bandwidth constraint. Due to its paramount importance onto the global system performance, this activity is hard to be fully automated.

One of the goals of cosynthesis is to simplify the interfacing with industrial standards and tools both for hw and sw development. Hence, there is an increasing effort in the research community in using standard formalisms to represent the synthesized system (e.g., VHDL) as well as to refine strategies able to predict the final product of the well assessed synthesis strategies. These data can be backannotated onto the system description and are useful to drive the design space exploration.

3.5 Coverification

A key issue in codesign is the possibility of concurrently verifying the interaction between hardware and software prior to committing to an implementation. Main characteristics to be inspected are functionality, performance, communication and constraints fulfillment. This activity can be performed at different abstraction levels, with different models and accuracy, and constitutes the background for all other codesign activities.

Coverification has several flavors, probably the former effort has been targeted to allow the designer to verify system consistency via simulation. Different tools, are present on the market, targeted for hw or sw: software simulators typically use functional models of the microprocessors and can be cycle-accurate as well as operate at the instruction level, while EDA environments for hw design use more time accurate models at the register-transfer or gate level. Such an heterogeneity in terms of accuracy (and consequently speed) and simulation technology has spurred the growing of *cosimulation* strategies, able to bring together and coordinate different simulator domains and tools; probably the best effort in this direction is represented by the Ptolemy environment [6]. However, in many occasions, the speed of hw and sw simulators is not sufficient for large scale runs, so that additional hw is used to speed up simulation. This strategy, called *coemulation*, uses programmable hardware (e.g., FPGAs) to implement the hardware part of the system, while the software runs on the target microprocessor through in-circuit emulation. In this case the speed of the obtained system is typically one order of magnitude smaller the coemulated system, hence they cannot be used for accurate debugging of time transient inspection.

Apart from functional or performance analysis, coverification covers also much more "semantic" analysis of the system, in particular an active research field aims at enabling the verification of system *properties* or to formally prove the equivalence of different hw/sw implementations, maybe obtained through restructuring of the original specification.

4. Current approaches and EDA environments

In the past few years, a number of institutions started to investigate specific aspects of codesign, and currently some prototype methodologies and CAD environments are becoming available within the research community. A brief taxonomy of the more mature approaches and projects is here reported.

The problem of cosimulation has been extensively addressed in the Ptolemy project [6] and Coware [9], while the verification of formal properties is one of the focus of the Polis [2] environment. Concerning the capturing of system specifications and design requirements, graphical formalisms embedded in prototype environments have been studied in the TOSCA [14, 15] and SpecSyn [3] projects. The activity of exploring different alternative designs at system-level is one of the main value added of SpecSyn, TOSCA and Co-Saw. The synthesis of software for embedded applications is the scope of SpecSyn, TOSCA, Co-Saw and Polis, while the activity of interfacing hw and sw is the main goal of Chinook [4]. By now, many approaches prefer to interface with existing environments for hw synthesis, e.g at the VHDL level, instead of defining a new development strategy. Distributed embedded systems are the reference architecture for [5, 6], whose focus is on performance modeling and software generation.

Some recent projects, partially funded by the EC focussed on codesign. The effort of INSYDE [8] was in the field of system specification and object oriented modeling techniques to unify hw and sw representations. SYDIS/COBRA [7] and CASTLE [13] aimed at defining a complete co-design flow, covering specification, verification, partitioning and synthesis. Another framework providing a complete codesign flow is TOSCA, where the issues of modeling and design space exploration has been extensively considered in the SEED project. SYDIS focused on design data integration considered two target architectures: ASIP and a single processor joined to a coprocessor.

Other important investigations have been carried out to realize the COSYMA and COSMOS/SOLAR [11] codesign systems, whose main goal is the partitioning and synthesis stages, and in the GRAPE [10] project where the problem of emulating a system for data-oriented and cycle-static applications, has been addressed.

Currently, there exists a strong interest from CAD vendors in the codesign discipline, their main effort, up to now, has been in integrating existing hw and sw design flow starting from the bottom line: hw/sw cosimulation.

5. Concluding remarks

The constant growing of the design complexity gap between the chip density and the ability to design complex systems, together with the reduction of design time are the main motivations behind codesign. Currently, the length of the design cycle ranges from 6 to 24 months. This gap slows down the development of really new products, the achievements of optimal realizations and requires broader design expertise and large design teams. Several strategies to control the complexity gap can be conceived, e.g.:

1. Concurrent development of hardware, software and mechanical parts of the system.
2. Reuse of standard parts in-house developed for other projects as well as cores provided by third parts (IP macrocells).
3. Designing at the higher abstraction levels, only at the level of virtual prototyping with the support of design automation tools to provide implementation. The focus is thus on product specification and solutions exploration.

Although codesign relies on all the aspects above reported, current maturity of methodologies and tools allows the designer to be supported only during activities 1) and partially 3).

This paper presented an overview of the open problems encountered during the design of an embedded system, and of the emerging methodology called codesign.

The research community is more and more getting aware that the success of each proposal requires a strong cooperation between university, EDA developers and Industries. This concept has been also the trigger of the RASSP Program [16], initially focused on signal processor-based military products, whose goal is to decrease the overall design-time, dramatically (at least of a 4X factor).

References

1. G. De Micheli, M.G. Sami editors, Hardware/Software Co-Design, NATO ASI Series, Series E: Applied Sciences - vol.310, Kluwer Academic Pub., The Netherlands, 1996.
2. F.Balarin et Al., Hardware-Software Co-Design of Embedded Systems, The POLIS approach Kluwer Academic Publishers, 1997.
3. D.Gajski, F.Vahid, S.Narayan, J.Gong, Specification and Design of Embedded Systems, Prentice Hall, 1994.
4. P.Chou, G.Borriello, The Chinook Hardware/Software Cosynthesis System, ISSS'95, Cannes, France, 1995.
5. J.Hou, W.Wolf, Process Partitioning for Distributed Embedded Systems, DAC'96, Las Vegas, Nevada, 1996.
6. Ptomely www site: http://ptolemy.eecs.berkeley.edu/
7. G.Koch, U.Kebschull, W.Rosenstiel, A Prototyping Environment for Hardware/Software Codesign in the COBRA Project, CODES/CASHE'94, Grenoble, France.
8. AAVV, A formal Approach to Hardware Software Codesign: The INSYDE Project, ECBS'96, March 1996.
9. K.Van Rompaey, D.verkest, I.Bolsens, H.De Man, CoWare – A Design Environment for Heterogeneous Hardware/Software Systems, Euro-Dac'96, Geneve, 1996.
10. M.adè, R.Lauwereins, J.A. Peperstraete, Hardware/Software Codesign with GRAPE, Int Workshop on Rapid System Prototyping, Chapel Hill, North Carolina, June, 1995.
11. T.Ben Ismail, A,A, Jerraya, Synthesis Steps and Design Models for Codesign, IEEE Computers, February 1995.
12. J.Henkel, R.Ernst, et alii, An Approach to the Adaption of Estimated Cost Parameters in the COSYMA System, Codes/CASHE'94, Grenoble, France, 1994.
13. Camposano R., Wilberg J. , Embedded System Design, Design Automation for Embedded Systems, Kluwer Academic Publishers, vol.1, n.1-2, pp.5-50, January 1996.
14. W.Fornaciari, F.Salice, D.Sciuto, A two-level Cosimulation Environment, IEEE Computer, pp. 109-111, Jun. 1997.
15. SEED www site: http://www.cefriel.it/eda/projects/seed/mainmenu.htm.
16. RASSP Project WWW site: http://rassp.scra.org/
17. J.K.Adams, D.E.Thomas, The Design of Mixed Hardware/Software Systems, DAC'96, Las Vegas, Nevada, 1996.
18. S. Edwards, et Al., Design of Embedded Systems: Formal Models, Validation and Synthesis, Proc. of the IEEE, vol.85, n.3, March 1997.
19. G. Gossens, et Al., Embedded Software in Real-Time Signal Processing Systems: Design Technologies, Proc. of the IEEE, vol.85, n.3, March 1997.
20. P. Paulin, et Al., Embedded Software in Real-Time Signal Processing Systems: Application and Architecture Trends, Proc. of the IEEE, vol.85, n.3, March 1997.
21. G. De Micheli, R. Gupta, Hardware Software Codesign, Proc. of the IEEE, vol.85, n.3, March 1997.

Hardware/Software Embedded System Specification and Design Using Ada and VHDL[1]

Adrian López[1], Maite Veiga[1] and Eugenio Villar[1]

[1] Microelectronics Engineering Group, TEISA Department, University of Cantabria, E.T.S.I.Industriales y Telecom., Avda. los Castros s/n, 39005 Santander, Spain
{adrian, maite, villar}@teisa.unican.es

Abstract. System specification is one of the main tasks in any HW/SW co-design methodology. Many languages are being used based on different underlying models. None of them has been developed specifically for general purpose, real-time, HW/SW embedded system specification and design. In this paper, Ada [1] is proposed for the specification of complex, real-time, embedded systems containing functions to be implemented either in hardware or software. Its suitability for this kind of application will be analyzed and its role in a complete HW-SW co-design methodology will be described. The co-design methodology proposed is based on the interrelated use of both Ada and VHDL. Both are standard languages with a very similar syntax, based on the same programming concepts.

1 Introduction

System specification represents a key step in any computer-aided-design methodology [2]. At the Register Transfer (RT) level, hardware specification evolved from an immature period in the 70s characterized by a very large number of different Hardware Description Languages (HDLs) being developed to the current mature situation characterized by the use of a few standard HDLs (basically VHDL and Verilog). At the system level, the situation is similar to that during the 70s at the RT-level: many languages are used in different HW-SW co-design methodologies based on different underlying models [2][3]. None of these languages has been developed specifically for general purpose, real-time, embedded system specification and design.

Specific languages are being used for specific applications. So, for instance, SDL and LOTOS are CCITT standard languages for telecommunication system specification. Silage is specialized in the specification of hardware digital signal processing systems. Esterel is based on the perfect synchrony hypothesis, which represents a formalization of the clock based (RT) paradigm being developed for the specification of reactive systems. Although they are well suited to the particular application each of them addresses, their use as general-purpose specification languages presents severe limitations.

---

[1] This work has been partially supported by INDRA-Espacio through the Esprit 26971 CoMES project.

Several graphical notations [2][3] have been proposed for system specification based on the state transition paradigm. One of the most classical is Petri Nets and its extensions. Another classical graphical specification notation is represented by StateCharts. StateCharts are an extension of the FSM model intended to facilitate the description of complex behavior. A further extension is represented by the SpecCharts which allow any arbitrary behavior to be associated to any state [2]. All these models have to be translated to a programming language for execution purposes. Their main advantage comes as graphical specification entries.

C is one of the most widely used languages for system specification. The reason for this derives more from its popularity as a programming language and the corresponding availability of compilers than from its features as a system specification language. In fact, C has several limitations when used in the specification of complex, real-time, embedded systems, particularly, its lack of support for concurrency. In order to overcome some of these limitations, several C-based specification languages have been proposed such as HardwareC [4] and C^x [5]. As academic languages, their spread and support are limited. In other cases, the designer is provided with library packages in addition to some syntactical and semantical constraints in order to allow the use of C/C++ as a specification language [6][7]. Java is being considered as an alternative in this sense. Although Java supports concurrent execution of multiple threads, it has been developed specially for distributed systems, not for real-time, embedded systems. Thus, the addition of missing features would require similar solutions as in the case of C/C++. An additional problem comes from the fact that Java imposes object orientation and Java classes are dynamically linked, complicating the analysis of the specification at compilation time [8]. New languages and notations are still being proposed [9].

Hardware designers using VHDL prefer to extend this language up to the system level. This fact highlights an important conclusion: the system specification and RT languages, if not the same, should be as similar as possible. Nevertheless, VHDL has severe limitations as a system specification language. The most important limitation of VHDL derives from the underlying, event-driven, logic simulation mechanism it is based on. At the system-level, exact timing is not yet known. It can vary dramatically depending on the final partition and implementation of both the hardware and the software parts. Only functional and/or domain timing restrictions in terms of minimum and/or maximum timing constraints among data are relevant. VHDL on the contrary, imposes exact timing, which, in most cases, implies an excessive over-specification. If simulation timing is considered, simulation results may become unreliable as they may depend on particular event synchronization. Moreover, the simulation time is unnecessarily long [10]. Concurrency is another essential feature supported by VHDL. Although data concurrency is fully supported by VHDL, control concurrency is only partially supported. Moreover, the communication mechanism is extremely simple. It is based on synchronous shared memory (signals). Although VHDL'93 also supports asynchronous shared memory based on shared variables, very few commercial simulators fully implement this feature.

Some authors propose specifying the system using several languages. This approach has as an advantage in that it is possible to choose the most suitable language for each system component. Although it is clearly an attractive approach from a research point of view, it is unrealistic from a commercial point of view. Both the users and the vendors reject the support of different languages and their corresponding interfaces and translators.

Currently, an international standardization effort is being carried out by the SLDL Committee of the EDA Industry Council, aimed at the development of an interoperable language environment for the specification and high-level design of microelectronics-based systems. Experiences from the currently used languages constitute an important input to this initiative. In this sense, a benchmark has been chosen in order to allow the comparison among different languages with respect to their suitability to model heterogeneous systems (i.e. modeling effort, simulation performance, reusability, etc.). The benchmark, a portal crane [11], will be used as an example in this paper.

A relationship can be found between the design methodology at any level and the language used as shown in Figure 1:

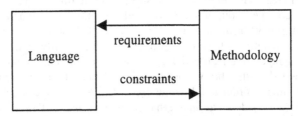

Fig. 1. Language-Methodology relationship. A language supports a certain methodology when it satisfies all the requirements imposed by the methodology while reducing the constraints on the methodology.

A standard language should be as general as possible, that is, it should be independent of any concrete methodology and/or technology. As a consequence, the language should impose as few constraints on the methodology as possible.

In this paper, Ada is proposed for the specification of complex, real-time, embedded systems containing functions to be implemented either in hardware or software. Its suitability for this kind of application will be analyzed and its role in a complete HW-SW co-design methodology will be described. The co-design methodology proposed is based on the interrelated use of both Ada and VHDL. In fact, the ternary Ada/VHDL/VHDL-AMS represents a coherent set of languages able to cover the design tasks from the specification of mixed analog-digital systems down to the final implementation as shown in Figure 2.

Ada was originally developed and has been used since for the design and implementation of 'traditional' (SW) real-time embedded systems. Nevertheless, the embedded systems that can be designed now impose new requirements on the specification language. These new requirements come basically from four main challenges. Firstly, the increasing complexity of today's microprocessors and associated real-time software. Secondly, the increasing complexity of the associated hardware performing all those tasks which for timing constraints or cost can not be allocated to the microprocessor. Thirdly, the increasing complexity of the hardware/software interface implementing the hardware/software communication mechanisms needed in these complex real-time applications. Fourthly, the increasing integration capability opening the way to the implementation of the whole system or parts of it, on a single chip as a System-On-Silicon (SOS). Thus, when analyzing the features of Ada as a HW/SW embedded system specification language, special emphasis has to be put on these new requirements. Specifically, interface synthesis, HW/SW co-simulation at different abstraction levels and HW synthesizability.

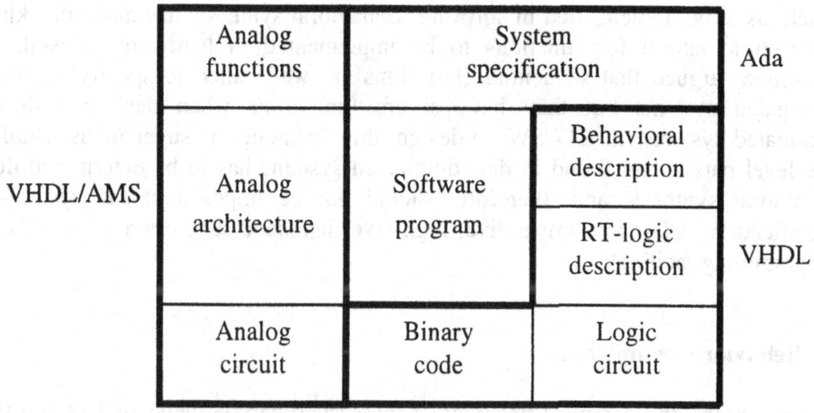
Analog functions
System specification
Ada
Behavioral description
VHDL/AMS
Analog architecture
Software program
RT-logic description
VHDL
Analog circuit
Binary code
Logic circuit

Fig. 2. Multi-level system description using Ada-VHDL-VHDL/AMS.

The structure of the paper will be as follows. In Section 2, Ada will be proposed as a HW/SW embedded system specification language covering most of the requirements imposed for this kind of application. In Section 3, the HW synthesizability of the language will be analyzed. In the next Section, the portal crane benchmark will be used to illustrate the proposed embedded system design methodology based on Ada and VHDL. Finally, some conclusions will be derived.

2 Ada as a HW/SW embedded system specification language

Although both software development and hardware design use relatively mature methodologies, co-design of systems composed of software and hardware functions currently constitutes an open and still unsolved problem. System specification represents one of the most important challenges in embedded system design. For the first time, digital design is confronted as a unified problem for which software and hardware functions become implementation alternatives for the same specification. This fact imposes a first, general requirement on the specification means; that it is capable of specifying in a natural way computational algorithms which will be partitioned and whose parts will be implemented either in hardware or software. That is possible because the algorithm is independent of its final implementation. Digital Signal Processing (DSP) is a good example of this statement. So, for instance, a Fast Fourier Transform can either be implemented in a microprocessor, a DSP processor or in hardware depending on the throughput required. It is an objective of any co-design tool to be able to identify the best implementation in each case from the same specification. Additional, more concrete requirements follow [2][7][12].

2.1 Programming constructs

In most cases, complex behavior can best be described using a sequential algorithm. In fact, system design can be seen essentially as a programming activity [7]. System specification by means of a programming language is particularly natural for those functions to be implemented in software. Behavioral synthesis has made this kind of description natural for functions to be implemented in hardware as well. It is sometimes argued that sequential algorithms are well suited to specifying control-dominated systems but they have severe limitations when dealing with data-dominated systems. In HW/SW co-design, this distinction is superfluous. Hardware low-level parallelism found in data-dominated systems has to be determined during behavioral synthesis and, therefore, should not be imposed at the system-level specification. Ada as an imperative, high-level language supports a wide variety of programming facilities.

2.2 Behavioral completion

In some cases, the complete behavior of the system can be better understood if this complete behavior, and the sub-behaviors in which it is divided reach a completion point, at which any computation has been executed and all the variables updated. Ada includes constructs, which ensure behavioral completion.

2.3 State transitions

In some cases, embedded systems are best conceptualized as having different states[2] of behavior. Each state may represent any arbitrary computation. In most cases, after state computation completion, the transition condition is evaluated and the next state decided. This description means is particularly natural for reactive systems [13] and is more a graphical, user-friendly interface than a proper specification mechanism. The graphical description can be easily translated to programming language code (i.e. Ada) for execution and analysis purposes using description styles similar to FSMs in VHDL.

2.4 Partition and hierarchy

Partition and hierarchy represent two of the most important means of handling complexity. Following the principle of "dividing and conquering", a problem that is too complex to be understood as a whole is decomposed in smaller pieces which are decomposed again until manageable components are found. The problem is then approached by ensuring that each component is behaving correctly and its composition makes the corresponding component in the higher level of the hierarchy behave correctly too. Two kinds of hierarchical partitions are desirable in the embedded system specification means: structural and behavioral. In general, the specification of a complex embedded system will require a mixture of both structural and behavioral hierarchical partitioning.

Structural partition and hierarchy is the capability to decompose the system into a set of interconnected components, which may have their own internal structure. As

---

[2] The term "state" is used here as a computation mode of an algorithm and, therefore, in a more general sense than the state in a Finite State Machine (FSM).

each component has its own behavior, structural partition is closely related to concurrency. Ada supports structural partitioning through tasks.

Behavioral partition and hierarchy is the capability to decompose the system behavior into distinct sub-behaviors, which may have their own internal behavioral partition and hierarchy. Functional partition and hierarchy is supported in Ada through packages, subprograms (procedures and functions) and blocks.

2.5 Concurrency

In most cases, a complex behavior can be better conceptualized as a set of concurrent subbehaviors. Concurrency is an important requirement of any specification means in order to support structural partitioning. Concurrency can be applied with different granularity. In a HW/SW co-specification, the thickest grain granularity is represented by task-level concurrency. Any behavior can be partitioned in different tasks. Finer grain granularity is represented by statement-level concurrency. Even finer grain granularity would be the operation-level concurrency in which, provided the data dependencies are satisfied, two operations can be performed sequentially or in parallel. Both statement-level and operation-level concurrency are analyzed and decided during behavioral synthesis. The finest grain granularity would be the bit-level concurrency, which is decided at the logic level.

There is always a possible tradeoff between sequential and concurrent implementations. Sequential implementations are, in general, slower but cheaper (in terms of number of gates and power consumption) while, concurrent implementations are, in general, faster but more expensive. Any synthesis tool at any level should be able to perform sequential-concurrent transformations exploring the design space for solutions satisfying the design requirements.

Software engineering indicates that the specification language should reflect the structure of the application domain. If the application domain contains inherent parallelism, then the design and implementation of the software product will be less error-prone, easier to verify and easier to adapt if concurrency is available in the specification language [8][14]. As the embedded system will contain concurrent operations, concurrency is an important feature of any HW/SW co-design specification means. Sequential computations are deterministic and may hide non-deterministic behavioral modes, which may appear in the final implementation. A concurrent specification may help to detect them and if necessary, to avoid them. Moreover, concurrency leads to more flexible specifications.

2.6 Non-determinism

Non-determinism refers to the capability of a system to react in an unpredictable way to a certain event. Two kinds of non-deterministic behaviors can be found when an embedded system is specified, functional non-determinism and temporal non-determinism. By functional non-determinism, the possibility of behaving in different ways under the same sequence of input patterns is understood. As mentioned before, a concurrent specification is non-deterministic as different results can be obtained depending on the order of execution of tasks and thus, it reflects more accurately any potential non-deterministic behavior in the final implementation. It is worth pointing out that an embedded system implementing HW and SW functions is concurrent by nature and, therefore, non-deterministic. In the general case, system behavior should be predictable, yielding the same results from the same inputs [7]. Thus, functional non-determinism constitutes an essential feature at the system specification level in order to detect it as early as possible and, if necessary, to avoid it. Temporal non-determinism is caused by the variability of the time spent by a certain computation. Support for temporal non-determinism is also an essential feature, as at the system-level, exact timing is not yet known.

2.7 Timing

By timing, we refer to the information about the temporal behavior of the system at a certain abstraction level. Timing information is one of the most important characteristics of the system being designed and, in fact, it can be used to conceptually identify the different levels of abstraction.

At the specification stage, no temporal information about the system is available and only the timing constraints to be imposed are defined. Timing constraints have to be analyzed for consistency in order to ensure an implementation exists which satisfies them [15].

Ada, as a programming language, is executed without any exact timing, thus accelerating the verification and debugging of the system specification. In order to support particular real-time constraints, it contains some time-related constructs. In an Ada-VHDL co-simulation environment, timing restrictions could be annotated and taken into account.

2.8 Communication

Ada tasks can communicate among themselves through three main mechanisms: shared variables, protected objects, and rendezvous. Based on these basic communication mechanisms, any other, more complex, communication and synchronization mechanism can be specified in a natural way (monitors, semaphores, channels, broadcasting, etc.). Provided an efficient implementation for the basic mechanisms exists, an efficient implementation for these other, more complex, derived communication and synchronization mechanisms will be ensured.

2.9 Synchronization

The simplest way in Ada for synchronizing tasks, is an accept statement without a body. Task synchronization can also be achieved through shared memory or protected objects. In addition to the synchronous communication mechanisms mentioned so far, Ada tasks may interact asynchronously.

2.10 Exceptions and interrupts

Reliable systems should work properly even if abnormal computation modes are reached due to malformed or unexpected input data, unexpected execution modes or hardware malfunctions. The specification should avoid such unexpected situations but, in order to be reliable, it should account for and be prepared for them. Such situations are called exceptions in Ada and the language provides mechanisms for dealing with them.

Interrupts can be explicitly described in the Ada specification. These interrupts will affect the whole system. During HW/SW partitioning, the corresponding interrupt handlers can be assigned either to SW or HW.

2.11 Object-Orientation

Object-oriented programming is currently a usual programming approach. Its extension to hardware design is currently under investigation based on an object-oriented extension of VHDL [16].

In addition to these requirements, the SLDL Committee has defined a further set of requirements and constraints to be imposed on the specification language:

2.12 Specify partial descriptions

The system specification language must be able to describe the information known at a certain step of the design process without the need for a complete description. Ada supports this through the separate compilation facility.

2.13 State things in a domain independent fashion

Ada satisfies this requirement as a standard, flexible language, independent of any concrete design methodology, application or technology.

2.14 Specify the value and the meaning of parametric values

Ada supports the definition of design requirements and constraints by the use of pragmas and attributes. Furthermore, an Ada specification can be made dependent on those parameters through generics and discriminants. In order to become standard and, therefore, be accepted by any tool, an embedded system specification annex should be developed without modifying the language itself. The annex could define additional pragmas, attributes, packages and restrictions with the objective of efficiently supporting HW/SW co-design.

2.15 Divide responsibility of the requirement among components

When a design requirement has been imposed on a system unit (i.e. input-output delay, maximum power consumption, etc.) and the system unit has been partitioned into several components, the general requirement will imply concrete requirements on each one of the components. Although this is a responsibility of the design tool being used, the language should be capable of applying the requirements to any relevant portion of the code. Ada pragmas and attributes can be used in this way.

2.16 Represent measurements and compare them to constraints

Although it would be a responsibility of the design tool to extract the actual properties of a certain implementation and compare them to the requirements and constraints imposed at the specification level, the language should facilitate the task. Thus, the Ada embedded systems annex proposed above could include backannotation mechanisms for the design requirements and constraints defined.

2.17 Track the satisfaction of a requirement or constraint

Annotated requirements and constraints can be passed to the lower-level tool when needed. When applying to software, they have to be moved directly to the compiler or to pre- or post-process tools. When applying to hardware, they have to be moved to the behavioral synthesis tool. In this sense, compatibility between the design requirements and constraints defined at the system level and at the behavioral level should be ensured.

2.18 Easy entry and manipulation of requirements and descriptions

There are several Ada features, which support this requirement. On the one hand, the modularity of the language based on subprograms, tasks, blocks and packages. Separate compilation also facilitates the isolation of pieces from the entire description. On the other hand, generics and discriminants facilitate manipulation and reuse of the code.

2.19 Execution or simulation of the specification

As stated above, Ada is a high-level, imperative, programming language supporting the specification of complex embedded systems for HW/SW co-design. There are many commercial tools available allowing code analysis, debugging, compilation, cross-compilation, etc. When the exact timing behavior of a module is known, the corresponding Ada code can be simulated inside a VHDL simulator.

3 Ada synthesizability

The aim of the system specification methodology is to permit the complete specification of embedded systems in Ada through a series of concurrent tasks and procedures, without introducing any type of restrictions on the language usage. The main advantage of this general approach is its flexibility. No syntactical constraint is imposed. Nevertheless, synthesis efficiency is always related to the synthesis tool capability to identify the implementation associated with the described behavior. This requires an implementation semantics in the specification used [20]. As a consequence, there will be some parts of the code, which due to the style in which they have been specified, could lead to unsuitable or inefficient implementations. In HW/SW co-design this is particularly probable in those tasks to be assigned to hardware which when described using computationally complex algorithms (i.e. code handling complex data structures, recursive functions, etc.) could lead to unsuitable implementations. It is a designer responsibility to use suitable description styles for the whole specification and, particularly, for those functions with a high probability to be allocated to hardware. In fact, an important aspect in Ada system specification is the definition of appropriate description styles.

Specification code generation with appropriate description style refers to both the syntactic as well as the semantic aspects of the code. On the one hand, a certain code may not admit any hardware implementation due to syntactical reasons. On the other hand, a certain code can be syntactically supported by the compiler or the hardware synthesis tool but may lead to inefficient implementations.

3.1 Specification structure

The system specification can be conceived as an entity with inputs and outputs as shown in Figure 3 a).

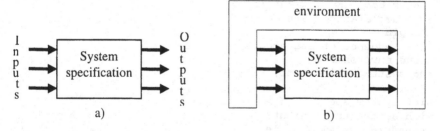

Fig. 3. Specification structure. a) System specification. b) The system and its environment.

In order to verify the specification under the operational conditions in which the system shall function, an environment or test-bench has to be developed. This environment has to produce the inputs to stimulate the system and has to store the outputs produced by the system as shown in Figure 3 b). As both the system specification and its environment have to operate concurrently, they have to be developed as Ada tasks activated by the main subprogram. When dealing with large programs, the complete Ada specification can be split into two packages used by the main procedure. Package "system_spec" contains the embedded system specification itself. Package "system_environment" generates the inputs to exercise the system and to store and/or monitor the data it produces. The system specification structure would be the following.

```
package system_spec
  -- declarative part
  task specification is
    entry input1 (…);
    pragma map_IO (input1, protocols.RS232);
    entry input2 (…);
    …
    entry output1 (…);
    …
  end specification;
end system_spec;

package body system_spec
-- declarative part
  task body specification is
  -- declarative part
  begin
  -- sequence of statements
  end specification;
end system_spec;

package system_environment
  -- declarative part
  task environment;
end system_environment;

package body system_environment
-- declarative part
  task body environment is
  -- declarative part
  begin
  -- sequence of statements
  end environment;
end system_environment;

with system_spec;
with system_environment;
procedure system_name is
begin
  null;
end system_name;
```

The entries of task "specification" in package "system_spec" allow easy identification of the inputs and outputs of the embedded system. They play a similar role to ports in a VHDL entity. While task "specification" is to be totally or partially designed, task "environment" is not. Thus, the description style for implementability, which will be commented later, applies for the former. For the latter, only the general recommendations to be followed when programming in Ada apply. Some restrictions have to be imposed on the Ada specification part to be implemented in hardware. The main ones will derive from the VHDL synthesis syntax and semantics of the behavioral synthesis tool. Regarding the Ada specification, three different situations arise. Those Ada features directly translatable to VHDL represent the first. These features do not present any problem and due to the syntactical similarities between Ada and VHDL only minor modifications will be needed. Those Ada features without any direct translation to behavioral VHDL but which with some modifications can be converted to VHDL code supported by the behavioral synthesis tool, represent the second. These features will be called indirectly supported. Those Ada features without possible translation to behavioral VHDL represent the third. Any Ada specification module containing this kind of unsupported features does not admit hardware implementation and has to be moved to software during partitioning.

3.2 Interface synthesis

After partitioning, the complete specification is divided in two parts. The first, containing all the tasks to be implemented in software and thus, to be executed by the processor[3]. The second part, containing all the tasks to be implemented in hardware and thus, to be executed concurrently by several hardware modules. Both the Ada software code and the behavioral VHDL code are obtained directly from the Ada specification. Nevertheless, in addition to the hardware and software algorithms extracted from the original specification, some additional code has to be added in order to ensure a correct implementation on the target architecture of all the communication among tasks contained in the specification. As the interface implementation directly affects the performance and cost of the whole system implementation, it has to be taken into account during the system specification itself and, therefore, it will be briefly described next. Two kinds of interfaces can be distinguished:

I/O Interface. This interface has to deal with the implementation of all the communication between the system and its environment through its inputs and outputs. The protocol and hardware to be used can be specified using pragmas as shown in Figure 4a). Usually, an interface pragma will be associated with a specific I/O hardware. If not directly specified, the most suitable I/O hardware has to be chosen. In any case, the I/O hardware can be either a soft VHDL synthesizable module or a hard module (a commercial off-the-shelf component or a silicon macro-cell).

In the case in which the data to read from or to write to the entry are managed by a task allocated to software, additional Ada code has to be added to the Ada software algorithm to ensure proper communication between the processor and the I/O hardware module. This additional code, called I/O driver, will be strongly dependent on the target architecture chosen and the communication protocol used.

HW/SW Interface. The second kind of interfaces refers to the correct implementation of the communication mechanisms among tasks contained in the Ada specification. Depending on the final allocation of tasks, four possible combinations of data transfers have to be considered:

- Data transfer from Hardware to Hardware.

---

[3] Tasks will be executed serially under the control of a scheduler.

- Data transfer from Software to Hardware.
- Data transfer from Hardware to Software.
- Data transfer from Software to Software.

If both tasks were implemented in software, there would be no need to design any specific interface. The Ada compiler would be directly responsible for ensuring the correct data transfers using the system resources.

If both tasks were allocated to hardware, the direct solution would be the use of dedicated connections. Synchronization between the FSMs implementing each VHDL process has to be ensured during behavioral synthesis [17]. If both FSMs are synchronized by construction, the data transfer could be done periodically at certain states. A second solution would make use of shared memory. If it is dedicated, that is, only used for storing a variable to which a task accesses in writing mode and another task accesses in reading mode, the situation is similar to the previous one. If the data memory is used, it is necessary to redefine the VHDL code to adapt to such a situation, which generally requires the implementation of additional bus arbitration hardware.

In the case of data transfers between HW and SW tasks and viceversa, modifications to the code (Ada and VHDL) will be necessary in order to ensure that the data dependencies are not violated. Depending on their characteristics (amount of data involved, frequency, timing constraints, etc.), communication can be done directly through the bus, through the data memory or by a specific hardware interface [18].

4 System specification example

In order to show the use of Ada as a HW/SW embedded system specification language, the portal crane benchmark will be used. We will roughly follow the MCSE methodology [13]. The starting point will be the Requirements Document describing the customer needs in terms of general functionality, input information to be processed, output information to be generated and design requirements and constraints imposed (timing constraints, cost constraints, size, weight, power consumption, reliability, maintainability, etc.).

Based on this information, a functional description is generated. In this design step, the functional architecture of the system, that is, the set of concurrent functions and the communication among them, is decided. The input and output data types as well as the internal data types are specified. Each function can be described as an Ada task. No code is needed at this stage, only the data movement among tasks is relevant. If some design decisions are already taken, they can be specified using pragmas. So, the functional architecture for the portal crane benchmark is composed of three tasks and three protected objects. The three tasks ('Control_task', 'Diagnosis' and 'Braking_Detector') model the functional behavior of the system. The 'Scheduler' protected object models the timing behavior. The protected objects 'Sensors' and 'Actuators' specify the I/O interface of the system.

Based on the number of tasks, their priorities, the relation among them and the estimation of their frequency and execution times, a Rate Monotonic Analysis (RMA) for schedulability can be done [19]. This is important information for the functional specification. In this design step, the specific functionality of each task is decided. If needed, a further partitioning of the more complex tasks can be performed. After the functionality of each task has been specified, the functional implementation process can start with the objective of developing the complete Ada code. Once the Ada specification has been developed, it can be debugged. Using relevant input sequences, the Ada specification can be profiled. The following information can be obtained: the number of times each task is activated; the maximum number of data stored in each memory; the utilization of each communication channel, etc. As both the domain and functional timing constraints are known, they can be propagated through the whole architecture and the timing constraints for each task and the bandwidth of each channel, analyzed. Based on this information, the HW/SW partition can be decided.

Table 1 shows the code size and the execution times obtained on a UltraSparc. It is clear that even using a small microprocessor, all the relevant tasks of the specification can be implemented in SW. Packages "Sensors" and "Actuators" will be implemented using USARTs. Additional code will be added for initialization and communication.

Table 1. Profiling results of the portal crane example.

	MEAN TIME	# EXECUTIONS	TOTAL TIME	ADA STATEMENTS
CONTROL	0,045 ms	15.534	699,03 ms	107
BRAKE	0,000264 ms	3.218	0,84955 ms	33
DIAGNOSIS	0,0003618 ms	32.162	11,64 ms	58

5 Conclusions

Ada is powerful enough for the specification of complex, embedded systems containing functions to be implemented either in hardware or software. It is particularly suited to real-time, reliable system specification and design. Its syntactical similarity to VHDL facilitates the development of a HW-SW co-design methodology using VHDL for hardware specification and design.

In this paper, Ada has been proposed as a HW/SW embedded system specification language covering most of the requirements imposed for this kind of application. The HW synthesizability of the language has been analyzed. The portal crane benchmark has been used to illustrate the proposed embedded system design methodology based on Ada and VHDL.

6 References

[1] "Information Technology, Programming Languages, Ada Reference Manual", International Standard ISO/IEC 8652:1995, January, 1995.
[2] D. D. Gajski, F. Vahid, S. Narayan and J. Gong: *"Specification and design of embedded systems"*, Prentice-Hall, 1994.
[3] F. Rammig: *"System level design"*, in "Fundamentals and standards in hardware description languages", edited by J. Mermet, Kluwer, 1993.
[4] R.K. Gupta and G. de Micheli: *"Hardware-software co-synthesis for digital systems"*, IEEE Design and Test of Computers, September, 1993.

370

[5] Ernst, R. and Henkel, J.: "Hardware-software co-design of embedded controlers based on hardware extraction", proc. of the IEEE International Workshop on HW/SW Co-design", September, 1992. 1992.

[6] H. Schwetman: "Using CSIM to model complex systems", proc. of the 1988 Winter Simulation Conference, 1988.

[7] R.K. Gupta and S. Liao: "Using a programming language for digital system design", IEEE Design and Test of Computers, April-June, 1997.

[8] R. Helaihel and K. Olukotun: "Java a a specification language for hardware-software systems", proc. of ICCAD'97, IEEE, 1997.

[9] P.H.A. van der Putten and J.P.M. Voeten: "Specification of Reactive hardware/software systems", CIP-Data Library Technishe Universiteit Eindhoven, 1997.

[10] E. Casino; P. Sánchez and E. Villar: "A high-level VHDL simulator", proc. of Spring VIUF'92, May, 1992.

[11] W. Nebel, G. Gorla and E. Moser: "Java, VHDL-AMS, Ada or C for system level specifications ?", Proc. of the Design, Automation and Test in Europe Conference 1999, IEEE, 1999.

[12] E. Villar: "Embedded system specification", in "Advanced techniques for embedded system design and test", ed. J. C. López; R. Hermida and W. Geisselhardt, Kluwer, 1998.

[13] J. P. Calvez: "Embedded real-time systems: A specification and design methodology", Wiley, 1993.

[14] A. Burns and A. Wellings: "Concurrency in Ada", Cambridge University Press, 1995.

[15] D.C. Ku and G. de Micheli: "High-level synthesis of ASICs under timing and synchronization constraints", Kluwer, 1992.

[16] W. Nebel and G. Schumacher: "Object-Oriented hardware modeling - Where to apply and what are the objects?", proc. of EuroDAC'96 with EuroVHDL'96, IEEE, September, 1996.

[17] Eles, P.; Kuchcinski, K.; Peng, Z. and Minea, M.: "Synthesis of VHDL concurrent processes", proc. of EuroDAC'94 with EuroVHDL'94, IEEE, September, 1994.

[18] Walkup, E. and Borriello, G.: "Automatic synthesis of device drivers for HW/SW co-design", proc. of the IEEE International Workshop on HW/SW Co-design", October, 1993.

[19] M.H. Klein, T. Ralya, B. Pollak, R. Obenza, and M. Gonzalez Harbour. "A practitioner's Handbook for Real-Time Analysis". Kluwer, 1993.

[20] E. Villar and P. Sánchez: "Synthesis applications of VHDL", in "Fundamentals and standards in hardware description languages", edited by J. Mermet, Kluwer, 1993.

Acknowledgment

The authors gratefully acknowledge the valuable contribution to the paper made by Dr. Michael González Harbour.

System on Chip Specification and Design Languages Standardization

Jean Mermet

ECSI & Laboratoire TIMA, Grenoble, France

jean.mermet@imag.fr

Abstract. This paper is aimed at summarizing the present international standardization activity in the domain of electronic systems' design languages. This activity is the ultimate evolution of the development of Hardware Description Languages, a process in which the author has been involved since the mid sixties.

A Short History of Standardization

Hardware Description Languages (HDL) started to be created in the 60s. In 1975 they were proliferating, which led to the creation of the *Computer Hardware Description Languages Conference* (CHDL) and the first attempt to an international standardization project, the CONLAN group, chaired by Pr. R. Piloty (U.Darmstadt).
In 1981, the CONLAN (CONsensus LANguage) report published was used extensively for the definition of VHDL. In 1982 the call of the DoD for the definition of a VHDL was classified the program, preventing non American teams to apply.
In Grenoble, CASCADE (5) extended CONLAN to encompass analogue behavior and then was implemented on top of CONLAN. In Darmstadt, R. Piloty realized with REGLAN a full CONLAN implementation (3).
Multi-languages with bridging semantics: CASCADE was an attempt to cover all design levels, from system to analogue/electrical, by merging 4 existing languages into a single one. All languages were redefined using CONLAN, which offered the bridging semantic.
But, finally, VHDL became an IEEE (and then a world-wide) standard in 1987. Then Verilog, a proprietary language acquired by CADENCE, was put in public domain and become another HDL standard, due to its market share. Then, after 10 years of work to produce a universally recognized standard HDL, designers had 2 standards.
The 90's were the time of the implementation of HDL's by Electronic Design Automation (EDA) tool providers and their dissemination world-wide. Although HDL existed already for more than 2 decades they had been used by a minority of large companies. Their synthesisable subsets, supported by commercial tools, made them a tool used by all designers. Extensions to VHDL appeared:

- *VHDL-Analogue and Mixed Signal (AMS):* among European requirements for VHDL93, there was a strong demand for mixed analogue/digital modeling and simulation. During the VUFE in Santander, the timeframe appeared too short to introduce this evolution into VHDL 93, then a new IEEE working group was created. VHDL/AMS, a new, VHDL-compatible, standard, has been stamped by the IEEE in 1999. VHDL-AMS is a true superset of VHDL which brings new concepts such as *nature* which relates to domain of application (electrical, mechanical, ..) the variables of the analogue model. VHDL-AMS can be used also at *system level*, to describe models and their environment with a continuous/discrete timing scheme.

- *Objective VHDL:* Objective-VHDL is an object-oriented extension of VHDL which was developed within the R&D ESPRIT project "REQUEST", mainly at university of Oldenburg. Objective VHDL is a true superset of VHDL with only two new keywords: *class, abstract.* A complete prototype of the Objective VHDL to VHDL translator was made in 1998.

- *VHDL+:* This VHDL extension was developed at ICL (UK) as an attempt to address some system level requirements not fulfilled by VHDL. The new concept brought by VHDL+ is that of *Interface* primary unit, which defines the communication between entities, can be re-used, and is multi-level.

Challenges for the Next Decade

It is clear that VHDL does not yet incorporate many of the features implemented in some of the ancestor languages cited above. Registers, Clocks, Finite State Machines, communication and synchronization mechanisms, object constructs, private data types, all these proven concepts could be requirements for VHDL 200X. Continuous and system level modeling capabilities are also lacking. The continuous modeling capability hopefully will come with VHDL-AMS, but system level description and modeling will not be provided only by VHDL extensions. VHDL is already a complex language and there is a limit to the increase of complexity that users can further accept and EDA tool providers implement.

Future design environments will have probably to accommodate a variety of different languages at a level ABOVE VHDL, but DEEPLY INTERFACED with it. The above mentioned VHDL extensions will only shorten the distance to these other languages and certainly facilitate the establishment of a seamless design flow, from system specification to circuit level, in a few years.

The Future of HDL's is not an HDL.

HDL's have made it possible to design multi-million gate chips and to follow the Moore's law over a third decade. But a paradigm shift has occurred: what is to be designed now is System on a Chip (SOC). SoC is no-longer hardware only, but more and more embedded software. Even if we restrict ourselves to hardware/software co-design and verification, there is today a Babel Tower situation among dozens of languages and formalisms, which recalls us the situation of HDL's in 1975, when it was decided to create CONLAN.

We need another CONLAN effort today at system level.

But this effort can last several years. In the meantime many of these languages will continue to be used beneficially in different application domains. And the design environments will have to be multi-languages for an undefined period of time.

To accommodate all these languages in a system design space, a standard set of notations is still to be defined, which will provide bridging semantics between different languages and computation models. Like in CONLAN, the goal would not be to define Yet Another Language, but to define the underlying semantics and provide the basic mechanisms to re-build the candidate system level languages on it.
This was the motivation for the EDA Roadmap Industry Council to rank with high priority the project of defining a "System Level Design Language: **SLDL**".

The Babel Tower (remake)

There are still many design languages that could be sorted in several categories:
- *Hardware description languages.* LAVA (hardware Haskell), Hardware-C, SPECCHARTS, VHDL, VERILOG, MIMOLA are some of them. Today, in Europe at least, its commercial support and numerous applications, its several extension developments, designate VHDL as the best candidate.
- *Protocol specification languages*: LOTOS and ESTELLE are ISO standards. SDL is an international standard of the CCITT used by hundreds of designers and beneficiating commercial suppor, at least from the companies: VERILOG and TELELOGIC. Several projects aim at translating SDL into synthesisable VHDL (10), (12), (17).
- *Synchronous languages*: In real-time applications,: ESTEREL, LUSTRE and SIGNAL are used and also Petri Nets and STATECHART. More than 20 variants of STATECHART exist. It is commercially supported. ESTEREL is also now supported by CADENCE,. The same is done by VERILOG with LUSTRE.
- *Parallel Programming languages:* The UK originated CSP, CCS, OCCAM fall in this category. These languages share with hardware the concept of concurrency and are still used, with proprietary tools, in conjunction with other languages, to specify embedded systems.
- *Programming languages*: C is usually the target language to describe the software modules in the design process. C++ is widely used to describe digital algorithms for DSP. JAVA is getting momentum in similar applications. Some supporters also push it as a system level candidate. But ADA hasalso supporters at system level.
- *Continuous modeling languages.* In this category MATLAB, remains the most popular commercial tool, used by many system level designers. In the European aerospace industry and in the automotive industry other languages are seeked like MODELICA (15) . VHDL/AMS has become an IEEE standard and has been implemented by LEDA and ANACAD/MENTOR.
- *Languages to model architectures.* Languages to model architectures are not so numerous. NML, initially created by IMEC and the university of Berlin, has been used in DSP systems. Script languages like TCL or PERL have also supporters who think that gluing sub-systems is the main function of an architectural language.
- *Mathematical notations.* VDM (an ISO standard) is based on set theory and predicate logic. Z close to VDM was developed mainly in UK. In France J.R Abrial developed B, which provides a mathematical foundation and semantics to cover both specifications and multi-level design refinement until implementation.

1- The System Level Design Language (SLDL) Project

The EDA industry is facing a crisis: they cannot verify large systems on a single silicon wafer. The SLDL working group is an informal international group of volunteers which was convened by the EDA Roadmap Industry Council. It is not a standardisation group but its charter is to produce a straw-man to be turned over to the appropriate standard body. The work was started in the form of several workshops aimed at collecting some of the existing notations. The first was held in Dallas (TX) and the second in Santa Clara (Cal). The following occurred in Europe, in Barga (I) and in Lausanne (CH). The high level of information exchange has led ECSI to transform this workshop into an annual event: the SSDL workshop.

System level specification is clearly a domain broader than System on Silicon, but a consensus appeared at the workshop in Barga (1997) that System on a Chip (SoC) with millions of digital gates but also analogue, RF, sensors, microwaves, batteries, micro-machine, optical devices.....and thousands of lines of software, was not restricting the scope at all but on the contrary was proposing a challenging goal for a few years. The group created 5 sub-committees :

- SoC requirements capture

This SC tries to characterize the variety of requirements (technical, economical, marketing....) which must be captured in the system specifications. The requirements must be expressed with no application domain bias, which means not using a notation primarily intended for a given domain (VHDL, C++,...).

- Design constraints capture and inheritance

Constraints say what the system must not do, complementing the requirements which say what to do.

These constraints must be propagated all along the design cycle and translated progressively into more and more precise technological constraints.

- System to component interface

This SC must define the transition from SLDL to each implementation domain (digital, analogue, software, mechanical...). This transition should preferably be automated or at least proven. The target is several domain specific languages (VHDL, C++, VHDL/AMS, Java,.....). Bridging semantics is needed here.

- Hardware / Software co-design

This TC has more practical and well identified problems of HW/SW partitioning optimization, HW/SW co-simulation, HW/SW interface and translation. Translating SDL or C into VHDL belongs to this rubrique.

- Formal semantics

Will SLDL be a merge of existing formalisms, based on some operational definition? Or will it be a fresh new construct derived from a solid mathematical foundation? Which existing formal mechanisms best address the definition of the SLDL semantics? These are questions that this SC would like to answer.

The goals of the SLDL group clearly overlaps some basic preoccupations of the VSI-alliance System Level Design Development Working Group (SLD/DWG). Meetings of this VSI DWG are organized in Europe in conjunction with the *SLDL/SSDL workshops.*

The System Level Design Language Committee:

(This paragraph borrows material from the EDA roadmap chapter on SLDL (3) edited by Dave Barton, SLDL committee chair)

Mission: The mission of the SLDL committee is to support the creation and/or standardization of a language or representation, or set of languages or representations, that will enable engineers to describe single and multi-chip silicon-based embedded systems to any desired degree of detail and that will allow engineers to verify and/or validate those systems with appropriate tools and techniques. The languages or representations will address systems under design and their operating environment, including software, mixed-signal, optical, and micro-electronic mechanical characteristics. The committee subgroups have produced:

1.1- Requirements and Constraints

An SLDL must be able to state what a system is. This has, historically, been split into two subjects: requirements, which deal with *what a system must do* (or the functions that it must perform), and *constraints,* which deal with things that a system *must not do*. Requirements specification and tracking is an integral part of system design. To support this process, SLDL must provide the ability to:

Specify partial descriptions.
Specify combined levels of abstraction.
A system may have different components described at different levels of abstraction.
Specify the value and the meaning of parametric values.
Many languages allow the user to attach parameters and attributes to the description. SLDL must allow the user to specify both the values and their meaning.
Divide ``responsibility" for a requirement between components.
Often several parts of the system must co-operate in the satisfaction of a requirement, or divide up the ``budget" of a constraint such as power consumption.
Track the satisfaction of a requirement or constraint.
The language must provide facilities to link the statement of the requirement with that portion of the description that satisfies the requirement.
State things in an implementation domain independent fashion.
Specify interfaces between components in different implementation domains.
Present digital and analogue languages allow the specification of the interface between analogue and digital components. SLDL must be able to specify these interfaces.
Develop components in different implementation domains in tandem.
(For example, designing hardware and software in tandem). This capability must be available for all combinations of implementation domains.

Moreover, **SLDL** should support:
The execution, or simulation, of the specification.
The easy entry and manipulation of requirements and descriptions.
Knowledge bases of requirements.
The identification of the business impact of various requirements and constraints.
The use of templates to fill in system requirements.
SLDL must be able to state requirements about all kinds of *properties of a system.*

Static. Dynamic. Temporal. Deterministic. Non-deterministic. Consistency properties Coupled properties. Environmental. Life cycle (Cost, schedule, ...) Performance. Structural. Behavioural. Dependability. Reliability. Availability. Maintainability. Performability. Safety. Testability. Controllability. Observability. Diagnosibility. Manufacturability. Usability of product.

1.2- System Level to Component Interfaces

Any systems description must eventually reduce to a series of implementable components that are connected in known ways, providing thus, the ability to make a transition from the systems level notation to languages which are specific to a given implementation domain. Components described in these component notations (such as VHDL or Verilog for digital electronics, Ada, C++, or Java for software, VHDL-AMS for analogue electronics, and so on) can be implemented directly by existing tools such as compilers, synthesizers, and layout tools.

The interface between the SLDL and the component notations is therefore of tremendous importance. Requirements on this interface are as follows:

- To map system level behavioural requirements to an implementable description.
- To reflect system level constraint requirements into the implementable component level domain(VHDL, Verilog, and C++).
- To provide the ability to pass information bottom up and back-annotate
- To map system level interface protocols into known or new ways of communication at the interface level.
- To describe a component abstractly, without making assumptions about the implementation domain.
- To express performance models for standard products. This is very much tied up with the issue of *intellectual property* and the ability to distribute working models (at various levels of efficiency) for components that do not give up intellectual property. The SLDL committee strongly recommends *continued interface with the VSI effort* in this area.
- To establish a structured mapping between an event at the systems level and an event, or a set of events, at the component level.
- To specify the interface between the SLDL description and component descriptions in domain specific languages (referred to as component synthesis).
- To be specifiable from the point of view of the interface alone. This means that we need to be able to view the system as a "black box".
- To capture and use "lessons learned" data gained by experience on other, similar systems. This implies the ability to *memorize the design knowledge.*

1.3- Formal Semantics

The role of formal semantics in SLDL is a dual one. In the first place, a language that is as general as SLDL and that will be used in as many different domains as SLDL must have a formal mathematical basis for its definition; an operational semantic such as that used for VHDL is not acceptable, since it narrows the applicability of SLDL to that implementation domain.

The second area is that of tools. Formal manipulation is becoming more and more useful in both hardware and software design. It is particularly useful in areas where

simulation and test have proven inadequate. This applies strongly to the Systems on Silicon domain, where systems have grown beyond the ability of simulators. Thus, a formal semantics is doubly important for SLDL.
It must have the following characteristics:
Sufficient power.
Domain theories.
Partial specifications.
Composable descriptions.
Extensibility.
Different Component Notations.
Views.

(*Note of the author: Looking at most of the above required qualities of the semantic notation it would be interesting to consider whether a notation like B could be appropriate as a mathematical foundation of SLDL*).

Phase 1 SLDL

A preliminary SLDL solution is needed as soon as possible by industry. Describing the full functionality of the system, and its components, is not required. What is most urgently required is the specification of ``cross-domain constraints" (*Timing constraints, Information flow between the components, Temporal abstraction*).
Constraints in the description must be *verifiable.* Tool support is needed.

The present working groups and subcommittees are:

- The Language Working Group: Chair, Perry Alexander (Perry.Alexander@uc.edu).
- The MoC Working Group: Co-Chairs, Todd Cook (toddc@improvsys.com), and Vijay Madisetti (vkm@ee.gatech.edu).
- The Usage Model subcommitee: Co-Chairs, Gary Panzer (panzer@bala.hac.com), and Giulio Gorla (Giulio.Gorla@italtel.it).
- The Implementation subcommittee: Co-Chairs, Victor Berman (vhberman@worldnet.att.net), and Jim Heaton (j.heaton@uk03.wins.icl.co.uk).
- The Bylaws subcommittee: Chair, Dennis Brophy (dennis_brophy@mentorg.com).
- The Requirements Capture subcommittee: Chair, Steve Grout (steve.grout@sematech.org).
-

Since ICCAD 98, the Requirements Capture subcommittee has been working in conjunction with the OVI Design Constraints working group on the definition of specific constraints, with a goal of contributing to a DAC99 demonstration. Once this work is done, they will branch out to more general constraint definitions.

The Full SLDL Solution

The full SLDL solution will meet all of the requirements set out in this document. The schedule for meeting this requirement is not clear at this time.

2- The VSI-Alliance System Level Design Development Working Group (SLD/DWG)

The VSI-alliance SLD-DWG was created from the beginning of VSI existence and chaired successively by M. Muller from ARM and Mark Genoe, from ALCATEL.
The European chairmanship reflects the importance of system companies in the European industry.

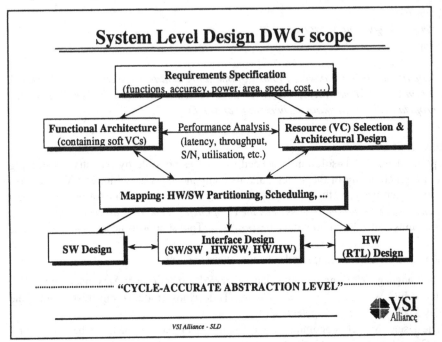

and interface was key in a model at system level, specially because functionality could be specified with several formalisms while interface had to be standard to allow *plug and play* and *re-use* (the goals of VSI-alliance). This interface must handle:

- HW to HW, SW to SW, HW to SW, SW to HW
- Functional Block to Protocol Block transaction layer
- Protocol Model Block abstraction mechanisms

Very soon an "Interface subgroup" Chaired by Chris Lennard from CADENCE, became active and produced a charter document which is presently reserved to VSI SLD-DWG members. The targeted deliverables of the group can be named however:

- "System-level interface-Behavior Documentation standard" a document which provides a standard way to describe a VC (Virtual Component) interface with any abstraction hierarchy with full property inheritance.
- "A standardized terminology and definitions"
- "An early adoption review program"
- "An interface description syntax". This sub-group has about 20 active members.

The **SLD Interface Standard Description** provides:
- A clean Definition of System Interface to separate VC function and interface
- Definition of System Interface Properties with transaction / attribute set
- A uniform Method for Interface Description which guarantees comprehensive documentation of interface behavior and a documentation format
- A hierarchical organization of VC System interfaces with clean method for linking the hierarchy and techniques to guaranty property inheritance.

The **System-Level Design Taxonomy and Terminology** document is the first deliverable of the SLD-DWG to be released publicly. The work started in Sept 97, based on the RASSP equivalent document.

Example of content: Token-based Performance Model
- *Definition:* "The Token-based Performance Model is a performance model of a multi-processor system's architecture. Measures associated with performance include response time and throughput of the system and the utilisation of its resources. Typically, the token-based performance model resolves the time for a multiprocessor networked system to perform major system functions. Data values are not modeled, except for control information. The structure of the system network is described down to the network node level. The internal structure of network switches, processor elements, shared memories, and I/O units is not described in a Token Based Performance Model. The primary purposes of a token-based performance model are to determine sufficiency of the following selections in meeting the system processing throughput and latency requirements: the number and type of processor elements, the size of memories and buffers, network topology (bus, ring, mesh, cube, tree, or custom configuration), network bandwidths and protocols, application partitioning, mapping, and scheduling of tasks onto processor elements, and flow control scheme."

The SLD Data Types Subgroup:
- Well-defined data types are essential for both the VC functional and interface
- The action point of this subgroup was agreed on in Feb 1998:

"To recommend a set of data-types and data representations for the import of user defined C/C++ simulation models into a system-level simulation environment.
The goal of this action is to obtain a format which will allow to mix and match different descriptions from different IP providers (external or internal), and to be able to simulate these models in any system level modeling, simulation.

Other SLD DWG Activities
- VC SLD Performance Modeling:
- VC Related Software aspects:

SW Taxonomy, ISS simulation environments with standard API, debugging of multi-core SoC, standard DSP, standard RTOS API...

III- The OVI Design Constraint Working Group

This paragraph uses material from "Group Charter, Scope and Deliverables" of May 22, 1998, edited by: Mark Hahn WG chair email: mhahn@cadence.com

"The *Design Constraints Working Group* is chartered with developing a *Design Constraint Specification Standard*. The standard, which encompasses a constraint description language, a constraint dictionary, and a constraint conceptual model, is intended for the prescription, representation, and preservation of the "*design intent*" throughout the *design cycle* of an electronic system or subsystem design. The design intent, typically expressed in a collection of constraints, assertions, and environment conditions, is the manifestation of system level design requirements other than functionality".... which is expressed in languages such as Verilog , VHDL or SLDL.
The key objectives of the Standard are to:

- Identify semantics and forms for expressing the design intent,
- Contribute to interoperability between tools.
- Apply uniformly across multiple tasks and constraint domains.
- Be compatible with existing standards (e.g. PDEF)
- Provide for automatic consistency checking between related constraints where possible.

Scope
"The standard should be language-independent, initially supporting chip and module level designs done in a mixture of Verilog, VHDL languages. Later work should add support for mixed-signal designs and corresponding design languages.
The standard should address required performance characteristics, implementation details, and descriptions of (as well as restrictions on) the environment in which the design is to be used.
The standard should be in consistent with exiting accredited public-domain standards. The working group will attempt to avoid overlapping efforts with other standard organizations, while achieve semantic consistency in the areas of overlap.

Constraint Domains
Constraint domain refers to different aspects of design objectives that need to be evaluated in tandem to observe the design tradeoffs best for the design over-all.
The constraint domains considered as within the scope of this standard are: Timing, Area, Clocking, Logic Architecture, Power, Physical Design, Signal Integrity and Test

Overlapping Standards
The group had identified areas of potential overlap with the efforts of other standard groups:

- The Physical Design Exchange Format (PDEF)
- Test constraints addressed by IEEE P1500 standard
- Constraints of the System Level Design Language Group
- Some board level constraints addressed by RAIL.

The DC-WG should work with these groups. to define the relationships between this DC-WG standard and their respective efforts.

Deliverables:
The working group is willing to issue:
A Constraints Conceptual Model
A document that outlines the conceptual model adopted by the working group provides an architectural framework the standard is to base upon.
A Constraint Dictionary
The dictionary is to provide standard terminology, structural relationship, and semantic definition of the generic constructs
A Constraint Description Language
A specification document for the language design will be provided, including a complete description of the syntax and semantic specific to each constraint.
A Golden Parser
A golden parser and syntax checking program for the above constraint description language will be provided. The program will be placed in the public domain.

The Design Constraints Description Language (OVI-VSIA-SLDL Joint Group)
The first meeting of the joint sub-committee between the Design Constraints Working Group and the System Level Design Language has been on Nov3, 1998.
The intent to work with other standardization groups, as it appeared clearly from the charter summarized above, was implemented with VSI-alliance first and the SLDL constraints sub-group with the common goal to:
- Define the general syntax and structure for the DC-WG constraint description language
- Define a conceptual model for constraints.
- Define a formal information model for various constraint domains

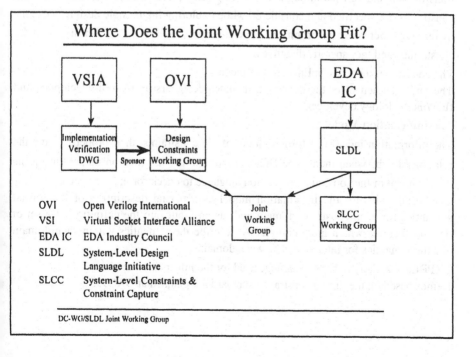

Where Does the Joint Working Group Fit?

VSIA	OVI	EDA IC

Implementation Verification DWG	Design Constraints Working Group	SLDL

Sponsor

Joint Working Group	SLCC Working Group

OVI   Open Verilog International
VSI   Virtual Socket Interface Alliance
EDA IC   EDA Industry Council
SLDL   System-Level Design Language Initiative
SLCC   System-Level Constraints & Constraint Capture

DC-WG/SLDL Joint Working Group

Beyond these common tasks each group will continue specific developments. The DC-WG will try to define a precise but informal constraint semantics and a specific syntax for a variety of different domains. The System Level Constraints and Constraint Capture sub group of SLDL will define a terminology and semantics for constraints applicable to system level design which are not addressed by the DC-WG and the SLDL group will address domain theories and create formal models of many aspects of each domain (including constraints), as well as the relationships between domains

The Constraints Language Syntax and Structure

This language is a definition of the syntactical rules which all constraint descriptions should follow

Ambit and IBM donations will be used as straw-man proposals, as they become available

Additional syntax will be needed to represent a variety of information beyond simple declarative constraints, such as:

- modeling tradeoffs between constraints
- distinguishing between absolute constraints and desirable properties
- self-defining constraints
- constraint transformations and dependencies

The Conceptual Model

The conceptual model should describe how constraints are specified, applied, refined, transformed, and verified throughout the design flow, how tradeoffs between different constraints are specified and considered while exploring the feasible design space, the differences between environment specifications, assertions in library models, constraints, and tool-specific directives.

The conceptual model is an English document.

The target audience for the document includes designers, EDA tool developers, and flow/methodology developers.

The Information Model

The information model is a formal model of the constraints, their properties, and the relationships between them. The DC-WG will use the information model during the development of the constraint description language to check for inconsistencies.

The SLDL will use the information model as a partial description of the formal semantics for each constraint domain and as an input into the definition of a set of domain theories which more completely describe the semantics within each domain and the semantics for interactions between domains.

EXPRESS is likely to be the language used for the information model

Demos based on the timing constraints standard are planned at DAC99.

IV- Multi-Language Environments for Co-Design

Among the 5 sub-committees of the SLDL we can consider that the HW/SW co-design and the system to component ones address short term goals while the 3 others have long term preoccupations.

The short term preoccupation is to identify, collect, recommend or provide tools that will enable system designers to implement their designs on a chip. This means defining a design re-use methodology, which is what VSI-alliance is all about, and defining more or less rigorous methods to interconnect tools used at different design levels of abstraction.

This is why many present works are targeting what they call « system level synthesis ». A NATO Advanced Study Institute, led by A. Jerraya and J. Mermet has established a state of the art of these works (Barga, Italy, Aug 1998) (14).

Other projects exist, around Esterel for example, with EC an extension of C with synchronization mechanisms translatable into Esterel (Lavagno). To be mentioned also is the project of the CADENCE lab in France to insert Esterel in their POLIS environment. Similarly the VERILOG team in Grenoble works on integrating LUSTRE in their Object-Geode environment.

Many of these multi-language environments exist now in large European companies designing systems. As an example, at Italtel, OCCAM, Objective-VHDL and C++ are used in conjunction with re-targetable code generators to implement Digital Signal Processors and embedded systems. But we cannot expect translators from one language to another, or synthesis from one level of abstraction down to a lower level (such as SDL to C++ or to VHDL) to provide a fully satisfactory solution until a common basic semantic definition for these different notations is created.

This definition must also solve the problem of merging different computation models through a rigorous general theory of events, intervals and sequences. There is still a great confusion among concepts in this domain, despite interesting presentations (15).

Synthesis itself is not enough. Abstraction mechanisms, allowing, for example, to induce from a VHDL synthesisable description a much more abstract model (for which the VHDL module is a specific implementation), are necessary to re-use legacy designs in a new system specification with some acceptable verification performances. Again, basic semantic foundation is called upon.

In conclusion, their is a clear need for a unifying foundation.

Many interesting works have tried, over the last 30 years, to give a sound theoretical foundation to the construction of large software systems. The domain of HDL's or SLDL's does not require different theories. It is clear that the advanced software concepts have been adapted after a certain delay to the specification of hardware. The tremendous speed of micro-electronics technology progress may have hidden this trend for a while: many difficult problems have not been solved, but just erased by the brute force of a doubling of performances every 18 months. But at the time of System-Chip design the unsolved problems re-appear and a look back to mathematical background imposes itself.

References

1. J.R. Abrial « The B-book . Assigning programs to meanings», Cambridge university press, 1996.
2. M. Barbacci, D. Borrione, D. Dietmeyer, F. Hill, R. Piloty, P. Skelly: «CONLAN Report», Lect. notes in Computer Science N° 151, Springer Verlag, 1983
3. David L. Barton « Systems Level Design Section of the Industry Standards Roadmap » The systems Level Description Language Committee
4. G.V. Bochman, Specification Languages for Communication Protocols, Proceedings of the Conference on Hadware Description Languages, April 1993
5. D. Borrione: « CASCADE », in « Fundamentals and Standards in Hardware Description Languages » KLUWER ACADEMIC, (1993).
6. R.T. Boute, « Fundamentals of Hardware Description Languages and Declarative Languages », in « Fundamentals and Standards in Hardware Description Languages » KLUWER ACADEMIC, (1993)
7. R. Braek, SDL Basics, Sintef Delab
8. K. Buchenrieder, A. Pyteel and C. Veith, Mapping StateCharts Models onto an FPGA Based ASIP Architecture, Proc. of EuroDAC with Euro-VHDL, September 1996
9. « CONLAN: a short review and critical comparison with VHDL ». IEEE Design & Test of computers. Sept 1992
10. J.M. Daveau, G. Fernandes Marchioro, C. Alberto Valderrama and A. Jerraya, *VHDL generation from SDL specifications*, IFIP 1997 .Chapman & Hall
11. Falkoff. A.D., Iverson. K.E., Sussenguth. E.H.: "Formal description of system/360" IBM sys. J. vol. 3, pp 198-262, 1964.
12. W. Glunz, T. Kruse, T. Rossel and D. Monjeau, Integrating SDL and VHDL for System Level Specification, Proceedings of the Conference on Hardware Description Languages, April 1993
13. D. Harel: Statecharts: A visual formalism for com-plex systems. Science of Computer Programming , 8, 1987
14. A. Jerraya, J. Mermet- editors. "System level synthesis" KLUWER ACADEMIC. Spring 1999.
15. E.Lee and A. Sangiovanni-Vincentelli, A Framework For Comparing Models Of Computation, IEEE Transactions on CAD, September 1998.
16. Modelica Version 1.1 - December 1998, Modelica Tutorial and Design Rationale, (HTML format) (Portable Document Format), updated (Modelica 1.1)
17. O. Pulkkinen and K. Krönlof, Integration of SDL and VHDL for High Level Digital Design, Proc. of EuroDAC with Euro-VHDL, September 1992.
18. Franz J. Rammig, « System Level Design », in « Fundamentals and Standards in Hardware Description Languages » KLUWER, (1993)
19. A, Sarma, Intro. to SDL-92, EURESCOM, G
20. VHDL modeling terminology and taxonomy , RASSP doc, Sept 9, 1996
21. E. Villar, Berrojo L, Sanchez P: « High-level synthesis and simulation with VHDL », Proc. of 2nd EuroVHDL Conf, Sockholm, Sept. 8-11, 1991,

An Incremental Recovery Cache
Supporting Software Fault Tolerance

P. Rogers* and A. J. Wellings

Department of Computer Science
University of York, York, YO1 5DD, UK
{progers, andy}@cs.york.ac.uk
+1 281 648 3165
*designated contact

Abstract. This paper focuses upon the requirement to save and restore application state as part of the execution of recovery blocks. Using the object-oriented features of the revised Ada language, we present a portable implementation of a state management scheme that is fully independent of applications. Results of the implementation of this mechanism are used to highlight both the strengths and weaknesses of some of the object-oriented features of Ada 95, particularly user-defined assignment.

Keywords: fault-tolerant systems, checkpointing, Ada, user-defined assignment

1 Introduction

Studies indicate that techniques for tolerating hardware faults are so effective that software *design errors* are the leading cause of all faults encountered [3]. Various techniques and mechanisms have been developed to address these *unanticipated* software faults. Thus the term "software fault tolerance" indicates tolerance of software faults, as opposed to the provision of hardware fault tolerance by means of software [1].

One of the main approaches for tolerating software faults is *recovery blocks* [4]. Recovery blocks are based on the concept of *design diversity*, i.e., the assumption that different designs (and thus implementations) will exhibit different faults (if any) for the same inputs and will, therefore, provide alternatives for each other. In the recovery block approach, a primary module and some number of alternates are implemented for a given unit of functionality; design diversity is incorporated via the alternate modules. The primary module is the only one executed under normal conditions. Only when an error is detected by an *acceptance test* do alternative modules execute. Alternatives are successively called, and the acceptance test successively applied against the results, until either a satisfactory result is obtained or no remaining alternates exist (in which case the failure is propagated).

Central to the concept is saving the current, valid state prior to execution of the primary module. This saved state is successively restored prior to the execution of each of the alternate modules. Variations on the basic model improve performance and unify tolerance to both software and hardware faults [6]. State saving and restoration are required, in any case.

The act of saving the state prior to entry of a recovery block is called "taking a checkpoint" [1]. Conceptually, the entire state of the application is saved, even values stored in secondary storage if they are directly accessible. To reduce the rather high associated run-time cost, an *incremental* checkpointing approach is possible, in which only those objects whose values are actually modified are stored. This approach is called a *recovery cache* (where "cache" means "hiding place" rather than a high speed buffering mechanism) [4]. This paper describes a software implementation of the incremental checkpointing mechanism. The implementation is application-independent, requiring little of application designers other than use of inheritance from an abstract base type we define. Additionally, the implementation provides enhanced performance by exploiting application-specific knowledge about what state to save. As such, it is a "partial" checkpointing scheme [1].

The goal of this paper is to show how Ada 95 can directly express state management in an application-independent mechanism. The object-oriented features of the language are used extensively to provide this independence. A secondary goal is to illustrate how the strengths and weaknesses of the object-oriented facilities, particularly those of user-defined assignment, affected the implementation. In Section 2, we describe an abstract interface for backward error recovery, and then in Section 3 we describe the semantics of an incremental checkpointing version of that abstract interface. Section 4 provides details of the implementation. We discuss related work in Section 5, and conclusions in Section 6. Section 7 indicates where the source code may be obtained.

2 Abstract Interface for Backward Error Recovery

Anderson and Lee describe basic facilities required to support *backward error recovery*, in which a previously-stored valid state is restored [1]. They define a "recovery point" as a restorable point in time at which a presumably valid application state existed. A backward error recovery mechanism can save and restore this state as necessary by saving appropriate information called "recovery data". In the terminology used by Anderson and Lee, saving the recovery data for a recovery point is called "establishing" the recovery point. "Restoring" the recovery point is the act of replacing the current state of the application with the state it occupied at the recovery point. They also indicate that a flexible mechanism should allow multiple recovery points to be available and, as a result, a means of discarding recovery points should be provided.

We represent the abstract interface for Anderson and Lee's basic recovery facilities in package Recovery_Point. The package exports an abstract tagged limited private type named Recovery_Data, fully declared in the private part as an extension to Limited_Controlled from package Ada.Finalization. The programmer may declare as many individual objects of the type as required; each will be identified by their object names. Three abstract procedures complete the interface for saving, restoring, and discarding recovery data.

```
with Ada.Finalization;
package Recovery_Point is
   type Recovery_Data is abstract tagged limited private;
   procedure Establish( This : in out Recovery_Data ) is abstract;
   procedure Restore  ( This : in out Recovery_Data ) is abstract;
   procedure Discard  ( This : in out Recovery_Data ) is abstract;
private
   type Recovery_Data is abstract
      new Ada.Finalization.Limited_Controlled with null record;
end Recovery_Point;
```

A central concept is that concrete descendants of type Recovery_Data represent the necessary information to manage recovery points, *not the actual application state to be managed*. Objects of application-specific types will represent that state as usual, although we will define another abstract root type for that purpose.

In the classic object-oriented paradigm, fault tolerance mechanisms based upon backward error recovery may use the abstraction defined by Recovery_Point without regard to which concrete implementation is actually provided. All calls to the abstract operations exported from package Recovery_Point are required by the language (i.e., by the compiler) to be dispatching calls to concrete extensions.

3 Incremental Backward Error Recovery

The recovery cache mechanism is an incremental checkpointing facility that provides better performance (both space and speed) than a basic checkpointing abstraction that saves and restores all values upon demand. Enhancements are achieved because recovery data are not allocated, managed, and reclaimed for recoverable application objects unless the values of those objects change.

Central to the incremental behavior is a *recovery region*. A recovery region is a sequence of statements delimited by calls to Establish and Discard (in that order). If no changes to the associated application objects take place between the beginning and ending of a region, no recovery action is necessary for that region. Therefore, the behavior of procedure Establish is fundamentally different from that of the basic checkpointing facility: instead of saving the value of application objects, a new recovery region is demarcated. Only when object values change *within* the active recovery region will recovery data be stored.

Furthermore, recovery data are only recorded for a recoverable object *the first time* the value of the object changes after the establishment of a new recovery region. This is because restoration of the recovery region restores the values that application objects had *prior* to the establishment of the new recovery region. Subsequent changes to the objects within that same recovery region need not be noted since only the previous value – the first and only one stored – is required to restore the previous state.

Using Anderson and Lee's example [1, pg. 193], consider the case of recovery point RP, and two recoverable objects, X and Y, as shown in Figure 1. The cache for RP contains two regions because Establish has been called twice for RP. After the first call to Establish, X is modified, resulting in a cache entry for X with the value of 10. A call to Restore at this point in the execution would therefore restore that value of X. After the second call to Establish, both X and Y are modified, so another cache entry is created. In this entry, X has a value of 30 and Y has a value of 20, so that the values of X and Y in the previous recovery point could be restored.

The other complexity introduced by the incremental behavior is that of discarding recovery regions. If there is only a single recovery region, procedure Discard simply reclaims the entries of the current recovery region (if any). This approach will not suffice if a previous recovery region exists because changes made to objects during the current recovery region (now being discarded) will not have been recorded in the previous region. Simply merging the two regions is not appropriate because each region might indeed have entries for a given recoverable object; the more recent entry should be discarded. Therefore, Discard supplements the entries in the previous region with those in the current region that are not also in the previous region. Discard has no effect if no recovery region is active.

Consider again Anderson and Lee's example shown in Figure 1. The cache for RP contains two regions because Establish has been called twice for RP. If Discard is now called, the cache entry at the top of the stack (containing values for both X and Y) will be deleted. However, Y has been changed since the first call to Establish, but the predecessor entry on the stack has no value for Y. Therefore, Discard will move the value {Y,20} into the predecessor region on the stack but will not move the value {X,30}.

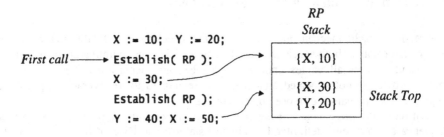

Figure 1 Example State (before call to Discard)

4 Concrete Implementation

A concrete implementation of the abstract interface with incremental behavior was straightforward except for three major areas. Specifically, assignment, finalization, and initialization were surprisingly difficult, due to the Ada model for manipulating non-limited types. The model is different from that of other languages that allow both redefinition of assignment and guaranteed initialization/finalization. We discuss the resulting difficulties after first describing the implementation details that cause the difficulties to arise.

4.1 The Recovery Cache

The concrete private type Recovery_Cache extends the abstract type Recovery_Data exported by package Recovery_Point. Procedures Establish, Restore, and Discard are, therefore, available as concrete implementations of the basic recovery interface. As explained in Section 3, a recovery cache is essentially a collection of recovery regions. A stack is appropriate for these regions because the recovery cache facility is intended for recovery blocks, in which recovery regions are strictly nested. Therefore, the full declaration in the private part is a record extension containing a stack. Each stack element contains a sequence of cache entries, each entry a combination of a stored value and a reference to the corresponding recoverable application object. Sequences are represented as lists since there is no upper bound on the number of recoverable objects supported. This representation (a stack of lists of cache entries) is essentially that of Anderson and Lee, introduced with the facility, and of Flaviu Cristian [2]. The full type in the private part is declared as an extension of Limited_Controlled for the sake of finalization. We discuss the use of finalization in Section 4.4.

4.2 Recoverable Application Types

Our concrete implementation exports a type named Recoverable to define the interface for recoverable application types.

```
type Any_Recovery_Cache is access all Recovery_Cache'Class;

type Recoverable( Recovery_Object : Any_Recovery_Cache ) is
   abstract tagged private;
```

The intent is to support state saving and restoring for objects of arbitrary, application-defined types by means of extensions to Recoverable. Since these extensions will be within the derivation class of Recoverable, dispatching allows our implementation to manipulate objects of application-defined types without having specific knowledge of them. Those familiar with object-oriented programming will recognize this approach as classic use of abstract types, inheritance, and dynamic dispatching.

Note that applications may define as many distinct extensions of the abstract type Recoverable as necessary; the implementation will allow individual objects of these types to be saved and restored as part of a recovery point manipulation. Specifically, whenever a call to one of Establish, Restore, or Discard occurs for a specified Recovery_Cache object, all objects (of types descended from Recoverable) designating that Recovery_Cache object may be manipulated. The programmer permanently specifies a Recovery_Cache object via the discriminant whenever a Recoverable application object is elaborated. All descendants of Recoverable inherit the discriminant and all such objects must specify their Recovery_Cache object.

Type Recoverable is fully defined in the private part as a descendant of type Controlled so it will have the facilities for user-defined assignment available. Concrete descendants defined by applications will then inherit the assignment semantics defined by our package. We discuss the implementation of assignment in Section 4.4.

4.3 Implementation-Specific Components

The types Recovery_Cache and Recoverable are defined by our implementation as type extensions with components necessary for the implementation. Those components associated with type Recoverable pose a difficulty for user-defined assignment and are described here as a result.

One of the differences from the logical representation of a stack of lists is fundamental to performance, and is, therefore, described by Anderson and Lee. Since recovery will be used relatively infrequently, normal execution must be optimized in preference to the recovery facilities. Hence, incremental assignment statements must be as efficient as possible. When recovery *is* used, recovery points will be discarded more frequently than they are restored, so procedure Discard should be as efficient as possible. The primary area of difficulty in both cases is the requirement to search the unbounded recovery region lists. The implementation of assignment must determine if an entry has already been placed in the current recovery region. For each entry in the current region, the implementation of Discard must *also* examine the previous region list to determine if an entry exists there. We expend additional storage to preclude these searches using one of the approaches Anderson and Lee describe. Specifically, recovery regions are associated with numbered levels corresponding to their depth in the stack; a dedicated value per Recovery_Cache object indicates the current level of that cache. Each recoverable application object has an associated numeric value indicating the recovery region in which the most recent cache entry for that object exists. The assignment implementation compares the level of the application object to the level of the associated Recovery_Cache object to see if a new cache entry is required. Similarly, prior to discarding the current region procedure Discard compares the fields to determine if any entries of the current region should be merged into the previous region. Thus each Recovery_Cache object has a numeric Current_Level component, and each recoverable application object has a numeric value named Max_Region_Entered.

Another component handles the differences between the lifetimes of Recoverable and Recovery_Cache objects. Procedure Restore traverses the recovery region list at the top of the stack such that the most recently cached values of the corresponding recoverable application objects are restored. However, we can only restore these values if we know that the corresponding application objects still exist. They might not exist because objects can be declared in nested declarative regions and because allocated objects can be manually deallocated. In those cases dangling references could remain in the Recovery_Cache data structures. Subsequent calls to procedure Restore could then attempt to use these invalid references, with unpredictable effects. To preclude dereferencing any dangling references we associate a Boolean flag, Known_Valid, with each recoverable application object. Each Known_Valid flag indicates whether or not the object is known to exist. Those objects for which Known_Valid is False are not restored. Setting and clearing the flag is described in the next section.

4.4 Assignment

After a call to Establish for a given Recovery_Cache object, the first assignment to an associated recoverable object will store the current value prior to taking on the new value. We use Ada's user-defined assignment to achieve this effect. Assignment using Ada's facilities was not entirely satisfactory in this case, although it does work.

User-Defined Assignment In Ada. The assignment operation may be indirectly redefined for descendants of type Controlled by overriding procedure Adjust and, depending upon the circumstances, procedure Finalize. (Type Recoverable is derived from Controlled.) In the canonical implementation, when an object of a controlled type is the target of an assignment statement Finalize is first called with that object passed as the parameter. Then a bit-wise copy of the right-hand-side value is copied into the target object. Finally Adjust is called with the target object as the parameter, providing an opportunity to finish the effect. Note that the compiler may use a temporary object instead of this direct approach, although typically a temporary will not be necessary.

However, Finalize and Adjust are also called for other reasons, both because of object destruction and because the assignment *operation* is invoked in a number of places, including, but not limited to, the assignment *statement*. For example, whenever a controlled object ceases to exist Finalize will be called, including both destruction for declared objects and deallocation for allocated objects. Values of controlled types returned by functions are considered objects too, and are finalized eventually. Procedure Adjust is called whenever a controlled value is assigned a value. For example, when an object is declared an initial value is assigned if it is provided. In this case Adjust is called, and Finalize is not (appropriately, since no prior value exists). Extension aggregates specifying a value for the ancestor part by means of the subtype name create a default-initialized object, and this object is Adjusted. Any design for Finalize and Adjust must work correctly in all these possible situations.

Effect of Assignment on Finalization. Although Adjust is the primary procedure associated with user-defined assignment, we must use procedure Finalize to save values for Recoverable subclasses during assignment statements. Finalize must be used because, by definition, the value to be incrementally stored is the *current* value, prior to the assignment of the new value. Adjust would be too late to store the current value since Adjust is called *after* the bit-wise copy of the right-hand side replaces the value of the target object. Also, Adjust is called in situations in which it would be inappropriate to store a value, for example in object declarations with explicit initial values.

Our implementation of Finalize for type Recoverable does not attempt to perform any storage reclamation since there is no way to distinguish calls due to assignment from calls due to object destruction. Some storage would not automatically be reclaimed because we can not declare all the necessary resources as simple record components directly within type Recoverable. For example, each object of a type derived from Recoverable has the Boolean flag Known_Valid to indicate whether or not the object is known to exist. Clearly we can not declare Known_Valid as a record component within type Recoverable since the flags would disappear with the very objects they are intended to indicate. Thus, we need the Known_Valid flag to exist *separately* from the corresponding application object. To accommodate that requirement we define a hidden type – the Descriptor – to maintain all such information about recoverable application objects; each Descriptor object is dedicated

392

to a single recoverable application object. Pointers held in the recovery region lists actually designate the Descriptors rather than the application objects themselves. To reclaim the storage allocated to Descriptors, the Finalize procedure for type Recovery_Cache automatically reclaims them rather than the Finalize for type Recoverable. This approach is safe because only those Recovery_Cache objects declared at the library level can be associated with the discriminants of recoverable application objects. Since any declared Recovery_Cache object must exist as long as the program, no application objects can "outlive" it.

The overall relationship of objects of types Descriptor, Recovery_Cache and Recoverable is depicted in Figure 2.

In addition to arranging for the Descriptors to be eventually reclaimed, we must also prevent use of the Descriptors after their corresponding application objects no longer exist. In particular, procedure Restore must not attempt to write a value to an object that no longer exists by dereferencing what is, in that case, a dangling reference within the Descriptor. Although we cannot know whether an invocation of Finalize is for object destruction or assignment, we *do* know that Adjust is not called when an object ceases to exist. Thus, we implement Finalize such that it performs the incremental assignment function and also marks the object as *potentially* nonexistent. Finalize sets the object Known_Valid flag in the Descriptor to False and Adjust resets it back to True. Adjust is not called if the application object really is about to be destroyed and the flag consequently remains False. Procedure Restore ignores those Descriptors whose Known_Valid flags are False.

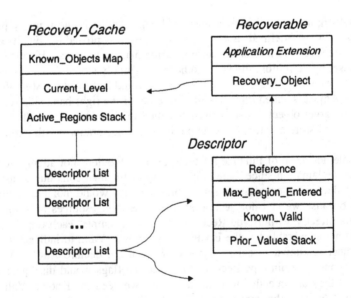

Figure 2. Data Structures

Maintaining Identities of Non-Limited Values. Any object that can be assigned a value by an assignment operation must be considered 'anonymous' in the sense that the *entire object* is overwritten by the bit-wise copy during assignment. Any individual 'identity' is lost, and therefore, assignment-compatible values must be considered freely substitutable with one-another. The Ada model for user-defined assignment supports this value transparency in that only the target of an assignment is passed to calls of Finalize and Adjust, rather than both the target and the source. All processing performed by those two procedures must be in terms of the single target object. Partial updates using information from both source and target are not possible for non-limited types.

The effect of this anonymity is that anything unique to a given object is difficult to maintain across assignments. For example, internal implementation components (e.g., inherited from the abstract type Recoverable) that should not be changed by assignment would have to be copied off to some shared temporary area by Finalize, and then copied back by Adjust. These internal components constitute the identity that is lost during the bit-wise copying of the assignment operation.

In the case of the incremental recovery cache, the identity of each recoverable application object is the reference to a dedicated Descriptor object and the component Max_Region_Entered. Neither should be overwritten by assignment. Some means of preserving these values must exist without the inefficiency of copying and the complexity of handling the various causes of invocation.

Instead of attempting to preserve internal components across assignments we use an identity that is permanent and unchanged by assignment: addresses. Each Recovery_Cache object has a mapping from the addresses of the objects it manages to the corresponding Descriptors. (Max_Region_Entered is placed within the Descriptor, along with all other such information.) For the sake of efficiency we use a hashed mapping, hashing the address of the actual parameter passed to Finalize and Adjust. These addresses are valid because Recoverable and its descendants are tagged types – they are always passed by reference so the formal parameters are not copies. Finalize and Adjust use this mapping to acquire a pointer to the corresponding Descriptor.

Effect Upon User Interface. The anonymity of non-limited objects actually has an effect upon the user interface. Since Adjust and Finalize are only passed the target of an assignment, the target must contain a reference to the associated Recovery_Cache object so that Adjust and Finalize can access the hashed Descriptor map. However, the reference to the Recovery_Cache object is yet another instance of identity not preserved by assignment. The access type discriminant associated with each Recoverable object exists to circumvent this loss of identity. Declarations of recoverable objects are thus required to specify the Recovery_Cache object that manages them. Although the discriminant might be overwritten, the compiler will raise Constraint_Error if the programmer attempts to assign objects with *different* discriminants, thereby preventing any effective changes. (Note that complete object assignment via an aggregate can not change the discriminant because there is no default provided.) Unfortunately this approach means that recoverable application objects can only be assigned to other recoverable application objects associated with the *same* Recovery_Cache object. A more dynamic approach allowing Recoverable objects to be associated with multiple Recovery_Cache objects is not feasible.

Effect Upon Error Detection. As mentioned, Finalize and Adjust are called for various situations in addition to assignment statements, including temporary objects, aggregates and initial values for object declarations. To ignore these cases Finalize and Adjust disregard those objects whose addresses are not bound within a hashed Descriptor map, effectively ignoring objects without a Descriptor. Unfortunately this approach means that we can not detect assignment of objects that have inadvertently not been allocated a Descriptor object via procedure Register. Not detecting the error is especially regrettable since the programmer is completely responsible for calling Register.

An alternative approach would be to generate Descriptors and bind them into the hash maps within Finalize, on demand. Although these unnecessary Descriptors would not cause failures since the Known_Valid flags would be False, a large number of such Descriptor objects might be allocated. Calls to Restore and Discard would visit each one to check Known_Valid, resulting in poor performance. The current approach seems to offer the best compromise.

4.5 Initializing Application Objects

The subprograms defined for type Ada.Finalization.Controlled (and for type Limited_Controlled) include procedure Initialize. Concrete overridings of Initialize are called automatically after a controlled object is created. However, the procedure is only called when necessary – when an initial value is not otherwise provided with the declaration of the controlled object. For *limited* controlled types, Initialize *is* always called since assignment is not allowed, including assignment of initial values.

However, the incremental recovery cache is predicated upon assignment so a limited type can not be used. As explained in Section 4.3, the implementation associates certain data structures with objects of concrete subclasses of type Recoverable. (These data structures are part of the recovery cache objects, not the recoverable application objects themselves.) We can not use Initialize to create these data structures because Initialize is not always called. Therefore, we define class-wide procedure Register for the purpose of initializing recoverable application objects, and raise exception Registration_Error when we can detect that such objects have not been registered. We chose not to name the procedure "Initialize" to avoid confusion with that of the controlled types.

5 Related Work

Rubira-Calsavara and Stroud's approach in C++ depends upon user-defined assignment as well [7]. In their scheme, all recoverable state is coalesced into one object (of one type) that is saved prior to execution of the recovery block variants. To preclude copying a potentially huge amount of data, users are expected to define a 'lazy' assignment per type, such that only when the value actually changes does a copy get created. All types would require this definition, including the predefined elementary types such as int and float. Our approach moves the complexity away from users to a central facility, but requires recoverable application types to be inherited from a type we define to have the incremental assignment semantics.

An alternative to the definition of explicit recovery and fault tolerance mechanisms is to extend the compiler or other tools so that support is entirely automated [5]. Within a given portion of program text, implementation-defined pragmas (compiler directives) would require the compiler to generate code such that a fault tolerance mechanism would be implemented. The central difference between this approach and ours is that the fault tolerance mechanism is directly expressed within the program source in our approach. The advantage of the compiler-extension approach is that users are not responsible for determining which objects require state saving and restoration. In our approach, recoverable application objects must be explicitly declared as such and associated with recovery points by the programmer, presenting the possibility of an oversight. Note, however, that a recovery block implementation – not the users – would make the calls to our routines, so there is no advantage to the compiler-generated approach in that regard. Furthermore, in either case the developer is responsible for indicating that a recovery mechanism is required. The principle advantage of the facilities we describe is that any Ada compiler can support them – no extended compilers or other special-purpose tools are required. Furthermore, with proper synchronization, the facilities described in this paper can be incorporated into fault tolerance mechanisms involving multiple threads of control. Wellings and Burns describe an atomic action mechanism using what is essentially the abstract recovery interface [8]. The compiler-generated approach would be very difficult to extend to this class of mechanism because such mechanisms are dynamic and not expressed entirely at compile-time.

6 Conclusions

We have demonstrated that Ada 95 can directly express Anderson and Lee's abstract recovery interface and can be used to produce an application-independent incremental recovery instance based upon augmented assignment. This is a valuable demonstration because Ada is widely used in applications with fault tolerance requirements and is generally touted as well-suited for that domain.

However, the implementation was complicated by Ada's model for initialization, finalization, and user-defined assignment. Specifically, all three facilities are shared among three procedures in a model that is based upon the substitutability of assignable values. As a result, it is difficult to preserve and manage object identity when assignment is required because the model is based on value anonymity. Other languages provide a different model, in which each of initialization, finalization, and assignment are separate constructs. For example, the entire behavior of the assignment operation is under programmer control. In that model only the necessary components are altered, preserving the values of the others and, hence, any identity associated with the target object. The Ada model for assignment uses a bit-wise copy and thus does not support both identity and assignment. Furthermore, because initial values may be supplied in various ways, initialization using any specific mechanism is not guaranteed for non-limited types. Identity is again the issue, in that there is no way to guarantee that a unique identity is created. Similarly, finalization is

396

complicated by the fact that the same routine (Finalize) is used in the Ada model for any object destruction, including those due to assignments.

The Ada model is certainly usable, since those abstractions not requiring identity are easily combined with user-defined assignment. Indeed, we found other concrete instances of the abstract Recovery_Point interface comparatively easy to implement because they did not require a redefinition of assignment; limited types were appropriate and, as a result, both initialization and finalization were straightforward. However, when both identity and assignment are required the facilities associated with the non-limited type Controlled are problematic.

7 Source Code

The source code for the packages presented in this paper can be obtained in a compressed tar formatted file in the UK at

    http://www.cs.york.ac.uk/~andy/state_restoration/recovery_cache.Z

The code is also available in the United States at

    http://www.classwide.com/products/freecode/recovery_cache.Z

and in Windows Zip format at

    http://www/classwide.com/products/freecode/recovery_cache.zip

We would like to thank Tucker Taft for suggesting the use of addresses and explaining the anonymous nature of non-limited types.

References

1. Anderson, T., Lee, P. A.: Fault Tolerance Principles and Practice. Prentice-Hall International (1981)
2. Cristian, F.: A Recovery Mechanism for Modular Software. Proc. IEEE Fourth International Conference on Software Engineering. Munich (1979) 42-50A
3. Gray, J.: Why Do Computers Stop And What Can Be Done About It? Proc. IEEE Fifth Symposium On Reliability In Distributed Software and Database Systems. (1986) 3-12
4. Horning, J. J., Lauer, H. C., Melliar-Smith, P. M., Randell, B.: A Program Structure For Error Detection and Recovery. In: E. Gelenbe and C. Kaiser (eds.): Lecture Notes In Computer Science, vol. 16. Springer-Verlag (1974) 171-187
5. Kermarrec, Y., Nana, L., Pautet, L.: Providing Fault-Tolerant Services To Distributed Ada95 Applications. Proc. ACM TRI-Ada'96. Philadelphia, Pennsylvania, USA (1996) 39-47
6. Kim, K. H.: The Distributed Recovery Block Scheme. In: M. Lyu (ed.) Software Fault Tolerance. Trends In Software, vol. 3. John Wiley & Sons (1995) 189-210
7. Rubira-Calsavara, C. M. F., Stroud, R. J.: Forward and Backward Error Recovery in C++. Object-Oriented Systems. 1,1 (1994) 61-86
8. Wellings, A., Burns, A.: Implementing Atomic Actions In Ada 95. IEEE Transactions On Software Engineering. 23,2 (1997) 107-123

Shared Recoverable Objects

Jörg Kienzle, Alfred Strohmeier

Swiss Federal Institute of Technology
Software Engineering Laboratory
1015 Lausanne Ecublens
Switzerland

email: {Joerg.Kienzle, Alfred.Strohmeier}@epfl.ch
phone: +41 (21) 693.42.37 – fax: +41 (21) 693.50.79

Abstract. This document describes an implementation of recoverable objects that can be accessed concurrently. After a brief description of the possible uses of recoverable objects and after reviewing some of the new features of Ada 95 used in the implementation, the design issues are discussed and the interface of the recoverable object class is presented. An example application using multitasking demonstrates its applicability.

Keywords. Recoverable Objects, Ada 95, Concurrency, Object-Oriented Programming, Controlled Types, Abort Deferred Regions, Transactions, Software Fault Tolerance.

1 Introduction

It is inconceivable that the role of fault tolerance in computing systems will diminish, its importance can only increase. There are clear indications of a widespread and growing demand for increased reliability in many areas. Fault tolerance techniques for coping with the occurrence and effects of hardware failures are now well established and form a vital part of any reliable computing system. Hence, *software fault tolerance* — the ability of software to cope with faults, especially design faults — is getting more and more important [1].

Various approaches (N-version programming, recovery blocks) have been proposed to address such unanticipated software faults. These mechanisms have been modified or extended to address concurrency (transactions, conversations, atomic actions). In most of these schemes, especially those using backward error recovery, it is often necessary to be able to undo the effects of a faulty computation, that is restoring the state of the application to a point where it was known to be correct. Objects offering such restoration capabilities in a concurrent environment are called *shared recoverable objects*.

This paper describes an implementation of shared recoverable objects for Ada 95 [2, 3]. The outline of the paper is as follows: section 2 describes recoverable objects in more detail and situates them with respect to various approaches for providing software fault tolerance; section 3 gives an overview of the important features of Ada 95 for the implementation of shared recoverable objects; section 4 presents the interface of the shared recoverable objects package and describes the offered functions; section 5 shows an example of how shared recoverable objects can be of help in an application using multitasking; section 6 exposes the internals of the implementation and the last section draws some conclusions and mentions future work.

2 Recoverable Objects

2.1 Terminology

A *recoverable object* is an object whose state can be saved and later on restored, if needed. Saving is sometimes also referred to as *taking/establishing a checkpoint/snapshot*; it is usually performed when the system, including the object to be saved, is in a consistent state. Once saved, the state of the object can be restored at any time. The reasons for restoration depend on the context in which the recoverable object is used.

It is possible to take several snapshots of an object, which means that it is possible to have multiple *versions* of the state of an object to which one can revert to. Branches are not allowed: each version has at a given time at most one parent and one child. The most recent version is called the *current* version.

Shared recoverable objects can be used by multiple tasks concurrently. Such tasks will be called *participant tasks*. Note that a shared recoverable object does neither provide nor impose any concurrency control between tasks accessing it. Consistent access to the data encapsulated in the object must be ensured by the application programmer.

2.2 Usage

Recoverable objects can be of use in a variety of different contexts, i.e. in applications that want to provide "undo" functionality (see "Example" in section 5). Before letting the user modify an object, a snapshot of its state is taken. If later on the user of the application is not satisfied with the results of his changes, the old state of the object can be restored. Multiple snapshots allow multiple levels of "undo".

More and more applications make use of multitasking to improve performance, or to provide better feedback and interaction to the user. Recoverable objects should therefore be designed with concurrency in mind.

Software fault tolerance techniques, especially those using backward error recovery such as recovery blocks and transaction-like systems can also make use of recoverable objects.

Recovery blocks [4] have been introduced as a software structuring mechanism providing software fault tolerance based on the concept of design diversity and backward error recovery. A recovery block consists of one or more alternatives implementing functionality, coupled with an acceptance test that determines whether an alternative has functioned correctly or not. Under normal conditions, only the first alternative is executed. Only if an error is detected by the acceptance test, other alternatives are tried successively. The typical syntax for expressing recovery blocks is as follows:

```
ensure <acceptance test> by <primary alternate>
else by <second alternate>
...
else by <n'th alternate>
else error
```

It is important to note that prior to execution of the primary alternate, a snapshot of the current state of the component is taken. When an alternative fails to pass the acceptance test, this state is restored, and the next alternative is tried. This is repeated until either an alternative succeeds, or there are no more alternatives available. In that case, the execution of the component is considered a failure and an error is propagated.

Recoverable objects can be very useful to a programmer of a recovery block. He can encapsulate the state of the component in one or several recoverable objects and take a snapshot before executing the primary alternative. If it fails the acceptance test, the state can be easily restored.

Transactions [5] are a well-known mechanism for structuring an application to provide data consistency in a concurrent environment and in the presence of failures. A transaction is a sequence of statements, whose execution is characterized by the famous ACID properties:

- *Atomicity*: A transaction gives an "all or nothing" guarantee: either all the state changes of the transaction are performed, or none are.

- *Consistency*: The execution of a transaction starting in a consistent state will produce another consistent state.

- *Isolation*: Transactions executing concurrently (*competitive* concurrency) are isolated from each other; the result must be the same as if they had been executed in some serial order.

- *Durability*: Once a transaction has terminated successfully, its effects are permanent, even when a failure occurs.

As with recovery blocks, recoverable objects can help providing atomicity of transactions. If the transaction aborts, the changes to the state of the application can be undone, provided that it is encapsulated in one or several recoverable objects and that a snapshot has been taken before entering the transaction. Nested transactions [6] can make use of nested snapshots.

Conversations [4], atomic actions [1] and finally coordinated atomic actions [7] can be seen as extensions of the basic transaction concept to cope with *cooperative* concurrency. In all three schemes, processes or tasks cooperate and potentially access shared data, that must be restored if an error occurs and if backward error recovery is used. Here again, recoverable objects are only useful if they can "live" in a concurrent environment.

3 Features of Ada 95

This section will describe two features of Ada 95 that are used extensively inside the implementation of shared recoverable objects, namely controlled types and task identification.

3.1 Controlled Types

Controlled types [2, 7.6] have been introduced in Ada 95 to facilitate resource management within abstract data types while preserving the abstraction. The language-defined package Ada.Finalization declares two abstract tagged types, Controlled and Limited_Controlled. A user-defined type derived from one of these two types inherits the operations Initialize, Finalize and (in case of the type Controlled) Adjust. These operations are somehow special, since they are automatically invoked in the following circumstances:

- Initialize — is invoked whenever an object of the controlled type is created and there is no explicit initialization.

- Finalize — is called just before a controlled object is destroyed, i.e. goes out of scope, is deallocated using an instantiation of Ada.Unchecked_Deallocation, or is overwritten during an assignment.

- Adjust — is invoked during an assignment just after the target object has been overwritten.

The default implementations of these three primitive operations do nothing at all. By overriding the inherited versions in the derived type, the application developer can precisely control object creation, destruction, and assignment. Especially the ability to associate automatic finalization actions with a data type is extremely important for Ada, given the orientation toward information hiding, coupled with the many ways that a scope may be exited in Ada (exceptions, exit, return, abort, asynchronous transfer of control).

3.2 Task Identification and Task Attributes

In order to identify instances of a task type, the language-defined package `Ada.Task_Identification` defines a `Task_ID` type. The operations provided in this package allow an application programmer to get the `Task_ID` of the current task, to abort tasks identified by a `Task_ID`, and to query information about the status of a task.

It is also possible to associate user-defined information with a task using the generic package `Ada.Task_Attributes`. The application programmer can attach a data type to each task in the system by instantiating the package:

```
package My_Task_Info is
   new Ada.Task_Attributes    (Attribute => My_Data_Type,
                               Initial_Value => My_Initial_Value);
```

The package provides functions to set and retrieve the value of the attribute associated with each task. Task attributes are of special interest when using controlled types: through their `Finalize` primitive operation application-defined actions can be performed on task abortion or termination.

4 Design Issues

4.1 Update Strategies

When implementing recoverable objects, one has to choose between two different strategies of updating the state of the object: *in-place* update and *deferred* update.

In-place Update

When using in-place update, only the current version of the recoverable object is visible and gets modified. The recoverable object can be represented as a list of versions of the state of the object (see figure 1), where all except the head of the list is hidden from the user. The different versions of the object are typically identified using a version number n. When a snapshot is taken, a copy of the current version is made and added to the list of hidden states; subsequent modifications are still performed on the current version. When a certain version must be restored, the corresponding state is copied from the list back to the current version.

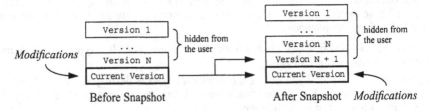

Figure 1: In-place Update

Typical operations that must be provided by an implementation using in-place update are:

- *Establish Checkpoint*: take a snapshot of the current state of the object (duplicate the current version of the state)
- *Discard Checkpoint (n)*: discard the version *n* (take the corresponding version out of the list)
- *Restore Checkpoint (n)*: restore the state of the object saved in version *n* by replacing the current state with the one stored in the version

Deferred Update

When using deferred update, a new version is created when a snapshot is taken and handed back to the user. Subsequent modifications are applied to this new version (see figure 2). Once the user is satisfied with his changes to the object, he can commit the modifications; this results in copying the new state back to the previous version.

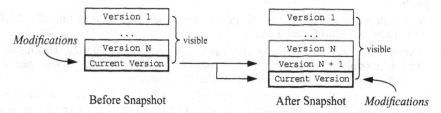

Figure 2: Deferred Update

In a deferred update scheme, the typical operations provided to the user are slightly different:

- *New State (S)*: duplicate the version *S* of the object and return the new version to the user
- *Discard State (S)*: discard version *S* (take the corresponding version out of the list)
- *Commit State (S)*: copy the contents of the version *S* of the object back over the contents of the parent version of *S* and then discard version *S* (take the corresponding version out of the list)

Update Strategies and Concurrency

It is highly advantageous to use a deferred update scheme when sharing recoverable objects between multiple tasks. Imagine a scenario where multiple tasks work on the same version of an object. Suddenly one of the tasks decides that it wants to revert to a previously saved state.

When using the in-place update scheme, calling *Restore Checkpoint* can lead to inconsistencies, because the other tasks don't know about the abort and will continue to work on the object as if it were still in the current state. To prevent such problems, the task must first communicate its decision to all other tasks. This synchronization of tasks is an additional burden for the application programmer.

With the deferred update scheme, the task that wants to revert to a previous version *S* can safely call *Discard State* on the current version, and then start working with version *S*, since all the versions of the object are visible. It can even create a new subversion of *S* if it wants to. In the mean time, the other tasks can continue with their work, and will be informed of the abort as soon as they try to commit their changes to the object.

In order to handle recovery correctly in the presence of concurrency, a recoverable object must know the number and identity of all the tasks that have manipulated it. It is the only way to know for instance when a version of the object can be discarded and the memory associated with it released. Hence, tasks must somehow register as users of a version of the recoverable object.

Rules for Recoverable Objects

Given these considerations, the following rules apply to shared recoverable objects:

- Several tasks can work with a version of the recoverable object concurrently. All but the task that created the version must explicitly register with the version as participants.

- Once a participant task has called *Discard State* on a version of the recoverable object, the version will be discarded regardless of the votes of the other participants.

- A version is considered committed and its state copied back to its parent only if *all* participant tasks call *Commit State*.

- A version can only have one non-discarded subversion at a given time. This means that it is possible to create a second subversion of a version only after at least one of the participants of the first version has called *Discard State*.

- Participants that disappear without calling *Commit State* or *Discard State* (deserters) are ignored. If the only participant of a version disappears, the version is discarded.

4.2 Interface

Following the previous arguments, this subsection describes the interface of the implementation of shared recoverable objects. The recoverable object class described below allows an application to transform arbitrary objects into recoverable objects. The package `Recoverable` declares an abstract tagged type `Recoverable_Object` with all the necessary functions for recovery:

```
package Recoverable is

    type Recoverable_Object is abstract tagged private;
    -- Although this type is not limited, assignment of versions
    -- is not allowed (Program_Error will be raised at run time)

    type Recoverable_Object_Ref is access all Recoverable_Object'Class;

    procedure New_State      (Object     : in Recoverable_Object_Ref;
                              New_Object : out Recoverable_Object_Ref);

    procedure Join_State     (Object : in Recoverable_Object_Ref);

    procedure Commit_State   (Object : in out Recoverable_Object_Ref;
                              Sync   : in Boolean := False);

    procedure Discard_State (Object : in out Recoverable_Object_Ref);

    type Object_Status_Type is
       (Undecided, Discarded, Committing);

    function Current_Status ( Object : in Recoverable_Object_Ref)
       return Object_Status_Type;

    Object_Discarded,
    Already_Created_Subversion,
    Task_Already_Joined,
    Task_Never_Joined,
```

```
       Cannot_Join_Original,
       Null_Object : exception;
   private
       ...
   end Recoverable;
```

Application programmers must write their own recoverable objects containing application dependent data using type extension:

```
type Recoverable_Data is new Recoverable.Recoverable_Object with
   record
       Data : Application_Data;
       ...
   end record;
```

The abstract tagged type Recoverable_Object is non-limited, and therefore all derived types must also be non-limited. Hence, recoverable objects can not contain any limited components. This drawback can be overcome by making the abstract Recoverable_Object type limited, and requiring the user to provide a *copy* procedure for the extended data type, or, following the approach described in [8], having the user write *flattening* and *reconstitute* operations that allow the user data to be copied using streams.

In order to share a recoverable object between multiple tasks, it must obviously be accessed by reference. This is why the procedures that provide recoverability all use references.

In the following subsections, the operations that allow the manipulation of recoverable objects will be presented. Note that all of the procedures and functions will raise the exception Null_Object if the user passes a non-valid pointer as a parameter.

4.2.1 New_State

```
       procedure New_State    (Object      : in Recoverable_Object_Ref;
                               New_Object  : out Recoverable_Object_Ref);
```

The New_State procedure must be used to establish a new version for the recoverable object Object. The object is duplicated, and a pointer to the new version is returned in New_Object. The task that calls this procedure is automatically added as a participant task for the new version of the object.

This procedure may raise the following exception:

- Already_Created_Subversion   is raised if the version pointed to by Object has already a subversion associated with it.

4.2.2 Join_State

```
       procedure Join_State    (Object : in Recoverable_Object_Ref);
```

If a task wants to participate in an already existing version, it must call Join_State, passing a reference to the version of the object. This will add the task to the list of participants.

The procedure may raise two different exceptions:

- Task_Already_Joined   is raised if the calling task is already registered as a participant of the version pointed to by Object.

4.2.3 Commit_State

```
       procedure Commit_State  (Object : in out Recoverable_Object_Ref;
                               Sync   : in Boolean := False);
```

By calling `Commit_State` a task states that it has successfully completed its modifications to the version of the object pointed to by `Object` and desires to commit these changes to the parent version. The parent version will be updated once *all* participating tasks have committed their changes. If the parameter `Sync` is set to true, the procedure will block the calling task until all other participant tasks have given their vote.

This procedure may raise the following exceptions:

- `Task_Never_Joined` is raised if the calling task is not a participant of the version pointed to by `Object`.
- `Object_Discarded` is raised if the parameter `Sync` is set to true and any of the other participating tasks calls `Discard_State` for the version pointed to by `Object`.

4.2.4 Discard_State

```
procedure Discard_State ( Object : in out Recoverable_Object_Ref);
```

With `Discard_State`, a task can cancel all its changes to the version of the object pointed to by `Object`. Once a participating task has called `Discard_State`, the state of the version will be discarded, regardless of the decisions of the other participating tasks.

The procedure may raise the following exception:

- `Task_Never_Joined` is raised if the calling task is not a participant of the version pointed to by `Object`.

4.2.5 Current_Status

```
function Current_Status ( Object : in Recoverable_Object_Ref)
       return Object_Status_Type;
```

This procedure allows a participant to get information about the current status of the version of the object pointed to by `Object`. Possible results are:

- `Discarded` — meaning that a participant has already called `Discard_State`,
- `Committing` — meaning that all other participants have called `Commit_State`,
- `Undecided` — otherwise.

5   Example

5.1 Introduction

The following section will present a small example application that manipulates digital images by applying so-called *filters*. Current digital image enhancement applications such as Adobe Photoshop® offer a huge variety of filters, including image sharpening or softening, stylizing, distortion, removal of dust and scratches, lightning, color adjustments, adding noise, applying textures, etc...

A filter can be seen as a function which is applied to each pixel of an image. The resulting pixel depends on the original pixel, the surrounding pixels, other global properties of the image and on parameters of the filter (i.e. for the *Gaussian Blur* filter, the radius of the pixel area is a parameter).

Some filters use very simple functions (i.e. inverting the picture), others can get very complicated. Image restoration filters such as edge detection or noise reduction filters

use discrete Fourier transforms to decompose an image into periodic structures —
moving the picture from the spacial to the frequency domain. This makes it easy to
remove certain frequencies from the image, noise being typically in the high frequency
range. Finally the spacial picture can be reconstructed using the inverse Fourier transform.

It is also much easier to calculate a convolution[1] in the frequency domain than in the
spacial domain, since it comes down to multiplying the Fourier transform of the original image with the Fourier transform of the convolution matrix.

5.2 Performance Considerations

The general formula calculating the two-dimensional Fourier transform of a $M \times N$
matrix with complex components is the following [9]:

$$F(u, v) = \frac{1}{\sqrt{MN}} \sum_{m=0}^{M-1} \sum_{n=0}^{N-1} e^{-\frac{2\pi jmu}{M}} e^{-\frac{2\pi jnv}{N}} f(m, n)$$

Applied directly, this formula is prohibitively expensive. If $M = N$, each pixel of the
image requires N^2 complex multiplications and $N^2 - 1$ complex additions, which
gives us an algorithmic complexity of N^4 for the entire picture. Using mathematical
transformations and precalculation of constants, the complexity can be reduced to
$N^2 \log N$, which still represents a considerable calculation effort.

With the emergence of multiprocessor systems in the personal computer area, current
image processing applications start to make use of the additional processing power to
boost the performance of filters. The following programming example will illustrate
how recoverable objects can be used in a multitasking environment to implement software fault tolerance and "undo" functionality.

5.3 Example Code

The first step is to define a type that can hold the image data. As shown in section 4.2,
type extension must be used to obtain a recoverable object containing application data.
The following package defines a new type `Recoverable_Picture` derived from the
type `Recoverable_Object`, adding a matrix of pixels to hold the color information of
the picture. The bounds of the picture can be specified at the moment of instantiation
through discriminants.

```
with Recoverable; use Recoverable;
package Recoverable_Picture is

    subtype Color_Span is Natural range 0 .. 255;
    type Pixel is record
        Red   : Color_Span := 0;
        Green : Color_Span := 0;
        Blue  : Color_Span := 0;
        Alpha : Color_Span := 0;
    end record;

    type Picture is array (Integer range <>, Integer range <>) of Pixel;

    type Recoverable_Picture ( Top    : Integer;
                               Left   : Integer;
```

---

1. A convolution is basically a function where the output value of the pixel depends on
its original value and the values of the surrounding pixels. Smoothing filters are typical
convolution examples.

```
                    Bottom : Integer;
                    Right  : Integer)
      is new Recoverable_Object with record
          Image : Picture (Left .. Right, Top .. Bottom);
      end record;

      type Recoverable_Picture_Ref is access all Recoverable_Picture'Class;

   end Recoverable_Picture;
```

The main procedure that implements the "undo" functionality is presented below:

```
   with Recoverable;          use Recoverable;
   with Recoverable.Picture;  use Recoverable.Picture;
   with Ada.Text_IO;          use Ada.Text_IO;

   procedure Photoshop is

      Original_Picture : Recoverable_Picture_Ref;
      Filtered_Picture : Recoverable_Picture_Ref;

      type Square is record
         Top    : Integer := 0;
         Left   : Integer := 0;
         Bottom : Integer := 0;
         Right  : Integer := 0;
      end record;

      Number_Of_Processors   : constant Positive := 5;
      Image_Square           : constant Square := (-4, -3, 4, 3);

      task type Filter_Task;

      task body Filter_Task is separate;
   begin
```

Now, the image must be allocated.

```
      Original_Picture := new Recoverable_Picture
                          ( Image_Square.Top, Image_Square.Left,
                            Image_Square.Bottom, Image_Square.Right);
```

The user of the application should now draw the contents of the image, or load an existing image from disk. Once he chooses to apply a filter to the image, a new version must be created.

```
      New_State  (Recoverable_Object_Ref (Original_Picture),
                  Recoverable_Object_Ref (Filtered_Picture));
```

The following block will create the tasks that actually perform the filtering. Note that the block is only exited when all of the Filter_Tasks have terminated.

```
      declare
         Tasks : array (1 .. Number_Of_Processors) of Filter_Task;
      begin
         null;
      end;
```

Now, we must check if the tasks have completed their work successfully. If not, the (probably incompletely) filtered picture must be discarded and an alert message should be displayed to the user.

```
      if Current_Status (Recoverable_Object_Ref (Filtered_Picture))
         /= Committing then

         Discard_State (Recoverable_Object_Ref (Filtered_Picture));
         Alert_User;

      else
```

Show the resulting picture to the user and ask him if he wants to keep the filtered picture, or undo the changes, then call Commit_State or Discard_State accordingly.

```
         if User_Accepts_Result then
            -- Make the changes definitive
            Commit_State (Recoverable_Object_Ref (Filtered_Picture));
```

```
        else
              -- Revert to the previous version
              Discard_State (Recoverable_Object_Ref (Filtered_Picture));
        end if;
    end if;
end Photoshop;
```

The actual filtering is done in the body of the `Filter_Tasks`. Lets assume there is a function that implements the desired filtering for one pixel using the interface:

```
function Filter_Pixel ( Source : Picture;
                        X, Y   : Integer)
       return Pixel;
```

A task that applies this filter on a square subregion of the image could be written the following way:

```
task body Filter_Task is
```

First we must initialize the local variables. This will be done using calls to a protected object[1].

```
    Source_Picture   : Recoverable_Picture_Ref   := Get_Source_Picture;
    Dest_Picture     : Recoverable_Picture_Ref   := Get_Dest_Picture;
    Subregion        : Square                     := Get_Subregion;
begin
```

Now we must tell the version of the recoverable object that we want to work with it.

```
    Join_State (Recoverable_Object_Ref (Dest_Picture));

    for Y in Subregion.Top .. Subregion.Bottom loop
      for X in Subregion.Left .. Subregion.Right loop
        Dest_Picture.Image (X, Y) :=
            Filter_Pixel (Source_Picture.Image, X, Y);
      end loop;
    end loop;
```

The filtering has been successful and we can commit the changes.

```
    Commit_State (Recoverable_Object_Ref (Dest_Picture));

exception

  when others =>
      Discard_State (Recoverable_Object_Ref (Dest_Picture));
      raise;
end;
```

Note that if the `Filter_Pixel` function raises an exception in one task, the current version of the picture is discarded, regardless of the decisions of the other participants. This avoids leaving the picture in an inconsistent state.

6 Implementation

This section will describe the basic structure of the implementation, and point out some of its subtleties.

---

1. The program code of the protected object is not shown here, but its implementation is straightforward.

From an implementation point of view, a recoverable object is essentially a doubly linked list of versions of the object. Each version contains a pointer to its parent and child version (if it exists), a field representing the current state of the version, and a list of the task IDs of all participant tasks (see fig. 3).

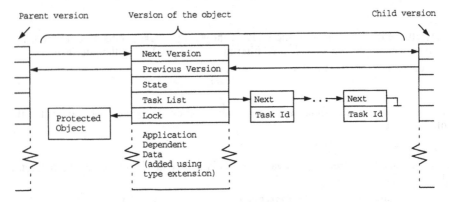

Figure 3: Recoverable Object Data Structures

Each version has a protected object providing simple Lock and Unlock operations associated with it, in order to protect it from concurrent accesses. It also defines an entry Wait_For_Participants that is used to block the participant tasks when they call Commit_State with synchronization.

```
protected type Recoverable_Object_Lock is

    entry Lock        ( L : in out Lock_Handler;
                        O : in Recoverable_Object_Ref);

    procedure Unlock ( L : in out Lock_Handler;
                        O : in Recoverable_Object_Ref);

    entry Wait_For_Participants;

    end Recoverable_Object_Lock;
```

By using a separate lock for each version of the object, concurrency is increased. Attention must be paid in the implementation of the Discard and Commit procedures, for they have to remove a version from the linked list. In order to prevent deadlocks, the locks of the parent, the version to be removed and the child version must be acquired in top-down order. That way, the bottom-most request will always complete.

The protected object cannot be directly included in the tagged type (see fig. 3), for this would make the type limited. It is important that assignment of versions be possible, since it is the only way to make copies of the application data added to the type using type extension. Copying is needed in the New_State procedure, when the new version of the object must be initialized with the contents of the old version, and in Commit_State, where the contents of the old version are replaced with the contents of the new one.

A user of the package on the other hand should not be allowed to make copies of the entire version of an object, for this could corrupt the recoverable object. Simply copying a version does not correctly allocate a new protected object, and it corrupts the doubly linked list of versions.

These problems can be overcome by making the Recoverable_Object type a controlled type. The Initialize and Finalize procedures take care of allocating and deallocating the protected object. The Adjust procedure is used to disallow copying of the entire version object outside of the recoverable objects package. To achieve this, the recoverable object type contains a private boolean value, which must be set to true in order to allow an assignment to complete. The Adjust procedure raises an exception if the flag is not set properly.

```
procedure Adjust (Object : in out Recoverable_Object) is
begin

   if Object.Copy_Allowed then
       Object.Copy_Allowed := False;
   else
       raise Program_Error;
   end if;

end Adjust;
```

Note that according to the Ada Reference Manual [2, 7.6.1(14)] it is a bounded error to raise an exception inside Adjust, but [2, 7.6.1(16)] states that when Adjust is invoked as part of an assignment operation, any other adjustments due to be performed are performed, and then Program_Error is raised, which is exactly what we want.

The recoverable objects presented here are designed to handle concurrent accesses, and should be useful in various forms of concurrency control mechanisms like transactions or conversations. Tasks working on behalf of an atomic action for instance can be aborted when an exception is raised in an other participant of the atomic action. We must therefore also consider ATC (Asynchronous Transfer of Control) when implementing the operations of recoverable objects to prohibit corruption of the internal data structures.

First of all we must ensure that all locks held by a task are always released when an ATC occurs. This is done by saving the fact that an object is locked in a controlled object Lock_Handler. Before acquiring the lock, an instance of the Lock_Handler type must be declared. Then, a reference to it is passed to the protected operation Lock. This guarantees atomicity of actual locking *and* saving of the fact that the version has been locked, since protected operations are abort deferred regions. The Finalize procedure of the Lock_Handler then takes care of releasing the locks as soon as the Lock_Handler instance ceases to exist, even in the presence of raised exceptions or ATCs.

The second problem with ATC is that aborting a task that is manipulating the recoverable object may leave the internal data structures in an inconsistent state. To avoid this, the modifications of the internal data structures must be performed in abort deferred regions. Unfortunately, it is not possible to use a protected object for that purpose, since potentially blocking calls such as acquiring a lock are not allowed from within a protected operation. The only portable way to create abort deferred regions is again using controlled types: the Initialize, Adjust and Finalize procedures of controlled types are abort deferred regions.

The procedure for transforming an operation having in and out parameters into an abort deferred operation is the following:

Controlled types have to be declared at the library level. Hence it is not possible to access the in and out parameters of the operation directly. They must be passed inside the controlled type itself, and therefore the controlled type must be declared as follows:

```
type Operation_Executor_Type is new Controlled with
   record
       In_Parameter_1 : In_Parameter_1_Type;
       --  ...
       In_Paramter_N : In_Parameter_N_Type;
```

```
        Out_Parameter_1 : Out_Parameter_1_Type;
        --   ...
        Out_Parameter_N : Out_Parameter_N_Type;
    end record;
```

The `Initialize` procedure cannot be used to execute the actual statements of the operation, since it is not possible to affect the in parameters to the type before `Initialize` is called. The `Finalize` procedure is not suitable either, since it is not possible to retrieve the out parameters before the instance of the type is deallocated. Hence the `Adjust` procedure must be used:

```
procedure Adjust (O : in out Operation_Executor_Type) is

begin
    --  The actual statements of the operation go here
    --  All occurences of In_Parameter_X must be replaced by
    --  O.In_Parameter_X, Out_Parameter_X by O.Out_Parameter_X

end Adjust;
```

The actual operation must be changed to:

```
procedure Operation ( In_Parameter_1 : in In_Parameter_1_Type;
                      Out_Parameter_1 : out Out_Parameter_1_Type) is

    Source, Destination : Operation_Executor_Type;

begin
    --  Affect the In parameters
    Source.In_Parameter_1 := In_Parameter_1;

    --  The actual statements will be executed inside the Adjust procedure
    Destination := Source;

    --  Retrieve the Out parameters
    Out_Parameter_1 := Destination.Out_Parameter_1;

end;
```

The last problem due to ATC is the deserter problem. A task that has joined a version of a recoverable object by calling `Join_State` but then terminates (or is aborted) without calling `Discard_State` or `Commit_State` first, will compromise the correct functioning of the recoverable object, since the version cannot be discarded, nor committed, until all participant tasks have given their vote. It is therefore necessary to detect deserter tasks.

This can be done by using a controlled task attribute that stores all the versions of all recoverable objects that a task has joined so far. If the task is aborted or terminates before it has called `Discard_State` or `Commit_State` for these versions, the `Finalize` procedure of the controlled attribute will inform the recoverable objects that the task has deserted.

7   Conclusion and Future Work

This paper describes an implementation of recoverable objects that supports concurrency. Application programmers can write their own recoverable objects by extending the `Recoverable_Object` root type.

It has been shown that when designing recoverable objects that can be accessed concurrently, a deferred update scheme should be preferred over an in-place update scheme. Implementation problems due to concurrency and corresponding solutions have been presented. Special attention must be paid to task abortion, for this can lead to corrupt data structures and memory leaks (deserter problem).

Future work in this direction include adding persistence functions to recoverable objects, making it possible to save the state of an object to stable storage and (automatically) restore it after a crash failure. Plans are then to implement some kind of concurrent transactional service built upon these abstractions.

8 Acknowledgments

The authors gratefully acknowledge the contributions of Alexander Romanovsky in the preparation of this paper, and want to thank Thomas Wolf for his excellent implementation suggestions.

References

[1] Lee, P. A.; Anderson, T.: "Fault Tolerance - Principles and Practice". In *Dependable Computing and Fault-Tolerant Systems*, volume 3, Springer Verlag, 2nd ed., 1990.

[2] Taft, S. T.; Duff, R. A. (Eds.): *International Standard ISO/IEC 8652:1995(E): Ada Reference Manual*. Lecture Notes in Computer Science **1246**, Springer Verlag, 1997.

[3] Barnes, J. (Ed.): *Ada 95 Rationale*. Lecture Notes in Computer Science **1247**, Springer Verlag, 1997.

[4] Randell, B.: "System structure for software fault tolerance". *IEEE Transactions on Software Engineering 1(2)*, pp. 220 – 232, 1975.

[5] Gray, J.; Reuter, A.: *Transaction Processing: Concepts and Techniques*. Morgan Kaufmann Publishers, San Mateo, California, 1993.

[6] Moss, J. E. B.: *Nested Transactions, An Approach to Reliable Computing*. Ph.D. Thesis, MIT, Cambridge, April 1981.

[7] Xu, J.; Randell, B.; Romanovsky, A.; Rubira, C. M. F.; Stroud, R. J.; Wu, Z.: "Fault Tolerance in Concurrent Object-Oriented Software through Coordinated Error Recovery". In *FTCS-25: 25th International Symposium on Fault Tolerant Computing*, pp. 499 – 509, Pasadena, California, 1995.

[8] Rogers, P.; Wellings, A. J.: "State Restoration In Ada 95: A Portable Approach to Supporting Software Fault Tolerance". *Technical Report YCS-98-297*, Department of Computer Science, University of York, York, UK, 1998.

[9] Jähne, B.: *Digital Image Processing, Concepts, Algorithms and Scientific Applications*. Springer, New York, 3rd ed., 1995.

Fault Tolerance by Transparent Replication for Distributed Ada 95

Thomas Wolf and Alfred Strohmeier

Swiss Federal Institute of Technology
Software Engineering Laboratory
1015 Lausanne Ecublens
Switzerland

e—mail: {Thomas.Wolf, Alfred.Strohmeier}@epfl.ch
phone: +41 (21) 693.42.37 — fax: +41 (21) 693.50.79

Abstract. This paper presents the foundations of RAPIDS ("Replicated Ada Partitions In Distributed Systems"), an implementation of the Distributed Systems Annex E incorporating the transparent replication of partitions in distributed Ada 95 applications. RAPIDS is a replication manager for semi–active replication based on a piecewise deterministic computation model. It guarantees replica consistency for arbitrary Ada 95 partitions despite the inherent non–determinism of multitasking, offering k–resilient partitions. The RAPIDS prototype is implemented for the GNAT compiler and evolved from its PCS, Garlic.

Keywords. Distributed Systems, Fault Tolerance, Non–Determinism, Piecewise Determinism, Replica Consistency, Semi–Active Replication.

1 Introduction

Measures for fault tolerance always introduce redundancy in the system. Examples are data redundancy (e.g., error–correcting codes), time redundancy (re–execution after a failure), or space redundancy (replication). Replication in particular is well suited for rendering nodes in a distributed application fault–tolerant, the idea being that if one replica of a node fails, the remaining replicas can continue to provide the node's services. The goal of replication for fault tolerance is thus the transparent masking of failures.

The main difficulty of replication of virtual nodes is maintaining the consistency of all the replicas. In Ada 95, this is further complicated by the inherent non–determinism. In section 2, we present our system model, before we examine the issue of non–determinism in detail in section 3. We show that this non–determinism cannot be exorcized even assuming that tasking was deterministic. In section 4, we briefly discuss our earlier attempt at replication in Ada 95 [Wol97] and show that it is inadequate for solving the problem of replication of non–deterministic partitions.

In section 5, we present a model of computation based on piecewise determinism [SY85, Eln93] that allows us to overcome this problem. Under the piecewise computation model, replica consistency can be ensured by coordinating the replicas using semi–active replication, which was pioneered in the Delta–4 project [Pow91]. In this scheme, all non–deterministic decisions are taken on one distinguished replica; all other replicas are forced to adopt that choice.

Section 6 gives a very brief overview of the implementation of RAPIDS [Wol98], a replica manager for transparent semi–active replication based on piecewise determinism for the GNAT compiler. We outline the basic structure of RAPIDS and indicate its interactions with other parts of the run–time support. A detailed presentation of RAPIDS' implementation is intended for a later paper.

The conclusion summarizes the main findings of our work and reports on the current state of RAPIDS.

2 The System Model

A distributed application in Ada 95 is composed of a set of virtual nodes (called "partitions") that themselves are indivisible as far as distribution is concerned and that execute on various physical nodes (computers), which may be heterogeneous [ISO95, E(6)]. The physical nodes are connected by a network, over which they communicate with each other. A partition in Ada 95 is a collection of library units, some of which constitute its interface towards the other partitions of the application. These well–defined interfaces are given by the specifications of certain library units that have to be marked in the source using special categorization pragmas.

Ada 95 distinguishes between active and passive partitions. Passive partitions are intended to model memory shared between virtual nodes, either physically or through a virtual distributed shared memory system, and have no thread of control associated with them. Their interface may contain remotely accessible data objects, which can be accessed by other (active) partitions. Active partitions *do* have a thread of control. Different active partitions communicate with each other only through their interface library units by means of remote procedure calls (RPCs, [BN84]). The language standard also defines ways for making dynamically bound remote calls through the use of remote access–to–procedure or remote access–to–class–wide types, but these too boil down ultimately to RPCs. Direct remote data access between active partitions does not exist in Ada 95.

Remote procedure calls are a communication abstraction built on top of simple message passing. They have "at most once" semantics. In Ada 95, the type safety is maintained even across RPCs because the compiler knows which subprograms are remotely callable (through the categorization pragmas) and hence can apply all the semantic checks to ensure the integrity of the distributed application, just like for local subprogram calls. The run–time support implements the message protocols underlying the RPC abstraction transparently in its Partition Communication Subsystem (PCS). The language standard strongly suggests [ISO95, E.5(24,25,28)] that a partition should handle incoming RPCs concurrently, each one in its own task.

Given this model defined by the language standard, we examine *transparent replication* for fault–tolerance assuming an asynchronous *heterogeneous* distributed system. The partitions of a distributed application do not share memory, but communicate only by RPC over the network through *reliable channels*[1]. Partitions are assumed to be subject to *crash failures* only (fail–silent behavior).

---

1. A message sent on a reliable channel will eventually be received by the recipient if both the sender and the receiver do not fail; if link failures are repaired eventually, this property can be implemented through message retransmissions.

We also assume to have a *view–synchronous* group communication system [Bir93] at our disposal. It supplies the group abstraction, i.e. consistent membership information and reliable multicast primitives with various ordering guarantees. The replicas of a partition form a view–synchronous group. With view synchrony, all correct group members have a consistent view of the group composition. As members join and leave the group (either voluntarily or because they fail or are suspected to have failed), this composition changes over time, leading to a sequence of views $V = \{V_0, ... V_i, V_{i+1}, ...\}$. The installation of a new view in the correct group members, i.e. the delivery of a new view, is called a *view change*. Communication in a view–synchronous group, i.e. the delivery of multicasts on the correct group members, is totally ordered with respect to view changes. This can be expressed more formally as:

- *View synchrony*: if one group member in view V_i delivers a multicast m and then view V_{i+1}, all group members in V_i that deliver V_{i+1} deliver m before V_{i+1}.

Note that this condition does *not* impose a total order on all multicasts: it only orders them with respect to view changes, i.e. all correct members in a view deliver the same set of multicasts in this view.

3 Non–Determinism in Ada 95

When the replicas of a partition are deterministic, the state machine approach of [Sch90] can be employed for active replication. Consistency between the replicas can then be ensured by satisfying two conditions:

- *Atomicity:* if one replica handles a request r, then all replicas do.
- *Order:* if one replica handles a request r_2 after having handled a request r_1, then all replicas handle r_2 only once they have handled r_1.

This guarantees that all replicas handle the same requests in the same order, and — since they are assumed to be deterministic — their states will evolve in a consistent way. When the replicas form a group, using totally ordered multicasts for requests ensures the above two conditions.

Request ordering alone is not sufficient to maintain replica consistency if the replicas are non–deterministic. Partitions in Ada 95 generally are multitasked, and task scheduling may well violate the order imposed on request handling, leading to diverging evolutions of replicas. Instead of ordering the delivery of requests, the state accesses performed by the requests must be ordered: all replicas must go through a *common sequence of state accesses*.

The non–determinism perceived at the language level in Ada 95 has several causes. The most obvious ones are all related to the behavior of the tasking system, for instance in the choice made in a selective accept statement. Explicit dependencies on time (`delay` statements) also are a source of non–determinism, in particular when used in the context of asynchronous transfers of control or timed entry calls. Because there is no global notion of time in a distributed Ada 95 application and because the physical nodes the replicas of a partition execute on may run at different speeds, timed entry calls may time out on one replica whilst succeeding on another.

Implicit timing dependencies — introduced e.g. by the use of time–sliced pre–emptive task scheduling, or by varying message delivery delays originating in the communication layer — may also cause executions on different replicas of a partition to diverge.

Even if one forbade the use of delays (e.g. through pragma Restrictions) in a partition that was to be replicated, it is *not* possible to side–step the problem of non–determinism simply by using deterministic task scheduling on all replicas, i.e., a scheduler that is guaranteed to make the same decisions on all replicas given the same sets of tasks. The problem is illustrated by fig. 1.

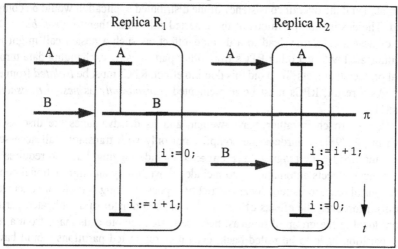

Fig. 1 Non–Determinism due to Delivery Delays

In this figure, two replicas of a multitasked partition both deliver two RPC requests A and B in the same order. Despite their using a deterministic task scheduler, their states diverge. At point π in fig. 1, the scheduler on replica R_1 has two tasks to schedule and decides to let B execute. On replica R_2, there is only the task for A at point π because the request B didn't arrive yet. As a result, R_2's scheduling differs from that on R_1, which may lead to state inconsistencies.

4 Transactions

One approach to synchronize the order of state accesses — short of executing all RPC requests strictly sequentially, which is not a viable option — would be based on the use of transactions.

We assume that state accesses are identified somehow, for instance through a new pragma Replicated the application developer uses to designate all global objects that are to be considered "state" [Wol97]. Instead of active replication, we use a passive replication scheme known as coordinator–cohort replication. One replica is singled out as the coordinator: it is the only one to handle requests. On the coordinator, the sequence of state accesses is logged. When a request is completed, this sequence of state accesses is reliably multicast to all cohorts, which then apply the state changes in the order recorded.

Upon a failure of the coordinator, one of the cohorts becomes the new coordinator. It has to restart requests from scratch as we cannot make the new coordinator continue at precisely the same point in the flow of control where the former coordinator failed[2]. Due to the non–determinism, re–execution might follow a different path in the control flow than the original execution on the former coordinator. If the former coordinator had made nested remote calls to yet other partitions, it is therefore not guaranteed that the new coordinator will redo them with the same parameters or that it will redo them at all. As a consequence, these nested remote calls must be undone before the new coordinator takes over, otherwise the "at most once" semantics of RPCs might be violated and the overall consistency of the distributed application would be compromised. The destination partitions of these nested calls must therefore *roll back*. Rollback of nested calls may lead to a domino–effect, as such a nested call might have communicated with yet other RPCs from other partitions by exchanging data through global protected objects. To avoid this domino effect, RPCs must be *isolated* from each other. As a result, RPCs must be implemented *transparently* as *nested transactions* [Mos81].

This approach is rather heavy–weight, and its disadvantages are discussed at length in [Wol98]. It burdens the compiler not only with translating all accesses to objects marked by the pragma Replicated to include logging, but also requires it to rewrite these objects automatically to include recoverability and transactional concurrency control (e.g., to include locks if strict two–phase locking is used for concurrency control). Moreover, the effects of a failure of the coordinator of a replicated partition are not local to the group of replicas: because nested remote calls made from a replicated partition have to be rolled back, even non–replicated partitions would have to implement RPCs as nested transactions.

The most serious problem with this idea of transparently implementing RPCs as nested transactions are deadlocks, though. As shown in fig. 2, the interactions between application–level scheduling implemented through the entry queues of protected objects and the constraints imposed by the serialization of transactions may lead to deadlocks that cannot be resolved transparently. We will show this assuming the use of strict two–phase locking for concurrency control; a similar argument can be made for concurrency control based on timestamp ordering (see [Wol98]).

In fig. 2, two concurrent RPCs, i.e., nested transactions, access two global protected objects x_1 and x_2. Both transactions first make a write access to one of the objects and then try to make an entry call on the other object. We assume that the barriers of these entry calls are such that they are open only when the write access of the other transaction occurred first. With the interleaving of operations shown in fig. 2, both transaction first execute their write accesses. Transaction t_1 then makes its entry call on object x_2 and is blocked despite the barrier being open because the object is locked by t_2. The same happens with transaction t_2 and object x_1. Suppose now that t_1 is aborted in an attempt to break the deadlock. At that moment, t_2 could basically pro-

---

2. In a heterogeneous system. In a homogeneous system, one could basically take a checkpoint including the program counter, tasking state, stacks, etc. However, taking such a checkpoint is far from evident in a multitasked environment, and even if it can be done, it might prove too costly to do each time the coordinator sends a message to some other partition.

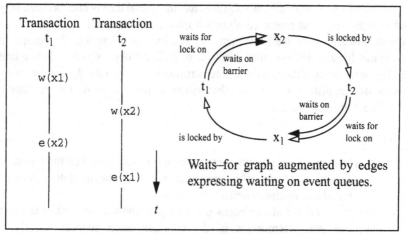

Fig. 2 An Unresolvable Deadlock

ceed with its entry call as t_1 no longer holds the lock of object x_2. However, t_2 will remain blocked because now the barrier is closed! (Recall that the assumption is that t_1's write access opens the barrier, but this write access has just been undone.)

As a result, this not at all uncommon case that works perfectly well in normal Ada 95 will always deadlock when the partition is replicated! Furthermore, the deadlock *cannot be broken*: one transaction will always be blocked by the two–phase locking rules while the other one will block on the application–defined entry barrier! The application must therefore be aware of this possibility and be written in such a way that these unbreakable deadlocks do not occur. Transactions cannot be used *transparently* to ensure consistency in a distributed application: they must be made visible to the application. How to best integrate transactions at the application level in Ada 95 is certainly an area worth exploring, but runs counter to our goal of offering fault tolerance by replication in a *transparent* manner.

5 Piecewise Determinism

We have therefore focused our attention on a more refined modeling of concurrent executions in Ada 95. In the piecewise deterministic computation model [SY85, Eln93], an execution is seen as a sequence of *deterministic state intervals* separated by *non–deterministically occurring events*.

This describes precisely executions in Ada 95. The language abstractions guarantee that any execution history in Ada 95 is *linearizable* [HW90]. The signaling model of Ada 95 [ISO95, 9.10(3–10)] requires that all concurrent accesses to an object be in fact sequential in some order, i.e., actions of different tasks on one and the same object are only allowed if the action of one task signals the action of the other task. This basically means that all global state that is to be accessed concurrently must be encapsulated in protected objects, or be protected by appropriate application–level synchronization using rendezvous[3], otherwise the partition is erroneous!

---

3. Special cases like a task writing a value into an unprotected object and then creating another task that reads it are also covered by the signaling model.

Without loss of generality, we assume that any global data is encapsulated in protected objects[4]. Because protected objects implement linearizability trivially through mutual exclusion, and because linearizability is a local property (i.e., the composition of individual linearizable execution histories of different objects yields again a linearizable history), the execution of the whole partition is linearizable. Any interleaving of piecewise deterministic state intervals that will occur in a correct Ada 95 partition will yield a global linearizable history.

5.1 Events

An execution history under piecewise determinism is characterized by the sequence of events that occur: the events describe the sequence of deterministic state intervals. We distinguish external and internal events.

External events occur at any interaction of a partition with the rest of the system and account for non–determinism in the communication support (cf. fig. 1 in section 3). They are:

- Delivery of an RPC request message sent by some other partition.
- Sending an RPC answer message back to the calling partition to return the results of a remote call.
- Sending an RPC request message to some other partition.
- Delivery of an RPC answer message from some other partition.

Internal events are all sources of non–determinism within a partition. They basically account for non–determinism in the tasking system and cover all signaling actions:

- The decision, which entry in a select statement is accepted.
- The outcome of timed and conditional entry calls.
- Entering and leaving protected actions, in particular locking and unlocking protected objects.
- Queueing and requeueing on entry calls.
- The creation, termination, and abortion of tasks.
- Abortion of an abortable part of an asynchronous select statement.
- Initialization, finalization, and assignments of controlled objects.

A special kind of internal events are local calls to subprograms whose results depend upon state outside the application, e.g. system calls. An example is the Clock function in the standard package Ada.Calendar, which returns an approximation of "wall clock" time. Such calls (and their results) also must be considered internal events.

5.2 Semi–Active Replication

The piecewise deterministic model lends itself well to semi–active replication [BHV+90] for coordinating the replicas. Semi–active replication has been introduced in the Delta–4 project [Pow91]. Replicas are organized as members of a group, and all replicas execute incoming RPC requests. One replica is designated the *leader*: it is

---

4. The case where a protected object acts as a lock for some unprotected data is functionally equivalent; synchronization through rendezvous also can be modeled by protected objects.

responsible for taking all non–deterministic decisions. These decisions are propagated to the other replicas — the *followers* — that then are forced to make the same choices.

Replica consistency with semi–active replication can thus be achieved by logging events on the leader. The leader then synchronizes its followers by sending them the events using a FIFO–ordered reliable multicast. The followers then replay the events as they occurred on the leader. As a result, all replicas will go through the same execution history, i.e, sequence of deterministic state intervals, and consequently state accesses will occur in the same order on all replicas.

5.3 Correctness

The correctness of this approach relies on the semantics of the programming language Ada 95. The signaling model guarantees that all state accesses are indeed separated by events and happen in different deterministic state intervals, because all signaling actions defined in the language standard are subsumed by the set of internal events. Thus, ordering state intervals (by ordering events) also orders concurrent accesses to objects.

Abortions in asynchronous select statements might basically cause the replicas' states to diverge if the abortion didn't happen at precisely the same logical moment during execution. Consider the example in fig. 3 below.

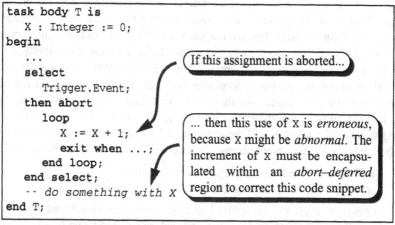

```
task body T is
   X : Integer := 0;
begin
   ...
   select
      Trigger.Event;
   then abort
      loop
         X := X + 1;
         exit when ...;
      end loop;
   end select;
   -- do something with X
end T;
```

If this assignment is aborted...

... then this use of X is *erroneous*, because X might be *abnormal*. The increment of X must be encapsulated within an *abort–deferred* region to correct this code snippet.

Fig. 3 Aborts in asynchronous select statements

The abortable part of this asynchronous select statement is started if the entry call on the protected object Trigger is not selected immediately or is requeued. If the triggering statement completes, the abortable part is aborted (provided it had been started and didn't complete already). This abortion might happen basically at any time, in the case of replication even at different times during the execution of the abortable part on any two replicas. Such asynchronous aborts may be problematic even in a centralized application, as even then it is nearly impossible to make sure the state accessed by the abortable part remains consistent in the face of abortion. Furthermore, if an assignment (other than to a controlled object, see below) is disrupted by the abortion, the target object of the assignment may become *abnormal* [ISO95, 9.8(21)], and any uses of values of abnormal objects are considered *erroneous* in the language standard [ISO95, 13.9.1]. The critical sections of abortable parts (in the sense of making modifications that might have an influence on the further execution) must therefore be implemented as *abort–deferred regions*. The language defines several constructs that defer abortion [ISO95, 9.8(6–11)], in particular, protected actions as well as initialization, finalization, and assignment of controlled objects cannot be aborted. The abortion takes place only once the abort–deferred construct is completed. The abort–deferred regions and also the possible triggers of such asynchronous aborts again are all subsumed by the above list of internal events. By replaying the event log on the followers, it is therefore guaranteed that an abort happens between the same two abort–deferred regions as on the leader, which is sufficient to maintain the semantics of Ada 95 given that any critical state modification in an abortable part is done within an abort–deferred region.

5.4 Replica Synchronization: Observable Events

Synchronizing the followers at each and every event that occurs on the leader would most probably be impractical: it would incur a prohibitively high performance overhead as internal events in particular are bound to occur very frequently. Fortunately, this is not necessary. As long as the effects of state intervals remain purely local to the leader, the followers need not be informed of any events. The followers must be brought up to date only when and if the effects become observable to the rest of the system. This leads to the notion of *observable events*: if the leader sends information to any other partition in the system (or outputs something), this data depends upon the precise sequence of state intervals executed, and followers must be guaranteed to go through the same sequence of state intervals in order to produce the same observable event. All other events have purely local effects — should the leader fail, the rest of the system is still in the same state as if they hadn't happened at all, and a follower, once it has become the new leader, may make its own, possibly different choices without disturbing the overall consistency of the application. Synchronization is therefore needed only before an observable event occurs. An observable event is one of the following:

- Sending an RPC answer message back to the client.
- Sending an RPC request message to some other partition.

Between observable events, the leader logs any occurrences of external and internal events by buffering them in an event log. Just before an observable event is about to happen, the leader multicasts this event log to the followers. Only then it may proceed and perform the observable event. We call the path of execution described by the event log an *extended state interval* as it my contain many simple state intervals together with the events relating them. Each observable event starts a new extended state interval. When a follower receives an event log from the leader, it proceeds with the execution, replaying the logged event outcomes and thereby recreating the extended state interval. It does not replay the initial observable event, though: since the leader already executed it, doing so would only result in a duplicate invocation. Instead, the followers will just use the logged outcome of the event. The leader is thus the only replica that ever interacts with the rest of the system. When an event occurs that is not in the log, this signifies that the whole log has been replayed, and the follower blocks until it receives the next event log from the leader, or until it becomes the new leader itself due to a failure of the former leader.

In general, the leader starts a new extended state interval each time an observable event occurs. But it is free to define additional points in the execution that also start new extended state intervals, i.e., that also make it send its event log to the followers. For instance, the leader can start a new extended state interval whenever its event log buffer threatens to overflow. This does not change the correctness of the approach, it just leads to a closer synchronization between the leader and the followers.

5.5 Failures

The failure of a follower is completely transparent. Because a follower never interacts with the rest of the system beyond the group of replicas, its failure cannot possibly have any effects on the distributed application. When a follower fails, it is simply excluded from the group.

Upon a failure of the leader, one of the followers must become the new leader[5]. It then resumes execution at the point the former leader had last communicated to the followers. It first re–executes any pending events in the event log. Once the event log is exhausted, the new leader simply continues executing, henceforth logging events as they occur and sending its event log to the remaining followers before each observable event.

Although the old leader may have progressed since it had sent its event log for the last time before its failure, the rule that synchronization must take place before any observable event ensures that any actions of the failed leader could not affect the system. This is similar to write–ahead logging in databases, where all necessary information for undoing or redoing an action must be in the log before the state may be updated. Here, the replicas must have received the leader's decisions that led to an observable event before the leader may execute this event. This is illustrated in fig. 4.

The leader L of a replicated partition started executing a request req_A, made a nested remote call req_B to some other partition P, waited for the result, and continued processing req_A before it finally failed. Just before it performed req_B (which is an observable event), it sent its event log for the extended state interval S_1 to its followers F_1 and F_2, which replay the log to execute S_1. When L fails, a view change occurs and follower F_1 becomes the new leader and continues execution from just after S_1. Note that the extended state interval S_3 may well be different from S_2 (except for the initial observable event req_B, which is guaranteed to be identical), but since S_2 could not possibly have affected any other part of the system except L itself, the application's overall state is still consistent.

Note that in the example in fig. 4, we assume that communication with a group of replicas is always by reliable multicast: even the reply rep_B is multicast from P to all replicas. F_1 therefore doesn't need to re–execute req_B at the very beginning of S_3 if the answer already arrived. If the view change due to the failure of L had occurred *before* rep_B had arrived, F_1 could *not* just wait for the reply: the former leader L might have

---

5. Any election algorithm (e.g. the bully algorithm) can be used to elect the new leader. In our case, the underlying group communication system delivers an ordered list of group members with each view change, and we simply choose the first replica in the list as the new leader.

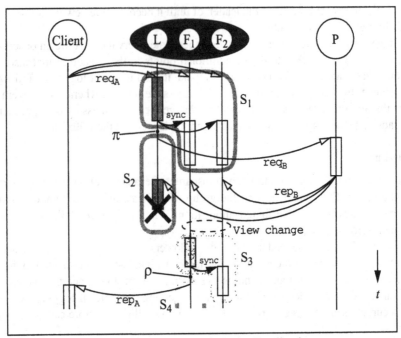

Fig. 4 Failures in Semi–Active Replication

failed at point π, i.e., after having synchronized the extended state interval S_1, but before having started S_2 by sending the RPC request req_B. Instead, the new leader F_1 has to (re–)do any observable event unless it can deduce that the event already had been done by the former leader (as is the case if it *did* receive the reply rep_B). This includes asynchronous RPCs, to which there are no replies. The same reasoning also applies to RPC answer messages sent by the leader. If F_1 fails after point ρ, F_2 will become the new leader. It cannot know whether or not F_1 already sent back rep_A to the client, so F_2 has no choice but execute the reply (again).

The above implies that partitions must be able to deal with *duplicate messages* for both incoming RPC requests and incoming RPC answers. Messages must therefore be tagged with unique, system–wide identifier. Repeated answer messages are simply ignored. If a request message is delivered several times, the request is only executed the first time. Repeated requests then return the result of the first invocation, which implies that results must be retained. Retained results must be eventually garbage collected to avoid memory leaks, which can be done by piggybacking with each message information about which RPC answers the sender already got from the receiver of the message. The receiver of the message can then discard these retained answers.

A follower encountering an observable event (i.e., at the very beginning of an extended state interval) during replay does not have to redo the action because it *knows* with absolute certainty that the leader did indeed perform the operation. Duplicate sending of messages can only occur if the leader fails after an observable event, but before the next synchronization.

6 RAPIDS: Replicated Ada Partitions In Distributed Systems

RAPIDS [Wol98] is an implementation of the semi–active replication scheme based on piecewise determinism (described in sections 5 and 5.2) for the GNAT compiler. It is implemented within the run–time support as part of the PCS and is therefore largely transparent to the application.

Rapids consists of a core implementing the event log, offering an interface for logging and replaying events and for transferring the event log from the leader to the followers. Actually, there are three interfaces:

- an internal one for use by Garlic [KPT95], GNAT's PCS, for logging and replaying external events, and
- an interface through callbacks which is used by GNAT's tasking support GNARL for logging and replaying internal events, and finally
- an interface in a child package of System.RPC for use by the standard libraries, which also may have to log and replay events (e.g., Ada.Calendar.Clock or file accesses).

Garlic has been modified to include unique message identifiers in all its messages and to do duplicate message detection. The necessary group communication has been added as a new protocol to Garlic. This protocol currently is only an interface to a third–party view–synchronous group communication system called Phoenix [MFSW95]. The tasking support GNARL has also been modified by adding callbacks to RAPIDS for logging and replaying of internal events. However, not all tasking is synchronized: RAPIDS only logs events for application tasks, but not for tasks used within the PCS itself. (The PCS must do different things on a leader or a follower!)

7 Conclusion

We have presented a method to transparently replicate Ada 95 partitions to achieve fault tolerance. The approach is based on a piecewise deterministic computation model and employs semi–active replication. It can offer k–resiliency for arbitrary partitions in heterogeneous distributed systems.

The implementation of this approach, called RAPIDS, is currently (Nov 1998) still in a prototype stage. It still needs serious optimization efforts, and it doesn't yet handle dynamically bound remote calls through remote access–to–subprogram or remote access–to–class–wide values. Also, events due to assignments of controlled types are not yet handled.

References

[BHV+90] Barrett, P. A.; Hilborne, A. M.; Veríssimo, P. et al.: "The Delta–4 Extra Performance Architecture XPA", in *Proceedings of the 20th International Symposium on Fault–Tolerant Computing Systems (FTCS–20)*, pp. 481 – 488, Newcastle upon Tyne, UK, June 1990.

[Bir93]   Birman, K. P.: "The Process Group Approach to Reliable Distributed Computing", *Communications of the ACM 36(12)*, Dec. 1993, pp. 37 – 53.

[BN84]   Birrell, A. D.; Nelson, B. J.: "Implementing Remote Procedure Calls",
            ACM Transactions on Computer Systems 2(1), 1984, pp. 39 – 59.

[Eln93]   Elnozahy, E. N.: *Manetho: Fault Tolerance in Distributed Systems using
            Rollback Recovery and Process Replication*, PhD Thesis, Rice University,
            Houston TX, USA, Oct. 1993.

[HW90]   Herlihy, M. P.; Wing, J. M.: "Linearizability: A Correctness Criterion for
            Concurrent Objects", *ACM Transactions on Programming Languages and
            Systems 12(3)*, July 1990, pp. 463 – 492.

[ISO95]   ISO: *International Standard ISO/IEC 8652:1995(E): Ada Reference Man-
            ual*, Lecture Notes in Computer Science **1246**, Springer Verlag, 1997; ISO,
            1995.

[KPT95]   Kermarrec, Y.; Pautet, L.; Tardieu, S.: "GARLIC: Generic Ada Reusable
            Library for Interpartition Communication", in *Proceedings of Tri-Ada '95*,
            pp. 263 – 269, Anaheim CA, USA, Nov. 1995.

[MFSW95]   Malloth, C.; Felber, P.; Schiper, A.; Wilhelm, U.: "Phoenix: A Toolkit for
            Building Fault–Tolerant, Distributed Applications in Large–Scale Net-
            works", in *Workshop on Parallel and Distributed Platforms in Industrial
            Products*, San Antonio TX, USA, Oct. 1995.

[Mos81]   Moss, J. E. B.: *Nested Transactions: An Approach to Reliable Distributed
            Computing*, PhD Thesis MIT/LCS/TR–260, MIT, Cambridge MA, USA,
            Apr. 1981.

[Pow91]   Powell, D. (Ed.): *Delta–4: A Generic Architecture for Dependable Distrib-
            uted Computing*, volume 1 of *ESPRIT Research Reports, Project 818/2252
            — Delta–4*, Springer Verlag, 1991.

[Sch90]   Schneider, F. B.: "Implementing Fault–Tolerant Services using the State
            Machine Approach", *ACM Computing Surveys 22(4)*, Dec. 1990,
            pp. 299 – 319.

[SY85]   Strom, R. E.; Yemini, S.: "Optimistic Recovery in Distributed Systems",
            ACM Transactions on Computer Systems 3(3), Aug. 1985, pp. 204 – 226.

[Wol97]   Wolf, T.: "Fault Tolerance in Distributed Ada 95", in *Proceedings of the
            8th International Real–Time Ada Workshop*, pp. 106 – 110, Ravenscar,
            UK, Apr. 1997, ACM Ada Letters **XVII**(5).

[Wol98]   Wolf, T.: *Replication of Non–Deterministic Objects*, PhD Thesis #1903,
            Swiss Federal Institute of Technology, Lausanne, Switzerland, Nov. 1998.

A Case Study in the Reuse of
On-board Embedded Real-Time Software

Tullio Vardanega[1], Gert Caspersen[2], and Jan Storbank Pedersen[2]

[1] European Space Agency Research & Technology Centre,
Keplerlaan 1, 2200 AG Noordwijk, Netherlands
tullio@ws.estec.esa.nl
[2] TERMA Elektronik AS,
Bregnerodvej 144, 3460 Birkerod, Denmark
{gec,jnp}@terma.com

Abstract. The rise of the 'cheaper, faster, better' mission paradigm increasingly challenges the industrial development of satellite systems. The novel paradigm will have a profound impact on the production of the real-time software embedded on board new-generation systems. This paper discusses how software reuse may fit in the rising development scenario and how reuse interacts with other important players in the picture, especially the software process model and the on-board software architecture.

1 The Rise of a New Project Paradigm

Similarly to a variety of other technology segments, the industrial development of satellite systems is confronted with the rise of the 'cheaper, faster, better' mission paradigm. The novel paradigm denotes the urge to attain increased operation capability, decreased power consumption, lower launch mass and shorter time to market. This trend will cause the future development scenario of on-board embedded real-time systems to be dominated by the demand to: (i) reduce the development schedule from the present 3-4 years to 18-24 months; (ii) deliver better mission product via increased autonomy and responsiveness of operation; (iii) support increasingly more software-intensive systems.

These demands have a vast impact on the architecture of the spacecraft bus, i.e. the module in charge of the control services on board the satellite. For example, the software size of those components is predicted to rise from the present 8-12,000 source statements to the 15-25,000 of new missions under the same language baseline. In the face of this event, the productivity of the software development process shall have to at least quadruple, for twice as big software will have to be delivered in half the time. Concurrently, the operation requirements placed on the software product will increase the functional complexity and the real-time criticality of the system, which will have to be attained within no less than the present envelope of dependability.

Earlier work (cf. [1, 2]) has argued that an iterative and incremental development process is better equipped than the traditional 'waterfall' model to cope with the increasing complexity of the product and the concurrent reduction of the development schedule. This paper concurs with this vision and takes it further towards industrial practice.

The envisioned process calls for a software architecture flexible enough to accommodate successive increments but also capable of assuring the integrity of the system and the convergence of the process. In our view, however, three further ingredients are required for a highly-productive realisation of the process: (i) an application model that favours the scalability of the architecture; (ii) a software reuse framework that accelerates the construction of systems in match with that application model; and (iii) enabling technology that supports the production of reusable, reliable and predictable software, with Ada [3, 4] playing a crucial rôle in this respect.

We recently reviewed the performance of a pilot development centred around those three ingredients in the frame of a project funded by the European Space Agency. This paper presents some of our findings.

2 Process Model

As outlined in [2], the process model assumed in this paper bases on two conceptual pillars: the design framework and the computational model.

The design framework covers the segment of the development process that spans from the software requirements phase to the detail design phase. Contrary to the classical waterfall model, the design framework contemplates the possibility of multiple, incremental iterations across phases. The notion of design framework aims to master the anticipated occurrence of feedback-based iterations in the design and verification of new-generation systems. The incremental nature of the process is the means to break the overall development down to (parallel) threads of sub-development, each characterised by bounded complexity and greater likelihood of faster completion.

The computational model assembles the notions that steer the iterative process within the design framework and lead it to convergence. Those notions defines: (a) the type of components to be used in the construction of the real-time architecture of the system, the means for the communication and synchronisation between them, and the concurrency paradigm assumed for their execution; (b) the execution properties and real-time attributes that characterise those components as well as the constraints placed on their use and interaction; and (c) an underpinning analytical model that allows the static analysis of the real-time behaviour of systems constructed in terms of those components. These definitions collectively determine the abstract view of the architectural support for predictability availed to the process. Suitable computational models support the construction of flexible yet statically verifiable architectures that fit in the incremental nature of the development and reduce the extent of real-time verification needed at integration testing.

On-board systems are inherently concurrent. A large proportion of new-generation systems will be even more so on account of the integration of an increasing number of control functions on a decreasing number of processing nodes. Our need is, thus, for a computational model that facilitates the controlled expression of that inherent concurrency.

Our choice originates from the definitions given in HRT-HOOD [5, 6] and bases on the principles of fixed priority preemptive scheduling [7, 8]. HRT-HOOD extends the base HOOD design method [9] in use at the European Space Agency by incorporating the abstractions supported by the revised tasking model of Ada 95 in the fashion prescribed by the 'Ravenscar profile' [10].

Our computational model contemplates: periodic objects that model time-triggered threaded activities; sporadic objects that model event-triggered threaded activities; and protected objects that model non-threaded structures for mutually exclusive access to shared data. The Ravenscar profile represents the most compact and efficient set of language primitives needed to implement our computational model. Architectures built in accordance with our computational model and implemented using the Ravenscar profile lend themselves to static timing analysis. Ref. [2] describes a set of static analysis techniques that support this notion.

3 Application Domain

Satellite systems typically perform their operation under the supervision of a control centre based on ground. The ground centre exercises its authority on the on-board system by the issue of telecommands (TC) and the reception of status and verification information contained in the response telemetries (TM) returned by the satellite. The servicing of the TC/TM flow between the ground centre and the orbiting satellite constitutes one fundamental function of the real-time software embedded in the spacecraft bus. This set of communication-related services is collectively termed Data Handling Control (DHC) system.

DHC services are typically executed in response to requests disjointly arriving from either the ground centre, for the processing of incoming TC, or on board, for the issue of TM or the servicing of other requests. Accordingly, DHC services have a predominantly sporadic, event-driven nature. Well-defined operation requirements normally bound the inter-arrival time of the triggering events for any given mission scenario. Additionally, DHC systems may also include a small number of naturally periodic activities. For example, the monitoring of selected on-board parameters with respect to mission-specific surveillance criteria, and the execution of any required corrective actions.

For traditional systems, the ground centre needs to maintain at all times the most accurate information about the status and operation of the spacecraft. New-generation autonomous systems tend to move part of the control responsibility to the space segment. Either way, the control activity assumes the minimisation in the latency and jitter incurred between the issue of a command and its actual execution on board. Most of the real-time requirements on DHC services should thus be regarded as mission-critical. Failure to meet any of these requirements may decrease the mission product or even compromise the mission.

4 Project Ingredients

4.1 Application Model

The European Space Agency's Packet Telemetry and Packet Telecommand Standards [11, 12] and the CCSDS Recommendations from which they are derived [13, 14] address the end-to-end transport of TC and TM data between user applications on ground and application processes on board. The European Space Agency's Packet Utilisation Standard (PUS) [15] complements and extends those standards by defining a packet-based interface for the execution of certain services by on-board application processes. The PUS defines those services by prescribing the service model (i.e. how the application processes are to behave on arrival of a given service request) and the inner structures of the associated TC and TM packets. In the absence of those definitions, mission teams traditionally opted to develop their own operational concept, along with a set of mission-specific TC and TM format layouts. That approach effectively prevented any practical reuse of DHC software as well as of electrical ground support equipment and control centre infrastructure. The PUS specifically emerged as an attempt to control the earlier ad-hoc approach to satellite operations.

In the context of the PUS, an application process is defined as an on-board entity capable of receiving TC packets and generating TM source packets. An application process is uniquely and statically identified for the entirety of a mission. No restrictions are placed on the mapping between application processes and the usual functional subdivision of a satellite into subsystems and payloads. We retain this basic definition and assume that multiple application processes may reside on the same processing node. The PUS operational model is shown in Figure 1.

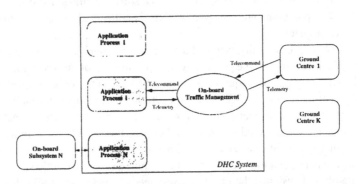

Fig. 1. Packet Utilisation Standard Operational Model.

The original definition of the PUS addressed the requirements arising from the commissioning and operation phase of the satellite life cycle as seen from the perspective of the ground centre(s). Recent work [16] has shown the usefulness of applying the PUS service model to the communications between on-board application processes without any necessary involvement of the ground. An on-going revision of the PUS standard is presently addressing the implications of this extension [17]. New space projects looking into autonomous operation of the spacecraft (e.g.: [18]) are also considering exploiting this potential.

Important advantages may be gained from the consistent application of the PUS service model throughout all phases of system definition and implementation. As shown in Fig. 1, a DHC architecture structured according to the partitioning implied by the PUS subdivides into a set of loosely-coupled application processes. This subdivision naturally reverberates across the development philosophy itself. Specification, implementation and verification of a DHC system thus conceived may in fact break down to progressive increments of sub-development, each addressing individual application processes or their next level of integration. This notion fits exceptionally well in the process model proposed in Ref.s [1] and [2].

4.2 Software Reuse Framework

Several key features of a PUS-compliant DHC software architecture emanate directly from the operational model shown in Fig. 1. First and foremost, the bulk of the software infrastructure in charge of on-board communications that adhere to the standard packet definitions may stay the same across missions. Moreover, the loosely-coupled character of the PUS operational model and the event-driven nature of the associated service model imply that the processing of independent commands may proceed in parallel throughout the system as a whole but also within individual application processes.

Consequently, the software architecture of application processes themselves naturally break down in two major components: a recurrent infrastructure for the support of the internal routing of commands and responses; and an application-specific implementation of the service capabilities to be provided by that application process.

These notions embody a vast amount of reuse potential. The on-board operations support software (OBOSS) system [16] was developed as a software reuse framework aimed to exploit that potential in the construction of PUS-based DHC software architectures.

OBOSS provides easily configurable support for packet-based message passing between the ground segment and on-board application processes. The DHC architecture promoted by OBOSS is loosely-coupled and naturally scalable. Control flow within OBOSS is predominantly event-driven, with an event corresponding to the arrival of a packet-encoded message from any source in the system. The communications architecture within OBOSS is a star configuration, based on mailboxes and packet-encoded messages, and centred around a Packet Router. The Packet Router determines the destination of the incoming message and deposits the packet in the mailbox of the relevant application process. OBOSS provides each application process with a local Packet Dispatcher that fetches the packet from the private mailbox and delivers it to the service capability concerned. OBOSS also allows application processes to operate as communications agents for on-board subsystems physically disjoint from the DHC. In that case, the DHC-resident application process embeds no service capability and simply forwards packets to and from the associated remote subsystem. Packet-encoded messages carry either commands for the execution of certain services within a given application process; or data produced from the execution thereof. A Ground Interface component transforms the source TC incoming from ground into internal packets carrying the corresponding command and passes them on to the Packet Router. Similarly, the Ground Interface receives from the Packet Router internal packets carrying responses directed to ground and transforms them into source TM. Fig. 2 depicts the main architectural components of a DHC software system based on OBOSS.

On top of the reference architecture depicted in Fig. 2 and the corresponding communications infrastructure, OBOSS provides a set of generic service capabilities that

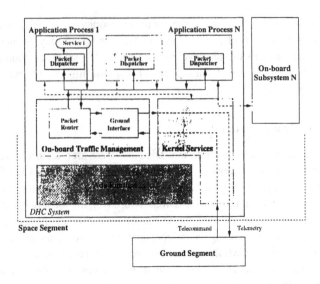

Fig. 2. Software Architecture Breakdown of DHC System based on OBOSS.

cover a subset of those specified in the PUS, and a vast amount of guidance information for the construction of mission-specific DHC systems.

Parameter configuration is the primary means offered by OBOSS to assemble reusable software artifacts into a coherent system architecture. The OBOSS parameters belong in three main categories: 'terminals', which interface individual application components to the OBOSS communications infrastructure; 'attributes', which capture specific functional characteristics of the individual component; and 'connectors', which encapsulate dependencies on the physical architecture of the DHC system under construction. The box tagged Kernel Services in Fig. 2 globally represents all the needed 'connectors'.

Fig. 3 depicts a simplified break-down of the software components that collectively constitute an application process embedding the incarnation of an OBOSS generic service capability. With respect to the cited parameter categories, Fig. 3 shows: a Packet Dispatcher ('terminal'), which delivers to the service incarnation incoming messages that carry commands for that service; a Packet Depositor ('terminal'), which forwards responses or commands generated by the service incarnation to the Packet Router; specific parameters ('attributes'), which define the characteristics of the service to be provided by the incarnation embedded in that particular application process: e.g.: unique identifier of the application process, service policy, service priority; a Bus Connector ('connector'), which interfaces the application process and the service incarnation to specific remote units on board the spacecraft.

4.3 Enabling Technology

Ada 83 [3] has been the programming language of choice for the vast majority of European Space Agency's space projects to date. On the availability of mature support for embedded targets, Ada 95 [4] will be the natural choice for future projects.

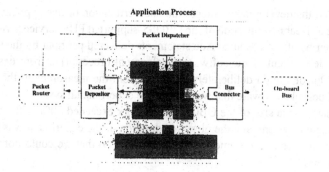

Fig. 3. Incarnation of OBOSS Service Capabilities in an Application Process.

The choice of Ada as enabling technology fits perfectly in the highly-productive process model sought by our experiment in several distinct respects. The OBOSS architecture embodies a vast amount of internal event-driven concurrency that needs to be controlled for efficiency, responsiveness and predictability. The loosely-coupled character of the OBOSS message-passing infrastructure needs to rely upon efficient asynchronous communications. The Ada implementation of the Ravenscar profile provides excellent support for both demands. Even though rarely used in on-board systems, Ada generics provide the most direct means to implement the OBOSS generic service capabilities. Accordingly, the desired characteristics of the service incarnation are simply specified as the actual parameters of the generic units concerned. One dimension of our experiment was expressly to assess the practicality of extensive use of Ada generics in resource-constrained on-board embedded real-time systems.

The strong industrial connotation of our undertaking dictated the use of Ada 83 technology equipped with support for the Ravenscar profile. As new technology becomes available, we also want to assess the benefit of transitioning the OBOSS implementation to Ada 95 in view of its greater expressive power and support for extendibility.

5 Evaluation

We recently conducted an experiment to evaluate the performance of a software development process centred around the ingredients described in section 4.

The idea behind the experiment was to engage a third-party team in the implementation of a sizeable proportion of a new-generation DHC system compliant with the PUS and based on the OBOSS software reuse framework. The third-party team had no prior knowledge about the PUS and no prior experience with OBOSS.

We selected several performance indicators and measured their evolution across the experiment. In the following we discuss some of the observations made during the experiment.

5.1 Productivity

The first dimension we looked into was the productivity rate achieved in the experiment with respect to typical values observed in industrial projects. The experiment encompassed the development, integration and verification of one application process embedding a sizeable proportion of the OBOSS-supported PUS services. We measured the rate in terms of 'new' source Ada statements delivered per hour by the team across a comparable segment of the software development process (i.e. from design to verification). Our definition deliberately excluded from the measurement the amount of unchanged bespoke software that was part of the experimental system. That precaution was necessary as the size of the OBOSS framework exceeded 70% of the total size of the experimental system, and the observed duration of the experiment was insufficient for the team to master the framework in its entirety, so that we could not regard it as truly 'delivered'.

Even with those precautions, we observed an important increase in productivity. We attributed the increase to several concurrent factors; in particular: (i) the lesser load imposed on the team by our incremental process; and (ii) the reduced design and integration effort incurred on adoption of the OBOSS architectural framework.

Fig. 4 relates the productivity attained in the experiment to the productivity band and width of observation for traditional (precursor) developments as well as recent commercial projects.

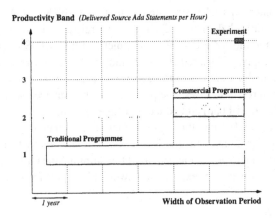

Fig. 4. Software Productivity Rate in Experiment vs Typical Space Projects.

5.2 Memory Size Requirements

The second dimension of our observation was the impact of the OBOSS reuse framework on the memory size requirements of the system. A certain inflation in code size is the inevitable 'dark' side of any ambitious reuse initiative. It certainly was in our experiment. In Table 1 we relate the code size of the experimental system based on OBOSS to a functionally comparable traditional DHC implementation. The notion of 'functionally comparable' is rather weak in this context, for no traditional DHC to our knowledge gets anywhere near the processing requirements induced by the PUS. Yet, we picked one last-generation traditional DHC as the reference term.

Table 1. Impact of OBOSS on Memory Budget: Code Size (in bytes)

component	traditional DHC 16-bit CISC	OBOSS-based DHC 32-bit RISC
Ada runtime	4,308	73,404
kernel services	21,470	53,313
communications services	6,492	76,112
application layer	18,788	79,028
total	51,058	281,856
inflation rate (normalised)	1.00	1.84

For the traditional DHC we considered the code breakdown on a 16-bit CISC space processor. For the OBOSS-based DHC we considered the experimental implementation on a new-generation RISC space processor. We then normalised the observed size increase to the 'natural' inflation rate incurred on the transition from 16-bit CISC to 32-bit RISC, which normally places in the region of 3.0. The breakdown components listed in Table 1 correspond to the main architectural blocks identified in Figure 2. The 'application layer' component denotes the equivalent of one application process embedding a sizeable proportion of the OBOSS-supported PUS services.

The experimental system was fully coded in Ada and executed on a standard runtime for the lack a 'Ravenscar-only' runtime suited for the target processor. The traditional system included a mixture of Ada and assembly and run on a custom (stripped down) version of the standard Ada runtime.

5.3 CPU Load Requirements

The subsequent dimension we looked into was the impact the OBOSS reuse framework had on the CPU load budget of the system. The circumstances described above made it difficult to establish a truly equivalent load scenario to relate against. Furthermore, the 'traditional' DHC operated on the basis of a fixed cyclic schedule, whereas OBOSS operates on preemptive scheduling. On account of this event, the nominal application scenario under consideration had: a 'worst-case' load, given by the fixed width of the DHC slot; and an 'actual' load, given by the effective utilisation of the DHC slot incurred in the scenario. We contrasted the figures thus determined to those respectively obtained from worst-case static analysis of the OBOSS-based system and from actual execution of the scenario.

Table 2 relates the values obtained in the two cases, after normalisation of the CPU power ratio between the two processors, which we estimated to a factor of 6 in favour of the 32-bit RISC.

5.4 Task Density

The decision to adopt the Ravenscar profile in the OBOSS implementation naturally resulted in raising the task density of the system to unprecedented levels. This was no

Table 2. Impact of OBOSS on Nominal CPU Load Budget (%).

CPU load	traditional DHC 16-bit CISC	OBOSS-based DHC 32-bit RISC	inflation rate (normalised)
worst-case	26.70	8.23	1.85
actual	7.01	7.54	6.45

great deal, for the expressive power and semantic contents of our computational model ensure full control of the induced concurrency. Yet, we found it crucial to demonstrate that well-defined bounds exist to the tasking population produced by an OBOSS-based system. In fact, those bounds can be expressed in a fairly elegant fashion, as follows.

Table 3. Definitions

TP total tasking population
CF communications framework component
AC application process interface component
SF service framework descriptor
AS application process service descriptor

Table 3 lists the structural components of OBOSS that feature internal concurrency. Eqn. 1 defines how those components contribute to the determination of the tasking population in an OBOSS-based system comprised of m application processes, denoted AP.

$$TP(m) = CF + AC + SF \times AS \times I_m \tag{1}$$

$$\text{where:} \quad SF = \begin{bmatrix} \tau_1 & \tau_2 & \tau_3 & \tau_4 & \tau_5 & \tau_6 & \tau_7 \\ \pi_1 & \pi_2 & \pi_3 & \pi_4 & \pi_5 & \pi_6 & \pi_7 \end{bmatrix} = \begin{bmatrix} 3 & 2 & 2 & 1 & 1 & 1 & 0 \\ 4 & 2 & 3 & 1 & 1 & 1 & 1 \end{bmatrix} \tag{2}$$

with τ_i and π_i respectively denoting the number of tasks and protected objects required to implement PUS service i for any given OBOSS implementation (currently in the range $[1..7]$);

$$CF = \begin{bmatrix} 3 \\ 7 \end{bmatrix} \quad \text{and} \quad AC = m \times \begin{bmatrix} 1 \\ 2 \end{bmatrix} \quad \text{using the same notation;} \tag{3}$$

$$AS = \begin{bmatrix} e_{1,1} & \cdots & e_{1,m} \\ & \cdots & \\ e_{6,1} & \cdots & e_{6,m} \\ n_1 & \cdots & n_m \end{bmatrix} \quad \text{with } e_{i,j} = \{ \begin{array}{l} 1 \text{ if AP}_j \text{ embeds service } i \\ 0 \text{ if AP}_j \text{ does not embed service } i; \end{array} \tag{4}$$

n_j is the number of packet stores used by AP_j; and I_m is an $[m \times 1]$ identity matrix.

With Eqn. 1 we easily determine the lower bound and the upper bound to the tasking population for all variants of OBOSS-based DHC systems that comply with the PUS.

The lower bound is obtained on a system comprised of one single application process (whereby $m = 1$) embedding no PUS services (whereby $AS = [0_{1,1}, \ldots, 0_{6,1}, 0_1]$), hence merely acting as destination of source TC and producer of source TM. The upper bound is obtained when every application process in the system embeds the whole set of PUS services supported by OBOSS (whereby $AS = [1_{1,1}, 1_1, \ldots, 1_{6,m}, 1_m]$). Eqn. 1 sets the lower-bound value to: $TP_{min} = [4, 9] + [1, 1]$, where the latter term accounts for the TC interpreter in the application process; and the upper-bound value to: $TP_{max}(m) = [(3 + m \times 11), (5 + m \times 15)]$. As an indicator of the predominant event-driven control flow in OBOSS, we note that all the tasks in term TP_{min} are classified as sporadic, whereas only $m \times 4$ periodic tasks contribute to term $TP_{max}(m)$.

6 Lessons Learned

The level of software productivity required by new-generation space projects compels industry to abandon the one-off product concept for the notion of 'product in a series'. Software reuse may play a crucial rôle in this transition.

OBOSS was conceived, designed and developed as a means to faster and progressively more reliable production of new-generation DHC software systems. The experimental observations discussed in section 5 indicate that this objective may be achieved, even in the case of inter-company reuse. The experiment showed that the software productivity, expressed in terms of new source Ada statements delivered per hour, may rise in excess of 4 times the traditional level and 2 times the performance of recent commercial projects (cf. Fig. 4). This productivity boost comes at a cost, though. The experiment highlighted some visible cost elements: the increase by a factor of 2 in the size of memory (cf. Table 1) as well as in the worst-case CPU load provisions (cf. Table 2). These indicators are important for on-board embedded systems that are subject to stringent resource constraints due, in part, to the material cost and, in part, to the proportional rise of the verification cost. In our view, the experimental results obtained in this respect yield modest concern. The impact on memory size needs to be assessed in the context of specific project economics: flight memory is normally a costly and spared resource; yet, the productivity increase and other architectural considerations may factor the extra cost off. The impact on CPU load is probably only of statistical interest in the face of the rising availability of more powerful space-qualified processors.

There are other, less visible costs that also need to be computed in the equation.

On-board embedded systems are exposed to levels of verification that require of the supplier the technical mastership of all components of the system, irrespective of their origin. This requirement may prove an unsurmountable hurdle as the implications it carries are not thoroughly understood at the start of the project. As well-structured as it may be, OBOSS brings along an unprecedented amount of flight-worthy bespoke software.

OBOSS represents up to 70% of a software-intensive new-generation DHC system. Thus, it takes a certain amount time to acquire a sufficient mastership of its internals and operation. The iterative and incremental nature of the proposed process model surely aids in spreading the 'learning curve' over an affordable time span. Yet, the effort needed to do so must be budgeted as an investment on a foreign product. This provision is likely to take a level of commitment that goes beyond the scope of the project itself. The major challenge facing OBOSS is, thus, to demonstrate its actual strategic convenience also in the case of inter-company reuse.

Disclaimer: The views expressed in this paper are those of the authors only and do not necessarily engage those of the European Space Agency.

References

1. Vardanega, T., van Katwijk, J.: Productive Engineering of Predictable Embedded Real-Time Systems: The Road to Maturity. Information and Software Technology, **40** (1998) 745–764.
2. Vardanega, T., van Katwijk, J.: A Software Process for the Construction of Predictable On-Board Embedded Real-Time Systems. Software - Practice and Experience, **29**:3 (1999) 1–32.
3. ISO, Ada Reference Manual. International Standardisation Organisation ISO/IEC JTC 1/SC22, Geneva, Switzerland (1987). ISO/IEC 8652:1987.
4. ISO, Ada Reference Manual. International Standardisation Organisation ISO/IEC JTC 1/SC22, Geneva, Switzerland (1995). ISO/IEC 8652:1995.
5. Burns, A., Wellings, A.: HRT-HOOD: A Structured Design Method for Hard Real-Time Systems. Real-Time Systems, **6** (1994) 73–114.
6. Burns, A., Wellings, A.: HRT-HOOD: A Structured Design Method for Hard Real-Time Systems. Elsevier Science, Amsterdam, Netherlands (1995).
7. Audsley, N., Burns, A., Richardson, M., Wellings, A.: Hard Real-Time Scheduling: The Deadline Monotonic Approach. Proc. Real-Time Operating Systems and Software, IEEE. **8** (1991) 127–132.
8. Audsley, N., Burns, A., Wellings, A.: Deadline Monotonic Scheduling Theory and Application. Control Engineering Practice, **1**:1 (1993) 71–78.
9. HTG, HOOD Reference Manual 3.1. HOOD Technical Group, Prentice Hall (1993).
10. Baker, T., Vardanega, T.: Session Summary: Tasking Profiles. Ada Letters, **XVII**:5 (1997) 5–7. Proc. 8th Int'l Real-Time Ada Workshop.
11. ESA, Packet Telemetry Standard. European Space Agency, Noordwijk, Netherlands, PSS-04-106: Issue 1 (1988). (http://esapub.esrin.esa.it/pss/pss-cat1.htm)
12. ESA, Packet Telecommand Standard. European Space Agency, Noordwijk, Netherlands, PSS-04-107: Issue 2 (1992). (http://esapub.esrin.esa.it/pss/pss-cat1.htm)
13. CCSDS, Telemetry Summary of Concept and Rationale. Consultative Committee for Space Data Systems, CCSDS 100.0-G-1: Issue 1 (1987). (http://www.ccsds.org/publications.html#telemetry)
14. CCSDS, Telecommand Summary of Concept and Service. Consultative Committee for Space Data Systems, CCSDS 200.0-G-6: Issue 6 (1987). (http://www.ccsds.org/publications.html#telecommand)
15. ESA, Packet Utilisation Standard. European Space Agency, Noordwijk, Netherlands, ESA PSS-07-101 Issue 1 (1994). (http://esapub.esrin.esa.it/pss/pss-cat1.htm)
16. CRI: Onboard Operations Support Software - Modules Users Manual. Deliverable on ES-TEC Contract 11277/94/NL/FM(SC), European Space Agency, Noordwijk, Netherlands (1997). (http://ftp.estec.esa.nl/pub/ws/wsd/oboss/www/oboss.html)
17. Parkes, A., Kaufeler, P., Merri, M., Valera, S., Vardanega, T.: The Future of the Packet Utilisation Standard. Proc. 1st ESA Workshop on Tracking, Telemetry and Command Systems, European Space Agency (1998).
18. Teston, F., Creasey, R., Van der Ha, J.: PROBA: ESA's Autonomy and Technology Demonstration Mission. Proc. Int'l Astronautical Congress, International Aeronautical Federation **48** (1997).

Development of
Flight Control Software in Ada:
Architecture and Design Issues and Approaches

Alfred Rosskopf

DaimlerChrysler Aerospace AG
Military Aircraft
P.O. Box 80 11 60, 81663 München, Germany

E-mail: alfred.rosskopf@m.dasa.de

Abstract. This paper discusses software architecture and design issues in the development of flight control software. After a short introduction to the flight control application domain, several design concepts and methods are described that have been applied and evaluated in an implementation of flight control laws for a fighter aircraft. The issues and approaches presented include: platform-independent software, object-oriented techniques, reusable components, design patterns and software design for multi-processor targets.

1 Introduction

This paper reports on experience from a research and technology project at DaimlerChrysler Aerospace. The objective of the project is an integrated process for the development of flight control laws for complex aircraft configurations. One component of this process is the development of control law software.

Various software technologies have been evaluated with respect to their applicability to - safety-critical - control law software. Control laws for a typical fighter aircraft have been implemented in Ada. The working title of the resulting experimental software is COLAda – Control Law Software in Ada. This paper presents some of the software concepts and methods applied and evaluated in the development of COLAda.

2   The Flight Control Application Domain

The following sections give a short overview of the flight control application domain. Various diagrams are used to give the reader an impression of typical architectures of flight control systems, flight control laws and the software in flight control computers.

Flight Control Systems and Flight Control Computers

Figure 1 shows a typical architecture of a Flight Control System (FCS) for a military aircraft (see e.g. [Collinson]).

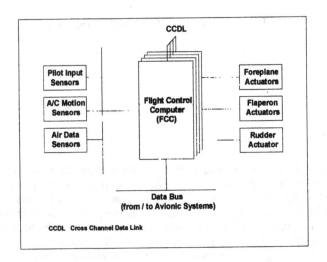

Fig. 1. Typical architecture of a Flight Control System

In figure 2 an example hardware architecture of a Flight Control Computer (FCC) is shown.

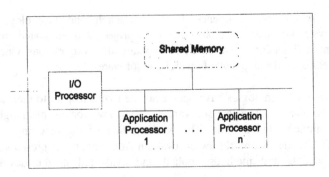

Fig. 2. Typical FCC hardware architecture

Flight Control Laws

Figure 3 is a simplified block diagram of typical (flight) control laws (CL) of a modern fighter aircraft. The diagram is derived from a description of the X-31A control law design (see [X-31A CL]). It illustrates the top-level design of the control laws, in terms of

- Basic components of the control laws
- Data flows between the components
- Inputs to and outputs from the control laws

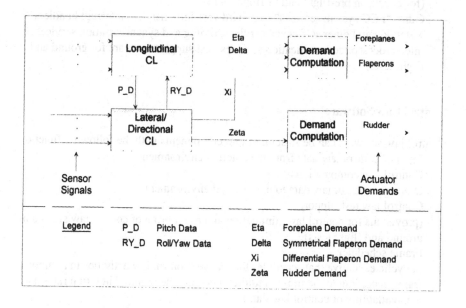

Fig. 3. Simplified block diagram of control laws

The main control law inputs (sensor signals) are the following:

- Pilot inceptors (stick, pedals, trim controls)
- Flow angles (Alpha, Beta)
- Rates and accelerations (P, Q, R, Nx, Ny, Nz)
- Air data (mach number, height, pressures, etc.)
- Configuration data (concerning tanks and stores)

The main control law outputs are the actuator demands for the aircraft's primary control surfaces, i.e. foreplane, flaperon and rudder demands. (Actuator demands for secondary control surfaces are not shown in the diagram.)

Flight Control Software

The software in a typical flight control computer includes the following functions:
- Input / output (I/O) for various types of I/O channels
  (e.g. data bus according to MIL-STD-1553B, analog I/O, discrete I/O, cross channel data link)
- Air data computations
- Control law software (see below)
- Redundancy management
  (e.g. voting and monitoring of redundant sensor signals and actuator demands)
- Built-in-test software
  (for checks in pre-flight and in-flight modes)
- Other "FCC system services" (e.g. hardware initialisation, interrupt handlers, watchdog and other self-check services, timing and synchronisation services, inter-processor communication services, test support software for ground and flight tests)

Control Law Software

Control law software can be structured into components with the following functions:
- Input of control law data from the external environment
- Control law computations
- Output of control law data to the external environment
- Control law test support
  (provisions for control law stimulation and monitoring of control law signals in ground and flight tests)
- Frame scheduler
  (a cyclic executive that schedules the various control law activities in a minor frame according to the timing requirements, i.e. the required iteration rates and the availability of control law data)

3 Design Issues and Approaches to Flight Control Software

The complexity of flight control systems for fly-by-wire aircraft demands advanced techniques for the production of the embedded software. This is valid for design and implementation as well as verification of the software (see also [Ro-Te]). Flight control software is a prominent example of safety-critical software. Ada is well suited for implementing safety-critical software (see [ISO 15942]) and in particular flight control software (see [Frisberg]).

In the following sections, design issues and approaches to the development of flight control software are discussed. Some of the concepts and methods applied to the development of control law software in Ada (COLAda) in a current research and technology project at DaimlerChrysler Aerospace are presented. These concepts are collectively refered to as the "COLAda approach" in the rest of the paper.

The COLAda approach to control law (CL) software can be characterised by the following software architecture and design concepts:

- Platform-independent CL software
- Object-oriented techniques for CL software
- Reusable components for CL software
- Design patterns for CL software
- Multi-processing design for CL software

Platform-Independent Control Law Software

It has been an essential goal of the COLAda approach to have *one* software implementation of control laws that can be run on *different* hardware platforms and in different runtime environments. This means that the *same* software that is used in development and simulation environments can also be used in the flight control computer. (Figure 4 shows five runtime environments where COLAda can be run.)

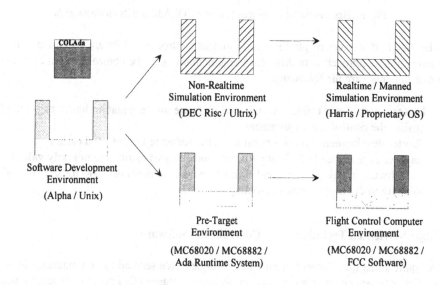

Fig. 4. Runtime environments of the COLAda software

To achieve the objective of platform-independent control law software suitable methods have to be applied during design and implementation, for example:

- Identifying the (inevitably) *environment-dependent* parts of the software and isolating them from the *environment-independent* core
- Designing a common software architecture suitable for all envisaged environments (see figure 5)
- Coding the control law software in Ada – without using any implementation-dependent features of the language

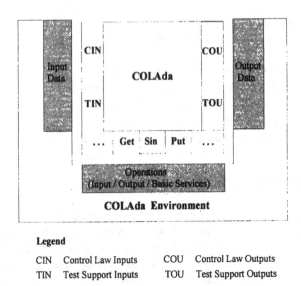

Legend

CIN	Control Law Inputs	COU	Control Law Outputs
TIN	Test Support Inputs	TOU	Test Support Outputs

Fig. 5. Basic external interfaces between COLAda and its environments

The major advantages of platform-independent control law software – compared to a conventional approach with different implementations of the control laws in different environments - are the following:

- Lower development effort – as only one software implementation has to be verified against the control law requirements
- Shorter development cycles – as errors in the software are detected earlier
- Improved quality and reliability – as test and analysis results are not only valid for the software in development and simulation environments but also for the "flying" software in the flight control computer

Object-Oriented Techniques for Control Law Software

For quite some time "object-oriented" techniques have seemed to be ubiquitous in the area of software engineering. However, in many instances this proves not to be much more than "lip service".

In the design of COLAda an attempt to exploit the potential of object-oriented techniques for control law software has been made. One of the design constraints that has been observed from the beginning is the required runtime efficiency of the software.

Various common elements of control laws, like for example different types of filters, limiters, faders etc., have been identified as candidate "objects". They have been designed and implemented as Abstract Data Types (ADTs) using the appropriate facilities of Ada (see [Ada 95]).

The following example (see figures 6, 7 and 8) outlines design and usage of filter "objects" within the control law software.

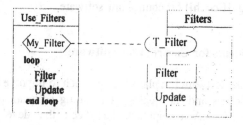

Fig. 6. Design diagram for package Filters

```
package Filters is

    type T_Filter is private    -- Object type
                                -- (Representation is hidden)
    procedure Filter (Filter : in out  T_Filter ;
                      Input  : in       T_Real   ;
                      Output :     out  T_Real   )

    procedure Update (Filter : in out  T_Filter)

    pragma Inline (Filter, Update) -- Avoid calling overhead
```

Fig. 7. Ada outline of package Filters

```
procedure Use_Filters is

    My_Filter  : T_Filter    -- Create a filter object

    loop
                            -- Apply filter object
        Filter (My_Filter, Input, Output)

        -- - - - - - - - - End of time-critical processing

        Update (My_Filter)   -- Update state of filter object
    end loop
```

Fig. 8. Ada outline of the usage of filter objects

The small example illustrates how the facilities of Ada for object-based design have been used in the design of COLAda. The additional use of classes and inheritance that would be possible with Ada 95 seems less natural and less appropriate for control law software. Through careful evaluation of design decisions (e.g. by inspecting the compiler-generated code for different design variants) it could be ensured that the required runtime efficiency is not compromised by the elegance of an object-based design. Thus it has been possible to exploit the major advantages of object-oriented techniques (see e.g. [Booch]) for control law software.

Reusable Components for Control Law Software

The attempt to reuse software is a plausible approach to improve both the productivity of software developers and the quality of resulting software products. One of the objectives of the COLAda approach has been the development of reusable components for control law software. They make it possible to compose certain parts of control law software from "off-the-shelf" building blocks (see figure 9).

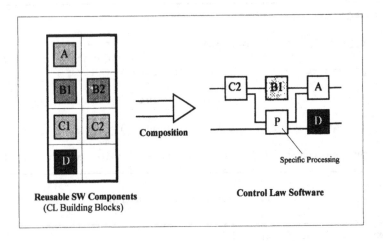

Fig. 9. Reusable components for control law software

In COLAda a number of control law elements have been identified as candidates for *reusable software components*, for example:

- Filter elements
- Limiter elements
- Fader and smoother elements
- Gain scheduling functions
- Control-law-specific math functions
- Test support elements (designed as "injector objects")

The chosen software design and implementation of these COLAda components should enable their reuse - at least in a control law software implementation with similar context. (This "context" is determined by the elements used in the control law design and by the implementation language.)

Obviously, for a "reusable software component" that is to be used in a safety-critical system more than the source code has to be available. The documentation of such a component must include the following additional items:

- A precise requirements specification
- Detailed design descriptions
- Complete test and analysis reports

Design Patterns for Control Law Software

Software reuse should not be restricted to the code level (code reuse). The reuse of higher level software products (i.e. of software designs or architectures) may also contribute to higher productivity and better software quality. Design patterns are a means of capturing the key aspects of design structures.

The COLAda approach has adopted the idea of design patterns and of domain-specific software architectures. The objective is to identify proved design patterns in the domain of control law software applications. The documentation of those patterns and of architectural aspects of control law software can help to produce a good design of a new control law application quicker (see figure 10).

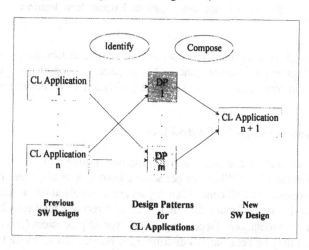

Fig. 10. Design patterns for control law software

The following example shows a design pattern that has been used to model the interface between COLAda and its different environments. The external input interface of COLAda (see figure 11) is the same for all environments and is defined by an Ada package specification (CL_Inputs). There are different bodies of this package, one for each environment (SDE/SIM/FCC). They implement the data transfer from the different data environments (again modeled by Ada packages) to

COLAda. This design pattern isolates the environment dependencies and supports the goal of environment-independent control law software.

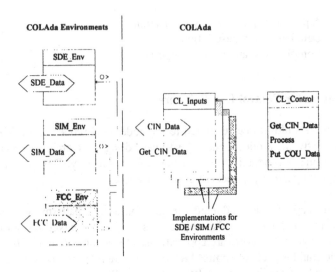

Fig. 11. Example design pattern: External Input Interface

Software design is a difficult process. A bad design causes many problems both during development and maintenance. Design patterns support the reuse of proved designs and can contribute to better software quality and lower development costs.

Multi-Processing Design for Control Law Software

Control law software is compute-intensive and needs quite a lot of processing power. A typical iteration rate of 80 cycles per second corresponds to a time frame length of 12.5 milliseconds. If not all control law inputs are available at the beginning of such a frame, a time interval of much less than 12.5 milliseconds may remain for certain - time-critical - computations. Depending on the type of processors (and co-processors) in the FCC, it may be necessary to distribute the control law software to two or more processors of a multi-processor architecture.

In the development of COLAda an FCC with a multi-processor hardware architecture (see figure 2) has been assumed. The control law software has been partitioned and allocated to two application processors of the FCC.

The structure of the control laws shown in the block diagram in figure 3 suggests a partitioning of the control law software where the longitudinal control laws are allocated to one processor and the lateral/directional control laws to a second one. It can also be seen that there are certain data dependencies (data flows) between various blocks of the control laws. This means that suitable mechanisms for synchronisation and communication between the distributed components of the control law software are required.

In order not to compromise the environment-independence of the control law software, an application-specific inter-processor communication package has been designed that is suitable both for the multi-processor FCC environment and also for single-processor environments (i.e. the software development and simulation environments, SDE and SIM). Environment-dependencies are isolated in the body of the communication package. It implements data exchange via shared memory for the FCC environment and uses mailbox and message passing services (built with the Ada tasking facilities) to support inter-task communication in single-processor environments.

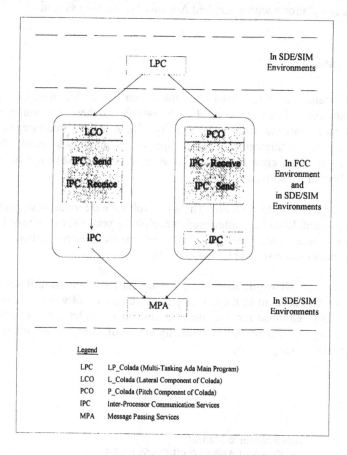

Fig. 12. Multi-processing / multi-tasking design of COLAda

Figure 12 illustrates the basic concurrency aspects of the design of COLAda: The two concurrent components of COLAda (LCO and PCO) can be part of two separate programs running on different processors. Or they can be run as cooperating tasks of a multi-tasking Ada program (LPC) running in a single-processor environment. In both cases the communication between the two components of the control law software (via the inter-processor communication services, IPC) is the same.

This multi-processor/multi-tasking design of COLAda offers the following major benefits:
- A suitable definition of the inter-processor communication services enables an efficient implementation in the FCC shared memory environment. (The compiler generated code consists only of a few machine instructions.)
- The synchronisation and communication between the two concurrent components of the control law software is the same both in the development and simulation environments and in the FCC environment.
- The multi-processor control law software is environment-independent. It can be run on any platform with a standard Ada runtime / tasking system.

4   Conclusion

The requirements for flight control software are manifold. Besides functional requirements (as defined by control law algorithms) there are numerous non-functional constraints that have to be satisfied. These include interface, timing and target hardware requirements. Further specific requirements result from the classification of flight control software as safety-critical, in particular the need for „analysability" of the software.

In the development of the COLAda flight control software additional quality goals have been persued. It has been attempted to exploit the potential of advanced software engineering concepts and methods, like platform-independent software, object-oriented techniques and software reuse concepts.

It is essential that all requirements and constraints for flight control software are already taken into account in the design phase. Numerous software architecture and design decisions determine not only the overall quality of safety-critical software but have also a large impact on the analysability and verifiability of the software - and therefore its fitness for purpose.

References

[Ada 95]   Ada Reference Manual,
                Int. Standard ANSI/ISO/IEC-8652:1995

[Booch]   G. Booch, Software Engineering with Ada,
                Benjamin/Cummings, Menlo Park, 1983

[Collinson]   R.P.G. Collinson, Introduction to Avionics,
               Chapman & Hall, London, 1996

[Frisberg]   Bo Frisberg, Ada in the JAS39 Gripen Flight Control System,
               Proc. Ada-Europe 98, LNCS 1411, Springer, 1998

[ISO 15942]   Guidance for the Use of the Ada Programming Language
               in High Integrity Systems,
               Draft of ISO/IEC TR 15942, 1998

[Ro-Te]   A. Rosskopf, T. Tempelmeier, Aspects of Flight Control Software:
               A Software Engineering Point of View,
               IFAC/IFIP Workshop on Real-Time Programming,
               Schloß Dagstuhl, Germany, June 1999

[X-31A CL]   H. Beh, G. Hofinger,
               Control Law Design of the Experimental Aircraft X-31A,
               ICAS Proceedings 1994 (Int. Council of Aeronautical Sciences),
               ISBN 1-56347-084-5

Author Index

Lecture Notes in Computer Science

For information about Vols. 1–1530
please contact your bookseller or Springer-Verlag